THE PROSE WORKS
OF
WILLIAM WORDSWORTH

THE PROSE WORKS OF
WILLIAM
WORDSWORTH

Edited by
W. J. B. OWEN
and
JANE WORTHINGTON SMYSER

VOLUME II

OXFORD
AT THE CLARENDON PRESS
1974

Oxford University Press, Ely House, London W. 1

GLASGOW NEW YORK TORONTO MELBOURNE WELLINGTON
CAPE TOWN IBADAN NAIROBI DAR ES SALAAM LUSAKA ADDIS ABABA
DELHI BOMBAY CALCUTTA MADRAS KARACHI LAHORE DACCA
KUALA LUMPUR SINGAPORE HONG KONG TOKYO

*Printed in Great Britain
at the University Press, Oxford
by Vivian Ridler
Printer to the University*

CONTENTS

ILLUSTRATIONS

VIII

REPLY TO 'MATHETES'

INTRODUCTION: GENERAL

COLERIDGE's letter to Southey of early November 1809 (*C.L.* iii. 260) prophesied of *The Friend*: '17. & 18. The foundations of Morality —Taste—in short, all the *principles* to get them over'. Accordingly (or perhaps by accident), *The Friend*, No. 17 (14 December 1809) was occupied by the contribution signed 'Mathetes' (μαθητής 'learner, pupil, disciple') which is reprinted in our Appendix, and by the early paragraphs (lines 1–159 of our text) of Wordsworth's 'Reply'. The original essay is attributed to John Wilson, and the 'Reply' to Wordsworth, in Dorothy Wordsworth to Lady Beaumont, 28 December 1809 (*M.Y.* i. 379): 'the 19th [*sic*] Number of the Friend . . . contains the continuation of my Brother's reply to Mathetes's letter. Mr Wilson sent the letter to Coleridge, and Coleridge requested my Brother to reply to it, he being at leisure, and disposed at that time to write something for the Friend.' Further details are given in Mary Gordon, *Christopher North* (Edinburgh, 1862), i. 130–1:

> In a letter I received from Dr. [Alexander] Blair, he says:—' "The Friend" was going on at that time—Coleridge living at Wordsworth's— Wordsworth making, and reading to us as he made them, the "Sonnets to the Tyrolese", first given in "The Friend;" and from Elleray that winter went "Mathetes."* I remember that De Quincey was with us at the time. He may have given some suggestions besides, but we certainly owed to him our signature.'

> * A letter on Education, the joint composition of Wilson and Blair, addressed to the editor of 'The Friend.'

This information is repeated, without significant addition, in Elsie Swann, *Christopher North* (Edinburgh, 1934), pp. 34–5. As Wordsworth's 'Reply' is hardly intelligible without reference to the original essay, we have printed this in our Appendix.

The early paragraphs of the 'Reply' appeared at the end of the seventeenth *Friend* (pp. 268–72), and must therefore have been written by 14 December 1809; the remainder appeared in No. 20 (4 January 1810; pp. 305–18). The delay in completing the work suggests that Wordsworth had not written all of it when the first instalment was published on 14 December 1809; indeed, it is not till 24 December that Coleridge informs John Brown, the printer of *The Friend*, that 'The Copy for No. 20 will be sent you by Tuesday's [26 December] Coach' (*C.L.* iii. 267); and Wordsworth tells Brown that the essay 'was sent off in a great hurry' (see Commentary, n. on 513–20, textual n.).

Some of the delay may have been caused by the rewriting of the opening of the second instalment, which is discussed in our observations on the text.

Wilson and Blair's paper is an intelligent, if somewhat hypothetical, discussion of the moral problems of adolescence, based on the assumptions that the present age is degenerate compared with the past, and that youth faces it with a more or less incurable optimism, which produces cumulatively an increasing, and generally unwarranted, admiration for the present. Not many of their points are directly answered by Wordsworth: he deals with the notions that the present age is degenerate (Mathetes, § 3 and *passim*); that a belief in general progress is not wholly justified (Mathetes, § 9); and that youth is in need of a teacher (Mathetes, §§ 16–17). His replies to these points are: that most ages are alike, in that they have peculiar merits and defects (*R.M.* 26–104); that a belief in progress is perhaps justified, but is more accurately replaced by a belief in a development, which, like the flow of a river, is towards an ultimate end even though its immediate direction may seem retrograde (105–206); and that reliance on a teacher has more disadvantages than advantages (550–650). The remainder of the essay (207–549) is concerned with a programme for the moral self-education of youth, which is now (208–18) admitted to be vulnerable to the seductions of an age which is likewise admitted (493–9) to be more or less degenerate. The programme is concerned with the choice between 'the World' and 'Intellectual Prowess' (278–301) which is to be directed by a return to Nature through the medium of Reason—a somewhat obscure discussion, the terms of which are inadequately defined, and which seems to be based on Wordsworth's own experience, in the middle nineties, of the healing power of Nature as *The Prelude* describes it. The general conclusion of this passage, that it is to youth's advantage to solve its own moral problems, and thus to acquire that clarity of vision which comes from seeing through one's own errors (500–49), leads Wordsworth to the rejection of Mathetes's request for a moral instructor such as himself.

Wordsworth's prose in this essay seems to have caught, either by design or accident, something of the intonation of Wilson and Blair's original paper. Thus the device of a series of nouns of the same grammatical value, all similarly qualified, as in *R.M.* 314–16: 'paths which . . . recesses which . . . beauty which . . . pathos which . . . sublimity to which'; or in *R.M.* 343–7: 'pleasures lying . . . as . . . Knowledge inhaled . . . like . . . dispositions stealing . . . like . . . images . . . rising up like . . . hopes plucked like . . .'—can be found in Mathetes, § 9: 'a perpetual acquisition . . . an unceasing progress . . . a perpetual unfolding'; § 11: 'Hope realizing . . . Ignorance dazzled . . . Power awakened . . . Enthusiasm kindling'; and cf. also § 14: 'There may be intellectual indolence' etc.; 'A reluctance to embrace' etc.; § 15: 'There are pleasures' etc. Note also the similarity in sentence-shape between *R.M.* 220–5: 'For Youth has [various qualities]; and, above all, Youth is rich' etc.; and Mathetes, § 15: 'There are pleasures . . . there are pursuits . . . above all there is' etc.

INTRODUCTION: TEXTUAL

THE *Reply to Mathetes* appeared first in *The Friend*, Nos. 17 and 20 (14 December 1809 and 4 January 1810). This printed text is manifestly in error from time to time (see especially textual notes to 281, 358, 413, 470, 513–20), and our text is therefore taken, as far as possible, from the incomplete manuscript of *The Friend* in the Forster collection, Victoria and Albert Museum (Forster MS. 112), in the hand of Mary Wordsworth. For a description of the manuscript see *The Friend*, ed. Barbara E. Rooke (London, 1969), ii. 379–87; we distinguish the first series of folios in the manuscript by the prefix 'Letters'. Deficiencies in the manuscript have been supplied from *The Friend*, as noted in our apparatus. The larger part of the text occurs on fs. 81–86ᵛ of the manuscript, beginning with cancelled passage [b] recorded in 207–8, textual n.; the replacement for this cancelled passage appears on Letters, f. 8, which also supplies lines 160–3 of our text ('The remarks . . . illustration.'), in the following terms:

(y)

Mr Brown,

    Sir

        The Sheet marked B has been received, and the Manuscript is in the following manner to be resumed.

THE FRIEND No 20

    The remarks, which [*etc., as text, as far as*] content the mind" &c as in the Manuscript and to proceed to the words "degrade that mind." (being the last of slip of paper marked 19).

    degrade that mind.

    But let me [*etc., as text, as far as*] fatal effects" &c as in the old Mss.—

The 'Sheet marked B' is f. 81 of the manuscript, which seems to have been returned by 'Mr Brown' (the printer of *The Friend*) to the author for emendation. The 'slip of paper marked 19' is f. 87 of the manuscript, containing lines 188–206 of our text ('has been . . . that mind.'), followed by cancelled passage [a] recorded in 207–8, textual n.; before the cancellation is an inserted instruction referring Brown to the letter 'marked y', i.e. Letters, f. 8 of the manuscript, cited above.

    These cancellations and replacements show that Wordsworth originally intended to conclude the first instalment of his essay with

f. 87 (including cancelled passage [a] and omitting, of course, the present lines 160–3 ['The remarks . . . illustration.']), and to begin the second instalment with cancelled passage [b]. He overestimated the space available to him for his first instalment in *The Friend*, No. 17, and had to make adjustments accordingly.[1]

On f. 88 of the manuscript appear instructions, ignored by Brown, for correcting lines 513–20:

> Mr Brown is requested to substitute the following for a sentence which he will find towards the latter part of the second sheet of the Essay marked No 18—which Essay begins with the words "In answer to the letter of Mathetes"—the sentence alluded to begins "In fact there are no conclusions relating to points which in any stage of life could admit of a doubt" for which print as follows "We may safely [*etc., as text, as far as*] for ever. Range &c."

See 513–20, textual n. On this page and on fs. 88–9 of the manuscript are early and emended drafts of *Epitaphs from Chiabrera*, VIII and IX, on which see W. J. B. Owen, 'Manuscript Variants of Wordsworth's Poems', *N. & Q.* cciii (1958), 308–10. On f. 89^v of the manuscript are instructions for correcting *R.M.* 636–43:

> The latter part of the *concluding* sentence of the Essay print thus. "when, in his character [*etc., as text, as far as*] Awful Power &c. *omit*[*t*]*ing* the *three preceeding* Stanzas—*omit* also the name at the end of the [? quotation].

Our apparatus records all emendations of importance which appear in the manuscript, and all variations between the manuscript and *The Friend*, Nos. 17 and 20. We find no evidence that the text of *R.M.* in later editions of *The Friend* has any Wordsworthian authority, and these editions have therefore been ignored in establishing the text.

---

[1] Miss Rooke's description of f. 87 as an 'insertion . . . in No 20' (ii. 385) is thus misleading in so far as it suggests that this passage is an afterthought.

[REPLY TO 'MATHETES']

THE Friend might rest satisfied that his exertions thus far have not
been wholly unprofitable, if no other proof had been given of their
influence, than that of having called forth the foregoing Letter, with
which he has been so much interested, that he could not deny himself
the pleasure of communicating it to his Readers.—In answer to his   5
Correspondent, it need scarcely here be repeated, that one of the main
purposes of his work is to weigh, honestly and thoughtfully, the moral
worth and intellectual power of the Age in which we live; to ascertain
our gain and our loss; to determine what we are in ourselves positively,
and what we are compared with our Ancestors; and thus, and by every   10
other means within his power, to discover what may be hoped for
future times, what and how lamentable are the evils to be feared, and
how far there is cause for fear. If this attempt should not be made
wholly in vain, my ingenuous Correspondent, and all who are in a
state of mind resembling that of which he gives so lively a picture, will   15
be enabled more readily and surely to distinguish false from legitimate
objects of admiration: and thus may the personal errors which he
would guard against, be more effectually prevented or removed, by
the developement of general truth for a general purpose, than by instructions specifically adapted to himself or to the Class of which he is   20
the able Representative. There is a life and spirit in knowledge which
we extract from truths scattered for the benefit of all, and which the
mind, by its own activity, has appropriated to itself—a life and a spirit,
which is seldom found in knowledge communicated by formal and
direct precepts, even when they are exalted and endeared by reverence   25
and love for the Teacher.

Nevertheless, though I trust that the assistance which my Correspondent has done me the honour to request, will in course of time
flow naturally from my labours, in a manner that will best serve him,
I cannot resist the inclination to connect, at present, with his Letter a   30
few remarks of direct application to the subject of it—*remarks*, I say,
for to such I shall confine myself, independent of the main point out of
which his complaint and request both proceed, I mean the assumed
inferiority of the present Age in moral dignity and intellectual power,
to those which have preceded it. For if the fact were true, that we had   35
even surpassed our Ancestors in the best of what is good, the main
part of the dangers and impediments which my Correspondent has

1–159 The Friend . . . *continued.*)] *From* The Friend, *pp. 268–72, which provides no
title: missing from* MS.

feelingly pourtrayed, could not cease to exist for minds like his, nor
indeed would they be much diminished; as they arise out of the Constitution of things, from the nature of Youth, from the laws that govern 40
the growth of the Faculties, and from the necessary condition of the
great body of Mankind. Let us throw ourselves back to the age of
Elizabeth, and call up to mind the Heroes, the Warriors, the Statesmen, the Poets, the Divines, and the Moral Philosophers, with which
the reign of the Virgin Queen was illustrated. Or if we be more 45
strongly attracted by the moral purity and greatness, and that sanctity
of civil and religious duty, with which the Tyranny of Charles the first
was struggled against, let us cast our eyes, in the hurry of admiration,
round that circle of glorious Patriots—but do not let us be persuaded,
that each of these, in his course of discipline, was uniformly helped 50
forward by those with whom he associated, or by those whose care it
was to direct him. Then as now existed objects, to which the wisest
attached undue importance; then as now judgment was misled by
factions and parties—time wasted in controversies fruitless, except as
far as they quickened the faculties; then as now Minds were venerated 55
or idolized, which owed their influence to the weakness of their
Contemporaries rather than to their own power. Then, though great
Actions were wrought, and great works in literature and science
produced, yet the general taste was capricious, fantastical, or grovel-
ling: and in this point as in all others, was Youth subject to delusion, 60
frequent in proportion to the liveliness of the sensibility, and strong
as the strength of the imagination. Every Age hath abounded in
instances of Parents, Kindred, and Friends, who, by indirect influence
of example, or by positive injunction and exhortation have diverted or
discouraged the Youth, who, in the simplicity and purity of Nature, 65
had determined to follow his intellectual genius through good and
through evil, and had devoted himself to knowledge, to the practice of
Virtue and the preservation of integrity, in slight of temporal rewards.
Above all, have not the common duties and cares of common life, at all
times exposed Men to injury, from causes whose action is the more 70
fatal from being silent and unremitting, and which, wherever it was
not jealously watched and steadily opposed, must have pressed upon
and consumed the diviner spirit?

    There are two errors, into which we easily slip when thinking of
past times. One lies in forgetting, in the excellence of what remains, 75
the large overbalance of worthlessness that has been swept away.
Ranging over the wide tracts of Antiquity, the situation of the Mind
may be likened to that of a Traveller* in some unpeopled part of

* Vide Ashe's Travels in America.

---

73 spirit? *Edd.*: spirit. *Friend.*

America, who is attracted to the burial place of one of the primitive Inhabitants. It is conspicuous upon an eminence, "a mount upon a mount!" He digs into it, and finds that it contains the bones of a Man of mighty stature: and he is tempted to give way to a belief, that as there were Giants in those days, so that all Men were Giants. But a second and wiser thought may suggest to him, that this Tomb would never have forced itself upon his notice, if it had not contained a Body that was distinguished from others, that of a Man who had been selected as a Chieftain or Ruler for the very reason that he surpassed the rest of his Tribe in stature, and who now lies thus conspicuously inhumed upon the mountain-top, while the bones of his Followers are laid unobtrusively together in their burrows upon the Plain below. The second habitual error is, that in this comparison of Ages we divide time merely into past and present, and place these in the balance to be weighed against each other, not considering that the present is in our estimation not more than a period of thirty years, or half a century at most, and that the past is a mighty accumulation of many such periods, perhaps the whole of recorded time, or at least the whole of that portion of it in which our own Country has been distinguished. We may illustrate this by the familiar use of the words Ancient and Modern, when applied to Poetry—what can be more inconsiderate or unjust than to compare a few existing Writers with the whole succession of their Progenitors? The delusion, from the moment that our thoughts are directed to it, seems too gross to deserve mention; yet Men will talk for hours upon Poetry, balancing against each other the words Ancient and Modern, and be unconscious that they have fallen into it.

These observations are not made as implying a dissent from the belief of my Correspondent, that the moral spirit and intellectual powers of this Country are declining; but to guard against *unqualified* admiration, even in cases where admiration has been rightly fixed, and to prevent that depression, which must necessarily follow, where the notion of the peculiar unfavourableness of the present times to dignity of mind, has been carried too far. For in proportion as we imagine obstacles to exist out of ourselves to retard our progress, will, in fact, our progress be retarded.—Deeming then, that in all ages an ardent mind will be baffled and led astray in the manner under contemplation, though in various degrees, I shall at present content myself with a few practical and desultory comments upon some of those general causes, to which my Correspondent justly attributes the errors in opinion, and the lowering or deadening of sentiment, to which ingenuous and aspiring Youth is exposed. And first, for the heart-cheering belief in the perpetual progress of the Species towards a point of unattainable perfection. If the present Age do indeed transcend the past in what is most beneficial and honorable, he that perceives this, being in no error, has no cause for complaint; but if it be not so, a Youth of genius might, it should seem, be preserved from any wrong influence of this faith, by an insight into a simple truth, namely, that it is not necessary, 125 in order to satisfy the desires of our Nature, or to reconcile us to the economy of Providence, that there should be at all times a continuous advance in what is of highest worth. In fact it is not, as a Writer of the present day has admirably observed, in the power of fiction, to pourtray in words, or of the imagination to conceive in spirit, Actions or 130 Characters of more exalted virtue, than those which thousands of years ago have existed upon earth, as we know from the records of authentic history. Such is the inherent dignity of human nature, that there belong to it sublimities of virtue which all men may attain, and which no man can transcend: And, though this be not true in an equal degree, of 135 intellectual power, yet in the persons of Plato, Demosthenes, and Homer,—and in those of Shakespeare, Milton, and lord Bacon,— were enshrined as much of the divinity of intellect as the inhabitants of this planet can hope will ever take up its abode among them. But the question is not of the power or worth of individual Minds, but of the 140 general moral or intellectual merits of an Age—or a People, or of the human Race. Be it so—let us allow and believe that there is a progress in the Species towards unattainable perfection, or whether this be so or not, that it is a necessity of a good and greatly gifted Nature to believe it—surely it does not follow, that this progress 145 should be constant in those virtues, and intellectual qualities, and in those departments of knowledge, which in themselves absolutely considered are of most value—things independant and in their degree indispensible. The progress of the Species neither is nor can be like that of a Roman road in a right line. It may be more justly compared to 150 that of a River, which both in its smaller reaches and larger turnings, is frequently forced back towards its fountains, by objects which cannot otherwise be eluded or overcome; yet with an accompanying impulse that will ensure its advancement hereafter, it is either gaining strength every hour, or conquering in secret some difficulty, by a labour that 155 contributes as effectually to further it in its course, as when it moves forward uninterrupted in a line, direct as that of the Roman road with which we began the comparison.

(*To be continued.*)

The remarks, which were called forth by the letter of Mathetes, 160 given in the 17th Number, concluded with a comparison of the progress of the human race to that of a river. We will now resume the subject, carrying on the same illustration. It suffices to content the mind, though there may be an apparent stagnation, or a retrograde movement in the Species, that something is doing which is necessary to be done, and 165 the effects of which, will in due time appear;—that something is unremittingly gaining, either in secret preparation or in open and triumphant progress. But in fact here, as every where, we are deceived by creations which the mind is compelled to make for itself: we speak of the Species not as an aggregate, but as endued with the form and 170 separate life of an Individual. But human kind, what is it else than myriads of rational beings in various degrees obedient to their Reason; some torpid, some aspiring, some in eager chace to the right hand, some to the left; these wasting down their moral nature, and those feeding it for immortality? A whole generation may appear even to 175 sleep, or may be exasperated with rage—they that compose it, tearing each other to pieces with more than brutal fury. It is enough for complacency and hope, that scattered and solitary minds are always labouring somewhere in the service of truth and virtue; and that by the sleep of the multitude, the energy of the multitude may be pre- 180 pared; and that by the fury of the people, the chains of the people may be broken. Happy moment was it for England when her Chaucer, who has rightly been called the morning star of her literature, appeared above the horizon—when her Wickliff, like the Sun, "shot orient beams" through the night of Romish superstition!—Yet may the dark- 185 ness and the desolating hurricane which immediately followed in the wars of York and Lancaster, be deemed in their turn a blessing, with which the Land has been visited.

May I return to the thought of progress, of accumulation, of increasing light or of any other image by which it may please us to represent 190 the improvement of the Species? The hundred years that followed the Usurpation of Henry the fourth, were a hurling-back of the mind of the Country, a delapidation, an extinction; yet institutions, laws, customs and habits, were then broken down, which would not have been so readily, nor perhaps so thoroughly destroyed by the gradual 195 influence of increasing knowledge; and under the oppression of which, if they had continued to exist, the Virtue and intellectual Prowess of the succeeding Century could not have appeared at all, much less could they have displayed themselves with that eager haste and with those beneficent triumphs which will to the end of time be looked back 200 upon with admiration and gratitude.

If the foregoing obvious distinctions be once clearly perceived, and

---

163–88 It suffices . . . the Land] *From* The Friend, *p. 305: missing from* MS.
198 could MS.²: would MS.   202 the foregoing . . . distinctions MS.²: this
. . . distinction to which I have adverted MS.

steadily kept in view,—I do not see why a belief in the progress of human Nature towards perfection should dispose a youthful Mind however enthusiastic to an undue admiration of his own Age, and thus 205 tend to degrade that mind.

But let me strike at once at the root of the evil complained of in my Correspondent's Letter.—Protection from any fatal effect of seductions and hindrances which opinion may throw in the way of pure and high-minded Youth can only be obtained with certainty at the same price 210 by which every thing great and good is obtained, namely, steady dependence upon voluntary and self-originating effort, and upon the practice of self-examination sincerely aimed at and rigourously enforced. But how is this to be expected from Youth? Is it not to demand the fruit when the blossom is barely put forth and is hourly at the mercy 215 of the frosts and winds? To expect from Youth these virtues and habits in that degree of excellence to which in mature years they *may* be carried would indeed be preposterous. Yet has Youth many helps and aptitudes, for the discharge of these difficult duties, which are with-drawn for the most part from the more advanced stages of Life. For 220 Youth has its own wealth and independence; it is rich in health of Body and animal Spirits, in its sensibility to the impressions of the natural Universe, in the conscious growth of Knowledge, in lively sympathy and familiar communion with the generous actions recorded in History and with the high passions of Poetry; and, above all, Youth is rich 225 in the possession of Time, and the accompanying consciousness of Freedom and Power. The Young Man feels that he stands at a distance from the Season when his harvest is to be reaped,—that he has Leisure and may look around—may defer both the choice and the execution of his purposes. If he makes an attempt and shall fail, new hopes im- 230 mediately rush in and new promises. Hence, in the happy confidence of

204 should MS.²: should [? necessarily] MS.   207–8 But let me . . . Letter.] *This sentence* (MS., *Letters, f. 8*) *replaces two deleted passages*:

[a; MS., f. 87] And assuredly little evil is to be apprehended from this quarter in a case like that of my Correspondent, who seems well aware of the many causes within and without [out MS.²] of himself, which are at work to check or turn him out of [from MS.²] that course which he feels was by Nature marked out [appointed MS.²] for him and along which he knows that it is his duty to advance.—But I must refer to [*To be continued* del.] [a future occasion *del.*] the rest of the remarks which I wished arising out of my Correspondents Letter to a future occasion.   MM

[b; MS., f. 81]   THE FRIEND No. 18
In answer to the letter of Mathetes, given in my last Number but one, I attempted to lop off one of the main branches from the evil which overshadowed [he described as overshadowing MS.²] his mind, and, if through want of skill too much time was employed in this service, I will now endeavour to make him and the general Reader amends by striking at the root of the tree at [? once].
216 of the frosts MS.: of frosts *Friend*.   218 preposterous MS.²: absurd and monstrous MS.   230 shall fail MS.²: have failed MS.   231–2 happy . . . Spirit MS.²: happiness of his Spirit MS.

his feelings and in the elasticity of his Spirit, neither worldly ambition, nor the love of praise nor dread of censure, nor the necessity of worldly maintenance, nor any of those causes which tempt or compel the mind habitually to look out of itself for support; neither these, nor the 235 passions of envy, fear, hatred, despondency, and the rankling of disappointed hopes (all which in after life give birth to and regulate the efforts of Men and determine their opinions)—have power to preside over the choice of the Young, if the disposition be not naturally bad, or the circumstances have not been in an uncommon degree unfavourable. 240

In contemplation, then, of this disinterested and free condition of the Youthful mind, I deem it in many points peculiarly capable of searching into itself, and of profiting by a few simple questions—such as these that follow. Am I chiefly gratified by the exertion of my power from the pure pleasure of intellectual activity, and from the knowledge 245 thereby acquired? In other words, to what degree do I value my faculties and my attainments for their own sakes? or are they chiefly prized by me on account of the distinction which they confer, or the superiority which they give me over others? Am I aware that immediate influence and a general acknowledgment of merit are no 250 necessary adjuncts of a successful adherence to study and meditation, in those departments of knowledge which are of most value to mankind?—that a recompence of honours and emoluments is far less to be expected—in fact, that there is little natural connection between them? Have I perceived this truth?—and, perceiving it, does the countenance 255 of philosophy continue to appear as bright and beautiful in my eyes?— has no haze bedimmed it? has no cloud passed over and hidden from me that look which was before so encouraging? Knowing that it is my duty, and feeling that it is my inclination, to mingle as a social Being with my fellow Men; prepared also to submit chearfully to the neces- 260 sity that will probably exist of relinquishing, for the purpose of gaining a livelihood, the greatest portion of my time to employments where I shall have little or no choice how or when I am to act; have I, at this moment, when I stand as it were upon the threshold of the busy world, a clear intuition of that preeminence in which virtue and truth (involv- 265 ing in this latter word the sanctities of religion) sit enthroned above all dominations and dignities which, in various degrees of exaltation, rule over the desires of Men?—Do I feel that, if their solemn Mandates shall be forgotten, or disregarded, or denied the obedience due to them when opposed to others, I shall not only have lived for no good 270 purpose, but that I shall have sacrificed my birth-right as a Rational

247 attainments MS.²: Knowledge MS.   254 little MS.²: no MS.
258 encouraging MS.²: gracious MS.   265 a clear MS.²: such a clear MS.
266 the sanctities MS.²: all the sanctities MS.

being; and that every other acquisition will be a bane and a disgrace to me? This is not spoken with reference to such sacrifices as present themselves to the Youthful imagination in the shape of crimes, acts by which the conscience is violated; such a thought, I know, would be recoiled from at once not without indignation; but I write in the Spirit of the ancient fable of Prodicus, representing the choice of Hercules.—Here is the WORLD, a female figure approaching at the head of a train of willing or giddy followers:—her air and deportment are at once careless, remiss, self-satisfied, and haughty:—and there is INTELLECTUAL PROWESS, with a pale cheek and severe brow, leading in chains Truth, her beautiful and modest Captive. The One makes her salutation with a discourse of ease, pleasure, freedom, and domestic tranquillity; or, if she invite to labour, it is labour in the busy and beaten track, with assurance of the complacent regards of Parents, Friends, and of those with whom we associate. The promise also may be upon her lip of the huzzas of the multitude, of the smile of Kings, and the munificent rewards of senates. The Other does not venture to hold forth any of these allurements; she does not conceal from him whom she addresses the impediments, the disappointments, the ignorance and prejudice which her Follower will have to encounter, if devoted, when duty calls, to active life; and if to contemplative, she lays nakedly before him a scheme of solitary and unremitting labour, a life of entire neglect perhaps, or assuredly a life exposed to scorn, insult, persecution, and hatred; but cheered by encouragement from a grateful few, by applauding Conscience, and by a prophetic anticipation, perhaps, of fame—a late though lasting consequence. Of these two, each in this manner soliciting you to become her Adherent, you doubt not which to prefer;—but oh! the thought of moment is not preference, but the *degree* of preference;—the passionate and pure choice, the inward sense of absolute and unchangeable devotion.

I spoke of a few simple questions—the question involved in this deliberation *is* simple; but at the same time it is high and awful: and I would gladly know whether an answer can be returned satisfactory to the mind.—We will for a moment suppose that it can not; that there is a startling and a hesitation.—Are we then to despond? to retire from all contest? and to reconcile ourselves at once to cares without generous hope, and to efforts in which there is no more Moral life than that which is found in the business and labours of the unfavoured and unaspiring Many? No—but, if the enquiry have not been on just grounds satisfactorily answered, we may refer confidently our Youth to that Nature of which he deems himself an enthusiastic follower, and one

275

280

285

290

295

300

305

310

281 severe MS.: serene *Friend.*   286–7 may be MS.²: is MS.   310 enquiry MS.²: question MS.

who wishes to continue no less faithful and enthusiastic.—We would tell him that there are paths which he has not trodden; recesses which he has not penetrated; that there is a beauty which he has not seen— 315 a pathos which he has not felt—a sublimity to which he hath not been raised. If he have trembled, because there has occasionally taken place in him a lapse of which he is conscious; if he foresee open or secret attacks which he has had intimations that he will neither be strong enough to resist, nor watchful enough to elude, let him not hastily 320 ascribe this weakness, this deficiency, and the painful apprehensions accompanying them, in any degree to the virtues or noble qualities with which Youth by Nature is furnished; but let him first be assured, before he looks about for the means of attaining the insight, the discriminating powers, and the confirmed wisdom of Manhood, that his 325 soul has more to demand of the appropriate excellences of Youth than Youth has yet supplied to it;—that the evil under which he labours is not a superabundance of the instincts and the animating spirit of that age, but a falling short, or a failure.—But what can he gain from this admonition? he cannot recal past time; he cannot begin his journey 330 afresh; he cannot untwist the links by which, in no undelightful harmony, images and sentiments are wedded in his mind. Granted that the sacred light of Childhood is and must be for him no more than a remembrance. He may, notwithstanding, be remanded to Nature; and with trust-worthy hopes; founded less upon his sentient than upon 335 his intellectual Being—to Nature, not as leading on insensibly to the society of Reason; but to Reason and Will, as leading back to the wisdom of Nature. A re-union, in this order accomplished, will bring reformation and timely support; and the two powers of Reason and Nature, thus reciprocally teacher and taught, may advance together 340 in a track to which there is no limit.

We have been discoursing (by implication at least) of Infancy, Childhood, Boyhood, and Youth—of pleasures lying upon the unfolding Intellect plenteously as morning dew-drops—of Knowledge inhaled insensibly like a fragrance—of dispositions stealing into the 345 Spirit like Music from unknown quarters—of images uncalled for and rising up like exhalations—of hopes plucked like beautiful wild flowers from the ruined tombs that border the high-ways of Antiquity to make a garland for a living forehead;—in a word, we have been treating of

332 *After* mind. MS. *deletes*: Aurora for him has risen, she has mounted her Car, the Clouds have coloured round the radiant Goddess—[? and] he has seen the Hours dance hand in hand before him [her MS.²], strewing the path with roses; he has seen the bright Company, and for him they are no longer in the Sky. Granted that the jocund and brief time is past—this gladness, this freshness, and this unsullied purity; and, if we must [may MS.²] speak of what we ourselves have felt [? and remember]

Nature as a Teacher of Truth through joy and through gladness, and 350
as a Creatress of the faculties by a process of smoothness and delight.
We have made no mention of fear, shame, sorrow, nor of ungovernable
and vexing thoughts; because, although these have been and have done
mighty service, they are overlooked in that stage of life when Youth is
passing into Manhood,—overlooked, or forgotten. We now apply for 355
succour, which we need, to a faculty that works after a different course:
that faculty is Reason: she gives much spontaneously but she seeks for
more; she works by thought, through feeling; yet in thought she
begins and ends.

A familiar incident may elucidate this contrast in the operations of 360
Nature, may render plain the manner in which a process of intellectual
improvement, the reverse of that which Nature pursues is by Reason
introduced.—There never perhaps existed a School-boy who, having
when he retired to rest carelessly blown out his candle, and having
chanced to notice as he lay upon his bed in the ensuing darkness the 365
sullen light which had survived the extinguished flame, did not, at
some time or other, watch that light as if his mind were bound to it by
a spell. It fades and revives—gathers to a point—seems as if it would
go out in a moment—again recovers its strength, nay becomes brighter
than before: it continues to shine with an endurance which in its 370
apparent weakness is a mystery—it protracts its existence so long,
clinging to the power which supports it, that the Observer, who had
lain down in his bed so easy-minded, becomes sad and melancholy:
his sympathies are touched—it is to him an intimation and an image
of departing human life;—the thought comes nearer to him—it is the 375
life of a venerated Parent, of a beloved Brother or Sister, or of an aged
Domestic; who are gone to the grave, or whose destiny it soon may be
thus to linger, thus to hang upon the last point of mortal existence,
thus finally to depart and be seen no more—This is Nature teaching
seriously and sweetly through the affections—melting the heart, and 380
through that instinct of tenderness, developing the understanding.—In
this instance the object of solicitude is the bodily life of another. Let us
accompany this same Boy to that period between Youth and Manhood
when a solicitude may be awakened for the moral life of himself.—Are
there any powers by which, beginning with a sense of inward decay 385
that affects not however the natural life, he could call up to mind the
same image and hang over it with an equal interest as a visible type
of his own perishing Spirit?—Oh! surely, if the being of the individual

---

356 succour, which MS.: succour which *Friend.*   358 in thought MS.: in
thoughts *Friend.*   360 operations MS.[2]: processes MS.   361–3 may
. . . introduced MS.[2]: MS. *illegible.*   362 improvement MS.: improvements
Friend.   366 flame MS.[2]: taper MS.   382 is MS.[2]: is awakened for
MS.   bodily MS.[2]: moral MS.   384 may be MS.[2]: is MS.

be under his own care—if it be his first care—if duty begin from the
point of accountableness to our Conscience, and, through that, to God   390
and human Nature;—if without such primary sense of duty, all
secondary care of Teacher, of Friend, or Parent, must be baseless and
fruitless; if, lastly, the motions of the Soul transcend in worth those of
the animal functions, nay give to them their sole value; then truly are
there such powers: and the image of the dying taper may be recalled   395
and contemplated, though with no sadness in the nerves, no disposition
to tears, no unconquerable sighs, yet with a melancholy in the soul,
a sinking inward into ourselves from thought to thought, a steady
remonstrance, and a high resolve.—Let then the Youth go back, as
occasion will permit, to Nature and to Solitude, thus admonished by   400
Reason, and relying upon this newly-acquired support. A world of
fresh sensations will gradually open upon him as his mind puts off its
infirmities, and as instead of being propelled restlessly towards others
in admiration or too hasty love, he makes it his prime business to
understand himself. New sensations, I affirm, will be opened out—   405
pure, and sanctioned by that reason which is their original Author:
and precious feelings of disinterested, that is self-disregarding, joy and
love may be regenerated and restored:—and, in this sense, he may be
said to measure back the track of life which he has trod.

In such disposition of mind let the Youth return to the visible   410
Universe; and to conversation with ancient Books; and to those, if
such there be, which in the present day breathe the ancient spirit: and
let him feed upon that beauty which unfolds itself, not to his eye as it
sees carelessly the things which cannot possibly go unseen and are
remembered or not as accident shall decide, but to the thinking mind;   415
which searches, discovers, and treasures up,—infusing by meditation
into the objects with which it converses an intellectual life; whereby
they remain planted in the memory, now, and for ever. Hitherto the
Youth, I suppose, has been content, for the most part, to look at his
own mind after the manner in which he ranges along the Stars in the   420
firmament with naked unaided sight: Let him now apply the telescope
of Art—to call the invisible Stars out of their hiding-places; and let
him endeavour to look through the system of his Being, with the organ
of Reason; summoned to penetrate, as far as it has power, in discovery
of the impelling forces and the governing laws.   425

389 be under MS.²: is under MS.   400 admonished MS.²: instructed and MS.
409 which he MS.: he *Friend*.   410 such disposition MS.²: this frame MS.
413 not to his eye MS.²: to his eye not MS.: *not* to his eye *Friend*.
419 been . . . at MS.²: looked at MS.   421 naked MS.²: the naked MS.
unaided sight MS.²: and unassisted eye MS.   423 system MS.²: whole
system MS.   Being MS.²: mind MS.   424–9 summoned . . . repose
MS.³: to whose power of [? penetration within limits] it can be [? assumed] [?] are
laid open the impelling [? forces] and the governing laws. These [?] are not

These expectations are not immoderate: they demand nothing more than the perception of a few plain truths; namely that Knowledge efficacious for the production of virtue, is the ultimate end of all effort, the sole dispenser of complacency and repose. A perception also is implied of the inherent superiority of Contemplation to Action. The FRIEND does not in this contradict his own words, where he has said heretofore, that "doubtless it is nobler to Act than to Think." In those words, it was his purpose to censure that barren Contemplation which rests satisfied with itself in cases where the thoughts are of such quality that they may be, and ought to be, embodied in Action. But he speaks now of the general superiority of thought to action;—as preceeding and governing all action that moves to salutary purposes: and, secondly, as leading to elevation, the absolute possession of the individual mind, and to a consistency or harmony of the Being within itself which no outward agency can reach, to disturb, or to impair:—and lastly, as producing works of pure science, or of the combined faculties of imagination, feeling, and reason;—works which, both from their independence in their origin upon accident, their nature, their duration, and the wide spread of their influence, are entitled rightly to take place of the noblest and most beneficent deeds of Heroes, Statesmen, Legislators, or Warriors.

Yet, beginning from the perception of this established superiority, we do not suppose that the Youth, whom we wish to guide and encourage, is to be insensible to those influences of Wealth, or Rank, or Station, by which the bulk of Mankind are swayed. Our eyes have not been fixed upon virtue which lies apart from human Nature, or transcends it. In fact there is no such Virtue. We neither suppose nor wish him to undervalue or slight these distinctions as modes of power, things that may enable him to be more useful to his Contemporaries; nor as gratifications that may confer dignity upon his living person; and, through him, upon those who love him; nor as they may connect his name, through a Family to be founded by his success, in a closer chain of gratitude with some portion of posterity; who shall speak of him, as among their Ancestry, with a more tender interest than the mere general bond of patriotism or humanity would supply. We suppose no

430
435
440
445
450
455
460

immoderate; they demand nothing more than the perception of a few simple [plain MS.²] truths; namely, that Knowledge [? in] which must be included [?] is [?]te end of all effort, the sole dis[?] of complacency and [?] MS.

431 in this MS.²: here MS.   433 purpose MS.²: object MS.   434 such MS.²: that MS.   435–6 he speaks MS.²: [? I speak] MS.   439–40 and to a . . . agency MS.²: which no outward violence MS.   440 disturb MS.²: destroy MS.   441 producing MS.²: producing [? outwardly] MS.   452 Virtue MS.²: Virtue; there may be [? holiness] or [? beatitude] for [? Christians but] there is no such Virtue for [? Men *or* ? Man] MS.   454 things MS.²: [? or] things MS.   455 gratifications that MS.²: they MS.   456 who MS.²: who may MS.

indifference to, much less a contempt of, these rewards; but let them have their due place; let it be ascertained, when the Soul is searched into, that they are only an auxiliary motive to exertion, never the principal or originating force. If this be too much to expect from a Youth who, I take for granted, possesses no ordinary endowments, 465 and whom circumstances with respect to the more dangerous passions have favoured, then, indeed, must the noble Spirit of the Country be wasted away: then would our Institutions be deplorable; and the Education prevalent among us utterly vile and debasing.

But the Correspondent, who drew forth these thoughts, has said 470 rightly that the character of the age may not without injustice be thus branded: he will not deny that, without speaking of other Countries, there is in these Islands, in the departments of Natural philosophy, of mechanic ingenuity, in the general activities of the country, and in the particular excellence of individual Minds in high Stations civil or 475 military, enough to excite admiration and love in the sober-minded, & more than enough to intoxicate the Youthful and inexperienced.— I will compare, then, an aspiring Youth, leaving the Schools in which he has been disciplined, and preparing to bear a part in the concerns of the World, I will compare him in this season of eager admiration, to a 480 newly-invested Knight appearing with his blank unsignalized Shield, upon some day of solemn tournament, at the Court of the Faery-Queen, as that Sovereignty was conceived to exist by the moral and imaginative genius of our divine Spenser. He does not himself immediately enter the lists as a Combatant, but he looks round him with a beating heart; 485 dazzled by the gorgeous pageantry, the banners, the impresses, the Ladies of overcoming beauty, the Persons of the Knights—now first seen by him, the fame of whose actions is carried by the Traveller, like Merchandize, through the World; and resounded upon the harp of the Minstrel.—But I am not at liberty to make this comparison. If a Youth 490 were to begin his career in such an Assemblage, with such examples to guide and to animate, it will be pleaded, there would be no cause for apprehension: he could not falter, he could not be misled. But ours is, notwithstanding its manifold excellences, a degenerate Age: and recreant Knights are among us, far outnumbering the true. A false 495 Gloriana in these days imposes worthless services, which they who perform them, in their blindness, know not to be such; and which are recompenced by rewards as worthless—yet eagerly grasped at, as if they were the immortal guerdon of Virtue.

I have in this declaration insensibly overstepped the limits which I 500

461 rewards MS.²: collateral rewards MS.   463 auxil[i]ary MS.²: accessary and additional MS.   465 possesses MS.²: is of MS.   470 the MS.²: my MS., *Friend.*

had determined not to pass:—let me be forgiven; for it is hope which hath carried me forward. In such a mixed assemblage as our age presents, with its genuine merit and its large overbalance of alloy, I may boldly ask into what errors, either with respect to Person or Thing, could a young Man fall, who has sincerely entered upon the 505 course of moral discipline which has been recommended, and to which the condition of youth, it has been proved, is favourable? His opinions could no where deceive him beyond the point to which, after a season, he would find that it was salutary for him to have been deceived. For, as that Man cannot set a right value upon health who has never known 510 sickness, nor feel the blessing of ease who has been through his life a stranger to pain, so can there be no confirmed and passionate love of truth for him who has not experienced the hollowness of error. We may safely affirm that, in relation to subjects which could in any stage of life admit of a doubt, to points which can fairly be called matter of 515 speculation or opinion, there is nothing whereupon the Mind reposes with a confidence equal to that with which it rests on those conclusions, by which truths have been established the direct opposite of errours once rapturously cherished and which have been passed through and are rejected for ever.—Range against each other as Advocates, oppose 520 as Combatants, two several Intellects, each strenuously asserting doctrines which he sincerely believes; but the one contending for the worth and beauty of that garment which the other has outgrown and cast away. Mark the superiority, the ease, the dignity, on the side of the more advanced Mind; how he overlooks his Subject, commands it 525 from centre to circumference; and hath the same thorough knowledge of the tenets which his Adversary, with impetuous zeal, but in confusion also and thrown off his guard at every turn of the argument, is labouring to maintain! If it be a question of the fine Arts (Poetry for instance) the riper mind not only sees that his Opponent is deceived; 530 but, what is of far more importance, sees *how* he is deceived. The imagination stands before him with all its imperfections laid open; as duped by shews, enslaved by words, corrupted by mistaken delicacy and false refinement,—as not having even attended with care to the reports

502 our MS.²: this MS.   505 young Man MS.²: youth MS.   507 the condition of youth MS.²: his condition MS.   508 to which MS.²: [? up *or* ? at] MS.   513–20 We may . . . for ever. MS.³: In fact, there are no conclusions, relating to points which in any stage of life could admit of a doubt, there is nothing that can be fairly called matter of speculation or opinion, upon which the mind can so confidently repose as those truths which are the direct opposite of errors once rapturously cherished, and which have been passed through and are rejected for ever. MS.: MS.² *as* MS.³, *except:* 516 whereupon MS.³: upon MS.²; 517 equal to MS.³: [? as firm as] MS.²; on MS.³: upon MS.²; 519 rapturously MS.³: fondly MS.²; and (*first*) MS.³: and now MS.². *There is no version of this passage in* Friend.   526 circumference MS.²: circumstance MS.

of the senses, and therefore deficient grossly in the rudiments of her 535
own power. He has noted how, as a supposed necessary condition, the
Understanding sleeps in order that the Fancy may dream. Studied in
the history of Society, and versed in the secret laws of thought, he can
pass regularly through all the gradations, can pierce infallibly all the
windings, which false taste through ages has pursued,—from the very 540
time when first, through inexperience, heedlessness, or affectation,
she took her departure from the side of Truth, her original parent.—
Can a disputant thus accoutred be withstood?—to whom, further, every
movement in the thoughts of his Antagonist is revealed by the light of
his own experience; who, therefore, sympathises with weakness gently, 545
and wins his way by forbearance; and hath, when needful, an irresistible
power of onset,—arising from gratitude to the truth which he vindi-
cates, not merely as a positive good for Mankind, but as his own
especial rescue and redemption.

   I might here conclude: but my Correspondent toward the close of 550
his letter, has written so feelingly upon the advantages to be derived,
in his estimation, from a living Instructor, that I must not leave this
part of the Subject without a word of direct notice. The FRIEND cited
some time ago a passage from the prose works of Milton, eloquently
describing the manner in which good and evil grow up together in the 555
field of the World almost inseparably; and insisting, consequently,
upon the knowledge and survey of vice as necessary to the constituting
of human virtue, and the scanning of Error to the confirmation of
Truth. If this be so, and I have been reasoning to the same effect in the
preceeding paragraph, the fact, and the thoughts which it may suggest, 560
will, if rightly applied, tend to moderate an anxiety for the guidance of
a more experienced or superior Mind. The advantage, where it is
possessed, is far from being an absolute good: nay, such a preceptor,
ever at hand, might prove an oppression not to be thrown off, and a
fatal hindrance. Grant that in the general tenor of his intercourse with 565
his Pupil he is forbearing and circumspect, inasmuch as he is rich in
that Knowledge (above all other necessary for a teacher) which cannot
exist without a liveliness of memory, preserving for him an unbroken
image of the winding, excursive, and often retrograde course along
which his own intellect has passed. Grant that, furnished with these 570
distinct remembrances, he wishes that the mind of his pupil should be
free to luxuriate in the enjoyments, loves, and admirations appropriate
to its age; that he is not in haste to kill what he knows will in due time

536–7 as a . . . sleeps MS.[2]: the Understanding sleeps as a necessary condition
MS.   537 in order that MS.[2]: that MS.   541–2 through . . . took
MS.[2]: she took MS.   543 Can a MS.[2]: Can such a MS.   550 toward
MS.: towards *Friend*.   556 inseparably MS.[2]: [? inseparately] MS.
561 anxiety MS.[2]: unreasonable anxiety MS.

die of itself; or be transmuted, and put on a nobler form and higher faculties, otherwise unattainable. In a word, that the Teacher is 575 governed habitually by the wisdom of Patience, waiting with pleasure. Yet, perceiving how much the outward help of Art can facilitate the progress of Nature, he may be betrayed into many unnecessary or pernicious mistakes where he deems his interference warranted by substantial experience. And, in spite of all his caution, remarks may 580 drop insensibly from him which shall wither in the mind of his pupil a generous sympathy, destroy a sentiment of approbation or dislike not merely innocent but salutary; and, for the inexperienced Disciple how many pleasures may be thus cut off, what joy, what admiration, and what love! While in their stead are introduced into the ingenuous 585 mind misgivings, a mistrust of its own evidence, dispositions to affect to feel where there can be no real feeling, indecisive judgements, a superstructure of opinions that has no base to support it, and words uttered by rote with the impertinence of a Parrot or a Mocking-bird, yet which may not be listened to with the same indifference, as they 590 cannot be heard without some feeling of moral disapprobation.

These results I contend, whatever may be the benefit to be derived from such an enlightened Teacher, are in their degree inevitable. And, by this process, humility and docile dispositions may exist towards the Master, endued as he is with the power which personal presence 595 confers; but at the same time they will be liable to overstep their due bounds, and to degenerate into passiveness and prostration of mind. This towards him; while, with respect to other living Men, nay even to the mighty Spirits of past times, there may be associated with such weakness a want of modesty and humility. Insensibly may steal in 600 presumption and a habit of sitting in judgement in cases where no sentiment ought to have existed but diffidence or veneration. Such virtues are the sacred attributes of Youth: its appropriate calling is not to distinguish in the fear of being deceived or degraded, not to analyze with scrupulous minuteness, but to accumulate in genial confidence; 605 its instinct, its safety, its benefit, its glory, is to love, to admire, to feel, and to labour. Nature has irrevocably decreed that our prime dependence in all stages of life after Infancy and Childhood have been passed through (nor do I know that this latter ought to be excepted) must be upon our own minds; and that the way to knowledge shall be long, 61 difficult, winding, and often times returning upon itself.

576 Patience MS.²: Nature MS.   *579* interference MS.²: intercourse MS.
581 shall MS.²: may MS.   *603* its appropriate calling is MS.²: it is
called upon by Nature MS.   *611* difficult, winding MS.²: and difficult,
and winding MS.   *After* itself. MS. *deletes:*—The hound may be led forth
by the Hunter, be cheared by his voice, animated by his presence; but he must
follow perseveringly by his own scent: if, the moment he is at a loss or foiled, the

What has been said is a mere sketch; and that only of a part of the interesting Country into which we have been led; but my Correspondent will be able to enter the paths that have been pointed out. Should he do this and advance steadily for a while, he needs not fear any deviations from the truth which will be finally injurious to him. He will not long have his admiration fixed upon unworthy objects; he will neither be clogged nor drawn aside by the love of friends or kindred, betraying his understanding through his affections; he will neither be bowed down by conventional arrangements of manners producing too often a lifeless decency; nor will the rock of his Spirit wear away in the endless beating of the waves of the World: neither will that portion of his own time, which he must surrender to labours by which his livelihood is to be earned or his social duties performed, be unprofitable to himself indirectly, while it is directly useful to others: for that time has been primarily surrendered through an act of obedience to a moral law established by himself, and therefore he moves then also along the orbit of perfect liberty.

Let it be remembered that the advice requested does not relate to the government of the more dangerous passions, or to the fundamental principles of right and wrong as acknowledged by the universal Conscience of Mankind. I may therefore assure my Youthful Correspondent, if he will endeavour to look into himself in the manner which I have exhorted him to do, that in him the wish will be realized, to him in due time the prayer granted, which was uttered by that living Teacher of whom he speaks with gratitude as of a Benefactor when, in his character of Philosophical Poet, having thought of Morality as implying in its essence voluntary obedience, and producing the effect of order, he transfers, in the transport of imagination, the law of Moral to physical Natures, and, having contemplated, through the medium of that order, all modes of existence as subservient to one spirit, concludes his address to the power of Duty in the following words:

> To humbler functions, awful Power!
> I call thee: I myself commend

615

620

625

630

635

640

Hunter is [be MS.²] ready to step in, and, having seen the course which the Game took, lays the Dog close at its heels, the Chase is deemed dishonorable, and the instinct of the Dog [animal MS.²] will be impaired or destroyed.

614–15 Should he do . . . advance MS.²: If he does . . . advances MS. 622 neither MS.²: nor MS.   623 labours MS.²: the labours MS. 636–42 when . . . words MS.³: thinking of morality as implying in its essence voluntary obedience, he transfers, in the rapture of imagination, the law of morality [moral MS.²] to physical natures, and, contemplating all modes of existence as subservient to one harmony he addresses [concludes his address to MS.²] the Power of Duty in the following words.

Here follow, deleted, lines 33–56 of Ode to Duty, *as in* P.W. *iv. 85–6, with the following variants*: 37 tires MS.²: MS. *illegible*; 39 name MS.²: aim MS.; 40 long MS.²: look MS.; 43 Of my own inborn wish; nor doubt MS.; 48 breed MS.²: breathe MS.

Unto thy guidance from this hour; 645
Oh, let my weakness have an end!
Give unto me, made lowly wise,
The spirit of self-sacrifice;
The confidence of reason give;
And in the light of truth thy Bondman let me live! 650

ΛΛΛ

651 ΛΛ ΛΛ MS.²: Wordsworth MS.

APPENDIX

LETTER OF 'MATHETES' (JOHN WILSON) TO *THE FRIEND*

(From *The Friend*, No. 17 (14 December 1809), pp. 257–68)

To the Editor of the Friend.

Sir,

[1] I hope you will not ascribe to presumption, the liberty I take in addressing you, on the subject of your Work. I feel deeply interested in the cause you have undertaken to support; and my object in writing this letter is to describe to you, in part from my own feelings, what I conceive to be the state of many minds, which may derive important advantage from your instructions.

[2] I speak, Sir, of those who, though bred up under our unfavourable System of Education, have yet held at times some intercourse with Nature, and with those great minds whose works have been moulded by the Spirit of Nature: who, therefore, when they pass from the Seclusion and Constraint of early Study, bring with them into the new scene of the world, much of the pure sensibility which is the spring of all that is greatly good in thought and action. To such the season of that entrance into the world is a season of fearful importance; not for the seduction of it's passions, but of it's opinions. Whatever be their intellectual powers, unless extraordinary circumstances in their lives have been so favourable to the growth of meditative genius, that their speculative opinions must spring out of their early feelings, their Minds are still at the mercy of fortune: they have no inward impulse steadily to propel them: and must trust to the chances of the world for a guide. And such is our present moral and intellectual State, that these chances are little else than variety of danger. There will be a thousand causes conspiring to complete the work of a false Education, and by enclosing the mind on every side from the influences of natural feeling, to degrade its inborn dignity, and finally bring the heart itself under subjection to a corrupted understanding. I am anxious to describe to you what I have experienced or seen of the dispositions and feelings that will aid every other Cause of danger, and tend to lay the Mind open to the infection of all those falsehoods in opinion and sentiment, which constitute the degeneracy of the age.

[3] Though it would not be difficult to prove, that the mind of the Country is much enervated since the days of her strength, and brought down from its moral dignity, it is not yet so forlorn of all good,—there is nothing in the face of the times so dark and saddening, and repulsive—as to shock the first feelings of a generous Spirit, and drive it at once to seek refuge in the elder ages of our greatness. There yet survives so much of the character bred up through long years of liberty, danger, and glory,

that even what this age produces bears traces of those that are past, and it still yields enough of beautiful, and splendid, and bold, to captivate an ardent but untutored imagination. And in this real excellence is the beginning of danger: for it is the first spring of that excessive admiration of the age which at last brings down to its own level a mind born above it. If there existed only the general disposition of all who are formed with a high capacity for good, to be rather credulous of excellence than suspiciously and severely just, the error would not be carried far:—but there are, to a young Mind, in this Country and at this time, numerous powerful causes concurring to inflame this disposition, till the excess of the affection above the worth of its object, is beyond all computation. To trace these causes it will be necessary to follow the history of a pure and noble mind from the first moment of that critical passage from seclusion to the world, which changes all the circumstances of its intellectual existence, shews it for the first time the real scene of living men, and calls up the new feeling of numerous relations by which it is to be connected with them.

[4] To the young adventurer in life, who enters upon his course with such a mind, every thing seems made for delusion. He comes with a spirit whose dearest feelings and highest thoughts have sprung up under the influences of Nature. He transfers to the realities of life the high wild fancies of visionary boyhood: he brings with him into the world the passions of solitary and untamed imagination, and hopes which he has learned from dreams. Those dreams have been of the great and wonderful, and lovely, of all which in these has yet been disclosed to him: his thoughts have dwelt among the wonders of Nature, and among the loftiest spirits of Men—Heroes, and Sages, and Saints;—those whose deeds, and thoughts, and hopes, were high above ordinary Mortality, have been the familiar Companions of his soul. To love and to admire has been the joy of his existence. Love and admiration are the pleasures he will demand of the world. For these he has searched eagerly into the ages that are gone: but with more ardent and peremptory expectation he requires them of that in which his own lot is cast:—for to look on life with hopes of happiness is a necessity of his nature, and to him there is no happiness but such as is surrounded with excellence.

[5] See first how this spirit will affect his judgment of moral character, in those with whom chance may connect him in the common relations of life. It is of those with whom he is to live, that his Soul first demands this food of her desires. From their conversation, their looks, their actions, their lives, she asks for excellence. To ask from all and to* ask in vain, would be too dismal to bear*: it would disturb him too deeply with doubt and perplexity, and fear. In this hope, and in the revolting of his thoughts from the possibility of disappointment, there is a preparation for self-delusion: there is an unconscious determination that his soul shall be satisfied; an obstinate will to find good everywhere. And thus his first study of mankind is a continued effort to read in them the expression of his own feelings. He catches at every uncertain shew and shadowy resemblance of

* too . . . hear *Friend*.

what he seeks; and unsuspicious in innocence, he is first won with those appearances of good which are in fact only false pretensions. But this error is not carried far: for there is a sort of instinct of rectitude, which like the pressure of a talisman given to baffle the illusions of enchantment, warns a pure mind against hypocrisy.—There is another delusion more difficult to resist and more slowly dissipated. It is when he finds, as he often will, some of the real features of excellence in the purity of their native form. For then his rapid imagination will gather round them all the kindred features that are wanting to perfect beauty; and make for him, where he could not find, the moral creature of his expectation:—peopling, even from this human world, his little circle of affection, with forms as fair as his heart desired for its love.

[6] But when, from the eminence of life which he has reached, he lifts up his eyes, and sends out his spirit to range over the great scene that is opening before him and around him,—the whole prospect of civilized life— so wide and so magnificent:—when he begins to contemplate, in their various stations of power or splendour, the leaders of mankind—those men on whose wisdom are hung the fortunes of nations—those whose genius and valour wield the heroism of a people;—or those, in no inferior "pride of place," whose sway is over the Mind of Society,—Chiefs in the realm of Imagination.—Interpreters of the Secrets of Nature,—Rulers of Human Opinion—what wonder, when he looks on all this living scene, that his heart should burn with strong affection, that he should feel that his own happiness will be for ever interwoven with the interests of mankind?— Here then the sanguine hope with which he looks on life, will again be blended with his passionate desire of excellence; and he will still be im- pelled to single out some, on whom his imagination and his hopes may repose. To whatever department of human thought or action his mind is turned with interest, either by the sway of public passion or by its own impulse—among Statesmen, and Warriors, and Philosophers, and Poets, he will distinguish some favoured names on which he may satisfy his admiration. And there, just as in the little circle of his own acquaintance, seizing eagerly on every merit they possess, he will supply more from his own credulous hope, completing real with imagined excellence, till living men, with all their imperfections, become to him the representatives of his perfect ideal creation:—Till, multiplying his objects of reverence, as he enlarges his prospect of life, he will have surrounded himself with idols of his own hands, and his imagination will seem to discern a glory in the Countenance of the Age, which is but the reflection of its own effulgence.

[7] He will possess, therefore, in the creative power of generous hope, a preparation for illusory and exaggerated admiration of the age in which he lives:—and this predisposition will meet with many favouring circum- stances, when he has grown up under a System of Education like ours, which (as perhaps all Education must that is placed in the hands of a dis- tinct and embodied Class, who therefore bring to it the peculiar and hereditary prejudices of their Order) has controuled his imagination to a reverence of former times, with an unjust contempt of his own.—For no

sooner does he break loose from this Controul, and begin to feel, as he contemplates the world for himself, how much there is surrounding him on all sides, that gratifies his noblest desires, than there springs up in him an indignant sense of injustice, both to the age and to his own mind: and he is impelled warmly and eagerly to give loose to the feelings that have been held in bondage, to seek out and to delight in finding excellence that will vindicate the insulted world, while it justifies too, his resentment of his own undue subjection, and exalts the value of his new-found liberty.

[8] Add to this, that secluded as he has been from knowledge, and, in the imprisoning circle of one System of ideas, cut off from his share in the thoughts and feelings that are stirring among men, he finds himself, at the first steps of his liberty, in a new intellectual world. Passions and powers which he knew not of, start up in his Soul. The human Mind, which he had seen but under one aspect, now presents to him a thousand unknown and beautiful forms. He sees it, in its varying powers, glancing over Nature with restless curiosity, and with impetuous energy striving for ever against the barriers which she has placed around it; sees it with divine power creating from dark materials living beauty, and fixing all its high and transported fancies in imperishable forms.—In the world of Knowledge, and Science, and Art, and Genius, he treads as a stranger:—in the confusion of new sensations, bewildered in delights, all seems beautiful; all seems admirable. And therefore he engages eagerly in the pursuit of false or insufficient Philosophy; he is won by the allurements of licentious Art; he follows with wonder the irregular transports of undisciplined Imagination.—Nor, where the objects of his admiration are worthy, is he yet skilful to distinguish between the acquisitions which the age has made for itself, and that large proportion of its wealth which it has only inherited: but in his delight of discovery and growing knowledge, all that is new to his own mind seems to him new-born to the world.—To himself every fresh idea appears instruction; every new exertion, acquisition of power: he seems just called to the consciousness of himself, and to his true place in the intellectual world; and gratitude and reverence towards those to whom he owes this recovery of his dignity, tends much to subject him to the dominion of minds that were not formed by Nature to be the leaders of opinion.

[9] All the tumult and glow of thought and imagination, which seizes on a mind of power in such a scene, tends irresistibly to bind it by stronger attachment of love and admiration to its own age. And there is one among the new emotions which belong to its entrance on the world—one—almost the noblest of all—in which this exaltation of the Age is essentially mingled. The faith in the perpetual progression of human nature towards perfection, gives birth to such lofty dreams, as secure to it the devout assent of Imagination; and it will be yet more grateful to a heart just opening to hope, flushed with the consciousness of new strength, and exulting in the prospect of destined achievements. There is, therefore, almost a Compulsion on generous and enthusiastic Spirits, as they trust that the future shall transcend the present, to believe that the present transcends

the past. It is only on an undue love and admiration of their own Age, that they can build their confidence in the amelioration of the human race. Nor is this faith,—which, in some shape, will always be the creed of virtue,—without apparent reason, even in the erroneous form in which the young adopt it. For there is a perpetual acquisition of knowledge and art,—an unceasing progress in many of the modes of exertion of the human mind,—a perpetual unfolding of virtues with the changing manners of society:—and it is not for a young mind to compare what is gained with what has passed away; to discern, that amidst the incessant intellectual activity of the race, the intellectual power of individual minds may be falling off;—and that amidst accumulating knowledge lofty Science may disappear:—and still less, to judge, in the more complicated moral character of a people, what is progression, and what is decline.

[10] Into a mind possessed with this persuasion of the perpetual progress of man, there may even imperceptibly steal both from the belief itself, and from many of the views on which it rests—something like a distrust of the wisdom of great men of former ages, and with the reverence—which no delusion will ever overpower in a pure mind—for their greatness, a fancied discernment of imperfection;—of incomplete excellence, which wanted for its accomplishment the advantages of later improvements: there will be a surprize, that so much should have been possible in times so ill prepared: and even the study of their works may be sometimes rather the curious research of a speculative Enquirer, than the devout contemplation of an Enthusiast; the watchful and obedient heart of a disciple listening to the inspiration of his Master.

[11] Here then is the power of delusion that will gather round the first steps of a youthful spirit, and throw enchantment over the world in which it is to dwell.—Hope realizing its own dreams:—Ignorance dazzled and ravished with sudden sunshine:—Power awakened and rejoicing in its own consciousness:—Enthusiasm kindling among multiplying images of greatness and beauty; and enamoured, above all, of one splendid error:—and, springing from all these, such a rapture of life and hope, and joy, that the soul, in the power of its happiness, transmutes things essentially repugnant to it, into the excellence of its own nature:—these are the spells that cheat the eye of the Mind with illusion. It is under these influences that a young man of ardent spirit gives all his love, and reverence, and zeal, to productions of Art, to theories of Science, to Opinions, to Systems of feeling, and to Characters distinguished in the World, that are far beneath his own original dignity.

[12] Now as this delusion springs not from his worse but his better nature, it seems as if there could be no warning to him from within of his danger: for even the impassioned joy which he draws at times from the works of Nature, and from those of her Mightier Sons, and which would startle him from a dream of unworthy passion, serves only to fix the infatuation:—for those deep emotions, proving to him that his heart is uncorrupted, justify to him *all* its workings, and his mind confiding and delighting in itself, yields to the guidance of its own blind impulses of

pleasure. His chance, therefore, of security, is the chance that the greater number of objects occurring to attract his honourable passions, may be worthy of them. But we have seen that the whole power of circumstances is collected to gather round him such objects and influences as will bend his high passions to unworthy enjoyment. He engages in it with a heart and understanding unspoiled: but they cannot long be misapplied with impunity. They are drawn gradually into closer sympathy with the falsehoods they have adopted, till, his very nature seeming to change under the Corruption, there disappears from it the capacity of those higher perceptions and pleasures to which he was born: and he is cast off from the communion of exalted minds, to live and to perish with the age to which he has surrendered himself.

[13] If minds under these circumstances of danger are preserved from decay and overthrow, it can seldom, I think, be to themselves that they owe their deliverance. It must be to a fortunate chance which places them under the influence of some more enlightened mind, from which they may first gain suspicion and afterwards wisdom. There is a Philosophy, which, leading them by the light of their best emotions to the principles which should give life to thought and law to genius, will discover to them in clear and perfect evidence, the falsehood of the Errors that have misled them; and restore them to themselves. And this Philosophy they will be willing to hear and wise to understand: but they must be led into its mysteries by some guiding hand; for they want the impulse or the power to penetrate of themselves the recesses.

[14] If a superior Mind should assume the protection of others just beginning to move among the dangers I have described, it would probably be found, that delusions springing from their own virtuous activity, were not the only difficulties to be encountered. Even after suspicion is awakened, the subjection to falsehood may be prolonged and deepened by many weaknesses both of the intellectual and moral nature; weaknesses that will sometimes shake the authority of acknowledged Truth.—There may be intellectual indolence; an indisposition in the mind to the effort of combining the ideas it actually possesses, and bringing into distinct form the knowledge, which in its elements is already its own:—there may be, where the heart resists the sway of opinion, misgivings and modest self-mistrust, in him who sees, that if he trusts his heart, he must slight the judgment of all around him:—there may be a too habitual yielding to authority, consisting, more than in indolence or diffidence, in a conscious helplessness, an incapacity of the mind to maintain itself in its own place against the weight of general opinion;—and there may be too indiscriminate, too undisciplined a sympathy with others, which by the mere infection of feeling will subdue the reason.—There must be a weakness in dejection to him who thinks, with sadness, if his faith be pure, how gross is the error of the multitude, and that multitude how vast:—A reluctance to embrace a creed that excludes so many whom he loves, so many whom his youth has revered:—a difficulty to his understanding to believe that those whom he knows to be, in much that is good and honourable, his

superiors, can be beneath him in this which is the most important of all:—
a sympathy pleading importunately at his heart to descend to the fellowship
of his brothers, and to take their wisdom and faith for his own.—How
often, when under the impulses of those solemn hours, in which he has felt
with clearer insight and deeper faith his sacred truths, he labours to win
to his own belief those whom he loves, will he be checked by their indifference or their laughter! and will he not bear back to his meditations a painful and disheartening sorrow,—a gloomy discontent in that faith which
takes in but a portion of those whom he wishes to include in all his blessings? Will he not be enfeebled by a distraction of inconsistent desires,
when he feels so strongly that the faith which fills his heart, the circles
within which he would embrace all he loves—would repose all his wishes
and hopes, and enjoyments, is yet incommensurate with his affections?

[15] Even when the Mind, strong in reason and just feeling united, and
relying on its strength, has attached itself to Truth, how much is there in
the course and accidents of life that is for ever silently at work for its
degradation. There are pleasures deemed harmless, that lay asleep the
recollections of innocence:—there are pursuits held honourable, or imposed by duty, that oppress the moral spirit:—above all there is that
perpetual connexion with ordinary minds in the common intercourse of
society;—that restless activity of frivolous conversation, where men of all
characters and all pursuits mixing together, nothing may be talked of that
is not of common interest to all—nothing, therefore, but those obvious
thoughts and feelings that float over the surface of things:—and all which
is drawn from the depth of Nature, all which impassioned feeling has made
original in thought, would be misplaced and obtrusive. The talent that is
allowed to shew itself is that which can repay admiration by furnishing
entertainment:—and the display to which it is invited is that which flatters
the vulgar pride of society, by abasing what is too high in excellence for
its sympathy. A dangerous seduction to talents—which would make language—that was given to exalt the soul by the fervid expression of its
pure emotions—the instrument of its degradation. And even when there
is, as the instance I have supposed, too much uprightness to choose so
dishonourable a triumph, there is a necessity of manners, by which every
one must be controled who mixes much in society, not to offend those with
whom he converses by his superiority; and whatever be the native spirit
of a mind, it is evident that this perpetual adaptation of itself to others—
this watchfulness against its own rising feelings, this studied sympathy
with mediocrity—must pollute and impoverish the sources of its strength.

[16] From much of its own weakness, and from all the errors of its misleading activities, may generous youth be rescued by the interposition of
an enlightened mind: and in some degree it may be guarded by instruction
against the injuries to which it is exposed in the world. *His* lot is happy
who owes this protection to friendship: who has found in a friend the
watchful guardian of his mind. He will not be deluded, having that light
to guide: he will not slumber, with that voice to inspire; he will not be
desponding or dejected, with that bosom to lean on.—But how many must

there be whom Heaven has left unprovided, except in their own strength; who must maintain themselves, unassisted and solitary, against their own infirmities and the opposition of the world! For such there may be yet a protector. If a Teacher should stand up in their generation conspicuous above the multitude in superior power, and yet more in the assertion and proclamation of disregarded Truth—to Him—to his cheering or summoning voice all hearts would turn, whose deep sensibility has been oppressed by the indifference, or misled by the seduction of the times. Of one such Teacher who has been given to our own age, you have described the power when you said, that in his annunciation of truths he seemed to speak in thunders. I believe that mighty voice has not been poured out in vain: that there are hearts that have received into their inmost depths all its varying tones: and that even now, there are many to whom the name of Wordsworth calls up the recollection of their weakness, and the consciousness of their strength.

[17] To give to the reason and eloquence of one Man, this complete control over the minds of others, it is necessary, I think, that he should be born in their own times. For thus whatever false opinion of pre-eminence is attached to the Age, becomes at once a title of reverence to him: and when with distinguished powers he sets himself apart from the Age, and above it as the Teacher of high but ill-understood truths, he will appear at once to a generous imagination, in the dignity of one whose superior mind outsteps the rapid progress of society, and will derive from illusion itself the power to disperse illusions. It is probable too, that he who labours under the errors I have described, might feel the power of Truth in a writer of another age, yet fail in applying the full force of his principles to his own times: but when he receives them from a living Teacher, there is no room for doubt or misapplication. It is the errors of his own generation that are denounced; and whatever authority he may acknowledge in the instructions of his Master, strikes, with inevitable force, at his veneration for the opinions and characters of his own times.—And finally, there will be gathered round a living Teacher, who speaks to the deeper soul, many feelings of human love, that will place the infirmities of the heart peculiarly under his controul; at the same time that they blend with and animate the attachment to his cause. So that there will flow from him something of the peculiar influence of a friend: while his doctrines will be embraced and asserted, and vindicated, with the ardent zeal of a disciple, such as can scarcely be carried back to distant times, or connected with voices that speak only from the grave.

[18] I have done what I proposed. I have related to you as much as I have had opportunities of knowing of the difficulties from within and from without, which may oppose the natural developement of true feeling and right opinion, in a mind formed with some capacity for good: and the resources which such a mind may derive from an enlightened contemporary writer.—If what I have said be just, it is certain that this influence will be felt more particularly in a work, adapted by its mode of publication, to address the feelings of the time, and to bring to its readers repeated admonition and repeated consolation.

[19] I have perhaps presumed too far in trespassing on your attention, and in giving way to my own thoughts: but I was unwilling to leave any thing unsaid which might induce you to consider with favour the request I was anxious to make, in the name of all whose state of mind I have described, that you would at times regard us more particularly in your instructions. I cannot judge to what degree it may be in your power to give the Truth you teach a controul over understandings that have matured their strength in error; but in our Class I am sure you will have docile learners.

MATHETES.

COMMENTARY

7–8. **moral** worth and intellectual power] Similar formulas occur at 34, 106–7, 197. Cf. *P. Exc.* 75: 'Of moral strength, and intellectual Power' ['Of virtue and of intellectual power', MS. B of *Recl.*, *P.W.* v. 338; cf. 'Virtue and intellectual Prowess', *R.M.* 197]; 'intellectual power' occurs also in *Prel.* XI. 43 and *Exc.* III. 700.

7–10. moral worth . . . Ancestors] See especially Mathetes, §§ 9–10.

16–17. distinguish . . . admiration] See especially Mathetes, § 11.

19–21. instructions . . . Representative] Requested in Mathetes, § 19.

25–6. even . . . Teacher] See Mathetes, §§ 16–17.

33–4. assumed inferiority] See Mathetes, §§ 2–3, 9–10.

34. moral dignity and intellectual power] Cf. *Exc.* II. 287: 'moral dignity, and strength of mind'.

37. dangers and impediments] No very specific ones are given by Mathetes, apart from an unwarranted admiration of the present age (*passim*), and 'false or insufficient Philosophy . . . licentious Art . . . undisciplined Imagination' (§ 8).

43–4. Of *Prel.* XI. 64: 'Sage, Patriot, Lover, Hero'; A²C and later texts: 'Sage, warrior, patriot, hero', de Selincourt observes (*Prel.*, p. 611): 'When Wordsworth first wrote the lines he would not allow the warrior, as distinct from the patriot, to be one of "the great family".' This passage, and 445–6, indicate that the change of view was accomplished by 1809. The 'Heroes, and Sages, and Saints' of the past are mentioned in Mathetes, § 4; 'Statesmen, and Warriors, and Philosophers, and Poets', in Mathetes, § 6.

45. illustrated] 'illuminated, made remarkable'. Cf. *Cintra*, 2798.

49. glorious Patriots] Such as 'The later Sidney, Marvel, Harrington,/ Young Vane, and Cyriac Skinner, Milton's Friend' (*Nat. Ind. and Lib.* I. xv. 3–4, MS. version; *P.W.* iii. 116); and Milton himself.

55–6. Minds . . . idolized] Cf. Mathetes, § 6.

59–60. the general taste . . . grovelling] Cf. *E.S.* 208–359; and for an instance of 'fantastical' taste from the period concerned see *E.E.* II. 235–46.

60. Youth subject to delusion] Cf. *E.S.* 27–53.

62–8. Every Age . . . rewards] Wordsworth perhaps remembers his own experience in the late seventeen-eighties and early seventeen-nineties.

78 ff., and 78, fn. Thomas Ashe, *Travels, in America, Performed in 1806, For the Purpose of Exploring the Rivers Alleghany, Monogahela, Ohio, and Mississippi, and Ascertaining the Produce and Condition of their Banks and*

Vicinity (3 vols., London, 1808). There are several accounts of Indian burial-places in this book, e.g. i. 78–86, 307–24; ii. 98–100, 195–202. Two passages draw attention to the size of the bones found:

[i. 318–19:] Judging from comparison and analogy, the being to whom these remains belonged could not have been less than seven foot high. That he was a king, sachem or chief of a very remote period there can be no manner of doubt. The distinction, ingenuity, labor, and care, with which he was buried, and the mausoleum constructed for him alone, on an eminence [cf. *R.M.* 80] above the multitude, and its disregarded dead [cf. *R.M.* 88–90] proclaims this beyond dispute. . . . [i. 321–2:] The remarkable size of the skeleton would signify that the Indians of every time were fond of associating in their chiefs, physical as well as mental endowments. That this king should unite a gigantic form [cf. *R.M.* 82–3] to wisdom and intrepidity of heart appears to have been ever their favourite principle . . . [ii. 200:] I consider mounds as the tumuli of kings and chieftains, and barrows [cf. *R.M.* 90] as sepulchres of the vulgar dead.

Giant remains had a local interest for Wordsworth: see Z. S. Fink, *The Early Wordsworthian Milieu* (Oxford, 1958), pp. 33–4.

80–1. "a mount . . . mount!"] *Paradise Lost*, V. 756–8: 'Satan [came] to his Royal seat / High on a Hill, far blazing, as a Mount / Rais'd on a Mount'.

83. Gen.6:4: 'There were giants in the earth in those days.'

90. burrows] 'barrows' in Ashe's *Travels*, ii. 200 (see n. on 78 ff. above), for which 'burrows' may be Wordsworth's or the printer's error. But since *burrow* is a recorded variant of *barrow*, it seems safer to retain the reading of *The Friend* in the absence of manuscript evidence to the contrary.

106–7. belief . . . declining] See Mathetes, § 3.

110–11. dignity of mind] So *Prel.* VI. 443.

113–14. ardent mind] So *Exc.* VII. 116.

119–21. belief . . . perfection] See Mathetes, §§ 9–10; *Cintra*, 3193–4; *P. Exc.* 122–3.

128. a Writer] We have not identified him.

137. lord Bacon] Cf. *Cintra*, 4238, textual n.

150–3. Cf. 569–70, 610–11. A similar image in *Prel.* IX. 1–9.

160–3. For the original layout of the essay at this point see 207–8, textual n., and Introd., pp. 7–8.

183. the morning-star of her literature] See *E.S.* 647, and n.

184–5. "shot orient beams"] Cf. *Misc. Son.* III. xliii (*P.W.* iii. 60): 'While beams of orient light shoot wide and high'. The source is *Paradise Lost*, VI. 12–15: 'now went forth the Morn . . . / Shot through with orient Beams'; cf. *P.L.* IV. 642–4: 'the Sun . . . spreads / His orient Beams'.

185–201. Cf. *Ecc. Son.* II. xvi (*P.W.* iii. 369); and, more generally, *Prel.* X. 423–30.

192–3. a hurling-back . . . Country] Wordsworth described the mind of Napoleon as 'lagging, in moral sentiment and knowledge, three hundred years behind the age in which it acts' (*Cintra*, 3760–2).

207–8, textual n. [b]. The 'last Number but one' with respect to *The Friend*, No. 18, was not No. 17, which contained the letter of Mathetes and the first section of our text. In the manuscript the '8' has possibly been altered from a '9'. Dorothy Wordsworth expected the second section to appear in No. 19 (*M.T.* i. 379), but in the same letter she corrected the reference to 'the next but one', i.e. No. 20, in which the second section actually appeared.

208. seductions] The 'seductions of [the world's] opinions' are mentioned in Mathetes, § 2.

222–4. sensibility . . . History] Cf. Mathetes, § 4: 'the young adventurer in life . . . comes with a spirit whose dearest feelings and highest thoughts have sprung up under the influences of Nature . . . his thoughts have dwelt among the wonders of Nature, and among the loftiest spirits of Men— Heroes, and Sages, and Saints.'

227. Freedom and Power] Cf. *P.L.B.* 350.

249–54. Cf. *E.S. passim*; *Cintra*, 3526–8: 'worldly distinctions and offices of command do not lie in the path—nor are they any part of the appropriate retinue—of Philosophy and Virtue.'

257–8. has no haze . . . look] Cf. *Exc.* VI. 703–4: 'oft / Hidden by clouds, and oft bedimmed by haze'.

266–7. enthroned above all dominations and dignities] Probably a verbal echo of *Paradise Lost*, V. 769: 'Thrones, Dominations, Princedomes, Vertues, Powers'.

277. fable of Prodicus] Xenophon, *Memorabilia*, II. i. 21–33. Only the general outline is followed in Wordsworth's adaptation. He owned 'Cebetis Tabula, Prodici Hercules, et Theophrasti Characteres Gr. et Lat., a J. Simpson, 8vo, Oxon., 1739' (Rydal Mount Catalogue, lot 409).

281. severe] See textual n. The word in the manuscript can be read as 'serene', but is more like 'severe', which suits the context better.

292–7. Cf. *P. 1815*, 333–44; *E.S.* 575–689.

308. Moral life] See n. on 416–17 below.

312. Nature . . . follower] See Mathetes, §§ 2, 4.

314–15. recesses . . . penetrated] Cf. Mathetes, § 13; *E.E.* II. 583–6.

316. pathos . . . sublimity] A conventional eighteenth-century antithesis. Cf. *E.S.* 741, and n.

331–2. untwist . . . mind] Milton, 'L'Allegro', 143–4: 'Untwisting all the chains that tie / The hidden soul of harmony'; 'links' is an echo of 'linked sweetness', 'L'Allegro', 140, and 'wedded' of 'Married', 'L'Allegro', 137.

332, textual n. what we ourselves have felt] Recorded in 'Ode: Intimations of Immortality' (*P.W.* iv. 279–85). Cf. 'the sacred light of Childhood' (333) and the 'celestial light' of 'Ode', 4. For the image of Aurora cf. *Prel.* VII. 531–2, and textual n. The detail here suggests that Wordsworth may have had in mind some painting of this conventional scene; see, for instance, Guido Reni's *Aurora*, reproduced in Rudolf Wittkower, *Art and Architecture in Italy, 1600 to 1750* (Pelican History of Art, Z 16; London, 1958), Plate 22.

334 ff. Nature and Reason are similarly associated in *Prel.* X. 605–10: 'Youth maintains . . . / Communion more direct and intimate / With Nature, and the inner strength she has, / And hence, oft-times, no less, with Reason too, / Than Age or Manhood, even.' In general, Wordsworth appears to be writing from recollection of his own experience in the middle nineties, when, after his enthusiasm for the achievements of the age (the French Revolution and Godwinian rationalism) had been found unjustified, 'Nature's Self . . . / Conducted me again to open day' (*Prel.* X. 922–4). In these circumstances, Nature 'Revived the feelings of my earlier life' (cf. *R.M.* 330–4, 408–9), and 'Gave me . . . strength and . . . knowledge full of peace' (cf. *R.M.* 427–9: 'Knowledge efficacious for the production of virtue . . . the sole dispenser of complacency and repose'). Again, with 'hopes . . . founded . . . upon his intellectual Being' (*R.M.* 335–6), cf. *Prel.* XII. 57–60 (of the same period): 'Again I took the intellectual eye / For my instructor, studious more to see / Great Truths, than touch and handle little ones. / Knowledge was given accordingly'. The process described here also seems parallel to that attributed to the 'favoured' child in *Prel.*, pp. 574–8, though 'Reason' is not there mentioned. See notes on 363 ff., 418–25 below. Cf. also *Exc.* IV. 260 ff.

343–4. unfolding Intellect] Cf. *Prel.* (1850), XII. 101: 'man's unfolding intellect'.

347. rising up like exhalations] *Paradise Lost*, I. 711: 'Rose like an exhalation'; and V. 185–6: 'Ye mists and exhalations that now rise / From hill or steaming lake', borrowed by Wordsworth in *Exc.* VI. 594–8, reading of MS.

348. tombs . . . Antiquity] Cf. *E.E.* I. 164–90; and for 'wild flowers' (347), cf. *E.E.* I. 170.

352. fear] On the value of 'the impressive discipline of fear' (*Prel.* I. 631) in the forming of the mind see especially various episodes in *Prel.* I, and others collected and discussed in Havens, ch. iii.

358–98. she works . . . to thought] Cf. the discussion of the 'simple and direct' and the 'complex and revolutionary' pathetic in *E.S.* 781–804, especially 796–9: 'There is also a meditative, as well as a human, pathos; an enthusiastic, as well as an ordinary, sorrow; a sadness that has its seat in the depths of *reason*, to which the mind cannot sink gently of itself—but to which it must descend by *treading the steps of thought*' (our italics). The earlier reaction to the taper indicates the 'pathetic' effect of an incident which is subsequently felt as an occasion of 'power'. The reactions to the taper somewhat resemble Wordsworth's reactions to the scenery of the Wye ('Tintern Abbey', 80–2, 88–93; *P.W.* ii. 261): the earlier, of 1793, marked by 'a feeling and a love / That had no need of a remoter charm, / By thought supplied'; and the later, of 1798, when Wordsworth had 'learned / To look on nature, not as in the hour / Of thoughtless youth; but hearing oftentimes / The still, sad music of humanity, / Nor harsh nor grating [cf. *R.M.* 396–7: 'no disposition to tears, no unconquerable sighs'], though of ample power / To chasten and subdue' [cf. *R.M.* 397–9: 'yet with a melancholy . . . resolve']. On the probable relation of the process involved to the doctrines of Roman Stoicism see Jane Worthington, *Wordsworth's Reading of Roman Prose* (New Haven, Conn., 1946), pp. 63–5.

363 ff. Cf. *Prel.*, p. 577, lines 225–7: 'The commonest images of nature . . . / A taper burning through the gloom of night' (parallel noted by de Selincourt).

388–9. Cf. 'Character of the Happy Warrior', 11 (*P.W.* iv. 86): 'makes his moral being his prime care'.

393. motions of the Soul] So *Exc.* III. 683.

412. the ancient spirit] So 'The Sailor's Mother', 7 (*P.W.* ii. 54).

413, textual n. The word 'not' is deleted after 'eye' and inserted above 'to', so that the crossing of the 't' of 'to' looks like an underscore, as the printer of *The Friend* took it.

416–17. At Cambridge Wordsworth 'gave a moral life' 'To every natural form' (*Prel.* III. 124–6). Cf. 'Moral life', 308.

417–18. whereby . . . for ever] Cf. *P. 1815*, 344, textual n.: 'a commutation and transfer of internal feelings, co-operating with external accidents, to plant, for immortality, images [conjoined impressions 1836] of sound and sight, in the celestial soil of the Imagination'.

418–25. Cf. *Prel.*, p. 575, lines 139–58, especially 144–5: 'he looks nearer, calls / The stars out of their shy retreats'; and 148–50: 'finally he takes / The optic tube of thought that patient men / Have furnished' (parallel noted by de Selincourt).

424–9, textual n. A letter on f. 89ᵛ of the manuscript, postmarked Kendal but of illegible date, deals with this passage:

I must further trouble Mr Brown to search for a passage in the M.S. (which I think will be found towards the end of the first, or beginning of the second Sheet) where he will find words to this effect "Knowledge in which word is included virtue" *for which print* "Knowledge efficacious for the production of Virtue" N.B. the Sentence ends [with the *del.*] or contains the words *complacency & repose*. I mention this that Mr B may not mistake the passage—

The reading of our text ('MS.³') is substituted for the original version ('MS.'), from 'summoned' (424) to 'discovery of the' (424–5) on the main manuscript, from 'impelling' (425) to 'Contemplation to' (430) on a pasted slip. The original version, beneath the slip, is heavily scored out as it is emended towards the final text; what can be recovered indicates that Wordsworth's changes were not of enormous significance.

427–9. Knowledge . . . repose] Cf. *Cintra*, 541–2: 'all knowledge of human nature leads ultimately to repose.' 'Complacency' = 'tranquil . . . satisfaction' (*O.E.D.*, sense 1), as in *Prel.* XI. 29 and *Recl.* I. i. 306.

429–46. Similarly *Cintra*, 3515–18: 'men of comprehensive sensibility and tutored genius . . . should [not] have vested in them political power.'

430 ff. *The Friend*, No. 6 (21 Sept. 1809), pp. 86–7:

I see, however, one favourable symptom in the minds of men at present. The notion of our measureless superiority in Good Sense to our Ancestors, is somewhat less fashionable, than at the commencement of the French Revolution: we hear less of the jargon of *this enlightened Age*. After having fatigued itself as Performer or Spectator of the giddy Figure-dance of political changes, Europe has seen the shallow Foundations of its self-complacent Faith give way; and we have now more reason to apprehend the stupor of Despondence, than the extravagances of idle Hope and unprincipled self-confidence. So grievously deceived by the showy mock theories of confident mock Thinkers, there seems a tendency in the public mind to shun all Thought, and to expect help from any quarter rather than from Seriousness and Reflection: as if some invisible Power would think for us, when we gave up the pretence of thinking for ourselves. But in the first place, did those, who opposed the theories of Innovators, conduct their *untheoretic* Opposition with more Wisdom or to a happier Result? And secondly, are Societies now constructed on Principles so few and so simple, that we could, even if we wished it, act as it were by *Instinct*, like our distant Forefathers in the infancy of States? Doubtless, to act is nobler than to think; but as the old man doth not become a Child by means of his second Childishness, as little can a Nation exempt itself from the necessity of thinking, which has once learnt to think.

438–9. the absolute . . . itself] See Worthington, p. 64.

444–5. to take place of] 'to take precedence of' (*O.E.D.*, s.v. *place*, sb., sense 27.c); so *Cintra*, 2889; *Subl. and Beaut.* 163.

445–6. Heroes . . . Warriors] See 43–4 and n.

470–2. But . . . branded] See Mathetes, § 3.

473–4. See the discussion of 'the improvement of experimental philosophy and the mechanic arts' in *Cintra*, 4238, textual n.

475–6. the particular . . . military] In view of Wordsworth's frequent condemnation of politicians and generals in *Cintra* (e.g. 2460 ff., 3321 ff., 3644–8, 3851–5), written a year before this passage, it is hard to guess whom he had in mind.

476. admiration and love] See Mathetes, § 4. Cf. 584–5 below; *Cintra*, 4333–4, and n.

477–80. See Mathetes, § 2.

480–1. a newly-invested . . . Shield] It is difficult to recall such a figure in *The Faerie Queene*.

494. manifold excellences] See Mathetes, § 3.

495. recreant Knights] *Faerie Queene*, I. iv. 41; II. vi. 28; v. xi. 46; VI. iii. 35, vi. 37, vii. 16.

495–6. A false Gloriana] Like the false Florimell of *F.Q.* III. viii ff.

513–20, textual n. See Introd., p. 7. Although the manuscript gives a clear direction after 'error.' (513) to 'see letter marked x' (i.e. f. 88 of the manuscript), the printer of *The Friend* ignored it and took account only of the deletion of the original reading. The 'letter marked x' proceeds after ' "Range &c." ' as follows: 'The above Essay was sent off in a great hurry & being written in a hand which Mr Brown is not used to it will require particular care to be taken in the printing—the word very ill written of which the first [letter *subs. for* word] is almost defaced is "blank unsignalized Shield" [*R.M.* 481]. Should this Essay not fill up a whole No. add the following [two epitaphs translated from Chiabrera]'.

534. false refinement] Cf. *P.L.B.* 119–20; *E.S.* 704.

534–5. not . . . senses] Cf. the discussion of the 'false and contradictory' natural descriptions of Dryden and Pope, *E.S.* 419–51.

536–7. Cf. *E.S.* 27–31.

550–2. See Mathetes, §§ 16–17.

553 ff. *The Friend*, No. 4 (7 Sept. 1809), p. 62, fn., cites two passages from Milton's *Areopagitica*. Wordsworth uses the first and last sentences of the first passage cited (Milton, *Works*, ed. Patterson *et al.*, iv (New York, 1931), 310–12): 'Good and evill we know in the field of this world grow up together almost inseparably . . . Since therefore the knowledge and survay of vice is in this world so necessary to the constituting of human vertue, and the scanning of error to the confirmation of truth, how can we more safely, and with lesse danger scout into the regions of sin and falsity then by reading all manner of tractats, and hearing all manner of reason?'

569–70. image . . . passed] Cf. 150–3, 610–11.

570–611. Cf. *E.S.* 37–44, on checking the reactions of the youthful mind to bad literature. In 1815 Wordsworth is less confident that error 'will in due time die of itself' (*R.M.* 573–4) or that 'errors always terminate of themselves in due season' (*E.S.* 44).

586–9. Cf. *P.L.B.* 679–86.

587. indecisive judgements] Cf. *Prel.* III. 215.

604–5. to analyze with scrupulous minuteness] Cf. *E.E.* I. 368–71.

618–19. clogged . . . affections] Cf. 62–8.

619–21. Cf. Mathetes, § 15.

627. orbit] Wordsworth thinks in terms of the astronomical image of 'Ode to Duty', 55–6, which he is about to quote (see 636–42, textual n.).

643–50. 'Ode to Duty', 57–64. See also 636–42, textual n.

651. The initials signing the work, hitherto printed 'M.M.', are in the manuscript clearly two inverted W's.

IX

ESSAYS UPON EPITAPHS

INTRODUCTION: GENERAL

THE first 'Essay upon Epitaphs' appeared originally, without Wordsworth's name, as a stop-gap essay in Coleridge's *The Friend* for
22 February 1810. At this moment 'Coleridge was in such bad spirits
that when the time came he was utterly unprovided'; and although
Wordsworth 'did not intend [his Essay] to be published now', it was
'ready' and so 'was sent off' to the printer (*M.T.* i. 391). By 28 February, if not earlier, Wordsworth had also written the second and
third Essays, which were to be held in reserve for a similar occasion
(*M.T.* i. 391); but the occasion never arose, since *The Friend* ceased
to appear shortly afterwards. Wordsworth reprinted the first Essay,
with revisions, as a note to *The Excursion* (1814), and, as with his other
works, continued to revise it in subsequent editions. In April 1812
Coleridge, 'at work on the supplemental Numbers' of *The Friend*,
hoped that 'Mr Wordsworth will transmit to me the two finishing
Essays on Epitaphs' and that Southey 'would immediately write to
Wordsworth & urge him to send them . . . or if he decline it, that
Southey should apprize me of it as soon as possible' (*C.L.* iii. 392).
Dorothy reported this request to William, who was in London in May
1812, and added that she had refused 'to send the Essays off without
your orders' (*M.T.* ii. 13). It seems likely, however, that her letter did
not reach him (*M.T.* ii. 18–19), and Wordsworth's attention must in
any case have been distracted almost immediately by efforts at personal
reconciliation with Coleridge and by the death of his daughter
Catherine. For whatever reason, the second and third Essays did not
appear in *The Friend* of 1812, and, except for some extended quotations
which Christopher Wordsworth made in his *Memoirs of William
Wordsworth* (1851), they remained unprinted until they appeared in
Grosart's edition of the *Prose Works* in 1876.

As early as 1799 Coleridge had discussed with Wordsworth 'Tombs
by the Roadside & Tombs in Church yards', and in the Essays Wordsworth draws some of his epitaphs from Coleridge's notes.[1] No doubt
these discussions remained in Wordsworth's mind, but, according to
the earliest text of Essay I, his interest in the poetics of the epitaph
arose from his study of the epitaphs of the Italian poet Gabriello
Chiabrera.[2] Apart from his general interest in Italian literature, which
he acquired at Cambridge, it is not clear what directed Wordsworth's
attention to this model. The published correspondence contains no

---

[1] See notes to *E.E.* I. 163–5; II. 129–36; III. 454–70.
[2] See *E.E.* I. 1, textual n.

reference to Chiabrera earlier than the date of the Essays (*M.T.* i. 388, 391). Essay II contains at least one passage in which the images are associated with the death of John Wordsworth, and another in Essay I may derive from Wordsworth's personal experience when, in 1805, he attempted 'to write a poem that should record my Brother's virtues and be worthy of his memory';[1] it is thus just possible that in his difficulty he turned to Chiabrera as a possible model.[2] But the point cannot be proved, and the poems on John Wordsworth which eventually emerged are far from resembling Chiabreran epitaphs.

In appending Essay I to *The Excursion*, Wordsworth drew attention to affinities between the Essay and Books V, VI, and VII of the poem, written, in part at least, about the same time as the Essays. It is difficult to find precise verbal parallels,[3] but parallels of mood and thought are obvious. Thus the Solitary's gloomy contrast between 'That which is done' and 'what is known / To reason, and by conscience is enjoined' (*Exc.* V. 250–61) echoes the essayist's contrast between the real vices and the reputed virtues of country people (*E.E.* II. 34 ff.). The Pastor's description of the two opposed aspects of the churchyard in April (*Exc.* V. 531 ff.) resembles Wordsworth's discussion of how 'qualities pass insensibly into their contraries' (*E.E.* I. 137). The unconscious virtue of the lowly is discussed in both *Exc.* V. 593–601 and *E.E.* II. 70–86; the obviousness of vice in both *Exc.* VI. 573–9 and *E.E.* II. 55–60. Wordsworth draws some phrases in *Exc.* VI from an epitaph by Gray which Essay III criticizes.[4] Apart from these specific resemblances, the portraits in these books of *The Excursion*, though hardly epitaphs, are often congruous with the recommendations for character-portrayal which the Essays provide. Indeed, such a portrait as that of the Pastor (*Exc.* V. 98–122) reads not unlike a Chiabreran epitaph.[5]

The existence of a substantial variant to Essay II (printed in Appendix I) that had not yet been worked into the main text, and the

---

[1] *E.T.*, p. 586; see notes to *E.E.* II. 43; I. 413–19.

[2] His interest in Italian literature had recently been newly aroused by his efforts to translate Michael Angelo's sonnets; see *E.T.*, pp. 517, 628 (Dec. 1804 and Oct. 1805); *P.W.* iii. 423.

[3] An exception is *Exc.* VI. 634–45, which reproduces in verse, often verbatim, *E.E.* II. 30–4; see n. ad loc.

[4] See n. to *E.E.* III. 269–71.

[5] Note the similarities of phrasing: *Exc.* V. 102: 'The shepherd of his flock', and *Chiabrera*, III. 6–7 (*P.W.* iv. 249): 'the Roman Shepherd / Gave to my charge Urbino's numerous flock'; *Exc.* V. 112–13: 'though born / Of knightly race', and *Chiabrera*, III. 3–4: 'I was born . . . of gentle blood'; *Exc.* V. 114–15: 'withdrew / From academic bowers', and *Chiabrera*, II. 2 (*P.W.* iv. 248): 'Drew TITUS from the depth of studious bowers'; *Exc.* V. 118: 'simple manners', and *Chiabrera*, VIII. 24 (*P.W.* iv. 253): 'mild manners'. Elsewhere: *Exc.* VII. 464: 'slow disease', and *Chiabrera*, IV. 31 (*P.W.* iv. 250).

inadequate punctuation of the manuscript of Essay III indicate that these two Essays at least were left not entirely finished;[1] and the content of the works suggests hasty composition. Wordsworth draws on convenient source-books for his examples when the arrangement of the Essays would hardly suggest it. For instance, he cites, with the air of one ranging widely over the many vicious epitaphs of the eighteenth century, two from Mason and one from Gray which he probably found printed one after the other on successive pages of Vicesimus Knox's *Elegant Extracts*.[2] In other instances he misinterprets his sources: he 'cannot resist the pleasure of transcribing the metrical part of an epitaph which formerly was inscribed in the church of St. Paul's', but fails to notice that Weever, his source, says that the epitaph engraved in the church was in Latin, and that the version given is 'thus Englished by *Iohn Stow*'.[3] Most astonishing, he assigns to Weever himself, as an example of 'sincerity' and as a 'simple effusion of the moment', the tribute to Sidney which Weever, in a phrase actually cited by Wordsworth, assigns to Camden, and which is, in fact, a quotation from Philemon Holland's Englishing of Camden's *Britannia*.[4]

Such details hardly affect Wordsworth's main themes, and the three interlinked Essays form a notable contribution to Romantic poetics.[5] The diction is sometimes Latinate and the sentences are involved, but we are rarely left groping for the meaning. The richness and aptness of the metaphors with which Wordsworth is able to illuminate difficult psychological concepts are particularly striking.[6]

[1] Afterthoughts rather clumsily inserted can be seen even in I. 470-8.
[2] See n. to *E.E.* III. 155.
[3] See *E.E.* III. 419-31, and n.
[4] See *E.E.* II. 339-52 and n. For other examples see notes on I. 9-14, 20-6.
[5] For fuller discussion, see W. J. B. Owen, *Wordsworth as Critic* (Toronto, 1969), pp. 115-50.
[6] See, for instance, II. 583-6; III. 162-4, 180-1.

INTRODUCTION: TEXTUAL

OUR text of *E.E.* I is from *Poetical Works* (1849–50), vi. 287–300 (Healey, item 151); and our apparatus records the variants between this, Wordsworth's final text, and earlier printings in the following: *The Friend*, No. 25 (22 February 1810), pp. 402–16 (cf. Healey, item 466); *The Excursion* (1814), pp. 430–46 (Healey, item 24); *The Excursion* (1820), pp. 431–50 (Healey, item 62); *Poetical Works* (1827), v. 400–19 (Healey, item 76); *Poetical Works* (1832), iv. 334–55 (Healey, item 83); *Poetical Works* (1836–7), vi. 351–72 (Healey, item 101); and *Poems* (1845), pp. 561–5 (Healey, item 135). A few corrected readings are drawn from Dorothy Wordsworth to Lady Beaumont, 28 February 1810 (*M.Y.* i. 391). We have found no manuscript version of this Essay.

Our text of *E.E.* II and III is from the manuscript (Prose 6) in the Wordsworth Library, Grasmere. For Essay II this is a leaflet of foolscap paper, 13 in. × 8¼ in., written on both sides of the page in the hand of Mary Wordsworth. It consists of six leaves, pp. 1–11; fol. 6ᵛ, p. [12] is blank, except for the following heading, not in the principal hand:

1

Essay on Epitaphs

A loose sheet, numbered '11' and then corrected to '13', contains the matter printed in our Appendix I. On its verso is the figure '2', apparently defining it as following after '1 Essay on Epitaphs'.

For Essay III the manuscript is a similar leaflet of the same paper, in the hand of Mary Wordsworth; the text fills six leaves, or twelve pages.

Although lacking some final corrections, the manuscript is a copy: see textual notes to II. 225 and III. 132, where the original reading is in each case a visual error; and III. 189–90, where the manuscript originally omitted six words by homœoteleuton.

Our apparatus records early variants and later insertions, our occasional corrections, and readings for which the deterioration of the manuscript has forced us to rely on Grosart's transcript (on one occasion confirmed from Christopher Wordsworth's quotations from *E.E.* III in his *Memoirs of William Wordsworth*). The punctuation of Essay II is mainly that of the manuscript, but occasionally editorial; that of the variant to Essay II, printed in Appendix I, and of Essay III, which are sometimes inadequately punctuated in the manuscript, is often editorial.

ESSAY UPON EPITAPHS.

It need scarcely be said, that an Epitaph presupposes a Monument, upon which it is to be engraven. Almost all Nations have wished that certain external signs should point out the places where their dead are interred. Among savage tribes unacquainted with letters this has mostly been done either by rude stones placed near the graves, or by 5 mounds of earth raised over them. This custom proceeded obviously from a twofold desire; first, to guard the remains of the deceased from irreverent approach or from savage violation: and, secondly, to preserve their memory. 'Never any,' says Camden, 'neglected burial but

In the texts of 1814 and later editions, the whole Essay is preceded by a note to 'The Excursion', V. 978, as follows:
'And whence that [this 1814–20] tribute? wherefore these regards?'
The sentiments and opinions here uttered are in unison with those expressed in the following Essay upon Epitaphs, which was furnished by me [by the author 1814–37] for Mr. Coleridge's periodical work, the Friend; and as they are dictated by a spirit congenial to that which pervades this and the two succeeding books, the sympathising reader will not be displeased to see the Essay here annexed.
    1 1810 *begins:*
In this, and some preceding Numbers, has been given a selection of Epitaphs from the Italian Poet CHIABRERA; in one instance imitated, and in the others carefully translated. The perusal of the original collection afforded me so much pleasure that I was induced to think upon the nature of that species of composition with more care than I had previously bestowed upon the Subject: the result of my reflections may perhaps be interesting to the Readers of THE FRIEND. An attempt will be made to unfold the Laws of Taste and Criticism systematically, as soon as certain topics, which have already been entered upon, shall be concluded: in the mean while, I wish to avail myself of the present occasion to tempt the more practised Reader into a short prelusive exercise of powers which he will hereafter be called upon to put forth in good earnest; and, in respect to those Persons who are unfamiliar with such speculations, my labour, in the present Essay, may be likened to that of a Teacher of Geology, who, to awaken the curiosity of his Pupils, and to induce them to prepare for the study of the inner constitution of the Planet, lectures with a few specimens of fossils and minerals in his hand, arranged in their several classes, and the beauty of which he points out to their attention.
    "To define an Epitaph," says Dr. Johnson, "is useless; every one knows that it is an inscription on a Tomb. An Epitaph, therefore, implies no particular character of writing, but may be composed in verse or prose. It is indeed commonly panegyrical; because we are seldom distinguished with a Stone but by our Friends; but it has no rule to restrain or mollify it, except this, that it ought not to be longer than common beholders may have leisure or patience to peruse." From this introduction the Critic immediately proceeds to a review of the metrical Epitaphs of Pope. This summary opinion is delivered with such laxity that, even on that account, the passage would not have deserved to be quoted, if it had not been forced upon the notice of our Countrymen, by the place which it occupies in the book entitled, "The Lives of the most eminent English Poets," by the same Writer. I now solicit the Reader's attention to a more comprehensive view of the subject; and shall endeavour to treat it with more precision.
    It needs scarcely be said, *etc.*
    1 need 1850: needs 1810–45.

some savage nations; as the Bactrians, which cast their dead to the 10
dogs; some varlet philosophers, as Diogenes, who desired to be
devoured of fishes; some dissolute courtiers, as Mæcenas, who was
wont to say, Non tumulum curo; sepelit natura relictos.

I'm careless of a grave:—Nature her dead will save.'

As soon as nations had learned the use of letters, epitaphs were 15
inscribed upon these monuments; in order that their intention might
be more surely and adequately fulfilled. I have derived monuments and
epitaphs from two sources of feeling: but these do in fact resolve themselves into one. The invention of epitaphs, Weever, in his Discourse of
Funeral Monuments, says rightly, 'proceeded from the presage or 20
fore-feeling of immortality, implanted in all men naturally, and is
referred to the scholars of Linus the Theban poet, who flourished about
the year of the world two thousand seven hundred; who first bewailed
this Linus their Master, when he was slain, in doleful verses, then
called of him Œlina, afterwards Epitaphia, for that they were first 25
sung at burials, after engraved upon the sepulchres.'

And, verily, without the consciousness of a principle of immortality
in the human soul, Man could never have had awakened in him the
desire to live in the remembrance of his fellows: mere love, or the
yearning of kind towards kind, could not have produced it. The dog or 30
horse perishes in the field, or in the stall, by the side of his companions,
and is incapable of anticipating the sorrow with which his surrounding
associates shall bemoan his death, or pine for his loss; he cannot pre-
conceive this regret, he can form no thought of it; and therefore cannot
possibly have a desire to leave such regret or remembrance behind him. 35
Add to the principle of love which exists in the inferior animals, the
faculty of reason which exists in Man alone; will the conjunction of
these account for the desire? Doubtless it is a necessary consequence of
this conjunction; yet not I think as a direct result, but only to be come
at through an intermediate thought, viz. that of an intimation or 40
assurance within us, that some part of our nature is imperishable. At
least the precedence, in order of birth, of one feeling to the other, is
unquestionable. If we look back upon the days of childhood, we shall
find that the time is not in remembrance when, with respect to our own
individual Being, the mind was without this assurance; whereas, the 45
wish to be remembered by our friends or kindred after death, or even
in absence, is, as we shall discover, a sensation that does not form itself
till the *social* feelings have been developed, and the Reason has connected itself with a wide range of objects. Forlorn, and cut off from
communication with the best part of his nature, must that man be, who 50
should derive the sense of immortality, as it exists in the mind of a

child, from the same unthinking gaiety or liveliness of animal spirits
with which the lamb in the meadow, or any other irrational creature
is endowed; who should ascribe it, in short, to blank ignorance in the
child; to an inability arising from the imperfect state of his faculties to   55
come, in any point of his being, into contact with a notion of death; or
to an unreflecting acquiescence in what had been instilled into him!
Has such an unfolder of the mysteries of nature, though he may have
forgotten his former self, ever noticed the early, obstinate, and un-
appeasable inquisitiveness of children upon the subject of origination?   60
This single fact proves outwardly the monstrousness of those sup-
positions: for, if we had no direct external testimony that the minds of
very young children meditate feelingly upon death and immortality,
these inquiries, which we all know they are perpetually making
concerning the *whence*, do necessarily include correspondent habits of   65
interrogation concerning the *whither*. Origin and tendency are notions
inseparably co-relative. Never did a child stand by the side of a running
stream, pondering within himself what power was the feeder of the
perpetual current, from what never-wearied sources the body of water
was supplied, but he must have been inevitably propelled to follow this   70
question by another: "Towards what abyss is it in progress? what
receptacle can contain the mighty influx?" And the spirit of the answer
must have been, though the word might be sea or ocean, accompanied
perhaps with an image gathered from a map, or from the real object in
nature—these might have been the *letter*, but the *spirit* of the answer   75
must have been *as* inevitably,—a receptacle without bounds or dimensions;—nothing less than infinity. We may, then, be justified in
asserting, that the sense of immortality, if not a co-existent and twin
birth with Reason, is among the earliest of her offspring: and we may
further assert, that from these conjoined, and under their countenance,   80
the human affections are gradually formed and opened out. This is not
the place to enter into the recesses of these investigations; but the
subject requires me here to make a plain avowal, that, for my own part,
it is to me inconceivable, that the sympathies of love towards each
other, which grow with our growth, could ever attain any new   85
strength, or even preserve the old, after we had received from the
outward senses the impression of death, and were in the habit of having
that impression daily renewed and its accompanying feeling brought
home to ourselves, and to those we love; if the same were not counteracted by those communications with our internal Being, which are   90
anterior to all these experiences, and with which revelation coincides,
and has through that coincidence alone (for otherwise it could not

57 had 1814: has 1810.   78 a 1814: *om.* 1810.   79 her 1814: its' [*sic*]
1810.

possess it) a power to affect us. I confess, with me the conviction is absolute, that, if the impression and sense of death were not thus counterbalanced, such a hollowness would pervade the whole system 95 of things, such a want of correspondence and consistency, a disproportion so astounding betwixt means and ends, that there could be no repose, no joy. Were we to grow up unfostered by this genial warmth, a frost would chill the spirit, so penetrating and powerful, that there could be no motions of the life of love; and infinitely less 100 could we have any wish to be remembered after we had passed away from a world in which each man had moved about like a shadow.—If, then, in a creature endowed with the faculties of foresight and reason, the social affections could not have unfolded themselves uncountenanced by the faith that Man is an immortal being; and if, consequently, 105 neither could the individual dying have had a desire to survive in the remembrance of his fellows, nor on their side could they have felt a wish to preserve for future times vestiges of the departed; it follows, as a final inference, that without the belief in immortality, wherein these several desires originate, neither monuments nor epitaphs, in 110 affectionate or laudatory commemoration of the deceased, could have existed in the world.

Simonides, it is related, upon landing in a strange country, found the corse of an unknown person lying by the sea-side; he buried it, and was honoured throughout Greece for the piety of that act. Another 115 ancient Philosopher, chancing to fix his eyes upon a dead body, regarded the same with slight, if not with contempt; saying, "See the shell of the flown bird!" But it is not to be supposed that the moral and tender-hearted Simonides was incapable of the lofty movements of thought, to which that other Sage gave way at the moment while his soul was 120 intent only upon the indestructible being; nor, on the other hand, that he, in whose sight a lifeless human body was of no more value than the worthless shell from which the living fowl had departed, would not, in a different mood of mind, have been affected by those earthly considerations which had incited the philosophic Poet to the performance 125 of that pious duty. And with regard to this latter we may be assured that, if he had been destitute of the capability of communing with the more exalted thoughts that appertain to human nature, he would have cared no more for the corse of the stranger than for the dead body of a seal or porpoise which might have been cast up by the waves. We 130 respect the corporeal frame of Man, not merely because it is the habitation of a rational, but of an immortal Soul. Each of these Sages

102–12 If, then . . . in the world. 1814: *om.* 1810.   121 nor 1814: or 1810.   126 duty. And with regard to this 1814: duty with respect to the 1810 [*corr. in M.Υ. i. 391*].

was in sympathy with the best feelings of our nature; feelings which, though they seem opposite to each other, have another and a finer connection than that of contrast.—It is a connection formed through 135 the subtle progress by which, both in the natural and the moral world, qualities pass insensibly into their contraries, and things revolve upon each other. As, in sailing upon the orb of this planet, a voyage towards the regions where the sun sets, conducts gradually to the quarter where we have been accustomed to behold it come forth at its rising; 140 and, in like manner, a voyage towards the east, the birth-place in our imagination of the morning, leads finally to the quarter where the sun is last seen when he departs from our eyes; so the contemplative Soul, travelling in the direction of mortality, advances to the country of everlasting life; and, in like manner, may she continue to explore those 145 cheerful tracts, till she is brought back, for her advantage and benefit, to the land of transitory things—of sorrow and of tears.

On a midway point, therefore, which commands the thoughts and feelings of the two Sages whom we have represented in contrast, does the Author of that species of composition, the laws of which it is our 150 present purpose to explain, take his stand. Accordingly, recurring to the twofold desire of guarding the remains of the deceased and preserving their memory, it may be said that a sepulchral monument is a tribute to a man as a human being; and that an epitaph (in the ordinary meaning attached to the word) includes this general feeling and 155 something more; and is a record to preserve the memory of the dead, as a tribute due to his individual worth, for a satisfaction to the sorrowing hearts of the survivors, and for the common benefit of the living: which record is to be accomplished, not in a general manner, but, where it can, in *close connection with the bodily remains of the* 160 *deceased:* and these, it may be added, among the modern nations of Europe, are deposited within, or contiguous to, their places of worship. In ancient times, as is well known, it was the custom to bury the dead beyond the walls of towns and cities; and among the Greeks and Romans they were frequently interred by the way-sides. 165

I could here pause with pleasure, and invite the Reader to indulge with me in contemplation of the advantages which must have attended such a practice. We might ruminate upon the beauty which the monuments, thus placed, must have borrowed from the surrounding images of nature—from the trees, the wild flowers, from a stream running 170 perhaps within sight or hearing, from the beaten road stretching its

152–3 desire . . . memory 1814: desire which has been deduced from the higher feeling, namely, the consciousness of immortality 1810: desire, namely, to guard the remains of the deceased, and to preserve their memory, which has been deduced from the higher feeling, the consciousness of immortality *M.Y. i. 391.*   160 but, where it can, 1814: but 1810.   168 We might 1827: I could 1810–20.

weary length hard by. Many tender similitudes must these objects
have presented to the mind of the traveller leaning upon one of the
tombs, or reposing in the coolness of its shade, whether he had halted
from weariness or in compliance with the invitation, 'Pause, Traveller!' 175
so often found upon the monuments. And to its epitaph also must have
been supplied strong appeals to visible appearances or immediate
impressions, lively and affecting analogies of life as a journey—death
as a sleep overcoming the tired wayfarer—of misfortune as a storm
that falls suddenly upon him—of beauty as a flower that passeth away, 180
or of innocent pleasure as one that may be gathered—of virtue that
standeth firm as a rock against the beating waves;—of hope 'undermined insensibly like the poplar by the side of the river that has fed it,'
or blasted in a moment like a pine-tree by the stroke of lightning upon
the mountain-top—of admonitions and heart-stirring remembrances, 185
like a refreshing breeze that comes without warning, or the taste of
the waters of an unexpected fountain. These, and similar suggestions,
must have given, formerly, to the language of the senseless stone a
voice enforced and endeared by the benignity of that nature with which
it was in unison.—We, in modern times, have lost much of these 190
advantages; and they are but in a small degree counterbalanced to the
inhabitants of large towns and cities, by the custom of depositing
the dead within, or contiguous to, their places of worship; however
splendid or imposing may be the appearance of those edifices, or
however interesting or salutary the recollections associated with them. 195
Even were it not true that tombs lose their monitory virtue when thus
obtruded upon the notice of men occupied with the cares of the world,
and too often sullied and defiled by those cares, yet still, when death
is in our thoughts, nothing can make amends for the want of the
soothing influences of nature, and for the absence of those types of 200
renovation and decay, which the fields and woods offer to the notice
of the serious and contemplative mind. To feel the force of this sentiment, let a man only compare in imagination the unsightly manner in
which our monuments are crowded together in the busy, noisy, un-
clean, and almost grassless church-yard of a large town, with the still 205
seclusion of a Turkish cemetery, in some remote place; and yet further
sanctified by the grove of cypress in which it is embosomed. Thoughts
in the same temper as these have already been expressed with true
sensibility by an ingenuous Poet of the present day. The subject of his
poem is "All Saints Church, Derby:" he has been deploring the for- 210
bidding and unseemly appearance of its burial-ground, and uttering a

175 with 1814: to 1810.   194 appearance 1827: appearances 1810–20.
209 ingenuous 1814: ingenious 1810 [*corr. in M.Y. i. 391*].   210–11 forbidding 1814: forbidden 1810.

wish, that in past times the practice had been adopted of interring the
inhabitants of large towns in the country:—

> 'Then in some rural, calm, sequestered spot,
> Where healing Nature her benignant look   215
> Ne'er changes, save at that lorn season, when,
> With tresses drooping o'er her sable stole,
> She yearly mourns the mortal doom of man,
> Her noblest work, (so Israel's virgins erst,
> With annual moan upon the mountains wept   220
> Their fairest gone,) there in that rural scene,
> So placid, so congenial to the wish
> The Christian feels, of peaceful rest within
> The silent grave, I would have stray'd.
>
> *   *   *   *
>
> —wandered forth, where the cold dew of heaven   225
> Lay on the humbler graves around, what time
> The pale moon gazed upon the turfy mounds,
> Pensive, as though like me, in lonely muse,
> 'Twere brooding on the dead inhumed beneath.
> There while with him, the holy man of Uz,   230
> O'er human destiny I sympathised,
> Counting the long, long periods prophecy
> Decrees to roll, ere the great day arrives
> Of resurrection, oft the blue-eyed Spring
> Had met me with her blossoms, as the Dove,   235
> Of old, returned with olive leaf, to cheer
> The Patriarch mourning o'er a world destroyed:
> And I would bless her visit; for to me
> 'Tis sweet to trace the consonance that links
> As one, the works of Nature and the word   240
> Of God.'—

JOHN EDWARDS.

A village church-yard, lying as it does in the lap of nature, may
indeed be most favourably contrasted with that of a town of crowded
population; and sepulture therein combines many of the best tendencies
which belong to the mode practised by the Ancients, with others 245
peculiar to itself. The sensations of pious cheerfulness, which attend
the celebration of the sabbath-day in rural places, are profitably
chastised by the sight of the graves of kindred and friends, gathered
together in that general home towards which the thoughtful yet happy

212 practice 1814: practices 1810.   224 stray'd [*or* strayed] 1810–32
recte: stayed 1837–50.

spectators themselves are journeying. Hence a parish-church, in the 250
stillness of the country, is a visible centre of a community of the living
and the dead; a point to which are habitually referred the nearest
concerns of both.

As, then, both in cities and in villages, the dead are deposited in close
connection with our places of worship, with us the composition of an 255
epitaph naturally turns, still more than among the nations of antiquity,
upon the most serious and solemn affections of the human mind; upon
departed worth—upon personal or social sorrow and admiration—
upon religion, individual and social—upon time, and upon eternity.
Accordingly, it suffices, in ordinary cases, to secure a composition of 260
this kind from censure, that it contain nothing that shall shock or be
inconsistent with this spirit.'But, to entitle an epitaph to praise, more
than this is necessary. It ought to contain some thought or feeling
belonging to the mortal or immortal part of our nature touchingly
expressed; and if that be done, however general or even trite the senti- 265
ment may be, every man of pure mind will read the words with
pleasure and gratitude. A husband bewails a wife; a parent breathes a
sigh of disappointed hope over a lost child; a son utters a sentiment of
filial reverence for a departed father or mother; a friend perhaps
inscribes an encomium recording the companionable qualities, or the 270
solid virtues, of the tenant of the grave, whose departure has left a
sadness upon his memory. This and a pious admonition to the living,
and a humble expression of Christian confidence in immortality, is the
language of a thousand church-yards; and it does not often happen that
anything, in a greater degree discriminate or appropriate to the dead 275
or to the living, is to be found in them. This want of discrimination
has been ascribed by Dr. Johnson, in his Essay upon the epitaphs of
Pope, to two causes; first, the scantiness of the objects of human praise;
and, secondly, the want of variety in the characters of men; or, to use
his own words, 'to the fact, that the greater part of mankind have no 280
character at all.' Such language may be holden without blame among
the generalities of common conversation; but does not become a critic
and a moralist speaking seriously upon a serious subject. The objects
of admiration in human-nature are not scanty, but abundant: and every
man has a character of his own, to the eye that has skill to perceive it. 285
The real cause of the acknowledged want of discrimination in sepulchral
memorials is this: That to analyse the characters of others, especially
of those whom we love, is not a common or natural employment of men
at any time. We are not anxious unerringly to understand the consti-

---

261 contain 1837: contains 1810–32.   277–8 Dr. Johnson . . . Pope 1814:
the Critic above quoted 1810.   279 the want 1814: to the want 1810.
281 Such language 1814: This is language which 1810.

tution of the minds of those who have soothed, who have cheered, who 290
have supported us: with whom we have been long and daily pleased or
delighted. The affections are their own justification. The light of love
in our hearts is a satisfactory evidence that there is a body of worth in
the minds of our friends or kindred, whence that light has proceeded.
We shrink from the thought of placing their merits and defects to be 295
weighed against each other in the nice balance of pure intellect; nor
do we find much temptation to detect the shades by which a good
quality or virtue is discriminated in them from an excellence known by
the same general name as it exists in the mind of another; and, least
of all, do we incline to these refinements when under the pressure of 300
sorrow, admiration, or regret, or when actuated by any of those feelings
which incite men to prolong the memory of their friends and kindred,
by records placed in the bosom of the all-uniting and equalising
receptacle of the dead.

The first requisite, then, in an Epitaph is, that it should speak, in a 305
tone which shall sink into the heart, the general language of humanity
as connected with the subject of death—the source from which an
epitaph proceeds—of death, and of life. To be born and to die are the
two points in which all men feel themselves to be in absolute coincidence. This general language may be uttered so strikingly as to 310
entitle an epitaph to high praise; yet it cannot lay claim to the highest
unless other excellencies be superadded. Passing through all intermediate steps, we will attempt to determine at once what these excellencies are, and wherein consists the perfection of this species of
composition.—It will be found to lie in a due proportion of the common 315
or universal feeling of humanity to sensations excited by a distinct and
clear conception, conveyed to the reader's mind, of the individual,
whose death is deplored and whose memory is to be preserved; at
least of his character as, after death, it appeared to those who loved
him and lament his loss. The general sympathy ought to be quickened, 320
provoked, and diversified, by particular thoughts, actions, images,—
circumstances of age, occupation, manner of life, prosperity which the
deceased had known, or adversity to which he had been subject; and
these ought to be bound together and solemnised into one harmony by
the general sympathy. The two powers should temper, restrain, and 325
exalt each other. The reader ought to know who and what the man
was whom he is called upon to think of with interest. A distinct conception should be given (implicitly where it can, rather than explicitly)
of the individual lamented.—But the writer of an epitaph is not an
anatomist, who dissects the internal frame of the mind; he is not even 330

a painter, who executes a portrait at leisure and in entire tranquillity: his delineation, we must remember, is performed by the side of the grave; and, what is more, the grave of one whom he loves and admires. What purity and brightness is that virtue clothed in, the image of which must no longer bless our living eyes! The character of a deceased 335 friend or beloved kinsman is not seen, no—nor ought to be seen, otherwise than as a tree through a tender haze or a luminous mist, that spiritualises and beautifies it; that takes away, indeed, but only to the end that the parts which are not abstracted may appear more dignified and lovely; may impress and affect the more. Shall we say, then, that 340 this is not truth, not a faithful image; and that, accordingly, the purposes of commemoration cannot be answered?—It *is* truth, and of the highest order; for, though doubtless things are not apparent which did exist; yet, the object being looked at through this medium, parts and proportions are brought into distinct view which before had been only 345 imperfectly or unconsciously seen: it is truth hallowed by love—the joint offspring of the worth of the dead and the affections of the living! This may easily be brought to the test. Let one, whose eyes have been sharpened by personal hostility to discover what was amiss in the character of a good man, hear the tidings of his death, and what a 350 change is wrought in a moment! Enmity melts away; and, as it disappears, unsightliness, disproportion, and deformity, vanish; and, through the influence of commiseration, a harmony of love and beauty succeeds. Bring such a man to the tombstone on which shall be inscribed an epitaph on his adversary, composed in the spirit which we 355 have recommended. Would he turn from it as from an idle tale? No;— the thoughtful look, the sigh, and perhaps the involuntary tear, would testify that it had a sane, a generous, and good meaning; and that on the writer's mind had remained an impression which was a true abstract of the character of the deceased; that his gifts and graces were 360 remembered in the simplicity in which they ought to be remembered. The composition and quality of the mind of a virtuous man, contemplated by the side of the grave where his body is mouldering, ought to appear, and be felt as something midway between what he was on earth walking about with his living frailties, and what he may be 365 presumed to be as a Spirit in heaven.

It suffices, therefore, that the trunk and the main branches of the worth of the deceased be boldly and unaffectedly represented. Any further detail, minutely and scrupulously pursued, especially if this be done with laborious and antithetic discriminations, must inevitably 370 frustrate its own purpose; forcing the passing Spectator to this conclusion,—either that the dead did not possess the merits ascribed to

336–7 otherwise 1814: other 1810.   356 No 1827: Ah! no 1810–20.

him, or that they who have raised a monument to his memory, and
must therefore be supposed to have been closely connected with him,
were incapable of perceiving those merits; or at least during the act of 375
composition had lost sight of them; for, the understanding having been
so busy in its petty occupation, how could the heart of the mourner be
other than cold? and in either of these cases, whether the fault be on the
part of the buried person or the survivors, the memorial is unaffecting
and profitless. 380

Much better is it to fall short in discrimination than to pursue it too
far, or to labour it unfeelingly. For in no place are we so much disposed
to dwell upon those points, of nature and condition, wherein all men
resemble each other, as in the temple where the universal Father is
worshipped, or by the side of the grave which gathers all human 385
Beings to itself, and 'equalises the lofty and the low.' We suffer and
we weep with the same heart; we love and are anxious for one another
in one spirit; our hopes look to the same quarter; and the virtues by
which we are all to be furthered and supported, as patience, meekness,
good-will, justice, temperance, and temperate desires, are in an equal 390
degree the concern of us all. Let an Epitaph, then, contain at least these
acknowledgments to our common nature; nor let the sense of their
importance be sacrificed to a balance of opposite qualities or minute
distinctions in individual character; which if they do not, (as will for
the most part be the case,) when examined, resolve themselves into a 395
trick of words, will, even when they are true and just, for the most part
be grievously out of place; for, as it is probable that few only have
explored these intricacies of human nature, so can the tracing of them
be interesting only to a few. But an epitaph is not a proud writing shut
up for the studious: it is exposed to all—to the wise and the most 400
ignorant; it is condescending, perspicuous, and lovingly solicits
regard; its story and admonitions are brief, that the thoughtless, the
busy, and indolent, may not be deterred, nor the impatient tired: the
stooping old man cons the engraven record like a second horn-book;—
the child is proud that he can read it;—and the stranger is introduced 405
through its mediation to the company of a friend: it is concerning all,
and for all:—in the church-yard it is open to the day; the sun looks
down upon the stone, and the rains of heaven beat against it.

Yet, though the writer who would excite sympathy is bound in this
case, more than in any other, to give proof that he himself has been 410
moved, it is to be remembered, that to raise a monument is a sober
and a reflective act; that the inscription which it bears is intended to be
permanent, and for universal perusal; and that, for this reason, the
thoughts and feelings expressed should be permanent also—liberated

390 justice, 1837: *om.* 1810–32.

from that weakness and anguish of sorrow which is in nature transitory, 415
and which with instinctive decency retires from notice. The passions
should be subdued, the emotions controlled; strong, indeed, but
nothing ungovernable or wholly involuntary. Seemliness requires this,
and truth requires it also: for how can the narrator otherwise be trusted?
Moreover, a grave is a tranquillising object: resignation in course of 420
time springs up from it as naturally as the wild flowers, besprinkling
the turf with which it may be covered, or gathering round the monument by which it is defended. The very form and substance of the
monument which has received the inscription, and the appearance of
the letters, testifying with what a slow and laborious hand they must 425
have been engraven, might seem to reproach the author who had given
way upon this occasion to transports of mind, or to quick turns of
conflicting passion; though the same might constitute the life and
beauty of a funeral oration or elegiac poem.

These sensations and judgments, acted upon perhaps unconsciously, 430
have been one of the main causes why epitaphs so often personate the
deceased, and represent him as speaking from his own tomb-stone. The
departed Mortal is introduced telling you himself that his pains are
gone; that a state of rest is come; and he conjures you to weep for him
no longer. He admonishes with the voice of one experienced in the 435
vanity of those affections which are confined to earthly objects, and
gives a verdict like a superior Being, performing the office of a judge,
who has no temptations to mislead him, and whose decision cannot but
be dispassionate. Thus is death disarmed of its sting, and affliction
unsubstantialised. By this tender fiction, the survivors bind themselves 440
to a sedater sorrow, and employ the intervention of the imagination in
order that the reason may speak her own language earlier than she
would otherwise have been enabled to do. This shadowy interposition
also harmoniously unites the two worlds of the living and the dead by
their appropriate affections. And it may be observed, that here we have 445
an additional proof of the propriety with which sepulchral inscriptions
were referred to the consciousness of immortality as their primal
source.

I do not speak with a wish to recommend that an epitaph should be
cast in this mould preferably to the still more common one, in which 450
what is said comes from the survivors directly; but rather to point out
how natural those feelings are which have induced men, in all states
and ranks of society, so frequently to adopt this mode. And this I have
done chiefly in order that the laws, which ought to govern the composition of the other, may be better understood. This latter mode, 455

418 involuntary 1810–14, 1827–50: involuntarily [*sic*] 1820.   445 it
may be observed 1832: I may observe 1810–27.

namely, that in which the survivors speak in their own persons, seems
to me upon the whole greatly preferable: as it admits a wider range of
notices; and, above all, because, excluding the fiction which is the
groundwork of the other, it rests upon a more solid basis.

Enough has been said to convey our notion of a perfect epitaph; but 460
it must be borne in mind that one is meant which will best answer the
general ends of that species of composition. According to the course
pointed out, the worth of private life, through all varieties of situation
and character, will be most honourably and profitably preserved in
memory. Nor would the model recommended less suit public men, in 465
all instances save of those persons who by the greatness of their
services in the employments of peace or war, or by the surpassing
excellence of their works in art, literature, or science, have made themselves not only universally known, but have filled the heart of their
country with everlasting gratitude. Yet I must here pause to correct 470
myself. In describing the general tenour of thought which epitaphs
ought to hold, I have omitted to say, that if it be the *actions* of a man,
or even some *one* conspicuous or beneficial act of local or general
utility, which have distinguished him, and excited a desire that he
should be remembered, then, of course, ought the attention to be 475
directed chiefly to those actions or that act: and such sentiments dwelt
upon as naturally arise out of them or it. Having made this necessary
distinction, I proceed.—The mighty benefactors of mankind, as they
are not only known by the immediate survivors, but will continue to be
known familiarly to latest posterity, do not stand in need of biographic 480
sketches, in such a place; nor of delineations of character to individualise
them. This is already done by their Works, in the memories of men.
Their naked names, and a grand comprehensive sentiment of civic
gratitude, patriotic love, or human admiration—or the utterance of
some elementary principle most essential in the constitution of true 485
virtue;—or a declaration touching that pious humility and self-
abasement, which are ever most profound as minds are most susceptible
of genuine exaltation—or an intuition, communicated in adequate
words, of the sublimity of intellectual power;—these are the only
tribute which can here be paid—the only offering that upon such an 490
altar would not be unworthy.

'What needs my Shakspeare for his honoured bones
The labour of an age in piled stones,
Or that his hallowed reliques should be hid
Under a star-ypointing pyramid?   495

461 borne in mind 1832: observed 1810–27.   466 save of 1814: save 1810.
474 have 1814: has 1810.   482 Works 1814: actions 1810.   486–8 —or
a declaration . . . exaltation— 1837: *om.* 1810–32.

Dear Son of Memory, great Heir of Fame,
What need'st thou such weak witness of thy name?
Thou in our wonder and astonishment
Hast built thyself a livelong monument,
And so sepulchred, in such pomp dost lie,   500
That kings for such a tomb would wish to die.'

[ESSAY UPON EPITAPHS, II]

Yet even these bones from insult to protect
Some frail memorial still erected nigh,
With uncouth rhymes and shapeless sculpture deck'd,
Implores the passing tribute of a sigh.

Their name, their years, spelt by the unletter'd Muse,   5
The place of fame and elegy supply,
And many a holy text around she strews,
That teach the rustic moralist to die.

———————

WHEN a Stranger has walked round a Country Church-yard and
glanced his eye over so many brief Chronicles, as the tomb-stones 10
usually contain, of faithful Wives, tender Husbands, dutiful Children,
and good Men of all classes; he will be tempted to exclaim, in the
language of one of the Characters of a modern Tale in a similar situation, "Where are all the *bad* People buried?" He may smile to himself
an answer to this question, and may regret that it has intruded upon 15
him so soon. For my own part such has been my lot. And, indeed, a
Man, who is in the habit of suffering his mind to be carried passively
towards truth as well as of going with conscious effort in search of it,
may be forgiven, if he has sometimes insensibly yielded to the delusion
of those flattering recitals, and found a pleasure in believing that the 20
prospect of real life had been as fair as it was in that picture represented. And such a transitory oversight will without difficulty be
forgiven by those who have observed a trivial fact in daily life, namely,
how apt, in a series of calm weather, we are to forget that rain and
storms have been, and will return, to interrupt any scheme of business 25
or pleasure which our minds are occupied in arranging. Amid the quiet
of a Church-yard thus decorated as it seemed by the hand of Memory,
and shining, if I may so say, in the light of love, I have been affected
by sensations akin to those which have risen in my mind while I have
been standing by the side of a smooth Sea, on a Summer's day. It is 30

The title is editorial: The Friend Nº 1 *heading in* MS.   18 with MS.²: in
MS.   22 without difficulty be MS.²: be readi MS.   24 rain MS.²:
rains MS.   27 as *Edd.*: at MS.   29–30 while . . . standing MS.²: while
standing MS.

such a happiness to have, in an unkind World, one Enclosure where
the voice of detraction is not heard; where the traces of evil inclinations
are unknown; where contentment prevails, and there is no jarring tone
in the peaceful Concert of amity and gratitude. I have been rouzed from
this reverie by a consciousness, suddenly flashing upon me, of the 35
anxieties, the perturbations, and, in many instances, the vices and
rancorous dispositions, by which the hearts of those who lie under so
smooth a surface and so fair an outside must have been agitated. The
image of an unruffled Sea has still remained; but my fancy has penetrated into the depths of that Sea—with accompanying thoughts of 40
Shipwreck, of the destruction of the Mariner's hopes, the bones of
drowned Men heaped together, monsters of the deep, and all the hideous
and confused sights which Clarence saw in his Dream!

Nevertheless, I have been able to return, (and who may not?) to a
steady contemplation of the benign influence of such a favourable 45
Register lying open to the eyes of all. Without being so far lulled as to
imagine I saw in a Village Church-yard the eye or central point of a
rural Arcadia, I have felt that with all the vague and general expressions of love, gratitude, and praise with which it is usually crowded,
it is a far more faithful representation of homely life as existing among 50
a Community in which circumstances have not been untoward, than
any report which might be made by a rigorous observer deficient in
that spirit of forbearance and those kindly prepossessions, without
which human life can in no condition be profitably looked at or described. For we must remember that it is the nature of Vice to force 55
itself upon notice, both in the act and by its consequences. Drunkenness,
cruelty, brutal manners, sensuality, impiety, thoughtless prodigality,
and idleness, are obstreperous while they are in the height and heyday
of their enjoyment; and, when that is passed away, long and obtrusive
is the train of misery which they draw after them. But, on the contrary, 60
the virtues, especially those of humble life, are retired; and many of the
highest must be sought for or they will be overlooked. Industry,
œconomy, temperance, and cleanliness, are indeed made obvious by
flourishing fields, rosy complexions, and smiling countenances; but
how few know anything of the trials to which Men in a lowly condition 65
are subject, or of the steady and triumphant manner in which those
trials are often sustained, but they themselves! The afflictions which
Peasants and rural Artizans have to struggle with are for the most part
secret; the tears which they wipe away, and the sighs which they

34 *After* gratitude. MS. *deletes*: The images of an [*cf.* 38–9]. 40 accompanying thoughts MS.²: thoughts MS. 41 Mariner's *Edd*.: Mariners MS.
50 as existing among MS.²: as it exists in MS. 51 circumstances MS.²:
their circumstances MS. 66 or of MS.²: of MS. 67 often sustained
MS.²: sustained MS. themselves! *Edd*.: themselves? MS.

stifle,—this is all a labour of privacy. In fact their victories are to them- 70
selves known only imperfectly: for it is inseparable from virtue, in the
pure sense of the word, to be unconscious of the might of her own
prowess. This is true of minds the most enlightened by reflection;
who have forecast what they may have to endure, and prepared themselves accordingly. It is true even of these, when they are called into 75
action, that they necessarily lose sight of their own accomplishments,
and support their conflicts in self-forgetfulness and humility. That
species of happy ignorance, which is the consequence of these noble
qualities, must exist still more frequently, and in a greater degree, in
those persons to whom duty has never been matter of laborious 80
speculation, and who have no intimations of the power to act and to
resist which is in them, till they are summoned to put it forth. I could
illustrate this by many examples, which are now before my eyes; but
it would detain me too long from my principal subject which was to
suggest reasons for believing that the encomiastic language of rural 85
Tomb-stones does not so far exceed reality as might lightly be supposed.
Doubtless, an inattentive or ill-disposed Observer, who should apply
to the surrounding Cottages the knowledge which he may possess of
any rural neighbourhood, would upon the first impulse confidently
report that there was little in their living Inhabitants which reflected 90
the concord and the virtue there dwelt upon so fondly. Much has been
said, in a former paper tending to correct this disposition; and which
will naturally combine with the present considerations. Besides, to
slight the uniform language of these memorials as on that account not
trustworthy would obviously be unjustifiable. Enter a Church-yard by 95
the Sea-coast, and you will be almost sure to find the Tomb-stones
crowded with metaphors taken from the Sea and a Sea-faring life.
These are uniformly in the same strain; but surely we ought not thence
to infer that the words are used of course without any heart-felt sense
of their propriety. Would not the contrary conclusion be right? But I 100
will adduce a fact which more than a hundred analogical arguments
will carry to the mind a conviction of the strength and sanctity of these
feelings which persons in humble stations of society connect with their
departed Friends & Kindred. We learn from the Statistical account of
Scotland that, in some districts, a general transfer of Inhabitants has 105

77 support MS.[2]: sustain MS.   79 still more MS.[2]: more MS.
80–1 laborious speculation MS.[2]: speculation MS.   84, 90 principal . . . there]
Altered from principle *and* their, *and underscored in pencil, perhaps only to indicate the*
errors of spelling.   95 *After* unjustifiable. MS. *deletes:* Finally let us reflect
that [?] we forget our afflictions or vexations when they have passed [?] true that
we are insensible to the height and depth of [?] are removed from us.   An experienced &c. [*cf.* 118–22]   101–4 which . . . Kindred MS.[2]: which will
[? place *or* ? plead] more strongly for my point than a hundred analogical arguments MS.

taken place; and that a great majority of those who live, and labour, and attend public worship in one part of the Country, are buried in another. Strong and inconquerable still continues to be the desire of all, that their bones should rest by the side of their forefathers, and very poor Persons provide that their bodies should be conveyed if necessary to 110 a great distance to obtain that last satisfaction. Nor can I refrain from saying that this natural interchange by which the living Inhabitants of a Parish have small knowledge of the dead who are buried in their Church-yards is grievously to be lamented wheresoever it exists. For it cannot fail to preclude not merely much but the best part of the 115 wholesome influence of that communion between living and dead which the conjunction in rural districts of the place of burial and place of worship tends so effectually to promote. Finally let us remember that if it be the nature of Man to be insensible to vexations and afflictions when they have passed away he is equally insensible to the height and 120 depth of his blessings till they are removed from him.

An experienced and well-regulated mind will not, therefore, be insensible to this monotonous language of sorrow and affectionate admiration; but will find under that veil a substance of individual truth. Yet, upon all Men, and upon such a mind in particular, an Epitaph must 125 strike with a gleam of pleasure, when the expression is of that kind which carries conviction to the heart at once that the Author was a sincere mourner, and that the Inhabitant of the Grave deserved to be so lamented. This may be done sometimes by a naked ejaculation; as in an instance which a friend of mine met with in a Church-yard in 130 Germany; thus literally translated. "Ah! they have laid in the Grave a brave Man—he was to me more than many!"

> Ach! sie haben
> Einen Braven
> Mann begraben—   135
> Mir war er mehr als viele.

An effect as pleasing is often produced by the recital of an affliction endured with fortitude, or of a privation submitted to with contentment;

111–12 Nor . . . natural MS.²: This unnatural MS.; *the* un- *of* unnatural *is deleted, in pencil, perhaps wrongly.*   116 wholesome *Edd.*: wholsome MS.   118 Finally MS.²: Finally with respect to the [   ] of persons in humble life towards their deceased Friends and Kindred MS. [*cf.* 102–4].   120 away MS.²: away from us MS.   height *Edd.*: heigth MS.   131 thus MS.²: it may be thus MS. laid MS.²: put into MS.   137 is often MS.²: may be MS.   138 fortitude, or MS.²: fortitude, MS.   *After* contentment; MS. *deletes*: [1] of resources by which the evil[?s] attendant upon it were diminished; [2] and the

or by a grateful display of the temporal blessings with which Providence had favoured the Deceased, and the happy course of life through   140
which he had passed. And where these individualities are untouched
upon it may still happen that the estate of man in his helplessness, in
his dependence upon his Maker or some other inherent of his nature
shall be movingly and profitably expressed. Every Reader will be able
to supply from his own observation instances of all these kinds, and it   145
will be more pleasing for him to refer to his memory than to have the
page crowded with unnecessary Quotations. I will however give one
or two from an old Book cited before. The following, of general
application, was a great favourite with our Forefathers.

> Farwel my Frendys, the tyd abidyth no man,   150
> I am departed hens, and so sal ye,
> But in this passage the best song I can
> Is *Requiem Eternam*, now Jesu grant it me.
> When I have ended all myn adversity
> Grant me in Paradys to have a mansion   155
> That shedst thy bloud for my redemption.

This Epitaph might seem to be of the age of Chaucer, for it has the
very tone and manner of his Prioress's Tale.

The next opens with a thought somewhat interrupting that complacency and gracious repose which the language and imagery of a   160
Church-yard tend to diffuse; but the truth is weighty, and will not be
less acceptable for the rudeness of the expression.

> When the bells be merrely roung
> And the Masse devoutly soung
> And the meate merrely eaten   165
> Then sall Robert Trappis his Wyffs and his Chyldren
>   be forgotten.

> Wherfor Jesu that of Mary sproung
> Set their soulys thy Saynts among
> Though it be undeservyd on their syde
> Yet good Lord let them evermor thy mercy abyde!   170

It is well known how fond our Ancestors were of a play upon the
Name of the deceased when it admitted of a double sense. The following is an instance of this propensity not idly indulged. It brings home
a general truth to the individual by the medium of a Pun, which will

148 following, MS.²: following is MS.   158 Prioress's *Edd.*: Prioresses
MS.   159 interrupting MS.²: discord- MS.   160 and [*first*] MS.²: that MS.
161 diffuse MS.²: convey MS.   *After* diffuse; MS. *deletes*: and which we before
contemplated with pleasure   171 were MS.²: were in their Epitaphs MS.
171–2 the Name . . . sense MS.³: words MS.: Names MS.².

be readily pardoned, for the sake of the image suggested by it, for the 175
happy mood of mind in which the Epitaph is composed, for the beauty
of the language, and for the sweetness of the versification, which indeed,
the date considered, is not a little curious—it is upon a man whose
name was Palmer. I have modernized the spelling in order that its
uncouthness may not interrupt the Reader's gratification.   180

> Palmers all our Fathers were
> I a *Palmer* lived here
> And travelled still till worn with age
> I ended this world's pilgrimage,
> On the blest Ascension-day   185
> In the chearful month of May;
> One thousand with four hundred seven,
> And took my journey hence to heaven.

With this join the following, which was formerly to be seen upon a
fair marble under the Portraiture of one of the Abbots of S! Albans.   190

> Hic quidem terra tegitur
> Peccati solvens debitum
> Cujus nomen non impositum
> In libro vitæ sit inscriptum.

The spirit of it may be thus given. "Here lies, covered by the Earth, 195
and paying his debt to sin, one whose Name is not set forth; may it be
inscribed in the book of Life!"

But these instances, of the humility, the pious faith, and simplicity
of our Forefathers have led me from the scene of our contemplations—
a Country Church-yard! and from the memorials at this day commonly 200
found in it. I began with noticing such as might be wholly uninteresting
from the uniformity of the language which they exhibit; because, without previously participating the truths upon which these general
attestations are founded, it is impossible to arrive at that state or
disposition of mind necessary to make those Epitaphs thoroughly felt 205
which have an especial recommendation. With the same view, I will
venture to say a few words upon another characteristic of these
Compositions almost equally striking; namely, the homeliness of some
of the inscriptions, the strangeness of the illustrative images, the
grotesque spelling, with the equivocal meaning often struck out by 210
it, and the quaint jingle of the rhymes. These have often excited regret
in serious minds, and provoked the unwilling to good-humoured
laughter. Yet, for my own part, without affecting any superior

180 Reader's *Edd.*: Readers MS.   189 upon a MS.²: under a MS.
197 inscribed MS.²: inserted MS.   206 especial MS.²: appropriate MS.

sanctity, I must say that I have been better satisfied with myself, when
in these evidences I have seen a proof how deeply the piety of the rude   215
Forefathers of the hamlet is seated in their natures, I mean how
habitual and constitutional it is, and how awful the feeling which they
attach to the situation of their departed Friends—a proof of this rather
than of their ignorance or of a deadness in their faculties to a sense of
the ridiculous. And that this deduction may be just, is rendered probable   220
by the frequent occurrence of passages, according to our present
notion, full as ludicrous, in the Writings of the most wise and learned
men of former ages, Divines or Poets, who in the earnestness of their
souls have applied metaphors and illustrations, taken either from
holy writ or from the usages of their own Country, in entire confidence   225
that the sacredness of the theme they were discussing would sanctify
the meanest object connected with it; or rather without ever conceiving
it was possible that a ludicrous thought could spring up in any mind
engaged in such meditations. And certainly, these odd and fantastic
combinations are not confined to Epitaphs of the Peasantry, or of the   230
lower orders of Society, but are perhaps still more commonly produced
among the higher, in a degree equally or more striking. For instance,
what shall we say to this upon Sir George Vane, the noted Secretary of
State to King Charles 1st?

> His Honour wonne i'th'field lies here in dust,   235
> His Honour got by grace shall never rust,
> The former fades, the latter shall fade never
> For why? He was Sr George once but St. George ever.

The date is 1679. When we reflect that the Father of this Personage
must have had his taste formed in the punning Court of James 1st and   240
that the Epitaph was composed at a time when our literature was stuffed
with quaint or out-of-the-way thoughts, it will seem not unlikely that
the Author prided himself upon what he might call a clever hit: I mean
that his better affections were less occupied with the several associations belonging to the two ideas than his vanity delighted with that   245
act of ingenuity by which they had been combined. But the first couplet
consists of a just thought naturally expressed: and I should rather
conclude the whole to be a work of honest simplicity; and that the
sense of worldly dignity associated with the title, in a degree habitual
to our Ancestors but which at this time we can but feebly sympathize   250
with, and the imaginative feeling involved, viz, the saintly and chival-
rous Name of the Champion of England, were unaffectedly linked

219 in MS.²: of MS.   223 ages MS.²: times MS.   225 usages
MS.²: images MS.   228 it was MS.²: it MS.   239 date MS.²: date of
this MS.

together: and that both were united and consolidated in the Author's mind, and in the minds of his contemporaries whom no doubt he had pleased, by a devout contemplation of a happy immortality, the reward 255 of the just.

At all events, leaving this particular case undecided, the general propriety of these notices cannot be doubted; and I gladly avail myself of this opportunity to place in a clear view the power and majesty of impassioned faith, whatever be its object: to shew how it subjugates 260 the lighter motions of the mind, and sweeps away superficial difference in things. And this I have done, not to lower the witling and the worldling in their own esteem, but with a wish to bring the ingenuous into still closer communion with those primary sensations of the human heart, which are the vital springs of sublime and pathetic composition, 265 in this and in every other kind. And, as from these primary sensations such composition speaks, so, unless correspondent ones listen promptly and submissively in the inner cell of the mind to whom it is addressed, the voice cannot be heard: its highest powers are wasted.

These suggestions may be further useful to establish a criterion of 270 sincerity, by which a Writer may be judged; and this is of high import. For, when a Man is treating an interesting subject, or one which he ought not to treat at all unless he be interested, no faults have such a killing power as those which prove that he is not in earnest, that he is acting a part, has leisure for affectation, and feels that without it he could 275 do nothing. This is one of the most odious of faults; because it shocks the moral sense: and is worse in a sepulchral inscription, precisely in the same degree as that mode of composition calls for sincerity more urgently than any other. And indeed, where the internal evidence proves that the Writer was moved, in other words where this charm 280 of sincerity lurks in the language of a Tombstone and secretly pervades it, there are no errors in style or manner for which it will not be, in some degree, a recompence; but without habits of reflection a test of this inward simplicity cannot be come at: and, as I have said, I am now writing with a hope to assist the well-disposed to attain it. 285

Let us take an instance where no one can be at a loss. The following Lines are said to have been written by the illustrious Marquis of Montrose with the point of his Sword, upon being informed of the death of his Master Charles 1st.

> Great, good, and just, could I but rate 290
> My griefs, and thy so rigid fate;

253 that both were MS.²: thus MS.   258 I gladly MS.²: I MS.
259 clear MS.²: clearer MS.   264 into MS.²: in MS.   286 Let us . . .
loss. MS.²: *om.* MS.   286–7 The . . . are MS.²: Take the following Lines MS.

I'd weep the world to such a strain,
As it should deluge once again.
But since thy loud-tongued blood demands supplies,
More from Briareus hands than Argus eyes,   295
I'll sing thy Obsequies with Trumpets sounds,
And write thy Epitaph with blood and wounds.

These funereal verses would certainly be wholly out of their place
upon a tombstone; but who can doubt that the Writer was transported
to the height of the occasion?— that he was moved as it became an   300
heroic Soldier, holding those Principles and opinions, to be moved?
His soul labours;—the most tremendous event in the history of the
Planet, namely, the Deluge, is brought before his imagination by the
physical image of tears,—a connection awful from its very remoteness
and from the slender bond that unites the ideas:—it passes into the 305
region of Fable likewise; for all modes of existence that forward his
purpose are to be pressed into the service. The whole is instinct with
spirit, and every word has its separate life; like the Chariot of the
Messiah, and the wheels of that Chariot, as they appeared to the
imagination of Milton aided by that of the Prophet Ezekiel. It had   310
power to move of itself but was conveyed by Cherubs.

> as with stars their bodies all
> And wings were set with eyes, with eyes the wheels
> Of Beryl, and careering fires between.

Compare with the above Verses of Montrose the following Epitaph   315
upon Sir Philip Sidney, which was formerly placed over his Grave in
S.t Paul's Church.

> England, Netherland, the Heavens, and the Arts,
> The Soldiers, and the World, have made six parts
> Of noble Sidney: for who will suppose   320
> That a small heap of Stones can Sidney enclose?
>
> England hath his Body, for she it fed,
> Netherland his Blood, in her defence shed:
> The Heavens have his Soul, the Arts have his Fame,
> The Soldiers the grief, the World his good Name.   325

There were many points in which the case of Sidney resembled that of
Charles 1.st: He was a Sovereign but of a nobler kind—a Sovereign in
the hearts of Men: and after his premature death he was truly, as he

---

299 transported MS.²: exalted MS.   301 Soldier MS.²: Man MS.
305 and from MS.²: and MS.   310 It MS.²: The Chariot MS.   312 as
Edd.: om. MS.   315 of MS.²: of the Marquis of MS.

hath been styled, "the world-mourned Sidney". So fondly did the admiration of his Contemporaries settle upon him, that the sudden 330 removal of a man so good, great, and thoroughly accomplished, wrought upon many even to repining, and to the questioning the dispensations of Providence. Yet he, whom Spenser and all the Men of Genius of his Age had tenderly bemoaned, is thus commemorated upon his Tombstone; and to add to the indignity, the memorial is nothing 335 more than the second-hand Coat of a French Commander! It is a servile translation from a French Epitaph, which, says Weever, "was by some English Wit happily imitated and ingeniously applied to the honour of our worthy Chieftain". Yet Weever, in a foregoing Paragraph thus expresses himself upon the same Subject; giving without his own 340 knowledge, in my opinion, an example of the manner in which such an Epitaph ought to have been composed.—"But here I cannot pass over in silence Sir Philip Sidney the elder brother, being (to use Camden's words) the glorious star of this family, a lively pattern of virtue, and the lovely joy of all the learned sort; who fighting valiantly with the 345 enemy before Zutphen in Gelderland, dyed manfully. This is that Sidney, whom, as God's will was, he should therefore be born into the world even to shew unto our age a sample of ancient virtues: so his good pleasure was, before any man looked for it, to call for him again, and take him out of the world, as being more worthy of heaven than 350 earth. Thus we may see perfect virtue suddenly vanisheth out of sight, and the best men continue not long."

There can be no need to analyse this simple effusion of the moment in order to contrast it with the laboured composition before given: the difference will flash upon the Reader at once. But I may say, it is not 355 likely that such a frigid composition as the former would have ever been applied to a Man whose death had so stirred up the hearts of his Contemporaries, if it had not been felt that something different from that nature which each Man carried in his own breast was in this case requisite; and that a certain *straining* of mind was inseparable from the 360 Subject. Accordingly, an Epitaph is adopted in which the Writer had turned from the genuine affections and their self-forgetting inspirations, to the end that his Understanding, or the faculty designated by the word *head* as opposed to *heart*, might curiously construct a fabric to be wondered at. Hyperbole in the language of Montrose is a mean instru- 365 ment made mighty because wielded by an afflicted Soul, and strangeness is here the order of Nature. Montrose stretched after remote

---

355 it MS.[2]: that it MS. 356 such a frigid MS.[2]: so frigid a MS.
359 carried MS.[2]: has carried MS. was in this case MS.[2]: was MS. 360 inseparable MS.[2]: necessary MS. 363 his MS.[2]: the MS. 365 of MS.[2]:
of the Marquis of MS.

things but was at the same time propelled towards them; the French
Writer goes deliberately in search of them; no wonder then if what
he brings home does not prove worth the carriage!   370
Let us return to an instance of common life. I quote it with reluctance,
not so much for its absurdity as that the expression in one place will
strike at first sight as little less than impious; and it is indeed, though
unintentionally so, most irreverent. But I know no other example that
will so forcibly illustrate the important truth I wish to establish. The   375
following Epitaph is to be found in a Church-yard in Westmorland
which the present Writer has reason to think of with interest as it contains the remains of some of his Ancestors and Kindred. The date is
1673.

> Under this Stone, Reader, inter'd doth lye,   380
> Beauty and virtue's true epitomy.
> At her appearance the noone-son
> Blush'd and shrunk in 'cause quite outdon.
> In her concenter'd did all graces dwell:
> God pluck'd my rose that he might take a smel.   385
> I'll say no more: But weeping wish I may
> Soone with thy dear chaste ashes com to lay.
> Sic efflevit Maritus

Can any thing go beyond this in extravagance? Yet, if the fundamental
thoughts be translated into a natural style, they will be found reason-   390
able and affecting—"The Woman who lies here interred, was in my
eyes a perfect image of beauty and virtue; she was to me a brighter
object than the Sun in heaven: God took her, who was my delight,
from this earth to bring her nearer to himself. Nothing further is
worthy to be said than that weeping I wish soon to lie by thy dear   395
chaste ashes—Thus did the Husband pour out his tears."
These verses are preceeded by a brief account of the Lady, in Latin
prose; in which the little that is said is the uncorrupted language of
affection. But, without this introductory communication, I should
myself have had no doubt, after recovering from the first shock of   400
surprize and disapprobation, that this man, notwithstanding his
extravagant expressions was a sincere mourner; and that his heart,
during the very act of composition, was moved. These fantastic images,
though they stain the writing, stained not his soul.—They did not even

369 goes deliberately MS.²: goes MS.   370 *After* carriage! MS. *deletes*:
In pursuance of the same general argument   371 life. MS.²: life which will
be found an extreme case indeed MS.   373–4 and it is . . . so, MS.²: though
unintentionally MS.   377 present Writer MS.²: Writer MS.   389 go
. . . extravagance MS.²: be more absurdity [*sic*] MS.   397 preceeded] *So
in* MS.   404 even *Grosart*: ev[*tear*] MS.

touch it; but hung like globules of rain suspended above a green leaf, 405
along which they may roll and leave no trace that they have passed
over it. This simple-hearted Man must have been betrayed by a common notion that what was natural in prose would be out of place in
verse;—that it is not the Muse which puts on the Garb but the Garb
which makes the Muse. And, having adopted this notion at a time when 410
vicious writings of this kind accorded with the public taste, it is
probable that, in the excess of his modesty, the blankness of his inexperience, and the intensity of his affection, he thought that the
further he wandered from nature in his language the more would he
honour his departed Consort, who now appeared to him to have sur- 415
passed humanity in the excellence of her endowments. The quality of
his fault and its very excess are both in favour of this conclusion.

Let us contrast this Epitaph with one taken from a celebrated Writer
of the last Century.

> *"To the memory of* Lucy Lyttleton, *Daughter &c*   420
> *who departed this life &c aged 29. Having employed*
> *the short time assigned to her here in the uniform*
> *practice of religion and virtue.*
>
> Made to engage all hearts, and charm all eyes;
> Though meek, magnanimous; though witty, wise;   425
> Polite, as all her life in courts had been;
> Yet good, as she the world had never seen;
> The noble fire of an exalted mind,
> With gentle female tenderness combined.
> Her speech was the melodious voice of love,   430
> Her song the warbling of the vernal grove;
> Her eloquence was sweeter than her song,
> Soft as her heart, and as her reason strong;
> Her form each beauty of the mind express'd,
> Her mind was Virtue by the Graces drest."   435

The prose part of this inscription has the appearance of being
intended for a Tomb-stone; but there is nothing in the verse that would
suggest such a thought. The composition is in the style of those laboured
portraits in words which we sometimes see placed at the bottom of a
print, to fill up lines of expression which the bungling Artist had left 440

407 betrayed MS.²: betrayed perhaps MS.   411 writings MS.²: Writers
MS.   accorded MS.²: adopted MS.   412 his [*first*] MS.²: this MS.   modesty,
MS.²: modesty, and MS.   412–13 inexperience MS.²: experience MS.
416 humanity MS.²: nature MS.   quality MS.²: nature MS.   418 with
MS.²: and MS.   436 has... being MS.²: appears MS.   438 in MS.²: of MS.

imperfect. We know from other evidence that Lord Lyttleton dearly loved his wife: he has indeed composed a monody to her memory which proves this, and that she was an amiable Woman; neither of which facts could have been gathered from these inscriptive Verses. This Epitaph would derive little advantage from being translated into 445 another style as the former was; for there is no under current, no skeleton or stamina, of thought and feeling. The Reader will perceive at once that nothing in the heart of the Writer had determined either the choice, the order, or the expression, of the ideas—that there is no interchange of action from within and from without—that the con- 450 nections are mechanical and arbitrary, and the lowest kind of these— Heart and Eyes—petty alliterations, as meek and magnanimous, witty and wise, combined with oppositions in thoughts where there is no necessary or natural opposition. These defects run through the whole; the only tolerable verse is, 455

"Her speech was the melodious voice of love."

Observe, the question is not which of these Epitaphs is better or worse; but which faults are of a worse *kind*. In the former case we have a Mourner whose soul is occupied by grief and urged forward by his admiration. He deems in his simplicity that no hyperbole can transcend 460 the perfections of her whom he has lost: for the version which I have given fairly demonstrates that, in spite of his outrageous expressions, the under current of his thoughts was natural and pure. We have therefore in him the example of a mind misled during the act of composition by false taste—to the highest possible degree; and, in that 465 of Lord Lyttleton, we have one of a feeling heart, not merely misled, but wholly laid asleep by the same power. Lord Lyttleton could not have written in this way upon such a subject, if he had not been seduced by the example of Pope, whose sparkling and tuneful manner had bewitched the men of letters his Contemporaries, and corrupted the 470 judgment of the Nation through all ranks of society.

441 other evidence MS.[2]: evidence MS. 442–3 memory which MS.[2]: memory MS. 445–7 This . . . perceive MS.[2]: In order that they may be more honestly compared with the extravagant Epitaph before given, let the Reader translate as was done in the former case the leading thoughts of this into other language; let him [? give] the skeleton or stamina as they really are, but this is not necessary. He will see MS. 449 the order MS.[2]: or the use MS. 453 combined MS.[2]: [? contained] MS. 467 power. MS.[2]: power and a [   ] of petty ingenuity put forth in it's stead. MS. 471 society. MS.[2]: society [? so] that a great portion of original Genius was necessary to embolden a Man to write faithfully to Nature upon any affecting subject if it belonged to a class of composition in which Pope had furnished examples. MS. *At this point follow the direction* New Paragraph *and, deleted, the words* Having mentioned (*replaced by* The course . . . brought us to). *In the right-hand margin, opposite* a feeling heart, not merely (466) *appears the word* Or *with two vertical lines about one inch long beneath it. Above the word* [? so] *in the passage recorded above is a mark of insertion. The alternative passage* I am anxious *etc. recorded in our Appendix was evidently to be inserted before the paragraph beginning at* 472.

The course which we have taken having brought us to the name of this distinguished Writer, I will in this place give a few observations upon his Epitaphs, the largest collection we have in our language, from the pen of any Writer of eminence. As the Epitaphs of Pope, and also those of Chiabrera, which occasioned this disquisition, are in metre, it may be proper here to enquire how far the notion of a perfect Epitaph, as given in a former Paper, may be modified by the choice of metre for the vehicle in preference to prose. If our opinions be just, it is manifest that the basis must remain the same in either case; and that the difference can only lie in the superstructure; and it is equally plain, that a judicious Man will be less disposed in this case than in any other to avail himself of the liberty given by metre to adopt phrases of fancy, or to enter into the more remote regions of illustrative imagery. For the occasion of writing an Epitaph is matter of fact in its intensity, and forbids more authoritatively than any other species of composition all modes of fiction, except those which the very strength of passion has created; which have been acknowledged by the human heart, and have become so familiar that they are converted into substantial realities. When I come to the Epitaphs of Chiabrera, I shall perhaps give instances in which I think he has not written under the impression of this truth: where the poetic imagery does not elevate, deepen, or refine the human passion, which it ought always to do or not to act at all, but excludes it. In a far greater degree are Pope's Epitaphs debased by faults into which he could not I think have fallen if he had written in prose as a plain Man, and not as a metrical Wit. I will transcribe from Pope's Epitaphs the one upon Mrs Corbet (who died of a Cancer); Dr Johnson having extolled it highly and pronounced it the best of the collection.

> Here rests a Woman, good without pretence,
> Blest with plain reason and with sober sense;
> No conquest she but o'er herself desir'd;
> No arts essayed, but not to be admir'd.
> Passion and pride were to her soul unknown,
> Convinc'd that virtue only is our own.
> So unaffected, so compos'd a mind,
> So firm, yet soft, so strong, yet so refin'd
> Heaven as it's purest gold by tortures tried
> The Saint sustain'd it, but the Woman died.

477 the MS.²: our MS.   490 shall perhaps MS.²: shall MS..   492 truth
MS.²: fact MS.   493 ought always to MS.²: might always MS.   495–6 in
prose MS.²: himself MS.   497 Cancer); MS.²: Cancer); in h MS.   498 having
MS.²: has MS.   highly and MS.²: and MS.

This *may* be the best of Pope's Epitaphs; but if the standard which we 510
have fixed be a just one it cannot be approved of. First, it must be
observed, that in the Epitaphs of this Writer the true impulse is always
wanting, and that his motions must of necessity be feeble. For he has
no other aim than to give a favourable *Portrait* of the Character of the
Deceased. Now mark the process by which this is performed. Nothing 515
is represented implicitly, that is, with its accompaniment of circumstances, or conveyed by its effects. The Author forgets that it is a
living creature that must interest us and not an intellectual Existence,
which a mere character is. Insensible to this distinction the brain of the
Writer is set at work to report as flatteringly as he may of the mind of 520
his subject; the good qualities are separately abstracted (can it be
otherwise than coldly and unfeelingly?) and put together again as
coldly and unfeelingly. The Epitaph now before us owes what exemption it may have from these defects in its general plan to the excruciating
disease of which the Lady died; but it too is liable to the same censure; 525
and is, like the rest, further objectionable in this: namely, that the
thoughts have their nature changed and moulded by the vicious
expression in which they are entangled, to an excess rendering them
wholly unfit for the place which they occupy.

"Here rests a Woman good without pretence   530
Blest with plain reason"
        —from which, *sober*
sense is not sufficiently distinguishable. This verse and a half, and the
one, *so unaffected, so composed a mind,* are characteristic, and the
expression is true to nature; but they are, if I may take the liberty of
saying it, the only parts of the Epitaph which have this merit. Minute 535
criticism is in its nature irksome; and, as commonly practised in books
and conversation, is both irksome and injurious. Yet every mind must
occasionally be exercised in this discipline, else it cannot learn the art
of bringing words rigorously to the test of thoughts; and these again
to a comparison with things, their archetypes; contemplated first in 540
themselves, and secondly in relation to each other; in all which processes the mind must be skilful, otherwise it will be perpetually
imposed upon. In the next couplet the word, *conquest*, is applied in a

510 *After* This MS. *deletes*: for aught I know   512 always] *Either underscored or, more likely, deleted in* MS.   515 mark MS.[2]: observe MS.   516 accompaniment MS.[2]: accompaniments MS.   517 effects. MS.[2]: effects [? but] the
brain of the Writer MS. [*cf.* 519–20].   518–19 an intellectual . . . character MS.[2]:
a mere intellectual Existence, which a character MS.   521 separately MS.[2]:
[? inseparably] MS.   523–4 exemption MS.[3]: [? objections] MS.: exception MS.[2].
525 died MS.[2]: died who is the subject of it MS.   it too . . . censure; MS.[2]: it
has too much of the same radical defect. MS.   530 "Here rests *Edd.*:
Here rest MS.   536–7 and, as . . . both MS.[2]: as . . . conversation, both
MS.   539 bringing MS.[2]: trying MS.

manner that would have been displeasing even from its triteness in a
copy of complimentary Verses to a fashionable Beauty; but to talk of 545
making conquests in an Epitaph is not to be endured. *No arts essayed,
but not to be admired*—are words expressing that she had recourse
to artifices to conceal her amiable and admirable qualities; and the
context implies that there was a merit in this; which surely no sane
mind would allow. But the meaning of the Author, simply and honestly 550
given, was nothing more than that she shunned admiration, probably
with a more apprehensive modesty than was common; and more than
this would have been inconsistent with the praise bestowed upon her—
that she had an unaffected mind. This couplet is further objectionable,
because the sense of love and peaceful admiration, which such a character 555
naturally inspires, is disturbed by an oblique and ill-timed stroke of
satire. She is not praised so much as others are blamed—and is degraded
by the Author in thus being made a covert or stalking-horse for gratifying a propensity the most abhorrent from her own nature. *"Passion
and pride were to her soul unknown"*—It cannot be meant that she had 560
no Passions, but that they were moderate and kept in subordination
to her reason; but the thought is not here expressed; nor is it clear that
a conviction in the understanding that *virtue only is our own*, though it
might suppress her pride, would be itself competent to govern or abate
many other affections and passions to which our frail nature is, and 565
ought, in various degrees, to be subject.—In fact, the Author appears
to have had no precise notion of his own meaning. If she was *"good
without pretence"* it seems unnecessary to say that she was not proud.
Dr Johnson, making an exception of the verse, *Convinced that virtue
only is our own*, praises this Epitaph for "containing nothing taken from 570
common places." Now in fact, as may be deduced from the principles of
this discourse, it is not only no fault but a primary requisite in an
Epitaph that it shall contain thoughts and feelings which are in their
substance common-place, and even trite. It is grounded upon the
universal intellectual property of man;—sensations which all men 575
have felt and feel in some degree daily and hourly;—truths whose very
interest and importance have caused them to be unattended to, as things
which could take care of themselves. But it is required that these truths
should be instinctively ejaculated, or should rise irresistibly from
circumstances; in a word that they should be uttered in such connection 580
as shall make it felt that they are not adopted—not spoken by rote, but
perceived in their whole compass with the freshness and clearness of an
original intuition. The Writer must introduce the truth with such

    546 essayed MS.²: *engaged* MS.   *564* to govern or MS.²: to MS.
570 only is our own MS.²: *is her own* MS.   *579* or should rise MS.²: and
sometimes as it were rising MS.   *581* are *Grosart*: MS. *torn*.

accompaniment as shall imply that he has mounted to the sources of things—penetrated the dark cavern from which the River that murmurs 585 in every one's ear has flowed from generation to generation. The line *"Virtue only is our own"*—is objectionable, not from the commonplaceness of the Truth, but from the vapid manner in which it is conveyed. A similar sentiment is expressed with appropriate dignity in an Epitaph by Chiabrera, where he makes the Archbishop of Urbino say 590 of himself, that he was

—"smitten by the great Ones of the world,
But did not fall; for Virtue braves all shocks,
Upon herself resting immoveably."

"So firm yet soft, so strong yet so refined"—these intellectual operations 595 (while they can be conceived of as operations of intellect at all, for in fact one half of the process is mechanical, words doing their own work, and one half of the line manufacturing the rest) remind me of the motions of a Posture-Master, or of a Man balancing a Sword upon his finger, which must be kept from falling at all hazards. *"The Saint sus-* 600 *tained it but the Woman died"*—Let us look steadily at this antithesis— the *Saint*, that is her soul strengthened by Religion supported the anguish of her disease with patience and resignation;—but the *Woman*, that is her *body*, (for if any thing else be meant by the word, woman, it contradicts the former part of the proposition and the passage is 605 nonsense) was overcome. Why was not this simply expressed; without playing with the Reader's fancy to the delusion and dishonour of his Understanding, by a trifling epigrammatic point? But alas! ages must pass away before men will have their eyes open to the beauty and majesty of Truth, and will be taught to venerate Poetry no further 610 than as She is a Handmaid pure as her Mistress—the noblest Handmaid in her train!

584 accompaniment MS.²: accompaniments MS.   590 Urbino *Edd.*: Albino MS.   595 *yet soft* MS.²: *so soft* MS.   600 hazards *Grosart*: hazar[*tear*] MS.   605 contradicts *Grosart*: con[*tear*]dicts MS.   606 Why *Grosart*: MS. *torn.*   607 fancy *Grosart*: fan[*tear*] MS.   610 be *Grosart*: MS. *torn.* 611 pure MS.²: as pure MS.

[ESSAY UPON EPITAPHS, III]

I VINDICATE the rights and dignity of Nature; and, as long as I condemn nothing without assigning reasons not lightly given, I cannot suffer any Individual, however highly and deservedly honoured by my Countrymen, to stand in my way. If my notions are right, the Epitaphs of Pope cannot well be too severely condemned: for not only 5 are they almost wholly destitute of those universal feelings and simple movements of mind which we have called for as indispensible, but they are little better than a tissue of false thoughts, languid and vague expression, unmeaning antithesis, and laborious attempts at discrimination. Pope's mind had been employed chiefly in observation upon the 10 vices and follies of men. Now, vice and folly are in contradiction with the moral principle which can never be extinguished in the mind: and, therefore, wanting this controul, are irregular, capricious, and inconsistent with themselves. If a man has once said, (see FRIEND No. 6) "Evil be thou my Good!" and has acted accordingly, however strenuous 15 may have been his adherence to this principle, it will be well known by those who have had an opportunity of observing him narrowly that there have been perpetual obliquities in his course; evil passions thwarting each other in various ways; and, now and then, revivals of his better nature, which check him for a short time or lead him to re- 20 measure his steps:—not to speak of the various necessities of counterfeiting virtue which the furtherance of his schemes will impose upon him, and the division which will be consequently introduced into his nature.

It is reasonable, then, that Cicero, when holding up Catiline to 25 detestation; and, (without going to such an extreme case) that Dryden and Pope, when they are describing Characters like Buckingham, Shaftsbury, Wharton, and the Duchess of Marlborough, should represent qualities and actions at war with each other and with themselves: and that the page should be suitably crowded with antithetical 30 expressions. But all this argues an obtuse moral sensibility and a consequent want of knowledge, if applied where virtue ought to be described in the language of affectionate admiration. In the mind of the truly great and good every thing that is of importance is at peace

The title is editorial: The Friend no 2 *heading in* MS.   4 If . . . right MS.²: If I am right in my notions concerning this species of composition MS.   9 unmeaning antithesis MS.²: antithesis MS.   14 No. 6 *Edd.*: No. [   ] MS.
15 *After* accordingly, MS. *deletes*: [?yet still]   16 by MS.²: to MS.
25 reasonable, then, MS.²: reasonable, MS.   30 be suitably MS.²: be MS.
31–2 argues . . . applied MS.²: applied MS.

with itself; all is stillness, sweetness, and stable grandeur. Accordingly 35
the contemplation of virtue is attended with repose. A lovely quality,
if its loveliness be clearly perceived, fastens the mind with absolute
sovereignty upon itself; permitting or inciting it to pass, by smooth
gradation or gentle transition, to some other kindred quality. Thus a
perfect image of meekness, (I refer to an instance before given) when 40
looked at by a tender mind in its happiest mood, might easily lead on
to the thought of magnanimity: for assuredly there is nothing in-
congruous in those virtues. But the mind would not then be separated
from the Person who is the object of its thoughts: it would still be
confined to that Person, or to others of the same general character; 45
that is, would be kept within the circle of qualities which range themselves quietly by each other's sides. Whereas, when meekness and
magnanimity are represented antithetically, the mind is not only
carried from the main object, but is compelled to turn to a subject in
which the quality exists divided from some other as noble, its natural 50
ally:—a painful feeling! that checks the course of love, and repels the
sweet thoughts that might be settling round the Person whom it was
the Author's wish to endear to us; but for whom, after this interruption,
we no longer care. If then a Man, whose duty it is to praise departed
excellence not without some sense of regret or sadness, to do this or 55
to be silent, should upon all occasions exhibit that mode of connecting
thoughts which is only natural while we are delineating vice under
certain relations, we may be assured that the nobler sympathies are
not alive in him; that he has no clear insight into the internal constitution of virtue; nor has himself been soothed, cheared, harmonized, 60
by those outward effects which follow every where her goings,—
declaring the presence of the invisible deity. And though it be true
that the most admirable of Men must fall far short of perfection, and
that the majority of those whose worth is commemorated upon their
Tomb-stones must have been Persons in whom good and evil were 65
intermixed in various proportions, and stood in various degrees of
opposition to each other, yet the reader will remember what has been
said before upon that medium of love, sorrow, and admiration through
which a departed friend is viewed: how it softens down or removes
these harshnesses and contradictions; which, moreover, must be sup- 70
posed never to have been grievous: for there can be no true love but

37 fastens MS.[2]: to fasten MS.   38 permitting MS.[2]: or permitting MS.
45 that Person MS.[2]: it MS.   49 carried MS.[2]: carried away MS.   55
this MS.[2]: that MS.   57 while . . . delineating MS.[2]: delineating MS.
59 into MS.[2]: of MS.   64–6 of those . . . and MS.[3]: whose worth is commemorated upon their Tomb-stones must be [must have been MS.[2]] intermixed
in various proportions, or MS.   68–9 through which . . . how it MS.[2]: which
MS.   70 harshnesses *Edd.*: harsnesses MS.   70–1 which . . . to MS.[3]:
while the same must be sup MS.: these moreover never can MS.[2].

between the good; and no Epitaph ought to be written upon a bad Man, except for a warning.

The purpose of the remarks given in the last Essay was chiefly to assist the reader in separating truth and sincerity from falsehood and affectation; presuming that if the unction of a devout heart be wanting every thing else is of no avail. It was shewn that a current of just thought and feeling may flow under a surface of illustrative imagery so impure as to produce an effect the opposite of that which was intended. Yet, though this fault may be carried to an intolerable *degree*, the reader will have gathered that in our estimation it is not *in kind* the most offensive and injurious. We have contrasted it in its excess with instances where the genuine current or vein was wholly wanting; where the thoughts and feelings had no vital union; but were artificially connected, or formally accumulated, in a manner that would imply discontinuity and feebleness of mind upon any occasion; but still more reprehensible here! I will proceed to give milder examples, not of this last kind but of the former; namely of failure from various causes where the groundwork is good.

> Take, holy earth! all that my soul holds dear:
> Take that best gift which Heaven so lately gave:
> To Bristol's fount I bore with trembling care,
> Her faded form. She bow'd to taste the wave—
> And died. Does youth, does beauty read the line?
> Does sympathetic fear their breasts alarm?
> Speak, dead Maria! breathe a strain divine;
> Even from the grave thou shalt have power to charm.
> Bid them be chaste, be innocent, like thee:
> Bid them in duty's sphere as meekly move:
> And if so fair, from vanity as free,
> As firm in friendship, and as fond in love;
> Tell them, tho tis an awful thing to die,
> ('Twas e'en to thee) yet, the dread path once trod;
> Heaven lifts its everlasting portals high,
> And bids "the pure in heart behold their God."

This Epitaph has much of what we have demanded: but it is debased in some instances by weakness of expression, in others by false prettiness.

79 impure MS.²: extravagant MS.   that which MS.²: what MS.   82 offensive and injurious MS.²: pernicious MS.   84 union MS.²: sympathy MS.   87 *After* here! MS. *deletes*: Yet still   87–88 milder examples MS.²: examples of failure, MS.   88 of this . . . of the] *Above each* of *is written* in; *the first group is rubbed with a pencil; in the second group only* of *is so rubbed.* 107 weakness . . . prettiness MS.²: weakness in others by false prettiness of expression MS.

"She bow'd to taste the wave and died." The plain truth was, she
drank the Bristol waters which failed to restore her, and her death soon
followed; but the expression involves a multitude of petty occupations   110
for the fancy: *"She bowed"*—was there any truth in this?—*"to taste the
wave,"* the water of a mineral spring which must have been drunk out
of a Goblet. Strange application of the word *Wave!* *"and died."* This
would have been a just expression if the water had killed her; but, as
it is, the tender thought involved in the disappointment of a hope   115
however faint is left unexpressed; and a shock of surprize is given,
entertaining perhaps to a light fancy, but to a steady mind unsatisfactory
—because false. *"Speak! dead Maria breathe a strain divine!"* This verse
flows nobly from the heart and the imagination; but perhaps it is not
one of those impassioned thoughts which should be fixed in language   120
upon a sepulchral stone. It is in its nature too poignant and transitory.
A Husband meditating by his Wife's grave would throw off such a
feeling, and would give voice to it; and it would be in its place in a
Monody to her Memory but, if I am not mistaken, ought to have been
suppressed here, or uttered after a different manner. The implied   125
impersonation of the Deceased (according to the tenor of what has
before been said) ought to have been more general and shadowy. *"And
if so fair, from vanity as free—As firm in friendship and as fond in love—
Tell them"*, these are two sweet verses, but the long suspension of the
sense excites the expectation of a thought less common than the   130
concluding one; and is an instance of a failure in doing what is most
needful and most difficult in an Epitaph to do; namely, to give to
universally received truths a pathos and spirit which shall re-admit
them into the soul like revelations of the moment.

I have said that this excellence is difficult to attain; and why? is it   135
because nature is weak?—no! Where the soul has been thoroughly
stricken, (and Heaven knows, the course of life has placed all men, at
some time or other, in that condition) there is never a want of *positive*
strength; but because the adversary of nature, (call that adversary Art
or by what name you will) is *comparatively* strong. The far-searching   140
influence of the power, which, for want of a better name, we will
denominate, Taste, is in nothing more evinced than in the changeful

---

108 *died."* Edd.: died," MS.   111 fancy: *Edd.*: fancy—MS.   113 application MS.²: this application MS.   118 false. *Edd.*: false—MS.   119 per-
haps] *Inserted in pencil, probably in Wordsworth's hand.*   125 uttered after
MS.²: clothed in MS.   128–9 *love . . .* verses MS.²: *love* are sweet verses MS.
129 *After* but MS. *deletes (in pencil)*: the word *fair* is misplaced [improper MS.²];
for unquestionably it was not intended that their title to [to receive MS.²] this
assurance should 'depend at all upon their personal beauty. In [Moreover, in
MS.²] this couplet and in what follows,   130 thought MS.²: sense MS.
132 namely MS.²: merely MS.   137 has MS.²: must have MS. (*but only* have
is deleted).   138 there Grosart: [*tear*]ere MS.   141 of the MS.²: of that MS.

character and complexion of that species of composition which we have
been reviewing. Upon a call so urgent, it might be expected that the
affections, the memory, and the imagination would be *constrained* to   145
speak their genuine language. Yet if the few specimens which have
been given in the course of this enquiry do not demonstrate the fact, the
Reader need only look into any collection of Epitaphs to be convinced
that the faults predominant in the literature of every age will be as
strongly reflected in the sepulchral inscriptions as any where; nay   150
perhaps more so, from the anxiety of the Author to do justice to the
occasion: and especially if the composition be in verse; for then it
comes more avowedly in the shape of a work of art; and, of course, is
more likely to be coloured by the works of art holden in most esteem
at the time. In a bulky Volume of Poetry entitled, ELEGANT EXTRACTS   155
in Verse, which must be known to most of my Readers, as it is circulated
every where and in fact constitutes at this day the poetical library of
our Schools, I find a number of Epitaphs, in verse, of the last century;
and there is scarcely one which is not thoroughly tainted by the artifices
which have overrun our writings in metre since the days of Dryden   160
and Pope. Energy, stillness, grandeur, tenderness, those feelings which
are the pure emanations of nature, those thoughts which have the
infinitude of truth, and those expressions which are not what the garb
is to the body but what the body is to the soul, themselves a constituent
part and power or function in the thought—all these are abandoned   165
for their opposites,—as if our Countrymen, through successive generations, had lost the sense of solemnity and pensiveness (not to speak of
deeper emotions) and resorted to the Tombs of their Forefathers and
Contemporaries only to be tickled and surprized. Would we not recoil
from such gratifications, in such a place, if the general literature of the   170
Country had not co-operated with other causes insidiously to weaken
our sensibilities and deprave our judgements? Doubtless, there are
shocks of event and circumstance, public and private, by which for all
minds the truths of Nature will be elicited; but sorrow for that Individual or people to whom these special interferences are necessary, to   175
bring them into communion with the inner spirit of things! for such
intercourse must be profitless in proportion as it is unfrequent, irregular,
and transient. Words are too awful an instrument for good and evil
to be trifled with: they hold above all other external powers a dominion
over thoughts. If words be not (recurring to a metaphor before used)   180
an incarnation of the thought but only a clothing for it, then surely will
they prove an ill gift; such a one as those poisoned vestments, read of

149 predominant . . . be MS.²: predominant will be MS.   151 from
MS.²: especially from MS.   175 or people to MS.²: to MS.   179 other
external MS.²: other MS.   181–2 it, . . . such MS.²: it, such MS.

in the stories of superstitious times, which had power to consume and to alienate from his right mind the victim who put them on. Language, if it do not uphold, and feed, and leave in quiet, like the power of 185 gravitation or the air we breathe, is a counter-spirit, unremittingly and noiselessly at work to derange, to subvert, to lay waste, to vitiate, and to dissolve. From a deep conviction then that the excellence of writing, whether in prose or verse, consists in a conjunction of Reason and Passion, a conjunction which must be of necessity benign; and that it 190 might be deduced from what has been said that the taste, intellectual Power, and morals of a Country are inseparably linked in mutual dependence, I have dwelt thus long upon this argument. And the occasion justifies me: for how could the tyranny of bad taste be brought home to the mind more aptly than by shewing in what degree the 195 feelings of nature yield to it when we are rendering to our friends this solemn testimony of our love? more forcibly than by giving proof that thoughts cannot, even upon this impulse, assume an outward life without a transmutation and a fall?

> "Epitaph on Miss Drummond in the Church of   200
> Brodsworth, Yorkshire
> Mason

> Here sleeps what once was beauty, once was grace;
> Grace, that with tenderness and sense combin'd
> To form that harmony of soul and face,   205
> Where beauty shines the mirror of the mind,
> Such was the maid, that in the morn of youth,
> In virgin innocence, in nature's pride,
> Blest with each art, that owes its charms to truth,
> Sunk in her Father's fond embrace, and died.   210
> He weeps: O venerate the holy tear!
> Faith lends her aid to ease affliction's load;
> The parent mourns his Child upon the bier,
> The christian yields an angel to his God."

The following is a translation from the Latin, communicated to a Lady 215 in her Childhood and by her preserved in memory. I regret that I have not seen the original.

189–90 of Reason . . . a conjunction which MS.²: which MS.   191 taste . . . and MS.²: taste, and MS.   195 aptly MS.²: forcibly MS.   197 more . . . proof MS.²: and MS.   199 fall? *Edd.*: fall. MS.   201 Brodsworth *Edd.*: Broadsworth MS.

She is gone—my beloved Daughter Eliza is gone,
Fair, chearful, benign, my child is gone.
Thee long to be regretted a Father mourns,   220
Regretted—but thanks to the most perfect God! not lost
For a happier age approaches
When again my child I shall behold
And live with thee for ever.

Mathew Dobson to his dear, engaging, happy Eliza   225

Who in the 18th year of her Age
Passed peaceably into heaven.

The former of these Epitaphs is very far from being the worst of its
kind, and on that account I have placed the two in contrast. Unquestionably, as the Father in the latter speaks in his own Person, the   230
situation is much more pathetic; but, making due allowance for this
advantage, who does not here feel a superior truth and sanctity, which
is not dependent upon this circumstance, but merely the result of the
expression and the connection of the thoughts? I am not so fortunate
as to have any knowledge of the Author of this affecting Composition,   235
but I much fear, if he had called in the assistance of English verse the
better to convey his thoughts, such sacrifices would, from various
influences, have been made *even by him*, that, though he might have
excited admiration in thousands, he would have truly moved no one.
The latter part of the following by Gray is almost the only instance,   240
among the metrical Epitaphs in our language of the last Century,
which I remember, of affecting thoughts rising naturally and keeping
themselves pure from vicious diction.

Epitaph on Mrs Clark.

———————

Lo! where the silent marble weeps,   245
A friend, a wife, a mother, sleeps;
A heart, within whose sacred cell
The peaceful virtues lov'd to dwell.
Affection warm, and love sincere,
And soft humanity were there.   250

228 The MS.²: Though the MS.   these MS.²: these two MS.   very far MS.²:
far MS.   228–9 the . . . account MS.²: an extreme case MS.   231–2 this
advantage MS.²: this MS.   239 would MS.²: would not MS.   240 instance
MS.²: instance where MS.   243 diction. MS.²: diction; and therefore retaining their appropriate power over the mind. MS.

In agony, in death resigned,
She felt the wound she left behind.
Her infant image, here below,
Sits smiling on a father's woe:
Whom what awaits, while yet he strays   255
Along the lonely vale of days?
A pang to secret sorrow dear;
A sigh, an unavailing tear,
Till time shall every grief remove,
With life, with memory, and with love.   260

I have been speaking of faults which are aggravated by temptations
thrown in the way of modern Writers when they compose in metre.
The first six lines of this Epitaph are vague and languid, more so than
I think would have been possible had it been written in prose. Yet
Gray, who was so happy in the remaining part, especially the last four 265
lines, has grievously failed *in prose*, upon a subject which it might have
been expected would have bound him indissolubly to the propriety of
Nature and comprehensive reason. I allude to the conclusion of the
Epitaph upon his Mother, where he says, "she was the careful tender
Mother of many Children, one of whom alone had the misfortune to 270
survive her." This is a searching thought, but wholly out of place. Had
it been said of an ideot, of a palsied child, or of an adult from any cause
dependent upon his Mother to a degree of helplessness which nothing
but maternal tenderness and watchfulness could answer, that he had
the misfortune to survive his Mother, the thought would have been 275
just. The same might also have been wrung from any Man (thinking
of himself) when his soul was smitten with compunction or remorse,
through the consciousness of a misdeed, from which he might have
been preserved (as he hopes or believes) by his Mother's prudence, by
her anxious care if longer continued or by the reverential fear of 280
offending or distressing her. But even then (unless accompanied with a
detail of extraordinary circumstances) if transferred to her monument,
it would have been mis-placed, as being too peculiar; and for reasons
which have been before alledged, namely, as too transitory and
poignant. But in an ordinary case, for a Man permanently and con- 285
spicuously to record that this was his fixed feeling; what is it but to
run counter to the course of nature, which has made it matter of

269–70 tender Mother MS.²: Mother MS.   271 but MS.²: but it is MS.
272 it been MS.²: any one MS.   276 The same might also MS.²: It also might
MS.   276–7 Man . . . himself) MS.²: Man MS.   278 through MS.²: from
MS.   he MS.²: he has a faith that he MS.   279 (as he . . . by MS.²: by MS.
280–1 reverential . . . distressing MS.²: reverence which he bore MS.   282–3 if
. . . monument, it MS.²: it MS.   283 as being . . . and MS.²: upon her
Monument MS.   284 as MS.²: as being MS.

expectation and congratulation that Parents should die before their Children? what is it, if searched to the bottom, but lurking and sickly selfishness? Does not the regret include a wish that the Mother should 290 have survived all her offspring, have witnessed that bitter desolation, where the order of things is disturbed and inverted? And finally does it not withdraw the attention of the Reader from the Subject to the Author of the Memorial, as one to be commiserated for his strangely unhappy condition, or to be condemned for the morbid constitution 295 of his feelings, or for his deficiency in judgment? A fault of the same kind, though less in degree, is found in the Epitaph of Pope upon Harcourt; of whom it is said that "he never gave his father grief but when he died." I need not point out how many situations there are in which such an expression of feeling would be natural and becoming; 300 but in a permanent Inscription things only should be admitted that have an enduring place in the mind: and a nice selection is required even among these. The Duke of Ormond said of his Son Ossory, "that he preferred his dead Son to any living Son in Christendom,"—a thought which (to adopt an expression used before) has the infinitude 305 of truth! But, though in this there is no momentary illusion, nothing fugitive, it would still have been unbecoming, had it been placed in open view over the Son's grave; inasmuch as such expression of it would have had an ostentatious air, and would have implied a disparagement of others. The sublimity of the sentiment consists in its being the 310 secret possession of the Father.

Having been engaged so long in the ungracious office of sitting in judgement where I have found so much more to censure than to approve, though wherever it was in my power, I have placed good by the side of evil, that the Reader might intuitively receive the truths 315 which I wished to communicate, I now turn back with pleasure to Chiabrera; of whose productions in this department the Reader of THE FRIEND may be enabled to form a judgment who has attentively perused the few specimens only which have been given. "An Epitaph" says Weever "is a superscription (either in verse or prose) or an astrict 320 pithie Diagram, writ, carved, or engraven, upon the tomb, grave, or sepulchre of the defunct, briefly declaring (*and that with a kind of commiseration*) the name, the age, the deserts, the dignities, the state, *the praises both of body and minde*, the good and bad fortunes in the life

293 attention of the Reader MS.²: readers attention MS.   296 in *Grosart*: MS. *torn*.   303 among MS.²: in MS.   308 the Son's MS.²: his MS. such . . . it MS.²: it MS.   309 and . . . implied MS.²: implying if displayed in that manner MS.   310 sublimity . . . sentiment MS.²: sublimity MS. 317–18 Reader . . . FRIEND MS.²: Reader MS.   319 only which MS.²: which MS.   have been MS.²: we have MS.   321 pithie *Edd.*: pithic MS.

and the manner and time of the death of the person therein interred." 325
This account of an Epitaph, which as far as it goes is just, was no doubt
taken by Weever from the Monuments of our own Country, and it
shews that in his conception an Epitaph was not to be an abstract
character of the deceased but an epitomized biography blended with
description by which an impression of the character was to be 330
conveyed. Bring forward the one incidental expression, a kind of commiseration, unite with it a concern on the part of the dead for the well-
being of the living made known by exhortation and admonition, and
let this commiseration and concern pervade and brood over the whole
so that what was peculiar to the individual shall still be subordinate 335
to a sense of what he had in common with the species—our notion of
a perfect Epitaph would then be realized, and it pleases me to say that
this is the very model upon which those of Chiabrera are for the most
part framed. Observe how exquisitely this is exemplified in the one
beginning "Pause courteous Stranger! Baldi supplicates" given in THE 340
FRIEND some weeks ago. The Subject of the Epitaph is introduced
intreating, not directly in his own Person but through the mouth of
the Author, that according to the religious belief of his Country a
Prayer for his soul might be preferred to the Redeemer of the World.
Placed in counterpoize with this right which he has in common with all 345
the dead, his individual earthly accomplishments appear light to his
funereal Biographer, as they did to the person of whom he speaks when
alive, nor could Chiabrera have ventured to touch upon them but under
the sanction of this previous acknowledgement. He then goes on to
say how various and profound was his learning and how deep a hold it 350
took upon his affections, but that he weaned himself from these things
as vanities and was devoted in later life exclusively to the divine truths
of the Gospel as the only knowledge in which he could find perfect rest.
Here we are thrown back upon the introductory supplication and made
to feel its especial propriety in this case: his life was long and every 355
part of it bore appropriate fruits; Urbino his birth-place might be
proud of him, and the Passenger who was entreated to pray for his
soul has a wish breathed for his welfare.—This composition is a perfect
whole; there is nothing arbitrary or mechanical, but it is an organized
body of which the members are bound together by a common life and 360
are all justly proportioned. If I had not gone so much into detail, I
should have given further instances of Chiabrera's Epitaphs, but I must

332–4 unite . . . concern MS.²: and let it MS.   336 species MS.²: species
and MS.   337 then be MS.²: be MS.   338 which those of MS.²: which
MS.   339 this MS.²: it MS.   340 Baldi *Edd.*: Balbi MS.   346 dead,
Edd.: dead: MS.   349 the MS.²: this MS.   356 fruits; *Edd.*: fruits.
MS.   Urbino *Edd.*: Urbina MS.

content myself with saying that if he had abstained from the introduction of heathen mythology of which he is lavish—an inexcusable
fault for an Inhabitant of a Christian country, yet admitting of some 365
palliation in an Italian who treads classic soil and has before his eyes
the ruins of the temples which were dedicated to those ficticious beings
as objects of worship by the majestic People, his Ancestors—had
omitted also some uncharacteristic particulars and had not on some
occasions forgotten that truth is the soul of passion, he would have left 370
his readers little to regret. I do not mean to say that higher and nobler
thoughts may not be found in sepulchral Inscriptions than his contain,
but he understood his work; the principles upon which he composed
are just. The Reader of "THE FRIEND" has had proofs of this; one shall
be given of his mixed manner, exemplifying some of the points in 375
which he has erred.

> O Lelius, beauteous flower of gentleness,
> The fair Aglaia's friend above all friends,
> O darling of the fascinating Loves,
> By what dire envy moved did Death uproot 380
> Thy days ere yet full blown, and what ill chance
> Hath robbed Savona of her noblest grace?
> She weeps for thee, and shall for ever weep,
> And if the fountain of her tears should fail,
> She would implore Sebeto to supply 385
> Her need; Sebeto sympathizing stream,
> Who on his margin saw thee close thine eyes
> On the chaste bosom of thy Lady dear.
> Ah what do riches, what does youth avail?
> Dust are our hopes; I weeping did inscribe 390
> In bitterness thy Monument, and pray
> Of every gentle Spirit bitterly
> To read the record with as copious tears.

This Epitaph is not without some tender thoughts, but a comparison
of it with the one upon the youthful Pozzobonelli (see FRIEND No 20) 395
will more clearly shew that Chiabrera has here neglected to ascertain
whether the passions expressed were in kind and degree a dispensation
of reason or at least commodities issued under her licence and authority.

367 ficticious] *So in* MS.   368 Ancestors— *Edd.*: Ancestors, that if he had
abstained from this fault MS.: Ancestors. MS.[2].   374 one MS.[2]: an Epitaph
MS.   381 ere *Edd.*: e'er MS.   385, 386 Sebeto . . . Sebeto *Edd.*:
Sabete . . . Sabete MS.   388 On MS.[2]: In MS.   395 No 20 *Edd.*: No
[   ] MS.

The Epitaphs of Chiabrera are twenty nine in number, all of them save two upon Men probably little known at this day in their own 400 Country and scarcely at all beyond the limits of it, and the reader is generally made acquainted with the moral and intellectual excellence which distinguished them by a brief history of the course of their lives or a selection of events and circumstances, and thus they are individualized; but in the two other instances—namely, those of Tasso and 405 Raphael—he enters into no particulars, but contents himself with four lines expressing one sentiment, upon the principle laid down in the former part of this discourse where the Subject of an Epitaph is a Man of prime note.

> Torquato Tasso rests within this Tomb: 410
> This Figure, weeping from her inmost heart,
> Is Poesy: from such impassioned grief
> Let every one conclude what this Man was.

The Epitaph which Chiabrera composed for himself has also an appropriate brevity and is distinguished for its grandeur, the sentiment 415 being the same as that which the Reader has before seen so happily enlarged upon.

As I am brought back to Men of first rate distinction and public Benefactors, I cannot resist the pleasure of transcribing the metrical part of an Epitaph which formerly was inscribed in the Church of 420 St. Paul's to that Bishop of London who prevailed with William the Conqueror to secure to the inhabitants of the City all the liberties and privileges which they had enjoyed in the time of Edward the Confessor.

> These marble Monuments to thee thy Citizens assigne,
> Rewards (O Father) farre unfit to those deserts of thine, 425
> Thee unto them a faithful friend, thy London people found,
> And to this towne of no small weight a stay both sure and sound.
> Their liberties restorde to them, by meanes of thee have beene,
> Their publicke weale by meanes of thee, large gifts have felt and seene,
> Thy riches, stocke, and beauty brave, one hour hath them supprest, 430
> Yet these thy virtues, and good deeds with us for ever rest.

Thus have I attempted to determine what a sepulchral Inscription ought to be, and taken at the same time a survey of what Epitaphs are

good and bad, and have shewn to what deficiencies in sensibility and
to what errors in taste and judgement most commonly are to be   435
ascribed.—It was my intention to have given a few specimens from
those of the Ancients but I have already I fear taken up too much of
the Reader's time. I have not animadverted upon such—alas! far too
numerous—as are reprehensible from the want of moral rectitude in
those who have composed them or given it to be understood that they   440
should be so composed: boastful and haughty panegyrics, ludicrously
contradicting the solid remembrance of those who knew the deceased,
shocking the common sense of mankind by their extravagance and
affronting the very altar with their impious falsehood. These I leave
to general scorn, not however without a general recommendation that   445
they who have offended or may be disposed to offend in this manner
would take into serious thought the heinousness of their transgression.

Upon reviewing what has been written, I think it better here to add
a few favourable specimens such as are ordinarily found in our Country
Church-Yards at this day. If those primary sensations upon which I have   450
dwelt so much be not stifled in the heart of the Reader, they will be
read with pleasure; otherwise neither these nor more exalted strains
can by him be truly interpreted.

Aged 87 and 83

Not more with silver hairs than virtue crown'd   455
The good old Pair take up this spot of ground:
Tread in their steps and you will surely find
Their Rest above, below their peace of mind.

At the Last day I'm sure I shall appear
To meet with Jesus Christ my Saviour dear,   460
Where I do hope to live with him in bliss;
Oh, what a joy in my last hour was this!

Aged 3 Month

What Christ said once he said to all:
Come unto me, ye Children small;   465
None shall do you any wrong,
For to my kingdom you belong.

---

448 written MS.²: said MS.

Aged 10 Weeks
The Babe was sucking at the breast
When God did call him to his rest.   470

In an obscure corner of a Country Church-yard I once espied, half-overgrown with Hemlock and Nettles, a very small Stone laid upon the ground, bearing nothing more than the name of the Deceased with the date of birth and death, importing that it was an Infant which had been born one day and died the following. I know not how far the 475
Reader may be in sympathy with me, but more awful thoughts of rights conferred, of hopes awakened, of remembrances stealing away or vanishing were imparted to my mind by that Inscription there before my eyes than by any other that it has ever been my lot to meet with upon a Tomb-stone.   480
     The most numerous class of sepulchral Inscriptions do indeed record nothing else but the name of the buried Person, but that he was born upon one day and died upon another. Addison in the Spectator making this observation says, "that he cannot look upon those registers of existence whether of brass or marble but as a kind of satire upon the 485
departed persons who had left no other memorial of them than that they were born and that they died." In certain moods of mind this is a natural reflection, yet not perhaps the most salutary which the appearance might give birth to. As in these registers the name is mostly associated with others of the same family, this is a prolonged companionship, 490
however shadowy; even a Tomb like this is a shrine to which the fancies of a scattered family may repair in pilgrimage; the thoughts of the individuals, without any communication with each other, must oftentimes meet here.—Such a frail memorial then is not without its tendency to keep families together; it feeds also local attachment, 495
which is the tap-root of the tree of Patriotism.
     I know not how I can withdraw more satisfactorily from this long disquisition than by offering to the Reader as a farewell memorial the following Verses, suggested to me by a concise Epitaph which I met with some time ago in one of the most retired vales among the 500
Mountains of Westmoreland. There is nothing in the detail of the

Poem which is not either founded upon the Epitaph or gathered from
enquiries concerning the Deceased made in the neighbourhood.

Beneath that Pine which rears its dusky head
Aloft, and covered by a plain blue stone   505
Briefly inscribed, a gentle Dalesman lies,
From whom in early childhood was withdrawn
The precious gift of hearing. He grew up
From year to year in loneliness of soul;
And this deep mountain valley was to him   510
Soundless, with all its streams. The bird of dawn
Did never rouze this Cottager from sleep
With startling summons: not for his delight
The vernal cuckoo shouted; not for him
Murmured the labouring bee. When stormy winds   515
Were working the broad bosom of the lake
Into a thousand, thousand sparkling waves,
Rocking the trees, or driving cloud on cloud
Along the sharp edge of yon lofty crags,
The agitated scene before his eye   520
Was silent as a picture: evermore
Were all things silent, wheresoe'er he moved.
Yet, by the solace of his own calm thoughts
Upheld, he duteously pursued the round
Of rural labours: the steep mountain side   525
Ascended with his staff and faithful dog.
The plough he guided, and the scythe he swayed;
And the ripe corn before his sickle fell
Among the jocund reapers. For himself,
All watchful and industrious as he was,   530
He wrought not; neither field nor flock he owned:
No wish for wealth had place within his mind;
Nor husband's love, nor father's hope or care.
Though born a younger Brother, need was none
That from the floor of his paternal home   535
He should depart to plant himself anew.
And when, mature in manhood, he beheld
His Parents laid in earth, no loss ensued
Of rights to him, but he remained well pleased,
By the pure bond of independent love   540
An inmate of a second family,
The fellow-labourer and friend of him

520 eye MS.²: eyes MS.   535 home MS.²: roof MS.

To whom the small inheritance had fallen.
Nor deem that his mild presence was a weight
That pressed upon his Brother's house, for books   545
Were ready comrades whom he could not tire,—
Of whose society the blameless Man
Was never satiate. Their familiar voice,
Even to old age, with unabated charm
Beguiled his leisure hours; refreshed his thoughts;   550
Beyond its natural elevation raised
His introverted spirit; and bestowed
Upon his life an outward dignity
Which all acknowledged. The dark winter night,
The stormy day, had each its own resource;   555
Song of the muses, sage historic tale,
Science severe, or word of holy writ
Announcing immortality and joy
To the assembled spirits of the just,
From imperfection and decay secure.   560
Thus soothed at home, thus busy in the field,
To no perverse suspicion he gave way,
No languor, peevishness, nor vain complaint:
And they who were about him did not fail
In reverence or in courtesy; they prized   565
His gentle manners: and his peaceful smiles,
The gleams of his slow-varying countenance,
Were met with answering sympathy and love.
—At length, when sixty years and five were told,
A slow disease insensibly consumed   570
The powers of nature; and a few short steps
Of friends and kindred bore him from his home
(Yon Cottage shaded by the woody crags)
To the profounder stillness of the grave.
Nor was his funeral denied the grace   575
Of many tears, virtuous and thoughtful grief;
Heart-sorrow rendered sweet by gratitude.
And now that monumental Stone preserves
His name, and unambitiously relates
How long, and by what kindly outward aids,   580
And in what pure contentedness of mind,
The sad privation was by him endured.

545 That . . . house MS.²: Upon his Brother's house MS.   550 refreshed MS.² (*inserted in pencil*): composed MS.   559 assembled MS.²:
exalted MS.

And yon tall Pine-tree, whose composing sound
Was wasted on the good Man's living ear,
Hath now its own peculiar sanctity;   585
And at the touch of every wandering breeze
Murmurs not idly o'er his peaceful grave.

APPENDIX

I

Oɴ a loose sheet of the manuscript appears the passage printed below, which Wordsworth had evidently considered inserting before *E.E.* II. 472 (see II. 471, textual n.). It is, however, impossible to insert it (as Grosart attempted to do), since lines 50–60 repeat approximately *E.E.* II. 445–54, and lines 62–3 repeat *E.E.* II. 467–8. These duplications make it clear that Wordsworth must have considered substituting the passage below for a passage in the main text which ends at 'society.' (II. 471), but the beginning of which is indeterminable, except that it must follow the quotation of Lyttleton's epitaph (II. 420–35). The passage, except for editorial punctuation, is as follows:

I am anxious not to be misunderstood. It has already been stated that in this species of composition, above every other, our sensations and judgment depend upon our opinion or feeling of the Author's state of mind. Literature is here so far identified with morals, the quality of the act so far determined by our notion of the aim and purpose of the   5
agent, that nothing can please us—however well executed in its kind —if we are persuaded that the primary virtues of sincerity, earnestness, and a real interest in the main object are wanting. Insensibility here shocks us and still more so if manifested by a Writer's going wholly out of his way in search of supposed beauties, which if he were truly 10
moved, he could set no value upon—could not even think of. We are struck in this case not merely with a sense of disproportion and unfitness, but we cannot refrain from attributing no small part of his intellectual to a moral demerit. And here the difficulties of the question begin: namely, in ascertaining what errors in the choice of, or the mode of 15
expressing, the thoughts most surely indicate the want of that which is most indispensable. Bad taste, whatever shape it may put on, is injurious to the heart and the understanding. If a man attaches much interest to the faculty of taste as it exists in himself and employs much time in those studies of which this faculty (I use the word *taste* in its 20
comprehensive, though most unjustifiable, sense) is reckoned the arbiter, certain it is his moral notions and dispositions must either be purified and strengthened, or corrupted and impaired. How can it

3 our MS.²: the MS.   11 even *Grosart*: [*tear*]ven MS.   12 dis[*tear*]roportion MS.   15 mode *Grosart*: [*tear*]ode MS.   17 is *Grosart*: MS. *torn*.   indispensable. *Edd.*: indispensable: MS.   22 arbiter, *Edd.*: arbiter. MS.

be otherwise when his ability to enter in the spirit of works in literature
must depend upon his feeling, his imagination, and his understanding— 25
that is, upon his recipient, upon his creative or active and upon his
judging powers, and upon the accuracy and compass of his knowledge—
in fine, upon all that makes up the moral and intellectual Man? What
is true of individuals is equally true of nations. Nevertheless, a man
called to a task in which he is not practised may have his expression 30
thoroughly defiled and clogged by the style prevalent in his age; yet
still through the force of circumstances that have roused him, his under
feeling may remain strong and pure. Yet this may be wholly concealed
from common view. Indeed, the favourite style of different ages is so
different and wanders so far from propriety that if it were not that first 35
rate writers in all nations and tongues are governed by common
principles, we might suppose that truth and nature were things not to
be looked for in books. Hence, to an unpractised reader the productions
of every age will present obstacles in various degrees hard to surmount.
A deformity of style, not the worst in itself but of that kind with which 40
he is least familiar, will, on the one hand, be most likely to render him
insensible to a pith and power which may be within; and, on the other
hand, he will be the least able to see through that sort of falsehood
which is most prevalent in the works of his own time. Many of my
readers—to apply these general observations to the present case—must 45
have derived much pleasure from the Epitaph of Lord Lyttleton, and
no doubt will be startled at the comparison I have made. But bring it
to the test recommended; it will then be found that its faults, though
not in degree so intolerable, are in kind more radical and deadly than
those of the strange composition with which it has been compared. It can 50
derive no advantage from being translated into another style; it would
not even admit of the process, for there is here no under-current, no
skeleton, or stamina of appropriate feeling. The attentive Reader will
perceive that nothing in the *heart* of the Writer had determined either
the choice, the order, or the expression of the ideas; that there is no 55
interchange of action from within or from without—no f[?], no stream.
In the absence of a constituent vital power, the connections are
mechanical and arbitrary, and the lowest kind of these: petty alliterations, as *meek* and *magnanimous*, combined with opposition in thoughts

---

25–8 upon . . . Man? MS.²: upon all that makes up the moral and intellectual
man upon his imagination his feeling & his MS. *In the deletion of the first version*
upon his (25) *was wrongly deleted.*   28 Man? *Edd.*: Man. MS.   30 called
Edd.: call MS.   32 through MS.²: from MS.   43 falsehood *Edd.*:
falshood MS.   56 *The tear in the* MS. *has removed about three letters; the word
may have been* flow.   57 connections *Edd.* (*cf. E.E.* II. 450–1): connecti[*tear*] MS.
58–9 alliterations *Edd.* (*cf. E.E.* II. 452): a[*tear*]terations MS.   59 thoughts
Edd. (*cf. E.E.* II. 453): thoug[*tear*] MS.

where there is no necessary or natural opposition. Then follow *voice,* 60
song, eloquence, form, mind, each enumerated by a separate act as if the
Author had been making a Catalogue Raisonné. Lord Lyttleton was a
Man of real sensibility and could not have written in this way

II

According to William Andrews, *Curious Epitaphs,* 2nd edn. (London,
1899), pp. 144–5, Wordsworth composed a prose epitaph for his
brother-in-law Henry Hutchinson. Andrews copied the inscription
from Hutchinson's gravestone in the churchyard of Kirk Braddan on
the Isle of Man, remarking that the inscription was then to be read
only with great difficulty, and 'in a few years [would] be effaced by the
effects of the weather on the tender stone'. The text is as follows:

In memory of HENRY HUTCHINSON, born at Penrith, Cumberland, 14th June 1769. At an early age he entered upon a Seafaring life
in the course of which, being of a thoughtful mind, he attained great
skill, and knowledge of his Profession, and endured in all climates
severe hardships with exemplary courage & fortitude. The latter part
of his life, was passed with a beloved Sister upon this Island. He
died at Douglas the 23rd of May 1839, much lamented by his Kindred
& Friends who have erected this stone to testify their sense of his mild
virtues & humble piety.

The epitaph was reprinted by Daniel Scott in a pamphlet entitled
Some Local and Other Epitaphs: Kirkyard Humours and Curiosities
(Penrith, 1899), p. 7, with a prefatory note to the effect that Scott's
article had first appeared in the *Penrith Observer,* 20 and 27 June 1899.

62 *After* Author MS. *deletes:* as a separate act as if the A

COMMENTARY

I

1, textual n. CHIABRERA] See II. 476, and n. Coleridge's 'imitation', '''Tis true, Idoloclastes Satyrane', based on Chiabrera's epitaph *'Per il Signor* AMBROSIO SALINERO', appeared in *The Friend*, No. 14 (23 Nov. 1809), p. 209. Cf. Wordsworth's translation, *P.W.* iv. 250–1.

An attempt will be made *etc.*] The Prospectus to *The Friend* (No. 1, 1 June 1809, p. 15), proposes as a subject 'The necessary Dependence of Taste on moral Impulses and Habits: and the Nature of Taste (relatively to Judgement in general and to Genius) defined, illustrated, and applied'. The main 'topic, which [had] already been entered upon' was 'Sketches and Fragments of the Life and Character of the late Admiral Sir Alexander Ball', begun in No. 19 (28 Dec. 1809) and continued in Nos. 21, 22, 26, and 27; in the last of these it is *'To be concluded in the next Number'*, which never appeared.

"To define *etc.*] From Johnson's Life of Pope; see *Lives*, iii. 254, where Hill's text reads: '. . . may be expected to have leisure and patience to peruse'.

7–8. Cf. Weever (see below, n. on 19), p. 5: 'a Monument . . . is a receptacle or sepulchre, purposely made, erected, or built, to receiue a dead corps, and to preserue the same from violation . . . And indeed these Funerall Monuments, in foregoing ages, were very fittingly called muniments, in that they did defend and fence the corpse of the defunct, which otherwise might haue beene pulled out of their graues by the sauage brutishnesse of wilde beasts.'

9–14. Camden, *Remaines Concerning Britain*, 6th edn. (London, 1657), p. 355:

> Neither have any neglected buriall, but some savage Nations, as Bactrians, (which cast the dead to their dogs) some varlet Philosophers, as *Diogenes* which desired to be devoured of fishes; some dissolute Courtiers as *Mecenas*, who vvas vvont to say.
>> *Non tumulum curo, sepelit natura relictos.*

But Wordsworth is following Weever (see below, n. on 19), p. 23:

> For neuer any (saith *Camden*) neglected buriall but some sauage nations; as Bactrians, which cast their dead to the dogs; some varlet Philosophers, as *Diogenes*, who desired to be devoured of fishes; some dissolute Courtiers, as *Mecænas* who was wont to say,
>> *Non tumulum curo sepelit natura relictos.*
>>> I'm carelesse of a graue:
>>> Nature her dead will saue.

We find no evidence that Wordsworth used Camden at all except through Weever's quotations. There is no truth in Grosart's suggestion (ii. 344)

that Wordsworth drew on *Wits Recreations. Containing . . . 160: Epitaphs
. . .* (London, 1641), which is in the Rydal Mount Catalogue.

19. Weever, in his Discourse] *Ancient Funerall Monuments within the
United Monarchie of Great Britaine, Ireland, and the Islands adiacent . . .
Whereunto is prefixed a Discourse of Funerall Monuments . . . Composed by
the Studie and Trauels of John Weever . . . London . . . 1631.* This work is
a major source of Wordsworth's Essays.

20–6. Weever, p. 9: 'The invention of Epitaphs proceeded from the
presage', etc., as in Wordsworth's text, except that Weever reads 'Ælina'
(25). But Weever is quoting without acknowledgement from Camden's
Remains (ed. 1657, p. 356), inserting after 'Linus' the fanciful gloss 'the
Theban poet, who flourished about the yeare of the world 2700'.

43 ff. Cf. Fenwick n. to the 'Intimations' Ode, *P.W.* iv. 463: 'Nothing
was more difficult for me in childhood than to admit the notion of death
as a state applicable to my own being. I have said elsewhere—

> "A simple child,
> That lightly draws its breath,
> And feels its life in every limb,
> What should it know of death!"—

But it was not so much from [feelings] of animal vivacity that *my* difficulty
came as from a sense of the indomitableness of the spirit within me.' Cf.
also a rejected fragment of *An Evening Walk, P.W.* i. 7:

> What tribes of happy youth have gambolled here,
> Nor in their wild mirth ever thought how near
> Their sensible warm motion was allied
> To the dull earth that crumbled at their side.
> Even now of that gay train who there pursue
> Their noisy sports with rapture ever new
> There are to whom the buoyant heart proclaims
> Death has no power oer their particular frames.

In *P.W.* iv. 466–7 the present passage is cited as parallel to ll. 119–21 of
the Ode: 'Thou, over whom thy Immortality / Broods like the Day, a
Master o'er a Slave, / A Presence which is not to be put by'. Cf. also *M.Y.*
ii. 189: 'This poem rests entirely upon two recollections of childhood, one
that of a splendour in the objects of sense which is passed away, and the
other an indisposition to be reduced to the law of death as applying to our own
particular case. A Reader who has not a vivid recollection of these feelings
having existed in his mind in childhood cannot understand that poem.'

67–77. Cf. *Prel.*, p. 572: the child's wonder at 'the River that flows on /
Perpetually, whence comes it, whither tends, / Going and never gone';
Exc. IV. 753–62; *The River Duddon*, Sonnets XXXII and XXXIII
(*P.W.* iii. 260).

113–15. Cf. 'I find it written', *P.W.* iii. 408. The source, as noted in
P.W. iii. 573, is either Valerius Maximus, *Facta et Dicta Memorabilia*,
I. vii, or Cicero, *de Divinatione*, I. xxvii. The Rydal Mount Catalogue lists

editions of Valerius Maximus of 1540 and 1650 (lots 445, 410). For 'tender-hearted Simonides' (118–19), cf. 'the tenderest Poet that could be' in the sonnet just cited, and 'Departing summer', 53–4 (*P.W.* iv. 100): 'One precious, tender-hearted, scroll / Of pure Simonides'.

115–16. Another ancient Philosopher] We have not found this anecdote in any of the expected classical sources.

161–2. Perhaps after Weever, p. 8: 'This order or custome of buriall without cities, continued amongst the Christians, vntill the time of *Gregory the great*, for as then the Monkes, Friers, and Priests . . . procured first, that the places of sepulture should bee adioyning vnto their Churches, and afterwards, they got licence to burie within Churches.'

163–5. Weever, p. 5: 'in foregoing ages . . . none were buried in Townes or Cities, but either in the fields, along the high way side (to put passengers in minde, that they were like those so interred, mortall).' Weever is adapting Camden, *Remains* (1657), p. 356. The latter part of the passage perhaps suggested to Wordsworth the ideas of 178–9. In 1799 Coleridge discussed with Wordsworth 'the question of Polytheism & Monotheism, of Tombs by the Roadside & Tombs in Church yards' (*C.N.B.* i. 1588, 494). Coleridge's notebooks record numerous epitaphs copied from stones which he himself had seen; frequently he notices the ways in which the natural surroundings modify the feelings with which the inscription is read, e.g. *C.N.B.* i. 255, 418, 450, 494–6, 548, 1267. See also *E.E.* II. 129–36; III. 454–70, and nn. thereon.

164–90. Cf. *R.M.* 347–8: 'hopes plucked like beautiful wild flowers from the ruined tombs that border the high-ways of Antiquity'.

182–3. 'undermined . . . fed it.'] We have not found the source of this quotation.

188. senseless stone] Perhaps after *Julius Caesar*, I. i. 39: 'You blocks, you stones, you worse than senseless things!'

209 ff. *All Saints' Church, Derby: a poem* (Derby, 1805), pp. 40–1. The matter summarized in 210–13 refers to foolish epitaphs of Roman Catholic times, now destroyed by the Reformation, and to Requiem Mass:

> But hence, these follies, light as laughter prov'd!
> Yes, they are gone—and oh that ages back,
> Some Champion of the church, had too prevail'd
> To close her vaults; and where unsightly now
> Her outer court its surface spreads, in heaps
> Trodden and bare and vile, to bid in peace
> The sylvan beauties of the garden bloom.
> Then in some *etc.*

The lines omitted after 224 are:

> now where,
> On columns ivy-wreath'd, o'er statues, urns,
> And obelisks, the Temple of the Dead,
> In Gothic state aspir'd; an open Pile;

While through inwoven arches, richly foil'd
With the dark verdure of intruding trees,
Or sombre windows where enamel'd forms
Of saints are seen, the dazzling glare of day
Came, solemniz'd, within; a twilight gloom,
Chilling, with awe sublime, the soul:—and now
Had wander'd forth *etc.*

At 224 the original reads 'stray'd', correctly followed by Wordsworth's texts until 1837. On John Edwards, see *P.W.* v. 449, n., and T. R. Potter, 'Three Neglected Derbyshire Worthies—John Edwards, John Allen, and Isaac Rowbottom', *The Reliquary*, xi (1871–2), 158–60. Cf. *M.T.* i. 470–1; ii. 213, 222.

In the Wordsworth Library, Grasmere, are preserved two letters, concerned primarily with *The Friend*, from John Edwards to Coleridge, dated 25 Sept. and 28 Oct. 1809. The second of these contains the following:

I have an unwearied pleasure in perusing & thinking on Wordsworth's poetry; & think his pamphlet exceeds all that have been written since Burke's on the french revolution. It is excellent in argument, beautiful in metaphors & similes, and sublime in its moral & philosophical strains. Such a work is a treat which I do not often enjoy. Of his poetry [I] have not now leisure to say what I feel: taken as a whole, I mean, reflecting on almost every individual poem, I cannot better express my sentiments than by applying his own words "Then gentle maiden, move along these shades,—In gentleness of heart, with gentle hand—Touch . . . for there is a Spirit in the woods" [words].

(The explanation of the pun is Edwards's.) Wordsworth, in including the quotation from and reference to Edwards here, may be returning these compliments.

263 ff. Cf. Johnson, *Essay on Epitaphs*, in *Works*, ed. Murphy (London, 1810), ii. 334:

The best subject for Epitaphs is private virtue; virtue exerted in the same circumstances in which the bulk of mankind are placed, and which, therefore, may admit of many imitators. He that has delivered his country from oppression, or freed the world from ignorance and errour, can excite the emulation of a very small number; but he that has repelled the temptations of poverty, and disdained to free himself from distress at the expense of his virtue, may animate multitudes, by his example, to the same firmness of heart and steadiness of resolution.

Wordsworth is said to have been ignorant of this essay when he wrote his own: see Christopher Wordsworth, *Memoirs of William Wordsworth* (London, 1851), i. 434.

276 ff. *Lives*, iii. 264:

The scantiness of human praises can scarcely be made more apparent than by remarking how often Pope has, in the few epitaphs which he composed, found it necessary to borrow from himself . . . [iii. 263–4:] The difficulty in writing epitaphs is to give a particular and appropriate praise. This, however, is not always to be performed, whatever be the diligence or ability of the writer, for the greater part of mankind 'have no character at all' [Pope, *Moral Essays*, II. 2], have little that distinguishes them from others equally good or bad, and therefore nothing can be said of them which may not be applied with equal propriety to a thousand more. It is indeed no great panegyrick that there is inclosed in this tomb one who was born in one year and died in another; yet many useful and amiable lives have been spent which yet leave little materials for any other memorial. These are, however, not the proper subjects of poetry, and whenever friendship or any other motive obliges a poet to write on such subjects, he must be forgiven if he sometimes wanders in generalities and utters the same praises over different tombs.

305 ff. Cf. II. 571 ff.

328. implicitly . . . rather than explicitly] Cf. II. 516, and n.

335–47. Cf. III. 67–70.

337. luminous mist] Cf. Coleridge, 'Dejection: An Ode', 62–3: 'This light, this glory, this fair luminous mist, / This beautiful and beauty-making power' (of 'Joy'). On mist as an analogue of the imagination in Wordsworth and Coleridge see Z. S. Fink, *The Early Wordsworthian Milieu* (Oxford, 1958), pp. 124–5.

375–6. Cf. II. 272–6.

386. 'equalises . . . low'] *Epitaphs translated from Chiabrera*, IV. 24 (*P.W.* iv. 250): 'one poor moment can suffice / To equalise the lofty and the low'. Cf. 'Personal Talk', 32 (*P.W.* iv. 74), and n. thereon, in *P.W.* iv. 415–16.

394–6. which . . . trick of words] For an example see II. 595–600.

409–29. Cf. III. 118–25, 271–85, 296–311.

413–19. Wordsworth is probably recalling his own experience in 1805, when he 'had a strong impulse to write a poem that should record my Brother's virtues and be worthy of his memory. I began to give vent to my feelings, with this view, but I was overpowered by my subject and could not proceed: I composed much, but it is all lost except a few lines, as it came from me in such a torrent that I was unable to remember it. . . . This work must therefore rest awhile till I am something calmer' (*E.Y.*, p. 586).

423–9. Wordsworth originally intended that his poem 'Written after the Death of Charles Lamb' (*P.W.* iv. 272–6) should be engraved as an epitaph on Lamb's stone (*L.Y.*, pp. 761–3). But as the poem grew in length, he recognized that it had in various ways gone beyond the limits of a public epitaph and had become instead an elegy for the printed page. In the poem itself (ll. 39–49) and in letters written while he was engaged in revision (*L.Y.*, pp. 761–4), Wordsworth distinguished the epitaph from the elegy much as he does here.

432–5. As in *Epitaphs from Chiabrera*, I, III, IV, and VI; the remaining six epitaphs translated by Wordsworth conform to 'the still more common [mould], in which what is said comes from the survivors directly' (450–1). See *P.W.* iv. 248 ff.

435–9. As in *Epitaphs from Chiabrera*, III and IV (*P.W.* iv. 249–50).

463. the worth of private life] See n. on 263 ff.

478 ff. Cf. Johnson, *Essay on Epitaphs*, in *Works*, ed. Murphy (London, 1810), ii. 328: 'It is not always necessary to recount the actions of a hero, or enumerate the writings of a philosopher; to imagine such informations necessary, is to detract from their characters, or to suppose their works mortal, or their achievements in danger of being forgotten. The bare name of such men answers every purpose of a long inscription.'

492–501. Milton, 'On Shakespear', omitting six lines after 'monument':

> For whilst to th' shame of slow-endeavouring art,
> Thy easie numbers flow, and that each heart
> Hath from the leaves of thy unvalu'd Book,
> Those Delphick lines with deep impression took,
> Then thou our fancy of it self bereaving,
> Dost make us Marble with too much conceaving.

II

1–8. Gray, *Elegy written in a Country Churchyard*, 77–84. These are two of four stanzas cited with particular approval in Johnson's Life of Gray (*Lives*, iii. 441–2). See also *Prel.* X. 496–500; *L.Y.*, p. 897.

10. brief Chronicles] *Hamlet*, II. ii. 555–6: '[actors] are the abstracts and brief chronicles of the time.'

13. a modern Tale] Lamb, *Rosamund Gray* (1798), in *Works*, ed. Hutchinson (London, 1908), i. 31–2; reading 'where be', etc.

24. a series of calm weather] Cf. 'Ode: Intimations of Immortality', 162 ff. (*P.W.* iv. 284): 'Hence in a season of calm weather . . . / Our Souls have sight of that immortal sea / Which brought us hither'. Note the imagery of the sea immediately following (30 ff.).

28. the light of love] Cf. I. 292.

30 ff. See n. on 24 above, and cf. the imagery of 'Elegiac Stanzas suggested by a Picture of Peele Castle' (*P.W.* iv. 258–60; written 1805, but recalling a visit to Rampside in 1794). Note especially 'Four summer weeks' ('Stanzas', 2) and 'on a Summer's day' (30); 'glassy sea' ('Stanzas', 4) and 'smooth Sea . . . unruffled Sea' (30, 39); also the change of imagery from calm to storm ('Stanzas', 44–52; *E.E.* II. 39–43).

30–4. *Exc.* VI. 634–45, is a versification of this passage: 'in the centre of a world whose soil / Is rank with all unkindness, compassed round / With such memorials, I have sometimes felt, / It was no momentary happiness / To have *one* Enclosure where the voice that speaks / In envy or detraction is not heard; / . . . where the traces / Of evil inclinations are unknown; / . . . and no jarring tone / Intrudes, the peaceful concert to disturb / Of amity and gratitude.'

34–8. Cf. the Solitary's contrast between 'That which is done' and 'what is known / To reason, and by conscience is enjoined', in *Exc.* V. 250–61.

42. monsters of the deep] *King Lear*, IV. ii. 50, caught up by association with 'the slimy bottom of the deep' in the passage from *Richard III* cited in our next note.

43. Clarence] *Richard III*, I. iii. 24–33. The imagery of shipwreck was associated in Wordsworth's mind with the death of John Wordsworth: see 'Elegiac Stanzas suggested by a Picture of Peele Castle', *passim*. A pamphlet on the loss of the *Earl of Abergavenny* was headed with 'a motto from Shakespeare from Clarence's dream' (*E.T.*, pp. 561, 565); Dorothy Wordsworth was 'too often haunted with dreadful images of Shipwrecks and the Sea when I am in bed and hear a stormy wind' (*E.T.*, p. 663); in 1808 Wordsworth declined an offer of accommodation from Wrangham on the grounds that 'since the loss of my dear Brother, we have all had such painful and melancholy thoughts connected with the ocean that nothing but a paramount necessity could make us live near it' (*M.T.* i. 212).

55 ff. Cf. *P. Bord.* 31–4: 'good actions being for the most part in their nature silent & regularly progressive, they do not present those sudden results which can afford a sufficient stimulus to a troubled mind. In processes of vice the effects are more frequently immediate, palpable, and extensive'; and *passim*. See also *Exc.* VI. 574–9.

70–86. The thought of this passage is akin to that of 'Ode to Duty' (*P.W.* iv. 83), 'Character of the Happy Warrior' (*P.W.* iv. 86; connected in Wordsworth's mind with John Wordsworth), and *Exc.* V–VII, especially V. 593–601.

91–2. Much . . . disposition] See I. 329–66.

104 ff. *A Statistical Account of Scotland, drawn up from the Communications of the Ministers of the Different Parishes. By Sir John Sinclair, Bart.* (21 vols., Edinburgh, 1791–9). Wordsworth's main points, that 'a general transfer of Inhabitants has taken place' (105–6), that it is 'the desire of all, that their bones should rest by the side of their forefathers' (108–9), and that 'a great distance' (111) is often involved, are to be found in the accounts of New port-Glasgow (v. 550), Weem (xii. 137), Borthwick (xiii. 632), Roxburgh (xix. 120), and Aberdeen (xix. 176–7). Many other entries record (as an apology for the unreliability or absence of parish registers of deaths) that strangers are buried inside, and parishioners outside, the parish, without giving reasons. The 'transfer of Inhabitants' is attributed mainly to the depopulation of the countryside by the growth of large farms and of industrial employment in the larger cities. We have found no authority for Wordsworth's statement that 'very poor Persons' (109–10) are particularly concerned; perhaps he merely inferred it from the obvious fact that most of the parishes discussed were indeed poor.

114–18. Cf. I. 242–53.

129–36. See Coleridge to Thomas Poole, 19 May 1799, in *C.L.* i. 515: 'I ought to say that in the Church Yard at Catlenberg I was pleased with the following Epitaph. "Johann Reimbold of Catlenburg.

Ach! sie haben	Ah! they have
Einen braven	Put a brave
Man begraben:	Man in Grave!
Vielen war er mehr.["]	He was more than Many!

This is word for word.' See also *C.N.B.* i. 418, and n. ad loc., where the epitaph is said to be 'an adaptation of a poem by Matthias Claudius *Bei dem Grabe meines Vaters*', and where Coleridge's translation is corrected ('To many he was more'). Wordsworth's version of the German is nearer to Coleridge's translation than to his version of the German. Contrary to Wordsworth's approval of the 'naked ejaculation', Johnson thought that 'exclamation seldom succeeds in our language, and I think it may be observed that the particle O! used at the beginning of a sentence always offends' (*Lives*, iii. 266).

150–6. Weever, p. 545: 'Here [at Baldock] is an ancient Monument, and an old Inscription which I often meete with.

> Farwel my frendys [etc., verbally as in text].'

There are variant versions in Weever, pp. 387, 610, 649; hence Wordsworth's 'a great favourite with our Forefathers' (149).

158. For Wordsworth's modernization of Chaucer's *Prioress's Tale* (1801, published 1820), see *P.W.* iv. 209–17.

163–70. Weever, p. 392. He adds after 'forgetten' (Wordsworth's 'forgotten', 166) the remark: 'Thus far *Stow*.' Wordsworth omits the last two lines: 'And of your cheritie, / For their soulys say a *Pater Noster* and an *Aue*.' Weever says that the epitaph is in St. Leonard's, Foster-lane. It is given in Camden, *Remaines* (1657), p. 384.

171 ff. Wordsworth achieves a periphrastic pun on a proper name in his 'Written after the Death of Charles Lamb', 23–4 (*P.W.* iv. 273): see his note of 1837 (ibid., p. 459), where he defends the pun by reference to the epitaph on Palmer.

181–8. Weever, pp. 331–2.

189–94. Weever, p. 556: 'I finde this Inscription following vpon a faire marble, vnder the pourtraiture of one of the Abbots, who modestly thus suppresseth his name.

> *Hic quidem* [etc., as in text].'

The translation is Wordsworth's. Johnson (*Lives*, iii. 257, 262) severely censures epitaphs which omit the name of the deceased.

213, 219–20, 222. laughter . . . sense of the ridiculous . . . full as ludicrous] Cf. *P.L.B.* 673–5: 'I have no doubt, that, in some instances, feelings, even of the ludicrous, may be given to my Readers by expressions which appeared to me tender and pathetic.'

215–16. rude Forefathers of the hamlet] Gray, *Elegy written in a Country Churchyard*, 16.

233–4. Wordsworth (or Mrs. Wordsworth) should have written 'the son of the noted Secretary of State'. If this is not a mere error of transcription (Wordsworth makes an accurate reference to Sir Henry Vane just below, 239 ff.), he may have misinterpreted the earlier part of the inscription, which is given in William Hutchinson, *The History and Antiquities of the*

County Palatine of Durham, iii (Carlisle, 1794), 168, as from the church of Long Newton:

HERE LIETH THE BODY OF S^{R.} GEORGE VANE INTERRED / MAY THE FIRST 1679 SECOND SON OF S^{R.} HENERY / VANE SOME TIME PRIN-CIPALL SECRETARY OF STATE / TO KING CHARLES THE FIRST. HE MARRIED ELIZABETH / THE HEIRESS OF Sr LYONELL MADDISON OF NEW-/ CASTLE UPON TYNE, BY WHOM HE HAD THIRTEENE / HOPEFULL CHILDREN viz FOURE SONS & NINE DAUGHTERS.

HIS HONOUR WONNE I'TH FIELD LIES HERE IN DUST
HIS HONOUR GOT BY GRACE SHALL NEVER RUST
  THE FORMER FADES, THE LATTER SHALL FAILE NEVER
FOR WHY, HE WAS S^{R.} GEORGE ONCE, B'T St GEORGE EVER.

Hutchinson was probably Wordsworth's source, since reference is made to the book, and the epitaph is quoted, in a manuscript of Dorothy Wordsworth's Journal. He may, however, have seen the inscription himself, since Long Newton is only a few miles from Sockburn-on-Tees, the home of Mary Hutchinson at the turn of the century. In 237 'fade' may be an error of Wordsworth's memory or of Mrs. Wordsworth's transcription.

239. the Father of this Personage] Sir Henry Vane the elder (1589–1655), Secretary of State from 1640.

265. sublime and pathetic] A conventional distinction: cf. *R.M.* 315–17: 'a pathos which he has not felt—a sublimity to which he hath not been raised'; *E.S.* 739–41: 'the profound and the exquisite in feeling, the lofty and universal in thought and imagination; or, in ordinary language, the pathetic and the sublime'; and *E.S.* 781–804.

267–9. unless . . . heard] Cf. *M.Y.* i. 146: even in 'worthy persons' other than 'London wits and witlings', the 'imagination has slept; and the voice which is the voice of my Poetry without Imagination cannot be heard'.

290–7. The only source of these lines which gives exactly Wordsworth's text and punctuation seems to be William Winstanley, *England's Worthies* (London, 1684; in the Rydal Mount Catalogue, lot 177), pp. 532–3 ('Life of James Marquess of Montross . . .'):

Some write, that though he had not the courteous invention of an Epitaph by any of his Friends to memorize him, that he was so zealous of the Fame of his great Master *Charles* the First, that with the point of his Sword he wrote these following lines.

> *Great, good, and just, could I but rate*
> *My griefs, and thy so ridgid fate;*
> *I'de weep the world to such a strain,*
> *As it should deluge once again.*
> *But since thy loud-tongu'd Bloud demands supplies,*
> *More from* Briareus *hands than* Argus *eyes,*
> *I'll sing thy Obsequies with Trumpets sounds,*
> *And write thy Epitaph with Bloud and Wounds.*

Montross.

308–14. *Paradise Lost*, VI. 754–6; Ezekiel, Ch. 1. The 'as' which we have restored in 312 is necessary to Milton's sense. For 'instinct with spirit' (307–8), see *Paradise Lost*, VI. 752, and cf. *Exc.* VII. 509.

315–25. Weever, p. 321.

327–8. a Sovereign . . . hearts of Men] Possibly after the biography in David Lloyd, *State Worthies* (London, 1670), p. 504: 'all serviceable men were entertained by him; and he among them a Prince, whose mind was great, but his spirit greater.' Lloyd's book is in Rydal Mount Catalogue, lot 177; it is referred to favourably by Coleridge in Oct. 1809 (*C.L.* iii. 241).

329. "the world-mourned Sidney"] The phrase is from Sylvester's *Dubartas his Second Weeke: Babylon. The Second Part of the Second Day of the II. Weeke*, line 664, in *Complete Works of Joshuah Sylvester*, ed. Grosart (privately printed, 1880), i. 144. Apart from this phrase and the reference to Du Bartas in *E.S.* 208 ff., there seems to be no evidence that Wordsworth had any direct knowledge of him; Wordsworth probably took the phrase from Winstanley's *England's Worthies* (see n. on 290–7 above), p. 220 ('The Life of Sir Philip Sidney'): 'Divine *Du Bartas* speaking of the most Learned of the English Nation, reckoneth him as one of the Chief, in these words:

> And (*world mourn'd*) Sidney, *warbling to the Thames*
> *His Swan-like tunes, so courts her coy proud streams,*
> *That (all with child with Fame) his Fame they bear*
> *To* Thetis *Lap, and* Thetis *every w[h]ere.*'

332–3. questioning the dispensations of Providence] e.g. st. 2 of 'The Dolefull Lay of Clorinda', in Spenser's *Astrophel* volume; see next n.

333–4. Spenser and all the Men of Genius] Wordsworth is thinking mainly of the collection of elegies headed by Spenser's *Astrophel* (1591). For other commemorative verses see S. A. Tannenbaum, *Sir Philip Sidney (A Concise Bibliography)* (New York, 1941), pp. 16 ff. Winstanley (see above, n. on 290–7), pp. 219–21, says: 'To recite the Commendations given him by several Authors, would of itself require a Volume: to rehearse some few not unpleasing to the Reader; *Heylin* in his Cosmography . . . *Stow* in his Annals . . . *Speed* in his Chronicle . . . Sir *Richard Baker* . . . the Poets, who offered whole Hecatombs of Verses in his praise . . . the Brittish Epigrammatist . . . Divine *Du Bartas* . . . Sir *John Harrington* . . . King *James* the First . . .'

336–9. Weever, p. 320:

Seigneur Des Accords in his booke entituled, *Les Bigarrures* . . . amongst many choice Epitaphs, hath one, selected out of the works of *Isaac du Bellay*, the French Poet, excellently composed, to the memory of *Sieur de Boniuet*, a great Commander in the warres; which by some English wit was happily imitated, and ingeniously applyed to the honour of this our worthy chiefetaine Sir *Philip*; written vpon a Tablet, and fastened to a pillar in S. Pauls Church London, the place of his buriall, as the sequele will more plainly shew.

Then follow du Bellay's *Epitaphe du Seigneur Bonivet* (see *Poésies françaises et latines de Joachim du Bellay*, ed. Courbet, Paris, 1919, i. 138–9), and an English translation (Weever's?) closely resembling the epitaph on Sidney. The information is also in Camden, *Remaines* (1657), p. 386.

339–52. Weever, p. 320. He is not, however, 'expressing himself', but quoting Camden's *Britannia* in the translation of Philemon Holland (London, 1637, p. 329): 'But Sir Philip, whom I cannot passe over in silence, beeing' etc., approximately as in our text. Wordsworth overlooks the scope of the parenthesis (343–4) in attributing the passage to Weever, and the 'simple effusion of the moment' (353) turns out to be a considered translation of Camden's Latin.

370. worth the carriage] Wordsworth probably remembers Johnson's account of the Metaphysical poets (*Lives*, i. 21): 'if their conceits were far-fetched, they were often worth the carriage.'

375–98. See Joseph Nicolson and Richard Burn, *The History and Antiquities of the Counties of Westmorland and Cumberland* (London, 1777), i. 405 (on Barton parish church): 'Upon a brass plate in the chancel is the following inscription:

' "Hic jacet Francisca Dawes, filia Thomæ Flecher de Strickland, armigeri, natu maxima; perquam charissima quidem et perdilecta uxor Lanceloti Dawes de Barton-Kirke, generosi. Quæ huic mundo, spe multo melioris, 23° Feb. valedixit: Anno ætatis suæ 23. Annoque D^{ni} 1673." '

The English verses follow, as in Wordsworth's text, apart from variants of spelling and punctuation. Richard Wordsworth of Sockbridge, the poet's grandfather, was buried in Barton church (Moorman, i. 8, n.). Here also were to be seen the arms of the Crackenthorpe family (Nicolson and Burn, i. 405).

407–10. Cf. *P.L.B.* 231–82, 482–6, 552–5; *Ap. L.B.* 58–62, 153–9; *E.E.* III. 152–5; III. 163–4 and n.

414. nature] 'natural expression'; see *P.L.B.* 360, and n.

420–35. See *A Complete Edition of the Poets of Great Britain*, ed. Anderson (London, 1795), x. 265. This was probably Wordsworth's source, not only because he regularly used this collection (see *M.Y.* i. 190), but also because the prose part of the epitaph is there printed in full, whereas it is rare in other editions of Lyttleton's poems. The full text of the prose reads: 'To the / Memory of Lucy Lyttleton, / Daughter of Hugh Fortescue of Filleigh, / In the county of Devon, Esq. / Father to the present Earl of Clinton, / By Lucy his wife, / The daughter of Matthew Lord Aylmer, / Who departed this life the 19th of Jan. 1746–7. / Aged twenty-nine, / Having employed the short time assigned to / her here / In the uniform practice of religion and virtue.' In 434 Anderson's text reads 'of her mind'.

442. a monody] *To the Memory of a Lady lately deceased. A Monody*, first published 1747. Reprinted in Anderson's *Poets of Great Britain*, x. 262. Some 'evidence that Lord Lyttleton dearly loved his wife' may be found

in a letter of Lyttleton's written during his wife's illness: see *The Works of George Lord Lyttleton*, 3rd edn. (London, 1776), iii. 320–2; and in Johnson's remark (*Lives*, iii. 449) that 'he appears to have lived [with her] in the highest degree of connubial felicity'.

449–50. no interchange . . . without] Verbally parallel to *Prel.* XII. 371 ff.: about 1793 Wordsworth began to see 'a new world . . . having for its base / That whence our dignity originates, / That which both gives it being and maintains / A balance, an ennobling interchange / Of action from within and from without'. In *The Prelude* Wordsworth means that the external universe is active, acting upon the mind which observes it, while the observing mind reciprocally acts upon the external universe. Here he appears to mean that the subject of an epitaph should similarly act upon the mind of the poet, and the poet's mind upon the subject of the epitaph.

453–4. oppositions . . . opposition] Cf. III. 36–73.

469–70. Cf. *E.S.* 382: Pope 'bewitched the nation by his melody'.

471, textual n. Nature] See n. on II. 534 below.

476. Chiabrera] Gabriello Chiabrera (1552–1638), lyric and would-be epic poet. For a convenient account see the article by Antonio Belloni in *Enciclopedia Italiana*, ix (Milan, 1931), 988. *The Friend*, No. 19 (28 Dec. 1809), contains Wordsworth's versions of two of his epitaphs, IV and VI in *P.W.* iv. 248 ff.; No. 20 (4 Jan. 1810) closes with VIII and IX; No. 25 (22 Feb. 1810) opens with II and III; *E.E.* I follows. Subsequent quotations in these notes are from *Delle Opere di Gabbriello Chiabrera Tomo Secondo* (Venice, 1782). Wordsworth owned this edition at some time, since his copy was to be sold by Sotheby on 23 June 1896; see W. J. B. Owen, 'Manuscript Variants of Wordsworth's Poems', *N. & Q.* cciii (1958), 308–10; and below, n. on III. 339–41.

478–9. According to William Andrews, *Curious Epitaphs*, 2nd edn. (London, 1899), pp. 144–5, Wordsworth composed a prose epitaph for his brother-in-law Henry Hutchinson. The text is given in our Appendix.

480–1. the difference . . . superstructure] Cf. II. 407–10 above, and n. ad loc.; III. 152–5.

491–2. instances . . . truth] See III. 363–98.

498–9. *Lives*, iii. 262: 'I have always considered this as the most valuable of Pope's epitaphs.'

500–9. See Pope's *Minor Poems*, ed. Ault and Butt (London, 1954), pp. 322–4. The inscription is in St. Margaret's, Westminster.

516. represented implicitly] Cf. I. 328; and for an outstanding example, see III. 471–80.

519. a mere character] A mere list of personal characteristics. Cf. III. 328–31: 'an abstract character of the deceased', distinguished from 'an epitomized biography blended with description by which an impression of the character was to be conveyed'. In such 'an epitomized biography', the 'character of the deceased' would be 'represented implicitly, that is, with

its accompaniment of circumstances, or conveyed by its effects' (II. 516–17). Wordsworth means that the generous actions of the deceased (for instance) should be given in the epitaph, rather than the mere statement that he was a generous man.

533. characteristic] Seems to mean, not 'characteristic of Pope's manner', but 'indicative of the character of the deceased'. Cf. III. 369: Chiabrera should have 'omitted . . . some uncharacteristic particulars'; *P. 1815*, 54–6: 'The characteristic and impassioned Epistle, of which Ovid and Pope have given examples'; *L.Y.*, p. 762: Chiabrera's 'Epitaphs are characteristic and circumstantial'; *L.Y.*, pp. 768–9: 'Mr Owen Ll[oyd]'s verses . . . are scarcely good or characteristic of the Subject [Charles Lamb].'

534. nature] 'natural feelings'. Cf. Arthur O. Lovejoy, *Essays in the History of Ideas* (Baltimore, Md., 1948), p. 70, sense 1 (a): 'Human nature, *i.e.*, possible or usual human behavior, the "natural" expression of the passions, in possible situations.'

535–7. Wordsworth is in fact following the model of Johnson in his discussion of Pope's epitaphs (*Lives*, iii. 254–72). The phrase 'Minute criticism' echoes *Lives*, iii. 254: 'The criticism upon Pope's *Epitaphs* . . . is placed here, being too minute and particular to be inserted in the Life.' See especially the discussion of the epitaphs on Dorset and Gay (*Lives*, iii. 254–6, 268–9). Cf. (for instance) 530–2 with *Lives*, iii. 268: 'The two parts of the first line ["Of manners gentle, of affections mild"] are only echoes of each other; *gentle manners* and *mild affections*, if they mean anything, must mean the same.'

569–71. *Lives*, iii. 262: 'There is scarce one line taken from commonplaces, unless it be that in which *only Virtue* is said to be *our own*.'

573–4. thoughts . . . common-place] Cf. I. 254 ff.

574–8. the universal . . . of themselves] Cf. *P.L.B.* 377–470; *M.Y.* ii. 238 (22 May 1815): 'One of my principal aims in the Ex^n: has been to put the commonplace truths, of the human affections especially, in an interesting point of view; and rather to remind men of their knowledge, as it lurks inoperative and unvalued in their own minds, than to attempt to convey recondite or refined truths.' See also the passage cited from *The Friend*, No. 5 (14 Sept. 1809), in Coleridge's characterization of Wordsworth's genius, *Biog. Lit.* i. 59–60; and an earlier version (1803) in *C.N.B.* i. 1622.

580–3. Cf. III. 132–4; *P.L.B.* 379–83.

589–94. Chiabrera, *Opere*, ii. 176, '*Per Monsignor* GIUSEPPE FERRERI *Arcivescovo di Urbino*', 10–12: 'Da' maggiori del Mondo io fui percosso,/Ma non cadei, che la virtù mantiensi/Saldamente appoggiata a se medesma'. The title indicates that emendation of the MS. reading 'Albino' (590) is necessary. For the complete text of Wordsworth's version, see *P.W.* iv. 249.

595–8. Cf. I. 394–6.

III

1. Nature] Either 'natural feelings' (cf. II. 534, and n.) or 'natural expression' (cf. II. 414, and n.). Since to Wordsworth language is the 'incarnation of the thought' (III. 181), the two concepts are not clearly distinguishable in this context.

14–15. *The Friend*, No. 6 (21 Sept. 1809), pp. 84–5:

Often have I reflected with awe on the great and disproportionate power, which an individual of no extraordinary talents or attainments may exert, by merely throwing off all restraint of Conscience. What then must not be the power, where an Individual, of consummate wickedness, can organize into the unity and rapidity of an individual will, all the natural and artificial forces of a populous and wicked nation? . . . it is not Vice, as Vice, which is thus mighty; but *systematic* Vice! . . . to him [*sic*] who has once said with his whole heart, Evil be thou my Good! has removed a world of Obstacles by the very decision, that he will have no Obstacles but those of force and brute matter . . . Happily for Mankind, however, the obstacles which a consistent evil mind no longer finds in itself, it finds in its own unsuitableness to Human nature.

The phrase which Wordsworth cites is, of course, originally from *Paradise Lost*, IV. 110.

25. Cicero] See, for instance, *In Catilinam*, ii. xi. 25:

Ex hac enim parte pudor pugnat, illinc petulantia; hinc pudicitia, illinc stuprum; hinc fides, illinc fraudatio; hinc pietas, illinc scelus; hinc constantia, illinc furor; hinc honestas, illinc turpitudo; hinc continentia, illinc libido; denique aequitas, temperantia, fortitudo, prudentia, virtutes omnes certant cum iniquitate, luxuria, ignavia, temeritate, cum vitiis omnibus; postremo copia cum egestate, bona ratio cum perdita, mens sana cum amentia, bona denique spes cum omnium rerum desperatione confligit.

26–8. Dryden and Pope . . . Marlborough] *Absolom and Achitophel*, 150–99, 544–68; *Moral Essays*, Epistle I. 174–209; Epistle II. 115–50. Wordsworth identifies Pope's Atossa, as commonly, with the Duchess of Marlborough; for the view that she represents the Duchess of Buckingham see *Poems of Alexander Pope*, III. ii, ed. F. W. Bateson (London, 1951), 155–64.

40. image . . . given] See the epitaph on Lucy Lyttleton, II. 420 ff.

54–62. Cf. Appendix, I. 4–14.

68. medium of love] See I. 335–47.

77–8. a current of just thought] Cf. II. 375–417.

83–4. instances . . . wanting] See II. 418–612.

90–105. Mason, 'Epitaph on Mrs. Mason, in the Cathedral at Bristol'. On Wordsworth's probable source see n. on 155 below.

116. a shock of surprize] Cf. *P. 1815*, 409: 'A flash of surprise' (of a fanciful image); and *Prel.* V. 407.

118–25. Cf. I. 409–29.

125–7. See I. 430–48, especially 443: 'This shadowy interposition'.

132–4. to give . . . moment] Cf. II. 574–83; *P.L.B.* 379–83: 'truth, not individual and local, but general, and operative; not standing upon external testimony, but carried alive into the heart by passion; truth which is its own testimony, which gives competence and confidence to the tribunal to which it appeals, and receives them from the same tribunal'.

139. nature] 'natural expression'; see II. 414, and n.

141–2. power . . . Taste] Cf. Appendix, I. 20–1: 'I use the word *taste* in its comprehensive, though most unjustifiable, sense'; and n. ad loc.

144–6. Upon a call . . . language] A case of the 'simple and direct' pathetic; cf. *E.S.* 781–6: 'As the pathetic participates of an *animal* sensation, it might seem—that, if the springs of this emotion were genuine, all men, possessed of competent knowledge of the facts and circumstances, would be instantaneously affected. And, doubtless, in the works of every true poet will be found passages of that species of excellence, which is proved by effects immediate and universal.'

152–5. and especially . . . at the time] Cf. II. 407–10, and n.

155. Elegant Extracts] Compiled by Vicesimus Knox. In the edition of 1805, entitled *Elegant Extracts; or, useful and entertaining Pieces of Poetry, Selected for the Improvement of Young Persons . . .*, the book has xvi + 1016 pages. On pp. 834–7 are epitaphs, including several by Pope. On pp. 836–7 occur, in succession, Mason's on Mrs. Mason (III. 90–105), Mason's on Miss Drummond (III. 200–14), and Gray's on Mrs. Clarke (III. 244–60). Rydal Mount Catalogue, lot 619, is 'Elegant Extracts in Verse, 8vo—(*no title*)'; the date of Wordsworth's copy is thus obscured. A copy used by Christopher Wordsworth is identified by Z. S. Fink, *The Early Wordsworthian Milieu* (Oxford, 1958), p. 75, as 'the so-called Dublin "third edition" of 1789'.

162–5. those thoughts . . . in the thought] Cf. III. 180–1, 304–6.

163–4. what the garb is to the body] A commonplace of neo-classic poetics: see, for instance, Dryden, *Essays*, i. 15, 52, 105, 170, 227; Pope, *Essay on Criticism*, 293–336, especially 318: 'Expression is the dress of thought'; Johnson, *Lives*, i. 31: the Metaphysical poets 'were in very little care to clothe their notions with elegance of dress'; i. 58–9: 'Language is the dress of thought; and as the noblest mien or most graceful action would be degraded and obscured by a garb appropriated to the gross employments of rusticks or mechanicks, so the most heroick sentiments will lose their efficacy . . . if they are conveyed by words used commonly upon low and trivial occasions.' Our textual note to III. 125 shows Wordsworth about to use the same metaphor and then rejecting it. His distinction is amplified in De Quincey's fourth essay on Style (1841), in *Collected Writings*, ed. Masson, x (Edinburgh, 1890), 229–30:

the more closely any exercise of mind is connected with . . . what is philosophically termed *subjective*,—precisely in that degree . . . does the style or the embodying of the thoughts cease to be a mere separable ornament, and in fact the more does the manner . . . become confluent with the matter. In saying this, we do but vary the form of what we once heard delivered on this subject by Mr. Wordsworth. His remark was . . . that it is in the highest degree unphilosophic to call language or diction "the *dress* of thoughts" . . . he would call it "the *incarnation* of thoughts." . . . Mr. Wordsworth was thinking, doubtless, of poetry like his own: viz. that which is eminently meditative. And the truth is apparent on consideration: for, if language were merely a dress, then you could separate the two; you could lay the thoughts on the left hand, the language on the right. But, generally speaking, you can no more deal thus with poetic thoughts than you can with soul and body. The union is too subtle, the intertexture too ineffable,—each co-existing not merely *with* the other, but each *in* and *through* the other. An image, for instance, a single word, often enters into a thought as a constituent part [cf. *E.E.* III. 164–5]. In short, the two elements are not united as a body with a separable dress, but as a mysterious incarnation.

To the same effect, ibid., p. 262.

164–5. themselves . . . thought] Cf. Wordsworth's note to 'The Thorn' (*P.W.* ii. 513): 'the interest which the mind attaches to words, not only as symbols of the passion, but as *things*, active and efficient, which are of themselves part of the passion'; *L.Y.*, p. 437: 'words are not a mere *vehicle*, but they are *powers* either to kill or to animate.'

172–4. Cf. *E.S.* 781–6, cited above, n. to III. 144–6.

182. poisoned vestments] For instance, the shirt of Nessus worn by Hercules (Sophocles, *Trachiniae*), or the poisoned robe sent by Medea to Jason's new bride (Euripides, *Medea*).

189–90. conjunction of Reason and Passion] Cf. I. 409 ff., especially 440–3.

191–3. taste . . . dependence] Cf. Appendix, I, *passim*; *P.L.B.* 40–56, 161–84; *E.S.*, *passim*.

196. nature] 'human nature'; cf. II. 534, and n.; *feelings of nature* = 'natural feelings'.

200–14. On Wordsworth's probable source, see n. on III. 155 above.

215. translation] We have not discovered the original of the epitaph or Wordsworth's source.

244–60. On the probable source see n. on III. 155 above. Standard texts of Gray read 'this silent' (245) and 'faith sincere' (249); and these are also the readings of *Elegant Extracts*. The first error may arise from a mishearing by Mrs. Wordsworth; the second probably derives from 'lov'd' (248), and may be hers or Wordsworth's.

268. Nature] See n. on III. 1 above.

comprehensive] 'all-embracing'?

269–71. See Gray, *Works . . . to which are added, Memoirs of his Life and Writings. By W. Mason, M.A.*, 4th edn. (London, 1807), ii. 82: 'IN THE VAULT BENEATH ARE DEPOSITED, / IN HOPE OF A JOYFUL RESURRECTION, / THE REMAINS OF / MARY ANTROBUS. / SHE DIED, UNMARRIED, NOV. V. MDCCXLIX. / AGED LXVI. / IN THE SAME PIOUS CONFIDENCE, / BESIDE HER

FRIEND AND SISTER, / HERE SLEEP THE REMAINS OF / DOROTHY GRAY, / WIDOW, THE CAREFUL TENDER MOTHER / OF MANY CHILDREN, ONE OF WHOM ALONE / HAD THE MISFORTUNE TO SURVIVE HER. / SHE DIED MARCH XI. MDCCLIII. / AGED LXVII.' Wordsworth seems to draw on phrases in this epitaph in a passage which appears in early texts of *Exc.* VI (*P.W.* v. 227): 'There a Husband sleeps, . . . in pious confidence / Of glorious resurrection'.

271–85, 296–311. Cf. I. 409–29.

297–8. Pope upon Harcourt] *Minor Poems*, ed. Ault and Butt (London, 1954), p. 242, lines 3–4: 'Who ne'er knew Joy, but Friendship might divide, / Or gave his Father grief, but when he dy'd.' The inscription is in Stanton Harcourt Church, Oxon.

303 ff. James Butler, first Duke of Ormonde (1610–88); Thomas Butler, Earl of Ossory (1634–80), eldest son of James, Duke of Ormonde. Wordsworth's source was probably Scott's notes to *Absolom and Achitophel* (*Works of John Dryden*, London, 1808, ix. 300): 'He [Ossory] died on the 30th July, 1680, aged forty-six years. The lamentation for his loss was general and excessive; the noble reply of his venerable father, to those who offered him consolation, is well known: "Since he had borne the death of his king, he could support," he said, "that of his child; and would rather have his dead son, than any living son in Christendom." ' Wordsworth had written to Scott in Jan. 1808, expressing a desire to 'see your notes on Dryden's political Poems, which are in my opinion far the best of his works' (*M.Y.* i. 191). Thomas Carte, *An History of the Life of James Duke of Ormonde* (London, 1736), ii. 507, gives a different and perhaps more authentic version, in which Ormonde's remark is presented as a sneer at a comforter suspected of insincerity. Hume, *History of England* (London, 1793), viii. 164, gives a version similar to Scott's, and was probably Scott's source.

305–6. infinitude of truth] Cf. III. 163.

317–19. For Wordsworth's versions of Chiabrera in *The Friend* see n. on II. 476 above.

319 ff. Weever, p. 8. The original reads: 'and that sometimes with a kinde of commiseration' and 'the good or bad fortunes in the life'. The italics are Wordsworth's; 'astrict' = 'brief, compressed'; 'pithic' (see 321, textual n.) seems to be Wordsworth's misreading of 'pithie', which in the copies of Weever inspected by us has a particularly blind -*e*, looking much like a -*c*.

332–3. unite . . . admonition] Cf. I. 430–48.

335–6. so that . . . species] Cf. I. 315 ff.

339–41. the one . . . ago] *P.W.* iv. 253. On the spelling of the proper name see W. J. B. Owen, 'Manuscript Variants of Wordsworth's Poems', *N. & Q.* cciii (1958), 308–10. The translation was first published in *The Friend*, No. 20 (4 Jan. 1810), p. 320. The original, headed '*Per il Signor* FERDINANDO BALBI', is in *Opere*, ii. 186.

356. Urbino] See textual n. The original reads: 'Urbino / Di lui s'onori', and there is nothing in the edition of 1782 to account for the error.

359. arbitary or mechanical] Cf. II. 451.

363–4. Cf. Johnson, *Lives,* iii. 261: 'To wish, *Peace to thy shade,* is too mythological to be admitted into a christian temple: the ancient worship has infected almost all our other compositions, and might therefore be contented to spare our epitaphs.'

369. uncharacteristic] See II. 533, and n.

375. some of the points] For instance, the personifications of Savona and Sebeto, and the untempered expression of grief.

377–93. A later version was published in 1837; see *P.W.* iv. 252. The errors there corrected (ibid., p. 449), it will be seen from our textual notes, are in the MS. The original, '*Per il Signor* LELIO PAVESE', is in *Opere,* ii. 184–5; there is nothing in the text of 1782 to account for the errors.

395. upon the youthful Pozzobonelli] 'Not without heavy grief of heart', *P.W.* iv. 252–3. First published in *The Friend,* No. 20 (4 Jan. 1810), p. 319. The original, '*Per Monsignor Abbate* FRANCESCO POZZOBONELLO', is in *Opere,* ii. 176–7.

400. upon Men] See textual n.

406. Raphael] '*Per il Signor* RA[F]AEL DI URBINO', in *Opere,* ii. 187: 'Per abbellir le immagini dipinte, / Alle vive imitar pose tal cura, / Che a belle far le vere sue natura,/Oggi vuole imitar le costui finte.'

406–9. Cf. I. 465–91.

410–13. Torquato Tasso] See *P.W.* iv. 377; never printed by Words-worth. The original, '*Per il Signor* TORQUATO TASSO', is in *Opere,* ii. 184: 'Torquato Tasso è quì sepolto: Questa, / Che dal profondo cor lagrime versa, / È Poesia: da così fatto pianto / Argomenti ciascun qual fu costui.'

414. Chiabrera's epitaph for himself is recorded in *Opere* (Venice, 1730), i. xxiii: 'AMICO Io vivendo cercava il conforto per lo Monte Parnaso. / Tu, meglio consigliato, fa di cercarlo sul Monte Calvario.' There is a vacant space in the MS. after 'enlarged upon' (417), where Wordsworth no doubt intended to insert a translation of the epitaph. The 'sentiment' (415) seems to be the mingling of the personal with 'a concern on the part of the dead for the well-being of the living' (332–3).

419–31. Weever, pp. 361–2:

I reade in the Catalogue of Bishops, and other writers . . . that *William* a Norman, who enioyed this Bishopricke in the Conquerours time, lieth here interred in the body of the Church. Vnto whom the City of London acknowledgeth it selfe greatly beholding, for that the king, by his meanes and instant suite, granted vnto them all kinde of liberties, in as ample manner as they enioyed them in the time of his predecessour *Ed.* the Confessour. [Document in Old English cited and translated.] In thankfulnesse hereof, the Citizens caused to be engrauen an Epitaph vpon his Tombe in Latine, thus Englished by *Iohn Stow.* [Prose part of the epitaph follows, then the verse as in text.] But this Tombe was long since either destroyed by time, or taken away vpon some occasion.

Wordsworth ignores the remark that the English version is Stow's.

434–6. have shewn . . . ascribed] The text here is barely intelligible, but may perhaps be construed: 'have shewn to what [causes] we are to ascribe deficiencies . . . and errors . . .'; or 'have shewn to what deficiencies . . . and to what [other causes] we are to ascribe errors . . .'. It is more likely that some such phrase as 'the defects of bad Epitaphs' is wanting after 'judgement'.

454–70. Coleridge apparently supplied Wordsworth with these four epitaphs. The first and fourth are in *C.N.B.* ii. 2982, and are there identified by Coleridge as having been seen in Ashby Church Yard, 6 Feb. 1807. Miss Coburn notes that Ashby-de-la-Zouch, Leics., is two miles from Coleorton, where Coleridge was then visiting the Wordsworths. In *C.N.B.* the first epitaph is headed: '83—and 87 years', and the fourth, which immediately precedes it, is headed: 'T.H. 25 July 1802. —/ Aged 10 weeks'. The second and third epitaphs are in *C.N.B.* i. 1267: the second begins: 'Here/ lyeth the Body of Elizabeth/ Bevan, who died the 3rd/ of June, 1725, aged 22 years'; the third begins: 'Here lyeth the Body of Sara & Hannah Jones the Daughters of Evan Jones & Jane his Wife./ Sara Jones died January the 19th, aged 2 years & 3 months/ Hannah Jones departed this Life the 8th day of September, 1746, aged 15 years.' Coleridge comments on the second: 'While I took the copy, the Groundsel showered its white Beard on me/ Groundsel & Fern on the grave, & the Thorns growing that had been bound over it'; he introduces the third: 'On a square Tomb as high as half up my Thigh, where the Tom Tits with their black velvet Caps showered down the lovely yewberries on me.' He saw these epitaphs in the churchyard of a 'White Church with grey Steeple a furlong or so from the Town [Laugharne, Carmarthenshire] near the bottom [of *del.*] on a Hillside.' The stone bearing the third could still be identified there in April 1963; it was then legible enough to indicate that Coleridge's transcript is fairly accurate, but he omitted the year, [?1739], after '19th'. Wordsworth followed this omission, and also miscopied the heading.

471–80. We have not discovered where Wordsworth saw this inscription.

483–7. Addison, *The Spectator*, ed. Donald F. Bond (Oxford, 1965), No. 26, i. 109.

499–503. Wordsworth saw the epitaph 'in the churchyard at the head of Haweswater' (*P.W.* v. 464), i.e. in Mardale churchyard, now submerged. All memorial stones were removed about 1938 from Mardale to the new churchyard at Shap. We are indebted to the Revd. T. E. H. Baily of Shap for this information, and for the following transcript of the epitaph: 'HERE LIETH THE BODY / OF THOMAS HOLME SON OF THE LATE HENRY / AND JANE HOLME OF CHAPEL HILL / HE WAS DEPRIVED OF THE SENSE OF HEARING / IN HIS YOUTH AND LIVED ABOUT 50 YEARS / WITHOUT THE

COMFORT OF HEARING ONE WORD / HE RECONCILED HIMSELF TO HIS MISFORTUNE BY / READING AND USEFUL EMPLOYMENT / WAS VERY TEMPERATE HONEST AND PEACEABLE / HE WAS WELL RESPECTED BY HIS NEIGHBOURS AND / RELATIONS AND DEPARTED THIS LIFE AFTER A SHORT / SICKNESS ON THE 22D OF MARCH 1773 AGED 67 YEARS.'

504–87. *Exc.* VII. 395–481. For the development of the text see *P.W.* v. 244–6.

COMMENTARY: APPENDIX

1–4. It has already . . . mind] See II. 270–85.

4. Literature . . . morals] Cf. *P.L.B.* 306–7, and n.

20–1. *taste* . . . sense] Cf. III. 141–2, and see the discussion in *E.S.* 718–23 ff.: 'TASTE . . . is a word which has been forced to extend its services far beyond the point to which philosophy would have confined them. It is a metaphor, taken from a *passive* sense of the human body, and transferred to things which are in their essence *not* passive,—to intellectual *acts* and *operations*' etc.

34. the favourite style of different ages] Cf. *P.L.B.*, 52–61.

36–7. common principles] Cf. *E.S.* 360–3: 'they whose opinions are much influenced by authority will often be tempted to think that there are no fixed principles in human nature for [poetry] to rest upon.'

48. the test recommended] Of translating it 'into another style' (51); see II. 445–7 and textual n.

X

A GUIDE THROUGH THE DISTRICT OF THE LAKES

INTRODUCTION: GENERAL

W H E N in 1809 Wordsworth agreed to supply an appropriate prose text to accompany Joseph Wilkinson's forthcoming publication of scenes drawn in the Lake District, he did so almost certainly for financial reasons. From 1809 until 1813, when Lord Lonsdale came to his assistance, Wordsworth was often in serious need of money to meet the demands of a growing family. In letters written during this period Dorothy particularly recognized with regret the necessity of William's having to earn money through some other means than poetry.[1] We do not know what the financial arrangement was between Wilkinson and Wordsworth, but in his letter of Dedication, 'To the Right Honourable Thomas Wallace, M.P., &c. &c. &c.', Wilkinson confessed that he was 'anxious for the success of this expensive undertaking', and it is not unlikely that one of his expenses was a fee for Wordsworth's assistance. Whatever the arrangement, it would seem that only a financial compensation could have persuaded Wordsworth in 1809 to do what a year before he had firmly refused to do. On 2 October 1808, in response to a letter from the Reverend J. Pering, who had recently visited the Lake District, Wordsworth made some remarks that are particularly interesting as coming from the future author of *The Guide to the Lakes*:

I am pleased to find that this beautiful country has made such an impression upon you as to induce you to record your feelings: but what shall I say to your request that I should communicate to you some description of the same objects?—Alas! you have but a faint notion how disagreeable writing, of all Sorts, is to me, except from the impulse of the moment. I must be my own Task master, or I can do nothing at all. Last Autumn I made a little Tour, with my wife, and she was very anxious that I should preserve the memory of it by a written account. I tried to comply with her entreaty, but an insuperable dullness came over me, and I could make no progress.

This simple and true statement I am sure you will deem a sufficient apology for not venturing upon a theme so boundless as this sublime and beautiful region.

Besides, you can easily conceive that objects may be too familiar to a Man, to leave him the power of describing them. This is the case with me in regard to these Lakes and mountains, which are my native Country, and among which I have passed the greatest part of my life: and really I should be utterly at a loss were I about to set myself to a formal delineation of them, or any part of them, where to begin, and where to end (*M.Y.* i. 271–2).

---

[1] *M.Y.* i. 325; see also Moorman, ii. 119–22, 156, 240–4.

That Wordsworth should accept Joseph Wilkinson as his 'Task master' for even the briefest time surely indicates some kind of financial hardship. Acquaintances of the Wordsworths for some years,[1] the Reverend Joseph Wilkinson and his wife were close friends of the Coleridges and Southeys. Until 1804, when they moved to Thetford, Norfolk, the Wilkinsons had resided at Ormathwaite, very near Greta Hall in Keswick. During his absences from home Coleridge, in letters to his wife, frequently asked to be remembered to his neighbours Mr. and Mrs. Wilkinson, and his daughter, Sara, born in 1802, was Mrs. Wilkinson's goddaughter.[2] Both Coleridge and Southey liked Wilkinson's drawings, mainly, it seems, for their fidelity to the scenes.[3]

When in the summer of 1809 Wilkinson decided that he wanted an accompanying text for his collection of engravings, he apparently first approached Coleridge. Preserved in the Wordsworth Library is an undated letter from Wilkinson addressed to Coleridge in Grasmere, where he had been staying since 14 June (*M.T.* i. 355); after giving a list of new subscribers for Coleridge's *Friend*, the 'first paper' of which he had read with pleasure, Wilkinson continued:

I am just returned from Town, where I have been making arrangements for my publication, and as I have seen some of Mr Greens numbers I will be obliged to you if you will tell our friend Wordsworth that no two works, descriptive of the same country can be more different, or less likely to interfere with each other, than his and mine. but I shall write to Mr Wordsworth in a few days more fully upon the subject when I hope either Mr W — or yourself, or both, will afford me the assistance I shall explain[,] to enable me to make my work more perfect and acceptable to the public than it otherwise would be.

From these remarks, we deduce that Coleridge, who was then pressed with work for *The Friend*, had suggested that Wordsworth, recently freed from intense activity over the printing of *Cintra*, should take on the assignment. But Wordsworth was obviously reluctant to abet any competition with his friend William Green of Ambleside, whose work he admired.[4] (Having published numerous sketches of the Lake scenery, Green in the summer of 1809 was preparing to bring out a volume of engravings, accompanied by a brief text.)[5] Once assured

---

[1] See *E.T.*, p. 344 n. 4; pp. 363, 372; *Journals*, i. 129, 148.

[2] *New Letters of Robert Southey*, ed. Kenneth Curry (New York, 1965), i. 421–4; *C.L.* ii. 786, 789, 939, 1130, 1140 (Griggs's index confuses Joseph Wilkinson with Thomas Wilkinson of Yanwath); L. N. Broughton, *Sara Coleridge and Henry Reed* (Ithaca, N.Y., 1937), pp. 90–1.

[3] *C.L.* ii. 978, 981; *C.N.B.* i. 1468; Southey, *Life and Correspondence* (1850), ii. 238.

[4] See our notes to *Guide*, 140 fn., and 412–16.

[5] The Introduction to Green's *Seventy-eight Studies from Nature* (London and Ambleside, 1809) is dated 1 August 1809; in the Introduction to his second volume,

that Green's interests would not be harmed, Wordsworth set to work for Wilkinson.

With the aid of subscribers, Wilkinson's *Select Views in Cumberland, Westmoreland, and Lancashire* (London, 1810) was privately published in twelve monthly instalments.[1] Today, library copies are usually bound, but the copy in the Wordsworth Library is a portfolio of forty-eight engravings, with the letterpress also unbound. According to the dates on the engravings, four were normally published on the first of the month (three were published in August and five in September).

Serial publication accounts for the fact that Wordsworth's 'Introduction' was published before he had finished writing some of the subsequent parts. In a letter to Catherine Clarkson, 18 November 1809, Dorothy writes (*M.Y*. i. 372): 'Sara [Hutchinson] has been kept almost constantly busy in transcribing: for William, and for "The Friend". . . . For William she has been transcribing the introduction to a collection of prints to be published by Mr. Wilkinson of Thetford. . . . I hope you will be interested with William's part of the work (he has only finished the general introduction, being unable to do the rest till he has seen the prints).' The published 'Introduction', which is now represented in our edition of the *Guide*, lines 501–2307 and textual notes, was in the hands of the Beaumonts probably well before 10 May 1810, on which day Wordsworth thanked Lady Beaumont for her praise of it, adding that, bad as the drawings were, he hoped 'that the Author and his Wife . . . may be spared any mortification from hearing them condemned severely by acknowledged judges'.[2] The dates of composition and publication for Wordsworth's remaining contributions to *Select Views* (i.e. 'Section I' and 'Section II') can be less precisely stated. Because there are no references to any of the engravings in 'Section I' ('Of the Best Time for Visiting the Lakes') and because we know that some of 'Section II' was written before mid March, we believe that 'Section I', like the 'Introduction', was written well in advance of publication. 'Section I', now represented in the *Guide* by 2308–406 and

A Description of Sixty Studies from Nature . . . Comprising a General Guide to the Beauties of the North of England (London, 1810), p. ix, he speaks of having published thirty sketches in 1808 and twelve more in 1809.

[1] For a bibliographical description see R. F. Metzdorf, *The Tinker Library* (New Haven, Conn., 1959), item no. 2337.

[2] *M.Y*. i. 404–5. Wordsworth's evaluation of the etchings is somewhat ambivalent: when he agreed to assist Wilkinson, he must have known what Wilkinson's artistry was like (see *Journals*, i. 166); in the 'Introduction', speaking of the work as a whole, he wrote that its purpose was to provide 'pleasing Sketches, and at the same time accurate Portraits of those scenes from which they are taken' (*Guide*, textual n. 528–31); in writing to Lady Beaumont, he admitted that those who were good judges of art would find the etchings 'intolerable' (*M.Y*. i. 404). Norman Nicholson in *The Lakers* (London, 1955), pp. 179–80, amply bears out Wordsworth's prediction of the response from good judges.

textual notes, is a very short section (one and a half folio pages) compared with 'Section II' (nine and a half folio pages). No manuscripts survive for either the 'Introduction' or 'Section I'; but for 'Section II', which we print separately on pp. 260–86, under the title *Select Views* (*S.V.*), some manuscripts do survive (they are described on pp. 137–43). Those that are in the hand of Sara Hutchinson must have been transcribed before the middle of March, when she left Grasmere for Wales (*M.Y.* i. 395); her hand is found as far along in 'Section II' as *S.V.* 200. This first part and some of the remaining parts of 'Section II' may have been written before mid December, for Wordsworth was 'at leisure' in the latter part of December to compose his 'Reply to Mathetes' (see p. 3) and by the end of February he had also finished the three 'Essays upon Epitaphs' (see p. 45). But, despite his early progress, he had to postpone his final writing for Wilkinson, and a year later, 12 November 1810, Dorothy spoke of work still to be done (*M.Y.* i. 449): 'in the evening Wm. employed me to compose a description or two for the finishing of his work for Wilkinson. It is a most irksome task to him, not being permitted to follow his own course, and I daresay you will find this latter part very flat.' Of Dorothy's descriptions we can identify, with some degree of certainty, only one: *Select Views*, 487–525 ('This Water . . . generations') is written in her hand and is, therefore, unique among the manuscripts for *Select Views*, although it is possible that another late 'description', lacking manuscript support for identification, may also be hers.

This last-minute composition reflects, no doubt, the delays and frustrations imposed upon Wordsworth by his having to wait for copies of Wilkinson's prints. Originally, the plan called for a number of shorter sections, each approximately the same length as 'Section I', rather than one long second section. For example, the manuscript for *S.V.* 136–200 is headed 'Section 5th / Windermere &c. in continuation'; although no manuscript survives for *S.V.* 201 ff., the single occurrence in the printed text of a subheading ('Ambleside', *S.V.* 201) must be a relic of a separate manuscript which would presumably have been headed 'Section 6th'. It was with this plan in mind that Wordsworth in the 'Introduction' promised to enter 'into detail in the several numbers of this publication' (*Guide*, textual n. 597). We do not know when or why it was decided to run the shorter sections together, but it could be that the sections were—at least in the eyes of Wilkinson— growing too long,[1] or were inappropriate to the monthly selection of

---

[1] Although we do not entirely understand Wordsworth's note to Wilkinson quoted in our description of MSS. Prose 20 (see p. 141), we suppose that Wordsworth, having arrived at *S.V.* 88, was foreseeing a need to print two of his sections for each of the six instalments still to come. Inasmuch as the manuscripts for *S.V.* 1–200 are much longer than the printed text, Wilkinson may have asked

drawings. As it is, the relationship between the text and the prints is not always congruent. In the table of 'CONTENTS' the drawings, listed by number and title, follow exactly the geographical sequence of Wordsworth's recommended tour, but the drawings themselves were not numbered, nor were they published in the order given in the table of Contents. We observe that in the printed text Wordsworth refers specifically to ten etchings published within the first four months, whereas he refers to only four published within the last eight months; yet from this fact we cannot conclude that when he was writing the early part of 'Section II', he had not seen the later ones, for the first explicit reference to a drawing (*S.V.* 85–6) is to 'Estwaite Water from below Bellemont', published 1 July. In composing a description of Grasmere, apparently intended to follow *S.V.* 307, Wordsworth refers in his manuscript to an etching 'of Grasmere Lake [?seen] from the edge of Easedale' (*S.V.*, textual n. 307/8), but no such etching was ever published, and probably for this reason the whole section on Grasmere was abandoned. Finally, a very strange effect stems from the fact that Wordsworth's name nowhere appears in the published work; yet in the printed text we find him speaking of views 'which I have given', as though he were the artist writing his own commentary. Fortunately, the surviving manuscripts help us to explain this misleading anonymity: on three occasions when the printed text employs the first person singular the manuscript employs the plural (*S.V.*, textual notes 464, 510, 705). We suspect that these alterations were the work of Wilkinson, whom Wordsworth in his letter to Lady Beaumont spoke of as a man 'not superabundant in good sense' (*M.Y.* i. 404).

In 1821 Wilkinson republished *Select Views*, this time with coloured versions of his engravings; except for the date, the title-page is the same as that of 1810. We have found no evidence that Wordsworth was even informed of this new edition, and accordingly our textual notes ignore it.[1]

Before he had finished his contributions to Wilkinson's first edition, Wordsworth was planning to publish a guide of his own. When Dorothy announced in her letter of 18 November 1809 that William had just completed the 'Introduction', she immediately added:

It is the only regular, and I may say *scientific* account of the present and past state and appearance of the country that has yet appeared. I think, if

Wordsworth to reduce the length and to run the sections into one; such a change in plan might explain why MS. Prose 24 (*S.V.* 89–200), though addressed as a letter to Wilkinson, was never mailed.

[1] In December 1811 Wilkinson had promised to send the Wordsworths his 'coloured prints', but from Dorothy's letter (*M.Y.* i. 526) there is no way of telling what prints these were.

he were to write a Guide to the Lakes and prefix this preface, it would sell better, and bring him more money than any of his higher labours. He has some thoughts of doing this; but do not mention it, as Mr. W's work should have its fair run. He mentioned to Mr. Wilkinson his scheme, to which I should think that Mr. W. will have no objection; as the Guide will, by calling Mr. W's publication to mind, after its first run, perhaps help to keep up the sale (*M.T.* i. 372).

Yet even this plan for a 'Guide to the Lakes' was not entirely a new one, for, as Mary Moorman (ii. 157) has pointed out, Wordsworth had told Lady Holland as early as August 1807 that he was 'preparing a manual to guide travelers in their tour amongst the Lakes'.[1] Mrs. Moorman thinks that this statement to Lady Holland strangely contradicts Wordsworth's firm rejection, in the following year, of Pering's request that he should write a description of the Lake District scenery, but the contradiction is surely more apparent than real. For Wordsworth 'a manual to guide travelers' would not have been the same thing as 'a formal delineation' of 'this sublime and beautiful region', to quote again from his letter to Pering. After successfully completing such a delineation in his 'Introduction' to Wilkinson's 'expensive undertaking', it is understandable that he should revive the notion of preparing a 'Guide' to fill out a separate—and possibly even more profitable—publication of his own.

Manuscripts in the Wordsworth Library show that he did, in fact, undertake such a composition. These manuscripts, which in our edition are entitled 'An Unpublished Tour' and 'The Sublime and the Beautiful', were all left unfinished; essentially, they are first, second, and occasionally third drafts for a work apparently soon abandoned. (For a description of the manuscripts, see pp. 137–49.) There is no date anywhere on the manuscripts, and we have found only one external reference to the work in progress, but we believe that the composition was not earlier than September 1811 and that it ceased about November 1812. The reason why we believe the manuscripts could not have been written before September 1811 is that, in writing about Donnerdale, Wordsworth incorporated into his new writing a part of an 1809 manuscript, transcribed for Wilkinson by Sara Hutchinson; in the course of expanding this section of the 'old letter'—for that is the way Wordsworth now refers to the manuscripts of *Select Views*—he adds details about the churchyard at Ulpha Kirk which he had acquired during a visit to it at the end of August or the beginning of September 1811. For example, in 1809, for *Select Views*, Wordsworth wrote of Ulpha Kirk: 'A pleasing Epitaph, the only one in the place if I

[1] *The Journal of Elizabeth Lady Holland,* ed. The Earl of Ilchester (London, 1908), ii. 231.

remember will be found affixed to the wall of the Church. This wild Count[ry was] once frequented by Druids . . .'; at this point the 'Unpublished Tour' manuscript was sewn directly over the 'old letter', and the passage was then expanded to include not only a quotation of the eight-line epitaph but also the following new information: 'This Tombstone, erected by a father to a Daughter who died at the age of one & twenty, is the only record in the Church yard, except that a Person has availed himself of the naked surface of a corner stone of the Chapel rudely to engrave thereon a brief notice of One who is buried near it. This wild country was once frequented by Druids . . .' (*U.T.* 472–7 and textual n. 461). Obviously, between 1809 and the writing of 'An Unpublished Tour' Wordsworth had not only revisited the church but also jotted down the epitaph and observed other details. This he did at the end of August or the beginning of September 1811 on his way home from a month spent at the seaside with his wife and two youngest children (see *M.Y.* i. 499–503). In recounting to Sara Hutchinson the homeward journey, Wordsworth wrote: 'Mary and I returned from Duddon Bridge, up the Duddon and through Seathwaite, the children with Fanny taking the direct road through Coniston. We dined in the Porch of Ulpha Kirk, and passed two Hours there and in the beautiful churchyard' (*M.Y.* i. 509). The two hours spent at Ulpha Kirk are clearly reflected in the expanded manuscript of 'An Unpublished Tour'.

How soon, or how long, it was after this visit to Ulpha Kirk that Wordsworth began writing his new guide we do not know, but by the following summer he must have written enough to tell Samuel Rogers something about it during the latter's visit to Windermere in August, when the two men were seeing each other often.[1] Sometime in the early winter Wordsworth wrote Rogers a letter which was all too promptly destroyed, as Rogers's reply on 9 January 1813 makes evident: 'Upon my return from the North Pole yesterday, I found your Letter lying upon my table to welcome me; & happy, I can truly say, I shall be to execute any Commission you may favor me with. You say the Work is in prose—&, so far I read—but unfortunately being called off in the middle of the letter, short as it was, when I returned, I found that my Sister by some unlucky mistake had burnt it. If you have not entrusted it to another, pray send it to me that I may begin my negotiation. I hope it is that which relates to your own Lakes & mountains. As for myself I have been idling away my life in the Highlands.'[2]

By the time this letter reached Grasmere, Wordsworth had already put aside his unfinished work. As he told Rogers in his prompt reply, the death of his son Thomas, 1 December, had caused him to 'defer' his

---

[1] See *M.Y.* ii. 42, 45.
[2] Rogers's unpublished letter is in the Wordsworth Library.

'intended Publication' (*M.T.* ii. 69). Another probable reason for indefinite deferment was that on 27 December he had accepted Lord Lonsdale's offer of £100, to be presented annually, until he could be appointed to the expected vacancy in the Stamp Office for Westmorland (*M.T.* ii. 53–4, 57). On 5 January Dorothy wrote to Catherine Clarkson that 'within the two last days' William had resumed work on *The Excursion*, or, as she still called it, *The Recluse* (*M.T.* ii. 64). Three days later, having received a draft for £100, Wordsworth wrote to Lord Lonsdale that this kindness would permit him to return to the writing of poetry, 'which for some time I could not have yielded to, on account of a task undertaken for profit. This I can now defer without imprudence till I can proceed with it more heartily than at present would be possible.'[1]

When Wordsworth began 'An Unpublished Tour', his intention apparently was merely to expand 'Section II' of *Select Views* and reprint the 'Introduction', just as Dorothy had from the first envisioned his doing. Thus early in 'An Unpublished Tour' (220), he reminds the reader of observations which had been more fully treated in the 'Introduction'. Following his first two short chapters there comes a manuscript direction which, though largely ignored, further indicates his original intention: 'Here take up Wilkinson Book' (*U.T.*, textual n. 203–6). That he was working with *Select Views* close at hand is evident from the fact that he does not hesitate to copy without change single sentences from the earlier text, and when he comes to the section on Donnerdale (*U.T.* 357–557 and textual notes), he turns directly to his old manuscripts for *Select Views* and incorporates them into the new ones. But with the section on Coniston Lake (*U.T.* 559 ff.) he abandons *Select Views*, perhaps because he found revision and expansion too tedious or too confining. Still, the main outline for a tour among the Lakes remains the same, beginning with Coniston and then proceeding to Windermere by way of Hawkshead, and there is every reason to think that he planned to follow thereafter the general itinerary set forth in 'Section II' of *Select Views*. In writing leisurely and freely about the neighbourhoods so familiar to him as a boy, Wordsworth allowed his chapters to grow out of all proportion with his early ones; for example, in Chapter two, he had managed to describe Lancaster in something less than twelve hundred words, but in his chapter on 'Hawkshead and the Ferry' he took approximately five times that number.

One part of 'An Unpublished Tour' is somewhat puzzling to us, partly because it is strangely isolated from the rest. The manuscript

---

[1] *M.T.* ii. 67. In a footnote the editors repeat the guess earlier hazarded by Moorman (ii. 242) that the 'task' was one of compiling 'an anthology of some kind'.

for the first draft of the section on Borrowdale (*U.T.* 1592–787) is physically like the other 'Unpublished Tour' manuscripts, but the second draft, unlike any of the others, is found in MSS. Verse 57, a notebook containing portions of *The Excursion*. Even more striking than this physical isolation is the fact that—to use the language of guide-books in Wordsworth's day—the tourist is not conducted to this spot; as a result, the section seems self-contained rather than a part of a continuing work. Recalling again Wordsworth's letter to Pering, we cannot help wondering whether this section was perhaps written in 1807, when after an excursion with Mary he had 'tried to comply with her entreaty' that he should 'preserve the memory of it by a written account'. The excursion that year had been 'to Wasdale, Ennerdale, Whitehaven, Cockermouth etc.' (*M.T.* i. 164), and we remember that Wordsworth recommends the route by Borrowdale for travellers going to Wasdale (*Guide*, 313–14). Because the writing throughout 'An Unpublished Tour' varies considerably from one part to another, we hesitate to make any judgement based on style, but the elaborate and rather artificial use of Michael Drayton, and the topographically irrelevant section on the gambling habits of the Borrowdale natives, make this section one of the least interesting for the reader, and so conceivably one of 'insuperable dullness' for the author, to quote once again from Wordsworth's letter to Pering.

Also standing apart from the beginning sections of 'An Unpublished Tour' is MSS. Prose 28, which the Wordsworth Library has entitled 'The Sublime and the Beautiful', a title we preserve. The beginning of this essay or chapter is lost, and though we are inclined to think that the loss was not extensive, we cannot be positive (see our n. to *Subl. and Beaut.* 1–58). Whether the essay should be identified as the beginning of a new work or a continuation of 'An Unpublished Tour' is also debatable. On the one hand, it seems to be a continuation because at the end of 'Hawkshead & the Ferry' the tourist has been led to the western shore of Windermere, and in 'The Sublime and the Beautiful' he is directed 'to turn his eyes . . . towards that cluster of Mountains at the Head of Windermere' (*Subl. and Beaut.* 56–7). On the other hand, Wordsworth now writes of the imagined tourist as one about to approach the mountains and to explore the valleys for the first time; speaking of 'the law of sublimity and that of beauty', he says that 'These shall be considered so far at least as they may be collected from the objects amongst which we are about to enter, viz., those of a mountainous region'. This remark seems to ignore the fact that, according to the arrangement of the tour, the traveller has already explored such then out-of-the-way places as Seathwaite in Donnerdale, Tilberthwaite, and Yewdale, as well as the more accessible Coniston.

In yet another way the essay seems a new beginning, for the mode of writing changes: in 'An Unpublished Tour' the mode is more varied, for it shifts back and forth between the topographical, the anecdotic, and the historical; in 'The Sublime and the Beautiful' the mode is almost entirely aesthetic and philosophical. It is as though Wordsworth had decided to write another kind of book, one which would be of value not only to the traveller in the Lake District but also to any philosophical mind interested in understanding the 'laws' under which objects, sublime or beautiful, are contemplated. A guide-book 'undertaken for profit' could easily be put aside unfinished, but when Wordsworth told Lord Lonsdale that he would 'defer' the book which he was then writing, he was speaking of a book which, like the 'Introduction' to *Select Views*, had grown into something more complex and of wider interest than a guide-book. Years later he continued to think about the possibility of taking up again the problems discussed in this final essay; in letters written to Jacob Fletcher in 1825 he not only repeated the main points of 'The Sublime and the Beautiful', but also twice spoke of his intention of illustrating them at large, or, as he put it in his letter of 6 April: 'I am far from thinking that I am able to write satisfactorily upon matters so subtle—yet I hope to make a trial.'[1]

Despite these hopes, Wordsworth, as far as we know, only once turned back to the manuscripts of 1811–12, and that was for a brief raid on the Seathwaite section of 'An Unpublished Tour', when he was composing his long note to be attached to Sonnets XVII and XVIII of *The River Duddon*. Part of the note (*P.W.* iii. 509–10) is a slightly revised and expanded version of 'An Unpublished Tour', 380–434. A more important addition to *The River Duddon, A Series of Sonnets: Vaudracour and Julia: and Other Poems* (London, 1820) is the *Topographical Description of the Country of the Lakes, In the North of England*, or the second edition of the *Guide* (cf. Healey, item 52). In a short prefatory note Wordsworth says that he is republishing the essay *'with emendations and additions . . . from a consciousness of its having been written in the same spirit which dictated several of the poems, and from a belief that it will tend materially to illustrate them'* (*Guide*, textual n. 500/1). The *Topographical Description* was praised by at least four important reviews,[2] and perhaps this good reception encouraged Wordsworth to publish his first separate edition in 1822.

As our textual notes show, Wordsworth made more additions and more extensive revisions for the second, third, fourth, and fifth

---

[1] *L.Y.*, p. 195; see also *L.Y.*, pp. 184–5, 194.
[2] Elsie Smith, *An Estimate of William Wordsworth* (Oxford, 1932) quotes *Blackwood's Edinburgh Magazine* (p. 321), *The Eclectic Review* (p. 324), *Gentleman's Magazine* (p. 326), and *The Monthly Review* (p. 329).

editions of the *Guide* than he did for any other piece of prose writing. To indicate as briefly and as prominently as possible the *major* changes, we resort to the following table:

Topographical Description of the Country of the
Lakes in the North of England (1820)

1. The removal of all references to Wilkinson's etchings; the omission of 'Section II'; the incorporation of 'Section I' into the single continuous essay.

2. The insertion of descriptive passages on the boundary-lines of the lakes (*Guide*, 858–906), and on the stranger's first experiences of mountainous scenery (2407–504), both passages showing the influence of the thought that had gone into 'The Sublime and the Beautiful'.

3. The insertion of comments on the tasteless 'improvements' made on the islands of Derwentwater and Windermere (1727–80), the comments on the changes at Windermere being an amplification of a part of 'Section II' (*S.V.* 152–72).

A Description of the Scenery of the Lakes in
the North of England (London, 1822)

1. Division into three main parts ('Description of the Scenery of the Lakes' (501–3), 'Miscellaneous Observations' (2308–9), 'Directions and Information for the Tourist' (textual n. 1–500)), with subordinate section headings for the first part (504–5, 1263–5, 1685–7).

2. The insertion of comments on the influence of climate (1132–73), a detailed comparison of Alpine scenery with that in the north of England (2505–788), and a revised version of Dorothy Wordsworth's account of her excursion up Scafell Pike (2793–906).

3. The addition of a severely spare final chapter, giving directions for a recommended tour (1–489 and textual notes), and drawing heavily on 'Section II' of *Select Views* (e.g. cf. *Guide*, 112–40 and *S.V.* 173–200; *Guide*, 184–9 and *S.V.* 15–21; *Guide*, 363–77 and *S.V.* 558–75; *Guide*, 389–489 and *S.V.* 580–712).

A Description of the Scenery of the Lakes in
the North of England (London, 1823)

1. The insertion of two new descriptions, one of the waterfowl (907–45) and one of night scenes (1216–62).

2. Amplifications of comments on the influences of climate (1174–215) and on the cultivated grounds in northern Italy (2611–37).

3. The insertion of a new division, 'Excursions to the Top of Scawfell and on the Banks of Ulswater' (2789–92), with its revised version of Dorothy Wordsworth's account of her Ullswater excursion in November 1805 (2958–3230).

*A Guide through the District of the Lakes in
the North of England* (Kendal and London, 1835)

1. An expansion of 'Directions and Information for the Tourist', which now becomes a prefatory division, on pages numbered [i]–xxiv (*Guide*, 1–500 and textual notes).

2. The addition of two quotations from 'the Author's Miscellaneous Poems' (*Guide*, 2907–49, 3230–325).

Besides these major changes, there were numerous smaller insertions, including fairly long footnotes, and countless minor emendations for stylistic reasons. Nevertheless, the *Guide* remains essentially a work of 1810, for in addition to the scattered use of portions of 'Section II', the major part of the *Guide* (501–2406) derives from *Select Views*.

In its separate editions the *Guide* became increasingly popular; 500 copies were printed for the edition of 1822, 1,000 copies for the edition of 1823, and 1,500 for the edition of 1835.[1] In a letter to Wordsworth, 27 September 1838, Hudson and Nicholson, the Kendal publishers of the 1835 edition, proposed that he should extend 'the directions to Tourists in the next Edition, which we think would materially increase the sale'. Apparently unwilling to perform again 'the humble and tedious task of supplying the Tourist with directions' (*Guide*, 9–10), Wordsworth allowed John Hudson to produce a new work, radically altering and expanding the 1835 edition and adding a great deal of new matter. Unpublished letters from Wordsworth to Hudson in 1842, now in the Wordsworth Library, show that Wordsworth took an active interest in the preparation of 'Hudson's *Guide*', as it came to be familiarly called:[2] he examined the proof sheets; helped persuade Professor Sedgwick to contribute an 'essay' on the geology of the district;[3] recommended that Thomas Gough, son of the blind botanist of Kendal, should draw up the botanical lists; and that either De Quincey or Hartley Coleridge should look over Nicholson's glossary of place-names with the hope of 'improving it'. Although his share in the profits from the three editions after 1835 was reduced from two-thirds to one-half, Wordsworth's income was well augmented by 'Hudson's *Guide*', and three years after his death Hudson was willing to extend 'the same terms' to Wordsworth's son William for the edition of 1854.[4]

---

[1] W. J. B. Owen, 'Costs, Sales, and Profits of Longman's Editions of Wordsworth', *The Library*, 5th Ser. xii (1957), 103; and J. Hudson's Statement (*Guide to the Lakes*) in the Wordsworth Library.

[2] *A Complete Guide to the Lakes, Comprising Minute Directions for the Tourist, With Mr. Wordsworth's Description of the Scenery of the Country, &c. And Three Letters on the Geology of the Lake District, by the Rev. Professor Sedgwick*, Edited by the Publisher (Kendal, 1842).   [3] See our note to *Guide*, 675–87.

[4] A statement from Hudson in September 1838 shows that Wordsworth had, from his own 1835 edition, received £29.17s.10d. whereas a statement of July 1849

Since its appearance in the two Victorian collections of Wordsworth's prose writings, one edited by Alexander B. Grosart (1876) and the other by William Knight (1896), the *Guide* has had several separate publications. Of these the first and most important is Ernest de Selincourt's scholarly edition, published in London in 1906. Although his textual notes are sometimes intentionally incomplete and very often erroneous,[1] we have found his critical notes valuable and helpful in many ways. In our own critical notes we have endeavoured always to cite him (E. de S.) when he has preceded us in correctly annotating the *Guide*; we have been silent about his failures to comment; and we have rarely—and then only for some good reason—drawn attention to misstatements. De Selincourt's Introduction contains a brief description of some of the many eighteenth- and early nineteenth-century writers who by their praises of the Lake District scenery had established a tradition, to which Wordsworth in 1810 was a comparative late-comer; but the main part of his Introduction is given over to a sympathetic appreciation of the *Guide* itself. Two comparatively recent publications are *A Guide Through the District of the Lakes*, Facsimile of the Definitive Fifth Edition (Malvern, England, 1948), with a four-paragraph Introduction by J. W. Lucas; and *A Guide Through the District of the Lakes* (London, 1951, and Bloomington, Ind., 1952), with a good critical Introduction (pp. 9–32) by W. M. Merchant.

shows that from Hudson's third edition of 1846 Wordsworth received £26.5s.2d. Except where otherwise noted, we have derived our information in this note and in the paragraph above from unpublished correspondence between Wordsworth and John Hudson, now in the Wordsworth Library.

[1] On the intentional omissions, see E. de S., p. [167]; the errors in textual collation may have come from his entrusting some of that work to others (see ibid. p. xxviii).

INTRODUCTION: TEXTUAL

T H E text for the *Guide* is that of the fifth edition, the last edition to be revised by Wordsworth: *A Guide through the District of the Lakes in the North of England* (Kendal and London, 1835). (For a bibliographical description, see Healey, item 93). The first edition, which appeared without the author's name, comprises three parts ('Introduction', 'Section I', and 'Section II') of Joseph Wilkinson's *Select Views in Cumberland, Westmoreland, and Lancashire* (London, 1810). Because one part ('Section II') differs extensively from the corresponding passages in the four subsequent editions, we print it separately, with its own textual notes, under the title *Select Views*. But the other two parts of this first edition are preserved in the text and textual apparatus of the *Guide*. Textual notes also include variants from the second, third, and fourth editions, and from one manuscript in the Wordsworth Library. We here give, in chronological order, all the sources represented in the textual notes to the *Guide*:

1810 = 'Introduction' and 'Section I' in Joseph Wilkinson, *Select Views in Cumberland, Westmoreland, and Lancashire* (London, 1810). (See Healey, item 489; for a more detailed bibliographical description, see R. F. Metzdorf, *The Tinker Library* (New Haven, Conn., 1959), item 2337.)

MS. = MS. Prose 30, written on a white or ivory paper, with a watermark of 1810, is an early version of 858–979 ('As the comparatively . . . internal springs'). The pages measure $7\frac{1}{2}$ in. wide × 12 in. long; pages [1^r]–[2^r] are filled, but there are only nine lines of text on page [2^v]. The hand in 858–79 ('As the . . . native wood') is Mary Wordsworth's, but thereafter it is probably Dorothy Wordsworth's. Giving matter not in *Select Views*, the manuscript must have been written for the 1820 edition, for it is often significantly like 1820 and unlike the three later editions (e.g. see textual nn., 886, 888, 890, 897–8, 900–3, 905, 947–8, 952–9). But it is also sometimes unique (e.g. see textual nn., 858, 863, 871, 878, 893, 950); either corrections were made in the proof sheets of 1820, or this manuscript was superseded by a revised copy now lost. (Once it is like 1822 and unlike 1820 (textual n., 865), and once it is like 1823 and unlike 1820 and 1822 (textual n., 951), but these two occurrences are no doubt accidental.)

1820 = *Topographical Description of the Country of the Lakes in the North of England*, in *The River Duddon . . . and Other Poems* (London, 1820), pp. [213]–[323]. (See Healey, item 52.)

1822 = *A Description of the Scenery of the Lakes in the North of England* (London, 1822). (See Healey, item 65.)

1823 = *A Description of the Scenery of the Lakes in the North of England* (London, 1823). (See Healey, item 73.)

Textual notes do not record our corrections of obvious misprints; nor do they record differences in spelling and punctuation, except where we alter the text of 1835 in favour of an earlier edition.

For the two parts of *Select Views* preserved in the text and textual notes of the *Guide*, no manuscript sources survive. But for that part ('Section II') which we print separately, manuscript variants do survive, and they are now published for the first time in our textual notes to *Select Views*. These manuscripts are almost inextricably related to other manuscripts, also in the Wordsworth Library, which constitute an unfinished work, hitherto unpublished. This unfinished work we now publish in two parts; for one part we choose the title 'An Unpublished Tour', and for the other part we retain the title 'The Sublime and the Beautiful', which the Library has given this manuscript. Before describing the individual manuscripts, we indicate by the following list the relationship between all the related manuscripts and Wordsworth's published and unpublished writings:

MSS. Prose 19: 'An Unpublished Tour' (*U.T.*), 1–356.
MSS. Prose 20: *Select Views* (*S.V.*), 1–21, 46–58, 66–76; *U.T.* 357–557; two parts of a note to *The River Duddon* (*P.W.* iii. 509–10, 515).
MSS. Prose 21: *U.T.* 558–812.
MSS. Prose 22: *U.T.* 812–1104.
MSS. Prose 23: *U.T.* 1105–591.
MS. Prose 24: *S.V.* 89–200.
MS. Prose 25: *S.V.* textual n., 307/8.
MSS. Prose 26: *S.V.* 382–413; *U.T.* (MS. *A*), 1592–787.
MSS. Prose 27: *S.V.* 576–724.
MSS. Prose 28: 'The Sublime and the Beautiful'.
MS. Prose 29: *S.V.* 414–525.
MSS. Prose 30: *Guide*, 858–979 (described above).
MSS. Verse 57: *U.T.* 1592–787; *U.T.*, textual n., 1591/2.

With MSS. Prose 19–30 Gordon Wordsworth, grandson of the poet, has left a note describing the condition of these manuscripts when he first came upon them: 'Tattered, torn, crumpled and subjected to frequent alterations and revisions the sheets of flimsy paper were found rolled up in an untidy bundle with all their sequence lost.' To Gordon Wordsworth the present editors are deeply indebted, for with patience and judicious care he sorted the manuscripts and arranged them in sequence. Except for ignoring deletions and early versions, he also transcribed in longhand MSS. Prose 19, 21, 22, 23, 25, 26, and those portions of MSS. Prose 20 and 24 which *Select Views* omitted entirely. His transcript, preserved with the manuscripts, has been extremely valuable to us, for the originals are often very difficult to decipher. Because it would increase too much the bulk of our textual notes, we have not indicated the numerous words, and even phrases, which his transcripts have helped us to read, nor do we note the occasional passages where we have been able to correct his reading. But wherever we are uncertain of the text, we give in our apparatus his tentative reading (G.W.), if it differs from ours.

With a few exceptions, the manuscripts are in several respects strikingly alike; by a description of those elements which are common to MSS. Prose 19, parts of 20, 21–3, 25–9, we shall reduce the length and complexity of our subsequent descriptions of the individual manuscripts. Where a manuscript differs in any way from the general rule, as summarized here, we shall, of course, describe in detail that difference.

Although Wordsworth's hand appears frequently, most of the manuscripts are in the hand of Mary Wordsworth. When Mary was serving as the amanuensis, her hand sometimes shows signs of haste and becomes difficult to read, and especially so when the dictation called for immediate revision; but at other times her hand is clear, and then there are signs either (*a*) that she is copying from an almost illegible first or second draft, which had been dictated to her or written out by Wordsworth himself; or (*b*) that she is taking dictation from a draft read to her by Wordsworth, who calls for occasional emendations in the course of dictating the draft. Wordsworth's hand, normally somewhat difficult, is here especially so; it is not unusual for one of these manuscripts to consist of several paragraphs dictated to Mary, then a few sentences in Wordsworth's hand, and then either new dictation, or an immediate copying by Mary of what Wordsworth had just written, followed by new dictation.

When the first draft, with its many false starts, its deletions and repetitions, and its reordering of identical phrases, is immediately rewritten in the same manuscript, we call the first draft MS. *A* and record its variants *only* when they contain matter that does not reappear in the rewritten copy. MS. *A* may vary in length from a whole separate page, as in MS. Prose 19^b, to a short paragraph or a few detached sentences. But it should be emphasized here that, with the exception of MSS. Prose 20^a–20^d and Prose 24, no manuscript is a clean copy, and, with the same two exceptions, all manuscripts are incomplete or unfinished in one way or another.

The bulk of the manuscripts is written on the same kind of paper: a light-weight bluish-grey paper, impressed with horizontal chain lines 1 in. apart, a watermark of 1806, and a simple design that looks somewhat like an anchor. The full sheet measured $17\frac{1}{4}$ in. wide × 21 in. long. From two such sheets where the cutting was incomplete (MSS. Prose 19[d] and 25), it is easy to see how the pages of various size were made: invariably the full sheet was folded horizontally at the middle and then slit or cut at the fold; after the cutting, the paper took half a dozen different forms:

1. A two-page unfolded half-sheet, $10\frac{1}{2}$ in. wide × $17\frac{1}{4}$ in. long.
2. A four-page leaflet, $8\frac{5}{8}$ in. wide × $10\frac{1}{2}$ in. long, made from a half-sheet folded once.
3. A six-page leaflet, $8\frac{5}{8}$ in. wide × $10\frac{1}{2}$ in. long, made by inserting a quarter-sheet into a four-page leaflet.
4. An eight-page leaflet, $8\frac{5}{8}$ in. wide × $10\frac{1}{2}$ in. long, made from the full sheet, after being cut, as usual, at the centre fold.
5. A sixteen-page leaflet, $8\frac{5}{8}$ in. wide × $10\frac{1}{2}$ in. long, made by folding together four half-sheets.
6. A quarter-sheet, made by cutting a half-sheet, or an irregular piece of paper torn or cut from either a full sheet or a half-sheet.

The measurements we have just given should be regarded as theoretical. If the paper had been cut exactly and folded evenly, the measurements would be correct, but actually slight variations in the cutting and folding, in addition to damages done to the edges by breaks and tears, have made almost all the pages slightly uneven: for example, the most commonly used four-page leaflet may have pages measuring $8\frac{1}{2}$ in. wide at the top and 8 in. wide at the bottom, or 10 in. long on the left margin and $10\frac{1}{4}$ in. long on the right. In our descriptions of the individual manuscripts, the paper and the form and size of the sheet or leaflet are all as we have here described, unless otherwise specified.

In our descriptions of the individual manuscripts, the arabic number (e.g. MSS. Prose 21) is the number assigned by the Wordsworth Library to a collection, or folder, of manuscripts. For convenience and clarity in referring to a particular manuscript within a collection, we attach to the Library number a superior lower case letter (e.g. MS. Prose 21[b]).

S.V. MANUSCRIPTS

MSS. Prose 20

MSS. Prose 20 are the most heterogeneous and complex of all the manuscripts: one part was originally written for *S.V.*; a second part, written for *U.T.*, adopts some of the first; a third part, which lies outside our province, consists of two short sections of the long note which Wordsworth attached to *The River Duddon*, XVII and XVIII (*P.W.* iii. 509–10, 515).

MSS. Prose 20ᵃ, 20ᵇ, 20ᶜ, 20ᵈ = four separate fragments, cut or neatly torn from what had once been a four-page leaflet, made from a folio of the same good white paper as was later used for MS. Prose 24. Like MS. Prose 24, the leaflet from which the four fragments derive was once a fair copy in the hand of Sara Hutchinson. From what remains, it is clear that the leaflet was folded and posted to Joseph Wilkinson. Returned to Wordsworth—perhaps because Wilkinson wanted it reduced in length (see our Introduction, fn. 1, p. 126)—the leaflet was opened flat and then cut or torn into separate pieces, probably at the time when Wordsworth was composing *U.T.* From the evidence of MS. Prose 24 it is clear that the original pages must have measured 9½ in. wide × 15 in. long. Of the four remaining fragments, two once made up the top 8 in. of page [1], and the other two, which are both very badly torn, made up the top 8 in. of page [2]; obviously then, 7 in. have been lost from the bottom of both pages.

MS. Prose 20ᵃ = An early version of *S.V.* 1–21 ('SECTION II . . . gradually and'), written on the two fragments from page [1ʳ]. It will be seen from our textual notes that the variants are few. The missing 7 in. of page [1ʳ] probably gave an early version of *S.V.* 21–46.

MS. Prose 20ᵇ = A longer version of *S.V.* 46–52 ('This little circular . . . accommodated'), written on the two fragments from page [1ᵛ]. From the way the manuscript text was being developed, we imagine that the text of the missing 7 in. not only completed the sonnet of which the first two lines are quoted at the end of *S.V.*, textual n. 52, but also described briefly the vale of Seathwaite, since *U.T.* 422–42, which echoes *S.V.* 46 ff., probably was not expanding that section of the printed text, but rather was drawing on that portion of Prose 20ᵇ which is now lost.

MS. Prose 20ᶜ = An early version of *S.V.* 52–8 ('Having satisfied . . . Church stands'), written on the two fragments from page [2ʳ]. MS. Prose 20ᶜ was later adopted to make up the actual text of *U.T.* 443–61; the adoption was effected by sewing the lower fragment of MS. Prose 20ᶜ to a sheet of *U.T.* To avoid twice printing the matter given in MS. Prose 20ᶜ—once as variants in the textual notes to *S.V.* 52–8 and then a second time as the text of *U.T.* 443–61—we simply direct the reader in the textual notes of *S.V.* to see instead the text and textual notes of *U.T.* The text contained in the missing 7 in. from page [2ʳ] is probably preserved in *U.T.* 477 ff. (see *U.T.*, textual n. 461), although there, of course, it is no longer identifiable.

MS. Prose 20ᵈ = An early version of *S.V.* 66–76 ('the sake of descending . . . carriage'), written on the upper fragment of page

[2ᵛ]. This early text of *S.V.* has also been adopted to make up a portion of the text of *U.T.* (539–57); this time the adoption was effected by the direction 'see old letter stitched to this sheet' (see *U.T.*, textual n. 539–40: from this note, it would seem that at the time of the sewing the two extant fragments of page [2] had not yet been separated from each other). Again to avoid twice printing the same matter, we direct the reader in the textual notes to *S.V.* to see instead the text and textual notes of *U.T.* The lower fragment of page [2ᵛ]— that is, the fragment which for the sake of the adopted *U.T.* text on the reverse side was sewn to a *U.T.* manuscript—was reserved for the address panel; it is stamped as having been posted at Kendal and was thus inscribed by Sara Hutchinson:

> To
> The Revᵈ Joseph Wilkinson
> Thetford
> Norfolk

Single Sheet

The missing 7 in. from page [2ᵛ] was probably blank, for the last line of the extant text of MS. Prose 20ᵈ appears as the last line of a 'chapter' in *U.T.*

In addition to the text of *S.V.*, all in the neat hand of Sara Hutchinson, there are two brief notes scratched on these fragments by Wordsworth himself. At the top of MS. Prose 20ᵃ, around the phrase 'Section 2', which forms part of the manuscript title (see *S.V.*, textual n. 1), he penned the following note to Wilkinson:

My dear Sir, Herewith is matter for two more numbers; I shall send for two additional ones in a couple of days.—You will probably judge best to print matter for two numbers with each month [? as] [? we] [? have] only six months before you and your numbers [? are] 12. Yours most truly, WW.

On MS. Prose 20ᵈ he added the other note to Wilkinson; although damaged by the sewing and tears, and cramped into a small space, the note can still be partly read:

My Bʳ Dʳ Wordsworth seeing by chance a specimen of your work put down his name there as a Subscriber, being so much pleased with it. Pray let a copy of as good impression as you can command be sent for [? his] to the Palace at Lambeth immediate[ly.] If [*tear*] been forwarded elsewhere [*tear*] received there.

MSS. Prose 20ᵉ and 20ᶠ = *U.T.* manuscripts, described below.

Although the two remaining manuscripts of MSS. Prose 20 have no connection with either *S.V.* or *U.T.*, we here briefly identify them for the sake of completeness: Prose 20ᵍ is a four-page leaflet, with pages measuring 6½ in. wide × 7½ in. long and bearing a watermark of 1815. In the hand of Mary Wordsworth, MS. Prose 20ᵍ begins '[His road *del.*] Traveller is thus' and ends 'a Tombstone with this inscription'; it was clearly written for Wordsworth's note to *The River Duddon*, XVII and XVIII (cf. *P.W.* iii. 509–10) MS. Prose 20ʰ is a single sheet, 5¾ in. wide × 7 in. long, numbered '56' on page [1ʳ] and '57' on page [1ᵛ]. In the hand of Mary Wordsworth, it begins 'He loved old customs' and ends 'wheel at which &c.'; it was written for the same *River Duddon* note as was MS. Prose 20ᵍ (cf. *P.W.* iii. 515).

MS. Prose 24

MS. Prose 24 = A fair copy, in the hand of Sara Hutchinson, of *S.V.* 89–200 ('The Tourist . . . are inexhaustible'). Much longer than the printed text, this version is written on a four-page leaflet made from a single folio of good heavy white paper; the pages measure 15 in. wide × 19 in. long, and are entirely filled, except for the middle panel of page [2ᵛ], which is reserved for the address:

> The Revᵈ Joseph Wilkinson
> Thetford
> Norfolk
>
> Single

The manuscript has not been stamped and it appears not to have been posted.

MS. Prose 25

MS. Prose 25 = *S.V.*, textual n. 307/8, written on an eight-page leaflet. Although none of this manuscript ever appeared in the printed text, its two explicit references to the 'Etchings' of *S.V.* make it certain that this description of Grasmere and the route north from Grasmere to Keswick was written for that volume. A first draft, the manuscript is written alternately—now by Wordsworth, now by Mary, and so on, to the end. Besides being sometimes almost illegible, the manuscript is badly damaged: a ragged hole near the top of page [1] has destroyed some phrases on both sides; from the top of page [2] a piece has been torn away along a slanting line to a depth of 2 in. on the outer margin. As noted above in our description of the paper, the full sheet was not completely cut at the fold, and as a result pages [3]–

[4] are still uncut at their tops, but the four pages of these two leaves are blank.

MSS. Prose 26

MS. Prose 26ᵃ = A *U.T.* manuscript, described below.

MS. Prose 26ᵇ = A first, or early, draft of *S.V.* 382–413 ('and on the plain . . . leisure to go in'), written on a two-page unfolded half-sheet. The upper half of page [1ʳ] is in Mary's hand, and the lower is almost entirely in Wordsworth's; page [1ᵛ] is blank.

MSS. Prose 27

MS. Prose 27ᵃ = A first, or possibly second, draft of *S.V.* 576-629 ('Having conducted . . . a more sublime'), written on a single sheet, raggedly torn from a half-sheet and left unfolded. The page measures approximately 8½ in. wide × approximately 9 in. to 9½ in. long. Except for a brief appearance of Wordsworth's hand on page [1ᵛ], both pages are in Mary's hand.

MS. Prose 27ᵇ = A first, or possibly second, draft of *S.V.* 629–724 ('combination of . . . discordant objects') is written on a four-page leaflet, unevenly torn from a full sheet; the pages measure 8½ in. wide × approximately 11½ in. long. Before the torn sheet was folded into a leaflet, approximately 1 in. of the torn top was folded downward over what are now pages [1ᵛ] and [2ʳ]; when Mary finished page [1ʳ], she turned the page and wrote on the top of the 1 in. fold of page [1ᵛ], and later on the top of the 1 in. fold of page [2ʳ]; under the fold of page [1ᵛ] is a deletion which derives from some other unknown text (see *S.V.*, textual n. 659). The concluding text on page [2ᵛ] fills only the top 2½ in. Except for a part of page [1ʳ] in Wordsworth's hand, the manuscript is in Mary's hand.

MS. Prose 29

MS. Prose 29 = A draft—in part, perhaps, the first—of *S.V.* 414–525 ('From the Vale . . . generations'), written on a four-page leaflet. Pages [1ʳ], [1ᵛ], and half of [2ʳ] are dictated to Mary, though strangely Dorothy appears briefly as the amanuensis on page [1ʳ] for *S.V.* 417–28 ('the Vale of . . . Crummock-water'). Thereafter the hand of Mary continues until midway on page [2ʳ], where Dorothy again takes over. This time, however, it seems from the kinds of manuscript corrections that she may be composing the text herself (i.e. *S.V.* 487-textual n. 525: 'This Water . . . the two princ'); in this connection, see our Introduction, p. 126.

U.T. MANUSCRIPTS

MSS. Prose 19

MS. Prose 19[a] = The text of *U.T.* 1–96 ('Upon the . . . advantage'), written on an unfolded half-sheet. The text fills page [1ʳ] and slightly over half of page [1ᵛ], which is numbered '2'; the lower half of page [1ᵛ] deletes a draft (MS. *A*) of *U.T.* 98–117 ('Lancaster . . . humanity &'). The hand is Mary's throughout.

MS. Prose 19[b] = A first draft (MS. *A*) of *U.T.* 117–65 ('have studiously . . . upon this'), written on an unfolded half-sheet. Except for a part of page [1ʳ], the hand on both pages is Wordsworth's. On page [1ʳ], Mary's hand strangely interrupts the continuity of Wordsworth's text to write a first draft (MS. *A*) of *U.T.* 202–6 ('The little . . . Lakes': cf. textual n. 203–6).

MS. Prose 19[c] = The text of *U.T.* 98–200 ('Lancaster . . . fashion"'), which fills a four-page leaflet. The hand is Mary's, except for Wordsworth's in MS. *A* of our textual nn. 104–8, 109.

MS. Prose 19[d] = The text of *U.T.* 202–356 ('The little . . . summer's sky'), written on an eight-page leaflet. Page [1ʳ] is numbered '4'; page [4ᵛ] is blank, except for a single sentence marked for insertion in *U.T.* 222–6 ('Conistone . . . backwards'). The hand is mainly Mary's, but Wordsworth writes the text of 261–85 ('In another . . . age') and MS. *A* in our textual n. 339–47.

MSS. Prose 20

MS. Prose 20[c] = The text of *U.T.* 443–61 ('The Traveller, having satisfied . . . Chapel stands': see *U.T.*, textual nn. 442/3 and 461, derived from a fragment written for *S.V.*, and described above.

MS. Prose 20[d] = The text of *U.T.* 539–57 ('the sake of descending . . . depth of quiet': see *U.T.*, textual n. 539–40), derived from a fragment written for *S.V.*, and described above.

MS. Prose 20[e] = The text for *U.T.* 461-textual n. 539–40 ('The following pleasing . . . On this account and for the sake of descending See old letter stitched to this sheet'), written on a four-page leaflet. The concluding text of MS. Prose 20[c], given in *U.T.*, textual n. 461, must be read under the sewing of MS. Prose 20[e]. Pages [1ʳ] and [1ᵛ] are full; the text ends about 2½ in. from the bottom of page [2ʳ]; page [2ᵛ] is blank. The hand is Mary's, except for Wordsworth's in 516–26 ('This building . . . the shore').

MS. Prose 20[f] = The text of *U.T.* 357–442 ('Donnerdale . . . whose decaying'), which fills a four-page leaflet. The hand is Mary's, except for Wordsworth's in 401–21 ('has consecrated . . . beneath him').

MSS. Prose 21

MS. Prose 21ᵃ = The text of *U.T.* 558–650 ('CONISTONE LAKE . . . not yet removed'), which fills a four-page leaflet. The hand is Mary's.

MS. Prose 21ᵇ = MS. *A* of *U.T.* 558–604 and 783, written on a four-page leaflet. Page [1ʳ], which gives MS. *A* as recorded in *U.T.*, textual n. 558, begins with Mary's hand, but is mainly in Wordsworth's; page [1ᵛ], which gives MS. *A* of *U.T.* 582–604 ('the clearness of . . . admiration') is in Wordsworth's hand; page [2ʳ] is blank, except for MS. *A*, as recorded in *U.T.*, textual n. 783, which is written in Mary's hand; page [2ᵛ] is blank.

MS. Prose 21ᶜ = The text of *U.T.* 650–709 ('so far from . . . crazy outhouses'), which fills a single sheet, 8¾ in. wide × 10½ in. long, cut from a half-sheet. The hand is Mary's.

MS. Prose 21ᵈ = The text of *U.T.* 709–31 ('might then be . . . No tragical story') and MS. *A* for *U.T.* 694–711, both written on a single sheet, approximately 8 in. wide × 7 in. long, roughly torn from a half-sheet. On page [1ʳ] Mary and Wordsworth alternately write MS. *A*; on page [1ᵛ] Mary's hand rewrites the conclusion of MS. Prose 21ᶜ (i.e. 708–9: 'Certain penurious . . . outhouses') and then continues with the text of 709–31.

MS. Prose 21ᵉ = The text of *U.T.* 731–812 ('No tragical story . . . is in part owing'), written on a four-page leaflet. Pages [1ʳ] and [1ᵛ] are filled; page [2ʳ], which gives only the text of 783–91, is largely blank; page [2ᵛ] is filled. The hand is Mary's, except for an occasional insertion by Wordsworth.

MSS. Prose 22

MS. Prose 22ᵃ = The text of *U.T.* 812–908 ('to a scantiness . . . her hand. To Tilberthwaite'), which fills a four-page leaflet. The hand is mainly Mary's, but Wordsworth writes 836–8 ('& will . . . confidence'), 868–80 ('Upon his . . . restless'), and 885–9 ('more affecting . . . stars').

MS. Prose 22ᵇ = MS. *A* of *U.T.* 908–57 ('To Tilberthwaite . . . infernal'), written on pages [1ʳ] and [1ᵛ] of a four-page leaflet. Page [2] is blank. Except for 908–15 ('To Tilberthwaite . . . Crag') in Mary's hand, the rest is in Wordsworth's.

MS. Prose 22ᵈ = The text of *U.T.* 968–1027 ('as we have already . . . in the same') and MS. *A* of *U.T.* 968–93, which together fill a four-page leaflet. Pages [1ʳ]–[2ʳ] are mainly in Mary's hand, although, in addition to short phrases here and there, Wordsworth writes a deleted passage on the top half of page [1ᵛ]; he also writes the text, on page [2ʳ], of 1020–7 ('It is . . . in the same'), and on page [2ᵛ] he writes all of MS. *A*, 968–93.

MS. Prose 22ᵉ = The text of *U.T.* 1027–104 ('manner, as if . . . a home'), written on a four-page leaflet. On page [1ʳ] Wordsworth completes the sentence he was writing at the bottom of MS. Prose 22ᵈ, page [2ʳ]; thereafter the hand is mainly Mary's, until Wordsworth writes the text of 1094–104 ('will be a . . . a home') on the bottom of page [2ʳ] and the top of page [2ᵛ]. The rest of page [2ᵛ] is blank.

MSS. Prose 23

MS. Prose 23ᵃ = The text of *U.T.* 1105–82 ('HAWKSHEAD . . . their feelings'), which fills a four-page leaflet. Page [1ʳ] is numbered '1'. The hand is Mary's, although Wordsworth's appears at least twice in passages deleted and then rewritten (e.g. see *U.T.*, textual nn. 1151 and 1179).

MS. Prose 23ᵇ = The text of *U.T.* 1183–6 ('A ¼ of a mile . . . have left') and the text of *U.T.* 1241–320 ('At the foot . . . a mystery'), which together fill a four-page leaflet. Page [1ʳ] is numbered '2'. The hand is Mary's.

On page [1ʳ] after the phrase 'Lake & Vale of Conistone we have left' (*U.T.* 1186), a large X is drawn, and the beginning of the sentence immediately following ('Nothing remarkable occurs till we come': *U.T.*, textual n. 1240) is deleted; the rest of the deleted sentence is marked by a second X, and is also later revised to read, 'At the foot of the hill within ½ a mile of Hawkshead stands . . .' (i.e. *U.T.* 1241); it is obvious to us (as it also was to Gordon Wordsworth in his transcript of MSS. Prose 23) that MS. Prose 23ᵍ, which was apparently written as an afterthought, is to be inserted at 1186; the text of *U.T.* 1187–240 derives, therefore, from MS. Prose 23ᵍ, which will be described below.

MS. Prose 23ᶜ = The text of *U.T.* 1320–85 ('If I have . . . gay feature'), written on a four-page leaflet. Page [1ʳ] is numbered '3'. We treat the numerous deletions and rewritings on pages [1ʳ] and [1ᵛ] as constituting MS. *A* of *U.T.* 1328–82. The hand is almost entirely Mary's.

In his transcript Gordon Wordsworth inserted at *U.T.* 1376, which occurs on page [2ʳ], the matter which we give in the first paragraph of *U.T.*, textual n. 1248–59. We find on the manuscript of page [2ᵛ] no markings to justify an insertion (cf. our textual nn. 1248–59 and 1376/7).

MS. Prose 23ᵈ = The text of *U.T.* 1386–478 ('But hurrying . . . wild time'), written on a four-page leaflet. Page [1ʳ] is numbered '4'. The hand is mainly Mary's, although Wordsworth writes the text of

1444–53 ('These beautiful . . . importance'), and the final deletion on page [2ᵛ], given in our textual n. 1478.

MS. Prose 23ᵉ = The text of *U.T.* 1479–591 ('a pretty range . . . Rydale head') is written on an eight-page leaflet. Page [1ʳ] is numbered '5'. On page [1ʳ] and the top of page [1ᵛ], Wordsworth writes the text of 1479–504 ('a pretty range . . . Esthwaite water'); it is mainly Mary's hand that writes the text of 1504–91 on pages [1ᵛ]–[3ʳ]; page [3ᵛ] is blank; on pages [4ʳ] and [4ᵛ] Wordsworth, and occasionally Mary, write MS. *A*, 1515–56 ('standing removed . . . uninhabitable').

MS. Prose 23ᶠ = The text of *U.T.*, textual n. 1248–59, written on a six-page leaflet. The single sheet, which is inserted into a four-page leaflet, was irregularly torn from a full sheet and measures 9 in. wide × 10½ in. long. Page [1] is blank; on page [2ʳ] Wordsworth writes a part of MS. *A*, textual n. 1248–59; on page [2ᵛ] Mary's hand writes another part of MS. *A*; on pages [3ʳ] and [3ᵛ] Mary's hand writes the final version of textual n. 1248–59 (i.e. the longer version which we punctuate and print first), except for the last three sentences ('These pleasures . . . consolation'), which are in Wordsworth's hand.

MS. Prose 23ᵍ = The text of *U.T.* 1187–240 ('A mile farther . . . naturally lead to'), written on a four-page leaflet. On page [1ʳ], except for 1227–8 ('who had disappeared . . . ground'), which is written in Mary's hand, the text of *U.T.* 1227–40 ('who had . . . lead to') is in Wordsworth's hand; on pages [1ᵛ] and [2ʳ], Mary's hand writes the text of *U.T.* 1187–227 ('A mile farther . . . unhappy Man'). Page [2ᵛ], which is alternately written in Mary's hand and Wordsworth's, gives MS. *A* of 1227–40.

MSS. Prose 26

MS. Prose 26ᵃ = MS. *A* of *U.T.* 1794–textual n. 1705–14 ('Borrowdale . . . the foreground'), written on a four-page leaflet. On page [1] Mary's hand writes MS. *A* of *U.T.* 1592–663 ('Borrowdale . . . to escape. At'); on page [2ʳ] her hand continues until 1687 ('their own ruggedness'); Wordsworth's hand then writes the last seven lines of page [2ʳ] and all page [2ᵛ], where MS. *A* concludes, as in *U.T.*, textual n. 1705–14.

MS. *A* of *U.T.* 1663–textual n. 1705–14 is, as a first draft, typical of other MSS. *A*, but the first part (1592–663) is a revised copy and therefore unique among MSS. *A*; we have treated it as MS. *A* only because a still later copy, with further revisions, exists in MS. Verse 57ᵃ; this copy is described below.

MS. Prose 26ᵇ = An *S.V.* manuscript, described above.

MSS. Verse 57

MS. Verse 57ᵃ = The text of *U.T.* 1592–787 ('Borrowdale . . . no virtue').

MS. Verse 57ᵇ = The text of *U.T.*, textual n. 1591/2.

MSS. Verse 57 is a handmade notebook, with pages measuring 5 in. wide × 8 in. long and watermarked 1802. With the cover missing and no title-page, we do not know which are the opening and which the closing pages of the notebook, for writing starts at both ends, although most of the notebook pages are blank. But at what we choose to call the front of the notebook, page [1ʳ] and page [1ᵛ] give a draft of *Exc.* III. 143–64; on pages [2ʳ]–[14ᵛ], Mary's hand writes the text of *U.T.* 1592–787. At the opposite end of the notebook, at least twenty-six pages have been cut away (from the stubs, these pages would seem to have contained verses from *Exc.*); on the first remaining page at this end, a torn page, in Wordsworth's hand, gives *Exc.* IV. 759–62; on the pages immediately following is the detached fragment that begins a description of the route from Ambleside to Keswick; this fragment we print in *U.T.*, textual n. 1591/2. (For de Selincourt's reference to this notebook, see his headnote to 'As when, upon the smooth pacific deep', *P.W.* v. 346.)

SUBL. AND BEAUT. MSS.

MSS. Prose 28

If they are compared to any first draft among the manuscripts of *S.V.* or *U.T.* (e.g. MSS. Prose 25, 19ᵇ, 22ᵇ, 23ᵉ), it is obvious that MSS. Prose 28 are at least a second or, more probably, a third draft. Although many of the emendations could have been inserted after Mary had finished copying an earlier draft, other emendations show that she was taking dictation, for it is as an amanuensis that she frequently strikes out a word or phrase and makes an immediate substitution on the same line. It is probable, then, that Wordsworth was dictating from a draft which antedated MSS. Prose 28. As is evident from our textual notes, the emendations are comparatively slight and there is actually only one attempt at new composition (see textual n. 107). Unless otherwise noted, the hand is Mary Wordsworth's.

MS. Prose 28ᵃ = The text of *Subl. and Beaut.* 1–58 ('amongst them . . . Pikes'), written on a four-page leaflet. Page [1ʳ] is numbered '1.3'; page [1ᵛ] is numbered '2.3'; page [2ʳ] is numbered '3.3'; page [2ᵛ] is unnumbered and blank, except for some pen-testing or a child's scrawl. After 'Pikes' 3 in. are left blank at the bottom of page [2ʳ]. (For our conjectures on the amount of text lost from the opening of MSS. Prose 28 see our n. to *Subl. and Beaut.* 1–58.)

MS. Prose 28^b = The text of *Subl. and Beaut.* 58–325 ('of Langdale . . . if this feeling'), written on a sixteen-page leaflet, made from four half-sheets. It is probable that three half-sheets were, at first, laid one on top of the other and folded to make a leaflet of twelve pages, and that the fourth and outer half-sheet was added later, when more pages were needed towards the end. This would explain why pages [1^r] and [1^v] are blank, whereas pages [8^r] and [8^v] of the same outer half-sheet are filled; it would also suggest that page [2^r], where the text begins with a deleted passage (see textual n. 39–58), was once the first page of the leaflet. Page [2^r] is numbered '4.3'; page [2^v] is numbered '4'; page [3^r] is numbered '5'; page [3^v] is numbered '6', and so on, without a break, to page [7^v], which is correctly numbered '14'. Between page '14' and the next page (i.e. page [8^r]), which is numbered '17', there is a gap in the text (see *Subl. and Beaut.* 280); we assume that a loose quarter-sheet, numbered '15' on the recto and '16' on the verso, had been here inserted and has since been lost. Page [8^v] is numbered '18'.

MS. Prose 28^c = The text of *Subl. and Beaut.* 325–68 ('should not . . . mind'), written on a quarter-sheet. Pages [1^r] and [1^v] are respectively numbered '19' and '20'. Wordsworth's hand, unusually clear, writes 345–52 ('But impediments . . . I might').

A

GUIDE

THROUGH THE

DISTRICT OF THE LAKES

IN

The North of England,

WITH

A DESCRIPTION OF THE SCENERY, &c.

FOR THE USE OF

TOURISTS AND RESIDENTS.

FIFTH EDITION,

WITH CONSIDERABLE ADDITIONS.

By WILLIAM WORDSWORTH.

KENDAL:

PUBLISHED BY HUDSON AND NICHOLSON,

AND IN LONDON BY

LONGMAN & CO., MOXON, AND WHITTAKER & CO.

1835.

CONTENTS.

DIRECTIONS AND INFORMATION FOR THE TOURIST.

DESCRIPTION OF THE SCENERY OF THE LAKES.

SECTION FIRST.

VIEW OF THE COUNTRY AS FORMED BY NATURE.

SECTION SECOND.

ASPECT OF THE COUNTRY AS AFFECTED BY ITS INHABITANTS.

SECTION THIRD.

CHANGES, AND RULES OF TASTE FOR PREVENTING THEIR BAD EFFECTS.

MISCELLANEOUS OBSERVATIONS.

EXCURSIONS

ODE.

ITINERARY.

DIRECTIONS AND INFORMATION
FOR
THE TOURIST.

In preparing this Manual, it was the Author's principal wish to furnish a Guide or Companion for the *Minds* of Persons of taste, and feeling 5 for Landscape, who might be inclined to explore the District of the Lakes with that degree of attention to which its beauty may fairly lay claim. For the more sure attainment, however, of this primary object, he will begin by undertaking the humble and tedious task of supplying the Tourist with directions how to approach the several scenes in their 10 best, or most convenient, order. But first, supposing the approach to be made from the south, and through Yorkshire, there are certain interesting spots which may be confidently recommended to his notice, if time can be spared before entering upon the Lake District; and the route may be changed in returning. 15

There are three approaches to the Lakes through Yorkshire; the least adviseable is the great north road by Catterick and Greta Bridge, and onwards to Penrith. The Traveller, however, taking this route, might halt at Greta Bridge, and be well recompenced if he can afford to give an hour or two to the banks of the Greta, and of the Tees, at 20 Rokeby. Barnard Castle also, about two miles up the Tees, is a striking object, and the main North Road might be rejoined at Bowes. Every one has heard of the great fall of the Tees above Middleham, interesting for its grandeur, as the avenue of rocks that leads to it, is to the geologist. But this place lies so far out of the way as scarcely to be 25 within the compass of our notice. It might, however, be visited by a Traveller on foot, or on horseback, who could rejoin the main road upon Stanemoor.

The second road leads through a more interesting tract of country, beginning at Ripon, from which place see Fountain's Abbey, and 30 thence by Hackfall, and Masham, to Jervaux Abbey, and up the vale of

1–500 *For the text of* 1810, *see S.V.* 1–725, *pp.* 260–86 *below; not in* 1820; *printed as the final chapter in* 1822 (*following* 2906, by moonlight); *and as the final chapter in* 1823 (*following* 3230, before midnight). 4–101 In preparing . . . WIN-DERMERE. 1835: A BRIEF notice shall here be given of particulars in the several Vales of which the Country is composed. We will begin, as before, with

WINDERMERE.

This Lake is approached, by Travellers from the South, about the middle of its eastern side, at Bowness, or by Orrest-head. 1822–3.

Wensley; turning aside before Askrigg is reached, to see Aysgarth-
force, upon the Ure; and again, near Hawes, to Hardraw Scar, of
which, with its waterfall, Turner has a fine drawing. Thence over the
fells to Sedbergh, and Kendal.   35

The third approach from Yorkshire is through Leeds. Four miles
beyond that town are the ruins of Kirkstall Abbey, should that road
to Skipton be chosen; but the other by Otley may be made much more
interesting by turning off at Addington to Bolton Bridge, for the sake
of visiting the Abbey and grounds. It would be well, however, for a 40
party previously to secure beds, if wanted, at the inn, as there is but
one, and it is much resorted to in summer.

The Traveller on foot, or horseback, would do well to follow the
banks of the Wharf upwards, to Burnsall, and thence cross over the
hills to Gordale—a noble scene, beautifully described in Gray's Tour, 45
and with which no one can be disappointed. Thence to Malham, where
there is a respectable village inn, and so on, by Malham Cove, to
Settle.

Travellers in carriages must go from Bolton Bridge to Skipton,
where they rejoin the main road; and should they be inclined to visit 50
Gordale, a tolerable road turns off beyond Skipton. Beyond Settle,
under Giggleswick Scar, the road passes an ebbing and flowing well,
worthy the notice of the Naturalist. Four miles to the right of Ingleton,
is Weathercote Cave, a fine object, but whoever diverges for this,
must return to Ingleton. Near Kirkby Lonsdale observe the view from 55
the bridge over the Lune, and descend to the channel of the river, and
by no means omit looking at the Vale of Lune from the Church-yard.

The journey towards the lake country through Lancashire, is, with
the exception of the Vale of the Ribble, at Preston, uninteresting; till
you come near Lancaster, and obtain a view of the fells and mountains 60
of Lancashire and Westmorland; with Lancaster Castle, and the Tower
of the Church seeming to make part of the Castle, in the foreground.

They who wish to see the celebrated ruins of Furness Abbey, and
are not afraid of crossing the Sands, may go from Lancaster to
Ulverston; from which place take the direct road to Dalton; but by all 65
means return through Urswick, for the sake of the view from the top
of the hill, before descending into the grounds of Conishead Priory.
From this quarter the Lakes would be advantageously approached
by Coniston; thence to Hawkshead, and by the Ferry over Windermere, to Bowness: a much better introduction than by going direct 70
from Coniston to Ambleside, which ought not to be done, as that would
greatly take off from the effect of Windermere.

Let us now go back to Lancaster. The direct road thence to Kendal is
22 miles, but by making a circuit of eight miles, the Vale of the Lune

to Kirkby Lonsdale will be included. The whole tract is pleasing; there   75
is one view mentioned by Gray and Mason especially so. In West's
Guide it is thus pointed out:—"About a quarter of a mile beyond the
third mile-stone, where the road makes a turn to the right, there is a
gate on the left which leads into a field where the station meant, will
be found." Thus far for those who approach the Lakes from the South.   80
Travellers from the North would do well to go from Carlisle by
Wigton, and proceed along the Lake of Bassenthwaite to Keswick; or,
if convenience should take them first to Penrith, it would still be
better to cross the country to Keswick, and begin with that vale, rather
than with Ulswater. It is worth while to mention, in this place, that   85
the banks of the river Eden, about Corby, are well worthy of notice,
both on account of their natural beauty, and the viaducts which have
recently been carried over the bed of the river, and over a neighbouring
ravine. In the Church of Wetheral, close by, is a fine piece of monumental sculpture by Nollekens. The scenes of Nunnery, upon the Eden,   90
or rather that part of them which is upon Croglin, a mountain stream
there falling into the Eden, are, in their way, unrivalled. But the
nearest road thither, from Corby, is so bad, that no one can be advised
to take it in a carriage. Nunnery may be reached from Corby by
making a circuit and crossing the Eden at Armathwaite bridge.   95
A portion of this road, however, is bad enough.
As much the greatest number of Lake Tourists begin by passing
from Kendal to Bowness, upon Windermere, our notices shall commence with that Lake. Bowness is situated upon its eastern side, and
at equal distance from each extremity of the Lake of   100

WINDERMERE.

The lower part of this Lake is rarely visited, but has many interesting
points of view, especially at Storrs Hall and at Fell-foot, where the
Coniston Mountains peer nobly over the western barrier, which elsewhere, along the whole Lake, is comparatively tame. To one also who   105
has ascended the hill from Graythwaite on the western side, the
Promontory called Rawlinson's Nab, Storrs Hall, and the Troutbeck
Mountains, about sun-set, make a splendid landscape. The view from
the Pleasure-house of the Station near the Ferry has suffered much
from Larch plantations; this mischief, however, is gradually dis-   110
appearing, and the Larches, under the management of the proprietor,

89–90 Wetheral . . . Nollekens *Edd.*: Wetherby . . . Nollekins 1835.
102 of this Lake 1835: *not in* 1822–3.   103 Storrs *Edd.*: Storr's 1822–35.
Fell-foot 1823: Fell-fort 1822.   106–7 Graythwaite . . . Storrs *Edd.*:
Grathwaite . . . Storr's 1822–35.   110–12 this mischief . . . wood. 1835: and
from other causes. 1822–3.

Mr. Curwen, are giving way to the native wood. Windermere ought to be seen both from its shores and from its surface. None of the other Lakes unfold so many fresh beauties to him who sails upon them. This is owing to its greater size, to the islands, and to its having *two* vales 115 at the head, with their accompanying mountains of nearly equal dignity. Nor can the grandeur of these two terminations be seen at once from any point, except from the bosom of the Lake. The Islands may be explored at any time of the day; but one bright unruffled evening, must, if possible, be set apart for the splendour, the stillness, 120 and solemnity of a three hour's voyage upon the higher division of the Lake, not omitting, towards the end of the excursion, to quit the expanse of water, and peep into the close and calm River at the head; which, in its quiet character, at such a time, appears rather like an overflow of the peaceful Lake itself, than to have any more immediate 125 connection with the rough mountains whence it has descended, or the turbulent torrents by which it is supplied. Many persons content themselves with what they see of Windermere during their progress in a boat from Bowness to the head of the Lake, walking thence to Ambleside. But the whole road from Bowness is rich in diversity of 130 pleasing or grand scenery; there is scarcely a field on the road side, which, if entered, would not give to the landscape some additional charm. Low-wood Inn, a mile from the head of Windermere, is a most pleasant halting-place; no inn in the whole district is so agreeably situated for water views and excursions; and the fields above it, and 135 the lane that leads to Troutbeck, present beautiful views towards each extremity of the Lake. From this place, and from

AMBLESIDE,

Rides may be taken in numerous directions, and the interesting walks are inexhaustible;* a few out of the main road may be particularized; 140 —the lane that leads from Ambleside to Skelgill; the ride, or walk by

---

* Mr. Green's Guide to the Lakes, in two vols., contains a complete Magazine of minute and accurate information of this kind, with the names of mountains, streams, &c.

---

115 islands, 1823: islands*, [*with footnote appended*]
    * This Lake has seventeen Islands. Among those that lie near the largest, formerly called "Great Holm," may be noticed "Lady Holm," so called from the Virgin who had formerly a Chapel or Oratory there. On the road from Kendal to the Great-boat, might lately, and perhaps may still be seen, the ruins of the Holy Cross; a place where the Pilgrims to this beautifully situated shrine, must have been in the habit of offering up their devotions.—Two other of these Islands are named from the lily of the valley, which grows there in profusion. 1822: to [*third*] 1823: *not in* 1822.   118 once 1823: the same time 1822.   any 1823: any one 1822.   133 most 1835: *not in* 1822–3.   134–5 no inn . . . excursions 1835: *not in* 1822–3.   141 from Ambleside to 1835: towards 1822–3.

Rothay Bridge, and up the stream under Loughrigg Fell, continued
on the western side of Rydal Lake, and along the fell to the foot of
Grasmere Lake, and thence round by the church of Grasmere; or,
turning round Loughrigg Fell by Loughrigg Tarn and the River 145
Brathay, back to Ambleside. From Ambleside is another charming
excursion by Clappersgate, where cross the Brathay, and proceed with
the river on the right to the hamlet of Skelwith-fold; when the houses
are passed, turn, before you descend the hill, through a gate on the
right, and from a rocky point is a fine view of the Brathay River, 150
Langdale Pikes, &c.; then proceed to Colwith-force, and up Little
Langdale to Blea Tarn. The scene in which this small piece of water
lies, suggested to the Author the following description, (given in his
Poem of the Excursion) supposing the spectator to look down upon it,
not from the road, but from one of its elevated sides. 155

"Behold!
Beneath our feet, a little lowly Vale,
A lowly Vale, and yet uplifted high
Among the mountains; even as if the spot

146 another 1835: a 1822–3.   147–83 by Clappersgate . . . most advantage 1835: by Skelwith-fold and Colwith-force up Little Langdale, Blea Tarn,
Dungeon-ghyll waterfall (if there be time) and down Great Langdale. Stock-ghyll-
force and Rydal waterfalls, every one hears of. In addition to the two vales at its
head [two Streams at its head with their Vales 1822], Windermere communicates
with two lateral Vallies, that of Troutbeck, distinguished by the mountains at its
head, by picturesque remains of cottage architecture, and by fine fore-grounds
formed by the steep and winding banks of the river [*cf.* 225–30]. The other, the
vale of Hawkshead, is seen to most advantage by the approach from the ferry over
Windermere—the Lake of Esthwaite, Hawkshead Church, and the cone of Langdale Pike in the distance [*cf.* 231–5]. There are delightful walks in that part of
Grasmere, called Easedale; and the Vale is advantageously seen from Butterlip
How. As this point is four miles on the way to Keswick, it may here be mentioned,
that, from the high road between Keswick and Ambleside, which passes along the
eastern side of the several Lakes of Rydal, Grasmere, and part of Wythburn, these
lakes are not seen to their best advantage, particularly Rydal, and Wythburn—the
lower half of which is entirely lost. If, therefore, the excursion from Ambleside has
not been taken, a traveller on foot or on horseback would be well recompensed by
quitting the high road at Rydal over Pelter Bridge,—proceeding on the western
side of the two Lakes to Grasmere Church; and, thence to Butterlip How. A second
deviation [*cf.* 272–83] may be made when he has advanced a little beyond the mile-
stone, the sixth short of Keswick, whence there is a fine view of Legberthwaite
[Legberthwaite *Edd.*: Legbertwhaite 1822–3], with Blencathara (commonly called
Saddleback) in front. Having previously enquired, at the inn near Wythburn
Chapel, the best way from this mile-stone to the bridge that divides the Lake, he
must cross it, and proceed, with the Lake on the right, to the Hamlet near its
termination, and rejoin the main road upon Shoulthwaite Moss, about four miles
from Keswick. These two deviations lengthen the journey something less than
three miles. Helvellyn [*cf.* 285–6] may be ascended from Dunmail-raise by a foot
Traveller, or from the Inn at Wythburn.

CONISTON.

The next principal Vale, that of Coniston, is best seen 1822-3.

Had been, from eldest time by wish of theirs,   160
So placed, to be shut out from all the world!
Urn-like it was in shape, deep as an Urn;
With rocks encompassed, save that to the South
Was one small opening, where a heath-clad ridge
Supplied a boundary less abrupt and close;   165
A quiet treeless nook,* with two green fields,
A liquid pool that glittered in the sun,
And one bare Dwelling; one Abode, no more!
It seemed the home of poverty and toil,
Though not of want: the little fields, made green   170
By husbandry of many thrifty years,
Paid cheerful tribute to the moorland House.
—There crows the Cock, single in his domain:
The small birds find in spring no thicket there
To shroud them; only from the neighbouring Vales   175
The Cuckoo, straggling up to the hill tops,
Shouteth faint tidings of some gladder place."

From this little Vale return towards Ambleside by Great Langdale,
stopping, if there be time, to see Dungeon-ghyll waterfall.
The Lake of   180

CONISTON

May be conveniently visited from Ambleside, but is seen to most
advantage by entering the country over the Sands from Lancaster.
The Stranger, from the moment he sets his foot on those Sands, seems
to leave the turmoil and traffic of the world behind him; and, cross- 185
ing the majestic plain whence the sea has retired, he beholds, rising
apparently from its base, the cluster of mountains among which he is
going to wander, and towards whose recesses, by the Vale of Coniston,
he is gradually and peacefully led. From the Inn at the head of Coniston
Lake, a leisurely Traveller might have much pleasure in looking into 190
Yewdale and Tilberthwaite, returning to his Inn from the head of
Yewdale by a mountain track which has the farm of Tarn Hows, a
little on the right: by this road is seen much the best view of Coniston
Lake from the south. At the head of Coniston Water there is an agree-

---

* No longer strictly applicable, on account of recent plantations.

---

183 from 1835: of 1822–3.   194–6 At the . . . Duddon 1835: From Coniston it is best to pass by Hawkshead to the Ferry of Windermere, instead of going
direct to Ambleside, which would bring the Traveller upon the head of the Lake,
and consequently with much injury to its effect. If the Lake of Coniston be visited

able Inn, from which an enterprising Tourist might go to the Vale of 195
the Duddon, over Walna Scar, down to Seathwaite, Newfield, and to
the rocks where the river issues from a narrow pass into the broad
Vale. The stream is very interesting for the space of a mile above this
point, and below, by Ulpha Kirk, till it enters the Sands, where it
is overlooked by the solitary Mountain Black Comb, the summit 200
of which, as that experienced surveyor, Colonel Mudge, declared,
commands a more extensive view than any point in Britain. Ireland he
saw more than once, but not when the sun was above the horizon.

> "Close by the Sea, lone sentinel,
>   Black-Comb his forward station keeps;   205
> He breaks the sea's tumultuous swell,—
>   And ponders o'er the level deeps.
>
> He listens to the bugle horn,
>   Where Eskdale's lovely valley bends;
> Eyes Walney's early fields of corn;   210
>   Sea-birds to Holker's woods he sends.
>
> Beneath his feet the sunk ship rests,
>   In Duddon Sands, its masts all bare:
> *   *   *   *   * "

The Minstrels of Windermere, by Chas. Farish, B.D.   215

The Tourist may either return to the Inn at Coniston by Broughton,
or, by turning to the left before he comes to that town, or, which would
be much better, he may cross from

ULPHA KIRK

Over Birker moor, to Birker-force, at the head of the finest ravine in 220
the country; and thence up the Vale of the Esk, by Hardknot and

from the upper end, it is scarcely worth while to proceed further than about a mile
and a half down its eastern shore, for the sake of the views on returning.

DONNERDALE, or the Vale of the Duddon (*er* signifies *upon*) and the adjoining
Vale of the ESK, are rarely visited by Travellers.—Donnerdale is best approached
by Coniston 1822-3.

201 Colonel 1835: the late Colonel 1822-3.   203 saw more 1835: saw
from it more 1822-3.   216-94 The Tourist . . . from, Buttermere. 1835:
Details of this Vale are to be found in the Author's Poem, "The River Duddon."

In the Vale of Esk is an interesting Waterfall, called Birker Force, that lies
apart; and, from the chasm, a fine mountain view of Scawfell. At the head of the
Vale are conspicuous Remains of a Roman Fortress.

WASTDALE.

Into this Dale are three horse-roads, viz. over the Stye from Borrowdale; a
short cut over a ridge of Scawfell, by Burnmoor Tarn, which road descends upon

Wrynose, back to Ambleside. Near the road, in ascending from Eskdale, are conspicuous remains of a Roman fortress. Details of the Duddon and Donnerdale are given in the Author's series of Sonnets upon the Duddon and in the accompanying Notes. In addition to its   225 two Vales at its head, Windermere communicates with two lateral Vallies; that of Troutbeck, distinguished by the mountains at its head—by picturesque remains of cottage architecture; and, towards the lower part, by bold foregrounds formed by the steep and winding banks of the river. This Vale, as before mentioned, may be most con-   230 veniently seen from Low Wood. The other lateral Valley, that of Hawkshead, is visited to most advantage, and most conveniently, from Bowness; crossing the Lake by the Ferry—then pass the two villages of Sawrey, and on quitting the latter, you have a fine view of the Lake of Esthwaite, and the cone of one of the Langdale Pikes in the distance.   235

Before you leave Ambleside give three minutes to looking at a passage of the brook which runs through the town; it is to be seen from a garden on the right bank of the stream, a few steps above the bridge —the garden at present is rented by Mrs. Airey.—Stockgill-force, upon the same stream, will have been mentioned to you as one of the   240 sights of the neighbourhood. And by a Tourist halting a few days in Ambleside, the *Nook* also might be visited; a spot where there is a bridge over Scandale-beck, which makes a pretty subject for the pencil. Lastly, for residents of a week or so at Ambleside, there are delightful rambles over every part of Loughrigg Fell and among the enclosures   245 on its sides; particularly about Loughrigg Tarn, and on its eastern side about Fox How and the properties adjoining to the northwards.

ROAD FROM AMBLESIDE TO KESWICK.

The Waterfalls of Rydal are pointed out to every one. But it ought to be observed here, that Rydal-mere is no where seen to advantage   250 the head of the Lake; and the principal entrance from the open country at its foot: this last is much the best approach. Wastdale is well worth the notice of the Traveller who is not afraid of fatigue; no part of the country is more distinguished by sublimity.

ENNERDALE.

This Vale and Lake, though presenting some bold features, are only to be taken as leading to something else:—the Vale may be approached by Pedestrians, at its head, from Wastdale; and also over the mountains from Buttermere; and, by an indifferent Carriage-road, either from Calder Bridge, or Loweswater.

THE VALE OF BUTTERMERE, &c.

We are again in the beaten track of the Lakes, I will therefore pass to

THE VALE OF KESWICK,

Which place is [one of 1823] the head-quarters of Tourists. 1822–3.

from the *main road*. Fine views of it may be had from Rydal Park; but these grounds, as well as those of Rydal Mount and Ivy Cottage, from which also it is viewed to advantage, are private. A foot road passing behind Rydal Mount and under Nab Scar to Grasmere, is very favourable to views of the Lake and the Vale, looking back towards Amble- 255 side. The horse road also, along the western side of the Lake, under Loughrigg fell, as before mentioned, does justice to the beauties of this small mere, of which the Traveller who keeps the high road is not at all aware.

GRASMERE. 260

There are two small Inns in the Vale of Grasmere, one near the Church, from which it may be conveniently explored in every direction, and a mountain walk taken up Easedale to Easedale Tarn, one of the finest tarns in the country, thence to Stickle Tarn, and to the top of Langdale Pikes. See also the Vale of Grasmere from Butterlip How. 265 A boat is kept by the innkeeper, and this circular Vale, in the solemnity of a fine evening, will make, from the bosom of the Lake, an impression that will be scarcely ever effaced.

The direct road from Grasmere to Keswick does not (as has been observed of Rydal Mere) shew to advantage Thirlmere, or Wythburn 270 Lake, with its surrounding mountains. By a Traveller proceeding at leisure, a deviation ought to be made from the main road, when he has advanced a little beyond the sixth mile-stone short of Keswick, from which point there is a noble view of the Vale of Legberthwaite, with Blencathra (commonly called Saddle-back) in front. Having previously 275 enquired, at the Inn near Wythburn Chapel, the best way from this mile-stone to the bridge that divides the Lake, he must cross it, and proceed with the Lake on the right, to the hamlet a little beyond its termination, and rejoin the main road upon Shoulthwaite Moss, about four miles from Keswick; or, if on foot, the Tourist may follow the 280 stream that issues from Thirlmere down the romantic Vale of St. John's, and so (enquiring the way at some cottage) to Keswick, by a circuit of little more than a mile. A more interesting tract of country is scarcely any where to be seen, than the road between Ambleside and Keswick, with the deviations that have been pointed out. Helvellyn may 285 be conveniently ascended from the Inn at Wythburn.

THE VALE OF KESWICK.

This Vale stretches, without winding, nearly North and South, from the head of Derwent Water to the foot of Bassenthwaite Lake. It communicates with Borrowdale on the South; with the river Greta, and 290 Thirlmere, on the East, with which the Traveller has become acquainted

on his way from Ambleside; and with the Vale of Newlands on the
West—which last Vale he may pass through, in going to, or returning
from, Buttermere. The best views of Keswick Lake are from Crow
Park; Frier's Crag; the Stable-field, close by; the Vicarage, and from   295
various points in taking the circuit of the Lake. More distant views,
and perhaps full as interesting, are from the side of Latrigg, from
Ormathwaite, and Applethwaite; and thence along the road at the foot
of Skiddaw towards Bassenthwaite, for about a quarter of a mile.
There are fine bird's eye views from the Castle-hill; from Ashness, on   300
the road to Watenlath, and by following the Watenlath stream downwards to the Cataract of Lodore. This Lake also, if the weather be fine,
ought to be circumnavigated. There are good views along the western
side of Bassenthwaite Lake, and from Armathwaite at its foot; but
the eastern side from the high road has little to recommend it. The   305
Traveller from Carlisle, approaching by way of Ireby, has, from the
old road on the top of Bassenthwaite-hawse, much the most striking
view of the Plain and Lake of Bassenthwaite, flanked by Skiddaw, and
terminated by Wallowcrag on the south-east of Derwent Lake; the
same point commands an extensive view of Solway Frith and the   310
Scotch Mountains. They who take the circuit of Derwent Lake, may
at the same time include Borrowdale, going as far as Bowder-
stone, or Rosthwaite. Borrowdale is also conveniently seen on the way
to Wastdale over Styhead; or, to Buttermere, by Seatoller and Honister Crag; or, going over the Stake, through Langdale, to Ambleside.   315
Buttermere may be visited by a shorter way through Newlands, but
though the descent upon the Vale of Buttermere, by this approach,
is very striking, as it also is to one entering by the head of the Vale,
under Honister Crag, yet, after all, the best entrance from Keswick
is from the lower part of the Vale, having gone over Whinlater to   320
Scale Hill, where there is a roomy Inn, with very good accommodation.
The Mountains of the Vale of

BUTTERMERE AND CRUMMOCK

Are no where so impressive as from the bosom of Crummock Water.
Scale-force, near it, is a fine chasm, with a lofty, though but slender,   325
fall of water.

From Scale Hill a pleasant walk may be taken to an eminence in

295–6 from various points in 1823: by 1822.   306–7 the old road on 1835:
not in 1822–3.   314 over Styhead 1835: *not in* 1822–3.   315 going
over . . . to Ambleside. 1835: over the Stye to Langdale, and Ambleside. 1822–3.
317–22 though the descent . . . accommodation. The 1835: the best approach is from
Scale-hill: the 1822–3.   322–4 the Vale of . . . no where 1835: this Vale
are nowhere 1822–3.   324 Water 1835: Lake 1822–3.   325–6 near
it, is . . . water. 1835: is a fine Waterfall. 1822–3.   327–43 From Scale
Hill . . . of Wastdale. 1835: *not in* 1822–3.

Mr. Marshall's woods, and another by crossing the bridge at the foot of the hill, upon which the Inn stands, and turning to the right, after the opposite hill has been ascended a little way, then follow the road 330 for half a mile or so that leads towards Lorton, looking back upon Crummock Water, &c., between the openings of the fences. Turn back and make your way to

LOWESWATER.

But this small Lake is only approached to advantage from the other 335 end; therefore any Traveller going by this road to Wastdale, must look back upon it. This road to Wastdale, after passing the village of Lamplugh Cross, presents suddenly a fine view of the Lake of Enner-dale, with its Mountains; and, six or seven miles beyond, leads down upon Calder Abbey. Little of this ruin is left, but that little is well 340 worthy of notice. At Calder Bridge are two comfortable Inns, and, a few miles beyond, accommodations may be had at the Strands, at the foot of Wastdale. Into

WASTDALE

Are three horse-roads, viz. over the Stye from Borrowdale; a short 345 cut from Eskdale by Burnmoor Tarn, which road descends upon the head of the Lake; and the principal entrance from the open country by the Strands at its foot. This last is much the best approach. Wastdale is well worth the notice of the Traveller who is not afraid of fatigue; no part of the country is more distinguished by sublimity. Wastwater may 350 also be visited from Ambleside; by going up Langdale, over Hard-knot and Wrynose—down Eskdale and by Irton Hall to the Strands; but this road can only be taken on foot, or on horseback, or in a cart.

We will conclude with

ULLSWATER, 355

As being, perhaps, upon the whole, the happiest combination of beauty and grandeur, which any of the Lakes affords. It lies not more than ten miles from Ambleside, and the Pass of Kirkstone and the descent

---

336 Wastdale *Edd.*: Wasdale 1835. 343–50 Into WASTDALE . . . sublimity. 1835: *cf. textual n.* 216–94. 350–3 Wastwater may . . . a cart. 1835: *not in* 1822–3. 354–63 We will conclude . . . magnificent view of 1835:

ULSWATER

Is finely approached from Keswick* by Matterdale and Lyulph's Tower into Gowbarrow Park;—a magnificent view is unfolded of [*with footnote appended*]

* Pedestrians and Travellers on horseback cross the lower part of St. John's Vale, but a carriage must go a few miles along Hutton Moor before it turns off. 1822–3.

from it are very impressive; but, notwithstanding, this Vale, like the others, loses much of its effect by being entered from the head: so that 360 it is better to go from Keswick through Matterdale, and descend upon Gowbarrow Park; you are thus brought at once upon a magnificent view of the two higher reaches of the Lake. Ara-force thunders down the Ghyll on the left, at a small distance from the road. If Ullswater be approached from Penrith, a mile and a half brings you to the winding 365 vale of Eamont, and the prospects increase in interest till you reach Patterdale; but the first four miles along Ullswater by this road are comparatively tame; and in order to see the lower part of the Lake to advantage, it is necessary to go round by Pooley Bridge, and to ride at least three miles along the Westmorland side of the water, towards 370 Martindale. The views, especially if you ascend from the road into the fields, are magnificent; yet this is only mentioned that the transient Visitant may know what exists; for it would be inconvenient to go in search of them. They who take this course of three or four miles *on foot*, should have a boat in readiness at the end of the walk, to carry them 375 across to the Cumberland side of the Lake, near Old Church, thence to pursue the road upwards to Patterdale. The Church-yard Yew-tree still survives at Old Church, but there are no remains of a Place of Worship, a New Chapel having been erected in a more central situation, which Chapel was consecrated by the then Bishop of Carlisle, when 380 on his way to crown Queen Elizabeth, he being the only Prelate who would undertake the office. It may be here mentioned that Bassenthwaite Chapel yet stands in a bay as sequestered as the Site of Old Church; such situations having been chosen in disturbed times to elude marauders. 385

The Trunk, or Body of the Vale of Ullswater need not be further noticed, as its beauties show themselves: but the curious Traveller may wish to know something of its tributary Streams.

At Dalemain, about three miles from Penrith, a Stream is crossed called the Dacre, or Dacor, which name it bore as early as the time of 390 the Venerable Bede. This stream does not enter the Lake, but joins the Eamont a mile below. It rises in the moorish Country about Penruddock, flows down a soft sequestered Valley, passing by the ancient mansions of Hutton John and Dacre Castle. The former is pleasantly situated, though of a character somewhat gloomy and 395 monastic, and from some of the fields near Dalemain, Dacre Castle, backed by the jagged summit of Saddle-back, with the Valley and Stream in front, forms a grand picture. There is no other stream that conducts to any glen or valley worthy of being mentioned, till we reach that which leads up to Ara-force, and thence into Matterdale, 400

378 still 1835: *not in* 1822–3.

before spoken of. Matterdale, though a wild and interesting spot, has no peculiar features that would make it worth the Stranger's while to go in search of them; but, in Gowbarrow Park, the lover of Nature might linger for hours. Here is a powerful Brook, which dashes among rocks through a deep glen, hung on every side with a rich and happy 405 intermixture of native wood; here are beds of luxuriant fern, aged hawthorns, and hollies decked with honeysuckles; and fallow-deer glancing and bounding over the lawns and through the thickets. These are the attractions of the retired views, or constitute a foreground for ever-varying pictures of the majestic Lake, forced to take a winding 410 course by bold promontories, and environed by mountains of sublime form, towering above each other. At the outlet of Gowbarrow Park, we reach a third stream, which flows through a little recess called Glencoin, where lurks a single house, yet visible from the road. Let the Artist or leisurely Traveller turn aside to it, for the buildings and 415 objects around them are romantic and picturesque. Having passed under the steeps of Styebarrow Crag, and the remains of its native woods, at Glenridding Bridge, a fourth Stream is crossed.

The opening on the side of Ullswater Vale, down which this Stream flows, is adorned with fertile fields, cottages, and natural groves, that 420 agreeably unite with the transverse views of the Lake; and the Stream, if followed up after the enclosures are left behind, will lead along bold water-breaks and waterfalls to a silent Tarn in the recesses of Helvellyn. This desolate spot was formerly haunted by eagles, that built in the precipice which forms its western barrier. These birds used to wheel 425 and hover round the head of the solitary angler. It also derives a melancholy interest from the fate of a young man, a stranger, who perished some years ago, by falling down the rocks in his attempt to cross over to Grasmere. His remains were discovered by means of a faithful dog that had lingered here for the space of three months, self- 430 supported, and probably retaining to the last an attachment to the skeleton of its master. But to return to the road in the main Vale of Ullswater.—At the head of the Lake (being now in Patterdale) we cross a fifth Stream, Grisdale Beck: this would conduct through a woody steep, where may be seen some unusually large ancient hollies, 435 up to the level area of the Valley of Grisdale; hence there is a path for foot-travellers, and along which a horse may be led, to Grasmere. A sublime combination of mountain forms appears in front while ascending the bed of this valley, and the impression increases till the path leads almost immediately under the projecting masses of Helvellyn. 440 Having retraced the banks of the Stream to Patterdale, and pursued the road up the main Dale, the next considerable stream would, if

419 this 1835: the 1822–3.

ascended in the same manner, conduct to Deep-dale, the character of which Valley may be conjectured from its name. It is terminated by a cove, a craggy and gloomy abyss, with precipitous sides; a faithful 445 receptacle of the snows that are driven into it, by the west wind, from the summit of Fairfield. Lastly, having gone along the western side of Brotherswater and passed Hartsop Hall, a Stream soon after issues from a cove richly decorated with native wood. This spot is, I believe, never explored by Travellers; but, from these sylvan and rocky recesses, who- 450 ever looks back on the gleaming surface of Brotherswater, or forward to the precipitous sides and lofty ridges of Dove Crag, &c., will be equally pleased with the beauty, the grandeur, and the wildness of the scenery.

Seven Glens or Vallies have been noticed, which branch off from the Cumberland side of the Vale. The opposite side has only two Streams 455 of any importance, one of which would lead up from the point where it crosses the Kirkstone-road, near the foot of Brotherswater, to the decaying hamlet of Hartsop, remarkable for its cottage architecture, and thence to Hayswater, much frequented by anglers. The other, coming down Martindale, enters Ullswater at Sandwyke, opposite to 460 Gowbarrow Park. No persons but such as come to Patterdale, merely to pass through it, should fail to walk as far as Blowick, the only enclosed land which on this side borders the higher part of the Lake. The axe has here indiscriminately levelled a rich wood of birches and oaks, that divided this favoured spot into a hundred pictures. It has yet 465 its land-locked bays, and rocky promontories; but those beautiful woods are gone, which *perfected* its seclusion; and scenes, that might formerly have been compared to an inexhaustible volume, are now spread before the eye in a single sheet,—magnificent indeed, but seemingly perused in a moment! From Blowick a narrow track conducts 470 along the craggy side of Place-fell, richly adorned with juniper, and sprinkled over with birches, to the village of Sandwyke, a few strag- gling houses, that with the small estates attached to them, occupy an opening opposite to Lyulph's Tower and Gowbarrow Park. In Martindale,* the road loses sight of the Lake, and leads over a steep 475

* See Page 247.

---

474 Park. In 1823: Park. This stream flows down Martindale, a valley deficient in richness, but interesting from its seclusion. In Vales of this character the general want of wood gives a peculiar interest to the scattered cottages, embowered in syca- mores; and few of the Mountain Chapels are more striking than this of Martindale, standing as it does in the centre of the Valley, with one dark yew-tree, and enclosed by "a bare ring of mossy wall." The name of Boardale, a deep, bare, and houseless Valley, which communicates with Martindale, shews that the wild Swine were once numerous in that nook; and Martindale Forest is yet one of the few spots in England ranged over by red deer. These are the descendants of the aboriginal herds. [*Cf. textual n.* 2907–3325; *cf. below* 3074–80; 3094–7; 3120–2.] In 1822.
475 Martindale,* [*with footnote appended*] 1823: Martindale 1822.

hill, bringing you again into view of Ullswater. Its lowest reach, four
miles in length, is before you; and the view terminated by the long
ridge of Cross Fell in the distance. Immediately under the eye is a deep-
indented bay, with a plot of fertile land, traversed by a small brook,
and rendered cheerful by two or three substantial houses of a more 480
ornamented and showy appearance than is usual in those wild spots.

From Pooley Bridge, at the foot of the Lake, Haweswater may be
conveniently visited. Haweswater is a lesser Ullswater, with this
advantage, that it remains undefiled by the intrusion of bad taste.

Lowther Castle is about four miles from Pooley Bridge, and, if 485
during this Tour the Stranger has complained, as he will have had
reason to do, of a want of majestic trees, he may be abundantly recompensed for his loss in the far-spreading woods which surround that
mansion. Visitants, for the most part, see little of the beauty of these
magnificent grounds, being content with the view from the Terrace; 490
but the whole course of the Lowther, from Askham to the bridge under
Brougham Hall, presents almost at every step some new feature of
river, woodland, and rocky landscape. A portion of this tract has, from
its beauty, acquired the name of the Elysian Fields;—but the course of
the stream can only be followed by the pedestrian.   495

NOTE.—*Vide* pp. 162–3.—About 200 yards beyond the last house on
the Keswick side of Rydal village the road is cut through a low wooded
rock, called Thrang Crag. The top of it, which is only a few steps on
the south side, affords the best view of the Vale which is to be had by
a Traveller who confines himself to the public road.   500

481 is 1835: *not in* 1822–3.   489–500 Visitants . . . public road. 1835: *not in*
1822–3.   500/1 *Verso of fly title in* 1820 (*see Healey, item 52*) *appears in italics
the following note: This Essay, which was published several years ago as an Introduction
to some Views of the Lakes, by the Rev. Joseph Wilkinson, (an expensive work, and necessarily of limited circulation,) is now, with emendations and additions, attached to these
volumes; from a consciousness of its having been written in the same spirit which dictated
several of the poems, and from a belief that it will tend materially to illustrate them.*

DESCRIPTION
OF THE
SCENERY OF THE LAKES.

SECTION FIRST.

At Lucerne, in Switzerland, is shewn a Model of the Alpine country which encompasses the Lake of the four Cantons. The Spectator ascends a little platform, and sees mountains, lakes, glaciers, rivers, woods, waterfalls, and vallies, with their cottages, and every other object contained in them, lying at his feet; all things being represented in their appropriate colours. It may be easily conceived that this exhibition affords an exquisite delight to the imagination, tempting it to wander at will from valley to valley, from mountain to mountain, through the deepest recesses of the Alps. But it supplies also a more substantial pleasure: for the sublime and beautiful region, with all its hidden treasures, and their bearings and relations to each other, is thereby comprehended and understood at once.

Something of this kind, without touching upon minute details and individualities which would only confuse and embarrass, will here be attempted, in respect to the Lakes in the north of England, and the vales and mountains enclosing and surrounding them. The delineation, if tolerably executed, will, in some instances, communicate to the traveller, who has already seen the objects, new information; and will

501-5 DESCRIPTION . . . BY NATURE. 1822: TOPOGRAPHICAL DE-SCRIPTION OF THE COUNTRY OF THE LAKES. 1820: INTRODUCTION. 1810. (*Cf. textual n.* 1–500.)   506 is shewn 1822: there existed, some years ago, 1820: there existed some years ago, and perhaps does still exist, 1810. 506–7 the Alpine . . . encompasses 1820: a large portion of the Alpine country en-compassing 1810.   508 ascends 1822: ascended 1810–20.   sees 1822: saw 1810–20.   510 contained in them 1820: which they contained 1810. 511 their appropriate 1820: their exact proportions and appropriate 1810. 512 affords 1822: afforded 1810–20.   tempting it 1822: which was thus tempted 1820: which was tempted 1810.   513 at will 1820: *not in* 1810. 514 supplies 1822: supplied 1810–20.   515 substantial 1820: solid and sub-stantial 1810.   516 bearings and relations 1820: relations and bearings 1810.   517 is 1822: was 1810–20.   518–19 without touching . . . embarrass 1822: (as far as it [it *not in* 1810] can be performed by words, which must needs be [most 1810] inadequately 1810–20.   519–21 here be at-tempted . . . them. The 1820: be attempted in the following introductory pages, with reference to the country which has furnished the subjects of the Drawings now offered to the public, adding to a verbal representation of its permanent features such appearances as are transitory from their dependence upon accidents of season and weather. This 1810.

assist in giving to his recollections a more orderly arrangement than his own opportunities of observing may have permitted him to make; 525 while it will be still more useful to the future traveller, by directing his attention at once to distinctions in things which, without such previous aid, a length of time only could enable him to discover. It is hoped, also, that this Essay may become generally serviceable, by leading to habits of more exact and considerate observation than, as far as the 530 writer knows, have hitherto been applied to local scenery.

To begin, then, with the main outlines of the country;—I know not how to give the reader a distinct image of these more readily, than by requesting him to place himself with me, in imagination, upon some given point; let it be the top of either of the mountains, Great Gavel, 535 or Scawfell; or, rather, let us suppose our station to be a cloud hanging midway between those two mountains, at not more than half a mile's distance from the summit of each, and not many yards above their highest elevation; we shall then see stretched at our feet a number of vallies, not fewer than eight, diverging from the point, on which we 540 are supposed to stand, like spokes from the nave of a wheel. First, we note, lying to the south-east, the vale of Langdale *, which will conduct the eye to the long lake of Winandermere, stretched nearly to the sea; or rather to the sands of the vast bay of Morcamb, serving here for the rim of this imaginary wheel;—let us trace it in a direction from the 545 south-east towards the south, and we shall next fix our eyes upon the vale of Coniston, running up likewise from the sea, but not (as all the other vallies do) to the nave of the wheel, and therefore it may be

---

* Anciently spelt Langden, and so called by the old inhabitants to this day—*dean*, from which the latter part of the word is derived, being in many parts of England a name for a valley.

---

524 in giving 1820: him to give 1810.   *525* make 1820: do 1810. *528–31* It is . . . scenery. 1820: And, as must be obvious, this general introduction will combine with the Etchings certain notices of things which, though they may not lie within the province of the pencil, cannot but tend to render its productions more interesting; especially in a case like the present, where a work wishes to recommend itself by a two-fold claim, viz. by furnishing pleasing Sketches, and at the same time accurate Portraits of those scenes from which they are taken. 1810. *532* outlines 1820: demarkation 1810.   *533* to 1820: I can 1810.   these 1820: this 1810.   more readily 1820: *not in* 1810.   *534* with me 1820: *not in* 1810.   *535* mountains, Great 1820: mountain of Great 1810. *536* us . . . our 1820: him . . . his 1810.   *537* those 1822: these 1820: the 1810.   *538* not many 1820: but a few 1810.   *539* we shall . . . our 1820: he will . . . his 1810.   *540* eight 1822: nine 1810–20.   *540–1* we are 1820: he is 1810.   *541* we 1820: he will 1810.   *542* n. *Not in* 1810–20. *543* the eye 1820: his eye 1810.   stretched 1820: stretching, as appears, 1810. *544* serving here 1820: which here serves 1810.   *545* let us 1820: *not in* 1810.   *546* we shall . . . our 1820: he will . . . his 1810.   *548* the nave 1820: the station which I have considered as the nave 1810.   *548–9* be not 1822: not be 1810–20.

not inaptly represented as a broken spoke sticking in the rim. Looking forth again, with an inclination towards the west, we see immediately 550 at our feet the vale of Duddon, in which is no lake, but a copious stream winding among fields, rocks, and mountains, and terminating its course in the sands of Duddon. The fourth vale, next to be observed, viz. that of the Esk, is of the same general character as the last, yet beautifully discriminated from it by peculiar features. Its stream passes 555 under the woody steep upon which stands Muncaster Castle, the ancient seat of the Penningtons, and after forming a short and narrow æstuary enters the sea below the small town of Ravenglass. Next, almost due west, look down into, and along the deep valley of Wast-dale, with its little chapel and half a dozen neat dwellings scattered 560 upon a plain of meadow and corn-ground intersected with stone walls apparently innumerable, like a large piece of lawless patch-work, or an array of mathematical figures, such as in the ancient schools of geometry might have been sportively and fantastically traced out upon sand. Beyond this little fertile plain lies, within a bed of steep 565 mountains, the long, narrow, stern, and desolate lake of Wastdale; and, beyond this, a dusky tract of level ground conducts the eye to the Irish Sea. The stream that issues from Wast-water is named the Irt, and falls into the æstuary of the river Esk. Next comes in view Enner-dale, with its lake of bold and somewhat savage shores. Its stream, 570 the Ehen or Enna, flowing through a soft and fertile country, passes the town of Egremont, and the ruins of the castle,—then, seeming, like the other rivers, to break through the barrier of sand thrown up by the winds on this tempestuous coast, enters the Irish Sea. The vale of Buttermere, with the lake and village of that name, and Crummock- 575 water, beyond, next present themselves. We will follow the main stream, the Coker, through the fertile and beautiful vale of Lorton, till it is lost in the Derwent, below the noble ruins of Cockermouth Castle. Lastly, Borrowdale, of which the vale of Keswick is only a continuation, stretching due north, brings us to a point nearly opposite 580 to the vale of Winandermere with which we began. From this it will

550–1 we see . . . feet 1823: immediately at our feet lies 1810–22. 551 stream 1820: river 1810. 553 vale 1822: valley 1810–20. next . . . observed 1820: which we shall next observe 1810. 554 the Esk 1822: Eskdale 1810–20. 555 peculiar features. 1820: features which, in the more minute details attached to the several parts of this work, will here-after be described. 1810. 555–8 Its stream . . . Ravenglass. 1822: *not in* 1810–20. 558 small 1823: little 1822. 559 into, and along 1822: upon, and into 1810–20. 560–1 dwellings scattered upon a 1822: scattered dwellings, a 1810–20. 565 a 1823: its 1810–22. 568–79 The stream . . . the vale 1822: The several vales of Ennerdale and Buttermere, with their Lakes, next present themselves; and lastly, the vale of Borrowdale, of which that 1810–20.

appear, that the image of a wheel, thus far exact, is little more than one half complete; but the deficiency on the eastern side may be supplied by the vales of Wytheburn, Ulswater, Hawswater, and the vale of Grasmere and Rydal; none of these, however, run up to the 585
central point between Great Gavel and Scawfell. From this, hitherto our central point, take a flight of not more than four or five miles eastward to the ridge of Helvellyn, and you will look down upon Wytheburn and St. John's Vale, which are a branch of the vale of Keswick; upon Ulswater, stretching due east:—and not far beyond to 590
the south-east (though from this point not visible) lie the vale and lake of Hawswater; and lastly, the vale of Grasmere, Rydal, and Ambleside, brings you back to Winandermere, thus completing, though on the eastern side in a somewhat irregular manner, the representative figure of the wheel. 595

Such, concisely given, is the general topographical view of the country of the Lakes in the north of England; and it may be observed, that, from the circumference to the centre, that is, from the sea or plain country to the mountain stations specified, there is—in the several ridges that enclose these vales, and divide them from each 600
other, I mean in the forms and surfaces, first of the swelling grounds, next of the hills and rocks, and lastly of the mountains—an ascent of almost regular gradation, from elegance and richness, to their highest point of grandeur and sublimity. It follows therefore from this, first, that these rocks, hills, and mountains, must present themselves to 605
view in stages rising above each other, the mountains clustering together towards the central point; and next, that an observer familiar with the several vales, must, from their various position in relation to the sun, have had before his eyes every possible embellishment of beauty, dignity, and splendour, which light and shadow can bestow 610
upon objects so diversified. For example, in the vale of Winandermere, if the spectator looks for gentle and lovely scenes, his eye is

582 wheel, thus 1820: wheel, which I have made use of, and which is thus 1810. little 1820: not much 1810.   583 one 1820: *not in* 1810.   587 four or five 1822: three or four 1810–20.   592 vale 1820: winding vale 1810.   594 a somewhat 1820: an 1810.   597 England; and it 1820: England. But it must be observed that the visits of travellers are for the most part confined to the Vales of Coniston, Winandermere with the intermediate country between Ambleside and Keswick, the Vale of Keswick itself, Buttermere, and Ulswater, which are the most easy of access, and indeed from their several characters most likely to repay general curiosity; though each of the other more retired vales, as will appear when we enter into detail in the several numbers of this publication, has its own appropriate beauties—all exquisite in their kind. This Introduction will be confined as much as possible to general remarks. And first, returning to the illustrative figure which has been employed, it 1810.
599 mountain stations specified 1820: mountains of Great Gavel and Scawfell 1810.   603 their 1822: the 1810–20.   604 and sublimity 1822: *not in* 1810–20.   606 view 1820: the view 1810.

turned towards the south; if for the grand, towards the north: in the
vale of Keswick, which (as hath been said) lies almost due north of this,
it is directly the reverse. Hence, when the sun is setting in summer   615
far to the north-west, it is seen, by the spectator from the shores or
breast of Winandermere, resting among the summits of the loftiest
mountains, some of which will perhaps be half or wholly hidden by
clouds, or by the blaze of light which the orb diffuses around it; and the
surface of the lake will reflect before the eye correspondent colours   620
through every variety of beauty, and through all degrees of splendour.
In the vale of Keswick, at the same period, the sun sets over the
humbler regions of the landscape, and showers down upon *them* the
radiance which at once veils and glorifies,—sending forth, meanwhile,
broad streams of rosy, crimson, purple, or golden light, towards the   625
grand mountains in the south and south-east, which, thus illuminated,
with all their projections and cavities, and with an intermixture of
solemn shadows, are seen distinctly through a cool and clear atmosphere. Of course, there is as marked a difference between the *noontide*
appearance of these two opposite vales. The bedimming haze that   630
overspreads the south, and the clear atmosphere and determined
shadows of the clouds in the north, at the same time of the day, are
each seen in these several vales, with a contrast as striking. The
reader will easily conceive in what degree the intermediate vales
partake of a kindred variety.   635

I do not indeed know any tract of country in which, within so narrow
a compass, may be found an equal variety in the influences of light and
shadow upon the sublime or beautiful features of landscape; and it is
owing to the combined circumstances to which the reader's attention
has been directed. From a point between Great Gavel and Scawfell,   640
a shepherd would not require more than an hour to descend into any
one of eight of the principal vales by which he would be surrounded;
and all the others lie (with the exception of Hawswater) at but a small
distance. Yet, though clustered together, every valley has its distinct
and separate character: in some instances, as if they had been formed   645
in studied contrast to each other, and in others with the united pleasing
differences and resemblances of a sisterly rivalship. This concentration
of interest gives to the country a decided superiority over the most
attractive districts of Scotland and Wales, especially for the pedestrian
traveller. In Scotland and Wales are found, undoubtedly, individual   650

634 will . . . conceive 1822: will . . . perceive 1820: perceiving [*sic*] 1810.
635 partake 1820: will partake [*sic*] 1810.   a kindred 1823: the same 1810–22.
638 sublime or beautiful 1820: grand or gentle 1810.   639–40 the reader's
. . . directed 1835: I have directed the reader's attention 1810–23.   640
between 1820: between the mountains of 1810.   643 at but a 1820: but at
a 1810.   644 clustered 1820: thus clustered 1810.

scenes, which, in their several kinds, cannot be excelled. But, in Scotland, particularly, what long tracts of desolate country intervene! so that the traveller, when he reaches a spot deservedly of great celebrity, would find it difficult to determine how much of his pleasure is owing to excellence inherent in the landscape itself; and how much 655 to an instantaneous recovery from an oppression left upon his spirits by the barrenness and desolation through which he has passed.

But to proceed with our survey;—and, first, of the MOUNTAINS. Their *forms* are endlessly diversified, sweeping easily or boldly in simple majesty, abrupt and precipitous, or soft and elegant. In magni- 660 tude and grandeur they are individually inferior to the most celebrated of those in some other parts of this island; but, in the combinations which they make, towering above each other, or lifting themselves in ridges like the waves of a tumultuous sea, and in the beauty and variety of their surfaces and colours, they are surpassed by none. 665

The general *surface* of the mountains is turf, rendered rich and green by the moisture of the climate. Sometimes the turf, as in the neighbour- hood of Newlands, is little broken, the whole covering being soft and downy pasturage. In other places rocks predominate; the soil is laid bare by torrents and burstings of water from the sides of the mountains 670 in heavy rains; and not unfrequently their perpendicular sides are seamed by ravines (formed also by rains and torrents) which, meeting in angular points, entrench and scar the surface with numerous figures like the letters W. and Y.

In the ridge that divides Eskdale from Wasdale, granite is found; 675 but the MOUNTAINS are for the most part composed of the stone by mineralogists termed schist, which, as you approach the plain country, gives place to lime-stone and free-stone; but schist being the substance of the mountains, the predominant *colour* of their *rocky* parts is bluish, or hoary grey—the general tint of the lichens with which the 680 bare stone is encrusted. With this blue or grey colour is frequently intermixed a red tinge, proceeding from the iron that interveins the stone, and impregnates the soil. The iron is the principle of

651 excelled 1820: surpassed 1810.   652 long tracts . . . country 1822: deso- late and unimpressive tracts of country almost perpetually 1810–20.   654 would find it difficult 1820: is often at a loss 1810.   658–9 But to . . . Their *forms* 1820: For the *forms* of these mountains I refer to the Etchings to which these pages are an Introduction, and from which it will appear that their outlines 1810. 661 they 1820: these mountains 1810.   665 colours 1820: their colours 1810.   666 rendered 1820: made 1810.   668 is 1820: in particular, is 1810.   671 not unfrequently 1822: occasionally 1810–20.   673 scar 1822: scar over 1810–20.   675–6 In the ridge . . . most part 1823: The Mountains are 1810–22.   678 place 1820: way 1810.   680 *not in* 1820: *not in* 1810.   681 or 1820: and 1810.   682–3 iron that . . . the soil. 1820: iron with which the stone is interveined and the soil in many places impregnated. 1810.

decomposition in these rocks; and hence, when they become pulverized, the elementary particles crumbling down, overspread in many places 685 the steep and almost precipitous sides of the mountains with an intermixture of colours, like the compound hues of a dove's neck. When in the heat of advancing summer, the fresh green tint of the herbage has somewhat faded, it is again revived by the appearance of the fern profusely spread over the same ground: and, upon this plant, more 690 than upon any thing else, do the changes which the seasons make in the colouring of the mountains depend. About the first week in October, the rich green, which prevailed through the whole summer, is usually passed away. The brilliant and various colours of the fern are then in harmony with the autumnal woods; bright yellow or lemon colour, 695 at the base of the mountains, melting gradually, through orange, to a dark russet brown towards the summits, where the plant, being more exposed to the weather, is in a more advanced state of decay. Neither heath nor furze are *generally* found upon the *sides* of these mountains, though in many places they are adorned by those plants, so beautiful 700 when in flower. We may add, that the mountains are of height sufficient to have the surface towards the summit softened by distance, and to imbibe the finest aërial hues. In common also with other mountains, their apparent forms and colours are perpetually changed by the clouds and vapours which float round them: the effect indeed of mist or haze, 705 in a country of this character, is like that of magic. I have seen six or seven ridges rising above each other, all created in a moment, by the vapours upon the side of a mountain, which, in its ordinary appearance, shewed not a projecting point to furnish even a hint for such an operation.

I will take this opportunity of observing, that they who have 710 studied the appearances of nature feel that the superiority, in point of visual interest, of mountainous over other countries—is more strikingly displayed in winter than in summer. This, as must be obvious, is partly owing to the *forms* of the mountains, which, of course, are not affected by the seasons; but also, in no small degree, to the greater 715 variety that exists in their winter than their summer *colouring*. This variety is such, and so harmoniously preserved, that it leaves little cause of regret when the splendour of autumn is passed away. The oak-coppices, upon the sides of the mountains, retain russet leaves; the

688 fresh green 1820: freshness of the green 1810.   690 over . . . ground 1822: every where 1810–20.   692 About 1820: By 1810.   693 prevailed 1820: was preserved 1810.   summer, is 1820: summer by the herbage and by this plant, has 1810.   694 away. The . . . the fern 1820: away; its brilliant and various colours of light yellow, orange, and brown 1810.   700–1 many places . . . flower 1835: many places . . . adorned by the rich hues of these plants 1823: some places they are richly adorned by them 1810–22.   702 summit 1823: summits 1810–22.   705 or 1820: and 1810.   716 that 1820: which 1810.   718–19 oak-coppices 1820: coppice woods 1810.

birch stands conspicuous with its silver stem and puce-coloured twigs; 720
the hollies, with green leaves and scarlet berries, have come forth to
view from among the deciduous trees, whose summer foliage had
concealed them: the ivy is now plentifully apparent upon the stems and
boughs of the trees, and upon the steep rocks. In place of the deep
summer-green of the herbage and fern, many rich colours play into 725
each other over the surface of the mountains; turf (the tints of which
are interchangeably tawny-green, olive, and brown,) beds of withered
fern, and grey rocks, being harmoniously blended together. The
mosses and lichens are never so fresh and flourishing as in winter, if it
be not a season of frost; and their minute beauties prodigally adorn the 730
foreground. Wherever we turn, we find these productions of nature,
to which winter is rather favourable than unkindly, scattered over the
walls, banks of earth, rocks, and stones, and upon the trunks of trees,
with the intermixture of several species of small fern, now green and
fresh; and, to the observing passenger, their forms and colours are a 735
source of inexhaustible admiration. Add to this the hoar-frost and
snow, with all the varieties they create, and which volumes would not
be sufficient to describe. I will content myself with one instance of the
colouring produced by snow, which may not be uninteresting to
painters. It is extracted from the memorandum-book of a friend; and 740
for its accuracy I can speak, having been an eye-witness of the appearance. "I observed," says he, "the beautiful effect of the drifted snow
upon the mountains, and the perfect *tone* of colour. From the top of the
mountains downwards a rich olive was produced by the powdery snow
and the grass, which olive was warmed with a little brown, and in this 745
way harmoniously combined, by insensible gradations, with the white.
The drifting took away the monotony of snow; and the whole vale of
Grasmere, seen from the terrace walk in Easedale, was as varied,
perhaps more so, than even in the pomp of autumn. In the distance
was Loughrigg-Fell, the basin-wall of the lake: this, from the summit 750
downward, was a rich orange-olive; then the lake of a bright olive-
green, nearly the same tint as the snow-powdered mountain tops and
high slopes in Easedale; and lastly, the church, with its firs, forming
the centre of the view. Next to the church came nine distinguishable

721–2 hollies, with . . . view 1820: hollies have come forth to view, with green
leaves and scarlet berries 1810.   723 plentifully 1820: *not in* 1810.
724 upon the steep 1822: among the woody 1810–20.   place 1810–23, *Edd.*:
places 1835.   deep 1822: uniform 1810–20.   726 the tints of which 1820:
whose tints 1810.   737 they 1820: which they 1810.   741 having been
1820: as I myself was 1810.   744 downwards 1820: downward 1810.
747 away the 1820: away all the 1810.   751 of a 1820: a 1810.   754 view.
Next 1820: view. The firs looked magnificent, and carried the eye back to some
firs in Brother's Wood on the left side of the lake (we are looking towards Loughrigg). Next 1810.   came 1822: with its firs came 1810–20.

8124368.2   N

hills, six of them with woody sides turned towards us, all of them oak-   755
copses with their bright red leaves and snow-powdered twigs; these
hills—so variously situated in relation to each other, and to the view
in general, so variously powdered, some only enough to give the
herbage a rich brown tint, one intensely white and lighting up all the
others—were yet so placed, as in the most inobtrusive manner to   760
harmonise by contrast with a perfect naked, snowless bleak summit in
the far distance."

Having spoken of the forms, surface, and colour of the mountains,
let us descend into the VALES. Though these have been represented
under the general image of the spokes of a wheel, they are, for the most   765
part, winding; the windings of many being abrupt and intricate. And,
it may be observed, that, in one circumstance, the general shape of
them all has been determined by that primitive conformation through
which so many became receptacles of lakes. For they are not formed,
as are most of the celebrated Welsh vallies, by an approximation of   770
the sloping bases of the opposite mountains towards each other,
leaving little more between than a channel for the passage of a hasty
river; but the bottom of these vallies is mostly a spacious and gently
declining area, apparently level as the floor of a temple, or the surface
of a lake, and broken in many cases, by rocks and hills, which rise up   775
like islands from the plain. In such of the vallies as make many windings, these level areas open upon the traveller in succession, divided
from each other sometimes by a mutual approximation of the hills,
leaving only passage for a river, sometimes by correspondent windings,
without such approximation; and sometimes by a bold advance of one   780
mountain towards that which is opposite it. It may here be observed
with propriety that the several rocks and hills, which have been
described as rising up like islands from the level area of the vale, have
regulated the choice of the inhabitants in the situation of their dwellings. Where none of these are found, and the inclination of the ground   785
is not sufficiently rapid easily to carry off the waters, (as in the higher
part of Langdale, for instance,) the houses are not sprinkled over the

757 hills—so 1820: hills all distinguishable indeed from the summit downward,
but none seen all the way down, so as to give the strongest sense of number with
unity; and these hills so 1810.   in relation 1822: *not in* 1810–20.   760 were
1820: and 1810.   762 distance." 1820: distance in the left—the variety of site,
of colour, of woodiness, of the situation of the woods, &c. &c. made it not merely
number with unity, but intricacy combined that activity of feeling, which intricacy
awakens, with the complacency and repose of perfect unity." 1810.   764 VALES
1822: VALLEYS 1810–20.   773 mostly 1823: for the most part 1810–22.
775 broken 1823: beautifully broken 1810–22.   776 In such . . . vallies as
1820: As the vallies 1810.   779 passage 1820: a passage 1810.   780 advance of 1810–23, *Errata*: advance, of 1835.   781 towards 1810–20, 1835:
toward 1822–3.   it 1835: to it 1810–23.   782 have been 1820: I have
1810.

middle of the vales, but confined to their sides, being placed merely so far up the mountain as to be protected from the floods. But where these rocks and hills have been scattered over the plain of the vale, (as in Grasmere, Donnerdale, Eskdale, &c.) the beauty which they give to the scene is much heightened by a single cottage, or cluster of cottages, that will be almost always found under them, or upon their sides; dryness and shelter having tempted the Dalesmen to fix their habitations there.

 I shall now speak of the LAKES of this country. The form of the lake is most perfect when, like Derwent-water, and some of the smaller lakes, it least resembles that of a river;—I mean, when being looked at from any given point where the whole may be seen at once, the width of it bears such proportion to the length, that, however the outline may be diversified by far-receding bays, it never assumes the shape of a river, and is contemplated with thát placid and quiet feeling which belongs peculiarly to the lake—as a body of still water under the influence of no current; reflecting therefore the clouds, the light, and all the imagery of the sky and surrounding hills; expressing also and making visible the changes of the atmosphere, and motions of the lightest breeze, and subject to agitation only from the winds—

> ————The visible scene
> Would enter unawares into his mind
> With all its solemn imagery, its rocks,
> Its woods, and that uncertain heaven received
> Into the bosom of the *steady* lake!

It must be noticed, as a favourable characteristic of the lakes of this country, that, though several of the largest, such as Winandermere, Ulswater, Hawswater, do, when the whole length of them is commanded from an elevated point, lose somewhat of the peculiar form of the lake, and assume the resemblance of a magnificent river; yet, as their shape is winding, (particularly that of Ulswater and Hawswater) when the view of the whole is obstructed by those barriers which determine the windings, and the spectator is confined to one reach, the appropriate feeling is revived; and one lake may thus in succession present to the eye the essential characteristic of many. But, though the forms of the large lakes have this advantage, it is nevertheless

---

788 of 1823: part of 1810–22. 789 be protected 1822: protect them 1810–20. 791 Donnerdale 1820: Seathwaite 1810. 792 that 1820: which 1810. 795 speak of 1820: say a few words concerning 1810. 800 far-receding 1822: far-shooting 1810–20. 805 motions 1820: motion 1810. 810 woods 1820: wood 1810. 814 do 1822: &c. do 1810–20. 815 lose 1810–23, *Edd.*: loose 1835. 821 to the eye 1820: *not in* 1810. 822-3 nevertheless favourable 1823: nevertheless a circumstance favourable 1820-2: a circumstance still more favourable 1810.

favourable to the beauty of the country that the largest of them are comparatively small; and that the same vale generally furnishes a succession of lakes, instead of being filled with one. The vales in North Wales, as 825 hath been observed, are not formed for the reception of lakes; those of Switzerland, Scotland, and this part of the North of England, *are* so formed; but, in Switzerland and Scotland, the proportion of diffused water is often too great, as at the lake of Geneva for instance, and in most of the Scotch lakes. No doubt it sounds magnificent and flatters 830 the imagination, to hear at a distance of expanses of water so many leagues in length and miles in width; and such ample room may be delightful to the fresh-water sailor, scudding with a lively breeze amid the rapidly-shifting scenery. But, who ever travelled along the banks of Loch-Lomond, variegated as the lower part is by islands, without 835 feeling that a speedier termination of the long vista of blank water would be acceptable; and without wishing for an interposition of green meadows, trees, and cottages, and a sparkling stream to run by his side? In fact, a notion of grandeur, as connected with magnitude, has seduced persons of taste into a general mistake upon this subject. It is 840 much more desirable, for the purposes of pleasure, that lakes should be numerous, and small or middle-sized, than large, not only for communication by walks and rides, but for variety, and for recurrence of similar appearances. To illustrate this by one instance:—how pleasing is it to have a ready and frequent opportunity of watching, at the outlet 845 of a lake, the stream pushing its way among the rocks in lively contrast with the stillness from which it has escaped; and how amusing to compare its noisy and turbulent motions with the gentle playfulness of the breezes, that may be starting up or wandering here and there over the faintly-rippled surface of the broad water! I may add, as a 850 general remark, that, in lakes of great width, the shores cannot be distinctly seen at the same time, and therefore contribute little to mutual illustration and ornament; and, if the opposite shores are out of sight of each other, like those of the American and Asiatic lakes, then unfortunately the traveller is reminded of a nobler object; he has the 855 blankness of a sea-prospect without the grandeur and accompanying sense of power.

823–4 comparatively 1820: *not in* 1810.   824 vale 1823: valley 1810–22.
825 with 1820: by 1810.   vales 1823: vallies 1810–22.   830 in 1820: *not in* 1810.   831 expanses 1820: such expanses 1810.   835 by 1820: with 1810.   836 feeling that 1820: wishing for 1810.   837 would be ... wishing 1820: *not in* 1810.   844 by 1820: only by 1810.   849 that 1820: which 1810.   851 remark, 1820: remark upon this subject, 1810. 853–4 and, if the . . . lakes 1822: and if, like the American and Asiatic lakes, the opposite shores are out of sight of each other 1810–20.   856 grandeur 1822: same grandeur 1810–20.

As the comparatively small size of the lakes in the North of England is favourable to the production of variegated landscape, their *boundary-line* also is for the most part gracefully or boldly indented. That uni- 860 formity which prevails in the primitive frame of the lower grounds among all chains or clusters of mountains where large bodies of still water are bedded, is broken by the *secondary* agents of nature, ever at work to supply the deficiences of the mould in which things were originally cast. Using the word *deficiences*, I do not speak with reference 865 to those stronger emotions which a region of mountains is peculiarly fitted to excite. The bases of those huge barriers may run for a long space in straight lines, and these parallel to each other; the opposite sides of a profound vale may ascend as exact counterparts, or in mutual reflection, like the billows of a troubled sea; and the impression be, 870 from its very simplicity, more awful and sublime. Sublimity is the result of Nature's first great dealings with the superficies of the earth; but the general tendency of her subsequent operations is towards the production of beauty, by a multiplicity of symmetrical parts uniting in a consistent whole. This is every where exemplified along the 875 margins of these lakes. Masses of rock, that have been precipitated from the heights into the area of waters, lie in some places like stranded ships; or have acquired the compact structure of jutting piers; or project in little peninsulas crested with native wood. The smallest rivulet—one whose silent influx is scarcely noticeable in a season of 880 dry weather—so faint is the dimple made by it on the surface of the smooth lake—will be found to have been not useless in shaping, by its

858–976 *Not in* 1810 *except for the passage given in textual n.* 990/1. 858 comparatively small 1820: *not in* MS. 863 broken 1820: counteracted MS. 865 Using MS.², 1822: It [needs MS.] need scarcely be observed that using MS., 1820. with 1820: only with MS. 866 those stronger emotions MS.³, 1820: those elevated MS.: beauty and MS.². mountains] *In* MS. *altered to* mountainous region *but then restored.* 867 excite MS.², 1820: produce MS. bases 1820: basis MS. 870 like 1820: as those of MS. troubled MS.², 1820: stormy MS. 871 more . . . sublime 1820: more capable of awakening sublime sensations MS.: akin to the sublime MS.². 872 of [*first*] MS.², 1820: of the MS. the superficies MS.², 1820: this planet as far as its materials lie MS. 873 tendency MS.², 1820: tendencies MS. 874 beauty, 1820–3, *Edd.*: beauty MS.: beauty; 1835. by a . . . parts MS.⁴, 1820: by the harmonious composition [of many & diverse features in one countenance MS.] of multiplied members in one body MS.²: [through *del.*] by multiplication of parts MS.³. *After* uniting MS. *deletes*: both in respect to form & colour 877 heights MS.², 1820: steeps MS. in some places 1823: frequently MS., 1820–2. 878 stranded ships 1820: the shattered hulks of stranded ships MS. acquired MS.², 1820: assume MS. 879 *After* wood MS. *deletes*: But permanent effects still more interesting have proceeded from the streams perpetually pouring down through the collateral recesses and Vallies. 880 *After* rivulet MS. *deletes*: among these, such a one as scarcely may have power 881 made by it 1820: which it makes MS.: made b[?] MS.². 881–2 on the surface of the smooth 1820: on the [margin *del.*] surface of MS.: upon the [still *del.*] smooth MS.². 882 useless] MS. *wrongly deletes.*

deposits of gravel and soil in time of flood, a curve that would not otherwise have existed. But the more powerful brooks, encroaching upon the
level of the lake, have, in course of time, given birth to ample pro-   885
montories of sweeping outline that contrasts boldly with the longi-
tudinal base of the steeps on the opposite shore; while their flat or
gently-sloping surfaces never fail to introduce, into the midst of
desolation and barrenness, the elements of fertility, even where the
habitations of men may not have been raised. These alluvial pro-   890
montories, however, threaten, in some places, to bisect the waters
which they have long adorned; and, in course of ages, they will cause
some of the lakes to dwindle into numerous and insignificant pools;
which, in their turn, will finally be filled up. But, checking these
intrusive calculations, let us rather be content with appearances as they   895
are, and pursue in imagination the meandering shores, whether rugged
steeps, admitting of no cultivation, descend into the water; or gently-
sloping lawns and woods, or flat and fertile meadows stretch between
the margin of the lake and the mountains. Among minuter recommendations will be noticed, especially along bays exposed to the   900
setting-in of strong winds, the curved rim of fine blue gravel, thrown
up in course of time by the waves, half of it perhaps gleaming from
under the water, and the corresponding half of a lighter hue; and in
other parts bordering the lake, groves, if I may so call them, of reeds
and bulrushes; or plots of water-lilies lifting up their large target-shaped   905
leaves to the breeze, while the white flower is heaving upon the wave.

884 But the MS.², 1820: But [altho *del.*] while MS.   886 of sweeping
outline that 1822: the sweeping line of which MS.: whose sweeping line often
MS.², 1820.   888 surfaces . . . fail 1822: surface . . . fails MS., 1820.
889 fertility MS.², 1820: fertility & beauty MS.   890 have 1822: happen
to have MS., 1820.   *After* raised. MS. *deletes*: [But the ch *del.*] But [? this *or* these]
action of Nature is unremitting action of Nature cannot be stopped at the point
where local beauty may begin to suffer injury, the   These 1820: The MS.
892 ages MS.², 1820: time MS.   893 some of the lakes 1820: them MS.
894–5 But . . . us rather 1822: But the man of taste will say, it is an impertinent
calculation that leads to such unwelcome conclusions;—let us rather 1820: [But
del.] The man of taste will [not thank me *del.*] say [that it *del.*] this is an impertinent calculation that leads to such unwelcome conclusions. [Leaving it to the
God of nature to take charge of her momentous ⟨? enormous⟩ processes *del.*] Let us
[humbly *del.*] rather MS.   896 shores, MS.², 1820: shores, sometimes under
mountains MS.   897 descend MS.², 1820: descend abruptly MS.   water
MS.², 1820: waters MS.   897–8 or gently-sloping 1822: or the shore is
formed by gently-sloping MS., 1820.   898 woods 1823: rich woods MS.,
1820–2.   or flat . . . stretch 1822: or by flat . . . stretching 1820: or by the
interposition of flat & fertile meadows [by the *del.*] MS.   900–3 will
be . . . lighter hue 1823: [we shall *del.* MS.] will be noted with pleasure the curved
rim of fine blue gravel [in many places *del.* MS.] thrown up by the waves, especially
in bays exposed to [to om. MS.] the setting-in of [stronger MS.] strong winds MS.,
1820.   903–4 and in . . . bordering 1823: and, bordering 1822: here and
there are found, bordering MS., 1820.   905 target-shaped 1822: circular
MS., 1820.   906 breeze MS.², 1820: breeze if it be stirring MS.

To these may naturally be added the birds that enliven the waters. Wild-ducks in spring-time hatch their young in the islands, and upon reedy shores;—the sand-piper, flitting along the stony margins, by its restless note attracts the eye to motions as restless:—upon some jutting rock, or at the edge of a smooth meadow, the stately heron may be descried with folded wings, that might seem to have caught their delicate hue from the blue waters, by the side of which she watches for her sustenance. In winter, the lakes are sometimes resorted to by wild swans; and in that season habitually by widgeons, goldings, and other aquatic fowl of the smaller species. Let me be allowed the aid of verse to describe the evolutions which these visitants sometimes perform, on a fine day towards the close of winter.

> Mark how the feather'd tenants of the flood,
> With grace of motion that might scarcely seem
> Inferior to angelical, prolong
> Their curious pastime! shaping in mid air
> (And sometimes with ambitious wing that soars
> High as the level of the mountain tops,)
> A circuit ampler than the lake beneath,
> Their own domain;—but ever, while intent
> On tracing and retracing that large round,
> Their jubilant activity evolves
> Hundreds of curves and circlets, to and fro,
> Upward and downward, progress intricate
> Yet unperplex'd, as if one spirit swayed
> Their indefatigable flight.—'Tis done—
> Ten times, or more, I fancied it had ceased;
> But lo! the vanish'd company again
> Ascending;—they approach—I hear their wings
> Faint, faint, at first, and then an eager sound
> Past in a moment—and as faint again!
> They tempt the sun to sport amid their plumes;
> They tempt the water or the gleaming ice,
> To shew them a fair image;—'tis themselves,
> Their own fair forms, upon the glimmering plain,
> Painted more soft and fair as they descend
> Almost to touch;—then up again aloft,
> Up with a sally and a flash of speed,
> As if they scorn'd both resting-place and rest!

The ISLANDS, dispersed among these lakes, are neither so

907–45 *Not in* MS., 1820–22.   945/6 M.S. 1823: *om.* 1835.   946 dispersed . . . lakes 1823: *not in* MS., 1820–2.

numerous nor so beautiful as might be expected from the account that
has been given of the manner in which the level areas of the vales are
so frequently diversified by rocks, hills, and hillocks, scattered over
them; nor are they ornamented (as are several of the lakes in Scotland   950
and Ireland) by the remains of castles or other places of defence; nor
with the still more interesting ruins of religious edifices. Every one
must regret that scarcely a vestige is left of the Oratory, consecrated
to the Virgin, which stood upon Chapel-Holm in Windermere, and
that the Chauntry has disappeared, where mass used to be sung, upon   955
St. Herbert's Island, Derwent-water. The islands of the last-mentioned
lake are neither fortunately placed nor of pleasing shape; but if the
wood upon them were managed with more taste, they might become
interesting features in the landscape. There is a beautiful cluster on
Winandermere; a pair pleasingly contrasted upon Rydal; nor must the   960
solitary green island of Grasmere be forgotten. In the bosom of each
of the lakes of Ennerdale and Devockwater is a single rock, which,
owing to its neighbourhood to the sea, is—

"The haunt of cormorants and sea-mews' clang,"

a music well suited to the stern and wild character of the several   965
scenes! It may be worth while here to mention (not as an object of
beauty, but of curiosity) that there occasionally appears above the
surface of Derwent-water, and always in the same place, a considerable
tract of spongy ground covered with aquatic plants, which is called
the Floating, but with more propriety might be named the Buoyant,   970
Island; and, on one of the pools near the lake of Esthwaite, may sometimes be seen a mossy Islet, with trees upon it, shifting about before
the wind, a lusus naturæ frequent on the great rivers of America, and
not unknown in other parts of the world.

————"fas habeas invisere Tiburis arva,   975
Albuneæque lacum, atque umbras terrasque natantes."*

* See that admirable Idyllium, the Catillus and Salia, of Landor.

947–8 that has been 1822: I have MS.², 1820: which I have MS.   950 several
1823: several islands 1820–2: sometimes the islands MS.   951 and Ireland 1822:
not in MS., 1820.   castles MS., 1823: old castles 1820–2.   951–2 nor with
. . . religious 1823: or of monastic MS., 1820–2.   952–9 Every one . . .
landscape. 1822: *not in* MS., 1820.   952–7 Every one . . . lake 1823: Those
upon Derwent-water 1822.   959 is 1822: is however MS., 1820.   on
1823: of islands on 1820–2: of islands at MS.   960 pair MS.², 1820: pair of
MS.   upon 1820: at MS.   961 of [*first*] MS., 1823: in 1822: at 1820.
964 sea-mews' MS., 1820–3, *Edd.*: sea-mew's 1835.   966–76 It may . . .
natantes."* 1823: *not in* MS., 1820–2.

This part of the subject may be concluded with observing—that, from the multitude of brooks and torrents that fall into these lakes, and of internal springs by which they are fed, and which circulate through them like veins, they are truly living lakes, *"vivi lacus;"* and are 980 thus discriminated from the stagnant and sullen pools frequent among mountains that have been formed by volcanoes, and from the shallow meres found in flat and fenny countries. The water is also of crystalline purity; so that, if it were not for the reflections of the incumbent mountains by which it is darkened, a delusion might be felt, by a 985 person resting quietly in a boat on the bosom of Winandermere or Derwent-water, similar to that which Carver so beautifully describes when he was floating alone in the middle of lake Erie or Ontario, and could almost have imagined that his boat was suspended in an element as pure as air, or rather that the air and water were one.   990

Having spoken of Lakes I must not omit to mention, as a kindred feature of this country, those bodies of still water called Tarns. In the economy of nature these are useful, as auxiliaries to Lakes; for if the whole quantity of water which falls upon the mountains in time of storm were poured down upon the plains without intervention, in 995 some quarters, of such receptacles, the habitable grounds would be much more subject than they are to inundation. But, as some of the

977 This part . . . observing MS., 1820: So much for the form and size of lakes in general as illustrative of these in particular.—Their size and forms being thus in general terms described, I may add 1810.   978 torrents that 1820: torrents which MS., 1810.   these lakes MS., 1820: them 1810.   979 *After* springs MS. *writes:* &c. (*Two thirds of the last manuscript page is left blank.*) 983 found 1820: which are found 1810.   983–4 of crystalline purity 1823: pure and crystalline 1810–22.   990/1 As to the shores, it will be understood that those of the lakes in this country are endlessly diversified; in some places mountains, that admit of no cultivation, descend abruptly into the water; in others the shore is formed by gently sloping lawns and rich woods, with the interposition of flat and fertile meadows between the margin of the lake and the mountains; in many places they are beautifully edged with a rim of blue gravel; here and there are found, bordering the lake, groves (if I may so call them) of reeds and bulrushes, or water-lilies lifting up the orb of their large leaves to the breeze, if it be stirring, while the white flower is heaving upon the wave. The Islands are neither so numerous, nor so beautiful, as might be expected from the account which I have given of the manner in which the level areas of the vales are so frequently diversified by rocks, hills, and hillocks, scattered over them: nor are they ornamented, as are sometimes the islands of the lakes in Scotland, by the remains of castles or other places of defence, or of monastic edifices. There is however a beautiful cluster of islands at Winandermere; a pair of pleasingly contrasted at Rydale; nor must the solitary green Island of Grasmere be forgotten. In the bosom of each of the lakes of Ennerdale and Devock-water is a single rock which owing to its neighbourhood to the sea, is

"The haunt of Cormorants and Sea-mews clang;"

a music well suited to the stern and wild character of the several scenes. 1810. (*Cf.* 896–906; 946–52; 959–66.)
992 called 1820: which are called 1810.   993–1004 In the economy . . . of rain 1823: *not in* 1810–22.

collateral brooks spend their fury, finding a free course toward and
also down the channel of the main stream of the vale before those that
have to pass through the higher tarns and lakes have filled their   1000
several basins, a gradual distribution is effected; and the waters thus
reserved, instead of uniting, to spread ravage and deformity, with
those which meet with no such detention, contribute to support, for a
length of time, the vigour of many streams without a fresh fall of rain.
Tarns are found in some of the vales, and are numerous upon the   1005
mountains. A Tarn, in a *Vale*, implies, for the most part, that the bed
of the vale is not happily formed; that the water of the brooks can
neither wholly escape, nor diffuse itself over a large area. Accordingly,
in such situations, Tarns are often surrounded by an unsightly tract of
boggy ground; but this is not always the case, and in the cultivated   1010
parts of the country, when the shores of the Tarn are determined, it
differs only from the Lake in being smaller, and in belonging mostly
to a smaller valley, or circular recess. Of this class of miniature lakes,
Loughrigg Tarn, near Grasmere, is the most beautiful example. It has
a margin of green firm meadows, of rocks, and rocky woods, a few   1015
reeds here, a little company of water-lilies there, with beds of gravel
or stone beyond; a tiny stream issuing neither briskly nor sluggishly
out of it; but its feeding rills, from the shortness of their course, so
small as to be scarcely visible. Five or six cottages are reflected in its
peaceful bosom; rocky and barren steeps rise up above the hanging   1020
enclosures; and the solemn pikes of Langdale overlook, from a distance,
the low cultivated ridge of land that forms the northern boundary of
this small, quiet, and fertile domain. The *mountain* Tarns can only be
recommended to the notice of the inquisitive traveller who has time to
spare. They are difficult of access and naked; yet some of them are, in   1025
their permanent forms, very grand; and there are accidents of things
which would make the meanest of them interesting. At all events,
one of these pools is an acceptable sight to the mountain wanderer;
not merely as an incident that diversifies the prospect, but as forming
in his mind a centre or conspicuous point to which objects, otherwise   1030
disconnected or insubordinated, may be referred. Some few have a
varied outline, with bold heath-clad promontories; and, as they mostly

998–9 toward and also 1835: *not in* 1823.   1002 uniting, to 1835: uniting
with those which meet with no such detention to 1823.   1002–3 deformity,
with . . . contribute 1835: deformity, contribute 1823.   1005 Tarns 1823:
These 1810–22.   vales 1823: vallies 1810–22.   numerous 1822: very numerous
1810–20.   1009–10 an unsightly . . . ground 1822: a tract of boggy ground
which has an unsightly appearance 1810–20.   1013 class of . . . lakes 1820:
miniature class of lakes 1810.   1015 a [*first*] 1820: its 1810.   1027 At
all events 1820: In the first place 1810.   1030 centre 1820: spot 1810.
1031 insubordinated 1835: unsubordinated 1810–23.

lie at the foot of a steep precipice, the water where the sun is not
shining upon it, appears black and sullen; and, round the margin, huge
stones and masses of rock are scattered; some defying conjecture as to   1035
the means by which they came thither; and others obviously fallen
from on high—the contribution of ages! A not unpleasing sadness is
induced by this perplexity, and these images of decay; while the
prospect of a body of pure water unattended with groves and other
cheerful rural images by which fresh water is usually accompanied,   1040
and unable to give furtherance to the meagre vegetation around it—
excites a sense of some repulsive power strongly put forth, and thus
deepens the melancholy natural to such scenes. Nor is the feeling of
solitude often more forcibly or more solemnly impressed than by the
side of one of these mountain pools: though desolate and forbidding,   1045
it seems a distinct place to repair to; yet where the visitants must be
rare, and there can be no disturbance. Water-fowl flock hither; and
the lonely Angler may here be seen; but the imagination, not content
with this scanty allowance of society, is tempted to attribute a voluntary
power to every change which takes place in such a spot, whether it be   1050
the breeze that wanders over the surface of the water, or the splendid
lights of evening resting upon it in the midst of awful precipices.

> "There, sometimes does a leaping fish
> Send through the tarn a lonely cheer;
> The crags repeat the raven's croak   1055
> In symphony austere:
> Thither the rainbow comes, the cloud,
> And mists that spread the flying shroud,
> And sunbeams, and the sounding blast."

It will be observed that this country is bounded on the south and   1060
west by the sea, which combines beautifully, from many elevated

1033–4 where the . . . upon it 1820: *not in* 1810.   1034–5 huge stones
and 1820: *not in* 1810.   1035–43 some defying . . . scenes. 1820: *not
in* 1810.   1036 thither 1822: there 1820.   1037–43 A not . . .
scenes. 1822: The sense, also, of some repulsive power strongly put forth—
excited by the prospect of a body of pure water . . . to give any furtherance to the
meagre vegetation around it—heightens the melancholy natural to such scenes.
1820.   1041 furtherance 1823: any furtherance 1822.   1043–4 Nor
is . . . forcibly or 1820: The feeling of solitude is seldom more strongly and 1810.
1048 here 1823: oftentimes here 1810–22.   1049 scanty allowance of
society 1820: *not in* 1810.   1052 resting 1820: that rest 1810.   awful 1820:
the awful 1810.   1053 does 1820: doth 1810.   1060–8 It will be . . .
have the streams 1822: Though this country is, on one side, bounded by the sea,
which combines beautifully, from some elevated points of view, with the inland
scenery; yet the æstuaries cannot pretend to vie with those of Scotland and Wales
[yet no where are found the grand estuaries which are common in Scotland and Wales
1810]:—the Lakes are such in the strict and usual sense of the word, being all of
fresh water; nor have the Rivers [rivers themselves 1810] 1810–20.   1061 west
Edd.: east 1822–35.

points, with the inland scenery; and, from the bay of Morcamb, the sloping shores and back-ground of distant mountains are seen, composing pictures equally distinguished for amenity and grandeur. But the æstuaries on this coast are in a great measure bare at low water*; and there is no instance of the sea running far up among the mountains, and mingling with the Lakes, which are such in the strict and usual sense of the word, being of fresh water. Nor have the streams, from the shortness of their course, time to acquire that body of water necessary to confer upon them much majesty. In fact, the most considerable, while they continue in the mountain and lake-country, are rather large brooks than rivers. The water is perfectly pellucid, through which in many places are seen, to a great depth, their beds of rock, or of blue gravel, which give to the water itself an exquisitely cerulean colour: this is particularly striking in the rivers Derwent and Duddon, which may be compared, such and so various are their beauties, to any two rivers of equal length of course in any country. The number of the torrents and smaller brooks is infinite, with their water-falls and water-breaks; and they need not here be described. I will only observe that, as many, even of the smallest rills, have either found, or made for themselves, recesses in the sides of the mountains or in the vales, they have tempted the primitive inhabitants to settle near them for shelter; and hence, cottages so placed, by seeming to withdraw from the eye, are the more endeared to the feelings.

The Woods consist chiefly of oak, ash, and birch, and here and there Wych-elm, with underwood of hazle, the white and black thorn, and hollies; in moist places alders and willows abound; and yews among the rocks. Formerly the whole country must have been covered with wood to a great height up the mountains; where native Scotch

1065

1070

1075

1080

1085

* In fact there is not an instance of a harbour on the Cumberland side of the Solway frith that is not dry at low water; that of Ravenglass, at the mouth of the Esk, as a natural harbour is much the best. The Sea appears to have been retiring slowly for ages from this coast. From Whitehaven to St. Bees extends a track of level ground, about five miles in length, which formerly must have been under salt water, so as to have made an island of the high ground that stretches between it and the Sea.

1064 amenity and grandeur 1823: grandeur and amenity 1822.   1066 water* 1835: water [*no note appended*] 1822–3.   1070–1 the most considerable [of them 1822] 1822–35: *not in* 1810–20.   1072 are 1822: they are 1810–20. 1076 may 1820: may confidently 1810.   1080 smallest 1835: smallest of these 1810–23.   1083 shelter 1820: household accommodation and for shelter 1810. 1083–4 cottages so . . . feelings 1822: the retirement and seclusion by which these cottages are endeared to the eye of the man of sensibility 1810–20. 1086 there 1820: there (though very rarely) 1810.   Wych-elm 1835: a species of elm 1810–23.   1087 in 1820: in the 1810.

firs* must have grown in great profusion, as they do in the northern 1090
part of Scotland to this day. But not one of these old inhabitants has
existed, perhaps, for some hundreds of years; the beautiful traces,
however, of the universal sylvan† appearance the country formerly
had, yet survive in the native coppice-woods that have been protected
by inclosures, and also in the forest-trees and hollies, which, though 1095
disappearing fast, are yet scattered both over the inclosed and uninclosed parts of the mountains. The same is expressed by the beauty
and intricacy with which the fields and coppice-woods are often intermingled: the plough of the first settlers having followed naturally the
veins of richer, dryer, or less stony soil; and thus it has shaped out an 1100
intermixture of wood and lawn, with a grace and wildness which it
would have been impossible for the hand of studied art to produce.
Other trees have been introduced within these last fifty years, such as
beeches, larches, limes, &c. and plantations of firs, seldom with
advantage, and often with great injury to the appearance of the country; 1105
but the sycamore (which I believe was brought into this island from
Germany, not more than two hundred years ago) has long been the
favourite of the cottagers; and, with the fir, has been chosen to screen
their dwellings; and is sometimes found in the fields whither the winds
or the waters may have carried its seeds. 1110

The want most felt, however, is that of timber trees. There are few
magnificent ones to be found near any of the lakes; and unless greater
care be taken, there will, in a short time, scarcely be left an ancient oak
that would repay the cost of felling. The neighbourhood of Rydal, notwithstanding the havoc which has been made, is yet nobly distinguished. 1115

---

* This species of fir is in character much superior to the American which has
usurped its place: Where the fir is planted for ornament, let it be by all means of
the aboriginal species, which can only be procured from the Scotch nurseries.
   † A squirrel (so I have heard the old people of Wytheburn say) might have
gone from their chapel to Keswick without alighting on the ground.

1090 firs* 1835: firs [*no note appended*] 1810–23.   1090–1 must have . . .
day. 1823: (as in the northern part of Scotland to this day) must have grown in
great profusion. 1810–22.   1091 not 1822: no 1810–20.   1091–2 has
existed, perhaps 1822: of the country remains, or perhaps has done 1810–20.
1092 the beautiful 1835: beautiful 1810–23.   1093 sylvan† 1823: sylvan [*no note
appended*] 1810–22.   the [*second*] 1820: which the 1810.   1094 yet . . . coppice-
woods that 1822: are yet seen, both in the native coppice-woods that [which 1810]
remain, and [which 1810] 1810–20.   1096 both over 1820: over both 1810.
1101 with a grace . . . which 1820: the grace . . . of which 1810.   1104 larches,
limes 1820: larches, elms, limes 1810.   firs 1835: Scotch firs 1810–23.
1108 fir 1835: Scotch fir 1810–23.   1109 dwellings; 1810–23, *Edd.*: dwellings:
1835.   1110 the waters 1835: waters 1810–23.   1111 want 1820: want
which is 1810.   few 1810–23, *Errata:* a few 1835.   1112 and 1820: and indeed
1810.   1113 ancient 1820: *not in* 1810.   1115 distinguished. 1820:
distinguished; and we have reason to hope, will long continue so. 1810.

In the woods of Lowther, also, is found an almost matchless store of ancient trees, and the majesty and wildness of the native forest.

　　Among the smaller vegetable ornaments must be reckoned the bilberry, a ground plant, never so beautiful as in early spring, when it is seen under bare or budding trees, that imperfectly intercept the 1120 sun-shine, covering the rocky knolls with a pure mantle of fresh verdure, more lively than the herbage of the open fields;—the broom that spreads luxuriantly along rough pastures, and in the month of June interveins the steep copses with its golden blossoms;—and the juniper, a rich evergreen, that thrives in spite of cattle, upon the 1125 uninclosed parts of the mountains:—the Dutch myrtle diffuses fragrance in moist places; and there is an endless variety of brilliant flowers in the fields and meadows, which, if the agriculture of the country were more carefully attended to, would disappear. Nor can I omit again to notice the lichens and mosses: their profusion, beauty, 1130 and variety, exceed those of any other country I have seen.

　　It may now be proper to say a few words respecting climate, and "skiey influences," in which this region, as far as the character of its landscapes is affected by them, may, upon the whole, be considered fortunate. The country is, indeed, subject to much bad weather, and it 1135 has been ascertained that twice as much rain falls here as in many parts of the island; but the number of black drizzling days, that blot out the face of things, is by no means *proportionally* great. Nor is a continuance of thick, flagging, damp air, so common as in the West of England and Ireland. The rain here comes down heartily, and is frequently suc- 1140 ceeded by clear, bright weather, when every brook is vocal, and every torrent sonorous; brooks and torrents, which are never muddy, even in the heaviest floods, except, after a drought, they happen to be defiled for a short time by waters that have swept along dusty roads, or have broken out into ploughed fields. Days of unsettled weather, 1145 with partial showers, are very frequent; but the showers, darkening, or brightening, as they fly from hill to hill, are not less grateful to the eye than finely interwoven passages of gay and sad music are touching to the ear. Vapours exhaling from the lakes and meadows after sun-rise, in a hot season, or, in moist weather, brooding upon the heights, or 1150 descending towards the valleys with inaudible motion, give a visionary

1116 is found an almost matchless store 1820: are found store [*sic*] 1810. 1117 ancient 1822: the grandest 1810–20.　　and the 1823: and all the 1810–22. 1118 ornaments 1822: ornaments provided here by nature 1820: ornaments which nature has here provided 1810.　　　1119–27 bilberry . . . there is an 1822: juniper, bilberry, and the broom-plant, with which the hills and woods abound; the Dutch myrtle in moist places; and the 1810–20.　　　1124 interveins 1823: intervenes [*sic*] 1822.　　　1130 mosses: their 1820: mosses, which, in 1810. 1132–265 *Not in* 1810–20.

character to everything around them; and are in themselves so beautiful, as to dispose us to enter into the feelings of those simple nations (such as the Laplanders of this day) by whom they are taken for guardian deities of the mountains; or to sympathise with others who have fancied these delicate apparitions to be the spirits of their departed ancestors. Akin to these are fleecy clouds resting upon the hill-tops; they are not easily managed in picture, with their accompaniments of blue sky; but how glorious are they in nature! how pregnant with imagination for the poet! and the height of the Cumbrian mountains is sufficient to exhibit daily and hourly instances of those mysterious attachments. Such clouds, cleaving to their stations, or lifting up suddenly their glittering heads from behind rocky barriers, or hurrying out of sight with speed of the sharpest edge—will often tempt an inhabitant to congratulate himself on belonging to a country of mists and clouds and storms, and make him think of the blank sky of Egypt, and of the cerulean vacancy of Italy, as an unanimated and even a sad spectacle. The atmosphere, however, as in every country subject to much rain, is frequently unfavourable to landscape, especially when keen winds succeed the rain which are apt to produce coldness, spottiness, and an unmeaning or repulsive detail in the distance; —a sunless frost, under a canopy of leaden and shapeless clouds, is, as far as it allows things to be seen, equally disagreeable.

It has been said that in human life there are moments worth ages. In a more subdued tone of sympathy may we affirm, that in the climate of England there are, for the lover of nature, days which are worth whole months,—I might say—even years. One of these favoured days sometimes occurs in spring-time, when that soft air is breathing over the blossoms and new-born verdure, which inspired Buchanan with his beautiful Ode to the first of May; the air, which, in the luxuriance of his fancy, he likens to that of the golden age,—to that which gives motion to the funereal cypresses on the banks of Lethe;—to the air which is to salute beatified spirits when expiatory fires shall have consumed the earth with all her habitations. But it is in autumn that days of such affecting influence most frequently intervene;—the atmosphere seems refined, and the sky rendered more crystalline, as the vivifying heat of the year abates; the lights and shadows are more delicate; the coloring is richer and more finely harmonized; and, in this season of stillness, the ear being unoccupied, or only gently excited, the sense of vision becomes more susceptible of its appropriate enjoyments. A resident in a country like this which we are treating of, will agree with me, that the presence of a lake is indispensable to exhibit in perfection the beauty of one of these days; and he must have

1155
1160
1165
1170
1175
1180
1185
1190

1168 every 1823: every other 1822.   1174–262 *Not in* 1822.

experienced, while looking on the unruffled waters, that the imagination, by their aid, is carried into recesses of feeling otherwise im-   1195
penetrable. The reason of this is, that the heavens are not only brought
down into the bosom of the earth, but that the earth is mainly looked at,
and thought of, through the medium of a purer element. The happiest
time is when the equinoxial gales are departed; but their fury may
probably be called to mind by the sight of a few shattered boughs,   1200
whose leaves do not differ in colour from the faded foliage of the
stately oaks from which these relics of the storm depend: all else
speaks of tranquillity;—not a breath of air, no restlessness of insects,
and not a moving object perceptible—except the clouds gliding in the
depths of the lake, or the traveller passing along, an inverted image,   1205
whose motion seems governed by the quiet of a time, to which its
archetype, the living person, is, perhaps, insensible:—or it may
happen, that the figure of one of the larger birds, a raven or a heron,
is crossing silently among the reflected clouds, while the voice of the
real bird, from the element aloft, gently awakens in the spectator the   1210
recollection of appetites and instincts, pursuits and occupations, that
deform and agitate the world,—yet have no power to prevent nature
from putting on an aspect capable of satisfying the most intense
cravings for the tranquil, the lovely, and the perfect, to which man, the
noblest of her creatures, is subject.   1215

Thus far, of climate, as influencing the feelings through its effect
on the objects of sense. We may add, that whatever has been said upon
the advantages derived to these scenes from a changeable atmosphere,
would apply, perhaps still more forcibly, to their appearance under the
varied solemnities of night. Milton, it will be remembered, has given   1220
a *clouded* moon to Paradise itself. In the night-season also, the narrowness of the vales, and comparative smallness of the lakes, are especially
adapted to bring surrounding objects home to the eye and to the heart.
The stars, taking their stations above the hill-tops, are contemplated
from a spot like the Abyssinian recess of Rasselas, with much more   1225
touching interest than they are likely to excite when looked at from
an open country with ordinary undulations: and it must be obvious,
that it is the *bays* only of large lakes that can present such contrasts of
light and shadow as those of smaller dimensions display from every
quarter. A deep contracted valley, with diffused waters, such a valley   1230
and plains level and wide as those of Chaldea, are the two extremes in
which the beauty of the heavens and their connexion with the earth are
most sensibly felt. Nor do the advantages I have been speaking of
imply here an exclusion of the aerial effects of distance. These are
insured by the height of the mountains, and are found, even in the   1235

1199 time 1823, *Errata*: times 1835.   1230 such a valley 1835: *not in* 1823.

narrowest vales, where they lengthen in perspective, or act (if the
expression may be used) as telescopes for the open country.

The subject would bear to be enlarged upon: but I will conclude this
section with a night-scene suggested by the Vale of Keswick. The
Fragment is well known; but it gratifies me to insert it, as the Writer   1240
was one of the first who led the way to a worthy admiration of this
country.

> "Now sunk the sun, now twilight sunk, and night
> Rode in her zenith; not a passing breeze
> Sigh'd to the grove, which in the midnight air   1245
> Stood motionless, and in the peaceful floods
> Inverted hung: for now the billows slept
> Along the shore, nor heav'd the deep; but spread
> A shining mirror to the moon's pale orb,
> Which, dim and waning, o'er the shadowy cliffs,   1250
> The solemn woods, and spiry mountain tops,
> Her glimmering faintness threw: now every eye,
> Oppress'd with toil, was drown'd in deep repose,
> Save that the unseen Shepherd in his watch,
> Propp'd on his crook, stood listening by the fold,   1255
> And gaz'd the starry vault, and pendant moon;
> Nor voice, nor sound, broke on the deep serene;
> But the soft murmur of swift-gushing rills,
> Forth issuing from the mountain's distant steep,
> (Unheard till now, and now scarce heard) proclaim'd   1260
> All things at rest, and imag'd the still voice
> Of quiet, whispering in the ear of night."*

* Dr. Brown, the author of this fragment, was from his infancy brought up in
Cumberland, and should have remembered that the practice of folding sheep by
night is unknown among these mountains, and that the image of the Shepherd upon
the watch is out of its place, and belongs only to countries, with a warmer climate,
that are subject to ravages from beasts of prey. It is pleasing to notice a dawn of
imaginative feeling in these verses. Tickel, a man of no common genius, chose, for
the subject of a Poem, Kensington Gardens, in preference to the Banks of the
Derwent, within a mile or two of which he was born. But this was in the reign of
Queen Anne, or George the first. Progress must have been made in the interval;
though the traces of it, except in the works of Thomson and Dyer, are not very
obvious.

1258 swift-gushing *Errata*: soft-gushing 1823–35.   1262 n. *Dr. Brown . . .
was from his infancy brought up in Cumberland 1835: *Dr. Brown . . . was a native
of Cumberland 1823.

SECTION SECOND.

ASPECT OF THE COUNTRY, AS AFFECTED BY ITS INHABITANTS.

1265

Hitherto I have chiefly spoken of the features by which nature has discriminated this country from others. I will now describe, in general terms, in what manner it is indebted to the hand of man. What I have to notice on this subject will emanate most easily and perspicuously from a description of the ancient and present inhabitants, their 1270 occupations, their condition of life, the distribution of landed property among them, and the tenure by which it is holden.

The reader will suffer me here to recall to his mind the shapes of the vallies, and their position with respect to each other, and the forms and substance of the intervening mountains. He will people the vallies 1275 with lakes and rivers: the coves and sides of the mountains with pools and torrents; and will bound half of the circle which we have contemplated by the sands of the sea, or by the sea itself. He will conceive that, from the point upon which he stood, he looks down upon this scene before the country had been penetrated by any inhabitants:—to 1280 vary his sensations, and to break in upon their stillness, he will form to himself an image of the tides visiting and re-visiting the friths, the main sea dashing against the bolder shore, the rivers pursuing their course to be lost in the mighty mass of waters. He may see or hear in fancy the winds sweeping over the lakes, or piping with a loud voice 1285 among the mountain peaks; and, lastly, may think of the primeval woods shedding and renewing their leaves with no human eye to notice, or human heart to regret or welcome the change. "When the first settlers entered this region (says an animated writer) they found it overspread with wood; forest trees, the fir, the oak, the ash, and the 1290 birch had skirted the fells, tufted the hills, and shaded the vallies, through centuries of silent solitude; the birds and beasts of prey reigned over the meeker species; and the *bellum inter omnia* maintained the balance of nature in the empire of beasts."

Such was the state and appearance of this region when the aboriginal 1295 colonists of the Celtic tribes were first driven or drawn towards it, and became joint tenants with the wolf, the boar, the wild bull, the red deer, and the leigh, a gigantic species of deer which has been long extinct; while the inaccessible crags were occupied by the falcon, the

1266 Hitherto 1823: Thus far 1810–22.   1273 suffer me here 1820: here suffer me 1810.   shapes 1820: description which I have given of the substance and form of these mountains, the shape 1810.   1274–5 and the . . . mountains 1820: *not in* 1810.   1276 coves and sides 1820: sides and coves 1810.   1279 stood 1822: before stood 1810–20.

raven, and the eagle. The inner parts were too secluded, and of too 1300 little value, to participate much of the benefit of Roman manners; and though these conquerors encouraged the Britons to the improvement of their lands in the plain country of Furness and Cumberland, they seem to have had little connexion with the mountains, except for military purposes, or in subservience to the profit they drew from the 1305 mines.

When the Romans retired from Great Britain, it is well known that these mountain-fastnesses furnished a protection to some unsubdued Britons, long after the more accessible and more fertile districts had been seized by the Saxon or Danish invader. A few, though distinct, 1310 traces of Roman forts or camps, as at Ambleside, and upon Dunmallet, and a few circles of rude stones attributed to the Druids,* are the

---

* It is not improbable that these circles were once numerous, and that many of them may yet endure in a perfect state, under no very deep covering of soil. A friend of the Author, while making a trench in a level piece of ground, not far from the banks of the Emont, but in no connection with that river, met with some stones which seemed to him formally arranged; this excited his curiosity, and proceeding, he uncovered a perfect circle of stones, from two to three or four feet high, with a *sanctum sanctorum*,—the whole a complete place of Druidical worship of small dimensions, having the same sort of relation to Stonehenge, Long Meg and her Daughters near the river Eden, and Karl Lofts near Shap (if this last be not Danish), that a rural chapel bears to a stately church, or to one of our noble cathedrals. This interesting little monument having passed, with the field in which it was found, into other hands, has been destroyed. It is much to be regretted, that the striking relic of antiquity at Shap has been in a great measure destroyed also.

The DAUGHTERS of LONG MEG are placed not in an oblong, as the STONES of SHAP, but in a perfect circle, eighty yards in diameter, and seventy-two in number, and from above three yards high, to less than so many feet: a little way out of the circle stands LONG MEG herself—a single stone eighteen feet high.

When the Author first saw this monument, he came upon it by surprize, therefore might over-rate its importance as an object; but he must say, that though it is not to be compared with Stonehenge, he has not seen any other remains of those dark ages, which can pretend to rival it in singularity and dignity of appearance.

> A weight of awe not easy to be borne
> Fell suddenly upon my spirit, cast
> From the dread bosom of the unknown past,
> When first I saw that sisterhood forlorn;—
> And Her, whose strength and stature seem to scorn
> The power of years—pre-eminent, and placed
> Apart, to overlook the circle vast.
> Speak, Giant-mother! tell it to the Morn,
> While she dispels the cumbrous shades of night;
> Let the Moon hear, emerging from a cloud,
> When, how, and wherefore, rose on British ground
> That wondrous Monument, whose mystic round
> Forth shadows, some have deemed, to mortal sight
> The inviolable God that tames the proud.

1304-5 except for . . . subservience 1820: which were not subservient 1810. 1312 and a few 1822: and two or three 1820: (erected probably to secure a quiet transfer of the ore from the mines) and two or three 1810.　　Druids,* 1822: Druids, [*no note appended*] 1810-20.　　　　　　1312 n. *In the second sentence,*

only vestiges that remain upon the surface of the country, of these ancient occupants; and, as the Saxons and Danes, who succeeded to the possession of the villages and hamlets which had been established 1315 by the Britons, seem at first to have confined themselves to the open country,—we may descend at once to times long posterior to the conquest by the Normans, when their feudal polity was regularly established. We may easily conceive that these narrow dales and mountain sides, choaked up as they must have been with wood, lying 1320 out of the way of communication with other parts of the Island, and upon the edge of a hostile kingdom, could have little attraction for the high-born and powerful; especially as the more open parts of the country furnished positions for castles and houses of defence, sufficient to repel any of those sudden attacks, which, in the then rude state of 1325 military knowledge, could be made upon them. Accordingly, the more retired regions (and to such I am now confining myself) must have been neglected or shunned even by the persons whose baronial or signorial rights extended over them, and left, doubtless, partly as a place of refuge for outlaws and robbers, and partly granted out for the 1330 more settled habitation of a few vassals following the employment of shepherds or woodlanders. Hence these lakes and inner vallies are unadorned by any remains of ancient grandeur, castles, or monastic

following sort of relation to, 1822 *reads*: the STONES OF SHAP, or LONG MEG and her DAUGHTERS, near the banks of the Eden, that a rural chapel bears to our noble cathedrals.

After the fourth sentence, ending destroyed also, 1822 *continues*: It is thus described in the History of Westmorland:—"Towards the south end of the village of Shap, near the turnpike road, on the east side thereof, there is a remarkable monument of antiquity; which is an area upwards of half a mile in length, and between twenty and thirty yards broad, encompassed with large stones (with which that country abounds), many of them three or four yards in diameter, at eight, ten, or twelve yards distance, which are of such immense height that no carriage now in use could support them. Undoubtedly this hath been a place of Druid worship, which they always performed in the open air, within this kind of enclosure, shaded with wood, as this place of old time appears to have been, although there is now scarce a tree to be seen, (*Shap-thorn* only excepted, planted on top of the hill for the direction of travellers). At the high end of this place of worship there is a circle of the like stones about eighteen feet in diameter, which was their *sanctum sanctorum*, (as it were), and place of sacrifice. The stone is a kind of granite, and when broken appears beautifully variegated with bright shining spots, like spar. The country people have blasted and carried away some of these stones, for the foundation-stones of buildings. In other places some have cut these stones (but with difficulty) for mill-stones. When polished they would make beautiful chimney-pieces." Some contend that this is a Danish monument. 1822 *here continues as in* 1823–35 (The DAUGHTERS *etc.*).

In the fifth line of verse: seem 1823: seems 1822.

1313 only 1820: only visible 1810.   1316 at first 1820: *not in* 1810.
1318 polity 1820: policy 1810.   1320 must have been 1820: would be 1810.
1322 could 1820: would 1810.   1327 to such 1822: observe, it is to these
1810–20.   1333 any 1822: any of the 1810–20.

edifices, which are only found upon the skirts of the country, as
Furness Abbey, Calder Abbey, the Priory of Lannercost, Gleaston   1335
Castle,—long ago a residence of the Flemings,—and the numerous
ancient castles of the Cliffords, the Lucys, and the Dacres. On the
southern side of these mountains, (especially in that part known by
the name of Furness Fells, which is more remote from the borders,) the
state of society would necessarily be more settled; though it also was   1340
fashioned, not a little, by its neighbourhood to a hostile kingdom. We
will, therefore, give a sketch of the economy of the Abbots in the
distribution of lands among their tenants, as similar plans were doubtless adopted by other Lords, and as the consequences have affected
the face of the country materially to the present day, being, in fact, one   1345
of the principal causes which give it such a striking superiority, in
beauty and interest, over all other parts of the island.

"When the Abbots of Furness," says an author before cited, "enfranchised their villains, and raised them to the dignity of customary
tenants, the lands, which they had cultivated for their lord, were   1350
divided into whole tenements; each of which, besides the customary
annual rent, was charged with the obligation of having in readiness a
man completely armed for the king's service on the borders, or elsewhere; each of these whole tenements was again subdivided into four
equal parts; each villain had one; and the party tenant contributed   1355
his share to the support of the man of arms, and of other burdens.
These divisions were not properly distinguished; the land remained
mixed; each tenant had a share through all the arable and meadow-
land, and common of pasture over all the wastes. These sub-tenements
were judged sufficient for the support of so many families; and no   1360
further division was permitted. These divisions and sub-divisions were
convenient at the time for which they were calculated: the land, so
parcelled out, was, of necessity more attended to, and the industry
greater, when more persons were to be supported by the produce of it.
The frontier of the kingdom, within which Furness was considered,   1365
was in a constant state of attack and defence; more hands, therefore,
were necessary to guard the coast, to repel an invasion from Scotland,
or make reprisals on the hostile neighbour. The dividing the lands in
such manner as has been shown, increased the number of inhabitants,
and kept them at home till called for: and, the land being mixed, and   1370
the several tenants united in equipping the plough, the absence of the
fourth man was no prejudice to the cultivation of his land, which was
committed to the care of three.

1334 of the 1822: of this 1810–20.   1336 long ago a 1820: the original
1810.   1337 the Lucys 1822: *not in* 1810–20.   1340–1 it also . . . little,
by 1822: it was . . . little, with the rest of the [this 1810] country by 1810–20.
1356 of arms 1835: at arms 1810–23.

"While the villains of Low Furness were thus distributed over the land, and employed in agriculture; those of High Furness were charged with the care of flocks and herds, to protect them from the wolves which lurked in the thickets, and in winter to browze them with the tender sprouts of hollies and ash. This custom was not till lately discontinued in High Furness; and holly-trees were carefully preserved for that purpose when all other wood was cleared off; large tracts of common being so covered with these trees, as to have the appearance of a forest of hollies. At the Shepherd's call, the flocks surrounded the holly-bush, and received the croppings at his hand, which they greedily nibbled up, bleating for more. The Abbots of Furness enfranchised these pastoral vassals, and permitted them to enclose *quillets* to their houses, for which they paid encroachment rent."— West's *Antiquities of Furness*.

However desirable, for the purposes of defence, a numerous population might be, it was not possible to make at once the same numerous allotments among the untilled vallies, and upon the sides of the mountains, as had been made in the cultivated plains. The enfranchised shepherd, or woodlander, having chosen there his place of residence, builds it of sods, or of the mountain-stone, and, with the permission of his lord, encloses, like Robinson Crusoe, a small croft or two immediately at his door for such animals as he wishes to protect. Others are happy to imitate his example, and avail themselves of the same privileges: and thus a population, mainly of Danish or Norse origin, as the dialect indicates, crept on towards the more secluded parts of the vallies. Chapels, daughters of some distant mother church, are first erected in the more open and fertile vales, as those of Bowness and Grasmere, offsets of Kendal: which again, after a period, as the settled population increases, become mother-churches to smaller edifices, planted, at length, in almost every dale throughout the country. The inclosures, formed by the tenantry, are for a long time confined to the home-steads; and the arable and meadow land of the vales is possessed in common field; the several portions being marked out by stones, bushes, or trees: which portions, where the custom has survived, to this day are called *dales*, from the word *deylen*, to distribute; but, while the valley was thus lying open, enclosures seem to have taken place upon the sides of the mountains; because the land there was not intermixed, and was of little comparative value; and, therefore, small opposition would be made to its being appropriated by those

1375

1380

1385

1390

1395

1400

1405

1410

1395 as 1822: chiefly as 1810–20.   1397–8 a population, mainly . . .
crept 1820: population creeps 1810.   1403 planted 1822: scattered 1810–20.
in almost every 1820: almost in every 1810.   1408 from the word 1820:
probably from the Belgic word 1810.   1409 valley 1820: vale 1810.

to whose habitations it was contiguous. Hence the singular appearance which the sides of many of these mountains exhibit, intersected, as they are, almost to the summit, with stone walls. When first erected, 1415 these stone fences must have little disfigured the face of the country; as part of the lines would every where be hidden by the quantity of native wood then remaining; and the lines would also be broken (as they still are) by the rocks which interrupt and vary their course. In the meadows, and in those parts of the lower grounds where the soil 1420 has not been sufficiently drained, and could not afford a stable foundation, there, when the increasing value of land, and the inconvenience suffered from intermixed plots of ground in common field, had induced each inhabitant to enclose his own, they were compelled to make the fences of alders, willows, and other trees. These, where the native 1425 wood had disappeared, have frequently enriched the vallies with a sylvan appearance; while the intricate intermixture of property has given to the fences a graceful irregularity, which, where large properties are prevalent, and large capitals employed in agriculture, is unknown. This sylvan appearance is heightened by the number of ash-trees 1430 planted in rows along the quick fences, and along the walls, for the purpose of browzing the cattle at the approach of winter. The branches are lopped off and strewn upon the pastures; and when the cattle have stripped them of the leaves, they are used for repairing the hedges or for fuel. 1435

We have thus seen a numerous body of Dalesmen creeping into possession of their home-steads, their little crofts, their mountain-enclosures; and, finally, the whole vale is visibly divided; except, perhaps, here and there some marshy ground, which, till fully drained, would not repay the trouble of enclosing. But these last partitions do 1440 not seem to have been general, till long after the pacification of the Borders, by the union of the two crowns: when the cause, which had first determined the distribution of land into such small parcels, had not only ceased,—but likewise a general improvement had taken place in the country, with a correspondent rise in the value of its produce. 1445 From the time of the union, it is certain that this species of feudal population must rapidly have diminished. That it was formerly much more numerous than it is at present, is evident from the multitude of tenements (I do not mean houses, but small divisions of land) which

---

1415 the 1822: their 1810–20.   walls. 1823: walls, of which the fences are always formed. 1810–22.   1416 these stone fences 1823: they 1810–22. 1430 heightened 1823: still further heightened 1810–22.   1431 planted 1822: which have been planted 1810–20.   1432 the cattle 1835: cattle 1810–23.   1433 strewn 1822: strewed 1810–20.   1434 the hedges 1835: hedges 1810–23.   1446 union 1820: union of the two kingdoms 1810. 1447 must rapidly have diminished 1822: would rapidly diminish 1810–20.

belonged formerly each to a several proprietor, and for which separate   1450
fines are paid to the manorial lord at this day. These are often in the
proportion of four to one of the present occupants. "Sir Launcelot
Threlkeld, who lived in the reign of Henry VII., was wont to say, he
had three noble houses, one for pleasure, Crosby, in Westmoreland,
where he had a park full of deer; one for profit and warmth, wherein   1455
to reside in winter, namely, Yanwith, nigh Penrith; and the third,
Threlkeld, (on the edge of the vale of Keswick), well stocked with
tenants to go with him to the wars." But, as I have said, from the union
of the two crowns, this numerous vassalage (their services not being
wanted) would rapidly diminish; various tenements would be united   1460
in one possessor; and the aboriginal houses, probably little better than
hovels, like the kraels of savages, or the huts of the Highlanders of
Scotland, would fall into decay, and the places of many be supplied by
substantial and comfortable buildings, a majority of which remain to
this day scattered over the vallies, and are often the only dwellings   1465
found in them.

From the time of the erection of these houses, till within the last
sixty years, the state of society, though no doubt slowly and gradually
improving, underwent no material change. Corn was grown in these
vales (through which no carriage-road had yet been made) sufficient   1470
upon each estate to furnish bread for each family, and no more: notwithstanding the union of several tenements, the possessions of each
inhabitant still being small, in the same field was seen an intermixture
of different crops; and the plough was interrupted by little rocks,
mostly overgrown with wood, or by spongy places, which the tillers   1475
of the soil had neither leisure nor capital to convert into firm land. The
storms and moisture of the climate induced them to sprinkle their
upland property with outhouses of native stone, as places of shelter
for their sheep, where, in tempestuous weather, food was distributed
to them. Every family spun from its own flock the wool with which it   1480
was clothed; a weaver was here and there found among them; and the
rest of their wants was supplied by the produce of the yarn, which they
carded and spun in their own houses, and carried to market, either
under their arms, or more frequently on pack-horses, a small train
taking their way weekly down the valley or over the mountains to the   1485
most commodious town. They had, as I have said, their rural chapel,
and of course their minister, in clothing or in manner of life, in no

---

1450 a 1822: its 1810-20.   1459 crowns 1820: kingdoms 1810.
1463 would 1822: would many of them 1810-20.   the places of many be 1822:
wholly disappear, while the place of others was 1810-20.   1465 often
1822: in many 1810-20.   1468 sixty 1822: fifty 1820: forty 1810.
1470 yet 1835: *not in* 1810-23.   1482 was 1822: were 1810-20.
1483 houses, and carried 1820: houses upon the large wheel, and carried it 1810.

respect differing from themselves, except on the Sabbath-day; this was the sole distinguished individual among them; every thing else, person and possession, exhibited a perfect equality, a community of 1490 shepherds and agriculturists, proprietors, for the most part, of the lands which they occupied and cultivated.

While the process above detailed was going on, the native forest must have been every where receding; but trees were planted for the sustenance of the flocks in winter,—such was then the rude state of 1495 agriculture; and, for the same cause, it was necessary that care should be taken of some part of the growth of the native woods. Accordingly, in Queen Elizabeth's time, this was so strongly felt, that a petition was made to the Crown, praying, "that the Blomaries in High Furness might be abolished, on account of the quantity of wood which was 1500 consumed in them for the use of the mines, to the great detriment of the cattle." But this same cause, about a hundred years after, produced effects directly contrary to those which had been deprecated. The re-establishment, at that period, of furnaces upon a large scale, made it the interest of the people to convert the steeper and more stony of the 1505 enclosures, sprinkled over with remains of the native forest, into close woods, which, when cattle and sheep were excluded, rapidly sowed and thickened themselves. The reader's attention has been directed to the cause by which tufts of wood, pasturage, meadow, and arable land, with its various produce, are intricately intermingled in the same field; 1510 and he will now see, in like manner, how enclosures entirely of wood, and those of cultivated ground, are blended all over the country under a law of similar wildness.

An historic detail has thus been given of the manner in which the hand of man has acted upon the surface of the inner regions of this 1515 mountainous country, as incorporated with and subservient to the powers and processes of nature. We will now take a view of the same agency—acting, within narrower bounds, for the production of the few works of art and accommodations of life which, in so simple a state of society, could be necessary. These are merely habitations of 1520 man and coverts for beasts, roads and bridges, and places of worship.

And to begin with the COTTAGES. They are scattered over the vallies, and under the hill sides, and on the rocks; and, even to this day, in the more retired dales, without any intrusion of more assuming buildings; 1525

> Cluster'd like stars some few, but single most,
> And lurking dimly in their shy retreats,

1493 forest 1820: Forests 1810.   1497 woods 1822: forest 1810–20.
1505 steeper 1820: steepest 1810.   1508 The reader's . . . directed 1822:
I have already directed the reader's attention 1810–20.   1515 this 1820: the
1810.   1523 even 1820: *not in* 1810.

> Or glancing on each other cheerful looks,
> Like separated stars with clouds between.　　　MS.

The dwelling-houses, and contiguous outhouses, are, in many instances, of the colour of the native rock, out of which they have been built; but, frequently the Dwelling or Fire-house, as it is ordinarily called, has been distinguished from the barn or byer by rough-cast and white wash, which, as the inhabitants are not hasty in renewing it, in a few years acquires, by the influence of weather, a tint at once sober and variegated. As these houses have been, from father to son, inhabited by persons engaged in the same occupations, yet necessarily with changes in their circumstances, they have received without incongruity additions and accommodations adapted to the needs of each successive occupant, who, being for the most part proprietor, was at liberty to follow his own fancy: so that these humble dwellings remind the contemplative spectator of a production of nature, and may (using a strong expression) rather be said to have grown than to have been erected;—to have risen, by an instinct of their own, out of the native rock—so little is there in them of formality, such is their wildness and beauty. Among the numerous recesses and projections in the walls and in the different stages of their roofs, are seen bold and harmonious effects of contrasted sunshine and shadow. It is a favourable circumstance, that the strong winds, which sweep down the vallies, induced the inhabitants, at a time when the materials for building were easily procured, to furnish many of these dwellings with substantial porches; and such as have not this defence, are seldom unprovided with a projection of two large slates over their thresholds. Nor will the singular beauty of the chimneys escape the eye of the attentive traveller. Sometimes a low chimney, almost upon a level with the roof, is overlaid with a slate, supported upon four slender pillars, to prevent the wind from driving the smoke down the chimney. Others are of a quadrangular shape, rising one or two feet above the roof; which low square is often surmounted by a tall cylinder, giving to the cottage chimney the most beautiful shape in which it is ever seen. Nor will it be too fanciful or refined to remark, that there is a pleasing harmony between a tall chimney of this circular form, and the living column of smoke, ascending from it through the still air. These dwellings, mostly built, as has

1530

1535

1540

1545

1550

1555

1560

1529 MS. 1820: *not in* 1810.　　　1532 Dwelling or . . . called 1823: dwelling-house 1810–22.　　　1533 or 1835: and 1810–23.　　　1535 weather 1820: the weather 1810.　　　1538–9 without incongruity 1823: *not in* 1810–22.　　　1547 bold and 1822: the boldest and most 1810–20.　　　1558 often 1820: *not in* 1810.　　　1561 that 1820: as a general principle, that 1810. 1562–3 ascending . . . air 1823: through the still air ascending from it 1810–22. 1563–4 mostly built . . . said 1822: as has been said, are built 1810–20.

been said, of rough unhewn stone, are roofed with slates, which were
rudely taken from the quarry before the present art of splitting them 1565
was understood, and are, therefore, rough and uneven in their surface,
so that both the coverings and sides of the houses have furnished places
of rest for the seeds of lichens, mosses, ferns, and flowers. Hence
buildings, which in their very form call to mind the processes of nature,
do thus, clothed in part with a vegetable garb, appear to be received 1570
into the bosom of the living principle of things, as it acts and exists
among the woods and fields; and, by their colour and their shape,
affectingly direct the thoughts to that tranquil course of nature and
simplicity, along which the humble-minded inhabitants have, through
so many generations, been led. Add the little garden with its shed for 1575
bee-hives, its small bed of pot-herbs, and its borders and patches of
flowers for Sunday posies, with sometimes a choice few too much
prized to be plucked; an orchard of proportioned size; a cheese-press,
often supported by some tree near the door; a cluster of embowering
sycamores for summer shade; with a tall fir, through which the winds 1580
sing when other trees are leafless; the little rill or household spout
murmuring in all seasons;—combine these incidents and images
together, and you have the representative idea of a mountain-cottage
in this country so beautifully formed in itself, and so richly adorned by
the hand of nature. 1585

Till within the last sixty years there was no communication between
any of these vales by carriage-roads; all bulky articles were transported
on pack-horses. Owing, however, to the population not being concen-
trated in villages, but scattered, the vallies themselves were intersected
as now by innumerable lanes and path-ways leading from house to 1590
house and from field to field. These lanes, where they are fenced by
stone walls, are mostly bordered with ashes, hazels, wild roses, and
beds of tall fern, at their base; while the walls themselves, if old, are
overspread with mosses, small ferns, wild strawberries, the geranium,
and lichens: and, if the wall happen to rest against a bank of earth, it is 1595
sometimes almost wholly concealed by a rich facing of stone-fern. It is
a great advantage to a traveller or resident, that these numerous lanes
and paths, if he be a zealous admirer of nature, will lead him on into all
the recesses of the country, so that the hidden treasures of its landscapes may, by an ever-ready guide, be laid open to his eyes. 1600

1564 are 1822: and they are 1810–20.   1566 and [*first*] 1820: and the slates
1810. 1566–7 surface, so that both 1823: surfaces, so that both 1820–2: surfaces.
Both 1810.   1570 clothed . ·. garb 1835: clothed with this vegetable garb
1820–3: by this vegetable garb with which they are cloathed 1810.   1576 bed
1835: beds 1810–23.   borders 1820: border 1810.   1580 fir 1835:
Scotch fir 1810–23.   1586 sixty 1822: fifty 1820: forty 1810.   1588 Owing,
however 1820: But, owing 1810.   1595 happen 1820: happens 1810.
1598 lead 1822: introduce him, nay, will lead 1810–20.

Likewise to the smallness of the several properties is owing the great number of bridges over the brooks and torrents, and the daring and graceful neglect of danger or accommodation with which so many of them are constructed, the rudeness of the forms of some, and their endless variety. But, when I speak of this rudeness, I must at the same 1605 time add, that many of these structures are in themselves models of elegance, as if they had been formed upon principles of the most thoughtful architecture. It is to be regretted that these monuments of the skill of our ancestors, and of that happy instinct by which consummate beauty was produced, are disappearing fast; but sufficient speci- 1610 mens remain* to give a high gratification to the man of genuine taste. Travellers who may not have been accustomed to pay attention to things so inobtrusive, will excuse me if I point out the proportion between the span and elevation of the arch, the lightness of the parapet, and the graceful manner in which its curve follows faithfully that of 1615 the arch.

Upon this subject I have nothing further to notice, except the PLACES OF WORSHIP, which have mostly a little school-house adjoining.† The architecture of these churches and chapels, where they have not been recently rebuilt or modernised, is of a style not less 1620

---

* Written some time ago. The injury done since, is more than could have been calculated upon.

Singula de nobis anni prædantur euntes. This is in the course of things; but why should the genius that directed the ancient architecture of these vales have deserted them? For the bridges, churches, mansions, cottages, and their richly fringed and flat-roofed outhouses, venerable as the grange of some old abbey, have been substituted structures, in which baldness only seems to have been studied, or plans of the most vulgar utility. But some improvement may be looked for in future; the gentry *recently* have copied the old models, and successful instances might be pointed out, if I could take the liberty.

† In some places scholars were formerly taught in the church, and at others the school-house was a sort of anti-chapel to the place of worship, being under the same roof; an arrangement which was abandoned as irreverent. It continues, however, to this day in Borrowdale. In the parish register of that chapelry is a notice, that a youth who had quitted the valley, and died in one of the towns on the coast of Cumberland, had requested that his body should be brought and interred at the foot of the pillar by which he had been accustomed to sit while a school-boy. One cannot but regret that parish registers so seldom contain any thing but bare names; in a few of this country, especially in that of Loweswater, I have found interesting notices of unusual natural occurrences—characters of the deceased, and particulars of their lives. There is no good reason why such memorials should not be frequent; these short and simple annals would in future ages become precious.

1609 happy 1820: happiness of 1810.　　　　1611 remain* 1823: remain [*no note appended*] 1810–22.　　　1611 n. *Near the end of the penultimate sentence* 1823 *reads:* on plans of　　　1612 Travellers . . . been 1822: Such travellers as may not be 1810–20.　　　1613 things so inobtrusive 1822: these things 1810–20. 1619 adjoining† 1822: adjoining [*no note appended*] 1810–20.　　　1619–24 The architecture . . . generally 1820: The lowliness and simple elegance of these churches and chapels, 1810.

appropriate and admirable than that of the dwelling-houses and other structures. How sacred the spirit by which our forefathers were directed! The *religio loci* is no where violated by these unstinted, yet unpretending, works of human hands. They exhibit generally a well-proportioned oblong, with a suitable porch, in some instances a 1625 steeple tower, and in others nothing more than a small belfry, in which one or two bells hang visibly. But these objects, though pleasing in their forms, must necessarily, more than others in rural scenery, derive their interest from the sentiments of piety and reverence for the modest virtues and simple manners of humble life with which they may 1630 be contemplated. A man must be very insensible who would not be touched with pleasure at the sight of the chapel of Buttermere, so strikingly expressing, by its diminutive size, how small must be the congregation there assembled, as it were, like one family; and proclaiming at the same time to the passenger, in connection with the 1635 surrounding mountains, the depth of that seclusion in which the people live, that has rendered necessary the building of a separate place of worship for so few. A patriot, calling to mind the images of the stately fabrics of Canterbury, York, or Westminster, will find a heart-felt satisfaction in presence of this lowly pile, as a monument of the wise 1640 institutions of our country, and as evidence of the all-pervading and paternal care of that venerable Establishment, of which it is, perhaps, the humblest daughter. The edifice is scarcely larger than many of the single stones or fragments of rock which are scattered near it.

We have thus far confined our observations on this division of the 1645 subject, to that part of these Dales which runs up far into the mountains.

As we descend towards the open country, we meet with halls and mansions, many of which have been places of defence against the incursions of the Scottish borderers; and they not unfrequently retain their towers and battlements. To these houses, parks are sometimes 1650 attached, and to their successive proprietors we chiefly owe whatever ornament is still left to the country of majestic timber. Through the

1623 violated 1822: outraged 1820.   1625 suitable 1820: *not in* 1810.
1627 visibly. But these objects, though 1820: visibly,—these are objects which, though 1810.   1628 others 1820: any others 1810.   1629 sentiments 1820: feelings 1810.   1632–3 so strikingly . . . size 1820: which by its diminutive size, so strikingly expresses 1810.   1634–5 proclaiming 1820: proclaims 1810.   1637 that 1820: which 1810.   1638 images 1820: image 1810.   1646 up far 1820: far up 1810.   1647–52 As we . . . majestic timber 1823: In addition to such objects as have been hitherto described, it may be mentioned that, as we descend towards the open part of the Vales, we meet with the remains of ancient Parks, and with old Mansions of more stately architecture; and it may be observed, that to these circumstances the country owes whatever ornament it retains of majestic and full-grown timber, as the remains of the park of the ancient family of the Ratcliffs at Derwent-water, Gowbray-park, and the venerable woods of Rydal. 1810–22.

open parts of the vales are scattered, also, houses of a middle rank between the pastoral cottage and the old hall residence of the knight or esquire. Such houses differ much from the rugged cottages before 1655 described, and are generally graced with a little court or garden in front, where may yet be seen specimens of those fantastic and quaint figures which our ancestors were fond of shaping out in yew-tree, holly, or box-wood. The passenger will sometimes smile at such elaborate display of petty art, while the house does not deign to look 1660 upon the natural beauty or the sublimity which its situation almost unavoidably commands.

Thus has been given a faithful description, the minuteness of which the reader will pardon, of the face of this country as it was, and had been through centuries, till within the last sixty years. Towards the 1665 head of these Dales was found a perfect Republic of Shepherds and Agriculturists, among whom the plough of each man was confined to the maintenance of his own family, or to the occasional accommodation of his neighbour.* Two or three cows furnished each family with milk and cheese. The chapel was the only edifice that presided over these 1670 dwellings, the supreme head of this pure Commonwealth; the members of which existed in the midst of a powerful empire, like an ideal society or an organized community, whose constitution had been imposed and regulated by the mountains which protected it. Neither high-born nobleman, knight, nor esquire, was here; but many of these 1675 humble sons of the hills had a consciousness that the land, which they walked over and tilled, had for more than five hundred years been possessed by men of their name and blood; and venerable was the transition, when a curious traveller, descending from the heart of the

* One of the most pleasing characteristics of manners in secluded and thinly-peopled districts, is a sense of the degree in which human happiness and comfort are dependent on the contingency of neighbourhood. This is implied by a rhyming adage common here, "*Friends are far, when neighbours are nar*" (near). This mutual helpfulness is not confined to out-of-doors work; but is ready upon all occasions. Formerly, if a person became sick, especially the mistress of a family, it was usual for those of the neighbours who were more particularly connected with the party by amicable offices, to visit the house, carrying a present; this practice, which is by no means obsolete, is called *owning* the family, and is regarded as a pledge of a disposition to be otherwise serviceable in a time of disability and distress.

1653 open parts 1820: more open part 1810.   are scattered, also, houses 1823: are scattered, with more spacious domains attached to them, houses 1820–2: also are scattered houses 1810.   1654 hall residence 1820: hall-residences 1810.   1654–5 knight or esquire. 1823: more wealthy *Estatesman*. 1820–2: more wealthy *estatesman* with more spacious domains attached to them. 1810. 1655–62 Such houses . . . commands 1823: *not in* 1810–22.   1665 sixty 1822: fifty 1820: forty 1810.   1669 neighbour.* 1822: neighbour. [*no note appended*] 1810–20.   1675 high-born . . . esquire 1822: Knight, nor Esquire [Squire 1810], nor high-born Nobleman 1810–20.

mountains, had come to some ancient manorial residence in the more   1680
open parts of the Vales, which, through the rights attached to its
proprietor, connected the almost visionary mountain republic he had
been contemplating with the substantial frame of society as existing in
the laws and constitution of a mighty empire.

SECTION THIRD.

CHANGES, AND RULES OF TASTE FOR PREVENTING THEIR
BAD EFFECTS.

1685

S u c h, as hath been said, was the appearance of things till within the
last sixty years. A practice, denominated Ornamental Gardening, was
at that time becoming prevalent over England. In union with an   1690
admiration of this art, and in some instances in opposition to it, had
been generated a relish for select parts of natural scenery: and Travellers, instead of confining their observations to Towns, Manufactories,
or Mines, began (a thing till then unheard of) to wander over the island
in search of sequestered spots, distinguished as they might accidently   1695
have learned, for the sublimity or beauty of the forms of Nature there
to be seen.—Dr. Brown, the celebrated Author of the Estimate of the
Manners and Principles of the Times, published a letter to a friend, in
which the attractions of the Vale of Keswick were delineated with a
powerful pencil, and the feeling of a genuine Enthusiast. Gray, the   1700
Poet, followed: he died soon after his forlorn and melancholy pilgrimage to the Vale of Keswick, and the record left behind him of what he
had seen and felt in this journey, excited that pensive interest with
which the human mind is ever disposed to listen to the farewell words
of a man of genius. The journal of Gray feelingly showed how the   1705
gloom of ill health and low spirits had been irradiated by objects, which
the Author's powers of mind enabled him to describe with distinctness
and unaffected simplicity. Every reader of this journal must have been

---

1681 through 1820: with 1810.   1682 he 1820: which he 1810.   1685–7 *Not*
in 1810–20.   1688 hath been 1822: I have 1810–20.   1688–9 the last
sixty 1822: these last fifty 1820: these last forty 1810.   1689 practice, 1823:
practice, by a strange abuse of terms, 1820–2: practice which by a strange abuse of
terms has been 1810.   1690 prevalent 1820: generally prevalent 1810.
1693 Manufactories 1820: Manufactures 1810.   1695–6 distinguished . . .
learned 1820: which they might have accidentally learnt were distinguished 1810.
1696 or 1820: and 1810.   1697–8 Estimate . . . Times, 1820: "Estimate . . .
Times," &c. 1810.   1701 followed: he 1820: followed; and the report, which
he gave, was circulated among his friends. He 1810.   1705 showed how
1820: recorded the manner in which 1810.   1706 objects 1820: objects most
beautiful and sublime 1810.   1708–10 Every . . . Grasmere 1820: The Vale
of Grasmere is thus happily discriminated at the close of his description 1810.

impressed with the words which conclude his notice of the Vale of
Grasmere:—"Not a single red tile, no flaring gentleman's house or   1710
garden-wall, breaks in upon the repose of this little unsuspected
paradise; but all is peace, rusticity, and happy poverty, in its neatest
and most becoming attire."

What is here so justly said of Grasmere applied almost equally to all
its sister Vales. It was well for the undisturbed pleasure of the Poet   1715
that he had no forebodings of the change which was soon to take place;
and it might have been hoped that these words, indicating how much
the charm of what *was*, depended upon what was *not*, would of themselves have preserved the ancient franchises of this and other kindred
mountain retirements from trespass; or (shall I dare to say?) would   1720
have secured scenes so consecrated from profanation. The lakes had
now become celebrated; visitors flocked hither from all parts of
England; the fancies of some were smitten so deeply, that they became
settlers; and the Islands of Derwentwater and Winandermere, as they
offered the strongest temptation, were the first places seized upon,   1725
and were instantly defaced by the intrusion.

The venerable wood that had grown for centuries round the small
house called St. Herbert's Hermitage, had indeed some years before
been felled by its native proprietor, and the whole island planted anew
with Scotch firs, left to spindle up by each other's side—a melancholy   1730
phalanx, defying the power of the winds, and disregarding the regret
of the spectator, who might otherwise have cheated himself into a
belief, that some of the decayed remains of those oaks, the place of
which was in this manner usurped, had been planted by the Hermit's
own hand. This sainted spot, however, suffered comparatively little   1735
injury. At the bidding of an alien improver, the Hind's Cottage, upon
Vicar's island, in the same lake, with its embowering sycamores and
cattle-shed, disappeared from the corner where they stood; and right

1709 which 1822: that 1820.   1710–11 flaring gentleman's . . . breaks 1820:
gentleman's flaring house or garden walls, break 1810.   1715 Poet 1820:
Poet's mind 1810.   1716 the change . . . soon 1820: what was so soon
after 1810.   1717–18 indicating . . . would of 1820: at once the dictate of a
sympathetic heart, a pure imagination, and a genuine taste, would almost of 1810.
1720 trespass; or 1820: trespass or intrusion, or 1810.   1722 visitors 1820:
the mania of ornamental gardening and prospect hunting had spread wide; visitors
1810.   1723 England 1820: the Island 1810.   some were . . . deeply 1820:
some of these were so strongly smitten 1810.   1724–6 the Islands . . . intrusion
1820: numerous violations soon ensued 1810.   1727–81 The venerable . . .
But, in truth, no one 1820: This beautiful country has, in a great variety of instances, suffered from the spirit of tasteless and capricious innovation. No one 1810.
1729 planted 1822: had been planted 1820.   1734 was 1822: is 1820.
1735 hand. This . . . comparatively 1822–3, *Edd.*: hand. Comparatively, however,
this sainted spot suffered 1820: hand: This . . . comparatively 1835.   1736–8
At the bidding . . . disappeared 1822: The Hind's Cottage upon . . . disappeared,
at the bidding of an alien improver 1820.   1738 stood 1822: had stood 1820.

in the middle, and upon the precise point of the island's highest
elevation, rose a tall square habitation, with four sides exposed, like 1740
an astronomer's observatory, or a warren-house reared upon an eminence for the detection of depredators, or, like the temple of Œolus,
where all the winds pay him obeisance. Round this novel structure,
but at a respectful distance, platoons of firs were stationed, as if to
protect their commander when weather and time should somewhat 1745
have shattered his strength. Within the narrow limits of this island
were typified also the state and strength of a kingdom, and its religion
as it had been, and was,—for neither was the druidical circle uncreated,
nor the church of the present establishment; nor the stately pier,
emblem of commerce and navigation; nor the fort to deal out thunder 1750
upon the approaching invader. The taste of a succeeding proprietor
rectified the mistakes as far as was practicable, and has ridded the spot
of its puerilities. The church, after having been docked of its steeple, is
applied, both ostensibly and really, to the purpose for which the body
of the pile was actually erected, namely, a boat-house; the fort is 1755
demolished; and, without indignation on the part of the spirits of the
ancient Druids who officiated at the circle upon the opposite hill, the
mimic arrangement of stones, with its *sanctum sanctorum*, has been
swept away.

The present instance has been singled out, extravagant as it is, 1760
because, unquestionably, this beautiful country has, in numerous other
places, suffered from the same spirit, though not clothed exactly in
the same form, nor active in an equal degree. It will be sufficient
here to utter a regret for the changes that have been made upon the
principal Island at Winandermere, and in its neighbourhood. What 1765
could be more unfortunate than the taste that suggested the paring
of the shores, and surrounding with an embankment this spot of
ground, the natural shape of which was so beautiful! An artificial
appearance has thus been given to the whole, while infinite varieties
of minute beauty have been destroyed. Could not the margin of this 1770
noble island be given back to nature? Winds and waves work with
a careless and graceful hand: and, should they in some places carry
away a portion of the soil, the trifling loss would be amply compensated by the additional spirit, dignity, and loveliness, which
these agents and the other powers of nature would soon communi- 1775
cate to what was left behind. As to the larch-plantations upon the
main shore,—they who remember the original appearance of the
rocky steeps, scattered over with native hollies and ash-trees, will

1741 astronomer's 1822: *not in* 1820.   1753 its [*first*] 1823: all its
1820–2.   1754 applied, 1820–3, *Edd.*: applied 1835.

8124368.2   P

be prepared to agree with what I shall have to say hereafter upon
plantations* in general.   1780

But, in truth, no one can now travel through the more frequented
tracts, without being offended, at almost every turn, by an introduction
of discordant objects, disturbing that peaceful harmony of form and
colour, which had been through a long lapse of ages most happily
preserved.   1785

All gross transgressions of this kind originate, doubtless, in a feeling
natural and honourable to the human mind, viz. the pleasure which it
receives from distinct ideas, and from the perception of order, regularity, and contrivance. Now, unpractised minds receive these impressions only from objects that are divided from each other by strong   1790
lines of demarcation; hence the delight with which such minds are
smitten by formality and harsh contrast. But I would beg of those who
are eager to create the means of such gratification, first carefully to
study what already exists; and they will find, in a country so lavishly
gifted by nature, an abundant variety of forms marked out with a   1795
precision that will satisfy their desires. Moreover, a new habit of
pleasure will be formed opposite to this, arising out of the perception
of the fine gradations by which in nature one thing passes away into
another, and the boundaries that constitute individuality disappear in
one instance only to be revived elsewhere under a more alluring form.   1800
The hill of Dunmallet, at the foot of Ulswater, was once divided into
different portions, by avenues of fir-trees, with a green and almost
perpendicular lane descending down the steep hill through each

---

*These are disappearing fast, under the management of the present Proprietor,
and native wood is resuming its place.

1780 plantations* 1835: plantations [*no note appended*] 1820–3.   1782 tracts,
without 1820: tracts, without finding at almost every turn the venerable and pure
simplicity of nature vitiated by some act of inconsiderate and impertinent art;
without 1810.   at almost every turn 1820: *not in* 1810, *but see note immediately
preceding*.   1783 disturbing 1820: disturbing every where 1810.   1786 originate, doubtless 1820: in matters of taste originate 1810.   1787–8 it receives
1820: we receive 1810.   1790–1 objects . . . demarcation 1820: objects
between which there exists eternally [*misprint for* externally?] a strong demarcation 1810.   1791 delight 1820: pleasure 1810.   1792–4 who are eager
. . . will find 1820: who, under the control of this craving for distinct ideas, are
hastily setting about the production of food by which it may be gratified, to temper
their impatience, to look carefully about them, to observe and to watch; and they
will find gradually growing within them a sense by which they will be enabled to
perceive 1810.   1795 abundant . . . marked 1820: ever-renewing variety of
forms which will be marked 1810.   1797 formed . . . arising 1820: forming in
the mind the opposite of this, viz., a habit arising 1810.   1800 revived elsewhere 1820: renewed in another 1810.   1801–2 The hill . . . portions 1820:
My meaning will at once be obvious to those who remember the hill of Dunmallet
at the foot of Ulswater divided into different portions, as it once was 1810.

avenue;—contrast this quaint appearance with the image of the same hill overgrown with self-planted wood,—each tree springing up in the situation best suited to its kind, and with that shape which the situation constrained or suffered it to take. What endless melting and playing into each other of forms and colours does the one offer to a mind at once attentive and active; and how insipid and lifeless, compared with it, appear those parts of the former exhibition with which a child, a peasant perhaps, or a citizen unfamiliar with natural imagery, would have been most delighted! **1805** **1810**

The disfigurement which this country has undergone, has not, however, proceeded wholly from the common feelings of human nature which have been referred to as the primary sources of bad taste in rural imagery; another cause must be added, that has chiefly shown itself in its effect upon buildings. I mean a warping of the natural mind occasioned by a consciousness that, this country being an object of general admiration, every new house would be looked at and commented upon either for approbation or censure. Hence all the deformity and ungracefulness that ever pursue the steps of constraint or affectation. Persons, who in Leicestershire or Northamptonshire would probably have built a modest dwelling like those of their sensible neighbours, have been turned out of their course; and, acting a part, no wonder if, having had little experience, they act it ill. The craving for prospect, also, which is immoderate, particularly in new settlers, has rendered it impossible that buildings, whatever might have been their architecture, should in most instances be ornamental to the landscape; rising as they do from the summits of naked hills in staring contrast to the snugness and privacy of the ancient houses. **1815** **1820** **1825** **1830**

No man is to be condemned for a desire to decorate his residence and possessions; feeling a disposition to applaud such an endeavour, I would show how the end may be best attained. The rule is simple; with respect to grounds—work, where you can, in the spirit of nature,

1804 contrast . . . appearance with 1820: who can recal to mind the delight with which they might as children have looked at this quaint appearance; and are enabled to contrast that remembrance with the pleasure which the more practiced eye of mature age would create for itself from 1810.   1806 situation [*second*] 1820: same situation 1810.   1810 the 1820: its 1810.   1813 The disfigurement 1822: I cannot, however, omit observing, that the disfigurement 1810–20. 1814 however 1822: *not in* 1810–20.   the 1822: those 1810–20.   1816 imagery 1822: scenery 1810–20.   that 1820: which 1810.   1817–18 a warping . . . consciousness 1820: a constraint or warping of the natural mind arising out of a sense 1810.   1821 that 1820: which 1810.   1822 Persons 1820: Men 1810.   1825–6 The craving . . . also 1820: Moreover, the craving for prospect 1810.   1829 rising . . . from 1820: starting . . . on 1810. 1831–3 No man . . . show how 1820: I do not condemn in any man a desire that his residence and possessions should draw upon them the approbation of the judicious; nor do I censure attempts to decorate them for that purpose. I rather applaud both the one and the other; and would shew in what manner 1810.

with an invisible hand of art. Planting, and a removal of wood, may 1835
thus, and thus only, be carried on with good effect; and the like may be
said of building, if Antiquity, who may be styled the co-partner and
sister of Nature, be not denied the respect to which she is entitled. I
have already spoken of the beautiful forms of the ancient mansions of
this country, and of the happy manner in which they harmonise with 1840
the forms of nature. Why cannot such be taken as a model, and modern
internal convenience be confined within their external grace and
dignity. Expense to be avoided, or difficulties to be overcome, may
prevent a close adherence to this model; still, however, it might be
followed to a certain degree in the style of architecture and in the 1845
choice of situation, if the thirst for prospect were mitigated by those
considerations of comfort, shelter, and convenience, which used to be
chiefly sought after. But should an aversion to old fashions unfortunately
exist, accompanied with a desire to transplant into the cold and stormy
North, the elegancies of a villa formed upon a model taken from 1850
countries with a milder climate, I will adduce a passage from an
English poet, the divine Spenser, which will show in what manner such
a plan may be realised without injury to the native beauty of these
scenes.

"Into that forest farre they thence him led,   1855
Where was their dwelling in a pleasant glade
With MOUNTAINS round about environed,
And MIGHTY WOODS which did the valley shade,
And like a stately theatre it made,
Spreading itself into a spacious plaine;   1860
And in the midst a little river plaide
Emongst the pumy stones which seem'd to 'plaine
With gentle murmure that his course they did restraine.

Beside the same a dainty place there lay,
Planted with mirtle trees and laurels green,   1865
In which the birds sang many a lovely lay
Of God's high praise, and of their sweet loves teene,
As it an earthly paradise had beene;
In whose *enclosed shadow* there was pight
A fair pavilion, *scarcely to be seen*,   1870
The which was all within most richly dight,
That greatest princes living it mote well delight."

1837 who 1820: which 1810.   1841 such 1822: these 1810–20.
1843–4 Expense . . . may prevent 1820: But, should expense . . . prevent 1810.
1844 however 1820: *not in* 1810.   1846 thirst 1820: craving 1810.
1862 pumy 1810–23, *Edd.*: puny 1835.   1870 pavilion 1810–23, *Edd.*: pavillion
1835.

Houses or mansions suited to a mountainous region, should be "not obvious, not obtrusive, but retired;" and the reasons for this rule, though they have been little adverted to, are evident. Mountainous 1875 countries, more frequently and forcibly than others, remind us of the power of the elements, as manifested in winds, snows, and torrents, and accordingly make the notion of exposure very unpleasing; while shelter and comfort are in proportion necessary and acceptable. Far-winding vallies difficult of access, and the feelings of simplicity habitu- 1880 ally connected with mountain retirements, prompt us to turn from ostentation as a thing there eminently unnatural and out of place. A mansion, amid such scenes, can never have sufficient dignity or interest to become principal in the landscape, and to render the mountains, lakes, or torrents, by which it may be surrounded, a subordinate part 1885 of the view. It is, I grant, easy to conceive, that an ancient castellated building, hanging over a precipice or raised upon an island, or the peninsula of a lake, like that of Kilchurn Castle, upon Loch Awe, may not want, whether deserted or inhabited, sufficient majesty to preside for a moment in the spectator's thoughts over the high mountains 1890 among which it is embosomed; but its titles are from antiquity—a power readily submitted to upon occasion as the vicegerent of Nature: it is respected, as having owed its existence to the necessities of things, as a monument of security in times of disturbance and danger long passed away,—as a record of the pomp and violence of passion, and a 1895 symbol of the wisdom of law;—it bears a countenance of authority, which is not impaired by decay.

> "Child of loud-throated war, the mountain-stream
> Roars in thy hearing; but thy hour of rest
> Is come, and thou art silent in thy age!"   1900

To such honours a modern edifice can lay no claim; and the puny efforts of elegance appear contemptible, when, in such situations, they are

---

1873 Houses . . . region 1820: I have been treating of the erection of houses or mansions suited to a grand and beautiful region; and I have laid it down as a position that they 1810.   1874 not obtrusive 1822: nor obtrusive 1810–20. rule 1820: *not in* 1810.   1877 manifested 1820: it is exhibited 1810.   1880 difficult 1820: which are difficult 1810.   the 1820: our 1810. 1880–1 habitually 1820: which are habitually 1810.   1884 to [*second*] 1822: *not in* 1810–20.   1886 view. 1820: view; nor are the grand features of nature to be absorbed by the puny efforts of human art. 1810.   1887 building 1820: mansion 1810.   1889 sufficient majesty 1820: that majesty which shall enable it 1810.   1892 readily . . . occasion 1820: which is readily . . . occasions 1810.   1893 necessities 1820: necessity 1810.   1898–1906 "Child of . . . or flat 1820: These honours render it worthy of its situation; and to which of these honours can a modern edifice pretend? Obtruding itself in rivalry with the grandeur of Nature, it only displays the presumption and caprice of its individual founder, or the class to which he belongs. But, in a flat or merely undulating 1810.   1900 age!" 1835: age!" MS.   1820–3.

obtruded in rivalship with the sublimities of Nature. But, towards the verge of a district like this of which we are treating, where the mountains subside into hills of moderate elevation, or in an undulating or flat country, a gentleman's mansion may, with propriety, become a principal feature in the landscape; and, itself being a work of art, works and traces of artificial ornament may, without censure, be extended around it, as they will be referred to the common centre, the house; the right of which to impress within certain limits a character of obvious ornament will not be denied, where no commanding forms of nature dispute it, or set it aside. Now, to a want of the perception of this difference, and to the causes before assigned, may chiefly be attributed the disfigurement which the Country of the Lakes has undergone, from persons who may have built, demolished, and planted, with full confidence, that every change and addition was or would become an improvement.

The principle that ought to determine the position, apparent size, and architecture of a house, viz. that it should be so constructed, and (if large) so much of it hidden, as to admit of its being gently incorporated into the scenery of nature—should also determine its colour. Sir Joshua Reynolds used to say, "If you would fix upon the best colour for your house, turn up a stone, or pluck up a handful of grass by the roots, and see what is the colour of the soil where the house is to stand, and let that be your choice." Of course, this precept given in conversation, could not have been meant to be taken literally. For example, in Low Furness, where the soil, from its strong impregnation with iron, is universally of a deep red, if this rule were strictly followed, the house also must be of a glaring red; in other places it must be of a sullen black; which would only be adding annoyance to annoyance. The rule, however, as a general guide, is good; and, in agricultural districts, where large tracts of soil are laid bare by the plough, particularly if (the face of the country being undulating) they are held up to view, this rule, though not to be implicitly adhered to, should never be lost sight of;—the colour of the house ought, if possible, to have a cast or shade of the colour of the soil. The principle is, that the house must harmonise with the surrounding landscape: accordingly, in mountainous countries, with still more confidence may it be said, "look at the rocks and those parts of the mountains where the soil is visible, and they will furnish a safe direction." Nevertheless, it will often happen that the rocks may bear so large a proportion to the

1911–12 no commanding . . . nature 1820: there are no conspicuous or commanding forms of Nature to 1810.　　1918 that 1820: which 1810.　　1921 into 1820: with 1810.　　　　　1935 of;—the 1820: of, that is, the 1810. 1936 principle 1810–22, *Errata*: principal 1823–35.　　1940 direction 1820: general direction 1810.

rest of the landscape, and may be of such a tone of colour, that the rule may not admit, even here, of being implicitly followed. For instance, the chief defect in the colouring of the Country of the Lakes (which is most strongly felt in the summer season) is an over-prevalence of a bluish tint, which the green of the herbage, the fern, and the woods, does not sufficiently counteract. If a house, therefore, should stand where this defect prevails, I have no hesitation in saying, that the colour of the neighbouring rocks would not be the best that could be chosen. A tint ought to be introduced approaching nearer to those which, in the technical language of painters, are called *warm*: this, if happily selected, would not disturb, but would animate the landscape. How often do we see this exemplified upon a small scale by the native cottages, in cases where the glare of white-wash has been subdued by time and enriched by weather-stains! No harshness is then seen; but one of these cottages, thus coloured, will often form a central point to a landscape by which the whole shall be connected, and an influence of pleasure diffused over all the objects that compose the picture. But where the cold blue tint of the rocks is enriched by the iron tinge, the colour cannot be too closely imitated; and it will be produced of itself by the stones hewn from the adjoining quarry, and by the mortar, which may be tempered with the most gravelly part of the soil. The pure blue gravel, from the bed of the river, is, however, more suitable to the mason's purpose, who will probably insist also that the house must be covered with rough-cast, otherwise it cannot be kept dry; if this advice be taken, the builder of taste will set about contriving such means as may enable him to come the nearest to the effect aimed at.

The supposed necessity of rough-cast to keep out rain in houses not built of hewn stone or brick, has tended greatly to injure English landscape, and the neighbourhood of these Lakes especially, by furnishing such apt occasion for whitening buildings. That white should be a favorite colour for rural residences is natural for many reasons. The mere aspect of cleanliness and neatness thus given, not only to an individual house, but, where the practice is general, to the whole face

1943 admit, even here 1820: even here admit 1810.   1947 counteract. If 1820: counteract. This blue tint proceeds from the diffused water, and still more from the rocks which the reader will remember are generally of this colour. If 1810. 1957 an 1820: the 1810.   1958 that compose the picture 1820: of which the picture is composed 1810.   1958-9 But where 1820: Where however 1810. 1959 enriched by 1820: animated by hues of 1810.   1962-4 The pure . . . insist also 1820: But, should the mason object to this, as they will do, and insist upon the mortar being tempered by blue gravel from the bed of the river, and say 1810.   1965 covered with 1820: *not in* 1810.   1965-6 if this . . . taken 1820: then 1810.   1971-3 That white . . . neatness 1820: I will therefore say a few words upon this subject; because many persons, not deficient in taste, are admirers of this colour for rural residences. The reasons are manifold; first, as is obvious, the air of cleanliness and neatness which is 1810.

of the country, produces moral associations so powerful, that, in many 1975
minds, they take place of all others. But what has already been said
upon the subject of cottages, must have convinced men of feeling and
imagination, that a human dwelling of the humblest class may be
rendered more deeply interesting to the affections, and far more
pleasing to the eye, by other influences, than a sprightly tone of colour 1980
spread over its outside. I do not, however, mean to deny, that a small
white building, embowered in trees, may, in some situations, be a
delightful and animating object—in no way injurious to the landscape;
but this only where it sparkles from the midst of a thick shade, and in
rare and solitary instances; especially if the country be itself rich and 1985
pleasing, and abound with grand forms. On the sides of bleak and
desolate moors, we are indeed thankful for the sight of white cottages
and white houses plentifully scattered, where, without these, perhaps
every thing would be cheerless: this is said, however, with hesitation,
and with a wilful sacrifice of some higher enjoyments. But I have 1990
certainly seen such buildings glittering at sunrise, and in wandering
lights, with no common pleasure. The continental traveller also will
remember, that the convents hanging from the rocks of the Rhine, the
Rhone, the Danube, or among the Appenines, or the mountains of
Spain, are not looked at with less complacency when, as is often the 1995
case, they happen to be of a brilliant white. But this is perhaps owing,
in no small degree, to the contrast of that lively colour with the gloom
of monastic life, and to the general want of rural residences of smiling
and attractive appearance, in those countries.

The objections to white, as a colour, in large spots or masses in 2000
landscape, especially in a mountainous country, are insurmountable.
In nature, pure white is scarcely ever found but in small objects, such
as flowers; or in those which are transitory, as the clouds, foam of
rivers, and snow. Mr. Gilpin, who notices this, has also recorded the
just remark of Mr. Locke, of N——, that white destroys the *gradations* 2005
of distance; and, therefore, an object of pure white can scarcely ever
be managed with good effect in landscape-painting. Five or six white
houses, scattered over a valley, by their obtrusiveness, dot the surface,
and divide it into triangles, or other mathematical figures, haunting
the eye, and disturbing that repose which might otherwise be perfect. 2010

1975 produces moral associations 1820: which moral associations are 1810.
1975–6 many minds 1822: the minds of many 1810–20.   1976 all others 1822:
every other relating to such objects 1810–20.   1978 dwelling 1823: habitation
1810–22.   1985 itself 1820: in itself 1810.   1986 abound with 1822:
full of 1810–20.   1987 we are 1820: one is 1810.   1990 with a . . .
enjoyments 1820: in the sleep of some of the higher faculties of the mind
1810.   1997–8 gloom of 1820: feeling of gloom associated with 1810.
2002 pure white 1820: it 1810.   2009–10 haunting . . . disturbing 1820:
which haunt . . . disturb 1810.

I have seen a single white house materially impair the majesty of a
mountain; cutting away, by a harsh separation, the whole of its base,
below the point on which the house stood. Thus was the apparent size
of the mountain reduced, not by the interposition of another object in
a manner to call forth the imagination, which will give more than the   2015
eye loses; but what had been abstracted in this case was left visible;
and the mountain appeared to take its beginning, or to rise, from the
line of the house, instead of its own natural base. But, if I may express
my own individual feeling, it is after sunset, at the coming on of twilight, that white objects are most to be complained of. The solemnity   2020
and quietness of nature at that time are always marred, and often
destroyed by them. When the ground is covered with snow, they are
of course inoffensive; and in moonshine they are always pleasing—it is
a tone of light with which they accord: and the dimness of the scene is
enlivened by an object at once conspicuous and cheerful. I will conclude   2025
this subject with noticing, that the cold, slaty colour, which many
persons, who have heard the white condemned, have adopted in its
stead, must be disapproved of for the reason already given. The flaring
yellow runs into the opposite extreme, and is still more censurable.
Upon the whole, the safest colour, for general use, is something   2030
between a cream and a dust-colour, commonly called stone colour;
—there are, among the Lakes, examples of this that need not be
pointed out. *

The principle taken as our guide, viz. that the house should be so
formed, and of such apparent size and colour, as to admit of its being   2035
gently incorporated with the works of nature, should also be applied
to the management of the grounds and plantations, and is here more
urgently needed; for it is from abuses in this department, far more even
than from the introduction of exotics in architecture (if the phrase may
be used), that this country has suffered. Larch and fir plantations have   2040
been spread, not merely with a view to profit, but in many instances
for the sake of ornament. To those who plant for profit, and are
thrusting every other tree out of the way, to make room for their
favourite, the larch, I would utter first a regret, that they should have
selected these lovely vales for their vegetable manufactory, when there   2045
is so much barren and irreclaimable land in the neighbouring moors,

* A proper colouring of houses is now becoming general. It is best that the
colouring material should be mixed with the rough-cast, and not laid on as a *wash*
afterwards.

2021 are 1820: is 1810.   2023 of course 1820: *not in* 1810.   2032 that
1820: which 1810.   2033 out.* 1835: out. [*no note appended*] 1810–23.
2034 taken as 1820: which we have taken for 1810.   2036 works 1823:
scenery 1810–22.   2041 spread, 1822: spread every where, 1810–20.
2046–7 in the . . . moors, and 1820: *not in* 1810.

and in other parts of the island, which might have been had for this purpose at a far cheaper rate. And I will also beg leave to represent to them, that they ought not to be carried away by flattering promises from the speedy growth of this tree; because in rich soils and sheltered 2050 situations, the wood, though it thrives fast, is full of sap, and of little value; and is, likewise, very subject to ravage from the attacks of insects, and from blight. Accordingly, in Scotland, where planting is much better understood, and carried on upon an incomparably larger scale than among us, good soil and sheltered situations are appropriated 2055 to the oak, the ash, and other deciduous trees; and the larch is now generally confined to barren and exposed ground. There the plant, which is a hardy one, is of slower growth; much less liable to injury; and the timber is of better quality. But the circumstances of many permit, and their taste leads them, to plant with little regard to profit; 2060 and there are others, less wealthy, who have such a lively feeling of the native beauty of these scenes, that they are laudably not unwilling to make some sacrifices to heighten it. Both these classes of persons, I would entreat to enquire of themselves wherein that beauty which they admire consists. They would then see that, after the feeling has 2065 been gratified that prompts us to gather round our dwelling a few flowers and shrubs, which from the circumstance of their not being native, may, by their very looks, remind us that they owe their existence to our hands, and their prosperity to our care; they will see that, after this natural desire has been provided for, the course of all beyond 2070 has been predetermined by the spirit of the place. Before I proceed, I will remind those who are not satisfied with the restraint thus laid upon them, that they are liable to a charge of inconsistency, when they are so eager to change the face of that country, whose native attractions, by the act of erecting their habitations in it, they have so em- 2075 phatically acknowledged. And surely there is not a single spot that would not have, if well managed, sufficient dignity to support itself, unaided by the productions of other climates, or by elaborate decorations which might be becoming elsewhere.

Having adverted to the feelings that justify the introduction of a few 2080

2056 other 1820: other native 1810.   2058 injury 1820: the injuries which I have mentioned 1810.   2059–60 the circumstances . . . and their 1822: there are many, whose circumstances permit them, and whose 1810–20. 2061 there are 1822: *not in* 1810–20.   2066 that 1820: which 1810. 2071–2 proceed . . . remind 1822: proceed with this subject, I will prepare my way with a remark of general application, by reminding 1810–20.   2074–5 whose native . . . act 1820: the native attractions of which by the art [*sic*] 1810. 2075–6 so emphatically 1820: emphatically and conspicuously 1810.   2076 not 1822: not in this country 1810–20.   2080 Having 1822: But to return;— having 1810–20.   feelings that 1822: considerations that 1820: considerations which 1810.

exotic plants, provided they be confined almost to the doors of the house, we may add, that a transition should be contrived, without abruptness, from these foreigners to the rest of the shrubs, which ought to be of the kinds scattered by Nature, through the woods— holly, broom, wild-rose, elder, dogberry, white and black thorn, &c. 2085 —either these only, or such as are carefully selected in consequence of their being united in form, and harmonising in colour with them, especially with respect to colour, when the tints are most diversified, as in autumn and spring. The various sorts of fruit-and-blossom- bearing trees usually found in orchards, to which may be added those 2090 of the woods,—namely, the wilding, black cherry tree, and wild cluster-cherry (here called heck-berry)—may be happily admitted as an intermediate link between the shrubs and the forest trees; which last ought almost entirely to be such as are natives of the country. Of the birch, one of the most beautiful of the native trees, it may be 2095 noticed, that, in dry and rocky situations, it outstrips even the larch, which many persons are tempted to plant merely on account of the speed of its growth. The Scotch fir is less attractive during its youth than any other plant; but, when full-grown, if it has had room to spread out its arms, it becomes a noble tree; and, by those who are 2100 disinterested enough to plant for posterity, it may be placed along with the sycamore near the house; for, from their massiveness, both these trees unite well with buildings, and in some situations with rocks also; having, in their forms and apparent substances, the effect of something intermediate betwixt the immoveableness and solidity of 2105 stone, and the spray and foliage of the lighter trees. If these general rules be just, what shall we say to whole acres of artificial shrubbery and exotic trees among rocks and dashing torrents, with their own wild wood in sight—where we have the whole contents of the nursery- man's catalogue jumbled together—colour at war with colour, and 2110 form with form?—among the most peaceful subjects of Nature's kingdom, everywhere discord, distraction, and bewilderment! But this deformity, bad as it is, is not so obtrusive as the small patches and large tracts of larch-plantations that are over-running the hill sides. To justify our condemnation of these, let us again recur to Nature. The 2115 process, by which she forms woods and forests, is as follows. Seeds are scattered indiscriminately by winds, brought by waters, and dropped

2087 being united 1835: uniting 1810–23.   2091 namely 1820: *not in* 1810. 2094 country. 1820: country, oak, ash, birch, mountain ash, &c. &c. 1810. 2098–102 The Scotch fir . . . sycamore 1823: Sycamore, and the Scotch fir (which, when it has room to spread out its arms, is a noble tree) may be placed with advantage 1810–22.   2102–3 both these trees 1823: they 1810–22. 2106 spray 1822: sprays 1810–20.   2114 over-running 1810–23, *Edd.*: overrunning 1835.

by birds. They perish, or produce, according as the soil and situation upon which they fall are suited to them: and under the same dependence, the seedling or the sucker, if not cropped by animals, (which Nature is often careful to prevent by fencing it about with brambles or other prickly shrubs) thrives, and the tree grows, sometimes single, taking its own shape without constraint, but for the most part compelled to conform itself to some law imposed upon it by its neighbours. From low and sheltered places, vegetation travels upwards to the more exposed; and the young plants are protected, and to a certain degree fashioned, by those that have preceded them. The continuous mass of foliage which would be thus produced, is broken by rocks, or by glades or open places, where the browzing of animals has prevented the growth of wood. As vegetation ascends, the winds begin also to bear their part in moulding the forms of the trees; but, thus mutually protected, trees, though not of the hardiest kind, are enabled to climb high up the mountains. Gradually, however, by the quality of the ground, and by increasing exposure, a stop is put to their ascent; the hardy trees only are left: those also, by little and little, give way—and a wild and irregular boundary is established, graceful in its outline, and never contemplated without some feeling, more or less distinct, of the powers of Nature by which it is imposed.

Contrast the liberty that encourages, and the law that limits, this joint work of nature and time, with the disheartening necessities, restrictions, and disadvantages, under which the artificial planter must proceed, even he whom long observation and fine feeling have best qualified for his task. In the first place his trees, however well chosen and adapted to their several situations, must generally start all at the same time; and this necessity would of itself prevent that fine connection of parts, that sympathy and organization, if I may so express myself, which pervades the whole of a natural wood, and appears to the eye in its single trees, its masses of foliage, and their various colours, when they are held up to view on the side of a mountain; or when, spread over a valley, they are looked down upon from an eminence. It is therefore impossible, under any circumstances, for the

(marginal line numbers: 2120, 2125, 2130, 2135, 2140, 2145, 2150)

2118 and situation 1822: *not in* 1810–20.   2119 are 1822: is 1810–20.
2120 the sucker 1823: sucker 1810–22.   2120–2 (which . . . shrubs) 1823: *not in* 1810–22.   2123 compelled 1820: being compelled 1810.   2127 that 1820: which 1810.   2128 be thus 1820: thus be 1810.   2133 quality 1820: nature 1810.   2134 a stop 1820: as top [*misprint*] 1810.   2135 those 1822: these 1810–20.   2136 graceful in . . . and 1820: which, while it is graceful in its outline, is 1810.   2138 is 1820: has been 1810.   2139 that encourages . . . this 1820: and law under which this is carried on, as a 1810.   2143 for his task 1820: to tread in the path of nature 1810.   2144 start all 1835: all start 1810–23.   2145 necessity 1822: circumstance 1810–20.   2147 appears 1820: which appears 1810.   2151 therefore 1823: then 1810–22.

artificial planter to rival the beauty of nature. But a moment's thought will show that, if ten thousand of this spiky tree, the larch, are stuck in at once upon the side of a hill, they can grow up into nothing but deformity; that, while they are suffered to stand, we shall look in vain for any of those appearances which are the chief sources of beauty in a natural wood. 2155

It must be acknowledged that the larch, till it has outgrown the size of a shrub, shows, when looked at singly, some elegance in form and appearance, especially in spring, decorated, as it then is, by the pink tassels of its blossoms; but, as a tree, it is less than any other pleasing: 2160 its branches (for *boughs* it has none) have no variety in the youth of the tree, and little dignity, even when it attains its full growth; *leaves* it cannot be said to have, consequently neither affords shade nor shelter. In spring the larch becomes green long before the native trees; and its green is so peculiar and vivid, that, finding nothing to harmonize with 2165 it, wherever it comes forth, a disagreeable speck is produced. In summer, when all other trees are in their pride, it is of a dingy lifeless hue; in autumn of a spiritless unvaried yellow, and in winter it is still more lamentably distinguished from every other deciduous tree of the forest, for they seem only to sleep, but the larch appears absolutely 2170 dead. If an attempt be made to mingle thickets, or a certain proportion of other forest-trees, with the larch, its horizontal branches intolerantly cut them down as with a scythe, or force them to spindle up to keep pace with it. The terminating spike renders it impossible that the several trees, where planted in numbers, should ever blend together 2175 so as to form a mass or masses of wood. Add thousands to tens of thousands, and the appearance is still the same—a collection of separate individual trees, obstinately presenting themselves as such; and which, from whatever point they are looked at, if but seen, may be counted upon the fingers. Sunshine, or shadow, has little power to adorn the 2180 surface of such a wood; and the trees not carrying up their heads, the wind raises among them no majestic undulations. It is indeed true, that, in countries where the larch is a native, and where, without

2155–6 we shall . . . beauty in 1820: an absolute and insurmountable obstacle will prevent the realization of any of those appearances which we have described as the chief cause of the beauty of 1810. 2159 shows 1820: has 1810. form 1820: its form 1810. 2160 decorated . . . then is 1820: when decorated 1810. 2165 the larch 1822: it 1810–20. 2167 wherever it . . . produced 1820: it makes a speck and deformity in the landscape 1810. 2169–72 in autumn . . . dead. 1820: and in winter appears absolutely dead. In this respect it is lamentably distinguished from every other tree of the forest. 1810. 2175 terminating spike 1822: spike in which it terminates 1810–20. 2175–6 the . . . numbers 1822: when it is planted in numbers, that the several trees 1810–20. 2179 obstinately presenting 1820: which obstinately present 1810. which 1820: *not in* 1810. 2183 raises 1820: produces 1810.

interruption, it may sweep from valley to valley, and from hill to hill,   2185
a sublime image may be produced by such a forest, in the same manner
as by one composed of any other single tree, to the spreading of which
no limits can be assigned. For sublimity will never be wanting, where
the sense of innumerable multitude is lost in, and alternates with, that
of intense unity; and to the ready perception of this effect, similarity and   2190
almost identity of individual form and monotony of colour contribute.
But this feeling is confined to the native immeasurable forest; no
artificial plantation can give it.

The foregoing observations will, I hope, (as nothing has been
condemned or recommended without a substantial reason) have some   2195
influence upon those who plant for ornament merely. To such as plant
for profit, I have already spoken. Let me then entreat that the native
deciduous trees may be left in complete possession of the lower ground;
and that plantations of larch, if introduced at all, may be confined to the
highest and most barren tracts. Interposition of rocks would there   2200
break the dreary uniformity of which we have been complaining; and
the winds would take hold of the trees, and imprint upon their shapes
a wildness congenial to their situation.

Having determined what kinds of trees must be wholly rejected, or
at least very sparingly used, by those who are unwilling to disfigure   2205
the country; and having shown what kinds ought to be chosen; I
should have given, if my limits had not already been overstepped, a
few practical rules for the manner in which trees ought to be disposed
in planting. But to this subject I should attach little importance, if
I could succeed in banishing such trees as introduce deformity, and   2210
could prevail upon the proprietor to confine himself, either to those
found in the native woods, or to such as accord with them. This is,
indeed, the main point; for, much as these scenes have been injured by
what has been taken from them—buildings, trees, and woods, either
through negligence, necessity, avarice, or caprice—it is not the re-   2215
movals, but the harsh *additions* that have been made, which are the
worst grievance—a standing and unavoidable annoyance. Often have
I felt this distinction, with mingled satisfaction and regret; for, if no
positive deformity or discordance be substituted or superinduced, such
is the benignity of Nature, that, take away from her beauty after   2220
beauty, and ornament after ornament, her appearance cannot be
marred—the scars, if any be left, will gradually disappear before

2196 merely 1820: mainly 1810.   such as 1822: those who 1810–20.
2200 highest and most 1820: higher and more 1810.   2207 my limits
. . . overstepped 1822: I had not already overstepped my limits 1810–20.
2211–12 those found in 1820: which form 1810.   2215–16 the removals 1822:
these removals 1810–20.   2222 marred 1820: lastingly marred 1810.

a healing spirit; and what remains will still be soothing and pleasing.—

> "Many hearts deplored 2225
> The fate of those old trees; and oft with pain
> The traveller at this day will stop and gaze
> On wrongs which nature scarcely seems to heed:
> For sheltered places, bosoms, nooks, and bays,
> And the pure mountains, and the gentle Tweed, 2230
> And the green silent pastures, yet remain."

There are few ancient woods left in this part of England upon which such indiscriminate ravage as is here "deplored," could now be committed. But, out of the numerous copses, fine woods might in time be raised, probably without sacrifice of profit, by leaving, at the periodical 2235 fellings, a due proportion of the healthiest trees to grow up into timber.—This plan has fortunately, in many instances, been adopted; and they, who have set the example, are entitled to the thanks of all persons of taste. As to the management of planting with reasonable attention to ornament, let the images of nature be your guide, and the 2240 whole secret lurks in a few words; thickets or underwoods—single trees—trees clustered or in groups—groves—unbroken woods, but with varied masses of foliage—glades—invisible or winding boundaries —in rocky districts, a seemly proportion of rock left wholly bare, and other parts half hidden—disagreeable objects concealed, and formal 2245 lines broken—trees climbing up to the horizon, and, in some places, ascending from its sharp edge, in which they are rooted, with the whole body of the tree appearing to stand in the clear sky—in other parts, woods surmounted by rocks utterly bare and naked, which add the sense of height, as if vegetation could not thither be carried, and im- 2250 press a feeling of duration, power of resistance, and security from change!

The author has been induced to speak thus at length, by a wish to preserve the native beauty of this delightful district, because still further changes in its appearance must inevitably follow, from the change of inhabitants and owners which is rapidly taking place.—About the 2255 same time that strangers began to be attracted to the country, and to feel a desire to settle in it, the difficulty, that would have stood in the way of their procuring situations, was lessened by an unfortunate alteration in the circumstances of the native peasantry, proceeding

2260

2223–4 pleasing.— 1820: pleasing.—"Many hearts;" says a living Poet speaking of a noble wood which had been felled in an interesting situation; 1810. 2233 as is here "deplored," 1820: *not in* 1810. 2235 without 1822: without any 1810–20. 2253 The author has 1835: I have 1810–23. by 1822: with 1810–20. 2254 further 1835: farther 1810–23. 2258 desire 1822: wish 1810–20.

from a cause which then began to operate, and is now felt in every house. The family of each man, whether *estatesman* or farmer, formerly had a twofold support; first, the produce of his lands and flocks; and, secondly, the profit drawn from the employment of the women and children, as manufacturers; spinning their own wool in their own 2265 houses (work chiefly done in the winter season), and carrying it to market for sale. Hence, however numerous the children, the income of the family kept pace with its increase. But, by the invention and universal application of machinery, this second resource has been cut off; the gains being so far reduced, as not to be sought after but by a few aged 2270 persons disabled from other employment. Doubtless, the invention of machinery has not been to these people a pure loss; for the profits arising from home-manufactures operated as a strong temptation to choose that mode of labour in neglect of husbandry. They also participate in the general benefit which the island has derived from the 2275 increased value of the produce of land, brought about by the establishment of manufactories, and in the consequent quickening of agricultural industry. But this is far from making them amends; and now that home-manufactures are nearly done away, though the women and children might, at many seasons of the year, employ themselves with advan- 2280 tage in the fields beyond what they are accustomed to do, yet still all possible exertion in this way cannot be rationally expected from persons whose agricultural knowledge is so confined, and, above all, where there must necessarily be so small a capital. The consequence, then, is—that proprietors and farmers being no longer able to maintain themselves 2285 upon small farms, several are united in one, and the buildings go to decay, or are destroyed; and that the lands of the *estatesmen* being mortgaged, and the owners constrained to part with them, they fall into the hands of wealthy purchasers, who in like manner unite and consolidate; and, if they wish to become residents, erect new mansions 2290 out of the ruins of the ancient cottages, whose little enclosures, with all the wild graces that grew out of them, disappear. The feudal tenure under which the estates are held has indeed done something towards checking this influx of new settlers; but so strong is the inclination, that these galling restraints are endured; and it is probable, that in a 2295 few years the country on the margin of the Lakes will fall almost entirely into the possession of gentry, either strangers or natives. It is then much to be wished, that a better taste should prevail among these

2264 drawn 1820: which was drawn 1810.   2266 work chiefly done 1820: which was done chiefly 1810.   2269 cut 1822: wholly cut 1820: almost wholly cut 1810.   2285 proprietors and 1822: *not in* 1810–20.   2286 in 1820: into 1810.   2292 that 1820: which 1810.   them, disappear 1820: them and around them, dissappear [*sic*] 1810.   2293 under which . . . held 1820: of these estates 1810.   2296 on the margin 1820: *not in* 1810.

new proprietors; and, as they cannot be expected to leave things to themselves, that skill and knowledge should prevent unnecessary 2300 deviations from that path of simplicity and beauty along which, without design and unconsciously, their humble predecessors have moved. In this wish the author will be joined by persons of pure taste throughout the whole island, who, by their visits (often repeated) to the Lakes in the North of England, testify that they deem the district a sort of 2305 national property, in which every man has a right and interest who has an eye to perceive and a heart to enjoy.

2301 along 1820: in 1810.   2304 in 1820: to [*sic*] 1810.   2307/8 The Writer may now express a hope that the end, which was proposed in the commencement of this Introduction, has not been wholly unattained; and that there is no impropriety in connecting these latter remarks with the Etchings now offered to the public. For it is certain that, if the evil complained of should continue to spread, these Vales, notwithstanding their lakes, rivers, torrents, and surrounding rocks and mountains, will lose their chief recommendation for the eye of the painter and the man of imagination and feeling. And, upon the present occasion, the Artist is bound to acknowledge that, if the fruit of his labours have any value, it is owing entirely to the models which he has had before him, in a country which retained till lately an appearance unimpaired of MAN and NATURE animated, as it were, by one spirit for the production of beauty, grace, and grandeur.

THE END. 1810: om. 1820–35.

MISCELLANEOUS
OBSERVATIONS

M R. W E S T, in his well-known Guide to the Lakes, recommends, as 2310 the best season for visiting this country, the interval from the beginning of June to the end of August; and, the two latter months being a time of vacation and leisure, it is almost exclusively in these that strangers resort hither. But that season is by no means the best; the colouring of the mountains and woods, unless where they are diversified by rocks, 2315 is of too unvaried a green; and, as a large portion of the vallies is allotted to hay-grass, some want of variety is found there also. The meadows, however, are sufficiently enlivened after hay-making begins, which is much later than in the southern part of the island. A stronger objection is rainy weather, setting in sometimes at this period with a 2320 vigour, and continuing with a perseverance, that may remind the disappointed and dejected traveller of those deluges of rain which fall

2308–9 MISCELLANEOUS OBSERVATIONS. 1822: *not in* 1820: SECTION I. OF THE BEST TIME FOR VISITING THE LAKES. 1810.   2309/10 A few words may not improperly be annexed, with an especial view to promote the enjoyment of the Tourist. And first, in respect to the Time when this Country can be seen to most advantage. 1820: In the Introduction to this Work a survey has been given of the face of the country, in which our English Lakes are situated which will not perhaps prove unserviceable even to Natives and Residents, however well acquainted with its appearance; as it will probably direct their attention to some objects which they have overlooked, and will exhibit others under relations of which they have been unconscious. I will now address myself more particularly to the Stranger and the Traveller; and, without attempting to give a formal Tour through the country, and without binding myself servilely to accompany the Etchings, I will attach to the Work such directions, descriptions, and remarks, as I hope will confer an additional interest upon the Views, and will also be of use to a person preparing for a first visit to these scenes, and during his progress through them.—To begin then with the time which he ought to choose:— 1810: *om.* 1822–35.   2310 in his . . . Lakes 1820: *not in* 1810.   2310–11 as the . . . country 1822: *not in* 1810–20.   2312 time 1822: season 1810– 20.   2313–14 it is almost . . . season is 1820: are those which are generally selected; but they are 1810.   2314 resort hither 1822: visit the Country 1820. 2314–18 the colouring . . . are sufficiently 1820: for the disadvantages belonging to them are many and great. The principal are, the monotonous green of the Mountains and of the Woods, and the embrowned colour of the grass in the Vallies. This however is variegated and 1810.   2314–16 the colouring . . . unvaried a 1822: there is a want of variety in the colouring of the mountains and woods; which, unless where they are diversified by rocks, are of a monotonous 1820. 2317 some 1822: a 1820.   2319 part 1820: parts 1810.   2319–20 A stronger objection 1820: An objection which will be more strongly felt 1810. 2320 setting in sometimes 1822: setting in often 1820: which often sets in 1810. 2321 continuing 1820: continues 1810.   2322 traveller of those 1820: Traveller of the wet season between the Tropics; or of those 1810.

among the Abyssinian mountains, for the annual supply of the Nile. The months of September and October (particularly October) are generally attended with much finer weather; and the scenery is then, beyond comparison, more diversified, more splendid, and beautiful; but, on the other hand, short days prevent long excursions, and sharp and chill gales are unfavourable to parties of pleasure out of doors. Nevertheless, to the sincere admirer of nature, who is in good health and spirits, and at liberty to make a choice, the six weeks following the 1st of September may be recommended in preference to July and August. For there is no inconvenience arising from the season which, to such a person, would not be amply compensated by the *autumnal* appearance of any of the more retired vallies, into which discordant plantations and unsuitable buildings have not yet found entrance.—In such spots, at this season, there is an admirable compass and proportion of natural harmony in colour, through the whole scale of objects; in the tender green of the after-grass upon the meadows, interspersed with islands of grey or mossy rock, crowned by shrubs and trees; in the irregular inclosures of standing corn, or stubble-fields, in like manner broken; in the mountain-sides glowing with fern of divers colours; in the calm blue lakes and river-pools; and in the foliage of the trees, through all the tints of autumn,—from the pale and brilliant yellow of the birch and ash, to the deep greens of the unfaded oak and alder, and of the ivy upon the rocks, upon the trees, and the cottages. Yet, as most travellers are either stinted, or stint themselves, for time, the space between the middle or last week in May, and the middle or last week of June, may be pointed out as affording the best combination of long days, fine weather, and variety of impressions. Few of the native trees are then in full leaf; but, for whatever may be wanting in depth of shade, more than an equivalent will be found in the diversity of foliage, in the blossoms of the fruit-and-berry-bearing trees which abound in the woods, and in the golden flowers of the broom and other shrubs, with which many of the copses are intervened. In those woods, also, and on these mountain-sides which have a northern aspect, and in

2325

2330

2335

2340

2345

2350

2355

2323–4 Nile. The 1820: Nile. Hence, as a very large majority of strangers visit the Lakes at this season, the country labours under the ill repute of being scarcely ever free of rain.—The 1810.   2326 diversified 1810–23, *Errata*: diversified 1835. 2329 Nevertheless, to 1820: Nevertheless the beauty of this country in Autumn so far surpasses that of Midsummer, that to 1810.   2333 compensated 1823: recompensed 1810–22.   2335 plantations 1810, 1823–35: plantation 1820–2. 2336 admirable 1820: admirable and affecting 1810.   2337 in colour 1822: in form and colour 1810–20.   2339 rock 1820: rocks 1810.   2342 lakes and 1820: Lakes or 1810.   2345 alder 1820: the alder 1810.   upon [*second*] 1820: *not in* 1810.   2347–8 the space . . . pointed out as 1823: I would recommend the space . . . last week of June, as 1810–22.   2350 then 1820: indeed then 1810.   2351 more 1820: far more 1810.   2354 intervened 1820: variegated 1810.   2355 these 1823: those 1810–22.

the deep dells, many of the spring-flowers still linger; while the open and sunny places are stocked with the flowers of the approaching summer. And, besides, is not an exquisite pleasure still untasted by him who has not heard the choir of linnets and thrushes chaunting their love-songs in the copses, woods, and hedge-rows of a mountainous 2360 country; safe from the birds of prey, which build in the inaccessible crags, and are at all hours seen or heard wheeling about in the air? The number of these formidable creatures is probably the cause, why, in the *narrow* vallies, there are no skylarks; as the destroyer would be enabled to dart upon them from the near and surrounding crags, before 2365 they could descend to their ground-nests for protection. It is not often that the nightingale resorts to these vales; but almost all the other tribes of our English warblers are numerous; and their notes, when listened to by the side of broad still waters, or when heard in unison with the murmuring of mountain-brooks, have the compass of their 2370 power enlarged accordingly. There is also an imaginative influence in the voice of the cuckoo, when that voice has taken possession of a deep mountain valley, very different from any thing which can be excited by the same sound in a flat country. Nor must a circumstance be omitted, which here renders the close of spring especially interesting; I mean 2375 the practice of bringing down the ewes from the mountains to yean in the vallies and enclosed grounds. The herbage being thus cropped as it springs, *that* first tender emerald green of the season, which would otherwise have lasted little more than a fortnight, is prolonged in the pastures and meadows for many weeks: while they are farther en- 2380 livened by the multitude of lambs bleating and skipping about. These sportive creatures, as they gather strength, are turned out upon the open mountains, and with their slender limbs, their snow-white colour, and their wild and light motions, beautifully accord or contrast with the rocks and lawns, upon which they must now begin to seek 2385 their food. And last, but not least, at this time the traveller will be sure

2356 spring-flowers 1820: earlier spring-flowers 1810.   2357 the approaching 1835: approaching 1810–23.   2363 these 1823: those 1810–22. probably 1820: *not in* 1810.   2366–7 It is not . . . the nightingale resorts [Nightingales resort 1820–2] to these vales 1820–35: Neither are Nightingales here to be heard 1810.   2370–1 the compass . . . accordingly 1820: much more power over the heart, and the imagination than in other places 1810.   2373 very 1820: which is very 1810.   2374 a circumstance be omitted 1820: I omit a circumstance 1810.   2377–8 herbage . . . it springs 1820: springing herbage being thus cropped 1810.   2378 emerald 1820: and emerald 1810. 2379 have lasted 1820: last 1810.   2381–2 about. These . . . creatures 1820: about; which 1810.   2385 rocks and lawns 1820: lawns and rocks 1810.   upon 1820: upon and among 1810.   2386–7 And last . . . inns. 1820: But, what is of most consequence, the Traveller at this season would be almost sure of having fine weather.—The opinion which I have given concerning the comparative advantages of the different times for visiting these Lakes, is founded upon a long acquaintance with the Country, and an intimate knowledge of its appearance at all seasons. But 1810.

of room and comfortable accommodation, even in the smaller inns. I am aware that few of those who may be inclined to profit by this recommendation will be able to do so, as the time and manner of an excursion of this kind are mostly regulated by circumstances which 2390 prevent an entire freedom of choice. It will therefore be more pleasant to observe, that, though the months of July and August are liable to many objections, yet it often happens that the weather, at this time, is not more wet and stormy than they, who are really capable of enjoying the sublime forms of nature in their utmost sublimity, would desire. 2395 For no traveller, provided he be in good health, and with any command of time, would have a just privilege to visit such scenes, if he could grudge the price of a little confinement among them, or interruption in his journey, for the sight or sound of a storm coming on or clearing away. Insensible must he be who would not congratulate himself upon 2400 the bold bursts of sunshine, the descending vapours, wandering lights and shadows, and the invigorated torrents and water-falls, with which broken weather, in a mountainous region, is accompanied. At such a time there is no cause to complain, either of the monotony of mid-summer colouring, or the glaring atmosphere of long, cloudless, and 2405 hot days.

Thus far concerning the respective advantages and disadvantages of the different seasons for visiting this country. As to the order in which objects are best seen—a lake being composed of water flowing from higher grounds, and expanding itself till its receptacle is filled 2410 to the brim,—it follows, that it will appear to most advantage when approached from its outlet, especially if the lake be in a mountainous country; for, by this way of approach, the traveller faces the grander features of the scene, and is gradually conducted into its most sublime recesses. Now, every one knows, that from amenity and beauty the 2415 transition to sublimity is easy and favourable; but the reverse is not

2388–9 inclined . . . recommendation 1820: satisfied with the reasons, by which this opinion is supported 1810.   2389 do so 1820: profit from what has been said 1810.   2390 are 1810, 1822–35: is 1820.   2391–2 pleasant to 1822: pleasant to me to 1810–20.   2393 many objections 1820: the objections which have been mentioned 1810.   often 1822: not unfrequently 1810–20.   2394 and 1820: or 1810.   2395 utmost 1820: height of 1810.   2396 be 1820: is 1810.   2399 for 1820: from 1810.   2400 Insensible . . . would not 1820: and he would 1810.   2401 wandering 1820: and wandering 1810.   2402 shadows, and 1820: shadows, 1810.   2404–6 there is . . . days. 1820: the monotony of midsummer colouring, and the want of variety caused by this, and by the glaring atmosphere of long, cloudless and hot days, is wholly removed. 1810. *Section I of* 1810 *here ends; for Section II, with which* 1810 *concludes, see pp.* 260–86 *below and cf. textual n.* 1–500.   2407–3325 *Not in* 1810.   2407–8 concerning . . . seasons 1835: respecting the most eligible season 1820–3.   2411 follows, 1822: follows from the nature of things, 1820.

so; for, after the faculties have been elevated, they are indisposed to humbler excitement. *

It is not likely that a mountain will be ascended without disappointment, if a wide range of prospect be the object, unless either the summit 2420 be reached before sun-rise, or the visitant remain there until the time of sun-set, and afterwards. The precipitous sides of the mountain, and the neighbouring summits, may be seen with effect under any atmosphere which allows them to be seen at all; but *he* is the most fortunate adventurer, who chances to be involved in vapours which open and 2425 let in an extent of country partially, or, dispersing suddenly, reveal the whole region from centre to circumference.

A stranger to a mountainous country may not be aware that his walk in the early morning ought to be taken on the eastern side of the vale, otherwise he will lose the morning light, first touching the tops and 2430 thence creeping down the sides of the opposite hills, as the sun ascends, or he may go to some central eminence, commanding both the shadows from the eastern, and the lights upon the western mountains. But, if the horizon line in the east be low, the western side may be taken for the sake of the reflections, upon the water, of light from the 2435 rising sun. In the evening, for like reasons, the contrary course should be taken.

After all, it is upon the *mind* which a traveller brings along with him that his acquisitions, whether of pleasure or profit, must principally depend.—May I be allowed a few words on this subject? 2440

Nothing is more injurious to genuine feeling than the practice of hastily and ungraciously depreciating the face of one country by comparing it with that of another. True it is Qui *bene* distinguit bene *docet*; yet fastidiousness is a wretched travelling companion; and the best guide to which, in matters of taste we can entrust ourselves, is a disposition 2445 to be pleased. For example, if a traveller be among the Alps, let him surrender up his mind to the fury of the gigantic torrents, and take delight in the contemplation of their almost irresistible violence, without

---

* The only instances to which the foregoing observations do not apply, are Derwent-water and Lowes-water. Derwent is distinguished from all the other Lakes by being *surrounded* with sublimity: the fantastic mountains of Borrowdale to the south, the solitary majesty of Skiddaw to the north, the bold steeps of Wallow-crag and Lodore to the east, and to the west the clustering mountains of New-lands. Lowes-water is tame at the head, but towards its outlet has a magnificent assemblage of mountains. Yet as far as respects the formation of such receptacles, the general observation holds good: neither Derwent nor Lowes-water derive any supplies from the streams of those mountains that dignify the landscape towards the outlets.

2417 elevated 1822: raised by communion with the sublime 1820.   2418 excitement. * 1822: excitement. [*no note appended*] 1820.   2428–37 *Not in* 1820. 2440 few words 1822: concluding word 1820.   on 1835: upon 1820–3.

complaining of the monotony of their foaming course, or being disgusted with the muddiness of the water—apparent even where it is violently agitated. In Cumberland and Westmorland, let not the comparative weakness of the streams prevent him from sympathising with such impetuosity as they possess; and, making the most of the present objects, let him, as he justly may do, observe with admiration the unrivalled brilliancy of the water, and that variety of motion, mood, and character, that arises out of the want of those resources by which the power of the streams in the Alps is supported.—Again, with respect to the mountains; though these are comparatively of diminutive size, though there is little of perpetual snow, and no voice of summer-avalanches is heard among them; and though traces left by the ravage of the elements are here comparatively rare and unimpressive, yet out of this very deficiency proceeds a sense of stability and permanence that is, to many minds, more grateful—

> "While the coarse rushes to the sweeping breeze
> Sigh forth their ancient melodies."

Among the Alps are few places that do not preclude this feeling of tranquil sublimity. Havoc, and ruin, and desolation, and encroachment, are everywhere more or less obtruded; and it is difficult, notwithstanding the naked loftiness of the *pikes*, and the snow-capped summits of the *mounts*, to escape from the depressing sensation, that the whole are in a rapid process of dissolution; and, were it not that the destructive agency must abate as the heights diminish, would, in time to come, be levelled with the plains. Nevertheless, I would relish to the utmost the demonstrations of every species of power at work to effect such changes.

From these general views let us descend a moment to detail. A stranger to mountain imagery naturally on his first arrival looks out for sublimity in every object that admits of it; and is almost always disappointed. For this disappointment there exists, I believe, no general preventive; nor is it desirable that there should. But with regard to one class of objects, there is a point in which injurious expectations may be easily corrected. It is generally supposed that waterfalls are scarcely worth being looked at except after much rain, and that, the more swoln the stream, the more fortunate the spectator; but this however is true only of large cataracts with sublime accompaniments; and not even of these without some drawbacks. In other

2450–1 even where . . . agitated 1822: wherever it is unagitated 1820.
2464 coarse 1820–3, *Edd.*: course 1835.   2465/6 *See the Ode, Pass of Kirkstone.* 1820: *om.* 1822–35.   2477 mountain imagery 1823: mountain-scenery 1820–2.   2485 however 1823: *not in* 1820–2.   2486–91 In other . . . observed that the principal 1823: The principal 1820–2.

instances, what becomes, at such a time, of that sense of refreshing coolness which can only be felt in dry and sunny weather, when the rocks, herbs, and flowers glisten with moisture diffused by the breath of the precipitous water? But, considering these things as objects of sight only, it may be observed that the principal charm of the smaller waterfalls or cascades consists in certain proportions of form and affinities of colour, among the component parts of the scene; and in the contrast maintained between the falling water and that which is apparently at rest, or rather settling gradually into quiet in the pool below. The beauty of such a scene, where there is naturally so much agitation, is also heightened, in a peculiar manner, by the *glimmering*, and, towards the verge of the pool, by the *steady*, reflection of the surrounding images. Now, all those delicate distinctions are destroyed by heavy floods, and the whole stream rushes along in foam and tumultuous confusion. A happy proportion of component parts is indeed noticeable among the landscapes of the North of England; and, in this characteristic essential to a perfect picture, they surpass the scenes of Scotland, and, in a still greater degree, those of Switzerland.

As a resident among the Lakes, I frequently hear the scenery of this country compared with that of the Alps; and therefore a few words shall be added to what has been incidentally said upon that subject.

If we could recall, to this region of lakes, the native pine-forests, with which many hundred years ago a large portion of the heights was covered, then, during spring and autumn, it might frequently, with much propriety, be compared to Switzerland,—the elements of the landscape would be the same—one country representing the other in miniature. Towns, villages, churches, rural seats, bridges and roads: green meadows and arable grounds, with their various produce, and deciduous woods of diversified foliage which occupy the vales and lower regions of the mountains, would, as in Switzerland, be divided by dark forests from ridges and round-topped heights covered with snow, and from pikes and sharp declivities imperfectly arrayed in the same glittering mantle: and the resemblance would be still more perfect on those days when vapours, resting upon, and floating around the summits, leave the elevation of the mountains less dependent upon the eye than on the imagination. But the pine-forests have wholly disappeared; and only during late spring and early autumn is realized here that assemblage of the imagery of different seasons, which is exhibited through the whole summer among the Alps,—winter in the

2490
2495
2500
2505
2510
2515
2520
2525

2496–7 The beauty . . . manner 1822: Peculiarly, also, is the beauty of such a scene, where there is naturally so much agitation, heightened here 1820. 2501 A happy 1822: I will conclude with observing, that a happy 1820. 2502 indeed 1822: generally 1820.   2504/5 THE END. 1820: *om.* 1822–35. 2505–3325 *Not in* 1820.   2513 Towns 1823: *not in* 1822.

distance,—and warmth, leafy woods, verdure and fertility at hand, and widely diffused.

Striking, then, from among the permanent materials of the landscape, that stage of vegetation which is occupied by pine-forests, and, above that, the perennial snows, we have mountains, the highest of which 2530 little exceed 3,000 feet, while some of the Alps do not fall short of 14,000 or 15,000, and 8,000 or 10,000 is not an uncommon elevation. Our tracts of wood and water are almost as diminutive in comparison; therefore, as far as sublimity is dependent upon absolute bulk and height, and atmospherical influences in connection with these, it is 2535 obvious, that there can be no rivalship. But a short residence among the British Mountains will furnish abundant proof, that, after a certain point of elevation, viz. that which allows of compact and fleecy clouds settling upon, or sweeping over, the summits, the sense of sublimity depends more upon form and relation of objects to each other than upon 2540 their actual magnitude; and, that an elevation of 3,000 feet is sufficient to call forth in a most impressive degree the creative, and magnifying, and softening powers of the atmosphere. Hence, on the score even of sublimity, the superiority of the Alps is by no means so great as might hastily be inferred;—and, as to the *beauty* of the lower regions of the 2545 Swiss Mountains, it is noticeable—that, as they are all regularly mown, their surface has nothing of that mellow tone and variety of hues by which mountain turf, that is never touched by the scythe, is distinguished. On the smooth and steep slopes of the Swiss hills, these plots of verdure do indeed agreeably unite their colour with that of the 2550 deciduous trees, or make a lively contrast with the dark green pine-groves that define them, and among which they run in endless variety of shapes—but this is most pleasing *at first sight*; the permanent gratification of the eye requires finer gradations of tone, and a more delicate blending of hues into each other. Besides, it is only in spring and late 2555 autumn that cattle animate by their presence the Swiss lawns; and, though the pastures of the higher regions where they feed during the summer are left in their natural state of flowery herbage, those pastures are so remote, that their texture and colour are of no consequence in the composition of any picture in which a lake of the Vales is a feature. 2560 Yet in those lofty regions, how vegetation is invigorated by the genial climate of that country! Among the luxuriant flowers there met with, groves, or forests, if I may so call them, of Monks-hood are frequently seen; the plant of deep, rich blue, and as tall as in our gardens; and

this at an elevation where, in Cumberland, Icelandic moss would only 2565
be found, or the stony summits be utterly bare.

We have, then, for the colouring of Switzerland, *principally* a vivid
green herbage, black woods, and dazzling snows, presented in masses
with a grandeur to which no one can be insensible; but not often
graduated by Nature into soothing harmony, and so ill suited to the 2570
pencil, that though abundance of good subjects may be there found,
they are not such as can be deemed *characteristic* of the country; nor is
this unfitness confined to colour: the forms of the mountains, though
many of them in some points of view the noblest that can be conceived,
are apt to run into spikes and needles, and present a jagged outline 2575
which has a mean effect, transferred to canvass. This must have been
felt by the ancient masters; for, if I am not mistaken, they have not
left a single landscape, the materials of which are taken from the
peculiar features of the Alps; yet Titian passed his life almost in their
neighbourhood; the Poussins and Claude must have been well acquain- 2580
ted with their aspects; and several admirable painters, as Tibaldi and
Luino, were born among the Italian Alps. A few experiments have
lately been made by Englishmen, but they only prove that courage,
skill, and judgment, may surmount any obstacles; and it may be safely
affirmed, that they who have done best in this bold adventure, will be 2585
the least likely to repeat the attempt. But, though our scenes are better
suited to painting than those of the Alps, I should be sorry to contemplate either country in reference to that art, further than as its fitness
or unfitness for the pencil renders it more or less pleasing to the eye of
the spectator, who has learned to observe and feel, chiefly from Nature 2590
herself.

Deeming the points in which Alpine imagery is superior to British
too obvious to be insisted upon, I will observe that the deciduous
woods, though in many places unapproachable by the axe, and triumphing in the pomp and prodigality of Nature, have, in general, * neither 2595
the variety nor beauty which would exist in those of the mountains of
Britain, if left to themselves. Magnificent walnut-trees grow upon the
plains of Switzerland; and fine trees, of that species, are found scattered
over the hill-sides: birches also grow here and there in luxuriant
beauty; but neither these, nor oaks, are ever a prevailing tree, nor can 2600
even be said to be common; and the oaks, as far as I had an opportunity
of observing, are greatly inferior to those of Britain. Among the
interior vallies the proportion of beeches and pines is so great that
other trees are scarcely noticeable; and surely such woods are at all
seasons much less agreeable than that rich and harmonious distribution 2605
of oak, ash, elm, birch, and alder, that formerly clothed the sides of

* The greatest variety of trees is found in the Valais.

Snowdon and Helvellyn; and of which no mean remains still survive at the head of Ulswater. On the Italian side of the Alps, chesnut and walnut-trees grow at a considerable height on the mountains; but, even there, the foliage is not equal in beauty to the "natural product" of this climate. In fact the sunshine of the South of Europe, so envied when heard of at a distance, is in many respects injurious to rural beauty, particularly as it incites to the cultivation of spots of ground which in colder climates would be left in the hands of nature, favouring at the same time the culture of plants that are more valuable on account of the fruit they produce to gratify the palate, than for affording pleasure to the eye, as materials of landscape. Take, for instance, the Promontory of Bellagio, so fortunate in its command of the three branches of the Lake of Como, yet the ridge of the Promontory itself, being for the most part covered with vines interspersed with olive trees, accords but ill with the vastness of the green unappropriated mountains, and derogates not a little from the sublimity of those finely contrasted pictures to which it is a fore-ground. The vine, when cultivated upon a large scale, notwithstanding all that may be said of it in poetry,* makes but a dull formal appearance in landscape; and the olive-tree (though one is loth to say so) is not more grateful to the eye than our common willow, which it much resembles; but the hoariness of hue, common to both, has in the aquatic plant an appropriate delicacy, harmonising with the situation in which it most delights. The same may no doubt be said of the olive among the dry rocks of Attica, but I am speaking of it as found in gardens and vineyards in the North of Italy. At Bellagio, what Englishman can resist the temptation of substituting, in his fancy, for these formal treasures of cultivation, the natural variety of one of our parks—its pastured lawns, coverts of hawthorn, of wild-rose, and honeysuckle, and the majesty of forest trees?—such wild graces as the banks of Derwent-water shewed in the time of the Ratcliffes; and Gowbarrow Park, Lowther, and Rydal do at this day.

* Lucretius has charmingly described a scene of this kind.

> "Inque dies magis in montem succedere sylvas
> Cogebant, infraque locum concedere cultis:
> Prata, lacus, rivos, segetes, vinetaque læta
> Collibus et campis ut haberent, atque olearum
> *Cærula* distinguens inter *plaga* currere posset
> Per tumulos, et convalleis, camposque profusa:
> Ut nunc esse vides vario distincta lepore
> Omnia, quæ pomis intersita dulcibus ornant,
> Arbustisque tenent felicibus obsita circum."

2610 "natural product" 1823: natural product 1822.   2611–37 In fact . . . at this day 1823: *not in* 1822.   2624 fn. tumulos . . . Arbustisque 1835: tumulus . . . Arbustique 1823.

As my object is. to reconcile a Briton to the scenery of his own country, though not at the expense of truth, I am not afraid of asserting that in many points of view our LAKES, also, are much more interest- 2640 ing than those of the Alps; first, as is implied above, from being more happily proportioned to the other features of the landscape; and next, both as being infinitely more pellucid, and less subject to agitation from the winds.* Como, (which may perhaps be styled the King of Lakes, as Lugano is certainly the Queen) is disturbed by a periodical 2645 wind blowing *from* the head in the morning, and *towards* it in the afternoon. The magnificent Lake of the four Cantons, especially its noblest division, called the Lake of Uri, is not only much agitated by winds, but in the night time is disturbed from the bottom, as I was told, and indeed as I witnessed, without any apparent commotion in the air; and 2650 when at rest, the water is not pure to the eye, but of a heavy green hue—as is that of all the other lakes, apparently according to the degree in which they are fed by melted snows. If the Lake of Geneva furnish an exception, this is probably owing to its vast extent, which allows the water to deposit its impurities. The water of the English lakes, on the 2655 contrary, being of a crystalline clearness, the reflections of the surrounding hills are frequently so lively, that it is scarcely possible to distinguish the point where the real object terminates, and its unsubstantial duplicate begins. The lower part of the Lake of Geneva, from its narrowness, must be much less subject to agitation than the 2660 higher divisions, and, as the water is clearer than that of the other Swiss Lakes, it will frequently exhibit this appearance, though it is scarcely possible in an equal degree. During two comprehensive tours among the Alps, I did not observe, except on one of the smaller lakes, between Lugano and Ponte Tresa, a single instance of those beautiful 2665 repetitions of surrounding objects on the bosom of the water, which are so frequently seen here: not to speak of the fine dazzling trembling

* It is remarkable that Como (as is probably the case with other Italian Lakes) is more troubled by storms in summer than in winter. Hence the propriety of the following verses.

> "Lari! margine ubique confragoso
> Nulli cœlicolum negas sacellum
> Picto pariete saxeoque tecto;
> Hinc miracula multa navitarum
> Audis, nec placido refellis ore,
> Sed nova usque paras, Noto vel Euro
> *Æstivas* quatientibus cavernas,
> Vel surgentis ab Adduæ cubili
> Cæco grandinis imbre provoluto."   LANDOR.

2644 winds.* 1823: winds. [*no note appended*] 1822.   2653 furnish 1823: furnishes 1822.   2662 will frequently 1823: may 1822.   2663 scarcely 1823: not 1822.   2666 surrounding objects 1823: the surrounding scenery 1822.

network, breezy motions, and streaks and circles of intermingled smooth and rippled water, which make the surface of our lakes a field of endless variety. But among the Alps, where every thing tends to the grand and the sublime, in surfaces as well as in forms, if the lakes do not court the placid reflections of land objects, those of first-rate magnitude make compensation, in some degree, by exhibiting those ever-changing fields of green, blue, and purple shadows or lights, (one scarcely knows which to name them) that call to mind a sea-prospect contemplated from a lofty cliff.

The subject of torrents and water-falls has already been touched upon; but it may be added that in Switzerland, the perpetual accompaniment of snow upon the higher regions takes much from the effect of foaming white streams; while, from their frequency, they obstruct each other's influence upon the mind of the spectator; and, in all cases, the effect of an individual cataract, excepting the great Fall of the Rhine at Schaffhausen, is diminished by the general fury of the stream of which it is a part.

Recurring to the reflections from still water, I will describe a singular phenomenon of this kind of which I was an eye-witness.

Walking by the side of Ulswater upon a calm September morning, I saw, deep within the bosom of the lake, a magnificent Castle, with towers and battlements, nothing could be more distinct than the whole edifice;—after gazing with delight upon it for some time, as upon a work of enchantment, I could not but regret that my previous knowledge of the place enabled me to account for the appearance. It was in fact the reflection of a pleasure-house called Lyulph's Tower—the towers and battlements magnified and so much changed in shape as not to be immediately recognized. In the meanwhile, the pleasure-house itself was altogether hidden from my view by a body of vapour stretching over it and along the hill-side on which it stands, but not so as to have intercepted its communication with the lake; and hence this novel and most impressive object, which, if I had been a stranger to the spot, would, from its being inexplicable, have long detained the mind in a state of pleasing astonishment.

Appearances of this kind, acting upon the credulity of early ages, may have given birth to, and favoured the belief in, stories of sub-aqueous palaces, gardens, and pleasure-grounds—the brilliant ornaments of Romance.

2670

2675

2680

2685

2690

2695

2700

2705

2669 make 1822–3, *Edd.*: makes 1835.   2672 objects, those 1822–3, *Edd.*: objects those 1835.   2678 in Switzerland 1823: *not in* 1822.   2680 obstruct 1823: obstruct in some degree 1822.   2702 Appearances 1823: An appearance 1822.   2703 and favoured the belief in, stories 1823: the stories 1822.

With this *inverted* scene I will couple a much more extraordinary phenomenon, which will shew how other elegant fancies may have had their origin, less in invention than in the actual processes of nature.

About eleven o'clock on the forenoon of a winter's day, coming suddenly, in company of a friend, into view of the Lake of Grasmere, 2710 we were alarmed by the sight of a newly-created Island; the transitory thought of the moment was, that it had been produced by an earthquake or some other convulsion of nature. Recovering from the alarm, which was greater than the reader can possibly sympathize with, but which was shared to its full extent by my companion, we proceeded to 2715 to examine the object before us. The elevation of this new island exceeded considerably that of the old one, its neighbour; it was like-wise larger in circumference, comprehending a space of about five acres; its surface rocky, speckled with snow, and sprinkled over with birch trees; it was divided towards the south from the other island by a 2720 narrow frith, and in like manner from the northern shore of the lake; on the east and west it was separated from the shore by a much larger space of smooth water.

Marvellous was the illusion! Comparing the new with the old Island, the surface of which is soft, green, and unvaried, I do not scruple 2725 to say that, as an object of sight, it was much the more distinct. "How little faith," we exclaimed, "is due to one sense, unless its evidence be confirmed by some of its fellows! What Stranger could possibly be persuaded that this, which we know to be an unsubstantial mockery, is *really* so; and that there exists only a single Island on this beautiful 2730 Lake?" At length the appearance underwent a gradual transmutation; it lost its prominence and passed into a glimmering and dim *inversion*, and then totally disappeared;—leaving behind it a clear open area of ice of the same dimensions. We now perceived that this bed of ice, which was thinly suffused with water, had produced the illusion, by 2735 reflecting and refracting (as persons skilled in optics would no doubt easily explain) a rocky and woody section of the opposite mountain named Silver-how.

Having dwelt so much upon the beauty of pure and still water, and pointed out the advantage which the Lakes of the North of England 2740 have in this particular over those of the Alps, it would be injustice not to advert to the sublimity that must often be given to Alpine scenes, by the agitations to which those vast bodies of diffused water are there subject. I have witnessed many tremendous thunder-storms among the Alps, and the most glorious effects of light and shadow; but I never 2745 happened to be present when any Lake was agitated by those hurricanes which I imagine must often torment them. If the commotions be at all proportionable to the expanse and depth of the waters, and the height of the surrounding mountains, then, if I may judge from what is frequently seen here, the exhibition must be awful and astonishing.— 2750 On this day, March 30, 1822, the winds have been acting upon the small Lake of Rydal, as if they had received command to carry its waters from their bed into the sky; the white billows in different quarters disappeared under clouds, or rather drifts, of spray, that were whirled along, and up into the air by scouring winds, charging each 2755 other in squadrons in every direction, upon the Lake. The spray, having been hurried aloft till it lost its consistency and whiteness, was driven along the mountain tops like flying showers that vanish in the distance. Frequently an eddying wind scooped the waters out of the basin, and forced them upwards in the very shape of an Icelandic 2760 Geyser, or boiling fountain, to the height of several hundred feet.

This small Mere of Rydal, from its position, is subject in a peculiar degree to these commotions. The present season, however, is unusually stormy;—great numbers of fish, two of them not less than 12 pounds weight, were a few days ago cast on the shores of Derwent-water by 2765 the force of the waves.

Lest, in the foregoing comparative estimate, I should be suspected of partiality to my native mountains, I will support my general opinion by the authority of Mr. West, whose Guide to the Lakes has been eminently serviceable to the Tourist for nearly 50 years. The Author, 2770 a Roman Catholic Clergyman, had passed much time abroad, and was well acquainted with the scenery of the Continent. He thus expresses himself: "They who intend to make the continental tour should begin here; as it will give, in miniature, an idea of what they are to meet with there, in traversing the Alps and Appenines; to which our 2775 northern mountains are not inferior in beauty of line, or variety of summit, number of lakes, and transparency of water; not in colouring of rock, or softness of turf; but in height and extent only. The mountains here are all accessible to the summit, and furnish prospects no less surprising, and with more variety, than the Alps themselves. The tops 2780 of the highest Alps are inaccessible, being covered with everlasting snow, which commencing at regular heights above the cultivated tracts, or wooded and verdant sides, form indeed the highest contrast in nature. For there may be seen all the variety of climate in one view. To this, however, we oppose the sight of the ocean, from the summits 2785 of all the higher mountains, as it appears intersected with promontories, decorated with islands, and animated with navigation."—West's *Guide*, p. 5.

2761 several hundred feet 1823: 800 or 900 feet 1822.   2786 promontories 1822–3, *Errata*: promontaries 1835.

EXCURSIONS

TO

THE TOP OF SCAWFELL AND ON THE BANKS OF
ULSWATER.

It was my intention, several years ago, to describe a regular tour through this country, taking the different scenes in the most favourable order; but after some progress had been made in the work it was 2795 abandoned from a conviction, that, if well executed, it would lessen the pleasure of the Traveller by anticipation, and, if the contrary, it would mislead him. The Reader may not, however, be displeased with the following extract from a letter to a Friend, giving an account of a visit to a summit of one of the highest of these mountains; of which I am 2800 reminded by the observations of Mr. West, and by reviewing what has been said of this district in comparison with the Alps.

Having left Rosthwaite in Borrowdale, on a bright morning in the first week of October, we ascended from Seathwaite to the top of the ridge, called Ash-course, and thence beheld three distinct views;—on 2805 one side, the continuous Vale of Borrowdale, Keswick, and Bassenthwaite,—with Skiddaw, Helvellyn, Saddle-back, and numerous other mountains,—and, in the distance, the Solway Frith and the Mountains of Scotland;—on the other side, and below us, the Langdale Pikes— their own vale below *them*;—Windermere,—and, far beyond Winder- 2810 mere, Ingleborough in Yorkshire. But how shall I speak of the deliciousness of the third prospect! At this time, *that* was most favoured by sunshine and shade. The green Vale of Esk—deep and green, with its glittering serpent stream, lay below us; and, on we looked to the Mountains near the Sea,—Black Comb pre-eminent,—and, still beyond, 2815 to the Sea itself, in dazzling brightness. Turning round we saw the Mountains of Wastdale in tumult; to our right, Great Gavel, the loftiest, a distinct, and *huge* form, though the middle of the mountain was, to our eyes, as its base.

We had attained the object of this journey; but our ambition now 2820 mounted higher. We saw the summit of Scaw-fell, apparently very near to us; and we shaped our course towards it; but, discovering that it could not be reached without first making a considerable descent, we resolved, instead, to aim at another point of the same mountain, called the *Pikes*, which I have since found has been estimated as higher than 2825 the summit bearing the name of Scawfell Head, where the Stone Man is built.

The sun had never once been overshadowed by a cloud during the whole of our progress from the centre of Borrowdale. On the summit of the Pike, which we gained after much toil, though with- 2830 out difficulty, there was not a breath of air to stir even the papers containing our refreshment, as they lay spread out upon a rock. The stillness seemed to be not of this world:—we paused, and kept silence to listen; and no sound could be heard: the Scawfell Cataracts were voiceless to us; and there was not an insect to hum in the air. The vales 2835 which we had seen from Ash-course lay yet in view; and, side by side with Eskdale, we now saw the sister Vale of Donnerdale terminated by the Duddon Sands. But the majesty of the mountains below, and close to us, is not to be conceived. We now beheld the whole mass of Great Gavel from its base,—the Den of Wastdale at our feet—a gulph 2840 immeasurable: Grasmire and the other mountains of Crummock— Ennerdale and its mountains; and the Sea beyond! We sat down to our repast, and gladly would we have tempered our beverage (for there was no spring or well near us) with such a supply of delicious water as we might have procured, had we been on the rival summit of Great 2845 Gavel; for on its highest point is a small triangular receptacle in the native rock, which, the shepherds say, is never dry. There we might have slaked our thirst plenteously with a pure and celestial liquid, for the cup or basin, it appears, has no other feeder than the dews of heaven, the showers, the vapours, the hoar frost, and the spotless snow. 2850

While we were gazing around, "Look," I exclaimed, "at yon ship upon the glittering sea!" "Is it a ship?" replied our shepherd-guide. "It can be nothing else," interposed my companion; "I cannot be mistaken, I am so accustomed to the appearance of ships at sea." The Guide dropped the argument; but, before a minute was gone, he 2855 quietly said, "Now look at your ship; it is changed into a horse." So indeed it was,—a horse with a gallant neck and head. We laughed heartily; and, I hope, when again inclined to be positive, I may remember the ship and the horse upon the glittering sea; and the calm confidence, yet submissiveness, of our wise Man of the Moun- 2860 tains, who certainly had more knowledge of clouds than we, whatever might be our knowledge of ships.

I know not how long we might have remained on the summit of the Pike, without a thought of moving, had not our Guide warned us that we must not linger; for a storm was coming. We looked in vain to 2865 espy the signs of it. Mountains, vales, and sea were touched with the clear light of the sun. "It is there," said he, pointing to the sea beyond

2842–3 We sat . . . and 1823: *not in* 1822.   2846 receptacle 1823: receptacle of water 1822.   2848 liquid 1823: beverage 1822.   2867 said he 1823: he said 1822.

Whitehaven, and there we perceived a light vapour unnoticeable but by a shepherd accustomed to watch all mountain bodings. We gazed around again, and yet again, unwilling to lose the remembrance of what lay before us in that lofty solitude; and then prepared to depart. Meanwhile the air changed to cold, and we saw that tiny vapours swelled into mighty masses of cloud which came boiling over the mountains. Great Gavel, Helvellyn, and Skiddaw, were wrapped in storm; yet Langdale, and the mountains in that quarter, remained all bright in sunshine. Soon the storm reached us; we sheltered under a crag; and almost as rapidly as it had come it passed away, and left us free to observe the struggles of gloom and sunshine in other quarters. Langdale now had its share, and the Pikes of Langdale were decorated by two splendid rainbows. Skiddaw also had his own rainbows. Before we again reached Ash-course every cloud had vanished from every summit. 2870 2875 2880

I ought to have mentioned that round the top of Scawfell-PIKE not a blade of grass is to be seen. Cushions or tufts of moss, parched and brown, appear between the huge blocks and stones that lie in heaps on all sides to a great distance, like skeletons or bones of the earth not needed at the creation, and there left to be covered with never-dying lichens, which the clouds and dews nourish; and adorn with colours of vivid and exquisite beauty. Flowers, the most brilliant feathers, and even gems, scarcely surpass in colouring some of those masses of stone, which no human eye beholds, except the shepherd or traveller be led thither by curiosity: and how seldom must this happen! For the other eminence is the one visited by the adventurous stranger; and the shepherd has no inducement to ascend the PIKE in quest of his sheep; no food being *there* to tempt them. 2885 2890 2895

We certainly were singularly favoured in the weather; for when we were seated on the summit, our conductor, turning his eyes thoughtfully round, said, "I do not know that in my whole life, I was ever, at any season of the year, so high upon the mountains on so *calm* a day." (It was the 7th of October.) Afterwards we had a spectacle of the grandeur of earth and heaven commingled; yet without terror. We knew that the storm would pass away;—for so our prophetic Guide had assured us. 2900

Before we reached Seathwaite in Borrowdale, a few stars had appeared, and we pursued our way down the Vale, to Rosthwaite, by moonlight. 2905

2880 his 1823: its 1822.   2884 Cushions 1823: A few cushions 1822. 2893 stranger 1823: Traveller 1822.   2895 no food being 1823: for no food is 1822.   2900-1 a spectacle . . . of earth 1823: the storm, which exhibited the grandeur of the earth 1822.   2901 heaven 1823: heavens 1822.   2902 the storm 1823: it 1822.

Scawfell and Helvellyn being the two Mountains of this region which will best repay the fatigue of ascending them, the following Verses may be here introduced with propriety. They are from the Author's Miscellaneous Poems.   2910

TO ——,

ON HER FIRST ASCENT TO THE SUMMIT OF HELVELLYN.

INMATE of a Mountain Dwelling,
Thou has clomb aloft, and gazed,   2915
From the watch-towers of Helvellyn;
Awed, delighted, and amazed!

Potent was the spell that bound thee
Not unwilling to obey;
For blue Ether's arms, flung round thee,   2920
Stilled the pantings of dismay.

Lo! the dwindled woods and meadows!
What a vast abyss is there!
Lo! the clouds, the solemn shadows,
And the glistenings—heavenly fair!   2925

And a record of commotion
Which a thousand ridges yield;
Ridge, and gulf, and distant ocean
Gleaming like a silver shield!

—Take thy flight;—possess, inherit   2930
Alps or Andes—they are thine!
With the morning's roseate Spirit,
Sweep their length of snowy line;

Or survey the bright dominions
In the gorgeous colours drest   2935
Flung from off the purple pinions,
Evening spreads throughout the west!

Thine are all the choral fountains
Warbling in each sparry vault
Of the untrodden lunar mountains;   2940
Listen to their songs!—or halt,

2907–3325 *Not in* 1822.   2907–49 *Not in* 1823.   2938 choral *Edd.*:
coral 1835.

To Niphates' top invited,
Whither spiteful Satan steered;
Or descend where the ark alighted,
When the green earth re-appeared: 2945

For the power of hills is on thee,
As was witnessed through thine eye
Then, when old Helvellyn won thee
To confess their majesty!

Having said so much of *points of view* to which few are likely to   2950
ascend, I am induced to subjoin an account of a short excursion through
more accessible parts of the country, made at a *time* when it is seldom
seen but by the inhabitants. As the journal was written for one acquainted with the general features of the country, only those effects and
appearances are dwelt upon, which are produced by the changeableness   2955
of the atmosphere, or belong to the season when the excursion was
made.

A.D. 1805.—On the 7th of November, on a damp and gloomy
morning, we left Grasmere Vale, intending to pass a few days on the
Banks of Ullswater. A mild and dry autumn had been unusually favour-   2960
able to the preservation and beauty of foliage; and, far advanced as the
season was, the trees on the larger Island of Rydal-mere retained a
splendour which did not need the heightening of sunshine. We noticed,
as we passed, that the line of the grey rocky shore of that island, shaggy
with variegated bushes and shrubs, and spotted and striped with   2965
purplish brown heath, indistinguishably blending with its image
reflected in the still water, produced a curious resemblance, both in
form and colour, to a richly-coated caterpillar, as it might appear
through a magnifying glass of extraordinary power. The mists
gathered as we went along: but, when we reached the top of Kirkstone,   2970
we were glad we had not been discouraged by the apprehension of bad
weather. Though not able to see a hundred yards before us, we were
more than contented. At such a time, and in such a place, every
scattered stone the size of one's head becomes a companion. Near the
top of the Pass is the remnant of an old wall, which (magnified,   2975
though obscured, by the vapour) might have been taken for a fragment
of some monument of ancient grandeur,—yet that same pile of stones
we had never before even observed. This situation, it must be allowed,
is not favourable to gaiety; but a pleasing hurry of spirits accompanies
the surprise occasioned by objects transformed, dilated, or distorted,   2980
as they are when seen through such a medium. Many of the fragments

2942 Niphates' *Edd.*: Niphate's 1835.   2950 *points* 1835: a *point* 1823.

of rock on the top and slopes of Kirkstone, and of similar places, are fantastic enough in themselves; but the full effect of such impressions can only be had in a state of weather when they are not likely to be *sought* for. It was not till we had descended considerably that the fields 2985 of Hartshope were seen, like a lake tinged by the reflection of sunny clouds: I mistook them for Brothers-water, but, soon after, we saw that Lake gleaming faintly with a steelly brightness,—then, as we continued to descend, appeared the brown oaks, and the birches of lively yellow—and the cottages—and the lowly Hall of Hartshope, with its 2990 long roof and ancient chimneys. During great part of our way to Patterdale, we had rain, or rather drizzling vapour; for there was never a drop upon our hair or clothes larger than the smallest pearls upon a lady's ring.

The following morning, incessant rain till 11 o'clock, when the sky 2995 began to clear, and we walked along the eastern shore of Ullswater towards the farm of Blowick. The wind blew strong, and drove the clouds forward, on the side of the mountain above our heads;—two storm-stiffened black yew-trees fixed our notice, seen through, or under the edge of, the flying mists,—four or five goats were bounding 3000 among the rocks;—the sheep moved about more quietly, or cowered beneath their sheltering places. This is the only part of the country where goats are now found;* but this morning, before we had seen these, I was reminded of that picturesque animal by two rams of mountain breed, both with Ammonian horns, and with beards majestic as 3005 that which Michael Angelo has given to his statue of Moses.—But to return; when our path had brought us to that part of the naked common which overlooks the woods and bush-besprinkled fields of Blowick, the lake, clouds, and mists were all in motion to the sound of sweeping winds;—the church and cottages of Patterdale scarcely visible, or seen 3010 only by fits between the shifting vapours. To the northward the scene was less visionary;—Place Fell steady and bold;—the whole lake driving onward like a great river—waves dancing round the small islands. The house at Blowick was the boundary of our walk; and we returned, lamenting to see a decaying and uncomfortable dwelling in a 3015 place where sublimity and beauty seemed to contend with each other. But these regrets were dispelled by a glance on the woods that clothe the opposite steeps of the lake. How exquisite was the mixture of sober and splendid hues! The general colouring of the trees was brown—rather that of ripe hazel nuts; but towards the water, there 3020 were yet beds of green, and in the highest parts of the wood, was

* A.D. 1805. These also have disappeared.

2992 there 1823, *Edd.*: their 1835.

abundance of yellow foliage, which, gleaming through a vapoury lustre, reminded us of masses of clouds, as you see them gathered together in the west, and touched with the golden light of the setting sun.

After dinner we walked up the Vale: I had never had an idea of its 3025 extent and width in passing along the public road on the other side. We followed the path that leads from house to house; two or three times it took us through some of those copses or groves that cover the little hillocks in the middle of the vale, making an intricate and pleasing intermixture of lawn and wood. Our fancies could not resist the 3030 temptation; and we fixed upon a spot for a cottage, which we began to build: and finished as easily as castles are raised in the air.—Visited the same spot in the evening. I shall say nothing of the moonlight aspect of the situation which had charmed us so much in the afternoon; but I wish you had been with us when, in returning to our friend's 3035 house, we espied his lady's large white dog, lying in the moonshine upon the round knoll under the old yew-tree in the garden, a romantic image—the dark tree and its dark shadow—and the elegant creature, as fair as a spirit! The torrents murmured softly: the mountains down which they were falling did not, to my sight, furnish a back-ground for 3040 this Ossianic picture; but I had a consciousness of the depth of the seclusion, and that mountains were embracing us on all sides; "I saw not, but I *felt* that they were there."

Friday, November 9th.—Rain, as yesterday, till 10 o'clock, when we took a boat to row down the lake. The day improved,—clouds and 3045 sunny gleams on the mountains. In the large bay under Place Fell, three fishermen were dragging a net,—a picturesque group beneath the high and bare crags! A raven was seen aloft; not hovering like the kite, for that is not the habit of the bird; but passing on with a straight-forward perseverance, and timing the motion of its wings to its own 3050 croaking. The waters were agitated; and the iron tone of the raven's voice, which strikes upon the ear at all times as the more dolorous from its regularity, was in fine keeping with the wild scene before our eyes. This carnivorous fowl is a great enemy to the lambs of these solitudes; I recollect frequently seeing, when a boy, bunches of un- 3055 fledged ravens suspended from the churchyard gates of H——, for which a reward of *so* much a head was given to the adventurous destroyer.—The fishermen drew their net ashore, and hundreds of fish were leaping in their prison. They were all of the kind called skellies, a sort of fresh-water herring, shoals of which may sometimes 3060 be seen dimpling or rippling the surface of the lake in calm weather. This species is not found, I believe, in any other of these lakes; nor, as far as I know, is the chevin, that *spiritless* fish, (though I am loth to call

3040 sight, 1823, *Edd.*: sight 1835.

it so, for it was a prime favourite with Isaac Walton,) which must
frequent Ullswater, as I have seen a large shoal passing into the lake   3065
from the river Eamont. *Here* are no pike, and the char are smaller than
those of the other lakes, and of inferior quality; but the grey trout
attains a very large size, sometimes weighing above twenty pounds.
This lordly creature seems to know that "retiredness is a piece of
majesty"; for it is scarcely ever caught, or even seen, except when it   3070
quits the depths of the lake in the spawning season, and runs up into
the streams, where it is too often destroyed in disregard of the law of
the land and of nature.

Quitted the boat in the bay of Sandwyke, and pursued our way
towards Martindale along a pleasant path—at first through a coppice,   3075
bordering the lake, then through green fields—and came to the
village, (if village it may be called, for the houses are few, and separated
from each other,) a sequestered spot, shut out from the view of the
lake. Crossed the one-arched bridge, below the chapel, with its "bare
ring of mossy wall," and single yew-tree. At the last house in the dale   3080
we were greeted by the master, who was sitting at his door, with a
flock of sheep collected round him, for the purpose of smearing them
with tar (according to the custom of the season) for protection against
the winter's cold. He invited us to enter, and view a room built by Mr.
Hasell for the accommodation of his friends at the annual chase of red   3085
deer in his forests at the head of these dales. The room is fitted up in the
sportsman's style, with a cupboard for bottles and glasses, with strong
chairs, and a dining-table; and ornamented with the horns of the stags
caught at these hunts for a succession of years—the length of the last
race each had run being recorded under his spreading antlers. The good   3090
woman treated us with oaten cake, new and crisp; and after this welcome refreshment and rest, we proceeded on our return to Patterdale
by a short cut over the mountains. On leaving the fields of Sandwyke,
while ascending by a gentle slope along the valley of Martindale, we
had occasion to observe that in thinly-peopled glens of this character   3095
the general want of wood gives a peculiar interest to the scattered
cottages embowered in sycamore. Towards its head, this valley splits
into two parts; and in one of these (that to the left) there is no house,
nor any building to be seen but a cattle-shed on the side of a hill, which
is sprinkled over with trees, evidently the remains of an extensive   3100
forest. Near the entrance of the other division stands the house where
we were entertained, and beyond the enclosures of that farm there are
no other. A few old trees remain, relics of the forest, a little stream
hastens, though with serpentine windings, through the uncultivated
hollow, where many cattle were pasturing. The cattle of this country   3105

3070 majesty"; 1823, *Edd.: quotation not closed* 1835.

are generally white, or light-coloured; but these were dark brown, or black, which heightened the resemblance this scene bears to many parts of the Highlands of Scotland.—While we paused to rest upon the hill-side, though well contented with the quiet every-day sounds—the lowing of cattle, bleating of sheep, and the very gentle murmuring of 3110 the valley stream, we could not but think what a grand effect the music of the bugle-horn would have among these mountains. It is still heard once every year, at the chase I have spoken of; a day of festivity for the inhabitants of this district except the poor deer, the most ancient of them all. Our ascent even to the top was very easy; when it was 3115 accomplished we had exceedingly fine views, some of the lofty Fells being resplendent with sunshine, and others partly shrouded by clouds. Ullswater, bordered by black steeps, was of dazzling bright-ness; the plain beyond Penrith smooth and bright, or rather gleamy, as the sea or sea sands. Looked down into Boardale, which, like Sty- 3120 barrow, has been named from the wild swine that formerly abounded here; but it has now no sylvan covert, being smooth and bare, a long, narrow, deep, cradle-shaped glen, lying so sheltered that one would be pleased to see it planted by human hands, there being a sufficiency of soil; and the trees would be sheltered almost like shrubs in a green- 3125 house.—After having walked some way along the top of the hill, came in view of Glenriddin and the mountains at the head of Grisdale.—Before we began to descend, turned aside to a small ruin, called at this day the chapel, where it is said the inhabitants of Martindale and Patterdale were accustomed to assemble for worship. There are now 3130 no traces from which you could infer for what use the building had been erected; the loose stones and the few which yet continue piled up resemble those which lie elsewhere on the mountain; but the shape of the building having been oblong, its remains differ from those of a common sheep-fold; and it has stood east and west. Scarcely did the 3135 Druids, when they fled to these fastnesses, perform their rites in any situation more exposed to disturbance from the elements. One cannot pass by without being reminded that the rustic psalmody must have had the accompaniment of many a wildly-whistling blast; and what dismal storms must have often drowned the voice of the preacher! 3140 As we descend, Patterdale opens upon the eye in grand simplicity, screened by mountains, and proceeding from two heads, Deepdale and Hartshope, where lies the little lake of Brotherswater, named in old maps Broaderwater, and probably rightly so; for Bassenthwaite-mere at this day, is familiarly called Broadwater; but the change in the 3145 appellation of this small lake or pool (if it be a corruption) may have been assisted by some melancholy accident similar to what happened

3136 fastnesses, 1823. *Edd.*: fastnesses 1835

about twenty years ago, when two brothers were drowned there, having gone out to take their holiday pleasure upon the ice on a new-year's day.   3150

A rough and precipitous peat track brought us down to our friend's house.—Another fine moonlight night; but a thick fog rising from the neighbouring river, enveloped the rocky and wood-crested knoll on which our fancy-cottage had been erected; and, under the damp cast upon my feelings, I consoled myself with moralising on the folly of hasty   3155 decisions in matters of importance, and the necessity of having at least one year's knowledge of a place before you realise airy suggestions in solid stone.

Saturday, November 10th. At the breakfast-table tidings reached us of the death of Lord Nelson, and of the victory at Trafalgar. Sequestered   3160 as we were from the sympathy of a crowd, we were shocked to hear that the bells had been ringing joyously at Penrith to celebrate the triumph. In the rebellion of the year 1745, people fled with their valuables from the open country to Patterdale, as a place of refuge secure from the incursions of strangers. At that time, news such as we   3165 had heard might have been long in penetrating so far into the recesses of the mountains; but now, as you know, the approach is easy, and the communication, in summer time, almost hourly: nor is this strange, for travellers after pleasure are become not less active, and more numerous than those who formerly left their homes for purposes of   3170 gain. The priest on the banks of the remotest stream of Lapland will talk familiarly of Buonaparte's last conquests, and discuss the progress of the French revolution, having acquired much of his information from adventurers impelled by curiosity alone.

The morning was clear and cheerful after a night of sharp frost. At   3175 10 o'clock we took our way on foot towards Pooley Bridge, on the same side of the lake we had coasted in a boat the day before.—Looked backwards to the south from our favourite station above Blowick. The dazzling sunbeams striking upon the church and village, while the earth was steaming with exhalations not traceable in other quarters,   3180 rendered their forms even more indistinct than the partial and flitting veil of unillumined vapour had done two days before. The grass on which we trod, and the trees in every thicket were dripping with melted hoar-frost. We observed the lemon-coloured leaves of the birches, as the breeze turned them to the sun, sparkle, or rather *flash*,   3185 like diamonds, and the leafless purple twigs were tipped with globes of shining crystal.

The day continued delightful, and unclouded to the end. I will not describe the country which we slowly travelled through, nor relate our adventures: and will only add, that on the afternoon of the 13th we   3190 returned along the banks of Ullswater by the usual road. The lake lay in deep repose after the agitations of a wet and stormy morning. The trees in Gowbarrow park were in that state when what is gained by the disclosure of their bark and branches compensates, almost, for the loss of foliage, exhibiting the variety which characterises the point of 3195 time between autumn and winter. The hawthorns were leafless; their round heads covered with rich red berries, and adorned with arches of green brambles, and eglantines hung with glossy hips; and the grey trunks of some of the ancient oaks, which in the summer season might have been regarded only for their venerable majesty, now attracted 3200 notice by a pretty embellishment of green mosses and fern intermixed with russet leaves retained by those slender outstarting twigs which the veteran tree would not have tolerated in his strength. The smooth silver branches of the ashes were bare; most of the alders as green as the Devonshire cottage-myrtle that weathers the snows of Christmas. 3205 —Will you accept it as some apology for my having dwelt so long on the woodland ornaments of these scenes—that artists speak of the trees on the banks of Ullswater, and especially along the bays of Stybarrow crags, as having a peculiar character of picturesque intricacy in their stems and branches, which their rocky stations and the mountain winds 3210 have combined to give them.

At the end of Gowbarrow park a large herd of deer were either moving slowly or standing still among the fern. I was sorry when a chance-companion, who had joined us by the way, startled them with a whistle, disturbing an image of grave simplicity and thoughtful 3215 enjoyment; for I could have fancied that those natives of this wild and beautiful region were partaking with us a sensation of the solemnity of the closing day. The sun had been set some time; and we could perceive that the light was fading away from the coves of Helvellyn, but the lake, under a luminous sky, was more brilliant than before.   3220

After tea at Patterdale, set out again:—a fine evening; the seven stars close to the mountain-top; all the stars seemed brighter than usual. The steeps were reflected in Brotherswater, and, above the lake, appeared like enormous black perpendicular walls. The Kirkstone torrents had been swoln by the rains, and now filled the mountain pass 3225 with their roaring, which added greatly to the solemnity of our walk. Behind us, when we had climbed to a great height, we saw one light, very distinct, in the vale, like a large red star—a solitary one in the gloomy region. The cheerfulness of the scene was in the sky above us.

Reached home a little before midnight. The following verses (from 3230 the Author's Miscellaneous Poems,) after what has just been read may be acceptable to the reader, by way of conclusion to this little Volume.

ODE.

THE PASS OF KIRKSTONE.   3235

1.

WITHIN the mind strong fancies work,
A deep delight the bosom thrills,
Oft as I pass along the fork
Of these fraternal hills: 3240
Where, save the rugged road, we find
No appanage of human kind;
Nor hint of man, if stone or rock
Seem not his handy-work to mock
By something cognizably shaped;   3245
Mockery—or model roughly hewn,
And left as if by earthquake strewn,
Or from the Flood escaped:
Altars for Druid service fit;
(But where no fire was ever lit,   3250
Unless the glow-worm to the skies
Thence offer nightly sacrifice;)
Wrinkled Egyptian monument;
Green moss-grown tower; or hoary tent;
Tents of a camp that never shall be raised;   3255
On which four thousand years have gazed!

2.

Ye plough-shares sparkling on the slopes!
Ye snow-white lambs that trip
Imprisoned 'mid the formal props   3260
Of restless ownership!
Ye trees, that may to-morrow fall
To feed the insatiate Prodigal!
Lawns, houses, chattels, groves, and fields,
All that the fertile valley shields;   3265
Wages of folly—baits of crime,—
Of life's uneasy game the stake,
Playthings that keep the eyes awake
Of drowsy, dotard Time;
O care! O guilt!—O vales and plains,   3270
Here, 'mid his own unvexed domains,

A Genius dwells, that can subdue
At once all memory of You,—
Most potent when mists veil the sky,
Mists that distort and magnify;   3275
While the coarse rushes, to the sweeping breeze,
Sigh forth their ancient melodies!

3.

List to those shriller notes!—*that* march
Perchance was on the blast,   3280
When through this Height's inverted arch,
Rome's earliest legion passed!
—They saw, adventurously impelled,
And older eyes than theirs beheld,
This block—and yon, whose Church-like frame   3285
Gives to the savage Pass its name.
Aspiring Road! that lov'st to hide
Thy daring in a vapoury bourn,
Not seldom may the hour return
When thou shalt be my Guide: 3290
And I (as often we find cause,
When life is at a weary pause,
And we have panted up the hill
Of duty with reluctant will)
Be thankful, even though tired and faint,   3295
For the rich bounties of Constraint;
Whence oft invigorating transports flow
That Choice lacked courage to bestow!

4.

My Soul was grateful for delight   3300
That wore a threatening brow;
A veil is lifted—can she slight
The scene that opens now?
Though habitation none appear,
The greenness tells, man must be there;   3305
The shelter—that the perspective
Is of the clime in which we live;
Where Toil pursues his daily round;
Where Pity sheds sweet tears, and Love,
In woodbine bower or birchen grove,   3310
Inflicts his tender wound.

3276 coarse *Edd.* [*cf. textual n.* 2464]: course 1835.

—Who comes not hither ne'er shall know
How beautiful the world below;
Nor can he guess how lightly leaps
The brook adown the rocky steeps.   3315
Farewell, thou desolate Domain!
Hope, pointing to the cultured Plain,
Carols like a shepherd boy;
And who is she?—Can that be Joy!
Who, with a sun-beam for her guide,   3320
Smoothly skims the meadows wide;
While Faith, from yonder opening cloud,
To hill and vale proclaims aloud,
"Whate'er the weak may dread, the wicked dare,   3325
Thy lot, O man, is good, thy portion fair!"

The Publishers, with permission of the Author,
have added the following

ITINERARY OF THE LAKES,

FOR THE USE OF TOURISTS.

STAGES.	Miles
Lancaster to Kendal, by Kirkby Lonsdale, ...	30
Lancaster to Kendal, by Burton, ...	22
Lancaster to Kendal, by Milnthorpe, ...	21
Lancaster to Ulverston, over Sands, ...	21
Lancaster to Ulverston, by Levens Bridge, . . .	35½
Ulverston to Hawkshead, by Coniston Water Head, . . .	19
Ulverston to Bowness, by Newby Bridge, . . .	17
Hawkshead to Ambleside, ...	5
Hawkshead to Bowness, ...	6
Kendal to Ambleside, ...	14
Kendal to Ambleside, by Bowness, ...	15
From and back to Ambleside, round the two Langdales, . .	18
Ambleside to Ullswater, ...	10
Ambleside to Keswick, ...	16¼
Keswick to Borrowdale, and round the Lake, . . .	12
Keswick to Borrowdale and Buttermere, ...	23
Keswick to Wastdale and Calder Bridge, ...	27
Calder Bridge to Buttermere and Keswick, . . .	29
Keswick, round Bassenthwaite Lake, ...	18
Keswick to Patterdale, Pooley Bridge, and Penrith, . . .	38
Keswick to Pooley Bridge and Penrith, ...	24
Keswick to Penrith, ...	17½
Whitehaven to Keswick, ...	27
Workington to Keswick, ...	21
Excursion from Penrith to Hawes Water, . . .	27
Carlisle to Penrith, ...	18
Penrith to Kendal, ...	26

ITINERARY.

Inns and Public Houses, when not mentioned, are marked thus.*

LANCASTER to KENDAL, by KIRKBY LONSDALE, 30 m.

Miles.		Miles.	Miles.		Miles.
5	Caton . . .	5	2	Tunstall . . .	13
2	Claughton . . .	7	2	Burrow . . .	15
2	Hornby* . . .	9	2	Kirkby Lonsdale .	17
2	Melling . . .	11	13	Kendal . . .	30

INNS.—*Lancaster*, King's Arms, Commercial Inn, Royal Oak.
INNS.—*Kirkby Lonsdale*, Rose and Crown, Green Dragon.

LANCASTER to KENDAL, by BURTON, 21¾ m.

10¾	Burton . . .	10¾		½	End Moor* . .	16
4¾	Crooklands* .	15½		5¾	Kendal . . .	21¾

INNS.—*Kendal*, King's Arms, Commercial Inn.—*Burton*, Royal Oak, King's Arms.

LANCASTER to KENDAL, by MILNTHORPE, 21¼ m.

2¾	Slyne* . . .	2¾	4	Hale* . . .	12
1¼	Bolton-le-Sands* .	4	½	Beethom* . . .	12½
2	Carnforth* .	6	1¼	Milnthorpe .	13¾
2	Junction of the Milnthorpe and Burton roads	8	1¼	Heversham* .	15
			1½	Levens-bridge .	16½
			4¾	Kendal . . .	21¼

INN.—*Milnthorpe*, Cross Keys.

LANCASTER to ULVERSTON, OVER SANDS, 21 m.

3½	Hest Bank* .	3½	1¼	Flookburgh* .	15
¼	Lancaster Sands .	3¾	¾	Cark . .	15¾
9	Kent's Bank .	12¾	¼	Leven Sands .	16
1	Lower Allithwaite .	13¾	5	Ulverston . .	21

INNS.—*Ulverston*, Sun Inn, Bradyll's Arms.

LANCASTER to ULVERSTON, by LEVENS BRIDGE, 35½ m.

12	Hale*	.	.	.	12	3	Lindal* . . . 23½
½	Beethom* .	.	.	12½	2	Newton* . . . 25½
1¼	Milnthorpe	.	.	13¾	2	Newby Bridge* . . 27½
1¼	Heversham*	.	.	15	2	Low Wood . . 29½
1½	Levens-bridge	.	.	16½	3	Greenodd . . . 32½
4	Witherslack*	.	.	20½	3	Ulverston . . . 35½

ULVERSTON to HAWKSHEAD, by CONISTON WATER-HEAD, 19 m.

6	Lowick-bridge	.	.	6	8	Coniston Water-Head* 16
2	Nibthwaite	.	.	8	3	Hawkshead . . 19

INN.—*Hawkshead*, Red Lion.

ULVERSTON to BOWNESS, by NEWBY-BRIDGE, 16 m.

3	Green Odd	.	.	3	2	Newby-bridge . . 8
3	Low Wood	.	.	6	8	Bowness . . . 16

INNS.—*Bowness*, White Lion, Crown Inn.

HAWKSHEAD to AMBLESIDE, 5 m.

HAWKSHEAD to BOWNESS, 5½ m.

2	Sawrey	.	.	.	2	1½ Bowness . . . 5½
2	Windermere-ferry*	.	4		

KENDAL to AMBLESIDE, 13½ m.

5	Staveley* .	.	.	5	1½	Troutbeck-bridge* . 10
1½	Ings Chapel	.	.	6½	2	Low Wood Inn . . 12
2	Orrest-head	.	.	8½	1½	Ambleside . . . 13½

INNS.—*Ambleside*, Salutation Hotel, Commercial Inn.

KENDAL to AMBLESIDE, by BOWNESS, 15 m.

4	Crook* .	.	.	4	2½	Troutbeck-bridge . 11½
2	Gilpin Bridge*	.	.	6	2	Low Wood Inn . . 13½
3	Bowness	.	.	9	1½	Ambleside . . . 15

A CIRCUIT from and back to AMBLESIDE, by LITTLE and GREAT LANGDALE, 18 m.

3	Skelwith-bridge*.	.	3	2	Langdale Chapel Stile*	13
2	Colwith Cascade .	.	5	5	By High Close and	
3	Blea Tarn .	.	8		Rydal to Ambleside .	18
3	Dungeon Ghyll .	.	11			

AMBLESIDE to ULLSWATER, 10 m.

4	Top of Kirkstone	.	4	3	Inn at Patterdale	. 10
3	Kirkstone Foot .	.	7			

AMBLESIDE to KESWICK, 16¼ m.

1½	Rydal . . .	1½	4	Smalthwaite-bridge	.	12¼
3½	Swan, Grasmere*	. 5	3	Castlerigg .	.	15¼
2	Dunmail Raise .	. 7	1	Keswick .	.	16¼
1¼	Nag's Head, Wythburn	8¼				

EXCURSIONS FROM KESWICK.

INNS.—*Keswick*, Royal Oak, Queen's Head.

To BORROWDALE, and ROUND THE LAKE, 12 m.

2	Barrow-house	.	. 2	1	Return to Grange	. 6
1	Lowdore .	.	· 3	4½	Portinscale	. 10½
1	Grange .	.	· 4	1½	Keswick .	. 12
1	Bowder Stone	.	· 5			

To BORROWDALE and BUTTERMERE.

5	Bowder Stone	.	. 5	4	Gatesgarth	. 12
1	Rosthwaite	.	. 6	2	Buttermere *	. 14
2	Seatoller .	.	. 8	9	Keswick, by Newlands .	23

TWO DAYS' EXCURSION TO WASTDALE, ENNER-DALE, and LOWES-WATER.

FIRST DAY.

6	Rosthwaite	.	. 6	6	Strands,* Nether Wast-	
2	Seatoller .	.	. 8		dale . . .	20
1	Seathwaite	.	. 9	4	Gosforth* .	. 24
3	Sty-head .	.	. 12	3	Calder Bridge* .	. 27
2	Wastdale-head .	.	14			

SECOND DAY.

7	Ennerdale Bridge	.	7	2	Scale-hill* .	.	.	16
3	Lamplugh Cross*	.	10	4	Buttermere*	.	.	20
4	Lowes Water	.	14	9	Keswick	.	.	29

KESWICK ROUND BASSENTHWAITE WATER.

8	Peel Wyke*	.	8	3	Bassenthwaite Sand-			
1	Ouse Bridge	.	9		bed	.	.	13
1	Castle Inn .	.	10	5	Keswick	.	.	18

KESWICK to PATTERDALE, and by POOLEY BRIDGE to PENRITH.

10	Springfield*	.	10	10	Pooley Bridge* through			
7	Gowbarrow Park	.	17		Gowbarrow Park	.		32
5	Patterdale*	.	22	6	Penrith	.	.	38

INNS.—*Penrith*, Crown Inn, The George.

KESWICK to POOLEY BRIDGE and PENRITH.

12	Penruddock*	.	12	3	Pooley Bridge	.	.	18
3	Dacre*	.	15	6	Penrith	.	.	24

KESWICK to PENRITH, 17½ m.

4	Threlkeld*	.	4	3½	Stainton* .	.	.	15
7½	Penruddock	.	11½	2½	Penrith	.	.	17½

WHITEHAVEN to KESWICK, 27 m.

2	Moresby .	.	2	5	Cockermouth	.	.	14
2	Distington	.	4	2½	Embleton .	.	.	16½
2	Winscales .	.	6	6½	Thornthwaite	.	.	23
3	Little Clifton	.	9	4	Keswick	.	.	27

INNS.—*Whitehaven*, Black Lion, Golden Lion, the Globe.
INNS.—*Cockermouth*, The Globe, The Sun.

WORKINGTON to KESWICK, 21 m.

The road joins that from Whitehaven to Keswick 4 miles from Workington.

INNS.—*Workington*, Green Dragon, New Crown, King's Arms.

EXCURSION from PENRITH to HAWESWATER.

5	Lowther, or Askham* .	5	
7	By Bampton* to Hawes Water . . .	12	
4	Return by Butterswick . . .	16	

5	Over Moor Dovack to Pooley . . .	21
6	By Dalemain to Penrith . . .	27

CARLISLE to PENRITH, 18 m.

2½	Carlton* . . .	2½	2	Plumpton* . .	13
7	Low Hesket* . .	9½	5	Penrith . . .	18
1½	High Hesket* . .	11			

INNS.—*Carlisle*, The Bush, Coffee House, King's Arms.

PENRITH to KENDAL, 26 m.

1	Eamont Bridge* . .	1	6¾	Hawse Foot* . .	17
1½	Clifton* . . .	2½	4	Plough Inn* . .	21
2	Hackthorpe * . .	4½	2½	Skelsmergh Stocks* .	23½
5¾	Shap . . .	10¼	2½	Kendal . . .	26

INNS.—*Shap*, Greyhound, King's Arms.

Kendal: Printed by Hudson and Nicholson.

APPENDIX I

[*Select Views*]

SECTION II.

I T is obvious that the point, from which a Stranger should begin this Tour, and the order in which it will be convenient to him to see the different Vales will depend upon this circumstance; viz: from what quarter of the Island he comes. If from Scotland, or by the way of 5 Stainmoor, it will suit him to start from Penrith, taking the scenery of Lowther in his way to Hawes-water. He will next visit Ullswater, &c. reversing the order which I shall point out as being in itself the best. Mr. West has judiciously directed those to whom it is convenient to proceed from Lancaster over the Sands; to take Furness Abbey in 10 their way, if so inclined; and then to advance by the Lake of Coniston. This is unquestionably the most favourable approach. The beautiful Lake of Coniston will thus be traced upwards from its outlet, the only way in which it can be seen, for the first time, without an entire yielding up of its most delightful appearances. And further, the Stranger, 15 from the moment he sets his foot upon the Sands, seems to leave the turmoil and the traffic of the world behind him; and crossing the majestic Plain from which the Sea has retired, he beholds, rising apparently from its base, that cluster of Mountains, among the recesses of which he is going to wander, and into which, by the Vale of Conis- 20 ton, he is gradually and peacefully introduced. The Lake and Vale of Coniston, approached in this manner, improve in appearance with every step. And I may here make this general remark, which, indeed the Reader may have deduced from the representation of the Country, given in the Introduction, that, wherever it is possible, these Lakes 25 and Vallies should be approached from the foot; otherwise most things will come upon the Spectator to great disadvantage. This general rule

1–725 *Cf. Guide,* 1–500.　　　1 SECTION II *S.V.*: Section 2 MS.　　　1/2 Of the points from which the Tour may be most advantageously commenced &c. &c. MS.: On the best approach to the Lakes &c. MS.²: *om. S.V.*　　　3 to him *S.V.*: for him MS.　　　6 start MS.², *S.V.*: begin [?] MS.　　　7 He will next *S.V.*: I suppose that I am addressing myself, not to those who are posting through the Country merely to snatch a slight view of two or three of the most celebrated scenes, but to such Persons as wish to be really acquainted with the most interesting parts of it. The Traveller from Scotland, or who has come by the way of Stainmoor will next MS.　　　8 out as being *S.V.*: out, and shall follow in detail as being MS.　　　10 Sands; MS., *Edd.*: sands *S.V.*　　　11 by *S.V.*: up MS. 12 approach MS.², *S.V.*: approach to the Lakes MS.　　　13 traced . . . outlet MS.², *S.V.*: [?] [?from] its foot MS.　　　18 from . . . beholds MS.², *S.V.*: [?] he sees MS.

applies, though not with equal force to all the Lakes, with the single exception of Lowes-water, which, lying in a direction opposite to the rest, has its most favourable aspects determined accordingly. 30

At the head of Coniston close to the water side is a small and comfortable Inn, which I would advise the Traveller, who is not part of a large company, and who does not look for a parade of accommodation, to make his head-quarters for two days. The first of these days, if the weather permit, may be agreeably passed in an excursion to the Vale 35 of Duddon, or Donnerdale, as part of it is called, and which name may with propriety be given to the whole. It lies over the high hill which bounds the Vale of Coniston on the West. This Valley is very rarely visited; but I recommend it with confidence to the notice of the Traveller of taste and feeling. It will be best approached by a road, 40 ascending from near the church of Coniston, which leads to that part of Donnerdale called Seathwaite. The road is so long and steep that the Traveller will be obliged to lead his horse a considerable part of it. The ascent and descent cannot I think be less than five miles; but, nothing can be found more beautiful than the scene, into which he will 45 be received at the bottom of the hill on the other side. This little circular Valley is a collateral compartment of the long winding Vale, through which flows the stream of Duddon; and its Brook finds its way to the River. Advancing, you will come to the lowly Chapel of Seathwaite, and a field or two beyond, is a Farm-house, where, though 50 there be no sign-board, or outward mark of an Inn, the Traveller who

47 *Before* is a collateral MS. Prose 20[b] *reads*: Person of common sensibility who should descend into this Valley towards the close of September while the aftergrass of the meadows is yet of a fresh green and the leaves of many of the trees faded but perhaps none fallen, will find this scene truly enchanting. [MS. *inserts a large* X.] The rocks, lawns, and woods, are intermingled with a felicity which I think is [equalled *del*.] surpassed in no other part of the Country; and there is one ivied Cottage which [surpasses *del*.] excels both in its form and colour any thing of the kind which I have ever seen—it is a bower of consummate beauty. The [*possibly altered to* This] little circular Vale in which the Traveller will now be embosomed   49 the River *S.V.*: that River MS. you *S.V.*: he MS.   50 field or two MS.², *S.V.*: little MS.   52 *After* accommodated MS. Prose 20[b] *continues*: with [a good Country dinner I *wrongly del*.] ought rather to say breakfast or luncheon; for he must be here in the morning, or he will scarcely have time to finish the days work which I have carved out for him. The meadows and woods of Seathwaite are rich, its appearance is [*tear*]ly undeformed by what Gray so well calls "scrubby plantations," or by mean and [?*del*.] pert houses of modern Architecture; and for the rocks that intersperse and surround it, I know not how I can give a better idea of them than by mentioning a saying which I heard from the Landlord of the Inn at this place. A Stranger some time ago found his way hither; having ordered his dinner he went out, and returning after a little time the [Landlord *del*.] Host in the frank manner of the Country said to him, "Well Sir you have been taking a walk then, which way have you been wandering?" The Traveller answered, "*I have been as* far *as it is finished*," an answer livelily expressing his sense of the chaotic appearance of one portion of the Scene. From the Inn, you will make your way [through *del*.] down the paths to the point where

can content himself with homely diet may be accommodated.—Having satisfied himself with strolling about Seathwaite, he will proceed down Donnerdale to Ulpha Kirk; and from this Church-yard he will have as grand a combination of mountain lines and forms as perhaps this coun- 55 try furnishes. The whole scene is inspirited by the sound and sight of the River rolling immediately below the steep ground upon the top of which the Church stands. From Ulpha Kirk proceed down the Vale towards Broughton. The same character of mingled wildness and culti- vation is still preserved. Rocky grounds, which must for ever forbid 60 the entrance of the plough, here and there, interrupt the cultivation; and in part or wholly fill up the bottom or sides of the Vale.—This beautiful Vale does not gradually disappear in a flat Plain, but termin- ates abruptly in a prospect of the Sands of Duddon, and of the Irish Sea. These are seen in conjunction with its River, and deep recesses of wood. 65 On this account, and for the sake of descending upon Seathwaite so advantageously, I have recommended in opposition to the general rule, that it should be approached from the upper part, rather than from its outlet. From Broughton return to Coniston by the nearest road. The morning of the next day may be employed in sailing upon, and looking 70 about the higher part of the Lake, and in strolling upon its Banks; and the other half in an excursion to the Valley of Yewdale (a branch of the Vale of Coniston) and round the sequestered Valley of Tilberthwaite, which may be considered as a remoter apartment of the Valley of Yew- dale. This excursion may be about five miles, and may be taken either 75 on foot or horse-back; but not in a carriage. From the Valley of Yew- dale having mounted to that of Tilberthwaite, with the Brook upon the right hand, pursue the road till it leads to the furthest of two Cottages; there, ask the way through the fields to an house called Holm-ground. If, on horse-back, alight there; and from a rocky and woody hill, 80 behind the house you will look down upon this wild, beautiful, and singularly secluded Valley. From Holm-ground return to the Inn at Coniston. Next day proceed to Hawkshead; and thence by the side of Estwaite looking back a little while after the road has left the Lake side

the [river *del.*] Duddon issues into the open and fertile Vale from the mouth of a narrow pass of desolate rocky mountains [into which the Duddon having left another open and pastoral division . . . has penetrated *del.*] through which strait the River flows for a considerable space having penetrated into it from another open and pastoral division of the Vale, something less than a mile above. [The river at this point of his journey has ⟨?⟩ by a living Poet *del.*]

Sonnet

O mountain Stream, the Shepherd and his Cot
Are privileg'd Inmates of deep Solitude:

52–8 Having satisfied . . . stands] *For S.V. variants in* MS. Prose 20ᶜ, *see U.T.* 443– 61 *and textual nn.*   66–76 the sake of . . . carriage] *For S.V. variants in* MS. Prose 20ᵈ, *see U.T.* 539–57 *and textual nn.*

upon a fine view (which will be found among these Etchings) of the   85
Lake of Estwaite. Thence, through the two Villages of Sawrey, you
come to the Ferry-house upon Windermere where are good accommodations for the night.

The Tourist has now reached Windermere, and has been introduced
in his road to some sequestered spots not exemplified in these Etchings,   90
but, which, if he wishes to have a complete knowledge of the various
features of this Country, he will be glad to have visited. Every thing
that is of consequence has been taken in its best order, except that the
first burst of the Vale of Windermere, though very interesting from
this approach, is much inferior to that which would have come upon   95
him had he descended by the road from Kendal. Before the Traveller,
whom I have thus far accompanied, enters the Peninsula, at the
extremity of which the Ferry House stands, it will be adviseable to
ascend to a Pleasure-house belonging to J. C. Curwen, Esq. which he
will see upon the side of the rocks on his left hand.—There is a gate,   100
and a person, attending at a little Lodge, or Cot adjoining, who will
conduct him. From this point he will look down upon the cluster of
Islands in the central part of the Lake, upon Bowness, Rayrigg, and
the Mountains of Troutbeck; and will have a prospect of the lower
division of this expanse of water to its extremity. The upper part is   105
hidden. The Pleasure house is happily situated, and is well in its kind,
but, without intending any harsh reflections on the contriver, from
whom it was purchased by its present Proprietor, it may be said that
he, who remembers the spot on which this building stands, and the
immediate surrounding grounds as they were less than thirty years   110
ago, will sigh for the coming of that day when Art, through every rank
of society, shall be taught to have more reverence for Nature. This
scene is, in its natural constitution, far too beautiful to require any
exotic or obtrusive embellishments, either of planting or architecture.

88/9 MS. Prose 24 *begins (om. S.V.):*

Section 4th
Upon Windermere &c.

89 and has *S.V.*: having MS.   90–1 not exemplified . . . but *S.V.: not in*
MS.   93 that the *S.V.*: that he must have had to look back for the view of
Esthwaite Water, given in the Etchings; and that the MS.   94 very interesting *S.V.*: interesting MS.   95 would have come MS.², *S.V.*: comes. MS.
96 him had he descended MS.², *S.V.*: you in descending MS.   99 belonging . . . Esq. *S.V.*: of Mr Curwens MS.: belonging to Mr Curwen MS.².
102 he MS.², *S.V.*: as is well known the Spectator MS.   106 The
S.V.: This MS.   situated *S.V.*: seated MS.   well *S.V.*: a good thing MS.
107 reflections on *S.V.*: reflection upon the taste of MS.   108 its present
Proprietor MS.², *S.V.*: Mr Curwen MS.   110 grounds MS.², *S.V.*: scenes
MS.   113 its MS., *Edd.*: it *S.V.*

With Winandermere a large majority of Visitants begin this Tour. 115
The ordinary course is from Kendal, by the nearest road to Bowness;
but I would recommend it to all persons, whatever may be their mode
of conveyance, or however large their party, when they shall have
reached the Turnpike-house, about a mile beyond Kendal, not to take,
as is commonly done, the road which leads directly to Bowness; but 120
that through Stavely: inasmuch as the break of prospect from Orrest-
head, where the road brings you to the first sight of Windermere, in
itself one of the finest things in the Tour, is much grander than as it
appears from the other road. This for two reasons; first, that you are
between two and three miles nearer the sublime mountains and large 125
expanse of water at the head of the Lake; and secondly that the new
houses and plantations, and the number of trim and artificial objects
with which the neighbourhood of Bowness is crowded, are so far removed from this point, as not to be individually offensive, as they melt
into the general mass of the Landscape. At the bottom of the hill, you 130
find a Guide-post; and, turning, abruptly to the left, will immediately
come in sight of the same general prospect which has been seen above,
from a point, which, as it is comparatively low, necessarily changes the
character of the scene. Thence on, through the close woods of Rayrigg,
to the bustling Inn of Bowness. 135

115 Winandermere *S.V.*: Windermere MS.   *After* Tour MS. *deletes*: and
what has thus far been said will to them be of little use and indeed what I have
to add of details collateral to the main subject will be perhaps of as little
121 break MS.², *S.V.*: [?burst] MS.   124 This for two *S.V.*: [This for two
del.] The latter, indeed is the better station for him who wishes for an instantaneous
map-like burst of the vale and lake, but the other, which opens somewhat gradually
is a much finer landscape; for two MS.   128 crowded *S.V.*: now crowded MS.
are so MS.², *S.V.*: are here so MS.   128–9 removed . . . to be *S.V.*: removed as
not to be from this point MS.   129 as they *S.V.*: and only MS.   130 *After*
Landscape MS. *deletes*: It has always appeared to me that a person of feeling mind,
beginning this excursion with Windermere and descending directly upon Bowness
would not only be disappointed but perhaps in no small degree disgusted with the
bustle, the parade, and drest-out appearance of so many of the objects immediately
around it, beautiful as the scene is in its own [natural constitution *del.*] original
composition. And it was this apprehension which swayed not a little with me, when
I directed the sincere votary to make his approach by the quiet way and entrance
over the Sands.   131 turning . . . left MS.², *S.V.*: turn . . . left, and MS.
immediately *S.V.*: soon MS.   134 scene *S.V.*: scene accordingly MS.
135/6 MS. *deletes*: The Reader, having now perceived the reasons upon which this
direction is founded, will suffer me to go back to Stavely—a Village which will
have opened upon him about four miles beyond Kendal. May the Writer of this be
permitted to say that his heart has never failed to be moved with pleasure, on [his
return *del.*] returning from the southern parts of the Island, at the sight of the fair
meadows, the pellucid and swift brook, and the rugged rocks, with which this
Village and its Church-tower are environed? For here it is that he has first recognized
the appropriate features of this beautiful Country, and felt himself once more
within the precincts of the home of his fancy and affections. As matter of general
interest, [I may add *del.*] it may be added that this Village has a claim, little known,
upon the regards of the Patriot, on account of a struggle that was made by a Band
of fearless and resolute Peasants who 200 years ago here pledged themselves to

defend the rights which they had inherited from their Forefathers. And, had not this struggle been attended with success, these Landscapes would have wanted the greatest part of the most interesting ornaments which they to this day possess, [and which I have dwelt so long upon in the Introduction *del.*] I allude to the Cottages, the partition of the Country into small Estates, and all those unaffected graces which arise out of that arrangement of property chiefly held by customary tenure, and out of that simple state of society which in the Introduction to this Work was described at length.—I will abridge, from Burns' History of West.ᵈ and Cumbᵈ, the interesting particulars of the case in which these Hampdens withstood the powerful Tyrants of their fields," their own Lords, who were led on, and urged on by no less a personage than their Sovereign James 1.ˢᵗ [MS. *inserts*: (*Print what follows in a smaller Type*)] "This King, after he had formed the resolution of laying aside Parlaments, was distressed for want of money, and, among other methods contrived for obtaining it, he laid a scheme to take all the crown lands in the Counties of West: and Cumb: into his own hands, upon the pretence that, as Border service had then ceased by the union of the two Kingdoms in his royal Person, the Estates were determined likewise, which the Tenants held by that service. And to keep himself in countenance he encouraged all the other Lords of Manors within the said Counties to take to themselves the absolute Estate of their several Tenants within their said Manors, and refuse to admit the heirs to their ancestor's Estate[s *del.*]. In consequence of this doctrine, the Prince of Wales, to whom the crown lands of these Counties were assigned, exhibited his Bill in Chancery denying the validity of the claim of Tenant-rights—the Tenants put in their answer: but, from the hazard of contesting with the King who had the judges both of law and equity at his devotion, and at the same time a good round sum in hand appearing to be not unacceptable to the Prince, the matter was compromised, and for the sum of £2700 he agreed to confirm unto them their custom, as set forth in their answer.—But as to the other Manors it did not rest here, but the Lords in several places ejected their tenants, and decrees both in the Chancery and in the Exchequer were obtained against them. The tenants still would not submit. Though the service had ceased the Border spirit remained, and they combined to defend each other by force if no other course should be effectual. A meeting was holden at Stavely, under colour of viewing a bridge, when they came to sundry resolutions to the above effect.—They chose an agent and manager, and, soon after, the King issued out against them a proclamation which was one of the most flagrant exertions of despotism that is to be met with in [the *del.*] English History. However the tenants did not despond. They drew up and published a remonstrance against the claim of the lords; complaining therein "That having peaceably enjoyed their tenements so long, it would be hard that some greedy eagle or devouring vulture should violently pull them out to miseries. The poor bird and weaker cattle (say they making use of an image natural to Mountaineers) are taught and encouraged, for maintenance of their ancient possession to resist others even to death though more able and strong by far than they are." And it was a common saying among them "If the devil be lord, I'll be tenant." Upon this the lords exhibited a bill against them in the Star chamber for a libel, charging them with assembling riotously at Stavely Chapel.—In short, the matter was battled in the Star chamber, and the King and his courts continued to proceed in the same unjust manner, not without gross inconsistency; for the King's letters and proclamations admit[ting *del.*] the existence of tenant-right founded upon Border-service but insist[ing *del.*] upon its abolition by the union of the Crowns, while the Court of [the *del.*] Star-chamber in their record deny that this right ever existed and consider the estates as occupied wholly at the will of the lord. But the lords seem to have been so convinced of the injustice of their own proceeding that compositions were made, and in several of these are clauses assuring and confirming to the tenants their estates descendable from Ancestor to Heir, as if the same before had been nothing but a pretence. Others purchased their tenements to freehold. ["*Edd.*]—[MS. *inserts*: (Here let the Printer resume the larger type)] The village of Stavely therefore is well worthy of a column to commemorate the resolution of these men. The spirit by which they were bound together may recal to the Passenger's mind more

I will not call upon the Reader to waste his time upon descriptions
of things, which every one makes a point of seeing, and of such as lie
open to the notice of the most inattentive Traveller. This, with respect
to a country now so well known, would be useless in itself; and would
be especially improper in a publication of this kind, the main purport   140
of which is, to exhibit scenes which lie apart from the beaten course of
observation.—Accordingly I shall chiefly expatiate upon those retired
spots, which have furnished subjects for the majority of these Etchings,
or upon others of the same character; and when I treat of the more
frequented scenes, I shall attempt little more than to point out qualities   145
by which they are characterized, which may easily escape the notice of
the cursory Spectator. The appearance of the neighbourhood of Bowness, within the last five and thirty years, has undergone many changes,
and most of these for the worse, for want of due attention to those
principles of taste, and those rules for planting and building in a country   150
of this kind, which have been discussed at large in the Introduction.

splendid efforts, those of the confederacy of Peasants that gave birth to the Swiss
Republic, or of the Magna Charta-Barons assembled at Runnymede.—I before
mentioned what connection this struggle has with the Landscapes of this [Country
del.] District, which is our present business. Two miles further stands Ings Chapel
[on the right *del.*] by the wayside: it was re-built by a Native of the place who went,
when a Boy, a poor Adventurer to London; afterwards, having realized a large
fortune as a Merchant at Leghorn, remitted from that place money for this pious
purpose, and also to purchase lands for the benefit of the poor. [In this Vale *del.*]
Here a House was [also *del.*] built by his orders, to receive him at his return;
[which *del.*] it is at this day called, Leghorn Hall. When he was preparing to sail for
England he died suddenly, and the suspicion still remains among the people of
the neighbourhood that [he *del.*] their Benefactor was poisoned, for the sake of his
wealth. The Chapel in the inside is very neat, floored with marble; and the Altar-
piece is enlaid with [different coloured *del.*] marble of various colours, which he
sent from Italy for that purpose. The ornaments about the Altar have been re-
painted not long ago in a stile which an intelligent Woman, the Wife of the Parish
Clerk, when she conducted me through the Church, complained of as being too
glaring for a sacred place.—Between Ings Chapel and Bowness there is nothing
that requires further notice.

136–200 *This section of* MS. Prose 24 *is headed:*

Section 5th
Windermere &c in continuation

136 will *S.V.*: shall MS.   141 scenes *S.V.*: interesting scenes MS.
142 Accordingly . . . expatiate *S.V.*: I therefore wish to hasten on to those
MS.: Accordingly I shall chiefly dwell MS.². 143 these MS., *S.V.*: the MS.².
144–5 when I . . . to point MS.², *S.V.*: to treat of Vales that will give me an
opportunity of pointing MS.   150 taste . . . for planting MS.², *S.V.*:
taste in planting MS.   151 *After* Introduction MS. *deletes*: Grievous would
be his disappointment who, unforewarned of these discordant changes, should first
come, in this quarter, to the side of this celebrated Lake, expecting to see realized
what Nature assisted by man, working for his own accommodation without design
to embellish, did formerly realize here—a perfect Landscape, or wilderness of
Landscapes, without deficiency or disturbance; surpassing those which the happiest
fancy, incited and soothed by the representations of painting and poetry and aided

The Islands of Windermere are beautifully shaped and intermingled. Upon the largest are a few fine old trees; but a great part of this delightful spot, when it first fell into the Improver's hand, was stuck over with trees that are here out of place; and, had the present 155 public-spirited Proprietor sufficient leisure amidst his important avocations to examine the principles which have been enforced in these pages, he would probably be induced to weed these foreigners out by little and little, and introduce more appropriate trees in their stead; such as would be pleasing to look at in their youth, and in maturity and 160 old age might succeed to those venerable natives which the axe has spared. The embankment also, which has been raised round this Island for the sake of preserving the land, could only, it should seem, have been necessary in a few exposed points; and the artificial appearance which this has given to the whole spot is much to be regretted; not to 165 speak of the infinite varieties of minute beauty which it must have destroyed. Could not the margin of this noble Island be given back to Nature? Winds and Waves work with a careless and graceful hand; and any thing which they take away would be amply compensated by the additional spirit, dignity and loveliness which these agents and the 170 other powers of Nature would soon communicate to what was left behind.

Windermere ought to be seen both from its shores and from its surface. None of the other Lakes unfold so many fresh beauties to him who sails upon them. This is owing to its greater size, to its Islands, and 175 to a circumstance in which this Lake differs from all the rest, viz. that of having two Vales at its head, with their accompanying mountains of nearly equal dignity. Nor can the whole grandeur of these two terminations be seen at the same time from any one point, except from the bosom of the Lake. The Islands may be explored at any time of the 180

by the choicest materials which the eye might have had an opportunity of gathering from living nature, could have prefigured to itself.—[MS. *continues undel.*] In addition to [which *del.*] what has been said on the subject of larch plantations with which this neighbourhood is now deformed, I am tempted here to observe, that all spiky trees have an especial bad effect upon the scenery in the narrow and deep vallies of a mountainous Country; for something of the same reason that spires, as has been delicately observed, are, in similar situations, an improper ornament for Churches. There is such a disagreeable contrast between the littleness of the taper form and the bulk and massiveness of the surrounding or incumbent Mountains. In an open or flat Country they are less objectionable, as they may be often referred to the sky, towards which, in manner of a Church spire, they tend or shoot, and from all communication with which, in a narrow valley, they are excluded.   155–7 had the . . . avocations *S.V.*: could the present public-spirited Proprietor spare from his important avocations time MS.   157–8 these pages *S.V.*: this little tract MS.   159 introduce MS.[2], *S.V.*: substitute MS.   164 artificial MS., *S.V.*: manufactured MS.[2].   172/3 I quit this favoured spot with regret. MS.: *om. S.V.*   179 point MS.[2], *S.V.*: point of view MS.

day; but one bright unruffled evening at least, must, if possible, be set apart for the splendour, the stillness and solemnity of a three hours voyage upon the higher division of the Lake, not omitting, towards the end of the excursion, to quit the expanse of water, and peep into the close and calm River at the head; which, in its quiet character, at such 185 a time, appears rather like an overflow of the peaceful Lake itself than to have any more immediate connection with the rough mountains from which it has descended, or the turbulent Torrents of which it is composed. Many persons content themselves with what they see of Windermere in their progress in a boat from Bowness to the head of 190 the Lake, walking thence to Ambleside; but this is doing things by halves. The whole road from Bowness is rich in diversity of pleasing or grand scenery; there is scarcely a field on the road side which, if it were entered, would not give to the Landscape some additional charm. Low-wood Inn, a mile from the head of Windermere is a pleasant 195 halting-place; and the fields above it, and the lane which leads to the Troutbeck, present beautiful views towards each extremity of the Lake. From this place, and still more conveniently from Ambleside, rides on horse-back or in carriages may be taken in almost every direction, and the interesting walks are inexhaustible. 200

AMBLESIDE, &c.

This Town or Market-village was formerly perhaps more rich in picturesque beauty, arising from a combination of rustic architecture and natural scenery than any small Town or Village in Great Britain. Many of the ancient buildings with their porches, projections, round 205 chimnies and galleries have been displaced to make way for the docked, featureless, and memberless edifices of modern architecture; which look as if fresh brought upon wheels from the Foundry, where they had been cast. Yet this Town, if carefully noticed, will still be found to retain such store of picturesque materials as will secure the praise of what it 210 once was from any suspicion of partiality. The Brook, which divides the Town ought to be explored along its channel; if the state of the stream

186 like *S.V.*: *not in* MS.   187 more immediate MS.², *S.V.*: other MS. 191 thence to MS.², *S.V.*: thence from MS.   192 diversity *S.V.*: interchange MS.   193 side which MS.², *S.V.*: side after you have left MS. 194–5 give . . . Low-wood *S.V.*: open out some additional recommendation to the Landscape. I shall only point out one Station, which would well reward the trouble of alighting and turning to it. It is close to Ecclerigg, the first house by the road side after you have left Troutbeck. Enter the gate of the fold-yard and turn to the left; and southwards you will look down upon a fine bay; and beyond it are promontories and part of a second bay, that of Bowness, and farther lies all the [beauty *del.*] richness of the Islands. This Landscape through the soft medium of hazy weather is seen to great advantage when the sun is hanging over it at noon-day.—Low-wood MS.   195 Windermere *S.V.*: the Lake MS.   196 which *S.V.*: that MS.

will permit. Below the Bridge is a Mill, and also an old Summer-house, with other old buildings, ivied Trunks of Trees, and mossy Stones, which have furnished subjects for many a picture; and above the 215 Bridge, though there are no Buildings, every step is interesting till the curious Traveller is stopped by the huge breastwork of Stock-gill Force. Within a quarter of a mile of Ambleside is a scene called the Nook, which deserves to be explored. It is to be found in Scandle Gill, the channel of the first Brook that comes down Scandle Fell to the 220 North of Ambleside. I need not describe the scene; its principal feature is a Bridge thrown over the Torrent. From this Bridge I wish it were in my power to recommend it to the Traveller to proceed northwards, along the slope of the hill-side, till he reaches the Park of Rydale; but this would be a trespass; for there is no path, and high and envious 225 stone walls interpose. We must therefore give up the best approach to some of the most glorious scenes in the world; this may be yet said, though not without painful regret for the havoc which has been made among them. Some hundreds of oaks are gone,

> "Whose boughs were mossed with age, 230
> "And high tops bald with dry antiquity,"

a majestic Forest covering a mountain side! into the recesses of which penetrated like a vision, Landscapes of rivers, broad waters, vallies, rocks and mountains:—The Lake of Rydale on the Northwest, with its Islands and rocky steeps, circular and deeply embosomed; and to the 235 South the long Valley of Ambleside and the gleaming Lake of Windermere. The noblest of these trees have been sacrificed; but the side of the hill, though thinned, is not wholly laid bare; and the Herons and Rooks that hover round this choice retreat have yet a remnant of their ancient roosting-place. The unfrequented spots, of which I have been 240 speaking may be visited, with permission from the Mansion, after the Water-fall has been seen.

Of places at a distance from Ambleside, but commodiously visited from that Village, Coniston may be first mentioned; though this Lake as I said before, will thus be approached to great disadvantage.—Next 245 comes Great Langdale, a Vale which should on no account be missed by him who has a true enjoyment of grand separate Forms composing a sublime Unity, austere but reconciled and rendered attractive to the affections by the deep serenity that is spread over every thing. There is no good carriage road through this Vale; nor ought that to be 250 regretted; for it would impair its solemnity: but the road is tolerable for about the distance of three miles from Ambleside, namely along the Vale of Brathay, and above the western banks of Loughrigg Tarn, and still further, to the entrance of Langdale itself: but the small and

peaceful Valley of Loughrigg is seen to much greater advantage from   255
the eastern side. When therefore you have quitted the River Brathay
enquire at the first house for the foot road, which will conduct you
round the lower extremity of the Tarn, and so on to its head, where,
at a little distance from the Tarn the path again leads to the publick
road and about a mile further conducts you to Langdale Chapel.—   260
A little way beyond this sequestered and simple place of worship is a
narrow passage on the right leading into a slate-quarry which has been
finely excavated. Pursuing this road a few hundred yards further, you
come in view of the noblest reach of this Vale, which I shall not attempt
to describe. Under the Precipice adjoining to the Pikes lies invisibly   265
Stickle Tarn, and thence descends a conspicuous Torrent down the
breast of the Mountain. Near this Torrent is Dungeon Gill Force,
which cannot be found without a Guide, who may be taken up at one
of the Cottages at the foot of the Mountain.

> "Into the chasm a mighty block   270
> Hath fallen, and made a bridge of rock;
> The gulph is deep below,
> And in a bason black and small
> Receives a lofty Waterfall."

At the head of Langdale is a passage over to the Borrowdale; but this   275
ought on no account to be taken by a person who has not seen the main
features of the country from their best approaches.—If the Traveller
has been zealous enough to advance as far as Dungeon-gill Force, let
him enquire for Blea Tarn; he may return by that circuit to Ambleside.
Blea Tarn is not an object of any beauty in itself, but it is situated in   280
a small, deep circular Valley of peculiar character; for it contains only
one Dwelling-house and two or three cultivated fields. Passing down
this Valley, fail not to look back now and then, and you will see Langdale Pikes, from behind the rocky steeps that form its north-eastern
boundary, lifting themselves, as if on tip-toe, to pry into it. Quitting   285
the Valley you will descend into little Langdale, and thence may proceed by Colwith Force and Bridge. Leaving Skelwith-Bridge on your
left, ascend with the road to Skelwith; and from a field on the northern
side of that small cluster of houses, you will look down upon a grand
view of the River Brathay, Elter-water and the mountains of Langdale,   290
&c. Thence proceed occasionally looking down the Brathay on the side
of the River opposite to that by which you had ascended in your way
to Loughrigg Tarn. The whole of this excursion may be as much as

18 miles, and would require a long morning to be devoted to the accomplishment. I will now mention only one more ride or walk from Ambleside. Go to the Bridge over the Rothay (of which a view is given in the Etchings), between Ambleside and Clappersgate. When you have crossed the Bridge, turn to a Gate on the right hand, and proceed with the road up the Valley of Ambleside, till you come opposite to the Village of Rydale; do not cross over to Rydale, but keep close to the Mountain on your left hand, with the River at a little distance on your right, till you come in view of Rydale Lake. Advance with the Lake on your right till you quit the Vale of Rydale, and come in view of Grasmere. Follow the road, which will conduct you round along the lower extremity of the Lake of Grasmere, till you reach the Church; thence into the main road back to Ambleside, looking behind you frequently.

295

300

305

307/8 *Apparently intended to follow immediately, or soon after,* 307, MS. Prose 25 *offers a badly preserved and sometimes barely legible description of Grasmere and Wythburn, or Thirlmere. We punctuate the parts not deleted.*

. . . [Immediately beneath is spread *del.*] the lake with a grassy island and its indented [shores *del.*] margins.

He [overlooks *del.*] looks down at the lake with its grassy island and indented shores [spread *del.*] immediately beneath him; beyond the lake in front [rising with *del.*] are seen ris[?ing with gent]le slope from its margins the cultivated ground in the body of the vale, with the Church [?and] little rocky and woody [?eminences] & cottages scattered on every side. Huge mountains [embosom *del.*] encircle this whole [and the sky rests upon ⟨it *del.*⟩ them and spreads itself over the whole valley *del.*], upon which the sky seems to rest, spreading itself in concave over the valley like a ceiling or roof. Nor is it in the power of words to tell how on a calm & solemn evening the Lake by the reflections of luminous clouds, blue ether, & the objects of earth which it receives into its bosom exalts and spiritualizes [⟨?gives⟩ depth *del.*] this quiet & lovely region, imparting the depth & immensity of the imperishable worlds of the imagination [to this quiet & lovely ⟨spot *del.*⟩ region ⟨which seems *del.*⟩ which without this accompaniment by its other *del.*] [to a spot more aptly framed to lay hold of the simple lowly human affections *del.*] to a scene which without this high recommendation would have appeared to want nothing, so exquisitely is it framed to lay hold of & gratify the simple & lowly human affections.

'tis the sense
Of majesty and beauty & repose,
A blended holiness of earth & sky,
Something that makes this individual spot,
This small Abiding-place of many men
A termination & a last retreat,
A Centre, come from wheresoe'er you will,
A Whole without dependence or defect,
Made for itself & happy in itself,
Perfect contentment, unity entire.

The road which slants along the steep side of Loughrigg fell is some too much elevated above the Vale, & the Traveller will do well as he advances to descend a little till he comes to that point which best pleases him.—[this is the *del.*] [Loughrigg fell rises abruptly from the foot of the Lake of Grasmere at the lower extremity of the Vale across which it runs & forms its southern barrier allowing the brook to steal out of the lake at one corner *del.*] The Spectator will not fail to congratulate himself upon the delicacy with which Nature interposing between the Lakes of

The two hours before sun-set are the most favourable time of the day for seeing the lower division of Wytheburne Lake, but it is advisable to choose the earlier part of this time, in order that the 310 Traveller may be enabled to descend into the Vale of Keswick while

Grasmere & Rydale this rocky & [? narrow] [*tear*] brook [whose course is so *del.*], short as its course is, & by the winding of the p[*tear*] along which it flows, has absolutely [divi *del.*] separated [& set apart the Vale of *del.*], both to the eye & to the feelings, the Vale of Grasmere from its neighbour, thus [giving to *del.*] stamping upon it that peculiar character which strikes the most rude & uncultivated minds of a Place, rather of a home or a world, in itself. [Instead of this mazy brook had *del.*] [Had the Lake of Rydale up wh⟨?⟩ *del.*] Had there been a continuation of lake where this Brook runs [and the feeling of unity which, ⟨?⟩ *del.*] the vale of Grasmere would have [been *del.*] appeared but another reach, or division, of a long tract of Country [nor could ⟨?⟩ *del.*], and the feeling of singularity and unity would not have existed [*or* existence ?] which sanctify all the beauties and renders the satisfaction of the spectacle complete. [*The conclusion of this paragraph is especially difficult to decipher.*]
    This Vale, which [we have beheld apparently ⟨?⟩ *del.*] appears to have laid itself open to our eyes [without reserve *del.*] in the grandeur & simplicity [of one impression where all is seen *del.*] of one impression where nothing is sensed to be withheld, has yet [? beauties *del.*] in reserve, for the delight of him who [will *del.*] has the inclination to go in quest [of them *del.*] of those attachments & dependences, recesses within recesses [the various beauties of which ⟨years of residence *del.*⟩ a wealth of *del.*], which after years of residence would still leave to the most curious investigator something new to discover. These scenes lie chiefly in a department or corner to the North West, known by the general name of Easedale & [divided by *del.*] separated from the body of the Vale by a little range of woody hills which run from the Mountain called Helm [west *del.*] to the western boundary of the Vale, admitting a passage for a small brook. In the first view of Grasmere, as described above, neither the Lake [? the rocks], nor the Mountains, nor the cultivated ground gave the predominating impression, but the Vale in the intenseness of its unity as composed of all these. In the inner compartments of [Grasmere *del.*] which I am now speaking, the rocky [character *del.*] features predominate, & [it is the boast of this *del.*] the pride of this Vale of G. is that [*deletions and emendations make the remainder of this paragraph barely legible; by a tear at the top of page* ⟨2ʳ⟩, *four or five lines are lost*] with a perfect simplicity of general effect arising from the grandeur of the [surrounding *del.*] Mountains, from the size and [? figure] of the Lake, from the space of cultivated ground besprinkled with cottages, and from the proportion and relation of all these objects to each other, while at the same time there [exists *del.*] lurks an endless intricacy and wildness [from *del.*] among the [rocks and woods and *del.*] rocky hills & hillocks with which this area of the vale is scattered over. [*Scattered phrases may be conjecturally read*: and ⟨? which⟩: on every side of the mountain by: they are enlivened and in many of the smaller compartments recesses on every side: The surrounding Mountains by which they are enclosed: Among these Etchings will be found a view of Grasmere Lake ⟨? seen⟩ from the edge of Easedale: I will quit the Vale of Grasmere]
    From Grasmere the Traveller ascends to Wythburn by [*altered to* ⟨? From Grasmere the Traveller proceeds towards Wythburn . . . to the north⟩] Dunmail raise gap, an opening in the shape of a huge inverted arch, the sides of which are formed by Steel fell on the left & on the right by Seat Sandal. Having passed the monumental heap of stones, he will come in view of the lake & vale of Wythburn extending thro' a long mountainous vista, terminated by Skiddaw & other mountains. [*Some deletions are*: Seat Sandal is: Helvellyn the side of which only is visible from the eastern boundary of the Vale & lake of Wythburn beyond: in the distance are the Mountains in the neighbourhood of Keswick: The high road runs along the edge of Wyth immediately under] Helvellyn forms the eastern Boundary of the vale of W. under which the high road runs along the [edge of *del.*] margin of the

the sun-beams are upon it. That this first impression of that Vale should be received under the most favourable circumstances, is very desirable; and therefore I do not recommend, as I should otherwise have done, that the Traveller, who has been guided by my directions 315 thus far, should lengthen his journey to Keswick still further, and follow the stream that issues out of Wytheburn Lake till it enters St. John's Vale, which he may do if he be on foot, keeping to the side of it almost all the way; and, if on horseback, he may return to it by a small circuit, after having crossed Shoulthwaite Moss. I should have 320 directed the Traveller in this case to proceed a mile and a half down St. John's Vale, and then to cross Naddle Fell, by St. John's Chapel, which would bring him into the road between Ambleside and Keswick, something better than two miles short of the latter place. This may easily be done, taking the lower division of Wytheburn earlier in the 325 afternoon than the time which I have recommended as the best.

We have now reached Keswick. I shall not attempt a general description of this celebrated Vale, because this has already been

---

Lake. The road then ascends a hill [⟨? returning⟩ from the Lake which *del.*] for a mile & a half perhaps & takes leave of the Lake [& when you come to the *del.*] & before you descend the hill on the opposite side, a little [before *del.*] beyond the sixth milestone, there opens upon you a noble view of the Vale of Legberthwaite with a peep of Saint Johns terminated by Saddleback. I have attended the Traveller to this point because it presents a most impressive Landscape, but here I must tell him that if he goes hence immediately forward to Keswick, he will leave the best parts of the Vale & Lake of Wythburn wholly unseen. On the left [adjoining to the road is *del.*] of the brow of this hill, from which he looks down upon Legberthwaite, & close to the roadside is a piece of rocky & rough ground into which at this place there was lately entrance by a Stile which I believe has been [*approximately five lines have been torn from the top of the page* ⟨2ᵛ⟩] . . . populous with houses & watered only by a small brook & a considerable portion of the [Lake & *del.*] Vale of Wythburn yet unseen by him, solitary, overbrowed by huge rocks & crags, and the whole bed of it filled by the unfrequented lake. In fact [the Traveller who keeps to the high road *del.*] this Lake would well repay the trouble of making the whole circuit of it, which may be done on foot or horseback, but as few persons [may be disposed to take the trouble *del.*] have time or inclination for this, I would recommend that the Traveller who [is constant in quest of the beauties of the Country should *del.*] have [*sic*] time & inclination to come by the high road to the brow of the hill which looks down into Legberthwaite for the sake of that View, & that he should descend the hill & at its base turn by a private road on the left [towards L⟨?⟩ Dale *del.*], which will bring him to an old mansion called Dale Park, from which he [may *del.*] will have no difficulty in finding [his *del.*] the bridge over the strait that divides Thirlmere into two parts. If he has leisure, it would be worth his while to go a mile or more along the side of this Lake [upwards *del.*] towards its head & return by the same road, but if not, he will proceed immediately downwards & [with *del.*] from different elevations will command many fine scenes. One [of which *del.*] of this lower division is given in the Etchings.
[*After a line drawn across the page, two incomplete sentences are set off by themselves:* I would next recommend as ⟨the best course for combining *del.*⟩ providing the most beauty with the least expense of time & trouble that the Traveller on foot or Horseback should: ⟨? Keeping⟩ as near to Stream ⟨*sic*⟩ that issues out of the lake as the ⟨? road⟩ will allow him.]

admirably performed by Dr. Brown, and by the Poet Gray; and the place is at this time very generally known. As the Views in this work 330 have been taken almost exclusively from retired spots in the *Ghylls*, or Gills, and smaller Vallies that branch off from the trunk of the Vale, it will be more appropriate to this publication, and will better suit its narrow limits, to say a few words upon them. And to begin with one of the smallest, Applethwaite (for Views of which see Nos. 22, 23, and 335 24). This is a hamlet of six or seven houses, hidden in a small recess at the foot of Skiddaw, and adorned by a little Brook, which, having descended from a great height in a silver line down the steep blue side of the Mountain, trickles past the doors of the Cottages. This concealed spot is very interesting as you approach from the bottom, with 340 your face towards the green and blue mass of Skiddaw; and is not less pleasing when, having advanced by a gentle slope for some space, you turn your head and look out from this chink or fissure, which is sprinkled with little orchards and trees, and behold the whole splendour of the upper and middle part of the Vale of Keswick, with its Lakes 345 and Mountains spread before your eyes. A small Spinning-mill has lately been erected here, and some of the old Cottages, with their picturesque appendages, are fallen into decay. This is to be regretted; for, these blemishes excepted, the scene is a rare and almost singular combination of minute and sequestered beauty, with splendid and ex- 350 tensive prospects. On the opposite side of the Vale of Keswick lie the Valley of Newlands, and the Village of Braithwaite, with its stream descending from a cove of the Mountain. From both these spots I have given Views, from which an idea of their features may be collected. Braithwaite lies at the foot of Whenlater, in the road to Lorton and 355 Cockermouth; and through Newlands passes the nearest road to Buttermere. Returning to the eastern side of the Vale of Keswick, we find the narrow and retired Valley of Watenlath, enclosed on each side and at the head by craggy Mountains. In the Mountains at the head, the stream rises, which forms the Cascade of Lodore. This, after flow- 360 ing a short way through a pastoral tract, falls into a small Lake or Tarn, which lies midway in the long Valley of Watenlath. At the point where the stream issues out of the Tarn, is a beautiful Bridge of one arch, and close beside the Bridge is a little Hamlet, a cluster of grey Cottages. There are no other dwellings in the Valley; and a more 365 secluded spot than this Hamlet cannot well be conceived: yet ascend a very little up the hill above it, and you have a most magnificent prospect of the Vale of Keswick, as far as Skiddaw; and, pursuing the Valley of Watenlath to its head, if you look back, the view of the little Valley itself, with its Lake, Bridge, and Cottages, is combined with 370 that of the majestic Vale beyond, so that each seems to be a part of the other. But the most considerable of the Dales which communicate with the Vale of Keswick by the Rivers which flow through them, are Borrowdale and St. John's. Of St. John's we have already spoken; and Borrowdale is in fact the head of the Vale of Keswick. It would be an endless task to attempt, by verbal descriptions, to guide the traveller among the infinite variety of beautiful or interesting objects which are found in the different reaches of the broad Valley itself, nor less so to attempt to lead him through its little recesses, its nooks, and tributary glens. I must content myself with saying, that this Valley surpasses all the others in variety. Rocks and Woods are intermingled on the hill-sides with profuse wildness; and on the plain below (for the area of the Valley, through all its windings is generally a level plain, out of which the Mountains rise as from their base,) the single Cottages and clusters of Houses are numerous; not glaringly spread before the eye, but unobtrusive as the rocks themselves, and mostly coloured like them. There is scarcely a Cottage that has not its own tuft of trees. The Yew-tree has been a favourite with the former Inhabitants of Borrow-dale; for many fine old Yew-trees yet remain near the Cottages, probably first planted for an ornament to their gardens, and now preserved as a shelter, and for the sake of their venerable appearance. But the noblest Yew-trees to be found here, are a cluster of three, with a fourth a little detached, which do not stand in connection with any houses; they are in that part of Borrowdale which is called Seathwaite, immediately under the entrance into the Lead-mines. Nothing of the kind can be conceived more solemn and impressive than the small gloomy grove formed by these trees.

The lower part of the Vale of Keswick is occupied by the Lake of Bassenthwaite; and he who coasts its western shore, will be well and

383 Valley MS., *S.V.*: vale MS.². 384 the single cottages MS.², *S.V.*: [? *del.*] gray cottages may be espec under MS. 385 before MS.², *S.V.*: out MS. 386 them. MS.², *S.V.*: them with moss & lichens and [?] MS. 387 There is MS.², *S.V.*: These cottages are MS. has MS.², *S.V.*: has for MS. 388 favourite MS.², *S.V.*: favourite tree MS. with the MS.², *S.V.*: of MS. 390 for MS., *S.V.*: as MS.². to *S.V.*: for MS. 391 *After* appearance MS. *deletes*: Speaking of [?]: But the first: Nor can I here forbear to mention a cluster of Yew trees [?] is that to be found in that part of Borrowdale which is called Seathwaite. 391–2 But the . . . here *S.V.*: But the finest trees of this kind MS. 392 a fourth MS.², *S.V.*: one MS. 394 they are *S.V.*: and are to be found MS. 395 the Lead-mines *S.V.*: a Lead mine MS. 398 The lower part MS.², *S.V.*: [?] it may be confidently recommended MS. is occupied *S.V.*: is so [?] MS. 399–406 and he . . . majesty from MS.², *S.V.*: and he . . . the western shore of the lake will be well recompensed by [the ⟨*Edd.*⟩] appearance of Skiddaw on this side of the lake and the vale at the foot. From Embleton which may be mentioned as the last . . . of Keswick [?] it is an extension of the [?] near the lower extremity of Bas-senthwaite Lake, a scene of humble & gentle character but deriving a [? majesty] from MS.

variously recompensed; and in particular by the appearance of Skid- 400
daw, rising immediately from the opposite side of the Lake. Following
this road, we cross the lower extremity of Embleton Vale. Embleton
may be mentioned as the last of the Vallies collateral to the main Vale
of Keswick. It unfolds on the west, near the foot of Bassenthwaite Lake,
a scene of humble and gentle character; but deriving animated beauty 405
from the Lake, and striking majesty from the Mountain of Skiddaw,
which is on this side broken and rugged, and of an aspect which is
forcibly contrasted with that with which it looks upon Derwent Lake.
The view of the whole vista of the Vale of Keswick from Armathwaite
and Ouze Bridge is magnificent; and the scenes upon the River Der- 410
went, as far as the grand ruins of Cockermouth Castle, are soft and
varied, and well worthy of the notice of the Pedestrian, who has leisure
to go in search of them.

From the Vale of Keswick, of which there is no need to say any thing
more, the Tourist usually proceeds to Buttermere, to which there are 415
three roads; the one through part of Borrowdale, which brings him
down into the Vale of Buttermere, at its head: but Borrowdale I suppose to have been already explored, a strong reason against choosing
this approach. Yet in justice to this road I must add, that the descent
into Gatesgarth, immediately under Honister Crag, causes one of the 420
sublimest impressions which this country can produce. The second road
leads through Newlands. The descent into Buttermere by this way is
solitary and grand; but the Vale of Newlands itself I suppose also to
have been visited in the Tour round the Lake of Keswick (which no
person of taste ought to omit), or in other rambles. It follows, then, 425
that the third is the road which I would recommend, namely, the carriage road, which leads over Whinlater, through part of the Vale of
Lorton, to the outlet of Crummock-water. Here was formerly an inn,
kept at a house called Scale Hill, an accommodation which I believe no
longer exists. It would, however, be ill-judged not to turn aside to 430

402 Vale. *S.V.*: vale (See No.). MS.   404 unfolds *S.V.*: leads MS.:
opens out MS.².   405 deriving animated *S.V.*: derives a spirited MS.
406 striking *S.V.*: *not in* MS.   407–8 which [*first*] . . .contrasted with that *S.V.*:
which appears [from this quarter *del.*] on this side [bold *del.*] broken & rugged and
of [?] exhibiting an aspect [strikingly contrasting *del.*] which is a striking contrast
to that with which MS.   409 view of *S.V.*: view up MS.   410 Ouze *S.V.*: the
neighbourhood of Ouze MS.   412 Pedestrian *S.V.*: Traveller MS.   414
to say MS.², *S.V.*: that we should [should *not del.*] MS.   415 Tourist MS.²,
S.V.: Traveller MS.   which *S.V.*: which place MS.   416 him *S.V.*:
you MS.   417 the Vale of Buttermere MS.², *S.V.*: Buttermere MS.   Borrowdale *S.V.*: half of MS.: the Borrowdale part of this Road MS.²   418 a
strong reason MS.², *S.V.*: which is one MS.   420 causes *S.V.*: affords MS.:
produces MS.².   421 produce *S.V.*: give MS.   422 way MS.², *S.V.*:
[? was] MS.   428 outlet MS.², *S.V.*: lower part MS.   formerly *S.V.*:
lately MS.   429 accommodation MS.², *S.V.*: accommodation for Travellers
MS.   I believe *S.V.*: *not in* MS.   430 ill-judged MS.², *S.V.*: a pity MS.

Scale Hill; the carriage or horses might be sent forward by the high-road, and ordered to wait till the Traveller rejoined them by the foot-path, which leads through the woods along the side of Crummock. This path presents noble scenes, looking up the Lake towards Buttermere. If the Traveller be desirous of visiting Lowes-water, instead of pro- 435 ceeding directly along this path, he must cross the Bridge over the Cocker, near Scale Hill, to which he must return after a walk or ride of three or four miles. I am not sure that the circuit of this Lake can be made on horseback; but every path and field in the neighbourhood would well repay the active exertions of the Pedestrian. Nor will the 440 most hasty Visitant fail to notice with pleasure, that community of attractive and substantial houses which are dispersed over the fertile inclosures at the foot of those rugged Mountains, and form a most impressive contrast with the humble and rude dwellings which are usually found at the head of these far-winding Dales. It must be men- 445 tioned also, that there is scarcely any thing finer than the view from a boat in the centre of Crummock-water. The scene is deep, and solemn, and lonely; and in no other spot is the majesty of the Mountains so irresistibly felt as an omnipresence, or so passively submitted to as a spirit incumbent upon the imagination. Near the head of 450 Crummock-water, on the right, is Scale Force, a Waterfal worthy of being visited, both for its own sake, and for the sublime View across the Lake, looking back in your ascent towards the Chasm. The Fall is perpendicular from an immense height, a slender stream faintly illu-minating a gloomy fissure. This spot is never seen to more advantage 455 than when it happens, that, while you are looking up through the Chasm towards the summit of the lofty Waterfal, large fleecy clouds, of dazzling brightness, suddenly ascend into view, and disappear silently upon the wind. The Village of Buttermere lies a mile and a half higher up the Vale, and of the intermediate country I have nothing 460 to say. It would be advisable, if time permit, that you should go as far up the Vale as Honister Crag; and if on horseback, or on foot, you may return to Keswick by Newlands.

437 to MS.², *S.V.*: & by MS.   438 the *S.V.*: a MS.   439 the *S.V.*: this MS.   441 Visitant *S.V.*: Traveller MS.   441–2 that commun-ity . . . substantial MS.², *S.V.*: the fertile inclosures & the substantial & attrac-tive MS.   442 are dispersed *S.V.*: sprinkle MS.   443–4 and form . . . contrast *S.V.*: contrasting most impressively MS.   446 finer *S.V.*: finer in the Country MS.   447 The scene is MS.², *S.V.*: it is an MS.   449 so irresistibly felt *S.V.*: felt more like MS.: so irresistingly felt MS.².   449–50 or so . . . to as MS.², *S.V.*: besetting & embracing the mind as MS.   451 on the right *S.V.*: in a Chasm on the right MS.   Scale MS.², *S.V.*: Scale hill MS.   453 Lake, looking back MS.³, *S.V.*: Lake which appears MS.: Lake which you will have MS.².   456 it happens . . . you are *S.V.*: *not in* MS.   457 Chasm MS.², *S.V.*: Carriage MS.   the summit MS.², *S.V.*: point where MS.   461 per-mit *S.V.*: would permit MS.   461–2 you . . . you *S.V.*: the Traveller . . . he MS.

The rest of the scenes in this part of the country of which I have given views, namely, those of Ennerdale and Wastdale, cannot, without a good deal of trouble, be approached in a carriage. For Foot-travellers, and for those who are not afraid of leading their horses through difficult ways, there is a road from Buttermere directly over the mountains to Ennerdale; there is also another road from the head of Buttermere to the head of Wastdale, without going into Borrowdale: but both Ennerdale and Wastdale are *best* seen by making a considerable circuit; namely, by retracing our steps to Scale Hill, and thence by Lowes-water and Lamplugh to Ennerdale. The first burst of Ennerdale from an eminence is very noble, and the mind is more alive to the impression, because we have quitted for a while the heart of the mountains, and been led through a tamer country. Ennerdale is bold and savage in its general aspect, though not destitute, towards the higher part of the Lake, of fertile and beautiful spots. From Ennerdale-Bridge to Calder-Bridge, the road leads over Cold Fell. The distance is six miles, a desolate tract, with the exception of the last half mile, through a narrow and well-wooded Valley, in which is a small, but beautiful fragment of Calder Abbey. The village lying close to Calder-Bridge has good inns, and the bed of the River about the Bridge is rocky and spirited. We are here in a plain country near to the sea, and therefore better prepared to enjoy the mountain sublimities of Wastdale, which soon begin to shew themselves, and grow upon us at every step, till we reach the margin of the Lake. This Water (for the Lakes are generally called *Waters* by the country people) is not so much as four miles in length, and becomes very narrow for the space of half a mile towards its outlet. On one side it is bordered by a continued straight line of high and almost perpendicular steeps, rising immediately from the Lake, without any bays or indentings. This is a very striking feature: for these steeps, or *screes* (as places of this kind are named), are not more distinguished by their height and extent,

464 I *S.V.*: we MS. 465 namely *S.V.*: viz MS. Wastdale *Edd.*: Wasdale MS.: Westdale *S.V.* 465–6 without . . . trouble *S.V.*: easily MS. 467 and *S.V.*: & also MS. 468–9 mountains *S.V.*: Mountain MS. 470 Wastdale MS., *Edd.*: Westdale *S.V.* 471 Wastdale *Edd.*: Wasdale MS.: Westdale *S.V.* 472 namely, by retracing *S.V.*: i.e. by reversing MS. and *S.V.*: *not in* MS. 474–5 the mind . . . have quitted *S.V.*: the Traveller feels it the more [from having previously descended into the tamer ⟨? Country⟩ *del.*] [from the circumstance of having *del.*] because he has quitted MS. 479–80 the road . . . tract *S.V.*: is about 6 miles of desolate Country MS. 482 Abbey *S.V.*: Abbey most unhappily elbowed by a large modern house MS. The village lying close to *S.V.*: C. Bridge a Village MS.: The village near MS.[2]. 484 We MS.[2], *S.V.*: You MS. 485–6 Wastdale MS., *Edd.*: Westdale *S.V.* 487–8 for the . . . *Waters S.V.*: for so the Lakes are commonly called MS. 489 very MS.[2], *S.V.*: exceedingly MS. 490 outlet MS.[2], *S.V.*: lower ext MS. 491 straight *S.V.*: *not in* MS. 492 bays or *S.V.*: *not in* MS.

than by the beautiful colours with which the pulverized rock, for ever 495
crumbling down their sides, overspreads them. The surface has the
apparent softness of the dove's neck, and (as was before mentioned, in
reference to spots of this kind,) resembles a dove's neck strongly in its
hues, and in the manner in which they are intermingled. On the other
side, Wast-water is bordered by knotty and projecting rocky moun- 500
tains, which, retiring in one place, admit the interposition of a few
green fields between them and the Lake, with a solitary farm-house.
From the termination of the Screes rises Scaw Fell, deemed higher
than Skiddaw, or Helvellyn, or any of the Mountains. The summit, as
seen from Wastdale, is bold and abrupt, and if you should quit the 505
Valley and ascend towards it, it appears, from the Cove beneath, like
the shattered walls or towers of an enormous edifice. Upon the summit
of one of those towers is a fragment of rock that looks like an eagle,
or a large owl, on that commanding eminence, stationary through all
seasons. The Views which I have given are from the shore about the 510
middle of Wast-water, from a point where the Vale appears to be
terminated by three large conical Mountains, Yewbarrow on the left,
Great Gavel in the centre, and Lingmoor on the right. About two miles
further is the Division of Wastdale Head, with its lowly Chapel. This
place formerly consisted of twenty tenements. It is now reduced to six. 515
This Valley has been described in the Introduction, as seen from the
summit of Great Gavel; but the Traveller will be pleased with a nearer
view of these pastoral dwellings, which in the inside are as comfortable
as their outside is beautiful and picturesque. A hospitable people live
here, and do not repine at the distance and the barriers which separate 520
them from the noisy world. Give them more sunshine and a richer soil,
and they would have little to complain of. The Stranger will observe
here and elsewhere large heaps of stones, like Sepulchral Barrows,
which have been collected from the fields and thrown together by the

495 with which the pulverized *S.V.*: [?] which the crumbling MS.: which
by the pulverized MS.[2].   496 overspreads them *S.V.*: they are overspread MS.   497 was before *S.V.*: before MS.   498 resembles . . .
neck *S.V.*: resembles it MS.   500 Wast-water *S.V.*: Wasdale MS.
503 higher MS.[2], *S.V.*: the highest M MS.   504 any *S.V.*: any other MS.
505 Wastdale *Edd.*: Wasdale MS.: Westdale *S.V.*   is bold MS.[3], *S.V.*: like the Ruins
of an enormous Edifice on which [?are] smaller rocks perched like owls on MS.:
the rocks of this mountain amongst them are MS.[2].   if you should *S.V.*: when
you MS.: climbing the mountain MS.[2]: if you [?should] MS.[3].   506 and
ascend *S.V.*: & you have ascended MS.: & ascended [*left uncorr.*] MS.[2].   507 or
towers *S.V.*: & ruins of an MS.: & towers MS.[2].   510 The Views which I . . .
are *S.V.*: The View which we have given is MS.   511 a point *S.V.*: this point
MS.: the point MS.[2].   514 Division *S.V.*: Hamlet MS.   Wastdale MS., *Edd.*:
Westdale *S.V.*   516 This Valley has *S.V.*: It has already MS.: The Valley has
MS.[2].   518 pastoral *S.V.*: snug & comfortable MS.: snug MS.[2].   are MS.[2],
S.V.: are still MS.   521 noisy *S.V.*: busy MS.   more MS.[2], *S.V.*: a little
more MS.   524 thrown MS.[2], *S.V.*: are [?] MS.

labours of many generations. From the summits either of Great Gavel, 525
or Scaw Fell, there are sublime prospects. Great Gavel may be proud
of the Vallies which it looks down into, and Scaw Fell of the dark
multitudinous Mountains, rising ridge above ridge, which it commands
on the one side, and of the extent of sea and sand spreading in a level
plain on the other. The ascent of Scaw Fell is easy, that of Great Gavel 530
laborious. I cannot deny myself the pleasure of adding, that on the
highest point of Great Gavel is a small triangular receptacle of water
in a rock. It is not a spring; yet the shepherds say that it is never dry:
certainly when I was there, during a season of drought, it was well
supplied with water. Here the Traveller may slake his thirst plen- 535
teously with a pure and celestial beverage; for it appears that this cup
or bason has no other feeder than the dews of heaven, the showers, the
vapours, the hoar frost, and the spotless snow. From Wastdale return
to Keswick by Stye-Head and Borrowdale. Take a look backwards
upon Wastdale, from the last point where it is visible. The long strait 540
vista of the Vale, and the sea beyond, apparent between the Mountains,
form a grand whole. A few steps further bring you to Stye-Head Tarn
(for which see No. 43). By the side of the Tarn, an eagle (I believe of
the ospray species) was killed last spring. Though large, it was very
light, and seemed exhausted by hunger. The stream which flows into 545
this Tarn comes from another, called Sprinkling Tarn, famous among
anglers for the finest trouts in the country. In rainy seasons there is
a magnificent waterfal formed by the stream which issues from Stye-
Head Tarn. You have it on your left as you descend into Seathwaite
division of Borrowdale. About a mile further down upon the left is that 550
cluster of yew-trees recommended to notice; thence through a succession of magnificent scenes to Keswick.

It remains that we should speak of Ullswater. There are two roads
by which this Lake may be visited from Keswick. That which is adapted
for Travellers on horseback, or on foot, crosses the lower part of St. 555
John's Vale, and brings you down through the Valley and scattered
Village of Matterdale into Gowbarrow Park, unfolding at once a magnificent view of the two higher reaches of the Lake. Airey Force
thunders down the *Ghyll*, or Gill, on the left, at a small distance from
the road; but you are separated from it by the Park-wall. In a carriage, 560
Ullswater is best approached from Penrith. A mile and a half brings
you to the winding Vale of Emont, and the prospects increase in
interest till you reach Patterdale; but the first four miles along Ullswater by this road are comparatively tame, and in order to see the
lower part of the Lake to advantage, it is absolutely necessary to go 565

525 labours *S.V.*: produce MS.: labour MS.[2]. *After* generations MS. *ends with an incomplete phrase*: Of the two princ   550 Borrowdale *Edd.*: Rovendale *S.V.*

round by Poolly-Bridge, and to ride at least three miles along the
Westmoreland side of the Water, towards Martindale. The Views
from this quarter, especially if you ascend from the road into the fields,
are magnificent; yet I only mention this that the transient Traveller
may know what exists; for it will be very inconvenient for him to go   570
in search of them. The person who takes this course of three or four
miles, which I am now recommending, *on foot*, should take care to have
a boat in readiness at the end of his walk, to carry him right across to
the Cumberland side, along which he may pursue his way upwards to
Patterdale.   575

Having conducted the Traveller hither, I shall treat no further of the
body of this celebrated Vale; but, for the same reasons which governed
me when I was speaking of Keswick, I shall confine myself to the Glens
and Vallies which branch off from it.

At Dalemain, about three miles from Penrith, a Stream is crossed,   580
called Dacre, which, rising in the moorish country about Penruddock,
flows down a soft sequestered Valley, passing by the ancient mansions
of Hutton John and Dacre Castle. The former is pleasantly situated,
though of a character somewhat gloomy and monastic; and from some
of the fields near Dalemain, Dacre Castle, backed by the jagged sum-   585
mit of Saddleback, and with the Valley and Stream in front of it, forms
a grand picture. There is no other stream that conducts us to any glen
or valley worthy of being mentioned, till you reach the one which leads
you up to Airey Force, and then into Matterdale, before spoken of.
Matterdale, though a wild and interesting spot, has no peculiar features   590
that would make it worth the Stranger's while to go in search of them;
but in Gowbarrow Park the lover of Nature might wish to linger for
hours. Here is a powerful Brook, which dashes among rocks through
a deep glen, hung on every side with a rich and happy intermixture of
native wood; here are beds of luxuriant fern, aged hawthorns, and   595
hollies decked with honeysuckles; and fallow-deer glancing and bounding over the lawns and through the thickets. These are the attractions
of the retired views, or constitute a fore-ground to ever-varying
pictures of the majestic Lake, forced to take a winding course by bold

576 hither MS.², *S.V.*: to this place MS.   treat MS.², *S.V.*: adopt with respect
to this celebrated Vale MS.   580 At Dalemain . . . Penrith *S.V.*: About 3
miles from Penrith [near *del.*] at Dalemain MS.   581 Dacre *S.V.*: the Dacre
MS.   582 passing by the *S.V.*: by the MS.: passing the MS.².   583 former
is pleasantly *S.V.*: former mansion is pleasingly MS.   585 Dacre Castle
MS.³, *S.V.*: the hamlet MS.: the [? village] MS.².   587 no other MS.², *S.V.*:
no Valley of importance or other MS.   588 the one MS.², *S.V.*: [? that *or*
the] stream MS.   leads *S.V.*: will lead MS.   589 then *S.V.*: thence MS.
590 Matterdale, though MS.², *S.V.*: Matterdale has no features MS.   a MS.²,
S.V.: as MS.   592 Gowbarrow MS.², *S.V.*: Gowbury MS.   593 Brook
MS.², *S.V.*: rocky brook MS.   which dashes *S.V.*: dashing MS.   594 a rich
MS.², *S.V.*: the richer MS.   599 majestic MS.², *S.V.*: winding MS.

promontories, and environed by mountains of sublime form, towering 600
above each other. Having passed under a plantation of larches, we
reach, at the outlet of Gowbarrow Park, a third Stream, which flows
through a little recess called Glencoin, in which lurks a single house,
yet visible from the road. Let the Artist and leisurely Traveller turn
aside to it, for the buildings and the objects around them are both 605
romantic and exquisitely picturesque. Having passed under the steeps
of Styebarrow Crag, and the remains of its native woods, you cross,
at Glenridding-Bridge, a fourth Stream, which, if followed up, would
lead to Red Tarn and the recesses of Helvellyn. The opening on the
side of Ullswater Vale, down which the Stream flows, is adorned with 610
fertile fields, cottages, and natural groves, which agreeably coalesce
with the transverse views of the Lake; and the Stream, if followed up
after the enclosures are left behind, will lead along bold water-breaks
and waterfals to a silent Tarn in the recesses of Helvellyn. This desolate spot was formerly haunted by eagles, that built in the precipice 615
which forms its western barrier. These birds used to wheel and hover
round the head of the solitary angler. It also now derives a melancholy
interest from the fate of a young man, a stranger, who perished here
a few years ago, by falling down the rocks in his attempt to cross over
to Grasmere. His remains were discovered by means of a faithful dog, 620
which had lingered here for the space of three months, self supported,
and probably retaining to the last an attachment to the skeleton of its
dead master. But to return to the road which we have left in the main
Vale of Ullswater.—At the head of the Lake (being now in Patterdale)
we cross a fifth Stream, Grisdale Beck; this conducts through a woody 625
steep, where may be seen some unusually large ancient hollies, up to

600 mountains MS.², *S.V.*: high Mountains MS.   601 Having passed MS.²,
S.V.: Passing MS.   a plantation of larches, we *S.V.*: an unsightly plantation of
larches by which a large tract of hill side is glaringly disfigured we MS.   602 reach,
at MS.², *S.V.*: reach a stream that flows MS.   603 in which lurks *S.V.*: here
stands MS.: here lurks MS.².   604 *After* road MS. *deletes*: it is well worthy
Artist and *S.V.*: painter or MS.   605 it, for the buildings *Edd.*: it for
the buildings, *S.V.*   the buildings and *S.V.*: the situation the buildings MS.
606 *After* picturesque MS. *deletes*: The fourth stream crosses about   607 its
native woods, you *S.V.*: its [hanging *del.*] native woods which [?we] have [seen
del.] noticed [?most un⟨?⟩ly *del.*] to be succeeded by a harsh & paltry intermixture
of [?] beeches scotch firs & larches [ingeniously *del.*] contrived as it were with a
perverse ingenuity to render disgusting one of the noblest scenes of this Island.
You MS.   608–9 which, if . . . Helvellyn *S.V.*: *del. in* MS., *which after* Helvellyn
continues to delete: The banks of this stream are fertile [?]   609 on *S.V.*: in
MS.   610 down MS.², *S.V.*: through MS.   611 which agreeably
coalesce *S.V.*: [from *del.*] [are *del.*] [the ⟨?⟩ of *del.*] which combine pleasingly MS.
612–13 and the Stream . . . will *S.V.*: and if followed . . . the stream will MS.
615 formerly MS.², *S.V.*: lately MS.   616 which *S.V.*: that MS.   barrier
MS.², *S.V.*: side MS.   617 now *S.V.*: *not in* MS.   621 lingered MS.²,
S.V.: watched the body till MS.   the space of *S.V.*: *not in* MS.   623 But to
return MS.², *S.V.*: Returning MS.   625 through *S.V.*: up MS.

the level area of the Valley of Grisdale; hence there is a path for Foot-travellers, and along which a horse may be led, but not without diffi-culty, to Grasmere. I know not any where a more sublime combination of mountain forms than those which appear in front, as we ascend 630 along the bed of this Valley; and the impression increases with every step till the path grows steep; and as we climb almost immediately under the projecting masses of Helvellyn, the mind is overcome with a sensation, which in some would amount to personal fear, and cannot but be awful even to those who are most familiar with the images of 635 duration, and power, and other kindred influences, by which mountain-ous countries controul or exalt the imaginations of men. It is not uninteresting to know, that in the last house but one of this Valley, separated, as it might seem, from all the ambition and troubles of the world, from its wars and commotions, was born the youth, who, in 640 Spain, took prisoner the Colonel of the Imperial Guard of Buonaparte. This favourite of the tyrant fled from the assault of our British moun-taineer, with his two attendants who escaped; but he himself was not so fortunate. Having retraced the banks of this stream to Patterdale, and pursued our way up the main Dale, the next considerable stream 645 which we cross, would, if ascended in the same manner, conduct us into Deepdale, the character of which Valley may be conjectured by its name. It is terminated by a cove, a craggy and gloomy abyss, with precipitous sides; a faithful receptacle of the snows, which are carried into it, by the west wind, from the summit of Fairfield. Lastly, having 650 gone along the western side of Brothers-water and passed Hartsop Hall, we are brought soon after to a stream which issues from a cove richly decorated with native wood. This spot is, I believe, never explored by Travellers; but whether from these sylvan and rocky recesses you look back on the gleaming surface of Brothers-water, or 655

627 area MS.², *S.V.*: plain MS.   hence there is *S.V.*: From hence is MS.   630 appear MS.², *S.V.*: front MS.   631 Valley MS.², *S.V.*: valley especially MS.   increases *S.V.*: strengthens MS.   632 as we climb MS.², *S.V.*: ascending MS.   633 overcome MS.², *S.V.*: overpowered MS.   634 which MS.², *S.V.*: with which MS.   635 even *S.V.*: *not in* MS.   638 the last house MS.², *S.V.*: this spot dw MS.   Valley *S.V.*: spot MS: Vale MS.².   639 separated *S.V.*: divided MS.   it *S.V.*: *not in* MS.   troubles MS.², *S.V.*: turmoil MS.   642 tyrant fled MS.², *S.V.*: Tyrant and his two attendants fled and was fin MS.   from MS.², *S.V.*: before MS.   642–3 mountaineer, with his two attendants MS., *Edd.*: mountaineer with his two attendants, *S.V.*   643 with his MS.², *S.V.*: he had MS.   644 fortunate *S.V.*: lucky MS.   645 pursued MS.², *S.V.*: pursuing MS.   647 Valley *S.V.*: *not in* MS.   conjectured *S.V.*: judged of MS.   648 cove MS.², *S.V.*: cove that [?] MS.   650 by the west MS.², *S.V.*: from the east MS.   651 gone . . . Water MS.³, *S.V.*: passed the western side of Brothers Lake MS.: crossed [?] Brothers Water on the west MS.².   and passed MS.³, *S.V.*: we [we *not del.*] pass MS.: & passed by MS.².   652 which *S.V.*: that MS.   653 This spot MS.², *S.V.*: a spot containing a [?] MS.

forward to the precipitous sides and lofty ridges of the mountains, you will be equally pleased with the beauty, the grandeur, and the wildness of the scenery.

We have thus noticed no less than seven Glens, or Vallies, which branch off from the western side of the long Vale which we have been 660 ascending. The opposite side has only two streams of any importance, one of which flows by the Village of Hartsop, near the foot of Brothers-water, and the other, coming down Martindale, enters Ullswater at Sandwyke, opposite to Gowbarrow Park. Of Martindale I shall say a few words, but I must first return to our head-quarters at the Village 665 of Patterdale. No persons, but such as come to this place merely to pass through it, should fail to walk a mile and a half down the side of the Lake opposite to that on which the high-road lies: they should proceed beyond the point where the inclosures terminate. I have already had too frequent reason to lament the changes which have been made in the 670 face of this country; and scarcely any where has a more grievous loss been sustained than upon the Farm of Blowick, the only enclosed land which on this side borders the higher part of the Lake. The axe has indiscriminately levelled a rich wood of birches and oaks, which, two or three years ago, varied this favoured spot into a thousand pictures. 675 It has yet its land-locked bays and promontories; but now those beautiful woods are gone, which clothed its lawns and *perfected* its seclusion. Who, then, will not regret that those scenes, which might formerly have been compared to an inexhaustible volume, are now spread before the eye in a single sheet, magnificent indeed, but seemingly perused 680 in a moment? From Blowick, a narrow track, by which a horse may be led, but with difficulty, conducts along the cragged side of Place Fell, richly adorned with juniper, and sprinkled over with birches, to the

656 precipitous sides *S.V.*: [?high] embosoming Mountains MS.: coves precipitous sides MS.². 659 which *S.V.*: that MS. *Before* that MS. *deletes*: But the streams of which flow into the Lake of Ullswater. *The deletion occurs under the fold at the top of page* [1ᵛ] *and does not cohere with the text.* 660 the long MS.², *S.V.*: that long MS. 661 has MS.², *S.V.*: is not [?] it is MS. *After* importance MS. *deletes*: I hasten 662 by MS.³, *S.V.*: near MS.: from [?] by MS.². 663 Ullswater MS.², *S.V.*: the Lake MS. 664 Of Martindale MS.², *S.V.*: Of this last stream and the valley of Martindale much might be said MS. 665 must MS.², *S.V.*: shall MS. 667 the side MS.², *S.V.*: the Eastern side [? continuing] MS. 670 reason *S.V.*: occasion MS. 670–1 in the face of *S.V.*: every where in MS. 672 Blowick MS., *S.V*: Blowyke MS.². the only MS.², *S.V.*: the last piece of MS. 674–5 two or three *S.V.*: a few MS. 675 varied *S.V.*: divided MS. spot MS.², *S.V.*: spot with its land locked bays & promontories MS. 676–7 but now . . . lawns and *S.V.*: & its lawns now naked but [the *del.*] Nature [which *del.*] by those beautiful woods had MS. 678 Who . . . regret that *S.V.*: & MS. 679 have been *S.V.*: be MS. an inexhaustible Volume MS.², *S.V.*: a Volume of numerous pages MS. 681 track MS., *Edd.*: tract *S.V.* by MS.², *S.V.*: along MS. 682 cragged *S.V.*: craggy MS.

Village of Sandwyke; a few straggling houses, which, with the small estates attached to them, occupy an opening opposite to Lyulph's 685 Tower and Gowbarrow Park. This stream flows down Martindale, a Valley deficient in richness, but interesting from its seclusion. In Vales of this character the general want of wood gives a peculiar interest to the scattered cottages, embowered in sycamores; and few of the Mountain Chapels are more striking than this of Martindale, standing as it 690 does in the centre of the Valley, with one dark yew-tree, and enclosed by "a bare ring of mossy wall." The name of Boardale, a bare, deep, and houseless Valley, which communicates with Martindale, shews that the wild swine were once numerous in that nook; and Martindale Forest is yet one of the few spots in England ranged over by red deer. 695 These are the descendants of the aboriginal herds. In Martindale, the road loses sight of the Lake, and leads over a steep hill, bringing you again into view of Ullswater. Its lowest reach, four miles in length, is before you; and the View is terminated by the long ridge of Cross Fell at a distance. Immediately under the eye is a deep-indented bay, with 700 a plot of fertile land by the side of it, traversed by a small brook, and rendered cheerful by two or three substantial houses of a more ornamental and shewy appearance than is usual in these wild spots. Poolly-Bridge, at the foot of the Lake, to which we have again returned, has a good inn; and from this place Hawes-water, which has furnished me 705 with the subject of an Etching, may be conveniently visited. Of Hawes-water I shall only say, that it is a lesser Ullswater, with this advantage, that it remains undefiled by the intrusion of bad taste.

Lowther Castle is about four miles from Poolly-Bridge, and if during this Tour the Stranger has complained, as he will have reason to do, 710 of a want of majestic trees, he may be abundantly recompensed for his loss in the far-spreading woods which surround that mansion.

684 a few . . . with MS.⁴, *S.V.*: These MS.: This cluster of [?houses] is seated in an opening MS.²: A few straggling houses which are MS.³. 685 attached to them *S.V.*: to which they are attached MS. opposite MS.², *S.V.*: in this side of the Lake MS. 686 flows MS.², *S.V.*: if followed up would MS. down *S.V.*: down from MS. *After* Martindale MS. *deletes*: & the road crosses the lower extremity 687 *After* seclusion MS. *deletes*: its solitary Chapel with a dark yew tree & a [?bare ring] of mossy wall. 689 embowered MS.², *S.V.*: with their tufts MS. and few MS.², *S.V.*: the Chapel MS. 692 The name of MS.², *S.V.*: a branch of MS. Boardale MS.², *S.V.*: Boardale a branch of Martin MS. bare, deep *S.V.*: deep bare MS. 693 which *S.V.*: that MS. 694 were MS., *S.V.*: was MS.². that nook *S.V.*: that mounta MS: that [that *not corr.*] nooks MS.². 694–5 Martindale Forest is MS.², *S.V.*: the Mountains are MS. 697 leads MS.², *S.V.*: conducts MS. 698 again *S.V.*: soon again MS. 700 at a distance MS.², *S.V.*: distant MS. deep-indented *S.V.*: bold MS.: deeply indented MS.². 701 *After* it MS. *deletes*: & [?] a few houses of a more shewy ornamented 705 me *S.V.*: us MS. 709 Castle *S.V.*: *not in* MS. 710 will have *S.V.*: will have had MS. 711 he *S.V.*: in the woods of Lowther he MS. recompensed MS.², *S.V.*: gratified MS. 712 in the . . . mansion *S.V.*: *not in* MS.

I must now express my hope, that the Reader of the foregoing pages will not blame me for having led him through unfrequented paths so much out of the common road. In this I have acted in con- 715 formity to the spirit of the Etchings, which are chiefly taken from sequestered scenes; and these must become every day more attractive in the eyes of the man of taste, unless juster notions and more appropriate feelings should find their way into the minds of those who, either from vanity, want of judgment, or some other cause, are rapidly 720 taking away the native beauties of such parts of this Country as are most frequented, or most easy of access; and who are disfiguring the Vales, and the Borders of the Lakes, by an accumulation of unsightly buildings and discordant objects.

THE END. 725

713–14 express . . . me for *S.V.*: take my leave of the Reader who will not I trust find fault with me for MS.   714–15 through unfrequented paths *S.V.*: *not in* MS.   717 sequestered scenes MS.², *S.V.*: the more sequestered parts of the Country & I have [? tried] further to [?] MS.   and these must MS.², *S.V.*: [which *del.*] & these are likely to MS.   more attractive *S.V.*: more interesting to the MS.: gain fresh attraction MS.².   718 taste MS.², *S.V.*: taste & feeling [? and] [?] the more accessible & celebrated scenes MS.   notions MS.², *S.V.*: notions should put MS.   719 feelings *S.V.*: feeling MS.   720 vanity, want of *S.V.*: avarice MS.: a sordid love of money vanity or [undeveloped *del.*] want of MS.².   or some other cause *S.V.*: *not in* MS.   721 such MS.², *S.V.*: the accessible MS.   722 frequented . . . access *S.V.*: easy of access or most celebrated MS.   are disfiguring *Edd.*: are even still more [deplorably ⟨?⟩antly *del.*] obviously & deplorably disfiguring [them with ⟨?⟩ irreverent *del.*] MS.: are disguising *S.V.*   723–4 the Lakes . . . buildings and *S.V.*: these Lakes by what they add, a never-ending [addition *del.*] accumulation of impertinent & MS.   725 THE END. *S.V.*: *not in* MS.

APPENDIX II
[An Unpublished Tour]

Upon the best Approach to the Lakes

It is obvious that the point from which a Stranger should begin this
Tour, and the order in which it will be convenient to see the different
Vales will depend upon this circumstance: from what quarter of the
Island he comes. If from Scotland through Carlisle, there are from this
City several ways of approach. Travellers in Carriages may proceed
by the shortest carriage-road to Keswick, which leads along the shore
of the Lake of Bassenthwaite, or they may go from Carlisle to Penrith,
in which case it will suit them, as it will also others who have come
from the South by way of Stainmoor, to start from Penrith, taking
Lowther in their way to Haweswater. A traveller with time upon his
hands would be well recompensed by making a curve which would
include Corby-Castle & Nunnery upon the Eden in his way to Penrith.
The scenery at Nunnery consists of two parts: the one upon the large
river Eden; the other upon a small stream, the Croglin, which making
a succession of water-falls flows into the Eden. The beauties of this
little stream have been rendered accessible at considerable expense
which is well repaid, for it is not easy any where to find a spot in which
so much attraction of this sort exists in so narrow a compass.

Persons on foot or on horseback may proceed direct from Carlisle
to Keswick by Rose Castle, & Roughton head & under Carrick fell
through Mungrisdale & Threlkeld. Rose Castle being an Episcopal residence has in consequence fortunately escaped those alterations in the
Buildings & gardens to which under the name of improvement it
would have been liable, had it been private property. The Castle stands
pleasantly upon ground that slopes gently to the river Caldew & commands an interesting view of the opposite woody bank of the river &
the stoney summit of Carrick fell beyond. But the peculiar recommendation here is the House itself—an ancient Building of red stone with
hanging gardens, an ivied Gateway, velvet lawns, old garden walls,

3 convenient MS.²: convenient to him MS.   4 circumstance: MS.²: circumstance; viz: MS.   5 through MS.²: by way of MS.   8 they MS.²: such
Travellers MS.   11 Lowther MS.²: the scenery of Lowther MS.   *After*
Haweswater MS. *deletes*: if they be inclined to visit the magnificent woods the wild
river scenery It is difficult to give directions [for *del.*] by which a Stranger may be
guided.   12 making MS.³: going MS.: taking MS.².   19 sort MS.²:
kind MS.   22 Mungrisdale *Edd.*: Grisdale MS.   24 gardens MS.²:
grounds MS.   25 had it MS.²: if it MS.   26 ground MS.²: a Lawn MS.
28 But the MS.²: It is MS.

trim flower-borders with stately & luxuriant flowers. This road from
Carlisle to Keswick may be passed, though not without some trouble,
in a single horse Chaise. It may be mentioned that at Caldbeck, a little
to the right of this road, is a beautiful stream with Limestone rocks &
caves, overhanging trees, pools & water breaks. At Sebergham, also 35
a Village upon the Caldew, is some wild-woodland & river scenery,
dignified by the neighbouring Mountain of Carrick. Having given
these preparatory directions to Persons approaching from Scotland,
they will proceed on their tour through the Lakes, reversing the order
which I shall point out as being in itself the best. But indeed for the 40
sake of seeing the different Vales in the order I shall propose, I strenuously recommend to all Persons approaching from Scotland or by
Stanemoor, if on foot or on horseback, to proceed through the woods
of Lowther to Haweswater & along the shore of that Lake, & through
Mardale & Long Sledale to Kendal, which will bring them not abso- 45
lutely to the best point to start from, but to one from which all the
principal scenes may be approached to the best advantage.

I will now address myself to Travellers coming from the South; &
premising that the best point to begin this tour from is Lancaster—&
the next to that, Kendal—I will mention a few scenes which in going 50
or returning may be visited without much trouble & are beautiful in
their kind. The nearest & best Carriage road from London to Kendal
is thro' Leeds & Craven, & this road, a few miles before you come to
Skipton, brings you to within 1/2 a mile's distance from an excellent
Inn at Bolton Bridge, from which may be visited a spot inferior to none 55
in England for beauty, the Ruins & grounds of Bolton Priory upon the
river Wharf. From this Place the Carriage Traveller must proceed to
Skipton, & would be well repaid by visiting Gordale Scar and Malham
Cove in the neighbourhood of Malham; & from Settle by making
another circuit in his way to Ingleton, Withercote Cave & Yordas 60
cave may be seen—the only things worth turning aside for in the
district of the Caves. But note that none of these objects, except Bolton
Priory, can be seen by Carriage Travellers without a considerable circuit & a good deal of trouble. Travellers on foot or on horseback may
go from Bolton Priory up the Wharf by Barden Tower & advance 65
along the banks of the river to Burnsall, where they will be directed
to Gordale by the nearest road. Thence to the Inn at Malham, &

---

36 is some] *wrongly deleted.*   40 But MS.[2]: & MS.   41 in the . . . propose MS.[2]: of this district to the best advantage MS.   41–2 strenuously MS.[2]:
should strenuously MS.   46 but to MS.[2]: but from one MS.   49 premising
MS.[3]: having stated MS.: stating MS.[2].   50 the next MS.[2]: the second best
MS.   in MS.[2]: eith MS.   51 may be visited MS.[2]: ought not to be negl
MS.   57 proceed MS.[2]: advance MS.   64 a good deal of MS.[2]: much MS.
66–7 be directed to MS.[2]: receive directions for MS.

thence to Settle, &c. Taking the Carriage Traveller up again at Kirby
Lonsdale, the view from the Churchyard may be recommended as particularly pleasing. From Kirby Lonsdale direct to Kendal is a distance   70
of 12 miles, but he who wishes & is able to do entire justice to the
Country will proceed down the rich Vale of Lune to Lancaster. 3 miles
short of Lancaster is the celebrated view which Mr Gray has recommended. Hackfall & Studley in Yorkshire lie not inconveniently for
south-country travellers going or returning; in either case Wensley   75
dale will be passed through. The whole tract of Country in that dale is
most agreeable; its particular features are the falls of the Ure, another
fall of water in a little Valley near Askrigg, & Hardraw Scar not far
from Hawes. Thence to Sedberg & Kendal.

I will conclude these introductory directions by recommending to   80
those who either going or returning may have occasion to cross Stanemoor to halt an hour at Greta Bridge. There is a pleasing walk of a
quarter of a mile along the side of the rocky channel of the river Greta
above the Bridge, & below it the grounds of Rokeby Hall are interesting—especially, the Bridge over the rocky strait into which the River   85
Tees is forced, with the adjoining remains of Egglestone Abbey. From
this place ascending by the side of the Tees for somewhat less than
2 miles, you are brought to the stately ruins of Barnard Castle, hanging
from a high perpendicular rock above the bed of the River. From
Barnard Castle to Bowes are 4 miles; at Bowes you join the main   90
Northern road, so that these interesting objects only take you 2 miles
about. Having finished these directions, pointing out beautiful spots
which may be commodiously visited by Travellers from the North or
the South, we will in the next Chapter take up the Tourist at Lancaster,
which is—as has been said before—the point whence a Tour of the   95
Lakes may be begun with the most advantage.

[Lancaster]

Lancaster with its Castle and the distant Mountains beyond present
a grand picture to a Person approaching from the South, but noble
as this landscape is, it is far inferior in its effect upon the mind to   100
the panorama view from the principal Tower of the Castle itself.

---

72 to MS.²: down MS.   73 view which MS.²: view distinguished MS.
75 either MS.²: which MS.   78 in MS.²: upon MS.   80 recommending
MS.²: observing MS.   84 Rokeby] *possibly* Rookby   84–5 interesting MS.²:
very interesting MS.   87 somewhat] *altered from* something   91 only
take you MS.²: do not require [?] MS.   92 pointing MS.²: which point MS.
beautiful MS.²: interesting MS.   95 point whence MS.²: best point from
which MS.   98 beyond MS.²: beyond it MS.   99 *After* South MS.
A deletes: The Steeple of the Church which for[?] [?] but the peculiar but noble as
this landscape is . . .   101 principal *Edd.*: central principal MS. (principal
was inserted and no deletion was made).

From this lofty station, or having ascended a few steps higher to the top of a little turret called John of Gaunt's chair, by which the tower is crested, the Spectator looks upon the inferior towers, courts, roofs, walls, battlements, & whole circumference of this vast edifice, & upon   105
the town, shipping, aqueduct, & Bridge—works of art sufficiently splendid for the situation which they occupy in the centre of a magnificent prospect of sea & land. After a hasty survey of the whole Scene, the Castle will naturally become the object of distinct attention.

We are accustomed to contemplate without regret the desolation   110
which time & circumstance have generally produced in buildings of this age and character—the very word 'Ruins' is a note of preparation for melancholy pleasure. But here antiquity is fresh & renovated, and the massy, formidable, and venerable aspect of castellated architecture unites in a stile worthy of the purpose to which the building is applied   115
with the neatness, airiness, & lightsomeness which modern humanity & taste have studiously introduced. In the several Courts immediately under the eye, the Debtors and various orders of Prisoners are seen pacing to & fro, amusing themselves or pursuing their occupations in the open air. The construction of their Prison-house makes it evident   120
that it is impossible for them to escape, & at the same time shews that no comfort or accommodation is wanting which their pitiable condition will allow. While the Spectator stands upon this eminence—the breezes passing by in freedom, & the clouds sailing at liberty over his head—the wide circumjacent region exhibits in the fields the cheerful-   125
ness & fertility, & in the Waters & Mountains the uncontroulable motions & the inexhaustible powers of Nature. The contrast is striking,

102–4 From . . . courts MS.⁴: From this lofty station the Spectator looks down MS.: From this Tower or from the still loftier station of the MS.²: From this lofty station, or having ascended a few steps higher to [the *del.*] a small turret named John of Gaunt's chair by which [it *undel.*] the Tower is crested. The Spectator looks down upon the inferior Towers, upon the courts MS.³. 104–8 the Spectator . . . land MS.: The Spectator looks down upon the Town & Shipping of Lancaster its River crossed by a stately Bridge and more stately Aqueduct [and *del.*] features of art which will strike his [?] amid the magnificence of the natural objects. MS. *A.*   109 the Castle . . . attention MS.²: the attention will at first settle upon the building itself MS. *A*: the attention will naturally settle upon the castle itself MS.   110 contemplate MS.²: survey MS. 111 generally MS.²: in most cases MS.   118–20 are seen . . . air MS.: you see & hear them walking about having the comfort of every accommodation which ample space MS. *A.*   123–4 the breezes . . . the clouds MS.²: and feels the breezes . . . and sees the clouds MS.   127–33 The contrast . . . necessary] *Two passages of* MS. *A read* (*we omit the erratic marks of deletion*): With this prospect immediately under your the eyes & with a feeling hanging about the heart & filling the imagination of the suffering misfortunes the privations & the offences sufferings & privations with this majestic display of the coercive Power which cruel Society is compelled to exercise from this as a central point: The grandeur of civil polity & the weakness & imperfections of society are here visibly & palpably expressed the one in union & the other in contrast to majesty of the elements & the other in

& it is impossible not to be touched by a depressing sympathy with
the unfortunate or guilty Captives under his eye. There is a counter-
poise, however, in the majesty of the building, by its appearance & 130
construction admirably fitted to announce & give effect to those coercive duties of civil polity which the infirmities of Men have rendered
necessary. But happy, if I may be here indulged in this course, are they
upon whose bodies neither the will of an arbitrary Ruler or the laws
of a justly offended country have imposed any restraints. What a sor- 135
rowful state is captivity, what a blessed one is liberty! Vain exclamation, whatever may have tempted us to utter it, if we forget that liberty
of body is a worthless or dangerous possession if the mind be enslaved
& that there is no true freedom but for him who is preserved by his own
exertion & by the blessing of Providence from the burden of inordinate 140
desires, sordid habits, & pining discontents, & unreasonable sorrows.
Then, & in that case only, is he at large, & in the presence of such a
scene as this may be entitled to give vent to his feelings in the impassioned language of the Poet:

> What more felicity can fall to Creature   145
> Than to enjoy delight with liberty,
> And to be the Lord of all the works of Nature,
> To reign in the Air from Earth to highest sky,
> To feed on flowers & weeds of glorious feature,
> To take whatever thing doth please the eye?   150
> Who rests not pleased with such happiness,
> Well worthy he to taste of wretchedness.

If the cells and different apartments of this Public building be
examined, they would be found excellently contrived for their several
purposes. Great expense has been laudably incurred in remodelling 155
the courts of justice under the direction of Mr Harrison the Architect,
but looking at these improvements with a view merely to the principles
of taste, I cannot forbear observing that an injury has been done: the
impression which the architecture on a first entrance would naturally

contrast to those creations of Almighty Wisdom in which however they The depressing sympathy that is felt by Contrast for the condition of the unfortunate or
guilty Captives, is counterpoised by the majesty of the edifice itself.

129 his eye. There MS.²: our eyes. But there MS.   133 course MS.³:
course of sentiment MS.: course [? *del.*] MS.².   137–8 liberty . . . if the MS.²:
there is no true freedom but of the MS.   139 is preserved MS.²: has preserved MS.   140 burden MS.²: thraldom MS.   142–3 is he . . . his
MS.²: are we . . . our MS.   143 feelings MS.²: feelings & MS.   154–5
their several purposes MS.: the purpose to which it is applied MS. *A.*   158
that an injury MS.²: that [? in one ⟨?⟩ to the architect] MS.

produce is in one of the rooms disturbed, or rather precluded, by two 160
portraits in the modern exhibition stile, hanging immediately above
the bench & representing the Persons of two Members for the County
—the one in a Black suit, the other in glaring regimentals. It may be
mentioned, as a general rule, that canvass being moveable & perishable, paintings upon this material somewhat painfully contrast with 165
the fixedness & durability of Masonry, & that, however interesting
for their own sakes, they can rarely be employed with advantage as
subsidiary to architecture in which dignity & grandeur are aimed at.
But in this instance the modern dresses are quite discordant with the
gothic stile of the room, & whatever claim the two Gentlemen here 170
represented might have upon the gratitude of the Country, & how far
soever the building itself might be indebted to their exertions &
liberality, the portraits, without any disrespect, may be said to occupy
a place which could only with propriety be filled by memorials or like-
nesses of Persons whom their Characters or stations have made gener- 175
ally interesting, the Sovereign for the time being, for instance, or those
of past ages by whose wisdom the constitution & jurisprudence of the
Country have been most benefitted—Alfred, or the worthies of the
Plantagenets, or William the third. Mr. H[arrison], the architect to
whom this County & that of Chester are so greatly indebted, has been 180
heard to say that he never received a compliment to his professional
skill so gratifying as a tribute of applause which was, without design,
paid him by a Peasant who in his presence, entering into one of these
rooms, passed with a deliberate step into the centre of it, & having
looked around took off his hat in sign of reverence that unequivocally 185
expressed the awe with which his mind was stricken. Mr Duppa, the
artist, seems, as appears from a note to his life of Michel Angelo, to
have been much impressed by another apartment of this Castle: "In
England," says he, "I have experienced a striking impression—from a
simple & unadorned room; not to make a comparison between it & the 190
St Maria degli Angeli, I mention it for the sake of instancing an example
of what may be obtained by simplicity & dimension without any other
aid. The room is in Lancaster Castle, appropriated to the use of the
prisoners, who for slight offenses are sentenced to a temporary confinement; it is about 63 feet long, having only 4 plain walls & making 195

165 contrast *Edd.*: contrasts MS.   170 gothic stile MS.²: gothic stone-
work & stile MS.   178 Alfred, or MS.²: Alfred for example, or Edward
the first or third or MS. *A*: Alfred for example the two Edwards or MS. *A*²:
Alfred Edward the G MS.   179 Mr. MS.²: It has been reported that Mr.
MS.   181 compliment *Edd.*: complement MS.   182 as a MS.²: as one MS.
184–5 having looked MS.²: looking MS.   185 off *Edd.*: of MS.
186 stricken *Edd.*: striken by the MS: striken MS.².   187 artist, seems
MS.²: artist in a note to his life of Michel Angelo highly commends one of [the
del.] them MS.   187–8 to have been MS.²: has been MS.

nearly the proportion of a double cube, & is remarkably illustrative of the true feeling of the great first principles of architecture; which are of so much importance, that when they are once felt & understood, it is not easy after to spoil the effect of grandeur, even by injudicious ornament or the caprice of fashion." 200

[The Sands and Furness Abbey]

The little inconvenience attached to a journey over the Sands, for in fine weather there is no danger, does not prevent me from advising with M[r.] West that from Lancaster the Traveller should proceed by that passage, as being the most eligible approach to the Country of the 205 Lakes. The beautiful Lake of Conistone will thus be traced upwards from its outlet, the only way in which it can be seen for the first time without injury amounting almost to an entire sacrifice of its most delightful appearances; & further the Stranger from the moment he sets his foot upon the Sands seems to leave the turmoil & the traffic of 210 the world behind him, & crossing this majestic Plain from which the Sea has retired & which in a few hours the Waters will cover again, he beholds rising apparently from its base that cluster of Mountains among the recesses of which he is going to wander, & into which by the Vale of Conistone he is gradually & peacefully introduced. The 215 Lake & Vale of C[onistone], approached in this manner, improve in appearance with every step.

And I may here make this general remark, which indeed the Reader may have deduced from the representation of the Country given in the Introduction, that, whenever it is possible, these Lakes & Vallies 220 should be approached from the foot; otherwise, most things will come upon the Spectator to great disadvantage. Conistone, Windermere, & Ulswater—these Lakes, in particular, suffer almost as much, at a first sight, in being approached from the head as an affecting Story would do, should the Reader begin with the last Chapter & read the whole 225 backwards. This general rule applies, tho' not with equal force, to all the Lakes, with the single exception of Lowes Water, which, lying in a direction opposite to the rest, has its most favourable aspects determined accordingly.

The detail of the ride over the Sands is well given in the notes 230 abridged from M[r] West. When the Traveller has reached Ulverston, he may be inclined to visit Furness Abbey. Concerning these noble remains, I can add nothing of importance to what will be found in the

---

199 after MS.[2]: afterwards MS.   203–6 from advising . . . Lakes MS.: from recommending that approach to the Lakes as being most eligible.—(Here take up Wilkinson Book) MS. *A*.   231 abridged MS.[2]: extracted MS. 232–3 Concerning . . . nothing MS.[3]: of this I have little MS.: Concerning this . . . I have [?] nothing MS.[2].

notes, but I cannot forbear to express regret for the delapidations
which have taken place within living memory, and particularly for the   235
fall of the Window Arch that fronted the visitor of the ruins in descending the valley. This arch, now gone, the span of which was long
preserved by its airy keystone, has been poetically denominated,

> The triumphal Arch of time.

And in a similar Spirit it has been boldly said that,   240

> Fountains Abbey, glorious in decay,
> Threatens to outlive the ravages of Time
> And bear the Cross till Christ shall come again.

Alas! as the present state shews, these are rather truths of the imagination than matters of fact. In the MS. from which the above Verses are   245
taken, I find the Author thus expressing himself on his approach to the
Ruins:

> Let us descend & on the sacred ground,
> With solemn, trembling, silent steps & slow,
> Tread softly, taste the consecrated brook   250
> That in meanders creeps along the Vale
> And in soft murmurs mourns the Abbey's fate.
> Thou plaintive brook, thy being still remains
> Framed by the Word divine, while the best works
> Of mortal Man lie mouldering in the dust.   255
> Sweet holy brook, whose cooling waters oft
> Did the parched Pilgrim quench & gave new life,
> What tho' thy Springs have been polluted long,
> Thou once wast holy. Thou art holy still.
> Let me taste freely of thy streams & live.   260

In another temper, contrasting melancholy images with chearful, the
Poet exclaims with equal spirit, calling to [? mind] the splendid domains
of the old Abbots:

> What herds of deer, brown, fallow, spotted, white,
> In these rich pastures, unmolested fed,   265
> Save when a festival with viands crowned,
> Far more luxurious than Apicius thine,

---

234 regret MS.²: my regret MS.   235 within MS.²: in my MS.   236 Window
MS.²: [? great] MS.   236–8 Window . . . keystone] *Deletions make the text
uncertain.*   240 boldly said that MS.²: not ill said [this *del.*] that the abbey
MS.   244 as the *Edd.*: as [the *del.*] MS.: as to MS.².   state MS.²: state of
these fabricks MS.   these MS.²: that these MS.   246 on his *Edd.*: on the
MS.: [on *del.*] his MS.².   246–7 to the Ruins MS.²: [?] this glorious Pile MS.
254 Framed MS.²: Made MS.   262 splendid MS.²: rich MS.

Called for the [? round] fat Haunch, to overload
The table with superfluous dainties heaped,
When Venus sate disguised like a Nun,   270
While Bacchus every mighty Goblet filled
With pure Falernian, with Burgundian grape,
With Lachrymae, Champain, & rich Tokay,
Till every Votary fired with generous wine
Devoutly drank the Toast: our Kingdom's here!   275

The Poet surveys with appropriate reflections the present state of the
Piscina, the Locutorium, the Prison, the Chapter House, Scriptorium,
Refectory, [?] & we will take leave of him with the following extract:

The walls that glowed with Tapestry, breathing life,
Are bare, save where the circling ivy twines   280
Around yon arches, nodding with the blasts.
The sun but faintly glimmers through the chinks
And shews the horrors of the gloomy cells,
Where the green lizard and the gilded newt
Lead unmolested lives & die by age.   285

Among these gloomy cells is one more terrible than the rest where the
wealth of the Abbey is reported to lie hid. Many Persons, as the tradition goes, have attempted to grope their way along the blind passage,
which leads to this treasure house, but in vain—lizards, vipers, adders,
huge toads, & monsters casting out flames from their wide jaws force   290
them to relinquish their purpose, & madness & death have been the
consequence of their fears. Yet the attempt, as the tradition goes, has
been renewed from age to age by fresh adventurers, so potent is the
imagination when the appetite of lucre is raging. Is it to be supposed
that these terrible consequences, attributed to such prying into the   295
abodes of darkness, arise in this case from a notion of sacrilege? Or are
they, according to the rules of poetic justice in a scheme of superstition,
nothing more than a fit penalty for unwarrantable curiosity, or intended to suppress the lurking dishonesty of seeking what is not the
searcher's own, though it does not in his feeling fairly belong to   300
another? Or, lastly, are these horrors intended to check the extravagances of those desires which would attain a great end by means wholly
disproportionate, or is there not a principle of malice in human nature

276 surveys MS.²: takes MS.   278 with the following extract MS.²:
by extracting from his work these verses MS.   288 grope MS.²: find MS.
292 as the tradition goes] *Inserted here and similarly inserted in* 287–8; *no deletion
was made.*   293 potent MS.³: ins[?] MS.: strong MS.².   295 that these
MS.²: that a notion of MS.   301 are these MS.²: is this MS.

which makes us delight in contrasts of this kind, where high blown
expectations of pride & pleasure go out, or pass suddenly into their   305
opposite realities of disappointment, pain, & terror?

The situation of this Monastery was in every respect singularly well
chosen: for security, as being in a remote corner of the Island & backed
by the Sea, from which, as the Scotch borderers did not venture
themselves upon that element, no danger was to be apprehended; for   310
accommodations of life, as the surrounding land is very fertile; and
for the moral advantages of sequestration & quiet. The buildings of the
Abbey must originally have stretched across the narrow Valley in
which it is placed, & the lofty towers must have almost overtopped its
sides—unless where surmounted by trees, but these, no doubt, existed   315
in abundance.

On either side, a wood
Of blackening pines, aye waving to & fro,
Sent forth a sleepy horror through the blood;
And where the Valley winded out, below,   320
The murmuring Main was heard, & scarcely heard, to flow.

So that in this respect the images of Nature would unite with the cloistral architecture to shut up the Soul within itself & to assist the
Devotee in the task of mortification & the relinquishment of worldly
pleasures; and in contrast to this seclusion, if a magnificent prospect   325
of Mountains & the plain of the Ocean may be supposed—in spite of
an oppressive routine of rites & ceremonies—not to have been lost
upon the mind, but to have contributed to devotional feeling by a display of the sublimest works of the Creator & by holding forth shadows
& sensible types or representations of that infinity which is the true   330
element & birthright of the human soul, an opportune station for
participating this advantage was not wanting. On the crown of an
eminence that rises immediately from the Abbey & is seen over all
Low Furness, stood a Beacon, whither, it pleases one to imagine, the
Meditative Monk might retire, not as a Scout or Watchman to look   335
forth in order to give alarm to his Companions [of] approaching

307 Monastery MS.²: Abbey MS.   309 did not venture MS.²: were [?]
themselves MS.   312 quiet. MS.²: privacy. The narrow Valley in which the
Abbey was placed MS.   314 have almost overtopped MS.²: have over
MS.   316 abundance MS.²: abundance one cannot but figure to oneself MS.
322 unite MS.²: combine MS.   324 worldly *Edd.*: wordly MS.   325 and
in MS.²: at the same time MS.   326 supposed MS.²: supposed to have had
any influence in exalting such minds MS.   328 devotional feeling MS.²: an
exaltation of MS.   330 sensible] *possibly del.*   representations MS.²: representations to the senses MS.   331 station MS.²: stations MS.   332 On
MS.²: From MS.   336 forth in order MS.²: forth for the prot MS.   336–7
[of *Edd.*] approaching danger MS.²: if danger were at hand MS. (*The* if *was left
unaltered in* MS.².)

danger, but to feed upon pious thoughts & to encourage that mood in
which melancholy—instead of depressing the spirit—acts as a power
that carries it upward to an elevation otherwise unattainable. Or if the
habitual listlessness & indolence of the cloister accompanied the soli- 340
tary visitant to this eminence, though too passive to seek for amusement in the creations of his own thoughts, he might still not be
insensible to the Changes in the appearances of things which Nature
would be carrying forward before his eyes. A gleam of light striking
upon the distant Towers of Lancaster, or a passing shower that con- 345
cealed them, might stir him—the one, to congratulation, the other,
to a sentiment of regret; and the line of clouds extended along the
mountainous ridge of the Isle of Man from one extremity to the other,
a body compact and stationary—but varying insensibly their colours &
their shapes—might furnish him with large materials for aerial Castle- 350
building with little cost to his own fancy. The power of the situation
in this respect reminds me again of Thomson.

> A pleasing land of drowsyhead it was,
> Of dreams that wave before the half-shut eye;
> And of airy castles in the clouds that pass,   355
> For ever flushing round a summer's sky.

Donnerdale

The head of Conistone Water may be confidently recommended as
the first halting-place to Travellers bent upon something more than
a mere transient observation of the most celebrated scenes of the 360
Country. Close by the Water-side & looking down the whole length
of the Lake stands an Inn, distinguished at present for its cleanliness
& comfort. Making this the head quarters, two days may be here
profitably & pleasantly passed. The first, if the weather permit, may

337 thoughts & MS.²: thoughts where [? elevation] of mind is ennobled MS.
337–9 in which . . . upward MS.²: in which elevation of spirit is not checked but
rather carried [? forward] & MS.   338 depressing . . . power MS.²: depressing is
a power MS.   339 it MS.²: the spirit MS.   339–47 Or if . . . other, to]
A version in MS. *A may be conjecturally read*: Or if indolence & listlessness of mind
[are supposed to *del.*] [not to *del.*] not relinquishing here that sway [which *undel.*]
[have been rendered habitual in the cloistral *del.*] which the cloister has rendered
habitual, accompanied the occasional visitant to this eminence if we may imagine
[? him when he ⟨?⟩] too passive to be disposed to amuse himself with the creations
of his own thoughts [as not *del.*] he still might not be insensible to the changes of
the distant scenery [around him *del.*] as [taking pleasure in *del.*] a [?] of light
that [revealed *del.*] rendered conspicuous the [? distant] towers of Lancaster Castle
or a transient [?] that concealed them—might stir him the one to congratulation
the other to [*blank*].   343–4 Nature would MS.³: Nature for the most part MS:
Nature at all seasons would MS.².   345 passing shower MS.³: cloud MS.:
vapour MS.².   349 insensibly MS.²: perpetually MS.   354 wave] *possibly*
wane   362 an MS.²: a most comfortable MS.   363 Making . . . quarters
MS.²: Here MS.

be employed in an excursion into Donnerdale by a stout Pedestrian, 365
or if horses can be procured.

Donnerdale is a name given to part of the Vales of Duddon, & the
whole might with propriety be so called, *Don* being a contraction of
the word *Duddon* & *er* in the composition of Names in this Country
signifying *upon*. Donnerdale lies wholly out of the beaten track, but 370
nothing is risked in recommending it to the Traveller of taste & feeling. It lies over the high hill that bounds the Vale of Conistone on the
West & will be best approached by a [?] road ascending from near the
Church of Conistone & leading into that division of the Vale called
Seathwaite. The road is so long and steep that the horse must be led 375
a considerable part of it. I think the ascent & descent cannot be less
than five miles, but nothing can be found more wild & beautiful than
the scene into which the Traveller will be received at the bottom of the
hill on the other side. It is an idle thing to lavish encomiastic epithets
upon these subjects, but I have no scruple in saying that any Person of 380
common sensibility who should descend into this Valley towards the
close of September, while the aftergrass of the meadows is yet of a
fresh green, with the leaves of many of the trees faded, but perhaps
none fallen, will find this scene truly enchanting. Near the foot of the
hill, the road, leading down a steep slope, passes close to the side of 385
a brook, foaming along its rugged channel; & at this point, elevated
enough to shew the various objects in the Valley & not so high as to
diminish their importance, the Stranger will instinctively halt. On the
foreground, a little below this station, a rude foot bridge is thrown
over the bed of this noisy brook. Russet & craggy hills of bold and 390
varied outline surround the valley, over which rocks, lawns, woods,
& buildings are scattered with exquisite felicity. But the style in which
the buildings are intermingled with each other & with the scenery
excites less admiration than the beauty of the buildings themselves.
The cottages in some places peep out from under the rocks hung with 395
trees, like hermitages whose scite has been chosen for the benefit of
sun-shine as well as shelter; in other instances, the dwelling house,

---

368 *Don* MS.²: the *Don* MS.   381 descend *Edd.*: descent MS.   381-4 *After
Valley* MS. Prose 20ᶠ *deletes*: towards . . . green & the leaves . . . find this—
After this deletion is written: see part of an old letter. (*Cf. S.V., textual n.* 47.)
Despite the direction to incorporate MS. Prose 20ᵇ, MS. Prose 20ᶠ *immediately rewrites the deletion and continues.*   385 leading . . . passes MS.²: leads . . .
& is brought MS.   392 scattered MS.²: scattered & intermingled MS.
394 *After* themselves MS. *deletes*: what deformity is almost everywhere produced
by modern farm houses & their dependences but [here *del.*] in this sequestered Valley
there are many barns & byers [which in their outward *del.*] whose appearance at a
little distance with the trees that embower and with the plants & shrubs that adorn
them call to mind the [beauty & *del.*] sanctity which is felt on beholding the beautiful remnants of ancient abbeys. *Under this deletion and centred as a title, although at
the bottom of page* [1ᵛ], *is the word*: Seathwaite

combining with the barn & byer, makes a cruciform structure, which,
with the foliage that embowers & the plants & mosses that encrust it,
calls to mind the sanctity which is felt on beholding the remains of 400
ancient abbeys. Time in most instances, & Nature every where, has
consecrated the humble works of man that are sprinkled over this peaceful valley: hence, a perfection & consummation of a beauty which could
not have been realized if aim or purpose which would have marred [?]
[? had] interfered with the course of convenience, utility, or necessity. 405
This unvitiated region stands in no need of the veil of twilight to soften
or disguise its features. It does not suffer from the broad light of mid-
day. As it glistens in the morning sun shine, it would fill the Spectator's
heart with gladsomeness. Looking from [the] station where he first
halts, he would feel an impatience to rove among its path ways, to be 410
greeted by the milkmaid, to wander from house to house, exchanging
words of courtesy as he passed the open doors; but, at evening, when
the sun is set, and a pearly light gleams from the western quarter
of the sky, and an answering light appears to gleam from the surface
of the smooth meadows; when the trees are dusky, but their various 415
kinds still distinguishable; when the cool air has condensed the blue
smoke rising from the cottages; when the dark mossy stones seem to
sleep in the bed of the brook foaming on every side of them; then,
he would be unwilling to move forward, both loath to relinquish
what he beholds and fearing to disturb by his approach the quietness 420
beneath him.

This little circular Valley is a collateral compartment to the long
winding Vale thro which flows the stream of Duddon, & its brook finds
its way to that River. Advancing, we come to the lowly Chapel of
Seathwaite with its small belfrey, its Yew-tree, its dial, & two or three 425
tombstones among the graves. One of these monuments bears upon
a brass plate the following Inscription: 'In memory of the Revd Robt
Walker, who died 25 June 1802, in the 93^[d] year of his age & 67th of
his Curacy at Seathwaite. Also of Anne his Wife, who died the 28th
of Jany 1800, in the 93^d year of her age.' The Parish Register also 430
contains the following Mem:—the only notice, beyond the bare list of
Baptisms, Marriages, & Funerals, that is to be found in it: 'Buried
June 28th. The Revd R. Walker. He was Curate of Seathwaite 66 years.

398 barn & byer MS.²: barns & byers MS.   399 mosses MS.²: shrubs MS.
400 remains MS.²: remnants MS.   404–5 realized . . . interfered] *Alterations
and insertions make the text uncertain.*   406 unvitiated MS.²: beautiful MS.
408 As it glistens MS.²: glistening MS.   409 from [the *Edd.*] station where
MS.²: from his station he will MS.   413 western MS.²: opposite MS.
425–6 two . . . graves MS.²: few graves. This [?] MS.   430–1 The Parish . . .
contains MS.²: In the Parish Register is MS.   432 Baptisms . . . Funerals
MS.²: Births . . . deaths MS.   433 *After* 28th MS. *inserts*: 18

He was a Man singular for his temperance, industry, & integrity.'
This brief encomium must, of necessity, be seen by few, & the meagre 435
Inscription upon the tombstone is perishable, for the brass plate is
already loosened from the Stone. Yet these Memorials, with the exception of a few letters preserved in an early Vol. of the Annual Register,
are, I believe, the only public Records that exist of this inestimable
Man, the remembrance of whom, even in that Valley to which he was 440
so long a blessing, will soon pass away, like that of the [? spreading]
tree that has been felled & whose decaying . . .

The Traveller, having satisfied himself with strolling about Seathwaite, will proceed down Donnerdale to Ulpha Kirk; and from the
Church-yard, looking into the Valley, he will have a grand arrange- 445
ment of mountain lines and forms. And to this I direct the attention
because, hitherto, [the] slight description given of this Vale has dwelt
chiefly upon its most striking [? character] viz: the rocks starting out
from, and roughening, its sides; or scattered ov[*tear*] The neighbouring
Vale of Eskdale is also diversified by rocks in the same [*tear*] manner, 450
yet with endless variations; and the Traveller will do well to fix his
[*tear*] upon three great classes into which these Vales may be divided:
first, [? those] like [*tear*]

In this second class, all sense of wild or beautiful littleness in the
parts is lost in the maj[*tear*] unity of the whole. The third division is 455
that which takes its *presiding* and *characteristic* impression neither from
the rocks nor from the mountains, but from the [*tear*] as the vale of
Windermere, Ulswater, &c.

---

435 meagre MS.²: scanty MS.   440 the remembrance MS.²: whose
memory MS.   442 whose decaying] MS. Prose 20ᶠ *ends on the last line of
page* [2ᵛ]; *the continuation is lost.*   442/3 MS. Prose 20ᶜ *begins:*

Section 3ᵈ
Donnerdale continued &c &c.

On the means by which U.T. here adopts a S.V. manuscript, see our description of MS.
Prose 20ᶜ.   443 The Traveller, having MS., *Edd.*: Having MS.². (*After the
subject of the sentence was deleted, no substitution was made; but see S.V.* 52–3.)
445-6 a grand [an *undel.*] arrangement . . . forms MS.²: as grand an arrangement of
mountain lines and forms as perhaps this Country furnishes MS.   446 the
attention MS.³: the Spectator's attention MS.: his attention MS.².   447 [the
Edd.] slight . . . has MS.²: in this slight description which has been given of
this Vale, I have MS.   453/4 *The lower fragment of* MS. Prose 20ᶜ *is so badly
torn that only incomplete phrases and partially completed words remain:*

Duddon a	ough there be nothing w	grandeur
	are they so constitu	
mountains	view, yet ~~where~~ the rocks	*ground*
intermixtu	river, give the predominating impression,	
those like	the upper part of Wastdale, where the pred	
impression	simple grandeur of the *mountains*, and from	
open area of	Vale in which there is nothing intricate or encumbered.	

To return to the Church-yard of Ulpha. The whole scene is
[inspirited] by the sound and sight of the river rolling immediately 460
below the steep ground [upon] the top of which the Chapel stands. The
following pleasing Epitaph will be found upon a stone affixed to the
Wall of the Chapel.

> Lo! here a Sister rests in peace,
> Worn out with pain & long disease. 465
> But now her tedious conflicts o'er,
> Disease & death can kill no more.
> Think, Reader, as thou passeth by,
> That Nature's birthright is to die.
> So raise to heaven thy pensive heart, 470
> Where dearest Friends will never part.

This Tombstone, erected by a father to a Daughter who died at the age
of one & twenty, is the only record in the Church yard, except that
a Person has availed himself of the naked surface of a corner stone of
the Chapel rudely to engrave thereon a brief notice of One who is 475
buried near it.

This wild country was once frequented by Druids, as appears from
one of those circles of upright stones, large and perfect, which we are
accustomed to call Druids Temples. This which I am now speaking of,
the People of the Country designate with characteristic feeling by the 480
name of Sunken Church; it lies at some distance to the South west
among the hills, & may be distinguished from the road leading from
this place & from Broughton over Stoneside to Bootle & Ravenglass.
By the bye, having mentioned this road, I cannot forbear to add that
it affords from the top of Stoneside a most magnificent burst of sea 485
prospect. The shore of Cumberland, belted with foam, the Isle of Man,
& the Scotch hills. This view, so noble in itself, comes upon the eye
of the Stranger with the strongest effects of contrasts, for in ascending
the hill & travelling over the wild moor with a dreary scene before
him, he will naturally have been tempted to look frequently back upon 490
the long & deeply sequestered Vale of the Duddon, & his mind will
revert with earnestness & his heart with regret to the sheltered

460 inspirited *Edd.* (*cf. S.V.* 56): inspir[*tear*] MS.   461 *After* stands MS.
Prose 20ᶜ *continues*: A pleasing Epitaph, the only one in the place if I remember
will be found affixed to the wall of the Church. This wild Count[ry was] once
frequented by Druids, as appears from one of those circles of upright stones. *After
the line ending with the word* remember, Prose 20ᶜ *was sewn to the top of page* [1ʳ] *of*
MS. Prose 20ᵉ, *which begins*: The following pleasing . . . *etc.*   472 Tombstone,
erected MS.²: tribute paid MS.   473 record MS.³: inscription MS.: grave
stone MS.².   474–5 of the Chapel MS.²: in the Building MS.   485 affords
MS.²: presents MS.   491 deeply sequestered MS.²: deep MS.   492 revert
MS.²: dwell MS.   to MS.²: upon MS.

privacy & the pastoral quiet which he had there left behind. All at once
these or any other meditations with which he may have been occupied ,
will be dispersed, for a single step will unfold to him the turbulent, or   495
sparkling & dancing Ocean, spread without limits, or with limits of
adequate grandeur, & displacing every placid sentiment & quiet
inclination by an influx of thoughts, turning upon hardship & enterprize, a homeless life, endless wanderings, & infinite dangers. Seduced
this far from my purpose—if I were guiding an Enthusiast—I would   500
say, Cast your eye upon Sunken Church in passing, & ascend to the
Top of the Mountain Black Coom, from which I can assert upon the
best authority, may be seen a more extensive view than any other
eminence in the Island affords.

Poem   505

   This preeminent command of prospect is owing to the situation of
the Mountain rising to such a height from the point of a promontory
at the Southern extremity of Cumberland. Black Coom, tho rising to
a great elevation, is, in this respect, surpassed by Schafell & several
other mountains in this region, but none of them are at all comparable   510
to it in bulk. I need not say that the view from its summit must be most
interesting, & such a Person as I have ventured to address would be
well repaid by making the circuit of its base, for on the southern side,
tho' comparatively tame on the north & west, it is bold & abrupt.
Under it lies, though not to be seen from the high road, the Castle of   515
Millom, standing upon the edge of Duddon Sands. This building,
though not grand or particularly interesting in itself, combines well
with the mountains and other features of the surrounding Landscape.
Contiguous to this Mansion, which is half decayed, yet one part of it
inhabited by Farmers, stands a Church, with its Churchyard pleasingly   520
darkened by surrounding trees that protect the consecrated ground &
spread over it an affecting stillness, that will be the more felt if any one
should be near to point out to the Visitant, among the few graves, that
part of the enclosure which is appropriate to the remains of those shipwrecked strangers whose bodies are from time to time cast up upon   525
the shore.

494 meditations MS.²: thoughts MS.   503 may be . . . view MS.²:
commands a view [of the *del.*] greater in extent MS.   505/6 *No verses are
given and only about three lines are left blank.*   507–8 the point . . . Cumberland MS.³: the [? projection] MS.: the extreme point of [the *del.*] a promontory of
Cumberland MS.².   508. *After* Cumberland MS. *deletes:* Among [? there is
none] to be compared in bulk with Black   509 is . . . surpassed MS.²: is
surpassed in height MS.   516 Millom *Edd.*: Milham MS.   standing upon
the edge MS.³: with as extensive L MS.: with its extensive Landscape MS.².
519 Mansion MS.²: Building MS.   520 stands MS.²: is MS.   522 will
be . . . if MS.²: is . . . when MS.   523 Visitant MS.²: Stranger MS.
524 enclosure MS.²: churchyard MS.

But this digression is already too long, & I hasten back to Ulpha Kirk, whence we will proceed down the Vale towards Broughton. The same character of blended wildness & cultivation is still preserved. Rocky grounds, which for ever forbid the entrance of the plough, interrupt here & there the cultivation & fill up in part or wholly the bottom or sides of the vale. Here also may be seen beautiful specimens of the manner in which the plough or the spade, following the veins & beds of the richer, drier, & more tractable soil, have fashioned fields & lawns & glades in intricate arrangements, out of the body of the native woods. This beautiful Valley does not die away gradually into a flat plain, but terminates abruptly in a prospect of the sands of Duddon, & of the Irish Sea, seen in conjunction with its river & deeply sheltered woody recesses. On this account, and for the sake of descending upon Seathwaite so advantageously, I have recommended, in opposition to the general rule, that it should be approached from the upper part rather than from its outlet.

From Broughton, return to Conistone by the nearest road. Should the day's work prove too much, comfortable lodging may be had at the neat little Town of Broughton. Assuming, however, that you are not obliged to pass the night at Broughton but can return to Conistone, the morning of the next day may be employed in sailing upon and looking about the higher part of the Lake, and in strolling upon its banks; and the other half, in an excursion up the valley of Yewdale (a branch of the Vale of Conistone) [and] round the sequestered Valley of Tilberthwaite, which may be considered as a remoter apart[ment of the] Valley of Yewdale. This excursion may be about five miles, and may be taken either [on foot or] horseback, but not in a Carriage. It will lead to crags of the boldest form, a dashing [*tear*]t, and happy-looking Cottages, fertile meadows, woody knolls without number, [*tear*]ng Coppices upon the hill sides, and through the whole is a seclusion and a depth of quiet.

530

535

540

545

550

555

CONISTONE LAKE

In a level & open Country the glories of the morning have their seat

528 Kirk MS.²: Church MS.   539–40 *After* descending MS. Prose 20ᵉ *writes*: see old letter stitched to this sheet. MS. Prose 20ᵈ, *to which we are thus directed, may once have been stitched to* this sheet, *but it is now loose (cf. textual n. 461).* 544 comfortable . . . be had MS.²: you may be comfortably lodged MS. 550–6 *The tear which had damaged* 449–53 (*see also textual n.* 453/4) *effects a similar damage to* 550–6. *The editorial interpolations in* 550–3 *are derived from* S.V., 73–6 (S.V. *omits* 553–7).   558 MS. *A* (MS. Prose 21ᵇ) *begins* (*we omit some of the more illegible deletions and insertions*):

Conistone Lake

As the most interesting part of the scenery lying immediately around Conistone [*cf.* 631 *ff.*] is upon the western side this Vale is therefore seen to most advantage

in the sky; among Mountainous recesses they appear rather to be 560
embodied in the earth itself. Who, then, wishing to be familiar with
the phenomena of such regions would not congratulate himself if, by
his early rising, he have gained the priviledge of witnessing the whole
progress & succession of beautiful changes which that time of the day
produces in the appearances of things, appearances the more touching 565
as they are so transitory. Let us then suppose that the shrill crowing
of the Cock, by which our sleep may have been broken, has not been
complained of as an annoyance; that looking forth from our chamber,
we see the promise of day to our wishes, the first steps of whose
progress are already noted upon the summits of the highest western 570
hills by a line of purple or rosy light as definite as the line of shadow
which points out the minute upon the face of a dial. Look again, & tho'
it has lost nothing of its precision, we perceive that it has become
broader, encroaching upon the shade & creeping slowly downwards
into the Valley. We now taste the freshness of the Season in the open 575
air, we stand by the margin of the still waters, our hearts are affected
by its quiet, & the smooth surface gives a pensive pleasure to the
faculty of seeing. But the eye is most strongly attracted towards the
Mountains; while we are conscious of our nearness to the sleeping
waters, it is lifted that way. As the morning advances, they look bright 580
& are refreshed; they are clothed as in a mantle of radiance that is
palpable but conceals nothing—it is transparent; & the clearness of the
atmosphere permits every wrinkle in the rugged surface of those huge
masses to be traced, so that, lasting as they assert themselves to be,
it is written upon their foreheads: we are perishable. But behold the 585

in the morning [when the light of the sun strikes upon it from the east *del.*] Let me
then advise the Stranger if fine weather favour him [to be early in his Boat & unencumbered by a hired Oarsman take his way down the middle of the Lake *del.*]
to rise so early as to give himself an opportunity of witnessing here the whole
succession of the transitory beauties [of morning *del.*] which that time of day
produces at all events he must not miss the first rosy purple beams of light . . .
succession of beautiful changes which that time of day produces in the appearance
of things . . . In a level & open country [*cf.* 559 *ff.*] the glories of morning have
their seat in the sky in a mountainous district they appear to be embodied in the
earth itself . . . he gains the privilege of [seeing *del.*] [noting *del.*] witnessing the
first purple glow of light striking upon the higher distant hills and making that
quarter [*cf.* 634] . . . with which that quarter will be [?] a small beginning—The
first steps in a descending scale of splendour which will reach by [? slow] [?] the
bottom of the valley . . .

560 among MS.[3]: to a Spectator embosomed MS.: to a Spectator shut up MS.[2].
566 so MS.[2]: the more MS.   571 as definite MS.[2]: with the presicion with
which the MS.   573 precision *Edd.*: presicion MS.   574 encroaching
MS.[2]: & has MS.   576 margin MS.[2]: side MS.   577 its MS.[2]: the MS.
578 most strongly attracted towards MS.[2]: chiefly turned to MS.   579 while
MS.[2]: and while MS.   580 advances MS.[2]: is advancing MS.   581 they
are clothed MS.[2]: where the splendour MS.   583 in the *Edd.*: in their MS.
(MS. *inserts* [583–4] of those huge masses *but* their *was left uncorrected.*)

Sun himself, whose splendour they have reflected long before the orb
became visible—spotless does that rising orb appear & unimpaired;
& feeling the contrast, we might almost be allowed for a moment to
resort to the language which the trans-atlantic Poet has given to the
Priest of the idolatrous Gibeonites & exclaim: 590

> Lashed by the flood, the hard rocks wear away;
> Worn by the storm, the lessening hills decay;
> Unchanged alone is thine exalted flame,
> From endless year to endless year the same;
> Thy splendours with immortal beauty shine,   595
> Roll round the eternal Heavens, & speak thy name divine.

But let us hearken to a still nobler voice & turn our minds to the Being
whom it worships.

> Thou Sun, of this great world both eye and soul,
> Acknowledge *Him* thy greater.   600

Then having ascended towards the utmost boundary of human thought,
the devotions of the morning may be sustained till the soul is satisfied,
& having adored the God of Nature as present in his works, let us be
content with the humbler service of admiration.

Familiar & wanting in dignity as are many of the topics that must   605
be treated of in this book, the Author will make no apology for these
serious apostrophes. We are upon the outset of a several days' journey
of pleasure, from which by the majority of those who undertake it
pleasure and amusement alone are desired. But to hurry forward with
the light-minded train from one distinguished spot to another is   610
nothing more than the prolongation of the labour of vanity, invigorated
& refreshed by a change of scene. What does he gain who proves by
the impatience of his motions & the listlessness of his appearance that
he is still whirled about by the eddy of fashion, & that its power is as
strong over him in the quiet Vales of Westmoreland as upon the noisy   615

587 that rising orb MS.³: it MS.: that object MS.².   605–35 Familiar . . .
beautiful] *It was perhaps the intention to delete these lines; a few broad lines of deletion
are irregularly drawn.*   605 & wanting MS.²: & therefore wanting MS.
topics MS.²: Subjects MS.   608 those who undertake it MS.²: Travellers
MS.   609 pleasure *Edd.*: pleasure alone MS. (*After the insertion of* and amusement alone *no deletion was made.*)   609–12 But to hurry . . . scene] MS. *makes
a series of deletions, some of which read*: but it is to little purpose that we wander
among Vales &: but it is to little purpose that we quit the crowded city & withdraw
from the bustle & [? cares] of life if a superficial entertainment of the eye be all that
we seek for & assuredly without a religious sentiment: but he is engaged in nothing
better than a labour of vanity: But it is nothing more than a prolongation of a labour
of vanity invigorated and refreshed by a change of scene [to quit the *del.*] to hurry
forward with the lightminded train of fashion from one distinguished spot to
another.   614 he is . . . fashion MS.²: the eddy of fashion has MS.

pavement of Grosvenor Square? Nay, to him who has come forth from his Counting house to enjoy a few weeks' summer's holiday & to interpose new objects between his mind & its labours & anxieties, to the Invalid who is hoping to recover his health, to the Artist who is eager to store his portfolio with outlines & colors, and to other Wanderers 620 whom the spirit of Youth has impelled to quit—not without an accompanying fear that they are playing the Truant—that office or Closet where he is intent upon the preparatory studies of less attractive professions, to each of these classes I will venture to say that Nature will be far more bountiful in granting what they severally look for if 625 he aspires at something beyond a superficial entertainment of the eye. The Soul of objects must be communicated with, & that intercourse can only be realized by some degree of the divine influence of a religious imagination.

    This prelude to an intended day's work, if seasonable any where, 630 has here from another cause an especial propriety, for the most interesting part of the scenery around Conistone Lake lies upon the western side, & the Vale, therefore, appears to most advantage in the morning when the light of the Sun strikes from the east upon that quarter where the objects are most beautiful. The Stranger then will do well to be 635 early in his boat, & let me advise him—if expert at the Oar—to take his way without the incumbrance of a hired assistant down the middle of the Lake when the Vapours are beginning to ascend & melt in the sunbeams, & before the breezes have risen to brush away the reflections in the water, disturbed by nothing but the motions of his own 640 boat or one of the barges creeping along the shore, which pass daily freighted with Slate from the Quarries of Yewdale or Tilberthwaite. Rowing down the Lake, he will have the advantage of fronting the objects which he would wish to have before him, & when he has gone something less than a mile, he will be inclined to halt in order that a 645 fixed picture may be impressed upon his mind. I will not anticipate any part of his pleasure by attempting to describe in words the materials & composition of this picture. It will be sufficient to observe that the

---

620 *After* colors MS. *deletes*: to each of these classes I will venture to say that Nature will be far more bountiful to [them *del.*] him in granting [them *del.*] the objects of [their several *del.*] his pursuits if religious inspirations [attend *del.*] be not unfrequently drawn from what he beholds and to [the *del.*] other [youthful Wanderer *del.*] Wanderers whom   625 what they . . . look for MS.²: the object of their several pursuits MS.   626 he aspires MS.²: they aspire MS. 628 some degree MS.²: religion MS.   630 This MS.²: After this MS. 635 *After* beautiful MS. *deletes*: Let me then advise the Stranger to be early in his boat & if expert at the oar unencumbered by a hired [Oarsman *del.*] assistant take his way down the middle   638 when MS.²: at a time when MS. 645 less than a mile, he will be *Edd.*: *after* less MS. *deletes*: than a mile he will *but then continues without deletion*: be less than a mile he will be   647 the materials MS.²: any part of MS.

Voyager will find himself resting upon the Watery plain of a Valley
seemingly shut up within its own barriers, as he is not yet removed so 650
far from the base of the rocky steeps by which Conistone is enclosed
to the North as to be brought into view of the summits of those lofty
Mountains Helvellyn & Fairfield, which clad in the aiery colors of
distance were conspicuous objects whilst he journeyed up by the lake
side from the South. Conistone is thus pleasingly distinguished from 655
the rest of the Lakes by seeming in this the most interesting part of it
to owe little of that effect of grandeur in which it is not deficient to the
positive bulk of the objects that surround it, their height or their
distance; and tho' nothing so strikingly impresses a sense of seclusion
as unusual depth, yet that feeling is here agreeably conveyed by gentler 660
means. For none of the boundaries of the Vale, except the mountain
of the Old Man, are of such height or importance as to aspire to a
communication with the neighbouring *Country*; every thing else seems
to belong exclusively to the place from which it is seen, & a heart-
satisfying privacy is unambitiously produced. Here also from the 665
superior advantages of possessing a Lake, the force of contrast is
almost as strikingly produced as in the parallel Vale of Seathwaite,
which I have already recommended to the Traveller's notice. Confine
the view to the knotty, [ferruginous] crags & you might imagine
yourself among the solitudes of Sweden; turn the eye to the smiling 670
Cottages & fertile enclosures & you feel at once you are in that
Country which the old Ballad writers have so well designated by the
name of merry England.

The Voyager whom we are accompanying in his progress down the
Lake, after a course of something less than 2 miles, will be brought to 675
Conistone Hall, an ancient half-ruined seat of the Flemings. Its ancient
architecture, its dignity & importance as a feudal head to the surrounding Cottages of the Yeomanry would have recommended it to his
notice if the building had [remained] undecayed, but nature has beautified the walls & roof with weeds & large masses of ivy, as if to make 680
amends for the injuries of time. Two of its large round Chimneys,
beautiful specimens of the Cylinder rising from a square, are completely covered by this green mantle; 2, being wholly bare, are of a
venerable grey colour, & one is half clad—a marked variety, as if
studied & produced by design. Loch Awe & Loch Leven & other 685

651 the rocky MS.²: those rocky MS.   by which MS.²: which enclose
MS.   652 the summits MS.²: those summits MS.   654 whilst MS.²:
to MS.   up MS.²: up the Vale MS.   660 conveyed by MS.²: produced by
other MS.   661 the boundaries MS.²: the barriers [?] side consist of a low
cultivated ridge on its MS.   669 ferruginous *Edd*.: frigeneous MS.
679 remained *Edd*.: *a word has been omitted from the top of a new page; we take the
suggestion of G. W.*

Scotch lakes are proud of their Castles, Killarney of its ruined Monastery, but our Traveller must condescend to pay particular attention to this humbler Edifice as, with the exception of a few of the village Churches, it is the most interesting piece of architecture these Lakes have to boast of—Grasmere Abbey having no existence but in the 690 pages of Romance, though the wreck of a sheep-fold has been more than once archly pointed out as its last remains by a Peasant in answer to questions eagerly put to him by Votaries whose heads were full of Sir E^d Newenden & the Recluse of the Lakes. And as it is the duty of a conscientious Guide both to tell what is to be found & to save un- 695 necessary trouble in seeking what is not to be found, I will avail myself of this opportunity to prevent further search after the Dwelling of Miss Evelyn & her ancient Uncle, to assure such female Readers as may have given too eager faith to the narratives of the Minerva Press that no such interesting Residence exists. 700

But to return to the realities of Conistone Hall. Its luxuriant hangings of ivy are cropped every winter by the farmer who inhabits the mansion, & distributed to his sheep, the sickly or feeble probably being preferred, as it is a species of food which browzing animals are fond of & is supposed to have a healing virtue. Many will join me in wishing 705 it were generally known that so beautiful a production may thus be made part of the farmer's annual dependence for winter nourishment. Certain penurious managers who were afraid of this insinuating creeper doing injury to their crazy outhouses might then be tempted to strike a balance of profit & loss, & spare the plant where it has 710 already gained footing. And what if they could be induced to cultivate it with the same view? We might then hope to see the paled ivy building its own bower, with the sanction of the President of the Board of Agriculture, against the sides of every unsightly Barn & Cowhouse in the Kingdom. Cottage Maidens sometimes introduce a spray of jasmine 715 from the outside of the casement to the interior of their apartment, & permit it to grow & spread there that they may have its blossoms in sight & be regaled by its odours. The rustic inmates of the beautiful fabric of Conistone Hall must take some pains to exclude the ivy from their chambers, or it would otherwise present itself as a bold intruder 720 &, not content with possession of the window, would advance till it had entwined the bedposts & decorated them like the Thyrsus of Bacchus. The Mansion being too large for the needs of farmers & part

693 put to him MS.²: put to him perhaps more than once MS.   Votaries MS.²: a band of Votaries MS.   694 Newenden *Edd*.: [? Newinden] MS.   699 too *Edd*.: to MS.   700 interesting Residence MS.²: structure MS.   705 healing MS.: restorative MS. *A*.   wishing MS.²: in the wish that MS.   716 apartment MS.²: apartment for the sake of the beauty of the shrub MS.   719–20 ivy from their [apartments *del*.] chambers or it MS.²: ivy as it MS.

of it having been accordingly suffered to fall into decay, the wind has
more free access to the inhabited quarters than the delicacy of modern 725
structures will allow, & on stormy nights the people are said to move
about with their candle under the protection of a lanthorn; when this
precaution is not taken, they are liable to be left suddenly in the dark
as they go along the passages, but I have never heard of [a] visionary
prevailing in this house as in [the] apparently coeval mansion of 730
Calgarth upon the Banks of Windermere. No tragical story is attached
to this abode, no ghost haunts it, they who have died here rest peaceably in their graves, & the living are unalarmed by the voice of the
waves dashing against the shore & by the wind moaning thro' the
remains of those aged sycamores which once bordered the bay & prom- 735
ontory, and in such a manner stretched their boughs over the margin
of the lake that a boat might have moved under their shade as along
a cloister.

Looking southward from our halting-place opposite Conistone Hall,
more than two miles further we have a small Island in distinct view and 740
that shall terminate our Voyage. Long before we reach it, Helvellyn
& Fairfield, rising at a distance above the northern boundaries of the
Vale, have given to it a new character, & on the west the Old Man has
assumed a bolder aspect, & contiguous to him rise the dark & aiery
precipices of Dow Crag—but our attention must now turn to the 745
Island itself. Tho' it has nothing in its form to recommend it, the
Botanist, the painter, & general lover of Nature will be delighted to
observe the marvellous variety of vegetable production—flowers,
plants, & trees which she has collected upon this seemingly forbidding
rock, the growth of the moist place & the dry, of the marsh & of the [?] 750
wilderness, of the hill & of the valley. We will take the eastern side,
keeping close to its shore, & row to the end of it; turning the point,
we find another little rocky island lurking as an appendage to the larger
one & shaping out, in conjunction with a bay at the extremity of the
larger one, a tiny piece of water into which are two small entrances 755
opposite each other—a smooth & intricate harbour, completely land-
locked. These rocks with their vegetable ornaments & the pool they
enclose make a foreground at once curious & beautiful to a noble

725 quarters MS.²: parts MS.   729 go MS.²: move MS.   a *Edd.*:
om. MS.   730 the *Edd.*: *om.* MS.   732 abode MS.²: place MS.   *After*
it MS. *deletes*: here as at Calgarth   732–3 peaceably MS.²: peacefully MS.
736 in such a manner MS.²: so MS.   740 more . . . further] *An insertion which*
possibly follows we have   *After* view MS. *deletes*: at [?] distance [?]   741
Helvellyn *Edd.*: Hellvellyn MS.   742 northern MS.²: southern MS.   749
she MS.²: Nature MS.   751 side MS.²: side of this small Island MS.
752 end MS.²: extremity MS.   turning MS.²: here we find a small MS.
755 tiny MS.²: little MS.   756 a smooth . . . completely MS.²: this
smooth & intricate harbour being completely [?] these openings [?] MS.

landscape; from the boat we look across the little harbour & across the
lake on the shore of which stands Oxness, a farm house embosomed in 760
dark trees, & a little to the right on the slope above hang two others, one
named Sunny bank, the whole grouping together into a small Hamlet
with [? slips] of winding road & a foaming stream dashing thro' it;
aloft are the bold outlines of the Old Man & the stern face of Dow
Crag & Walney Scar. But the foreground is peculiar & would be 765
remarkable for its beauty at all times and seasons; but if a breeze be
rippling the open part of the lake across which the eye is directed &
white waves passing by in succession like a fleet of Swans, it would be
truly charming in the month of September to see this sheltered pool
reflecting the rocks & trees which protect it, & glowing with colors 770
suffused from the purple heath, the russet or green mosses, & the
lemon-tinted leaves of the young ash when it has been nipped by the
first frosts of Autumn.

I promised to give my Voyager leave to return when he reached this
point, but it may be worth his while to row a little further & to round 775
the promontory upon the main shore, near the extremity of which these
2 small Islands lie. The view is far less interesting, but the abrupt
rocky shore advances as a foreground for a picture composed chiefly
of the same materials. Leaving my Companion to remeasure his course
to Water-head Inn, I shall be happy to rejoin him in the afternoon and 780
to recommend a *Walk* which I hope will prove as agreeable as his
morning's excursion upon the Water.

The principal feeders of Conistone Lake are two small brooks,
named Church beck & Yewdale beck, which, running parallel to each
other thro' the slope of cultivated ground interposed between the 785
Village of Church Conistone & the Lake, fall into it on the Western
side, something more than 1/2 a mile from its head. Let the Stranger
follow the high road from the Inn towards the Church of Conistone,
& either of these streams, as soon as he is brought to its banks, will
serve as a guide to an agreeable Walk. Of the more distant one, 790
Church beck, I shall barely say . . .

But we will now take the other stream as our guide & pursue our
way up Yewdale. On the left are huge crags, bold and abrupt; on the

759 look across MS.²: look over MS.   763 slips] *G. W. reads:* strips
stream *Edd.*: streaming MS.   771 *After* heath MS. *deletes:* & the
golden or lemon [? leaves] tinted   774 leave MS.²: liberty MS.
783 The principal . . . brooks MS.: The principal feeder of a Lake is almost in
all instances found at [its *del.*] the head & the stream [falls *del.*] steals [? impercep-
tibly] into the Lake [?] barely lifted above [the level of the Lake *del.*] its [?] surface.
At Conistone are two small brooks its MS. *A.*   787 *After* head MS. *deletes:*
each of these streams will serve as a guide to an agreeable walk.   789–90
will serve MS.²: may be taken MS.   791/2 *Two-thirds of the page is left blank.*
792 take MS.²: turn up MS

right the boundary is tame, a low woody ridge with no variety of outline; the bottom of the Vale is a flat oblong area which the industry of 795
Man might render beautiful. In few situations has nature [held] out
stronger inducements for the occupant to exert himself, & one is at
a loss to consider by what succession of untoward accidents a large
space of ground so sheltered, level, & well watered can have continued
to this day in a worse than aboriginal state. Many acres of excellent 800
soil are disfigured by swampy ground & overrun with plants of the
moor & the marsh, beautiful in themselves but disagreeable upon
ground which, if properly drained, as it might be at no great expence,
would become green meadow & fertile cornfield. When we have
advanced something less than a mile, we see in the face of a Farm that 805
extends over the plain of the Valley how happily this improvement has
been wrought & with what advantage to the passing Traveller. The
crags look more stern & awful hanging over fields green, neat, &
[? unencumbered], & the fields appear more bright & fertile than other
fields from a like effect of contrast. This backwardness in drawing by 810
improvement from the Lands of the Valley the wealth which they are
capable of bestowing is in part owing to a scantiness of capital, partly
to a constitutional indisposition towards novel enterprize—a common
failure among people who live in solitude—& not a little to a preference which man naturally feels for a pastoral life. The Sheep which 815
range upon the Mountains interest the affections more than a lifeless
crop; the profit they bring is not put off to a distant time, & falls in
according to the wants of the house by commodious detail. The labours
of the Shepherd also have the attractions of an amusement which in
a mountainous country is not languid & effeminate, but full of hardship, 820
effort, & danger, & diversified by the fluctuations of hope & fear. The
crags of Yewdale are apparently inaccessible, so steep, rough, & stony,
& the sheep-dogs after the service of a year or two must be changed, as
their feet are so worn by the surface which they have to scale that they
flinch from the pain & the labour. Yet at certain seasons of the year 825
these apparently impracticable precipices are daily ascended by the
Shepherds, whom a long sloping path, in some places visible, conducts

    796 held *Edd.*: *om.* MS.   801 swampy ground MS. *A, Edd.*: [?
swampy *or* swamps] MS.   803 as MS.²: which MS.   805 something
MS.²: up the Vale MS.   808 hanging over MS.²: from being contrasted
with MS.   812 owing] MS. Prose 21 *ends*; MS. Prose 22 *begins*: to a [want
del.] scantiness   812–13 partly to a MS.²: partly to the MS.   813–14 indisposition . . . solitude [who live in solitude *is perhaps del.*] MS.²: want of
[of *undel.*] enterprize to which people who live in solitude are peculiarly subject MS.
819 the Shepherd MS.²: this provider MS.   which MS.²: & not of the MS.
821 effort MS.²: peril MS.   diversified MS.²: enlivened MS.   824 the surface MS.²: the steepness & roughness of the surface MS.   827 conducts
MS.²: conducts him MS.

to the summit. Look upwards & imagine that you see what I happen
to know might a short while since have frequently been seen from this
bottom—the figure of a Shepherd climbing up this path and bearing   830
his son upon his shoulders. You will conjecture from the appearance
that the boy is yet too young to sustain the toil of an ascent so long &
steep, but there is not a sheep in this heath-bred & heath-going flock
the countenance of which is not perfectly known to him; & as soon as
the pair have reached the top of the eminence, he will slip from the back   835
of his panting father, & will either trip by his side over the plain or
commence his almost independent operations with vigor & a fearless
confidence. It must be allowed that the best culture is that which does
most good to the human heart, & seeing in these pastoral employments upon the rugged hills so pleasing & salutary an exercise of the   840
domestic affections, let us be permitted even by the agriculturalist, the
Statesman, & the Œconomist—to set one thing against another—
to look with indulgence upon the neglect from which the fields below
have suffered.

At the termination of this steep line of Rock is an opening through   845
which we mount towards Tilberthwaite, with a stream on our right
descending from that Valley to join the brook of Yewdale. The pass is
narrow & barren, & the aspect of Holmfell on the opposite side of the
river is bold, tho' less so than that part of it called Raven Crag which
fronted us as we came up the plain of Yewdale. The transitions of   850
Nature are always happily contrived; variety is never purchased at the
price of harsh contrast; a single step of ascent in this instance carries
us out of the limits of barrenness & shews a small circular area of
fertile fields, with woody hills rising from its level & around it. But
the sterile crags are not left behind; they have only receded further   855
from each other to admit this kindly receptacle for a few habitations
of men. The boundary which fronts us is low, & the high mountains
of Grasmere tower above it, softened by the colors of distance.

830 bottom MS.²: [? pla] MS.   and bearing MS.²: with MS.   832 toil
MS.²: labor MS.   833 this . . . flock MS.²: his father's flock MS.   834–5
as soon as the pair MS.²: when they MS.   835–6 the back of MS.²: his father's back
MS.   836 *After* will MS. *deletes*: commence his operations upon the plain with
vigor   838 It must be allowed MS.²: We must allow MS.   839–40 these
pastoral employments MS.²: this case [case *undel*.] MS.   843 neglect MS.²:
comp neglect MS.   845 At MS.²: From MS.   Rock MS.²: crag which forms
the western boundary of Yewdale we ascend with the road [? having the] MS.
847 descending MS.³: which has descended MS.: which is descending MS.².
848 *After* Holmfell MS. *deletes*: generally   849 is bold MS.²: [? unusually]
bold MS.   850 fronted us MS.²: fronts Yewdale & is MS.   came up MS.²:
ascended MS.   851 *After* contrived MS. *deletes*: [? either *or* whether] by
gentle gradations   852 a MS.²: here a MS.   in this instance] *possibly
inserted after* step   853 area of MS.³: plain with MS.: plain of fert MS.².
856 kindly MS.²: quiet MS.   857 boundary MS.²: narrow boundary of this
sequestered spot MS.

I am conducting the Traveller hither early in the afternoon; it may, therefore, happen that in the broad light of day this Vale may derive 860 [no] peculiar interest from the appearance of these distant Mountains, but it lies within the power of words to exercise an imperfect command over times & seasons, and the several charms of morning, noontide, evening, & moonlight may in some degree be reflected in language. Fortunate then should I be if through long familiarity with these scenes 865 I am enabled upon occasions to assist my Companion in representing to himself aspects of things more favourable than may chance to be before his eyes. Upon his entrance into this little valley, I would willingly afford him the help of my own memory so that he might hear, as I have done, its brook murmuring in deeper stillness and see its 870 circle of woods and dewy fields with the first dimness of Evening settled upon them. An upright column of blue smoke is mounting in air above the roof of the most distant cottage; a little beyond, the clear sky seems incorporated with the shadowy foliage of a few trees rising from the edge of a dusky rock. And what a [? pensive] radiance is afar 875 off upon the distance, what a solemnity & majesty of the departed sun glowing upon the crags and on the turf of those lofty mountains, a [? twilight illumination], an abated splendour! We recognize it as a bequest of the [departed] sun which ripens [the] harvest of the earth and guides its restless Inhabitant thro' the round of his daily occupa- 880 tions. Yet in the bedarkened recess from which this remote glory is distinctly beheld, the Spectator is touched by the sight—as it were a descent of something heavenly upon earth, vouchsafed to aid his imagination in determining the texture of the everlasting regions & what kind of substance it is which the feet of angels tread upon, more 885

---

860 *After* that MS. *deletes*: there may be nothing peculiarly favourable in 861 no peculiar *Edd.*: *as a result of the deletion in* 860 *the* MS. *reads*: derive peculiarly interest *After* Mountains MS. *deletes*: but [it is my wish *del.*] wishing occasionally [to suggest by *del.*] to exercise by words imperfect command over times and seasons that my Companion should see by the light of 863 *After* seasons MS. *deletes*: & sharing with my Companion as far as I can the stores of long experience I would wish to enable him to see by the light of his own conceptions the most favourable 865 Fortunate MS.²: Happy MS. scenes MS.²: scenes & MS. 866 occasions MS.²: some occasions MS. Companion MS.²: Reader MS. 867 aspects MS.²: the most favourable aspects MS. 869 afford him the help MS.²: lend him the light MS. 870 deeper stillness MS.²: the stillness of evening MS. 871 Evening MS.²: twilight MS. 872 settled] *possibly* settling 875 radiance MS.²: glory MS. 876 *After* distance MS. *deletes*: the light of departed] *possibly* departing 879 departed *Edd.*: departure MS. the harvest *Edd.*: our harvest MS.: harvest MS.². 880 its restless Inhabitant MS.²: the restless creature Man MS. 881 in MS.²: from MS. remote MS.²: distant MS. 882 Spectator is touched MS.²: imagination is affected MS. 883 vouchsafed to aid his] *Perhaps as a substitution,* MS. *lightly inserts above*: not wholly overpowering the 884 determining MS.²: conceiving MS. regions MS.²: heavens MS.

affecting to the mind of sublunary & mortal Man than what has been conceived by a divine [? genius]:

> That broad & ample way whose dust is gold
> And pavement stars.

Here I confess that I stand in need of the indulgence of my Reader, 890 as I feel some difficulty in bringing myself back to the appearances of an ordinary day. Tho' this sequestered spot is at all times beautiful, it is, however, disfigured by slate quarries which were softened or hidden by the dusky medium thro' which we have been looking at it; & as we cannot escape the sight of the rubbish thrown up out of them, we will 895 recompense ourselves by peeping into one, the mouth of which as we enter the Valley of Tilberthwaite is upon our left hand. A dark underground passage conducts to a huge excavation where he who has made his way through the blind level is glad to have sight again of the clouds & sky above his head. The walls of this quarry are on side smooth & 900 upright as a hay stack shorn by the Knife. The height of this mass of Rock is now awful & will soon be immense—not less than 50 yards; & as the Spectator looks up towards the fringe of birch wood upon the top of it, agitated by every breeze, he cannot fail to admire the careless bounty with which Nature scatters her ornaments & will be smitten 905 with the contrast here exhibited by the light & solid, the sensitive & impassive works of her hand.

To Tilberthwaite & the adjoining Vales of Langdale many a Town & Village all over England are indebted for the blue roofs that adorn them, this district being either richer in slate, or situated more con- 910 veniently for the removal of it, than any other part of the Country. The Quarry we have just now entered has the advantage of being quite easy of access, but there are others of more curious & striking appearance— particularly one high up the hills about a mile from this place & named Blessy Crag. As it would extend our walk too much to visit this spot, 915 I will [? attempt] to convey an idea of it by description. The quarrymen

887 a divine genius MS.²: the poet of MS.   888 *Before* That MS. *inserts:* [? 7ᵗʰ Bᵏ]   890 Here I confess that MS.²: I confess that [? scenes] here MS. 891 as MS.²: & MS.   892 *After* day MS. *deletes:* The quality that from many points of view disfigures this sequestered spot   895 thrown MS.³: which they MS.: which has been MS.².   896 *After* ourselves MS. *deletes:* as well as we can   898 *After* where MS. *deletes:* we are glad to have 899 have] *wrongly del.*   900 his MS.²: our MS.   on side] *G. W. thinks that the intention was:* on one side. *The* o *of* on *is smeared and the intention may have been to correct to:* in side   901 upright MS.²: perpendicular MS.   902 awful MS.²: great MS.   905 smitten MS.²: struck MS.   909 England MS.: the Island MS. *A.*   910 slate, or MS.²: the materials or better MS.   912 has the . . . being MS.²: is MS.   916–20 The quarrymen . . . top MS.²: There

working downwards have scooped out a vast cave of which the sides
are not smooth & perpendicular, but rugged with large ledges &
masses, & bend over, leaving a comparatively small opening to the sky
at the top. This apartment has been wrought into a depth of little less 920
than fifty yards by means of two levels with which the side of the Fell
has been successively pierced at different heights. As you look from
the bottom of the quarry, the mouth of the higher level makes a gloomy
spot half way up the blue side of the huge rotunda, within which a few
industrious Men carry on their work from morning to evening in a 925
cool air & by a sober light; but the most powerful impression would
be received if for a first sight of this labour of several generations you
should be conducted to the brink of the opening at the top; if you can
bear to look down from that station, the depth will appear much
magnified to the sense and more so to the imagination, and the gloom 930
cast over the persons of the workmen & every other object distinguishable at the bottom seems—not less than the distance—to soften
and to affect the tinkling noise made by the implements of labour &
every other sound that ascends from the abyss.

The way of life and occupations of a Quarry-man apparently partake 935
more of melancholy than even those of the Miner; so many instances
occur of men being crushed to death by masses of stone and earth falling in upon them, & of life, eye-sight, & limbs being lost from want
of due caution in the process of blasting the rocks by Gunpowder that
the danger may be deemed greater & the drudgery is certainly heavier; 940
for the Miner seldom continues at work more than six hours at a time
but the Quarry man allows himself no more indulgence in this respect

the Quarrymen have given to their work the shape of a vast cave scooped out of the
bottom of the mountain. The sides are not perpendicular [?] smooth as in the one
before spoken of but [? left rugged] with large ledges & masses bend over leaving
a comparatively small [? arch] opening to the sky at the top MS. *A*: Here Quarrymen have given to their work the shape of a vast cave[scooped out of the body of
the mountain *del.*] [here *del.*] The sides are not smooth & perpendicular but [left
del.] rugged with large . . . opening to the top MS. *The corrected version is difficult
to decipher and our reading is uncertain.*

920–6 This apartment . . . light] If the [?] peeps into the abyss it can only be
for a moment labour is here carried on from morning to evening in a cool & calm
air and by a sober light. This vast [?] which calls to mind the grandeur of the
most celebrated natural caverns [? and] [which for *del.*] little less than 50 yards deep
has been wrought into a depth of little less than 50 yards [by *del.*] which to a level
of which the side of the fell has been [? scooped] MS. *A*.   920 apartment
MS.²: vast apartment which calls to mind the grandeur of the most celebrated
natural caverns MS.   922 *After* heights MS. *deletes*: so that a large space
of the outside of the Fell is covered by the rubbish cast up [out of *del.*] from
them &   look MS.²: look up MS.   924 within which] MS. *lightly inserts*
above: where   927 received MS.²: received by him who MS.   930 more
MS.²: much more MS.   931–2 persons . . . distinguishable MS.²: objects
plainly distinguishable MS.   935 way MS.²: course MS.   940 greater . . .
certainly heavier MS.²: equal . . . greater MS.

than the Day-labourer in husbandry. Both employments afford considerable room for the exercise of ingenuity in procuring, with the smallest waste of time & labour, the several objects of their quest, but   945
in the quarry prevails but a small portion of those fluctuations of hope & fear which enliven the recesses of the mine. And it does not seem so unpleasant a necessity to quit for a few hours the light of day altogether as to be obliged to work in the Quarries, excavating the earth amid damp & gloom from morning to evening. Yet this may not be   950
a true estimate, for I remember once to have heard a miner say of himself & his companions that they were a quiet kind of people, considering so much of their time was passed underground. He felt that their condition was unnatural &, therefore, not favourable to humane or social conduct, and that darkness & dim tapers, and [?dusky] faces,   955
and labour never cheered by the sun had a tendency to breed savage tempers and dispositions somewhat infernal.

The Quarry at the mouth of Tilberthwaite will afford the Stranger an easy opportunity of observing the ingenious process of splitting the slate-stone into thin & light plates, an art which—as appears from the   960

943–57 Both employments . . . infernal MS.: In the [process of *del.*] course to be pursued for procuring with the least waste of labour the metal, such is the name given to these Strata of Rock [from *del.*] which are fit for the purpose of being split into slate—there is [no doubt *del.*] much room for [ingenuity *del.*] judgement and contrivance [The humblest labourer *del.*] even The most [?] & inexperienced must feel pleasure in exercising his mind and pride in giving his opinion. In this respect [he is upon a par with the Miner *del.*] [The ⟨?⟩ employments are ⟨?⟩ *del.*] but in the Quarry prevails but a small portion of those [fluctuations of *del.*] hope and fears which [spread so much of life *del.*] [enliven *del.*] animate the gloomy recesses of the Mine, and which the meanest drudge [?] [the common *del.*] labourer of [whose menial labour is ⟨?⟩ by their benefactions *del.*] cannot but [?] even when he knows that he must have little benefit from that gain. I remember once to have heard a Miner say of himself and his Companions that they were a quiet kind of people considering so much of their time had passed underground. [The knowledge of *del.*] Feeling [that labour underwent by the light of *del.*] that their condition was unnatural or not subject to the alternation of night & day of light and darkness, and not less that they who carried on their work were [shut out of *del.*] in the midst of the [?] saw little of its humanizing influence and the scene of their labours [?] is in the bowels of the earth might naturally be expected to be of a savage temper and disposition somewhat infernal. MS. *A.*   943–4 considerable MS.²: much MS.   945 smallest MS.²: least MS.   947 recesses MS.²: [?gloomy] recesses MS.   does not MS.²: seems better MS.   949 as to MS.²: than to MS.   953 that MS.²: that in this respect MS.   955 *After* conduct, and MS. *deletes*: might be   tapers MS.²: light MS.   dusky MS.²: sooty MS.   955–6 *After* faces *and again after* sun MS. *deletes*: might be expected   957 *After* infernal MS. *deletes*: I have been led into this comparison by the [objects *del.*] quarries of Tilberthwaite & the frequent traces of [?mining excavations] which [meet *del.*] the Wanderer meets with upon these hill sides every where are to be found the mouths of passages into [mines *del.*] the bowels of the earth some of which are of ancient date and have evidently been made before the application of gunpowder the blasting   960 slate-stone MS.²: slate [?block] MS.   plates, an art which MS.²: plates which has not been long known in the Country much above 1/2 a century MS.

thick & heavy covering of all the Buildings but those of modern date—
has not been long known in the country. Things are not to be valued
merely in reference to picturesque beauty, especially in this mountainous & romantic [? region], else one might be permitted to regret that
this delicate art should ever have been invented; for by means of it,   965
trim & [? spruce] roof[? s] upon the surface of which no seed can find a
[? rest or haven] will in time be substituted for those moss-grown and
fern-clad coverings which, as we have already noticed, harmoniously
unite the Cottages & outhouses with the rocks & trees among which
they are placed, & represent Nature to the fancy as having an interest   970
in adorning the Habitations of her Children. Across the front of this
Quarry flows the main stream of the Valley of Tilberthwaite, descending from a gill on the left which at a short distance appears to be
terminated abruptly by a blue precipice. But this gill has, in fact, a
much longer course. The bed of its brook is rugged, so rugged that it   975
cannot be traced, but opposite the mouth of the Quarry is to be seen
a mountain road leading to the Copper Mine above, & having ascended
by this road, the curious Stranger will be brought to the brink of a
steep, from which he will have an opportunity of looking down & he
will not look down without emotion into the cleft thro' which this   980
brook flows. Among sensations of sublimity there is one class produced
by images of duration, [or] impassiveness, by the sight of rocks of everlasting granite, or basaltic columns, a barrier upon which the furious
winds or the devouring sea are without injury resisted. In the chasm
above which we are now standing, Nature has employed contrary   985
means to seize upon the imagination: the predominating impression
being of decay & change, & danger & irregular power, & havoc &
insecurity. Permanence is indeed seated here but it is upon a shattered

961 thick MS.²: rough & thick MS.   all the MS.²: most of the MS.
963 picturesque MS.²: picturesque & romantic MS.   965 should MS.²:
had MS.   965-7 for by means . . . substituted MS.³: for in time [?]
smooth & delicate coverings will MS.: for in time it will displace all those
moss grown roofs rugged roofs MS.².   967 rest or haven] *G. W. reads*:
restingplace   968 coverings MS.²: coverings of cottages & houses MS.
969 unite MS.²: blend MS.   975 bed MS.²: channel MS.   brook
MS.²: river MS.   977 having ascended MS.²: by taking this road MS.
979 *After* down MS. *deletes*: with [? con]   981 Among . . . there is
MS.²: Sensations of sublimity are MS.   982 or *Edd.*: MS. *inserts* impassiveness *above* duration *and makes no deletion.*   984 are without
injury resisted MS.²: appear to make no impression MS.   985 above which
we MS.²: now before us MS.   contrary MS.²: other MS.   986 *After*
imagination MS. *deletes*: among [?]   988 *After* insecurity MS. *deletes*: It is
an awful [state *del.*] thing [to look down from a high Mountain *del.*] having ascending [*sic*] a huge hill in a clear light to come to an eminence from which [you *del.*]
we suddenly look down upon [a *del.*] the solid clouds fermenting & rolling, opening
& closing beneath our eyes, with gleams of the [earth *del.*] green fields & waters
[of earth *del.*] hastily afforded & instantaneously withdrawn, so that to the sight
not at all & scarcely to the consciousness does the world in which we live & breathe

and unquiet Throne. The Brook will continue to flow as it has done for ages, bewildered in the time of its feeble condition among the ruins   990
which it has caused in the season of its strength, & overwhelmed by the rock & earth which have fallen into its channel when the mouldering sides of the chasm have been no longer able to support the weight. The skeletons & bones, as one might almost say, of trees which have been buried in rubbish are brought to light again by the power of the   995
Waters that have bleached them. In other places trees are lying which have been recently felled by the axe & are dismantled of their boughs, but the trunk is left because it would not repay the labour necessary for its removal. Rocks, Stones, Trees, & Boughs, & Earth, living Plants & dead, lie prostrate & heaped upon each other in the wildest   1000
disorder, recalling to mind the state of a field of battle after a murderous conflict; & the fleeces of sheep & the bones of these & other animals that have perished in the gulph are scattered here & there; & tho' in themselves minute objects, they do not fail to heighten the desolation of the scene.   1005

I began by describing the general character of this hidden spot as it appears when looked down into from the edge of one of its lofty banks, but I have insensibly slipped into notice of those minute features which cannot be seen distinctly & with full effect unless the Traveller make his way to the head of the gill, & there descending into it, track the   1010
brook downward as far as he is able to proceed; but I will not omit one image which will be met with upon the edge of the steep bank. I allude to a Yew tree, the root of which clasps a mass of rock & earth of the weight of many Tons, & with small help from another tree of the same kind growing below supports it in air. Probably some root   1015
of this higher tree, acting like a wedge, may have contributed to separate at first the suspended mass from the main precipice, but at present it is scarcely possible to look at this sight without attributing

[see *del.*] continue to be the world to which we have been accustomed & to which we belong. But a gust of wind will some times almost instantaneously disperse the whole of this [celestial *del.*] unearthly machinery, or it will dissolve insensibly, and the Spctor is left standing [melancholy *del.*] in dejection upon the [rock *del.*] eminence & wondering at himself like one betrayed. He almost regrets the elevation of [? thought] to which he has been lifted because the Power that raised him ceases to maintain him there. But [among such *del.*] appearances of action such as [these we are treating of *del.*] are found in the course of this torrent though they do not at first sight possess & [overwhelm *del.*] overpower the mind like the fleeting spectacle which we have brought into comparison with them, are capable nevertheless of raising it to a high pitch of feeling & enjoyment, [which makes *del.*] an emotion that makes amends by being more durable than the other for what is wanting in intensity.

992 rock MS.²: weight of rock MS.   have *Edd.*: has MS.   997 their boughs MS.: the branches MS. *A.*   999–1000 Rocks . . . lie MS.²: These materials are lying MS.   1003 gulph MS.: chasm MS. *A.*   1011 will MS.²: can MS.   1014 many MS.²: several MS.   1018 this sight MS ²: the [? means] in which it clasps & supports it MS.

a feeling & a will to the fibres which embrace the hanging rock & prevent it from falling. It is remarkable that some person passing with an axe has attempted to cut through the Root by which the detached rock hangs, but he has desisted without making much progress in his work, either from weariness or apprehension of danger to himself. Continuing your way a little higher up along the edge of the steep, you see a slender Birch tree which somewhat fantastically stands with its two main Roots astride a little cleft or crevice, and seems to support a piece of rock in the same manner, as if aping with its delicate & feminine powers the ability of the eugh, its strong & hardy neighbour. A little higher up, the gill is divided into 2 branches, one of which is terminated by a respectable water-fall. It is an awful & . . .

Having tracked the brook to the water-fall, the interest belonging to it ceases, but we see before us a range of mountains fronted with black steeps & precipices, the summits of which would form noble stations for beholding scenes of clouds & vapours, such as we have been contemplating. One of these is called Hen crag, impassable for the foot of man, & along the ledges of its precipices the fox finds protection, but not security. Another is named Swallow crag; & it is remarkable that the swallows gathering together before their migration are often seen hovering in large flocks round this steep & airy height, tho' there is no apparent reason why, in preference to any neighbouring eminence, it should be frequented by these birds at such time. But it is probable that the Crag has derived its name from the circumstance. A still higher point of the fell is named Weather lam. The most obvious derivation would be from lamb & wether, belonging to sheep, but the last syllable is doubtless a corruption, &, like the Wetter horn of the Alps, the name is probably taken from the storms to which this highest point is exposed.

Scattered all over the ground which we now tread are to be found the entrances of mines long since abandoned; some of these passages are like natural crevices of rock, which might lead a wild beast to a place of security, & so strait that there is scarcely room for the person of a man to enter, except sideways. Their appearance shews that they have been made with wearisome & almost hopeless labour, before the

1020

1025

1030

1035

1040

1045

1050

1029 *After* divided MS. *deletes*: & one   1030 awful &] *Approximately one and a half lines are left blank*.   1032 before us MS.²: in front MS.   a range MS.³: several MS.: abrupt line MS.².   1034 for beholding MS.²: from which to look down upon MS.   1037 Another MS.²: The other MS. 1039 height MS.²: crag [& it *del*.] which probably has derived its name from this circumstance   1043 *After* Weather lam MS. *deletes*: This name [would *del*.] might lead one to suppose   1044 lamb MS.²: sheep MS.   1045 syllable MS.²: syllable of the name MS.   doubtless MS.²: probably MS.   1048 tread MS.²: are MS.   1049 *After* abandoned MS. *deletes*: having   1050 are like MS.²: are dark & narrow MS.   1051 strait MS.²: narrow MS.

application of gunpowder had facilitated these operations. A tradition prevails here that the miners of those ages, before they quitted their work at night, used to pile faggots of wood, which they had felled from the adjoining masses & heights then covered with forest trees, & that they left the fire burning in order that the heat might split the rocks & soften them for the hammer, drawing in a humble way from this rude process that kind of assistance which Hannibal was reported to have derived from the powers of vinegar in his passage over the Alps. If this was really the practice of the miners, it will account for the disappearance, on the higher regions of the mountains, of tracts of wood which by their situation would otherwise, perhaps, have been preserved to this day from destruction. (Note)—

Returning by the same way, we descend pleasingly upon the Valley of Tilberthwaite. It may be worth while to ask at the first cottage the way across the Valley to Holmground; & from a rocky hill, overgrown with copsewood, immediately behind that farm house, there is another good view of the green area of this Valley, to which the busy quarries, though they disfigure the scene to the eye, & the occasional report of the rocks blasted by gunpowder scarcely seem a disturbance. Descend again towards Yewdale, having the brook on the right, & turning with the road to the left, advance along the head of Yewdale under Raven crag; enquire at the Cottages, near which you will observe a tall & picturesque Yew tree, for the road which leads up by Tarn how gill to Conistone. At the top of the hill, you will come suddenly upon a view of the whole length of Coniston Water from a most favourable point of elevation. This is a singular & beautiful burst of prospect, & I much wish that my companion could have been brought to it without directions or previous knowledge of what he was about to see. But I must here observe, once for all, that these anticipations, undesirable as they are, must be submitted to, & I am confident that a Traveller who has a true relish for the beauties of landscape would much rather be introduced to a scene of this kind under such unavoidable disadvantages than miss it altogether, which otherwise he almost certainly would have

1055

1060

1065

1070

1075

1080

1085

1054 facilitated *Edd.*: felicitated MS.   1057–8 that they left MS.[2]: to leave MS.
1058 split MS.[2]: last & soften & MS.   1061 powers MS.[2]: softening powers MS.
1063 on MS.[2]: from MS.   1063–4 which . . . preserved MS.[3]: growing in situations which would otherwise have MS.: which by their being difficult of access would have perhaps saved them MS.[2].   1065 (Note)—] *No note was attached.*
1067 *After* Tilberthwaite MS. *deletes*: seen   1068–9 rocky hill . . . behind MS.[2]: woody hill above MS.   1070 area MS.[2]: fields MS.   *After* Valley MS. *deletes*: a [? pocket]   1078–9 from a . . . elevation MS.[2]: seen from an elevation sufficiently high to command a view of the objects MS.
1079 *After* prospect MS. *deletes*: and some time will elapse before a person who has come upon it unawares   1080–1 without directions MS.[2]: by accident MS.
1083 I am MS.[2]: it is [? surely] MS.   a Traveller MS.[2]: the Traveller MS.
1086 otherwise MS.[2]: without [? word *or* warn] MS.

done; for I myself had rambled thro' the Country from time to time for more than thirty years before accident conducted me to this spot. At the foot of the rugged slope, but with a green meadow between, stands by the margin of the Lake the Inn from which we began a walk that has led us through a variety of rough, austere, solitary, &, in some places, savage spots. This smooth plain of waters, therefore, & the soft sunny fields, & woodlands besprinkled with cheerful Dwellings, & low hills melting away in the hues of distance will be a sight peculiarly acceptable for a contrast, and at the conclusion of a long day, spent in the various labours of what may have produced a grateful weariness of body, will dispose & incline the mind to gentleness & quiet; and in such mood, after having satisfied himself with this prospect—not less remarkable for its singleness & simplicity as a whole than for the sweetness & variety of its detail—the Stranger, with congratulatory feelings and a quickened step, will advance to the Cottage Inn standing before him upon the edge of the lake, a resting place which we may already suppose to have acquired in his estimation something of the attractions of a home.

HAWKSHEAD & THE FERRY

Want of time, impatience to be forward, & other causes will hurry the great Body of Tourists past this first halting-place which I have recommended. But I hope the account of these excursions from the beaten track will not be found uninteresting in the perusal, even by such as do not visit the spots described. We now fall in with the ordinary road & proceed to Windermere by way of Hawkshead.

Before we leave the plain of the Vale of Conistone, we pass a house, the appearance of which shews that it has formerly been the Residence of a substantial yeoman or Estatesman. The Building is irregular & being somewhat neglected & decayed is the more picturesque on that account. Tall fir trees rise up around it with stems naked as masts, &

1090

1095

1100

1105

1110

1115

1087 for I myself MS.²: myself having MS.   1089 At the foot MS.²: Immediately below at the foot of MS.   of] *wrongly del.*   1090 margin MS.²: side MS. 1090–1 a walk that MS.²: our walk & to which MS.   1091 a variety of MS.²: many MS.   solitary MS.²: unpeopled MS.   1093 cheerful Dwellings MS.²: Cottages MS.   1094 *After* distance MS. *deletes*: and that one Cottage [upon *del.*] to which we are approaching   1095 day MS.²: days labour MS. 1098 this prospect MS.²: a minute observation MS.   1101 Inn MS.²: Inn which he sees MS.   1102 *After* lake MS. *deletes*: and which   resting place MS.²: a harbour MS.   1104 attractions MS.²: [? quality] MS.   1106–7 will . . . Tourists MS.²: will have hurried most Travellers MS.   1108 recommended MS.²: recommended to them MS.   1109 *After* perusal MS. *deletes*: while to such as proceed more leisurely MS.   1112 Before we leave MS.²: Ascending the hill from Conistone Lake MS.   Vale MS.²: Valley MS.   a house MS.⁴: some MS.: an old substantial MS.²: a Farm MS.³. *Faintly inserted in pencil is*: a not noble

the umbrella-like shade of their tops spreads a gloom & majesty over
the humble fabric & the old fashioned garden. It is curious to observe
here (& elsewhere) what pains has been taken to clip the yew trees into
grotesque forms. One of these before us has been fashioned into a rude   1120
likeness of a Man presenting a fowling-piece, as if to alarm the Traveller passing along the road. We should not be justified in concluding
that the beautiful or stately growth of the forest in their natural shape
had no attractions for the eyes of our ancestors who were so studious
to disfigure, by the shears, those trees which, being planted by the side   1125
of their own doors, came the most frequently under their notice. This
waywardness is in truth a step in the progress of refinement by a tie
less gross than that of necessity: Man is thus connected with living
Nature.

Yet in a Country so beautifully framed & prodigally adorned one   1130
cannot but be surprized at these instances of a busy propensity; & the
perverseness with which the dwellings often turn their backs upon the
finest Landscapes, even when there is not an excuse of catching a little
sunshine, seems to shew that—though utter insensibility or absolute
indifference to the general forms of Nature does not exist in any state   1135
of society, however rude—a relish for fine combinations of Landscape
is assuredly an acquired taste. Of this cool contempt for the proffered
bounty of Nature we have a striking instance as we ascend the hill.
A little above the Cottage just passed, stands a gentleman's House,
preferring a view across the road & a blank hill side, with a patch [of]   1140
northern sky, to a noble prospect of the Lake stretching southward

1118 humble MS.²: ancient MS.   1119 *After* trees MS. *deletes*: of this
1120 grotesque MS.²: fantastic MS.   *After* fashioned MS. *deletes*: a [? rude]
[?] seat   1122 concluding MS.²: inferring MS.   1123 *After* that MS.
deletes: a tree   1124 who were so MS.³: who took from MS.: who took so
much pains MS.².   1126 *After* notice MS. *deletes*: Yet this [innocent perverseness *del.*] busy propensity of which numerous instances are extant in [these
Valleys which *del.*] this [beautiful *del.*] Country [which Nature has ⟨beautifully
del.⟩ framed so beautifully & prodigally *del.*] beautifully framed & prodigally
adorned by nature. [Combined with *del.*] This and the perverseness with which the
dwellings often turn their backs upon the most beautiful landscapes even where
there is not the excuse of a little sunshine seems to shew that [the admiration of
del.] though [indifference *del.*] insensibility or indifference to the [grand and
beautiful productions & *del.*] general forms of nature does not exist in a state of
society however rude that a relish for fine combinations of Landscapes is an acquired
taste. So capacious is the human mind that it can find space for things widely
separated from each other in spirit & character & a liking for these uncouth
[? fancies] may consist with an admiration of the wild & careless graces of the
woods & fields. *Cf. textual n.* 1179.   1131 instances MS.²: uncouth [*faintly
del. with pencil*] instances MS.   1134 shew] *Faintly altered in pencil to*: shews
1136 a relish *Edd.*: that a relish MS.   1138 the hill MS.³: the hill with
the road from the Cottage just past MS.: along the hill side MS.².   1140
preferring MS.²: fronting the road MS.   of *Edd.*: *om.* MS.   1141 prospect
MS.²: view MS.

& which, tho' hidden from the house, may be seen from an alcove in the
pleasure ground behind, at a short distance from the door. There are,
I know, many persons not insensible to the beauties of scenery who,
in the choice of a scite for their residence, would rather avoid than seek 1145
a fine prospect from their windows, even if it could be procured with
a southern aspect & without the price of exposure to bleak winds. They
think that it is more desirable to be tempted out of doors in search of
entertainment of this kind, & apprehend that the best display of
Nature's wealth would tire the mind, if constantly obtruded on the 1150
sight. But this weariness or indifference cannot ensue without a defect
in the mind itself, for a landscape is a living thing, & the varieties of
nature—infinite in themselves—are no where more affectingly exhibited than in the visionary regions of distance. How many splendid
appearances of the sun rising or setting upon the sea or among distant 1155
mountain tops—how many phenomena of lights & shadows, of glorious vapours, & showers & storms coming in & clearing up are lost to
those who have no chance of seeing these changes but when wandering
out of doors! The most soothing house prospect is not an adequate
recompence for the scanty allowance which from its seclusion it must 1160
necessarily yield of these grand exhibitions. In the choice of a situation,
let sunshine & shelter be deemed indispensable, for tho' they may not
be necessary to youth & to those who are in vigourous health, yet
accidents of sickness & the unavoidable chillness of old age require this
comfort & protection. But if where a comprehensive picture, visible 1165
from the window & brought even to the fire side, may be united with
these primary recommendations, it is an error not to accept what the
situation offers, tho' the reasons for the refusal may not actually imply
what they will certainly have the appearance of—a sullenness against
Nature. I have already contended that we are bound by the laws of 1170
taste not to disfigure a beautiful Country, or break in upon its composure by flaring edifices placed injuriously to the feelings of others
for supposed advantages of our own; & I have already protested
against that craving for extensive prospect which would prompt the
builder to fix his habitation where it may stare & be stared at, after the 1175

1142 & which, tho' MS.[3]: & which is planted out behind MS.: but which MS.[2].
1143 *After* ground MS. *deletes*: a few hundred [? yards]   at *Edd.*: in at MS.
door MS.[2]: house door MS.   1144 scenery MS.[2]: Nature MS.   1148
more desirable MS.[2]: better MS.   1149 the best display MS.[2]: the most
beautiful exhibitions MS.   1151 *After* sight MS. *deletes*: but [this effect
cannot *del.*] though I have already protested . . . *and continues as in* 1173–8, *where
we will record the variants.*   ensue without MS.[2]: follow w MS.   1156
lights & shadows MS.[2]: storms & [? meteors] MS.   1167 not to accept MS.[2]:
to turn away from MS.   1172 placed injuriously MS.[2]: improperly placed
MS.   1173 own; & *Edd.*: own. & MS.   1175 where MS.[2]: upon a hill
top or high on a naked hill side where MS.   after MS.[2]: in MS.

manner of a trio of houses in a certain county which, from the absurdity of their appearance in this respect, have been severally nick-named by the Country-people Glare-at-'em, Glare-thro'-'em, & Glare-o'er-'em. With those, therefore, to whom I am recommending extent of prospect, this opinion will have a better chance of being listened to, and the 1180 giver of it may claim credit for sharing their aversion to this kind of exposure & for sympathy with the modesty of their feelings.

A 1/4 of a mile higher up the hill, near some Cottages called Hollinbank, will be found, both above & below the road, excellent points from which to take a last view of the Lake & Vale of Conistone we 1185 have left.

A mile farther on, we begin to descend into the Vale of Hawkshead, having from the high ground a sight of the upper part of Windermere stretching to the left. In the first cluster of houses we come to, named Hawkshead hill, stands a meeting-house by the road side, belonging 1190 to a congregation of Anabaptists, called by the Country people who are not of their own persuasion 'Whigs'. The Building is mean, & on the outside has so little to distinguish it as a place of worship that one might think it had been so constructed in an intolerant age for the purpose of avoiding notice; but this Conventicle is endowed with Lands 1195 that produce a respectable income for the Minister. I [? point] the Passenger's attention to that object because this is the only establishment of the kind that I know of among these Mountains. Behind runs a streamlet which is occasionally diverted into a reservoir wherein Adults are dipped, some coming from a considerable distance for this 1200 purpose. A little detached from the building lies also a small Cemetery,

1176 certain MS.²: neighbouring MS.   1178 o'er-'em. MS.²: o'er-en; yet MS.   1179 With those, therefore MS.²: I may therefore claim credit with MS.   *After* extent of *there occurs a heavily deleted passage, giving a first draft of* 1126–9 (This waywardness . . . Nature); *it may be conjecturally read*: This waywardness [? and] the [?] it is never the less in the spirit a step in the progress of refinement; a [?] link that connects man with the [?] nature By his own activity [? any man] in this connection, by a tie less gross than that of necessity has [?]   1179–80 prospect MS.²: prospect from their windows as many MS. 1181 sharing MS.²: being in sympathy MS.   1183 near some Cottages called MS.²: at a place called MS.   1186–241 *At* 1186 *the text of* MS. Prose 23ᵇ *originally continued with the matter now given in* 1241–320; *but* MS. Prose 23ᵍ, *written as an afterthought, was clearly intended for insertion here, and accordingly* 1187–240 *derives from* MS. Prose 23ᵍ (*see our description of* MSS. Prose 23 *and see also textual n.* 1240).   1189 come to MS.²: come to on the left MS.   1190 *After* road side MS. *deletes*: which having little of the appearance   1192 *After* 'Whigs' MS. *deletes*: behind this   1194 think MS.²: think that MS.   so constructed MS.²: erected MS.   1195–6 but this . . . produce MS.²: Lands are settled upon the Minister doing duty here from which proceeds MS.   1196 point MS.²: mention this MS.   1198 among *Edd.*: in MS.: [among *del.*] MS.²   1198–9 runs a *Edd.*: [? there *or* this] is a [small Cemetery reservoir *del.*] runs streamlet MS.   1201 *After* purpose MS. *deletes*: not [?]ing which occasions, does not meet with much [? respect] from the minds [?]   detached MS.²: detached only MS.

with one low headstone in the centre. The inscription is scarcely to
be traced on account of the lichens that have crept over the stone.
This obscure burial place is of a character peculiarly melancholy. The
ground is humbly fenced, like [? any] of the neighbouring fields, & not
a tree planted to dignify or adorn it. But among this little company of
graves, how much mortal weariness is laid at rest, how many anxieties
are stilled, what tender scruples & fearful apprehensions removed
forever!

To this congregation, who [?] [? devout worship], belonged many
years ago a Man oppressed by religious melancholy, whose residence
was at the head of the wild valley of Langdale. One day he rose up
from the table where he had been reading his Bible & dropped some
words intimating that he should be seen no more. It is remarkable that
those who heard him speak to this effect were not induced from apprehension of some ill consequence to follow his steps. But as he did not
return, search was made after him when too late, & continued both in
his own neighbourhood & thro distant parts of the Country; no tidings
could be gained of him. It happened, however, that long after while
a Shepherd was passing along the bank of a rugged gill near the head
of Langdale, his dog brought from below a bone which the Shepherd
might not perhaps have noticed, but a Person who was with him suggested that it belonged, as he phrased it, to the body of a Christian.
Upon this, they descended into the ghyll, & other human bones were
found that had been cast up by the torrent among the rocks & bushes.
These were carefully collected up, & it not being doubted that they
were the remains of this unhappy Man who had disappeared, they
were brought to be interred in this burial ground. As the circumstances
had made much impression in the neighbourhood, a large company
attended, and a sermon was delivered from the text "How can these dry
bones be quickened". Doubtless, the Preacher, in treating the subject

1205

1210

1215

1220

1225

1230

1202–3 is scarcely . . . stone MS.²: is difficult to read almost overgrown with
lichens—this is a solitary & melancholy spot MS.   1204 burial place
MS.²: burial place with the small company of graves which it contains has a
MS.   1205 any MS.²: one MS.   1205–6 not a tree] *The top of page*
[2ʳ] *of* MS. Prose 23ᵍ *is torn down the centre for about 2 in. Because* 1206 *ff. was*
written after the tear occurred, nothing of the text was here lost. But before the tear
occurred, the top of the page had been used for an early draft of 1556–9: [upon *del.*]
where the summit of it [*tear*] large [*tear*] poized in the firmament with [*tear*]
openings in them thro which [pale lights find their *del.*] a [?] finds its way to the
still bosom of [the Lake *del.*]   1206 dignify *Edd.*: dignity MS.   1207 is
MS.²: here is MS.   1217 him MS.²: the Man MS.   1217–18 & continued . . .
& thro MS.²: not only in his own neighbourhood but in MS.   1220 along
MS.²: by MS.   1224 they . . . ghyll MS.²: search was made MS.
1225 among] *altered from* amongst   1226 collected MS.²: gathered MS.
1230 delivered from the text MS.²: delivered upon the occasion from the text MS.:
preached by the Minister upon the occasion from the words as I have been told
MS. *A.*

of the resurrection of the Body, would not overlook upon this occasion that most sublime passage of Ezekiel where the Prophet speaks of himself as set down in the valley of dry Bones. "And he said unto me, Son of Man, can these bones live? And I answered, O Lord God, Thou knowest." 1235

Proceeding, we are soon after greeted by the white Church of Hawkshead standing conspicuously on a Hill, a chearful salutation & particularly so for those whose minds it may relieve from such serious reflections as the [*blank*] House of worship which we have left & its appurtenances will naturally lead to. 1240

At the foot of the hill within 1/2 a mile of Hawkshead stands by the road side an ancient Building, named Hawkshead hall, which yet retains in the stone work of the windows & gateways some interesting fragments of gothic architecture. In this house the Abbot of Furness kept residence by one or more Monks, who performed divine service in the 1245 Church & other parochial duties in that neighbourhood. There still remains a court room over the gate-way where the bailiff of Hawkshead held court & distributed justice in the name of the Abbot.

1232 would not overlook MS.²: would remind his [? listeners *del.*] [? hearers] MS. 1235 *After* Thou knowest." MS. *deletes:* At that time the Minister of this congregation of Anabaptists used to preach once a month in a private House in Langdale, a [labour that *del.*] must have been attended with great [? effects *or* efforts] [as he was zealous in the discharge of his duty & *del.*] as the place [which *del.*] stood in [? much] need of such attention [? As] the [?] benefits [of the established Church had scarcely been extended *del.*] [?] For though a Chapel of the Church of England existed there, the stipend not being more than five pounds per Annum, unless the Incumbent Clergyman [had *del.*] were a man of extraordinary character it was not likely that he would be competent to the discharge of his duty 1237–40 a chearful salutation . . . lead to] MS. *A gives numerous rewritings, almost all in Wordsworth's hand; without noting all the deletions, we record, in chronological order, some of these drafts:* a striking contrast to the obscure and forlorn House of Worship which we have left. At the foot of the hill within half a mile of Hawkshead a [?] embowering in trees and opposite to an antient Building [*cf. textual n.* 1240]: a chearing sight particularly to those who may be occupied by serious reflexions: may have turned aside to visit the [?] & baptismal reservoir belonging to this forlorn House of Worship: & whose minds are occupied with such serious reflexions as those images will naturally lead to: a chearful salutation particularly as it is scarcely possible to have: A chearful salutation & particularly so for those whose minds it may relieve from such serious reflections as the [forlorn *del.*] obscure House of Worship & its appurtenances which we have left naturally lead to. 1240 *After* lead to. *Wordsworth's hand immediately writes (we omit the deletions):* At the foot of the hill pleasantly [? embowered] in trees stands an antient Building *This continuation clearly marks the end of the insertion and leads us back to* 1186, *or* MS. Prose 23ᵇ, *where the text reads:* . . . Vale of Conistone [. Nothing remarkable occurs till we come *del.*] we have left. At the foot of the hill within 1/2 mile of Hawkshead [where we may notice on the left an ancient *del.*] stands by the road side an ancient Building [*cf.* 1241–2]. 1242 Building, named MS.²: Building on the left called MS. 1243 stone work of MS.²: window MS. 1248–59 MS. Prose 23ᶠ, *written as an afterthought, contains matter apparently intended for insertion somewhere around here, but unlike* 1187–240, *it was never worked into the text. Because the final version, which we give first, is a long one, we will punctuate it, as we normally punctuate other U.T. manuscripts:*

The situation of Hawkshead is excellent but its aspect, notwithstanding, from this quarter is far from agreeable. How much grace might not towns of this compass easily derive from a few trees intermingled with the houses, softening the glare of whitewashed walls & connecting the smoke which ascends from the chimneys with soothing images of rural seclusion & quietness! But this little Town, as we [approach it from this *del.*] are approaching it, appears a mere accumulation of naked buildings, unfurnished even with gardens to unite it with the country. The Church, also in itself a pleasing object happily placed, has within these few years been strangely disfigured by the erection of a Vestry, the roof of which runs in a line with the lower roof of the Church. This excrescence cuts off the lower base of the Steeple so that all the lightness which that part of the structure possessed [has been *del.*], as being in shape [for *del.*] distinctly separated from the body of the Church, is destroyed, nor has pains been taken to make the window uniform with those of the Church that run in a line with it. In a book of this kind one chief purpose of which is by commenting upon the face of the Country, as we pass along it, to endeavour to preserve its natural beauty & [establishing *del.*] to establish at the same time principals of taste which may extend their influence beyond the district which furnished the occasion for illustrating them, this notice will not be deemed insignificant, especially by those who feel a debt of gratitude to our ancestors for the rich inheritance of sacred architure [*sic*] which they have [transmitted MS. *A, Edd.: om.* MS.] to us. Besides it is difficult not to apprehend that there may be a decay of piety among those who when alterations & additions are called for in [such *del.*] structures raised with munificence & nice attention, execute them so carelessly, or in so mean & discordant a style as shews that the [chief thing aimed at *del.*] point most attended to was saving of expence. [In truth *del.*] We may confidently affirm none of the fine arts—if Poetry be excepted which is a spirit in the mind, a thing sui generis—have so much pleasurable & even valuable feeling dependent upon them as architecture. There is not a building, however [low *del.*] vulgar the purposes to which it may be applied, that will not admit of being constructed according to proportions [from *del.*] [by *del.*] which the mind may receive [delight *del.*] a [? *del.*] which [gratifies *del.*] These pleasures also are a free gift, presented to us without search in all moods and upon all occasions; and [on the contrary *del.*] in like manner, which further [proves *del.*] shews the comparative importance of architecture, the disgust which its productions excite, if bad, cannot be escaped. [In fact *del.*] In the present state of this art, it is painful to think how much the [pleasures *del.*] encouragements of a new taste in the Country lie at the mercy of the builder. There [There is *del.*] This dignity also belongs to Architecture: that it is not an imitative art, but a necessary appendage to human existence, that its works are incorporated with those of Nature, & that there is no combination of her forms the beauty or grandeur of which may not be heightened by [*the remaining text is uncertain*] the presence of some edifice subservient to the safety, the comfort of men, or [expressing *del.*] telling with sublimity or lowliness his dependence on his Maker, his hope, & his consolation.

An earlier version, also in the hand of Mary Wordsworth, reads: The situation of this little town is excellent but its appearance notwithstanding from this quarter is [unattractive *del.*] far from agreeable it is a mere accumulation of naked [houses *del.*] buildings no gardens unite it with the Country [no *del.*] [? for] a few trees intermingling with the houses soften the glare of the White washed fronts walls [*sic*] or break the horizontal line of their roofs or connect the smoke which ascends from the Chimneys with soothing images of rural seclusion & quietness The Church also in itself a pleasing object happily placed has been within these few years strangely disfigured by the erection of a Vestry the roof of which runs in a line with the lower roof of the Church cutting off the base of the Steeple so that all the lightness which that part of the structure possessed as being in shape distinctly separated from top to bottom of the body of the Church is destroyed nor has pains been taken to make the window of this excrescence uniform with those of the Church which run in a line with it In a [work *del.*] Book of this kind [these observations will one of the main purposes of which is to comment upon the face of the Country ⟨? wh⟩ are *del.*] one of the chief purposes of which is by commenting upon the face of the Country as we pass along [with a view to prevent⟨?⟩ *del.*] to save it from being

Passing over Gallow-barrow, a low hill probably so named from its
having formerly been a place where criminals were executed under   1250
the jurisdiction of the Abbot, we arrive at the little Market Town of
Hawkshead, pleasantly situated at the foot of a range of small cultivated or woody hills rising irregularly behind each other & backed by
a ridge of bare fells. On the top of the hill which screens the Town
stands the Church, overlooking the Valley, the southern extremity of   1255
which is filled by a Lake called Esthwaite water. Immediately under
the Church yard on the eastern side stands the Grammar School house,
founded & liberally endowed by Archbishop Sandes, a Native of this
neighbourhood.

The munificence of this Prelate & the partiality which would natur-   1260
ally be felt by those amongst whom he had been born for one who rose
to so high a station in the Church would perhaps have some tendency
to reconcile the rude people of this district to the changes made by the
reformation, from which at first they had been extremely averse, not
only for reasons generally felt through the nation, [but also] on account   1265
of their attachment to their ancient Lords, the Abbots of Furness. A
fisherman in this town, who stiled himself the Earl of Poverty, was one
of the most conspicuous leaders in the famous pilgrimage of Grace

further disfigured & to establish principles of taste which may extend their influence beyond the district which furnishes the present occasion for illustrating them
these [observations *del.*] notices will not [appear too minute *del.*] be deemed insignificant especially to those [who with the Author may rank architecture place
architecture with the first rank of the fine arts *del.*]

A first draft contains mainly disconnected and repetitious bits: but thought of
gratitude . . . we remember [? how] much we are indebted to our [fathers *del.*]
ancestors for the rich inheritance of sacred Architecture [to which both in Town &
in village *del.*] which they have transmitted to us. A want of taste is certainly
shown & it is difficult not to apprehend . . . None of the fine arts are so important
as Architecture [its productions are *del.*] there is not a building before us at all
seasons Numerous are the purposes to which it is applied [?] will not admit of being
constructed according to proportions . . . at once [gratify *del.*] please their eye &
their Intellect The productions of this art are everywhere exposed to us and unless
. . . In the Country they are incorporated with the work of Nature . . . None of the
fine arts have so much pleasurable & even valuable feeling dependent upon them
as architecture and none are so imperfect Their encouragements which to men of
taste may lie almost at the mercy of this Art. There is not a building however mean
the purpose for which it [? may] be applied that will not admit of being constructed
according to proposes [*sic*] that will [not equally *del.*] delight the mind.

1249 Gallow-barrow MS.[2]: Gallow-barrow hill & [?] MS.   named MS.[2]:
named during MS.   1251 little MS.[2]: small MS.   1252 *After* Hawkshead
MS. *deletes*: [which presides over it with its *del.*] seated under a hill upon the top
of which stands a handsome Church having a tower and double roof and making
an object that with sufficient dignity presides over this short & narrow Vale.
Immediately Under [the Church *del.*] the hill on the eastern side of the Church
stands the School-house founded & liberally endowed by archbishop Sandes a
Native of this neighbourhood.   1253 irregularly MS.[2]: irregularly in [? stages]
MS.   1255 Valley MS.[2]: Valley towards MS.   1260 *After* Prelate MS.
deletes: the high station he rose to in the Church the dignity   1264 had
been MS.[2]: were MS.   1265 but also *Edd.*: *om.* MS.

which disturbed the northern Counties in the time of Henry the Eight. How far this neighbourhood was committed in that insurrection & with what regret the people then looked back upon the institutions that had been destroyed may be inferred from a perusal of the following Summons from the chief Captains of the Commonalty assembled in pilgrimage: 1270

"To the Commyns of Hawkside Parish, Bailiffs, or Constables, with all the Hamletts of the same. 1275

Welbeloved we greet you well; whereas our brother Poverty, (the fisherman above spoken of) & our brother Rogers goith forward, is openly for the aide & assistance of your faith & holy church & for the reformation of such abbeys & monasteries, now dissolved & suppressed without any just cause. Wherefore gudde brethers, forasmuch as our sayd brederyn hath send to us for ayde & help, wee do not only effectually desire you, but also under the paine of deadly sinne we commaunde you, evry of you, to be at the stoke greene beside Hawkeside kirke, the Saturday next, being the xxviii day of October, by xi of the clock, in your best array; as you will make answer before the heigh judge at the dreadful day of dome, & in the payne of pulling downe your houses, & leasing of your gudd[? s], & your bodies to be at the Capteyns will: for at the place afforesaid, then & there, yee & we shall take further directions concerning our faith, so far decayed, & for gudde & laudable customes of the country, & such naughty inventions & strange articles now accepted & admitted, so that our said brothers bee subdued, they are lyke to goe furthwards to utter undoing of the comynwealth." 1280 1285 1290

What particular spot of ground the illiterate Sansculottes & Luddites of that day were invited & commanded to meet upon, in order to reinforce their Brother Poverty, I am unable to point out, but, thanks to the good Archbishop, Stoke green is probably now lost in the Schoolmaster's Orchard or in some enclosure that has since daily resounded with more agreeable tumults than prevailed in that discontented assembly—the noise of a numerous band of happy Schoolboys engaged in their sports & gamesome contests. 1295 1300

1269 in the time of MS.²: in Henry the eighth MS. 1271 with what regret MS.²: what interest the People took in MS. 1272 from MS.²: by MS. 1273 *After* Summons MS. *deletes*: No 1295 *After* ground MS. *deletes*: [under the *del.*] in the neighbourhood of the Church was fixed upon for the place of meeting where 1297 point out MS.²: say MS. 1300 more agreeable MS.²: other MS. than *Edd.*: then MS. 1301–2 engaged in MS.²: occupied with MS. 1302 *After* contests MS. *deletes*: [? along] [? From] Caprice & fashion are suffered to [? interfere] in the most serious concerns of body & mind [a physician shall lose *del.*] the practice of a physician shall fall away without any abatement of industry on his part or proof [given *del.*] afforded of want of skill

Along the eastern end of the Church runs a stone seat, a place of
resort for the old people of the Town, for the sickly, & those who have
leisure to look about them. Here sitting in the shade or in the sun, 1305
they talk over their concerns, & a few years back were amused by the
gambols & exercises of more than a 100 Schoolboys, some playing
soberly on the hill top near them, while others were intent upon more
boisterous diversions in the fields beneath. This public seat has indeed
many recommendations, & if those who frequent it cast their eyes upon 1310
the lofty Mountains which rise above the immediate boundary of this
Vale towards the North, they will there often behold movements &
changes of a more slow & tranquil character, which, however, it
requires some degree of imagination to take an interest in. Upon a
Summer afternoon cast with shadows of the clouds, deep & determined, 1315
the fells of Kirkstone & Rydale head appear from this seat like a tract
of chosen ground upon which detachments of a silent army are
maneuvering; positions are taken up and relinquished; the Spectacle
is entertaining & the law by which the changes are governed is a
mystery. If I have lingered too long upon this favorite old resting 1320
place, the Reader will excuse a partiality produced by the recollections
of more than 10 years of Boyhood & Youth passed in this Valley,
a period during which neither the eye was inattentive nor the imagination torpid.

    Within the Church is a stone Monument erected to the Parents of 1325
Archbishop Sandys, who are represented as recumbent figures side by
side, a latin inscription running like a band round the square Tablet
upon which they are laid. Nor can I omit noticing that the Church
contains a plain marble slab sacred to the memory of Eliz. Smith,
buried here a few years ago.   1330

    1305 *After* them MS. *deletes*: to   1307 *After* Schoolboys MS. *deletes*: spread
over the ground [below them *del.*] beneath their eyes   1308 soberly MS.[2]:
soberly at their side MS.   while MS.[2]: & MS.   1309 diversions MS.[2]:
amusements MS.   *After* beneath MS. *deletes*: [? Improvements] & changes little
[? obscure] of a more tranquil character [carried out by *del.*] & which perhaps it
requires some degree of imagination to take an interest in are   1309–20 This
public ... mystery] *Possibly deleted.*   1312 behold MS.[2]: be entertained by MS.
1313 more slow MS.[2]: very different MS.   1314–18 Upon a . . . maneuvering
MS[3].: From this seat upon a summer afternoon [when the shadows of the clouds
are deep and determined MS.[2]] the fells of Kirkstone & Rydale head often look
like a vast tract of chosen ground upon which detachments of a silent army of sun-
beams & shadows are maneuvering MS.   1316–18 seat like a tract of chosen
ground . . . are maneuvering; positions *Edd.* (*cf. preceding note*). MS. *seems to read*:
seat [?] upon which detachments of a silent army maneuvering upon a tract of
chosen ground—positions   1318 relinquished MS.[2]: relinquished by a law
which MS.   1320–1 old resting place MS.[2]: ground MS.   1321 a MS.[2]:
my MS.   1324 *After* torpid MS. *deletes*: Before we quit Hawkshead it may
be worth while to add that   1325 Within MS.[2]: In MS.   is MS.[2]: [?] seen
MS.   1328–9 the Church contains MS.: there is MS. *A.*   1329 sacred
MS.: *not in* MS. *A.*   *After* Smith MS. *A deletes*: a young Person of admirable

Of this extraordinary young Person memoirs have been published, & from them & from [her] own letters & compositions it appears that her acquisitions in learning & science were such as would have done honour to professed Scholars, & what is more remarkable were made in secret by unassisted efforts, triumphing over difficulties which to a 1335 less ardent zeal would have been insuperable. Till after her death the measure of these attainments was unknown to those with whom she daily conversed & even to her most intimate friends, so that she appears to have walked thro' the world by the side of her companions like a being of superior Nature—in no unworthy disguise but still that 1340 of human shape—who is not discovered till the wings that declare him to be of celestial origin are unfolded at his departure, & he is gone & hath left sadness & unavailing regret behind. This lamented young woman dwelt in the earlier part of her youth on the banks of the Wye, & the regret which by a mind tenderly alive to the beautiful in every 1345 thing must have been felt upon being compelled to relinquish the treasures of that favourite spot was, in course of time, alleviated by new attachments to scenes of nature still more beautiful & sublime, which her residence in this Country gave her an opportunity of form-ing. The loftiest peaks that were accessible to female feet had been 1350 trodden by her light steps, & the deepest dells were not unknown to

accomplishments, and acquisitions [? &] learning not [?] who died a few years ago at [? Newl *del.*] Conistone [her father's ⟨residence *del.*⟩ house in ⟨?⟩ It is generally known that a reverse in fortune compelled this family to quit their ⟨residence *del.*⟩ abode upon the banks of the Wye & the regret which in ⟨?⟩ This painful oc⟨?⟩ ⟨? sacrificed⟩ in relinquishing ⟨?⟩ of that MS. *A²*] & was buried here That regret which a mind [so *del.*] tenderly alive to the beautiful in every thing must have felt in being compelled to quit the family residence on the banks of the Wye was in course of time alleviated by [an opportunity *del.*] new attachments to scenes of Nature still more beautiful & sublime which her residence in this Country gave her an opportunity of forming—to the strength of these attachments [she *del.*] this lamented young woman gave in her last illness a most affecting testimony—it is recorded that, when in a state of threatening debility she was inhaling the fresh air within a tent placed upon a knoll by the side of Coniston Water & [the conversation ⟨? turned⟩ upon the ⟨? propriety⟩] [the ⟨? trial⟩ of a milder climate was recommended to her &] for the restoration of her health a milder climate was recommended & it happened that she was pressed to submit to this trial one day while in a state of [threatening *del.*] alarming debility she was inhaling the fresh air within a tent placed upon a knoll by the side of Conistone Waters, & in view of one of the loveliest of those scenes which we have passed thro' [a climate which *del.*] she was pressed to submit to this [? trial] fixing her glistening eyes [were fixed *del.*] upon the beautiful landscape, with an earnestness & even an impatience of voice & manner almost unnatural to her character she answered that if she could not be well with such a heavenly sight before her [eyes *del.*] she could be well no where
    1332 her *Edd.*: *om.* MS.   compositions MS.²: fragments MS.   1335 *After* efforts MS. *deletes*: supported with great [?]   triumphing MS.²: triumphed MS.   1337 measure MS.²: extent MS.   was MS.²: were MS.   to those MS.²: to her acquaintances MS.   1339 appears MS.²: appears in this respect MS.   1340 a being MS.²: a celestial MS.   1341 shape MS.²: being MS.   1342 gone MS.³: taken MS.: departed MS.².

her, & every nook of the scenes in the neighbourhood of Coniston
thro' which I have led my Companion was especially to [*sic*] her affections. To the strength of these attachments she gave in her last illness
a most moving testimony. For the restoration of her health, a milder   1355
climate had been recommended, & it happened one day while in a state
of alarming debility she was inhaling the fresh air, within a tent placed
at a small distance from her father's house upon a knoll on the sloping
bank of Conistone Water, she was pressed to submit to this trial. To
which entreaty, fixing her glistening eyes upon the landscape, one of   1360
the loveliest that the Vale affords, with an earnestness & even an
impatience of voice & manner almost unnatural in her character, the
sufferer answered that if she could not be well with such a heavenly
sight before her, she could be well no where.

I have already noticed that the northern boundary of Hawkshead is   1365
overlooked by the Heights of Ambleside & Rydale; & leaving the
Church yard & Town, as we cross the Vale on our way toward the
Ferry house of Windermere, we see that its western barrier is overtopped by the mountain called the Old Man, whose rugged bosom,
with the waterfalls which it embraces, enlivens & sets off by contrasts   1370
the smooth lake & fertile fields of Conistone, & whose summit crowns
that picture which, if it did not supply earthly hope to this dying
Maiden, at least soothed her pain, lifted up her spirits, & through the
medium of perishable things reminded her, as by a faint reflexion, of
regions maintained by the love of the Almighty in secure & undecaying   1375
beauty.

This Vale of Hawkshead is one of that class which within their own
limits contain nothing but what is of humble character, yet possess
considerable dignity borrowed from communication with Mountains
that belong to other Vales. Looking back when we have reached the   1380
Lake of Esthwaite, we see that Langdale Pikes have reared themselves

---

1352 *After* scenes MS. *deletes*: we have   1359 *After* Water MS. *deletes*:
& is in view of one of the most lovely [landscapes *del.*] scenes which the Vale affords.
1362–3 the sufferer MS.[2]: she MS.   1365 Hawkshead MS.[2]: this Vale MS.
1366 the Heights MS.[2]: the Mountains [of *del.*] above Ambleside & Rydale & as
taking MS.   1367 toward MS.[2]: to MS.   1369 the mountain MS.[2]: the
Fells of Coniston & in particular by the Old Man the Mountain which embosoms
the waterfalls & rocks that MS.   1370 *After* waterfalls MS. *deletes*: [? running]
1371 & whose summit MS.[2]: & that summit of which MS.   1372 *After* which
MS. *deletes*: soothed the heart of this   *After* hope MS. *deletes*: at least soothed
this troubled spirit   1373 pain MS.[2]: pain & MS.   through MS.[2]: by MS.
1376/7 *G. W. inserts the matter given at the beginning of our textual n. 1248–59.*
Nothing that we can see in the text or on the manuscript justifies an insertion here.
1377 that class which within MS.[2]: those which in MS.   1378 nothing . . .
character MS.[2]: few objects but those [?] which are of humble character but which
have MS.   1380 when we have reached MS.[2]: we see that as we approach
MS.   1381 reared MS.[2]: lifted MS.

into notice. One of them from this point takes the form of a sugar loaf &, not less for its singularity than its majesty, makes an interesting background to a beautiful landscape, of which the white church of Hawkshead is a gay feature.   1385

But hurrying forward to this scene, I have passed without notice a pool at the head of the Lake where if the wind had been up & had suddenly veered, we might have been startled by the sight of a curiosity—a floating grove in full sail. This moving Island does not appear & disappear, like the buoyant wonder of Derwent water, but navigates 1390 at all seasons the surface of this small pool, the trees that grow upon it serving it as masts & sails. There is no mystery in the origin of this unusual appearance, as it is plain that the platform with the trees upon it has been detached from the spungy ground that borders the pool & the winds will not suffer it to be reunited to the shore. I have not 1395 learned whether it increases in compass or diminishes.

Adjoining to this Pool, which is named Priest-pot, perhaps from some Ecclesiastic having been drowned in it, formerly stood a gibbet, upon which the body of some atrocious Criminal had been hung in Chains near the spot where his crime had been committed. Part of the 1400 Irons & some of the wood work remained in my memory. Think of a human figure tossing about in the air in one of these sweet Valleys. 'Tis an object sufficiently fearful & repulsive upon Hounslow heath or in the solitudes of Salisbury Plain, but in a populous enclosure like this where no one could look round without being crossed by the sight— 1405 what a dismal annoyance! It seems as if no sense of humanity, no feeling for rural beauty could have existed in the minds of those who among their woods & fields could tolerate such a spectacle. At that time the marshy ground at the head of this lake used to resound with the doleful cry of the Bittern, which, by the bye, has never been heard in its 1410

1382 One of MS.²: The form MS.   1386 But . . . scene MS.: But I have neglected to mention in its place a pool MS. *A*: But in my hastening forward to this scene MS. *A²*.   1387–9 Lake where . . . floating MS., MS. *A²*: Lake surrounded with spungy ground a piece of Water in no wise remarkable but that it contains a floating MS. *A*.   1389–90 grove in . . . but MS., MS. *A²*: [island *del.*] Grove not one that appears like the famous one of Derwent Water MS. *A*. 1390 navigates MS., MS. *A²*: sails about MS. A.   1391 at all seasons MS.²: at all times MS.: *not in* MS. *A*.   *After* pool MS. *A deletes*: as the wind shifts   1393 unusual appearance MS., MS. *A⁴*: moving Curiosity MS. *A*: appearance MS. *A²*: phenom MS. *A³*.   1398 in it MS.²: there MS. gibbet MS.²: gibbet of which some of the wood work MS.   1399 atrocious *Edd.*: 'attrocious MS.   had been MS.²: had [? for] been MS.   1401 Think MS.²: I should MS.   1402 in the air MS.²: [with the *del.*] upon the wind MS.   1403 'Tis an object MS.²: [how melancholy *del.*] tis a sight MS. or] *wrongly deleted*.   1404 Plain, but MS.²: Plain or upon Hounslow heath MS.   a MS.²: an MS.   this MS.²: [? this *or* that] valley MS.   1405 no one could MS.²: it must have been impossible to look round MS.   being crossed MS.²: seeing it MS.

ancient haunts since the great frost in 1740. This sound, blending with
the whistling of the Hawk repairing hither from distant crags & the
croaking of the carrion Crow & the Raven attracted by the suspended
corpse, must have made a dismal chorus for the ears of Passengers,
while the circumstances of the murder were yet fresh in memory, 1415
approaching along the several lanes which meet near the point where
the gibbet stood. The heads of traitors, should the times unfortunately
breed such offenders, would no longer be stuck up upon Temple Bar,
nor their Quarters dispersed to strike terror from the gates of provin-
cial Cities, & it would be well if this odious custom of exposing the 1420
Bodies of Criminals, of whatever description, were abandoned & all
traces of this relic of barbarism had disappeared from the land. If such
an exhibition, thro' long familiarity with it, can be looked at with
indifference by the innocent & good, there is surely nothing gained,
but such an effect is rather to be deplored. Whom can the ignominy 1425
of this exposure deter from wickedness? Surely not those from whose
hand the most inhuman cruelties are to be apprehended! There is no
place which a hardened villain would prefer for the perpetration of a
murder to the foot of a gibbet, if it lay within his choice. He would
select that very place in pride & bravado; & by such unaccountable 1430
impulses sometimes is man driven to action, & his unhappy mind is so
subject to be visited by perverse thoughts that evil in the worst degree
is often committed which would never have been dreamt of but for the
injudicious means used to prevent it.

No vestiges probably now remain of the object which led me to these 1435
reflections, but I should be sorry to think that the pool is no longer
frequented by a pair of beautiful Swans, long lived creatures which
haunted it for many years & which sailing about on a windy day by the
side of the floating Island would have made a romantic picture for the
entertainment of any eye. This faithful pair & another pair equally 1440
faithful to each other divided the domain of Esthwaite Water & the
pools & streams at the head & foot of it equally between them. An

---

1413–14 suspended corpse MS.²: dead body MS.   1417 *After* stood MS.
deletes: It would be well if all traces of this odious   1418 stuck up
MS.²: exposed MS.   1419 from MS.²: upon MS.   1422 this relic
MS.²: it MS.   *After* land MS. *deletes*: This practice is a [? reproach] to humanity
& a reproach to civilization   1424 there is MS.²: then it is MS.
1425 deplored MS.²: regretted MS.   1427 most inhuman cruelties MS.²:
worst crime MS.   1428 would prefer MS.²: would with so much pride &
bravado select MS.   1429 if it . . . choice MS.³: where the MS.: if he had
a MS.².   1430 that very place MS.²: the place MS.   unaccountable
MS.²: strange MS.   1431 *After* action, & MS. *deletes*: so it often is
1432 perverse thoughts MS.²: thoughts the opposite of those which MS.
1435 No vestiges MS.²: [No *del*.] [all *del*.] No vestiges of th MS.   1437 long
MS.²: [? most] MS.   1440 pair & MS.²: pair if still in existence MS.

instance was never known of either couple encroaching upon the rights
of the other. These beautiful Birds were a striking ornament to this
small lake. The tranquil habits of swans and their gentle [? moods] suit   1445
the stillness of diffused water, so that these animals seemed placed
more appropriately to their Natures and more happily upon lakes,
where the element is kept within bounds, than upon Rivers subject to
impetuous floods. Tame Swans were brought to Windermere, & the
breed of them encouraged there several years ago. Upon [that] plain   1450
of water, so large in a general view, these inhabitants of the surface
were insignificant, [but] meandering along the creeks & bays, there
they appeared objects of importance. Upon Windermere they became
numerous; their trespasses upon the fields bordering the lake being
complained of, the breed was destroyed. Those of Esthwaite, fortu-   1455
nately for themselves & their admirers, did not multiply; being so few
in numbers, their depredations were allowed, & in the hard season of
winter several Persons took delight in occasionally carrying them food.
I am writing of the Vale of Hawkshead from memory, & I will suppose
that my old acquaintances, the faithful swans, are still in existence or   1460
that others have taken their place, enlivening the fore ground of the
picture by the Lakeside to which we shall return. Their towering wings
& snow white plumage harmonize with the white Church of Hawkshead, standing at some distance upon the hill & leading the eye to the
hoary pikes of Langdale by which the horizon is bounded.   1465
At the point where we have turned back upon this view, lies a slip
of poor cultivated land, not much wider than the road itself. By this

1443 couple encroaching MS.²: pair trespassing MS.   1445 The *Edd.*: &
the MS.: Their MS.².   *After* swans MS. *deletes*: suits the placid [?]   gentle
moods] *possibly* gentleness   1450 Upon that plain *Edd.*: That plain MS.:
Upon plain MS.².   1451 *After* water MS. *deletes*: is too large   1451–2
these . . . were MS.²: [? they became] MS.   1452 *After* insignificant MS. *deletes*:
but they were often seen to great advantage sailing about in little fleets
but *Edd.*: and MS. *Cf. preceding note.*   1453 they [*second*] MS.²: the breed MS.
1454 *After* numerous MS. *deletes*: & the breed was destroyed in consequence of
complaints made by the property owners of fields bordering the lake that property
was injured [?]   1454–5 being complained of, MS.²: were complained of &
MS.   1455–6 fortunately] *wrongly deleted.*   1456 multiply MS.²: breed in
this number from there MS.   1461 enlivening MS.²: beautifying MS.
1463 harmonize MS.²: harmonizing MS.   1465 horizon MS.²: Landscape
MS.   1466 At the point where MS.: In front of the MS.² (*inserted and not
deleted, but left incomplete in sense*).   1467 poor MS.²: enclosed MS.   *After*
itself MS. *deletes*: divides the road from the water not wider than the water [*sic*]
itself   1467–504 By this appropriation . . . imagined.] *Our transcription is not
always certain, for the deletions, insertions, and rewritings are not clearly distinguishable, and phrases are often barely legible. Underneath the deletions and insertions the
first version can be read with some certainty*: By this enclosure [has been *del.*]
recently made, agriculture has gained little [by it *del.*] & liberty & taste have
lost much. In the wall that bounds this obnoxious enclosure is yet to be seen
the [fr *del.*] [remnant *del.*] of a decaying yew tree in within [*sic*] which some
contemplative [person *del.*] Man had formerly erected a seat capable of holding

appropriation, which has not long been made, agriculture has gained little, & liberty & taste have lost much, for it has shortened a pleasant line of communication [?] [?] which the road on this side [? makes] with   1470
the lake. In the wall that bounds this obnoxious enclosure is yet to be seen the remnant of a decaying Yew tree within which some contemplative Man erected a seat. Here a wayworn traveller might have found a grateful resting-place, protected from the wind or the sun, for the boughs had been trained to bend round the seat and almost embrace   1475
the Person who might occupy the seat within, allowing only an opening for the beautiful landscape. The narrow space between the yew tree & the Lake was scattered over with juniper, furze, heath, & wild time, a pretty range of nature's free ground ill exchanged for a worthless, misshapen field whose smooth surface renders more conspicuous the   1480
meagreness of the soil. These notices are minute, but to the loss [? in] the mind of such a Man as probably constructed the arbour that I have described might be [? considerable] among Life's little changes, & prove a cause of daily regret.

Advancing, we come to the point where the Road for a short space   1485
still lies open to the Lake shore. The traveller may pause and, if on foot, he will be inclined to stretch himself on the slopes back of the common, where he may look round him at liberty, in a situation which, though it be low, will distinctly shew him the character of this Vale. We have already classed it among those of minor interest which make   1490
up for the deficiencies within [their] own circuit by borrowing grandeur & boldness from a distance, and we have slightly sketched the principal features in the view towards the North. [? From] The eastern side of the lake is [?] [? distant] a [? tame] ridge almost covered with

only one person from which the solitary humour of the framer may not unfairly be inferred. Here a wayworn traveller might have found a grateful resting-place for standing by the road side it held out a [?]tious invitation [junipers *del.*] and protected from the wind [& *del.*] or the sun for the boughs had been trained to bend round the seat and almost embrace the Person sitting within allowing only an opening for the beautiful Landscape. The narrow space between the [seat *del.*] Yew tree & the Lake was scattered over with juniper furze heath & wild time.

1469 *After* lost much MS. *deletes:* for it has destroyed a pleasant communication of the high road with   1478 *After* time MS. *deletes:* [? This *or* these] primeval [? growth] converted into misshapened fields whose comparatively smooth surface renders more crude the meagreness of the soil   1481 *After* loss MS. *deletes:* which these changes   in] *possibly* to   1483 might be MS.[2]: & who could MS.   changes MS.[2]: [? things] MS.   1485 Advancing MS.[2]: As MS.   1486 *After* shore MS. *deletes:* we may look round us and repose at liberty here   1488 look MS.[2]: repose MS.   *After* liberty MS. *deletes:* We have already [slightly sketched *del.*] classed this Valley and [? their] the principal features as The view towards the north those which wanting bold & [? dignified] features within their [proper *del.*] own circuit must supply the deficiencies   1490 those MS.[2]: those vales MS.   1491 their own *Edd.*: own MS.   1491–2 grandeur] *G. W. reads:* greatness   1494 tame] *G. W. reads:* bare (*cf.* 1576.)   almost MS.[2]: chiefly MS.

coppice woods, but as we are travelling immediately along its base, 1495
[? we see] too little of this formless ridge to complain of it. The
Western side is formed as if in contrast to this, being entirely broken
from top to bottom into smooth [? round]-topped hills, which have a
remarkable softness of appearance. These hills, with the hedge rows
intersecting them in various directions, and several patches of wood 1500
in different positions upon all of them, impress, as has been observed,
upon that side of the vale a peculiar character, and form some of
the most delightful sheltered situations for houses that can well be
imagined. There are no islands in Esthwaite water. But it has the
further particularity of 2 large round peninsulas on opposite sides of 1505
the Lake, one of which by the form & the manner in which it is attached
to the shore seems to have reminded some one's fancy of the human
ear, for it is called Strickland-ears—perhaps instead of Strickland's ear
the *s* being transferred to the end of the designation that the word may
pass more easily off the tongue.   1510
    The ancient inhabitants have been attracted by the fitness & beauty
of those scites for houses with which the Stranger whose words we
have quoted was smitten, & he might have added to his description
that the ground which he praises is scattered over with chearful &
modest dwellings, standing removed from each other at distances that 1515
allow a domain of land to each sufficient for the maintenance of the
family, yet of that small compass which indicates the moderate desires

1495 but as we are MS.²: as we have been MS.   immediately MS.²: now MS.
its base MS.²: the base of it MS.   1496 we see *Edd.* (*G. W. reads* we see,
*probably because the context calls for something like that, but we do not find these words
in the manuscript. There seems to be one short illegible word.*)   formless ridge] *G. W.*
reads: formality   1499 the] *possibly* their   1501 as has been MS.²: as
some one MS.   1504 in Esthwaite MS.²: upon this Lake MS.   But it MS.²:
but two MS.   1505 *After* large *part of a* MS. *deletion reads:* [? grand *del.*] round
peninsulas these [?] are attached to the shore one of these called Strickland ears as
if the shape & the manner in which it is attached to the shore [?] to have reminded
someone's fancy of human ears One of these called Strickland ears probably [for
del.] instead of Stricklands ear the s being [? transferred] to the end of the word
[? because] it passes more easily off the tongue   1511 attracted by MS.²:
struck with MS.   1514–56 MS. *A is so heavy with deletions and rewritings of
identical phrases and sentences that we will record only those variants which differ markedly
from the revised version in* MS. Prose 23ᵉ.   1514–15 the ground . . . removed
MS.: for the sides of none of those lakes [? have as *del.*] were graced with houses
more suitable in shape & size to their situations or more happily distributed—standing removed MS. *A.*   1514 chearful MS.²: happy looking MS.   1515 *After*
dwellings MS. *deletes:* a [foreigner *del.*] house whose [size *del.*] [? stature *del.*]
figure & appearance proclaim it to be of foreign extraction has indeed lately sprung
among them. [one may be permitted to regret this intrusion as the habitation
which it supplanted *del.*] it has not only supplanted an ancient habitation of most
becoming appearance but has destroyed [interfered with a ⟨?⟩ the ⟨?⟩ *del.*] injuring
[*altered from* injured] the characteristic beauty of the whole scene   1517 family
MS.: household MS. *A.*   yet MS.²: but MS.   which indicates the moderate
MS.²: that seems to express the moderate MS.: that seemed to express [? respect
for *del.*] the moderate MS. *A.*

of the owner & affords the advantages, without the annoyance, of neighbourhood. But the *perfection* in which this characteristic beauty was here exhibited no longer exists; the old habitations of the country are beginning to be supplanted by fabrics which from their size require —what is not always to be obtained—an enlargement of boundary which did not press too closely upon their unambitious predecessors; & under these circumstances, that stile of building & arrangement of ground have been introduced that bespeak a transition from one state of society to another awkwardly & uneasily performed. Here within a circuit where the space of land capable of cultivation is so confined, one may be permitted to repine at such change, both for the suitableness, harmony, & happy equality that have been displaced, & for the disproportions & deformities which mark its commencement & will attend its progress.

They who peruse these pages at a distance from the scene may think that we have already lingered too long in a Vale of so little celebrity. By what has been said, I have wished to mark the character of Esthwaite lake as an individual spot, but the chief interest pertaining to it and to other lakes of the same class is of a general nature. Its waters are pure & crystalline; the breezes have room to play upon its surface, & the strong winds to agitate its depths. No finer net-work is woven than that which light airs frame of its liquid materials, & when its restlessness causes it to sparkle in the sunshine with diamonds, their myriads are not less brilliant than those which deck the stately breast of Windermere or Loch Lomond.

1520

1525

1530

1535

1540

1518 & MS.²: & assuredly MS., MS. *A.*   1519 *After* neighbourhood MS. *A deletes*: Such at least was the happy equality of [?] that nature & society had produced   1521–5 fabrics . . . ground MS.: fabrics [?had require *del.*] for their size require the enlargement all over which they cannot always obtain the destruction of boundaries that did not press too closely upon their humble [*or* ?humbler] predecessors MS. *A.*   1522 obtained MS.²: obtained with MS.   1524 that MS.²: the MS.   1527 land MS.²: ground MS.   1530 disproportions MS.²: gross disproportions MS: flagrant disproportions MS. *A.*   1533 in a Vale MS.: by the side of this Lake MS. *A.*   celebrity. MS.²: celebrity in MS. 1534–5 Esthwaite MS.²: this Lake and MS.   1535 lake MS.²: water MS. 1536 it MS.²: this Lake MS.   *After* it MS. *deletes*: of that   *After* nature MS. *A deletes*: The traveller by A.side will not fail to   1537 crystalline *Edd.*: christeline MS.   1537–42 its surface . . . Lomond] *Some versions of* MS. *A read*: its surface and the network which [faint *del.*] light airs and breath of wind weave upon its restless bos: the points of light which sparkle: diamonds which sparkle in the sun[?shine]: frame of its liquid materials along its surface [is as fine as that which *del.*] equals in fineness that which is woven for the ample surface of Windermere: The myriads of its and [its diamonds *del.*] & its sparkling points of light [?]ts unnumbered [?] as bright as those the sun on [?waterfall *del.*] 1538 No MS.²: The MS.   1539 *After* materials MS. *deletes*: [equals *del.*] is not less fine [*altered to* fineness] than that which is woven for the ample [*blank*] of Windermere or Loch Lomond   1540 sunshine MS.²: sun MS. 1541–2 the stately breast of MS.²: the breast of the most stately Waters MS.

I need not speak of the Water fowl that resort to it from remote regions in winter, nor of the Swallows that wheel round it in summer & are reflected in its smooth mirror, nor of the Boats that glide along 1545 its [? even] bosom, nor of the sports of angling, bathing, or skating, which in the several seasons enliven it from centre to circumference. Imagine to yourself the change which the variegated scene in front of which we are now resting undergoes when the abstractions of twilight have begun to take place among its forms, & when its colours retire 1550 before the shadows of approaching night; those numerous hills, which we now behold rising side by side & above each other on the opposite shore, pass gradually away from the sight till at length, with their cottages & fields & single trees, they have departed altogether, & the whole tract of ground assumes the appearance of one uniform mass, 1555 black & steep as a wall, insurmountable & uninhabitable. Above the summit, large clouds are perhaps poised in the firmament, with openings in them thro' which a radiance overshooting the gloom projected from the precipice finds its way to the still bosom of the lake.

Mid the dark steep's repose the shadowy streams, 1560
As touch'd with dawning moonlight['s] hoary gleams
Where'er the faint breeze is stirring on the deep,
Soft o'er the surface the pale lustres creep
Pursuing & pursued; at once the bright
Gains on the shade, the shade upon the light. 1565
Fair Spirits are abroad in sportive chase
Brushing with lucid wands the Water's face,
Wide field of calm delight in which they frame
The pensive measures of a noiseless game.

At the entrance of the Village of Sawrey, we take our leave of the 1570 Vale of Esthwaite, but first looking back, we see the Langdale Pikes

1543 resort MS.²: come MS.   1544 in winter MS.²: to enliven it in winter MS.   Swallows MS.²: wheeling Swallows [which *del.*] that in summer MS. 1545 the Boats MS.²: the few boats MS. *A.*   1547 *After* which MS. *A deletes*: draw the inhabitants of   1548 change MS.²: appearance of MS.: appearance of the scene MS. *A.*   variegated MS.²: many featured MS.   in front of MS.²: near MS.   1549 resting MS., MS. *A*²: resting at the approach of twilight MS. *A.*   1550 have begun MS.²: are beginning MS.   among its forms MS., MS. *A*²: upon it MS. *A.*   its colours MS.: its gay & diversified coulors [*sic*] MS. *A.*   retire MS.³: are fading MS.: [? retiring] MS.²: are subdued by [?] shadows MS. *A.*   1552 we now behold MS.²: we have described as MS. 1553 gradually MS.²: imperceptibly MS.   1554 departed altogether MS.²: disappeared altogether MS.: wholly disappeared MS. *A.*   1554–6 the whole . . . mass, black MS.²: the whole becomes [to the eye MS. *A*] one gloomy mass [black MS. *A*] steep MS., MS. *A.*   1557 summit MS.²: summit of this gloomy precipice MS.   1560 streams MS.²: gleams MS.   1561 with dawning MS.²: with hoary MS.   moonlight's *Edd.*: moonlight MS.   1564 Pursuing & pursued MS.³: 'Tis restless magic all MS.: with [*blank*] interchange MS.². 1571 but MS.²: & here MS.

towering above the intervening hills, more conspicuous than before & in connection with a more splendid plain of Water, but the Town & Church of Hawkshead are now hidden from the view. In justice to this Vale I must say that of all approaches to it that from Coniston is the worst; we entered upon it cross wise & fronting the tame ridge, which forms its eastern boundary; and pursuing our way by the Lake side, if we had not looked back, we must have missed the most interesting combinations of scenery. Approached lengthways either from Ambleside on the North or from the South by either side of the lake, the Vale of Hawkshead wants neither beauty nor dignity. They who may have time will be repaid by making the Tour of the Lake; it is seen to advantage from the top of a small hill, over which the road passes about a 1/4 of a mile from Hawkshead on the side opposite to that which we have taken; & when the last farm house on that side of the Vale is reached, it would be well to ascend some height the road which there branches off toward Ulverstone. The Lake from both these points is boldly broken by its peninsulas; the former view is well closed by Gommer's How, a [? communicating] Fell that rises from the farther shore of Windermere, & the latter by the capacious [? bosom] of Rydale head.

1575

1580

1585

1590

Borrowdale

"Where dost thou lie, thou thinly peopled green,
Thou nameless lawn, & Village yet unseen,

1572 towering MS.[2]: still towering MS.   conspicuous MS.[2]: conspicuously MS.   1575 Coniston MS.[2]: Coniston along which our road has led us MS. 1578 missed MS.[2]: lost MS.   1580 South MS.[2]: Ferry house at Windermere on the MS.   1581 Hawkshead wants . . . dignity] MS.[2] *deletes but makes no substitution*: Hawkshead appears [?] MS.   They MS.[2]: It is a MS. 1582 *After* Lake MS. *deletes*: & upon reconsideration I do not scruple to advise those   1583 over MS.[3]: on the MS.: about MS.[2].   1587 toward MS.[2]: to [*undel.*] MS.   both MS.[2]: this MS.   1589 *After* How MS. *deletes*: which Mountain rises from the: belonging to the eastern bank   communicating] *G. W. reads*: considerable rises MS.[2]: makes [?] MS.   1591/2 *In* MSS. Verse 57 *Wordsworth began a description of a tour from Ambleside to Keswick. Because he quickly abandoned it, we regard the fragment as the equivalent of a deletion, and merely record it here, as appropriately following the approach to Windermere and preceding the description of Borrowdale; the first two paragraphs below are in Mary Wordsworth's hand*:

From Ambleside to Keswick [enquires *del.*] [says *del.*] (explains the bustling leader of a party of Tourists, glancing his eye carelessly on the map in his hand or casting a look towards the clouds for information concerning the state of the weather) is how far? 16 miles. Is there any thing worthy of notice on the road? Nothing but what all Travellers see as they pass along—will probably be the answer of mine host of the Salutation if the question be asked at the height of the season & he is anxious to have his horses back again for a fresh job & the Post boy will confirm the [observation *del.*] asseveration if necessary for it being a point of feeling with him to hate all stoppages for which he does not receive extra pay. Humanity for his horses also will interfere if his [judg *del.*] mind be unbiassed by

Where sons, contented with their native ground,   1595
Ne'er wandered further than ten furlongs round
And the tann'd Peasant & his ruddy bride
Were born together & together died."

Surely if the Poet had beheld Borrowdale with the sun shining upon it, he would have exclaimed, this is the very spot which I have long 1600 sighed for, or this is the true lurking place of romantic felicity. Hither his Lycoris would instantly have been invited. After possession taken in her name of the newly discovered region, with all due rights & ceremonies, hither she would have been summoned to reign in uninterrupted peace over all the beauty that surrounds her. Alas, the love- 1605 sick Author of this empassioned ejaculation lived in the days of Queen Anne & King William, & chaunted at great length & in courtly strains the praises of Kensington gardens: Strange choice for a Man whose heart was rural, who had been educated into the possession of a fine ballad fancy, & whose birthplace was within a short walk of the banks 1610 of one of the most romantic rivers in the world, this very Derwent,

selfish expectation & the[ir *del.*] patient & solid claims to consideration of his old companions will be more regarded than the curiosity of a Stranger which he deems odd and fantastic.
    But are there not some celebrated Waterfalls not far from the road? Oh yes, Sir, I had forgotten them replies the [the *Edd.*: to MS.] veracious informant apparently [anxious *del.*] thankful to be set right you must allight [*sic*] in the Village of Rydal & they may be seen in 1/2 an hour. That 1/2 hour is given to the purpose for usage & fashion require it & for the rest of the journey the Party are contented with what they can collect [? for the *del.*] by their eyes some from the barouche box others from their seat in the open Landau with occasional upstandings upon especial summons or with the presentations through the windows of a close Chariot as the several vehicles are [driven *del.*] whirled along at the rate of 7 miles an hour.
    Wordsworth's hand writes an earlier version of the end of the fragment: and for the rest of the journey the party [proceed *del.*] are contented with what they can collect with their eyes from the barouch box, [and *del.*] others [with occa *del.*] from the seat of the open Landau, with occasional upstandings upon especial invitation or with such [appearances *del.*] as [?] presentations of through the loopholes of a close Chariot as the several vehicles whirl along at the rate of 7 miles an hour—But if the Author is to proceed at this rate what must become of the Book which he has undertaken to write—or [if you will *del.*]—to make—No—shall he [?] the next act [?] he has his staff in his hand—the satchel by his side, [as ⟨?⟩ *del.*] or his knapsack at his back [*the rest is illegible*].
    1599–614 Surely . . . must be, MS.: When the Poet asked himself this question wishing [to be directed to a spot *del.*] in a fit of love-sick imagination for a reality that might correspond with the image of his [fancy *del.*] mind & where he & the Object of his passion might consume their lives in romantic felicity he would have been satisfied if [directed *del.*] from the more open country where he himself was born he had traced upward the River Derwent [from the ⟨?⟩ *del.*] till he [reached the ⟨? fertile⟩ *del.*] approached its source among the recesses of Borrowdale [which were *del.*] a region at that time [almost wholly shut out from the *del.*] not only removed as it still is MS. *A*.   1602 taken MS.²: would have been taken MS.
1603 region] *possibly* regions   1604–5 uninterrupted peace MS.²: endless peace & unenvied glory MS.   1609 who . . . possession of MS.²: who possessing MS.

which if he had traced it upwards, would have conducted him to these
fascinating recesses, at that time not only removed as they still are,
& ever must be, from the broad high way of traffic & business, but
unpenetrated by general or even accidental curiosity. Doubtless the   1615
solitude of a plain might have satisfied such cravings as completely;
a Man may live as much lost to the world, both in reality & to his own
belief, in a level or in an undulating district that affords no commanding
elevation as in any composition of country whatever; but this is not an
impression of first sight, & if the Forest of Arden was spread over a   1620
flat region, the favourite solitudes of Greece were constructed of other
materials:

> —'This corner of Arcadia here,
> This little angle of the world you see,
> Which hath shut out of door all earth beside   1625
> And is barred up with mountains & with rocks,
> Has had no intertrading with the rest
> Of men, nor yet will have, but here alone,
> Quite out of fortune's way & underneath
> Ambition & desire that weighs them not,   1630
> They live still as in the golden age
> Whenas the world was in its pupilage.'

The Poet Gray, not fifty years ago, though a road for wheeled
carriages had at that time been opened out to connect Borrowdale with
Keswick, could not, as he travelled along, preserve himself from being   1635
daunted by the large masses of fallen rock, scattered about on every
side, & by others hanging from the heights above, as if at any moment
they might be loosened from their hold by the slightest disturbance in
the air. 'Non ragioniam di lor ma guarda e passa', was the exhortation
which the recollection of his feelings suggested, the extravagant   1640
apprehensions of a mind somewhat weakened by ill health. But certainly the passage must originally have been most difficult, if it be true,
what I have often heard, that the inhabitants of this Vale were in the

1613 fascinating *Edd.*: facinating MS.   1615 *After* curiosity MS. *A
erratically inserts some nearly illegible phrases, which may be conjecturally read*: For
But if the forest in Arden were spread the Solitude of Greece were constructed
or this the   1626 is MS., MS. *A²*: are MS. *A.*   1633 not fifty MS.: a
little more than forty MS. *A.*   1635 as he travelled along MS.: *not in* MS.
A.   1637 & by MS. *A, Edd.*: & from MS.   1638 loosened MS., MS.
A²: detached MS. *A.*   1639–41 was the . . . apprehensions MS.²: This is the
extravagance of a mind MS. *A*: This is the [extravagant MS. *A²*] apprehension
of a delicate MS., MS. *A²*.   1641–2 But . . . difficult MS.: but certain it is that
[in former times *del.*] before his time this passage must have been most difficult and
consequently Borrowdale [? to all *del.*] apparently cut off from all communication
with the world MS. *A.*   1643 the inhabitants of this Vale MS.: the inhabitants
of Borrowdale MS. *A*: its inhabitants MS. *A²*.

practice of attending the market of Ambleside in preference to that of Keswick. It is certain that to Ambleside they were accustomed to carry 1645 the yarn which had been spun in their houses over a succession of rough & high ridges that divide Stonethwaite from Grasmere, where are faint traces of a path called footman's-gate & not far distant from it may be discerned some vestiges of a road by which Horses might have ascended, though not without considerable ingenuity & courage both 1650 on their part & that of their conductors.

While they existed with these natural impediments to communication with their neighbours, whose experience was comparatively more diversified, the Inhabitants of Borrowdale fell under the reproach of being stupidly ignorant & implicitly credulous. The inharmonious 1655 name of *Gowk*, coupled with the word Borrowdale, designated the natives of this Valley, & the old story of a contrivance of the graver Inhabitants to detain a Cuckoo, that had made its appearance among them, by enclosing it within a wall served to insinuate what more than Gothamites must they be, who having such ramparts thrown round 1660 them by Nature could imagine that any petty addition from their labours would assist in confining a winged creature, to whom the space above his head was open & who was willing to escape. At present the people of Borrowdale do not appear less knowing or less capable of suiting their means to their ends than any of their neighbours, while 1665

1644 practice MS.², MS. *A*: habit MS.   market MS.², MS. *A*: markets MS.
1646–7 the yarn . . . over a [high & ⟨?⟩*del.*] succession . . . that divide MS.: their Yarn over a high ridge that divides MS. *A*.   1648 not . . . from it MS., MS. *A*²: not far from which MS. *A*.   1649 discerned MS.: discovered MS. *A*. a road MS., MS. *A*²: a horse road MS. *A*.   1650 ascended . . . ingenuity MS.: passed though with no little ingenuity MS. *A*.   1652 While . . . natural MS., MS. *A*³: Thus separated by natural MS. *A*: While they existed almost wholly MS. *A*². 1652–3 impediments to communication MS.²: barriers rendering it difficult for them to [have communication MS. *A*] communicate MS., MS. *A*².   1653–4 whose . . . diversified MS.: who had an experience comparatively more various MS. *A*. 1654 the reproach MS., MS. *A*²: a stigma MS. *A*.   1655 being . . . credulous MS.: extreme ignorance & simplicity a stigma which through change of circumstance is now going out of memory MS. *A*.   1656–8 coupled . . . Cuckoo, that MS.: was often coupled [to *del.*] with the [name of *del.*] word Borrowdale & applied to the natives of the Valley [& stories *del.*] [& the old Gothamite story of walling *del.*] an the [*sic*] old story of a [wall *del.*] [a resolution *del.*] contrivance of the graver part of the Inhabitants to [? take *del.*] detain a coucoo which MS. *A*.   1659 enclosing . . . wall MS.²: wailing it in MS., MS. *A*.   served MS.³: was [? famili] MS.: was applied MS.².   1659–62 served . . . creature MS.: was [maliciously *del.*] applied to these [secluded Mountaineers *del.*] sequestered Dalesmen [At present they do not appear in any quality of mind or body or in attainments at all inferior to their Neighbours *del.*] Dalesmen in a malicious spirit that meant to insinuate what more than Gothamites must these be, who having such "barriers" [erected *del.*] thrown round them by Nature [to *del.*] imagine that any petty addition of theirs could be more efficacious to confine a creature MS. *A*.   1662 space MS., MS. *A*²: region MS. *A*.   1664 appear MS.²: appear to be MS., MS. *A*.   1664–5 less . . . any of MS.: in attainments or in any qualities of mind or body at all inferior to MS. *A*.

the region which they inhabit may be said to surpass in variety &
beauty any other part of the Country.

I will not attempt to describe it by rule & compass, but will venture
to affirm that if the old topographer Michael Drayton had summoned
this Vale to a contest with the proudest of Albion, while he would not   1670
have suffered it, in resounding its own panegyric, to be silent upon the
peculiarity of its wealthy mines of Black lead, the song would have
been lengthened out by applauding the store of more poetical images
which its dominion contains or commands. Schafell or Great Gavel
would have been invited to act as Umpire, & Borrowdale, setting forth   1675
her own beauties, would have availed herself of the little central hill
of Rosthwaite; she would have called on him to speak for her, & to
declare with what pleasure he looks over the ivied cottages & Hamlets,
clustering round & under him for protection, to the three grand divisions of which her domain is composed. The little Hill, encouraged by   1680
this election, would have been introduced declaring that no spot in the
world presented a scene more attractive than lay before him when he
looked eastward in the morning over Stonethwaite, gracefully winding
a plain of cornfields & green meadows under threatening rocks & precipices, which cannot be seen without wonder that they do not mar or   1685
destroy a surface so soft & smooth, instead of guarding it as a cherished
contrast to their own ruggedness. Southward I behold Seathwaite, &

1666 may be said to surpass MS.: surpasses MS. *A*: may be said perhaps to surpass MS. *A²*.   1668–9 I will . . . that if MS.: Borrowdale is a [? three] [?]
Valley looked at from the central hill above Rosthwaite presents to the eye three
grand divisions which may be called forks to which that hill is the common centre
MS. *A*: If MS. *A²*.   1669 old MS.²: old poetical MS. *A*, MS.   Drayton
had MS.: Drayton [had *del.*] who called upon so many Rivers Mountains & Vallies
to [pronounce their own panegyrics *del.*] [contend with each other for *del.*] prefer
their claims for admiration [? and *del.*] in rivalship with each other had MS. *A*.
summoned MS. *A*, MS.²: summoned in his happiest manner MS.   1670 to a
contest MS.: MS. *A almost illegibly deletes*: to a [?] put in its claim in like manner
though: to the same kind of contest MS. *A²*.   1671 suffered it MS., MS. *A²*:
forgotten [?] MS. *A*.   resounding MS.: pronouncing MS. *A*.   1672 mines
of Black lead MS.: black lead mines MS. *A*.   1672–3 the song . . . out MS.,
MS. *A²*: he would have lengthened out its song MS. *A*.   1673 by applauding
the store MS.: in applauding the inexhaustible store MS. *A*.   1674–9 [The
central MS.] Schafell . . . for protection MS.²: The Umpire [would have been
called upon *del.*] invited to take his station upon the central hill [of
del.] above Rosthwaite & thence to look over the ivied cottages of the hamlet
which had clustered round & under it for protection MS. *A*.   1675 & Borrowdale MS.²: & to listen to praises MS.   1678 over MS.²: upon MS.   1680 her
MS.: the MS. *A*.   1680–3 The little . . . over Stonethwaite MS.: [His
eye *del.*] would have been directed [? *del.*] eastward to Stonethwaite MS. *A*.
1684 a plain of MS.: its fertile plain [under *del.*] of MS. *A*.   1684–5 precipices . . . be seen MS.: abrupt precipices [that seem jealously to guard a ⟨? surface⟩
Soft & smooth ⟨*altered from* Softness & smoothness⟩ *del.*] which [so strikingly contrast with their own ruggedness *del.*] cannot be looked at MS. *A*.   1686 cherished]
not in MS. *A*.   1687 Southward *Edd.*: [? Northward] MS.   1687–90 Southward . . . birthplace MS.: Seathwaite the southern division of the Vale would

with a loud voice will sing the praises of its torrents, in stormy weather
spouting from its lofty sides & clearing like rival leapers the obstacles
opposed to them. Seathwaite, the birthplace of Derwent, little dis- 1690
coloured by tempestuous seasons & at other times the most pellucid
of all rivers. Seathwaite, where Nature has raised a temple of everlasting Yew trees & hollowed out a nook beautified by the hamlet of
Seatoller. Triumphantly would he have boasted of the treasures not
concealed from him toward the North. The rocks & woods guarding 1695
the entrance of Borrowdale rival the Trossachs or Loch Katrine in
intricate enchantment. Castle crag, springing out from the midst of
them, crowned with the antiquated circle of a Roman encampment;
beneath, the huge mass of Bowder Stone, lying like a stranded Vessel
whose hour of danger is no more. And behold the Eagle upon the wing, 1700
retaining her empire when that ambitious People who adopted her
image for their standard have for ages been but a name, and the Bull
heard from a distance is provoking himself in the meadows of Stonethwaite till he is maddened by the reverberations of his own bellow.
Before this point of the contest, Borrowdale would have resumed her 1705
own encomium and would have continued luxuriating in the attractions of her heights & hollows. Her tributary glen of Watenlath would
have been commended for that littleness which is a grace, as it aids

have been praised [as the ⟨? source⟩ of Derwent the most pellucid of all rivers *del.*]
for the torrents which in stormy weather spout from its lofty sides [which seem
del.] clearing like an experienced leaper the barrier opposed to them, and as the
birthplace MS. *A*.

    1690 the birthplace MS.², MS. *A*.: play-ground MS.   1691 pellucid MS.
A, *Edd.*: pelucid MS.   1692–3 Seathwaite [that contains MS.], where . . .
a nook MS.²: Nor would its everlasting yew trees have been forgotten nor that
enviable nook MS. *A*.   1694–7 Triumphantly would he have [recorded
his ⟨? northern⟩ MS.] boasted . . . Castle crag MS.²: To the north in the compartment of [?] triumphantly would have been pointed out the [intricate *del.*]
rocks & woods that rival the trossachs in intricacy and guard the entrance of
Borrowdale. And Castle Crag MS. *A*.   1695 North *Edd.*: South MS.
1697 out from MS.: up from MS. *A*.   1699 beneath, the MS.: Beneath
lies MS. *A*.   mass MS., MS. *A*²: hulk MS. *A*.   1699–1700 lying . . . no
more MS.: like the hulk [of *Edd.*] a stranded vessel MS. *A*.   1700–2 And
behold the Eagle [soaring above & en MS.] upon . . . but a MS.²: The Eagle is
soaring above retaining his Empire when the [? adventurous] people who adopted
his image for their Standard are but a MS. *A*.   1704 maddened MS.: rendered
half mad MS. *A*.   bellow MS.: bellowing MS. *A*.   1705 Before MS.²:
Long Before MS.   1705–14 MS. *A concludes, in the hand of Wordsworth,
with the following*: [Such are the *del.*] Will the reader accept with indulgence this
rapid survey of the objects of admiration or wonder which a poetical topographer
would enlarge upon in sounding the praises of Borrowdale without speaking of the
[adjoining & tributary *del.*] small glen of Watenlath whose littleness is a grace as it
aids concealment or of the [majesty of *del.*] mountain of Skiddaw & the lake of
Derwent, both, from many points brought within the range of his eye whose
curiosity leads him to ascend the sides of the hills in which Borrowdale is immediately embosomed, and [adding *del.*] [? distances] to rich landscapes of which the
vast hollows of Borrowdale is the foreground

concealment. She would have laid claim to [? illustrations] from the spacious Lake of Derwent, and distant Skiddaw brought within the range of the ascending Shepherd's eye, and would have concluded by exclaiming: my vast excavation fears not to be seen from numberless points that command the distant ocean with all its sunshine & its sunless blackness.

But we live in a timid age of taste, and he who would escape censure must confine himself to a humbler strain. The characteristics of this vale are so well adapted to make their way to the human heart that I was pleased, without being surprized, when I read in The Register of its births, its Marriages, and its deaths a few words attached to the name of a young man, which recorded that having quitted Borrowdale to establish himself in a seaport Town of Cumberland, he was there seized with a mortal sickness & before his death expressed a wish that his remains might be carried back to his native Vale & deposited in the School (a division of the Chapel), at the foot of a pillar that neighboured his accustomed seat among his happy companions.

With this little anecdote drawn from an obscure source, I might conclude, but the lover of truth will forgive me, though he may be startled, when he is informed that among the inhabitants of this deeply

1710 Lake of Derwent MS.²: Derwentwater MS.   1711 ascending Shepherd's MS.²: the Shepherd who ascends MS.   and would MS.²: & finally MS. 1712 excavation MS.²: hollow MS.   fears not to be MS.²: does not shrink from being MS.   1713 all its sunshine MS.²: fields of light MS.   1715 he MS.³: it MS.: if I MS.².   1716 must confine MS.²: I must descend MS. characteristics MS.²: beauties MS.   1717 well adapted MS.²: manifold and MS.   1719 a few words MS.²: of a Youth MS.   1720 Borrowdale MS.²: this native Vale MS.   1724–5 that neighboured . . . companions MS.²: close to which he had been accustomed to sit while a School boy MS. 1728–87 *This portion of the* MS. *revises and expands an early draft immediately preceding it; omitting most of the rewritings and deletions, we here record this draft*: the inhabitants of this deeply sequestered spot have not been more able than the rest of mankind to resist the temptations to which circumstances have exposed them. The bounty of their mines was a bane to their: among the inhabitants of this deeply sequestered spot the agitations of gaming were prevalent. This Arcadia in outward appearance was heretofore plentifully stocked with pilferers & gamesters: the book of Hoyle . . . occurrence [*almost identical with* 1730–2]: In fact, the discovery of the vein of black lead unsettled the peaceful spirit of Borrowdale & broke in upon the [regularity *del.*] even tenor of its pastoral & rural labours. This mineral rose to so high a price that the beds of the torrents were eagerly explored for a substance that had been slighted as of no value & which was neither protected by any interest attached to its name nor for the uses to which the Possessors could apply it. Hence more than hesperian watchfulness was necessary to guard their property & some of the stoutest of the Youth of Borrowdale were brought to their graves by maladies caught in night watchings to acquire what the laws of: to acquire from the mouth of the mine a product: to acquire [? about *or* above] the tempting [? shop] a product of nature which the laws of the land had assigned to others. These precautions have ceased. Such pains-taking was often successful & extravagant hopes & comparatively inordinate desires with a train [of *Edd.*] novel & reprehensible indulgences were the unavoidable consequences of such incitement. It can scarcely . . . [almost

sequestered spot the agitations of gaming were prevalent in an extraordinary degree, that the book of Hoyle was a favourite study of the 1730
wealthier Yeomen, & that if 30 or 40 Guineas were won & lost in
the course of one evening at whist, it was no unusual occurrence. The
Chamois chaser of Switzerland, an enslaved adherent of fortune, daily
stakes his life against a few pieces of silver, the value of the creature
which he chases. He is a noble kind of gamester, & it affords corre- 1735
spondent pleasure to follow him through those perils which he does
not doubt will one day terminate in his death; his presence dignifies
the objects thro' which he pursues his career. So in no small degree
does a Cumbrian Shepherd attending upon his flock among the mountains, but the Card Table, however desperate its hazards to the purse, 1740
however pregnant its issues with exaltation or dejection, furnishes an
unacceptable object in the foreground of the landscapes of Borrowdale.

> His Sires, perchance, in Fairy land might dwell,
> Sicilian groves or Vales of Arcady,
> But *he*, I ween, was of the *north country*.   1745

In short, he was a human being, & attractive as may be the moral
sentiments which greeted us on our entrance into Borrowdale, we shall
be less inclined to [? shrink] from these unobvious realities if we reflect
that a love of violent emotions, a delight in the fluctuations of hope &
fear, & an eagerness to attain an object through means more [? promis- 1750
ing to the passionate than the ⟨?⟩] are indispensible stimulants to
prevent tranquillity from settling into stagnation & ease into listlessness; that without their intervention, content would be undermined by
indifference & indifference sink under the weight of apathy.

It is superfluous to enquire how habits & dispositions by which 1755
mankind are distinguished in all states of society & in every condition
acquired an unusual strength in this particular spot. But it seems not
improbable that a material which the Reader is daily holding in his
hand in the familiar shape of a Pencil may have contributed to produce
these local injuries in this remote part of the island. The mineral 1760
known by the name of wad, or black lead, notwithstanding its repute

identical *with* 1779–87, *except for* precious mineral *instead of* valuable ore *in*
1782–3].
    Immediately following, at the top of an otherwise blank page, Wordsworth writes:
To forsake mischief & to defy [? danger] when the evil may be [? eluded] or overcome, all Men

1732 unusual MS.²: uncommon MS.   1733 an enslaved MS.²: a bold MS.
daily *Edd.*: who daily MS.   1736 those perils] *altered from* [? the perils]
1738 So MS.²: Some portion of this MS.   1741 exaltation MS.²: joy MS.
1754 under MS.²: with MS.   1755 is MS.²: seems MS.   how MS.²: why
MS.   1759 contributed MS.²: contributed greatly MS.   1760 injuries
MS.²: effects MS.

for medicinal virtues, was long deemed not too precious to be applied to a purpose for which the most coarse material of colouring would have answered as well: viz., that of marking Sheep. But with the spread of refinements thro' the nations of Europe, it rose to so high a price 1765 that the beds of the torrents were eagerly explored for it, & more than Hesperian watchfulness became necessary on the part of the owners to guard from depredation a property which was not like the precious metals protected by an interest attached to its name, nor by the uses to which it had been applied by those to whose hands chance & nature 1770 had often presented it. Strange stories are told of the desperate attempts to rob the Stewards of the accumulated ore, & many of the stoutest Youth of Borrowdale were brought to their graves by maladies caught in night watchings about the Mouth of the mine to acquire a product of the mountains which the laws of the land had assigned to 1775 others. This pains-taking was often successful, & extravagant expectations & comparatively inordinate longings with a train of novel & reprehensible indulgences could not [but] be the consequence of these irregular incitements. It can scarcely be said any longer to exist, but the little cottage gardens of Borrowdale at this day frequently remind 1780 those who cultivate them of the trespasses & adventures of their predecessors by surrendering up to the spade small pieces of this valuable ore, which must have been secreted in the soil without having been found again. A deterioration of morals thus derived may remind the serious reader of the clause in our daily prayer, "Lead us not into 1785 temptation, but deliver us from evil"—as if temptation were the greatest of evils, & yet without trial there can be no virtue.

1763 of MS.²: for MS.   1764 with the spread MS.³: it rose [in course MS.] at length MS.².   1767 became MS.²: was MS.   1772 rob the Stewards MS.²: tear from the Mine MS.   1773 were brought MS.²: are known MS.   1777 longings MS.²: desires MS.   1778 but] *inadvertently om.*   1778–9 these . . . incitements] *possibly* this . . . incitement 1784 morals MS.²: manners & morals MS.   may MS.²: will MS.   1787 evils MS.²: all evils MS.

APPENDIX III

[The Sublime and the Beautiful]

. . . amongst them. It is not likely that a person so situated, provided his imagination be exercised by other intercourse, as it ought to be, will become, by any continuance of familiarity, insensible to sublime impressions from the scenes around him. Nay, it is certain that his conceptions of the sublime, far from being dulled or narrowed by   5
commonness or frequency, will be rendered more lively & comprehensive by more accurate observation and by encreasing knowledge. Yet, tho' this effect will take place with respect to grandeur, it will be much more strikingly felt in the influences of beauty. Neither the immediate nor final cause of this need here be examined; yet we may observe that,   10
though it is impossible that a mind can be in a healthy state that is not frequently and strongly moved both by sublimity and beauty, it is more dependent for its daily well-being upon the love & gentleness which accompany the one, than upon the exaltation or awe which are created by the other.—Hence, as we advance in life, we can escape upon the   15
invitation of our more placid & gentle nature from those obtrusive qualities in an object sublime in its general character; which qualities, at an earlier age, precluded imperiously the perception of beauty which that object if contemplated under another relation would have been capable of imparting. I need not observe to persons at all conversant in   20
these speculations that I take for granted that the same object may be both sublime & beautiful; or, speaking more accurately, that it may have the power of affecting us both with the sense of beauty & the sense of sublimity; tho' (as for such Readers I need not add) the mind cannot be affected by both these sensations at the same time, for they   25
are not only different from, but opposite to, each other. Now a Person unfamiliar with the appearances of a Mountainous Country is, with

1 them. MS.²: them & [? hence] [? the *or* ? tho] MS.   2 be exercised MS.²,
Edd.: be cultivated MS.³: have been exercised MS.³.   5 far . . . dulled MS.³:
so far from dulling his pleasure [sensibility MS.²] MS.   6 will MS.²: it
will MS. *An insertion above the deletion may be conjecturally read*: as the health [?]
every kind is   8–9 will . . . beauty MS.²: is in beauty MS.   9 beauty
MS.²: beauty upon his mind MS.   13 well-being *Edd.*: welfare MS.: wel-
being MS.².   15 life MS.²: life those more obvious featur MS.   17–18 which
qualities at an earlier age [ex MS.³] precluded imperiously the MS.⁴: which
may have [prevented MS.] excluded the MS.².   18–19 which that object . . .
been MS.²: which if contemplated under another relation it is MS.   21 the
same MS.²: an MS.   25 time, for *Edd.*: time for, MS.   26 other. Now
MS.²: other. The primary element in the sense of beauty is a distinct perception of
parts MS.   Person MS.²: Stranger MS.   27 unfamiliar MS.³: unf MS.: who
MS.².   is, with MS.³: stands MS.: is in MS.².

respect to its more conspicuous sublime features, in a situation resembling that of a Man of mature years when he looked upon such objects with the eye of childhood or youth. There appears to be something 30 ungracious in this observation; yet it is nevertheless true, & the fact is mentioned both for its connection with the present work & for the importance of the general truth. Sensations of beauty & sublimity impress us very early in life; nor is it easy to determine which have precedence in point of time, & to which the sensibility of the mind in 35 its natural constitution is more alive. But it may be confidently affirmed that, where the beautiful & the sublime co-exist in the same object, if that object be new to us, the sublime always precedes the beautiful in making us conscious of its presence—but all this may be both tedious & uninstructive to the Reader, as I have not explained what I mean 40 by either of the words *sublime* or *beautiful*; nor is this the place to enter into a general disquisition upon the subject, or to attempt to clear away the errors by which it has been clouded.—But as I am persuaded that it is of infinite importance to the noblest feelings of the Mind & to its very highest powers that the forms of Nature should be accurately 45 contemplated, &, if described, described in language that shall prove that we understand the several grand constitutional laws under which it has been ordained that these objects should everlastingly affect the mind, I shall deem myself justified in calling the Reader, upon the present humble occasion, to attend to a few words which shall be said upon two 50 of these principal laws: the law of sublimity and that of beauty. These shall be considered so far at least as they may be collected from the objects amongst which we are about to enter, viz., those of a mountainous region—and to begin with the sublime as it exists in such landscape. 55

Let me then invite the Reader to turn his eyes with me towards that cluster of Mountains at the Head of Windermere; it is probable that they will settle ere long upon the Pikes of Langdale & the black preci-

29 of a Man MS.³: of a child MS.: in which MS.².   33 truth] *Possibly* truths *as originally written; the downward stroke at the end of the word may be either part of the* s *or a mark of deletion.*   39–58 making us ... Pikes MS. Prose 28ᵃ: MS. Prose 28ᵇ *deletes*: making us conscious of its presence. This is so strikingly true with respect to the forms of Nature that the qualities of beauty will almost be entirely overlooked by a Spectator in an object where they may exist [are *undel.* MS.²] [involved MS.²] in a sublime object with which he may be unfamiliar. [As I do not⟨mean *del.*⟩ wish to weary the Reader with dry & abstract *undel.*] speculations I will at once refer to the [a MS.²] mountainous Country, as into such we are about to enter, in illustration of my notions of the sublime as it exists in landscape. [Let us *undel.*] fix [turn MS.²] our eyes together upon [towards MS.²] that cluster of mountains at the head of Windermere they [it MS.²] is probable that they will settle ere [long upon the Pikes *undel.*]   42 into *Edd.*: upon into MS. 44 noblest ... Mind MS.²: the mind MS.   46 described, MS.²: described in appropriate lang MS.   49 deem *Edd.*: deemed MS.   52 so far at least as MS.³: so far as MS.: not in so far MS.².   57–8 it ... they MS.²: they MS.

pice contiguous to them.—If these objects be so distant that, while we look at them, they are only thought of as the crown of a comprehen- 60 sive Landscape; if our minds be not perverted by false theories, unless those mountains be seen under some accidents of nature, we shall receive from them a grand impression, and nothing more. But if they be looked at from a point which has brought us so near that the mountain is almost the sole object before our eyes, yet not so near but that 65 the whole of it is visible, we shall be impressed with a sensation of sublimity.—And if this is analyzed, the body of this sensation would be found to resolve itself into three component parts: a sense of individual form or forms; a sense of duration; and a sense of power. The whole complex impression is made up of these elementary parts, & the 70 effect depends upon their co-existence. For, if any one of them were abstracted, the others would be deprived of their power to affect.

I first enumerated individuality of form; this individual form was then invested with qualities and powers, ending with duration. Duration is evidently an element of the sublime; but think of it without 75 reference to individual form, and we shall perceive that it has no power to affect the mind. Cast your eye, for example, upon any commonplace ridge or eminence that cannot be separated, without some effort of the mind, from the general mass of the planet; you may be persuaded, nay, convinced, that it has borne that shape as long as or longer than Cader 80 Idris, or Snowdon, or the Pikes of Langdale that are before us; and the mind is wholly unmoved by the thought; and the only way in which such an object can affect us, contemplated under the notion of duration, is when the faint sense which we have of its individuality is lost in the general sense of duration belonging to the Earth itself. Prominent 85 individual form must, therefore, be conjoined with duration, in order that Objects of this kind may impress a sense of sublimity; and, in the works of Man, this conjunction is, for obvious reasons, of itself sufficient for the purpose. But in works of Nature it is not so: with these must be combined impressions of power, to a sympathy with & a 90

63 receive MS.²: pro[?] receive MS.   66 visible, *Edd.*: visible: if this be analyzed MS: visible: MS.².   67 And if this is MS.³: This if MS.: and if this were MS.².   would MS.²: will MS.   68 three MS.²: four MS. 69 *After* forms MS. *deletes*: —of motion, abrupt, rapid or precipitous as expressed by the [? lin *del.*] outlines of the mountain before us   73 individuality of form MS.²: individual form MS.   ,   80 than MS.²: than the pikes MS. 80–1 Cader Idris *Edd.*: Caderideris MS.   84–5 in the general sense MS.²: under the feeling MS.   85 Prominent MS.²: [? to] MS.   86 conjoined MS.²: combined MS.   87 may impress a MS.²: must be conjoined to impress us with the MS.   87–8 and . . . Man MS.²: but in the works of Nature MS. 89 with MS.²: but MS.   90 *After* power MS. *deletes*: as produced by lines [? for] the production of pleasure & pain, good or evil change for the overcoming of resistance and the production of change for fear, for pleasure and pain, for good and for evil. These feelings are conveyed.

participation of which the mind must be elevated—or to a dread and awe of which, as existing out of itself, it must be subdued. A mountain being a stationary object is enabled to effect this in connection with duration and individual form, by the sense of motion which in the mind accompanies the lines by which the Mountain itself is shaped out.   95
These lines may either be abrupt and precipitous, by which danger & sudden change is expressed; or they may flow into each other like the waves of the sea, and, by involving in such image a feeling of self-propagation infinitely continuous and without cognizable beginning, these lines may thus convey to the Mind sensations not less sublime   100
than those which were excited by their opposites, the abrupt and the precipitous. And, to compleat this sense of power expressed by these permanent objects, add the torrents which take their rise within its bosom, & roll foaming down its sides; the clouds which it attracts; the stature with which it appears to reach the sky; the storms with which   105
it arms itself; the triumphant ostentation with which its snows defy the sun, &c.

92 subdued MS.².: [?drea]ded MS.   92–3 A mountain . . . this in MS.².: A stationary object as a mountain is, is enabled to MS.   96–7 danger & sudden change is MS.².: sudden danger is MS.   99 beginning MS.².: beginning or termination MS.   100 to the Mind sensations not less MS.².: to the Mind by these causes sensations which are the reverse of [?this as] MS.   102 *After* precipitous *a caret and an* X *would seem to indicate a place for an insertion, but we can find nothing marked for insertion.*   to compleat MS.².: lastly MS. *After* power MS. *deletes:* is imparted to the mind [by mountains from ⟨?the⟩ torrents *del.*] [by ⟨?that⟩ *del.*] by the individual Mountain or a cluster of Mountains [from the *del.*] at the head of Langdale which we have been contemplating, by 104 sides; *Edd.:* sides, MS.   it attracts MS.².: gather round it MS.   104–6 the clouds . . . the triumphant *Edd.:* by the clouds . . . by the stature . . . by the storms . . . by the triumphant MS.   105 sky; *Edd.:* sky— MS.   107 *After at least two false starts at a new paragraph, the* MS. *draws a broad line below the paragraph ending at* 107; *above this line and immediately after* the sun, &c., *the phrase* Thus has been *is inserted. This insertion makes it clear that everything below the line, whether deleted or not, is to be regarded as a deletion, for the revised text begins again on the next page of the* MS. *with the same phrase,* Thus has been. *The first part of the deleted matter has so many marks of deletion and insertion that the chronology and continuity of the variants cannot be positively asserted, but the deleted and undeleted sentences seem to have been developed in the following way:*

And the power of these outlines convey the feelings of danger & sudden change or by dim analogies to active [power *del.*] force as expressed by the [?to] parts of the human body such as shoulders or head or neck [exceeding heigh *del.*] is invigorated when the outlines by which these perturbed & violent sensations are [included *del.*] [intimated by individual form *del.*] are contrasted with the serenity, the depth & evanescence of form in MS. .

these outlines also affect us not merely by sensations referable to motion but by dim analogies which they bear to such parts of organized bodies as height of stature head neck shoulders back breast &c. [as the seats and instruments of active force *del.*] which are dignified in our estimation as being the seats & instruments of active force MS.².

the influence of these lines is heightened if the mountain before us be not overtopped by or included in others [it *del.*] but does itself [form the ho *del.*] form a boundary of the horizon for thus all these turbulent or awful sensations of power

Thus has been given an analysis of the attributes or qualities the co-existence of which gives to a Mountain the power of affecting the mind with a sensation of sublimity. The capability of perceiving these 110 qualities, & the degree in which they are perceived, will of course depend upon the state or condition of the mind, with respect to habits, knowledge, & powers, which is brought within the reach of their influence. It is to be remembered that I have been speaking of a visible object; & it might seem that when I required duration to be combined 115 with individual form, more was required than was necessary; for a native of a mountainous country, looking back upon his childhood, will remember how frequently he has been impressed by a sensation of sublimity from a precipice, in which awe or personal apprehension were the predominant feelings of his mind, & from which the milder 120 influence of duration seemed to be excluded. And it is true that the relative proportions in which we are affected by the qualities of these objects are different at different periods of our lives; yet there cannot be a doubt that upon all ages they act conjointly. The precipitous form of an individual cloud which a Child has been taught by tales & pictures 125 to think of as sufficiently solid to support a substantial body, & upon which he finds it easy to conceive himself as seated, in imagination, and thus to invest it with some portion of the terror which belongs to the precipice, would affect him very languidly, &, surely, much more from the knowledge which he has of its evanescence than from the less 130 degree in which it excites in him feelings of dread. Familiarity with these objects tends very much to mitigate & to destroy the power which they have to produce the sensation of sublimity as dependent upon personal fear or upon wonder; a comprehensive awe takes the place of the one, and a religious admiration of the other, & the condi- 135 tion of the mind is exalted accordingly.—Yet it cannot be doubted that a Child or an unpracticed person whose mind is possessed by the sight of a lofty precipice, with its attire of hanging rocks & starting trees, &c., has been visited by a sense of sublimity, if personal fear & surprize or wonder have not been carried beyond certain bounds. For whatever 140 suspends the comparing power of the mind & possesses it with a feeling

are excited in immediate contrast with the fathomless depth & the serenity of the sky or in contrast of another [*altered from* other] kind the permanent mountain's individual form is opposed to the fleeting or changeful [change *del.*] clouds which pass over it or lastly the sense of grandeur which it excites is heightened by the powers of the atmosphere [with *del.*] that are visibly allied with it MS.[3].

108 qualities MS.[2]: qualities by which MS.   110 capability MS.[2]: power MS.
115 object; *Edd.*: object, MS.   120 from MS.[2]: [? on *or* in] MS.   121 excluded. And *Edd.*: excluded & MS.   123 different [*first*] MS.[2]: very different
MS.   127 he finds it easy MS.[2]: it [? seems] [? easy] MS.   133–4 as
dependent upon MS.[2]: by MS.   134 upon [*second*] MS.[2]: by MS.   139 if
MS.[2]: [? then] MS.   141 power] *possibly* powers

or image of intense unity, without a conscious contemplation of parts, has produced that state of the mind which is the consummation of the sublime.—But if personal fear be strained beyond a certain point, this sensation is destroyed, for there are two ideas that divide & distract   145
the attention of the Spectator with an accompanying repulsion or a wish in the soul [that] they should be divided: the object exciting the fear & the subject in which it is excited. And this leads me to a remark which will remove the main difficulties of this investigation. Power awakens the sublime either when it rouses us to a sympathetic energy   150
& calls upon the mind to grasp at something towards which it can make approaches but which it is incapable of attaining—yet so that it participates force which is acting upon it; or, 2dly, by producing a humiliation or prostration of the mind before some external agency which it presumes not to make an effort to participate, but is absorbed in the   155
contemplation of the might in the external power, &, as far as it has any consciousness of itself, its grandeur subsists in the naked fact of being conscious of external Power at once awful & immeasurable; so that, in both cases, the head & the front of the sensation is intense unity. But if that Power which is exalted above our sympathy impresses   160
the mind with personal fear, so as the sensation becomes more lively than the impression or thought of the exciting cause, then self-consideration & all its accompanying littleness takes place of the sublime, & wholly excludes it. Or if the object contemplated be of a spiritual nature, as that of the Supreme Being, for instance (though few minds,   165
I will hope, are so far degraded that with reference to the Deity they can be affected by sensations of personal fear, such as a precipice, a conflagration, a torrent, or a shipwreck might excite), yet it may be confidently affirmed that no sublimity can be raised by the contemplation of such power when it presses upon us with pain and individual   170
fear to a degree which takes precedence in our thoughts [over] the power itself. For connect with such sensations the notion of infinity, or any other ideas of a sublime nature which different religious sects have connected with it: the feeling of self being still predominant, the condition of the mind would be mean & abject.—Accordingly Belial,   175

145 ideas MS.²: objects MS.   146 with an MS.³, MS.: by MS.².   or MS.²: [? with] MS.   147 that *Edd.*: *om.* MS.   149 of MS.²: which have hung around this subject MS.   153 force MS.²: [? that] power MS.   157-8 the naked . . . conscious MS.²: being capable MS.   158 Power MS.²: Power so [? aw] MS.   160 if MS.²: when MS.   impresses MS.³: has impressed MS.: should be thought of as having MS.².   169 raised MS.²: excited MS. 171 precedence in our thoughts MS.²: precedence [? for] MS.   over *Edd.*: over *is perhaps written on top of the smeared deletion.*   172 the notion of infinity MS.²: of infinity [? to] MS.   174 it MS.²: them MS.   the feeling of self being MS.²: as the feeling of self is MS.

the most sensual spirit of the fallen Angels, tho' speaking of himself & his Companions as full of pain, yet adds:

> Who would lose those thoughts
> Which wander thro' Eternity?

The thoughts are not chained down by anguish, but they are free, and 180 tolerate neither limit nor circumscription. Though by the opinions of many religious sects, not less than by many other examples, it is lamentably shewn how industrious Man is in perverting & degrading his mind, yet such is its inherent dignity that, like that of the fallen Spirit as exhibited by the Philosophic & religious Poet, he is per- 185 petually thwarted & baffled & rescued in his own despite.

But to return: Whence comes it, then, that that external power, to a union or communion with which we feel that we can make no approximation while it produces humiliation & submission, reverence or adoration, & all those sensations which may be denominated pas- 190 sive, does nevertheless place the mind in a state that is truly sublime? As I have said before, this is done by the notion or image of intense unity, with which the Soul is occupied or possessed.—But how is this produced or supported, &, when it remits, & the mind is distinctly conscious of his own being & existence, whence comes it that it will- 195 ingly & naturally relapses into the same state? The cause of this is either that our physical nature has only to a certain degree been endangered, or that our moral Nature has not in the least degree been violated.—The point beyond which apprehensions for our physical nature consistent with sublimity may be carried, has been ascertained; 200 &, with respect to power acting upon our moral or spiritual nature, by awakening energy either that would resist or that [? hopes] to participate, the sublime is called forth. But if the Power contemplated be of that kind which neither admits of the notion of resistance or participation, then it may be confidently said that, unless the apprehensions 205 which it excites terminate in repose, there can be no sublimity, & that this sense of repose is the result of reason & the moral law. Could this be abstracted & the reliance upon it taken away, no species of Power that was absolute over the mind could beget a sublime sensation; but, on the contrary, it could never be thought of without fear and 210 degradation.

---

181 tolerate MS.²: admit MS.   neither limit MS.²: no limit to their MS. Though MS.²: Though Man has been MS.   190 or MS.²: & MS.   192 the notion MS.²: the intense MS.   193 But MS.²: but when this remits & the consciousness MS.   197 either that MS.²: that MS.   199 beyond which MS.³: [?] in [of MS.²] which MS.   200 *After* nature MS. *deletes*: may be [? ascer]tained   201 to power MS.²: to our m MS.

I have been seduced to treat the subject more generally than I had at first proposed; if I have been so fortunate as to make myself understood, what has been said will be forgiven. Let us now contract the speculation, & confine it to the sublime as it exists in a mountainous 215 Country, & to the manner in which it makes itself felt. I enumerated the qualities which must be perceived in a Mountain before a sense of sublimity can be received from it. Individuality of form is the primary requisite; and the form must be of that character that deeply impresses the sense of power. And power produces the sublime either as it is 220 thought of as a thing to be dreaded, to be resisted, or that can be participated. To what degree consistent with sublimity power may be dreaded has been ascertained; but as power, contemplated as something to be opposed or resisted, implies a twofold agency of which the mind is conscious, this state seems to be irreconcilable to what has 225 been said concerning the consummation of sublimity, which, as has been determined, exists in the extinction of the comparing power of the mind, & in intense unity. But the fact is, there is no sublimity excited by the contemplation of power thought of as a thing to be resisted & which the moral law enjoins us to resist, saving only as far 230 as the mind, either by glances or continuously, conceives that that power may be overcome or rendered evanescent, and as far as it feels itself tending towards the unity that exists in security or absolute triumph.—(When power is thought of under a mode which we can & do participate, the sublime sensation consists in a manifest ap[p]roxima- 235 tion towards absolute unity.) If the resistance contemplated be of a passive nature (such, for example, as the Rock in the middle of the fall of the Rhine at Chafhausen, as opposed for countless ages to that mighty mass of Waters), there are undoubtedly here before us two distinct images & thoughts; & there is a most complex instrumentality 240 acting upon the senses, such as the roar of the Water, the fury of the foam, &c.; and an instrumentality still more comprehensive, furnished by the imagination, & drawn from the length of the River's course, the Mountains from which it rises, the various countries thro' which it flows, & the distant Seas in which its waters are lost. These images & 245

216 enumerated *Edd.*: ennumerated MS.   217 perceived MS.²: recognized MS.   218 Individuality MS.²: Before MS.   220 power. MS.²: power either to MS.   221 thing MS.²: thing either MS.   or that *Edd.*: or to that MS.   223 contemplated MS.²: to be resisted MS.   223–4 as something . . . implies MS.³: as [opposed & resisted MS.²] something to be resisted it might seem that the notion of resistance implies MS.   224 agency MS.³: agency it should seem MS.: agency it seems MS.².   225 what MS.²: that which MS.   229 power . . . to be MS.²: power that may be MS.   234 *After* triumph MS. *deletes*: —It therefore appears that in which   under a mode MS.²: as a thing MS.   241 acting MS.²: employed MS.   242 and . . . comprehensive MS.²: & a still more comprehensive MS.

thoughts will, in such a place, be present to the mind, either personally
or by representative abstractions more or less vivid.—Yet to return
to the rock & the Waterfall: these objects will be found to have exalted
the mind to the highest state of sublimity when they are thought of in
that state of opposition & yet reconcilement, analogous to parallel lines 250
in mathematics, which, being infinitely prolonged, can never come
nearer to each other; & hence, tho' the images & feelings above
enumerated have exerted a preparative influence upon the mind, the
absolute crown of the impression is infinity, which is a modification of
unity. 255

Having had the image of a mighty River before us, I cannot but, in
connection with it, observe that the main source of all the difficulties
& errors which have attended these disquisitions is that the attention
of those who have been engaged in them has been primarily & chiefly ⸱
fixed upon external objects & their powers, qualities, & properties, & 260
not upon the mind itself, and the laws by which it is acted upon. Hence
the endless disputes about the characters of objects, and the absolute
denial on the part of many that sublimity or beauty exists. To talk of
an object as being sublime or beautiful in itself, without references
to some subject by whom that sublimity or beauty is perceived, is 265
absurd; nor is it of the slightest importance to mankind whether there
be any object with which their minds are conversant that Men would
universally agree (after having ascertained that the words were used
in the same sense) to denominate sublime or beautiful. It is enough that
there are, both in moral qualities & in the forms of the external uni- 270
verse, such qualities & powers as have affected Men, in different states
of civilization & without communication with each other, with similar
sensations either of the sublime or beautiful. The true province of the
philosopher is not to grope about in the external world &, when he has
perceived or detected in an object such or such a quality or power, to 275
set himself to the task of persuading the world that such is a sublime
or beautiful object, but to look into his own mind & determine the law
by which he is affected.—He will then find that the same object has
power to affect him in various manners at different times; so that,
ludicrous as it . . . . . . to power as governed some where by the 280

255 *After* unity. MS. *deletes:* Lastly when power is thought of under a mode
263 To talk of MS.²: It is a matter of no importance whether there be in Nature
MS.   267 with which *Edd.*: which which MS.   Men MS.²: they MS.
271 as have affected MS.²: as have the power of comp MS.   272 civilization
MS.²: civilization with similar MS.   275 object MS.²: object or quality MS.
279 so that MS.²: so that the [? might] MS.   280 *Page* [7ᵛ] *of* MS. Prose 28ᵇ,
which the MS. *numbers* 14, *ends at* ludicrous as it; *page* [8ʳ] *is numbered* 17 *and
begins* to power as governed. *Presumably a loose quarter sheet, numbered* 15 *on the
recto and* 16 *on the verso, was once here inserted and has since been lost.*

intelligence of law & reason, and lastly to the transcendent sympathies which have been vouchsafed to her with the calmness of eternity.

Thus, then, is apparent how various are the *means* by which we are conducted to the same end—the elevation of our being; & the practical influences to be drawn from this are most important, but I shall con-   285
sider them only with reference to the forms of nature which have occasioned this disquisition.

I have already given a faint sketch of the manner in which a familiarity with these objects acts upon the minds of men of cultivated imagination. I will now suppose a person of mature age to be introduced   290
amongst them for the first time. I will not imagine him to be a man particularly conversant with pictures, nor an enthusiast in poetry; but he shall be modest & unpresumptuous, one who has not been insensible to impressions of grandeur from the universal or less local appearances & forms of nature (such as the sky, the clouds, the heavenly bodies,   295
rivers, trees, & perhaps the Ocean), & coming hither desirous to have his knowledge increased & the means of exalting himself in thought & feeling multiplied & extended. I can easily conceive that such a man, in his first intercourse with these objects, might be grievously disappointed, &, if that intercourse should be short, might depart without   300
being raised from that depression which such disappointment might reasonably cause. Such would have been the condition of the most eminent of our English Painters if his visits to the sublime pictures in the Vatican & the Cistine Chapel had not been repeated till the sense of strangeness had worn off, till the twilight of novelty began to dispel,   305
and he was made conscious of the mighty difference between seeing & perceiving. I have heard of a Lady, a native of the Orcades (which naked solitudes from her birth she had never quitted), whose imagination, endeavouring to compleat whatever had been left imperfect in pictures & books, had feasted in representing to itself the forms of   310
trees. With delight did she look forward to the day when it would be permitted to her to behold the reality, & to learn by experience how far its grandeur or beauty surpassed the conceptions which she had formed—but sad & heavy was her disappointment when this wish was

282 which *Edd.*: which which MS.   285 this MS.²: this as applicable to
MS.   285 shall MS.²: shall nevertheless MS.   modest MS.²: a Man of
candour MS.   *After* unpresumptuous MS. *deletes*: willing & wishing to be pleased
& desirous to have his mind opened out & exalted   297 knowledge MS.²:
mind MS.   increased MS.²: extended MS.   in MS.²: into MS.   299 might
MS.²: should MS.   306 and he was MS.²: & the veil was uplifted by which
MS.   307 *After* perceiving MS. *deletes*: [?] are the associations   which MS.²:
who in those MS.   308 solitudes from MS.³: solitudes beyond the limits she
had MS.: solitudes which MS.².   308–9 whose imagination MS.³: who had
feasted her imagination [& MS.²] in MS.   311 *After* trees MS. *deletes*: & in
connecting with those pictures of her mind completing whatever had been left imperfect by pictures & books to bring (*Wordsworth's hand writes* completing . . . bring).

satisfied. A journey to a fertile Vale in the South of Scotland gave her ³¹⁵
an opportunity of seeing some of the finest trees in the Island; but she
beheld them without pleasure or emotion, & complained that, compared with the grandeur of the living & ever-varying ocean in all the
changes & appearances & powers of which she was thoroughly versed
—that a tree or a wood were objects insipid and lifeless.—Something ³²⁰
of a like disappointment, or perhaps a kind of blank & stupid wonder
(one of the most oppressive of sensations), might be felt by one who
had passed his life in the plains of Lincolnshire & should be suddenly
transported to the recesses of Borrowdale or Glencoe. And if this
feeling should not burthen his mind, innumerable are the impressions ³²⁵
which may exclude him from a communication with the sublime in the
midst of objects eminently capable of exciting that feeling: he may be
depressed by the image of barrenness; or the chaotic appearance of
crags heaped together, or seemingly ready to fall upon each other, may
excite in him sensations as uncomfortable as those with which he would ³³⁰
look upon an edifice that the Builder had left unfinished; & many of the
forms before his eyes, by associations of outward likeness, merely may
recal to his mind mean or undignified works of art; & every where
might he be haunted or disturbed by a sense of incongruity, either light
& trivial, or resembling in kind that intermixture of the terrible & ³³⁵
the ludicrous which dramatists who understand the constitution of the
human mind have not unfrequently represented when they introduce
a character disturbed by an agency supernatural or horrible to a degree
beyond what the mind is prepared to expect from the ordinary course
of human calamities or afflictions. So that it appears that even those ³⁴⁰
impressions that do most easily make their way to the human mind,
such as I deem those of the sublime to be, cannot be received from an
object however eminently qualified to impart them, without a preparatory intercourse with that object or with others of the same kind.

315 *After* satisfied MS. *deletes*: she had an opportunity some of [*sic*] the finest
trees in the Island upon   318 in MS.²: with MS.   320 tree or
MS.³: tree & doubtless MS.: tree [?] MS.².   objects MS.²: an object MS.
324 recesses MS.²: plains MS.   And MS.²: or MS.   326 with MS.²:
of MS.   328 *After* barrenness MS. *deletes*: perplexed by a sense of
confusion   329 together MS.²: upon each other MS.   332 *After*
likeness MS. *deletes*: which [? I *or* h]   335 trivial MS.²: ludicrous MS.
335–6 that . . . dramatists MS.²: tho' in [? course] not in degree those which
dramatists MS.   338 disturbed MS.²: affected MS.   339 prepared
MS.²: thought MS.   341 impressions MS.³: sensations MS.: thoughts
MS.².   342–4 cannot . . . intercourse MS.³: do nevertheless demand a [previous
exercise & discipline & *del*.] certain degree of exercise discipline & familiarity if
not with the individual object at least with the [class *del*.] species of objects to
which it belongs unlike a [? cer] [?] cannot [make this *del*.] be imparted by an
object MS.: cannot [be *del*.] easily be perceived without a process of learning to
see and to feel & a certain degree of intercourse MS.².   344 intercourse with
MS.²: intercourse either with MS.   object MS.²: class of objects MS.

But impediments arising merely from novelty or inexperience in a   345
well disposed mind disappear gradually and assuredly. Yet, though it
will not be long before the Stranger will become conscious of the sublime where the power to raise it eminently exists, yet, if I may judge
from my own experience, it is only very slowly that the mind is opened
out to a perception of images of Beauty co-existing in the same object   350
with those of sublimity. As I have explained at large what I mean by
the word sublimity, I might with propriety here proceed to treat of
beauty, & to explain in what manner I conceive the mind to be affected
when it has a sense of the beautiful. But I cannot pass from the sublime
without guarding the ingenuous reader against those caprices of vanity   355
& presumption derived from false teachers in the philosophy of the
fine arts & of taste, which Painters, connesieurs, & amateurs are perpetually interposing between the light of nature & their own minds.
Powerful indeed must be the spells by which such an eclipse is to be
removed; but nothing is wanting, save humility, modesty, diffidence,   360
& an habitual, kindly, & confident communion with Nature, to prevent
such a darkness from ever being superinduced. 'Oh', says one of these
tutored spectators, 'what a scene should we have before us here upon
the shores of Windermere, if we could but strike out those pikes of
Langdale by which it is terminated; they are so intensely *picturesque*   365
that their presence excludes from the mind all sense of the sublime.'
Extravagant as such an ejaculation is, it has been heard from the
mouths of Persons who pass for intelligent men of cultivated mind.

345 inexperience MS.²: inexperience do MS.   347 Stranger MS.²: mind MS.
348 raise MS.²: excite MS.   351–2 As . . . here MS.³: I might here with
propriety MS.: As . . . I might here with propriety MS.².   353 explain
MS.²: define MS.   *After* affected MS. *deletes*: by an object which supposing us
to speak   356 derived MS.²: which have been derived MS.   in the MS.²:
in the fine MS.   philosophy *Edd.*: phylosophy MS.   357 which Painters
. . . are MS.²: with which artists Connesieurs & amateurs have narrowed MS.
359 Powerful . . . spells MS.²: I know not by what spells MS.   359–60 is
. . . removed MS.²: may be removed MS.   361 with Nature MS.²: with &
reliance upon Nature and MS.   363 tutored spectators MS.³: ripened connesieurs from MS.: ripened connesieurs, come on a visit to MS.².   scene MS.²:
sublime scene MS.   364 out those *Edd.*: out of the land [scene MS.²] yon
MS.: out of those MS.³.   365 they are so *Edd.*: they are peculiar & so MS.:
they so MS.².   367 been MS.²: been frequently MS.   368 Persons . . .
men MS.²: more than one Person who passes for an intelligent man MS.

APPENDIX IV

Origins of *Guide*, 2803–906 and 2958–3230

(from Dorothy Wordsworth's Journal)

WHEN in 1822 and again in 1823 Wordsworth further extended the conclusion of the *Guide*, he drew on a notebook of Dorothy Wordsworth's which is now catalogued in the Wordsworth Library as *Journals*, MS. 13. Among other things, this notebook contains the earliest extant versions of the *Guide*, 2803–906 (the Scafell Pike Excursion) and 2958–3230 (the Ullswater Excursion). No manuscript containing Wordsworth's final and extensive revisions has survived, but the early stages of his work appear in Dorothy's notebook. Primarily to preserve Wordsworth's initial alterations, we here present a textually annotated edition of the two Excursions as they appear in *Journals*, MS. 13. There is, of course, a secondary advantage in having Dorothy's original versions in the same volume with the *Guide*, where they appear in a radically altered form.

Before describing *Journals*, MS. 13, we should mention two other extant manuscripts, each containing one of Dorothy's two Excursions. Of these manuscripts, the earlier is a revised copy of the Ullswater Excursion. This sixteen-page manuscript, entirely in Dorothy's hand, is among the Coleorton papers (MA 1581) in the Pierpont Morgan Library, New York. Undoubtedly made for Lady Beaumont, it is a corrected transcript of MS. 13, for all its variants—and they are fairly numerous—effect either stylistic improvement or greater accuracy; in this manuscript (hereafter referred to as the Coleorton manuscript), Dorothy also occasionally omitted details too local in interest for a reader outside the family. Although it is undated, it was probably made soon after Dorothy had finished her own journal entry; certainly, it reflects none of the revisions for the 1823 edition of the *Guide* made directly on the pages of the Ullswater Excursion in MS. 13. The other extant manuscript is a slightly shorter transcript of the Scafell Pike Excursion, now among the Dorothy Wordsworth *Letters* (October 1818) in the Wordsworth Library. Unsigned and in an unidentified hand, all of it is enclosed in quotation marks; on a page reserved for it, there appears in a second unidentified hand the following superscription: 'Ellesmere January three 1819 / Miss Hutchinson / Hindwell / Radnor / per [?Kenyon]'.

As might be expected, neither of these manuscripts was used by Wordsworth when he was preparing his text for the *Guide*, and accordingly we will ignore both manuscripts in our textual apparatus, except where MS. 13 is either so badly torn or so heavily deleted that the only possible reading must be derived from one or the other of these better-preserved documents.

Journals, MS. 13 is a hand-sewn notebook, bound in brown wrapping paper. At the front are 3 folios, each measuring 7 in. wide × 8¾ in. long; these 6 pages of cheap thin paper bear a watermark of 1816. They are followed by 11 folios, of better paper, folded to produce 44 pages (7¾ in. wide × 9¾ in. long). Then come 4 folios of the same cheap paper as was used for the 3 folios at the front; at the very end is a small loose fragment, badly torn. Thus MS. 13 comprises 58 pages sewn into a note-book, in addition to one loose fragment from the end of the notebook.

The contents of the notebook are as follows: pp. [1]–[5], with the 1816 watermark, are written in the hurried hand of Dorothy; with their numer-ous false starts and deletions, they look like pages written at Words-worth's dictation. These pages contain new and disparate paragraphs for the Ullswater Excursion, as well as rewritings of a few paragraphs in Dorothy's original version; the matter on these 5 pages clearly moves in the direction of the *Guide*. Page [6] is blank. Pages [7]–[17] contain copies of some of Dorothy's own verses and have no bearing on the *Guide*. Pages [18]–[20] contain two revised drafts for the opening of the Ullswater Excursion; mainly written in Dorothy's hurried hand, there are a few phrases in Wordsworth's hand; like those on the first 5 pages, these revisions also approximate the *Guide*, or are identical with it. Pages [21]–[34] contain the earliest extant version of the Ullswater Excursion; it is perhaps not the original, for in the course of writing it out, Dorothy makes very few corrections. But also on these pages are numerous deletions and emendations which, moving in the direction of the *Guide* or identical with it, were made much later; of these, a few are in Wordsworth's hand, but the majority seem to be in Dorothy's. Pages [35]–[46] contain two prose narratives of Dorothy's, neither of which bears on the *Guide*. Pages [47]–[58], together with the small fragment torn from the end of the notebook, contain the earliest extant account of Dorothy's excursion up Scafell Pike; they are headed 'A.D. 1818—From a letter to Mr Johnson'. Here too it is usually easy to discriminate between corrections made by Dorothy while she was in the process of making her own extract from her letter to Johnson and corrections made a few years later when the 1822 *Guide* was being prepared.

Differences too numerous to comment upon individually will be found between our edition of Dorothy's Ullswater Excursion and two earlier editions made, respectively, by W. A. Knight and Ernest de Selincourt; we may, however, indicate briefly the main reasons for these differences. In the *Transactions of the Wordsworth Society*, No. 5 (1883), pp. 103–10 and later in his edition of Dorothy's *Journals* (London, 1897), ii. 153–60, Knight published generous selections from the Ullswater Excursion; he used either the Coleorton manuscript or a transcript of selections made from it by someone else for his use (cf. *Transactions*, No. 5 (1883), p. 8). De Selincourt, on the other hand, used MS. 13 in the Wordsworth Library; apparently unaware of the Coleorton manuscript and despite his statement that 'The *Excursion on the Banks of Ullswater* (1805), of which Professor Knight printed an abbreviated version, is here given complete from Dorothy's manuscript' (*Journals*, i. xiv), he sometimes silently followed Knight's edition. Thus, for example, where MS. 13 (Ullswater Excursion, 101–2) reads 'crossed the one-arched Bridge below the Church, with its "bare ring of mossy wall" ', de Selincourt (i. 416) turned to Knight's edition of the Coleorton manuscript and followed that reading: 'crossed the one-arched bridge above the Church; a beautiful view of the church with its "bare ring of mossy wall" '. Or, to cite another example, where Knight's edition of the Coleorton manuscript read 'The stars in succession took their stations on the mountain-tops', de Selincourt (i. 422) followed Knight, although the sentence does not appear in MS. 13 (cf. Ullswater Excursion, 284). Other differences between de Selincourt's edition of Dorothy's two Excursions and our edition derive from his having occasionally substituted for Dorothy's corrected version the late emendations made expressly for the *Guide*. Examples of these discrepancies between his edition and ours need not be given here, since they may be traced in our textual notes.

But differences between our text of the Scafell Pike Excursion, 152–63, and that of *M.T.* ii. 503 also call for a brief comment. The editors of *M.T.* indicate that the manuscript source of Letter 518 (D. W. to William Johnson, 21 October 1818) is '*WL transcript* [*possibly in John Carter's hand*]'. This headnote, with the editors' brackets, must denote the transcript which we have described above as being in an unidentified hand and bearing on the address panel the date 'January three 1819', for the editors do transcribe from this manuscript the final sentence, a sentence which occurs below the panel. But they state incorrectly that a portion of this 1819 transcript had been published by de Selincourt in *Journals*, i. 425–30 (headnote in *M.T.* ii. 499); they err further by publishing a text which follows, except for the final sentence, de Selincourt's edition of pages [47]–[58] in *Journals*, MS. 13. This fact explains why when damage to this earlier manuscript causes us to turn to the 1819 transcript, our text of the Scafell Pike Excursion at 152–63 differs from that of *M.T.* ii. 503.

Because Wordsworth's deletions and emendations in *Journals*, MS. 13 are comparatively slight and sometimes erratic and incomplete, we will reverse our usual procedure in editing a manuscript: rather than taking the last corrected version as the text and recording early variants in the notes, we will instead take as the text Dorothy's corrected version, and give in the notes (1) her variants and (2) the later alterations made for the *Guide*. In our textual notes we employ the following abbreviations:

D = Dorothy's original versions in MS. 13.

G = Late revisions made expressly for the *Guide* and written directly over D.

W = New paragraphs and rewritings for the *Guide* on pp. [1]–[5] and [18]–[20] in MS. 13.

C = The Coleorton manuscript in the Pierpont Morgan Library.

J = The 1819 transcript, in an unidentified hand, of Dorothy's letter to William Johnson

I

[Scafell Pike Excursion]

A.D. 1818—From a letter to Mr Johnson

SIR GEORGE & LADY BEAUMONT spent a few days with us lately, & I
accompanied them to Keswick. M^r & Mrs Wilberforce & their Family
happened to be at K. at the same time, & we all dined together in the
romantic Vale of Borrowdale, at the house of a female Friend, an un-   5
married Lady, who, bewitched with the charms of the rocks, & streams, &
Mountains, belonging to that secluded spot, has there built herself a house,
and, though she is admirably fitted for society, & has as much enjoyment
when surrounded by her Friends as any one *can* have her chearfulness has
never flagged, though she has lived more than the year round alone in   10
Borrowdale, at six miles distance from Keswick, with bad roads between—
You will guess that she has resources within herself—Such indeed she
has—She is a painter & labours hard in depicting the beauties of her
favorite Vale; she is also fond of Music and of reading; and has a reflecting
mind: besides, (though before she lived in Borrowdale she was no great   15
walker) she is become an active Climber of the hills, & I must tell you of
a feat that she & I performed on Wednesday the 7th of this month. I
remained in Borrowdale after Sir G. & Lady B. and the Wilberforces were
gone, & Miss Barker proposed that the next day she & I should go to
Seathwaite beyond the Black lead mines at the head of Borrowdale, &   20
thence up a Mountain called at the top *Ash Course,* which we suppose may
be a corruption of *Esk Hawes,* as it is a settling between the Mountains
over which the People are accustomed to pass between Eskdale and
Borrowdale; & such settlings are generally called by the name of "the
Hawes"—as Grisdale Hawes—Buttermere Hawes—from the German   25
word Hals, the neck. At the top of Ash Course Miss Barker had promised
me that I should see a most magnificent prospect; but we had some miles
to travel to the foot of the Mountain, and accordingly we went thither in
a cart—Miss Barker, her Maid, & myself: We departed before nine
o'clock. The sun shone; the sky was clear and blue; and light and shade   30
fell in masses upon the mountains; the fields below glittered with the dew,
where the beams of the sun could reach them; and every little stream
tumbling down the hills seemed to add to the chearfulness of the scene.
    We left our Cart at Seathwaite and proceeded, with a man to carry our
provisions, and a kind Neighbour of Miss Barker's, a Statesman & Shep-   35
herd of the Vale, as our companion & Guide. We found ourselves at the
top of Ash Course without a weary limb, having had the fresh air of

5 Friend D: *an unknown hand inserts, without making a deletion,* Miss Barker
7 belonging to D: of G.   9 her Friends D: Friends G.   19 that
the . . . go D²: to me that we should go the next day D.   23–4 People . . .
Borrowdale D²: People of Eskdale are accustomed to pass on their way to Borrowdale D.   26 the neck D: (neck) G.   27 me D: *del.* G.   most D:
del. G.   34 Seathwaite D²: Stonethwaite D.

autumn to help us up by its invigorating effects, & the sweet warmth of the unclouded sun to tempt us to sit and rest by the way. From the top of Ash Course I beheld a prospect which would indeed have amply repaid me 40 for a toilsome journey, if such it had been; and a sense of thankfulness for the continuance of that vigour of body, which enabled me to climb the high Mountain, as in the days of my youth, inspiring me with fresh chearfulness, added a delight, a charm to the contemplation of the magnificent scenes before me which I cannot describe—Still less can I tell you the 45 glories of what we saw. Three views, each distinct in its kind, we saw at once—the Vale of Borrowdale, of Keswick, of Bassenthwaite—Skiddaw, Saddleback, Helvellyn, numerous other Mountains, and, still beyond, the Solway Frith, and the Mountains of Scotland.

Nearer to us on the other side, and below us were the Langdale Pikes— 50 their own Vale below *them*,—Windermere—and, far beyond, after a long long distance we saw Ingleborough in Yorkshire.—But how shall I speak of the deliciousness of the third prospect! At this time *that* was the most favoured by sun & shade. The green Vale of Esk—deep & green, with its glittering serpent stream was below us; and on we looked to the Moun- 55 tains near the sea—Black Comb & others—and still beyond, to the Sea itself in dazzling brightness. Turning round we saw the Mountains of Wasdale in tumult; and Great Gavel, though the middle of the Mountain was to us as its base, looked very grand.

We had attained the object of our journey; but our ambition mounted 60 higher. We saw the summit of Scaw Fell, as it seemed, very near to us: we were, indeed, three parts up that Mountain, & thither we determined to go—We found the distance greater than it had appeared to us; but our courage did not fail; however, when we came nearer we perceived that, in order to attain that summit which had invited us forward, we must make 65 a great dip, and that the ascent afterwards would be exceedingly steep & difficult, so that we might have been benighted if we had attempted it; therefore, unwillingly, we gave it up, and resolved, instead, to ascend another pike of the same Mountain, called *the Pikes* & which, I have since found, the Measurers of Mountains estimate as higher than the larger 70 summit which bears the name of Scaw Fell, & where the Stone *Man* is built, which we, at the time, considered as the point of highest honour.— The Sun had never once been overshadowed by a cloud during the whole of our progress from the centre of Borrowdale; at the summit of the Pike there was not a breath of air to stir even the papers which we spread out 75

38 by its . . . effects D: by its . . . powers G: *del*. G².   39–46 *Pencilled vertical lines suggest that* G² *intended*: From the top of Ash Course we beheld Three views. . . .   40 I . . . me D: we . . . us G.   43 me with D: *del*. G. 45 which I . . . describe D: *del*. G.   50 us D²: them D.   51 beyond D beyond Windermere G.   52 we saw D: *del*. G.   53 deliciousness D: peculiar deliciousness G.   54 sun D: sunshine G.   57 *After* brightness D *deletes*: At this same station, (making as it might be called a 4ᵗʰ division or prospect) 62 & D: *del*. G.   63–4 We . . . perceived that D: *del*. G.   65 in order D: but in order G.   which . . . forward D: *del*. G.   must make D: have [?] *inserted, but no deletion is made* G.   66 and D: and seeing G.   69 pike D: point G.   72 which we . . . honour D: *del*. G.

containing our food.—There we ate our dinner in summer warmth; and the stillness seemed to be not of this world.—We paused & kept silence to listen, & not a sound of any kind was to be heard.—We were far out of the reach of the Cataracts of Scaw Fell; & not an insect was there to hum in the air. The Vales which I have before described lay in view; and,   80 side by side with Eskdale, we now saw the sister Vale of Donnerdale terminated by the Duddon Sands. But the majesty of the Mountains below us & close to us is not to be conceived. We now beheld the whole Mass of Great Gavel from its base—the Den of Wasdale at our feet, the Gulph immeasureable—Grassmire & the other mountains of Crummock—Enner-   85 dale & *its* mountains; and the Sea beyond.

While we were looking round after dinner our Guide said to us that we must not linger long; for we should have a storm. We looked in vain to espy the traces of it; for mountains, vales, & the sea were all touched with the clear light of the sun—"It is there," he said, pointing to the sea beyond   90 Whitehaven; and, sure enough, we there perceived a light cloud, or mist, unnoticeable but by a Shepherd, accustomed to watch all mountain bodings—We gazed around again, & yet again, fearful to lose the remembrance of what lay before us in that lofty solitude; and then prepared to depart. Meanwhile the air changed to cold, and we saw that tiny vapour   95 swelled into mighty Masses of cloud which came boiling over the Mountains. Great Gavel, Helvellyn, & Skiddaw were wrapped in storm; yet Langdale, & the Mountains in that quarter were all bright with sunshine— Soon the storm reached us; we sheltered under a crag; and, almost as rapidly as it had come, it passed away, and left us free to observe the   100 goings-on of storm and sunshine in other quarters—Langdale had now its share, and the Pikes were decorated by two splendid rainbows; Skiddaw also had its Rainbows, but we were truly glad to see *them* & the clouds disappear from *that mountain*, as we knew that M^r & Mrs Wilberforce & their Family (if they kept the intention which they had formed when they   105 parted from us the night before) must certainly be upon Skiddaw at that very time—and so it was. They were there, and had much more rain than we had; we, indeed, were hardly at all wetted; and before we found ourselves again upon that part of the Mountain called Ash Course every cloud had vanished from every summit.—Do not think we here gave up our   110 spirit of enterprise. No! I had heard much of the grandeur of the view of Wasdale from Stye Head, the point from which Wasdale is first seen in coming by the road from Borrowdale; but though I had been in Wasdale I had not seen what was so much talked of by Travellers. Down to that Pass (for we were yet far above it) we bent our course by the side of   115 Ruddle Gill, a very deep red chasm in the Mountains, which begins at a

76 food . . . dinner in D: refreshment which we ate in G.   78–9 out of D: above G.   80 which I have D: *del*. G.   82–3 below us D: below G. 87 to us D: *del*. G.   89 the sea D: sea G.   95 that tiny D: the tiny G.   103 its D: its own G.   104–5 M^r . . . Family D: some Friends of ours *inserted, but no deletion is made* G.   107–14 and so . . . Travellers D: G *deletes and erratically inserts* we [?returned] on our return   111 No! D: *del*. G.   the grandeur of D: *del*. G.

spring—that spring forms a stream, which must, at times, be a mighty Torrent, as is evident from the Channel which it has wrought out—Thence by Sprinkling Tarn to Stye head; & there we sate & looked down into Wasdale. We were now upon Great Gavel which rose high above us. Opposite was Scaw Fell, and we heard the roaring of the stream, from one of the ravines of that Mountain, which, though the bending of Wasdale Head lay between *us* and Scaw Fell, we could look into, as it were, and the depth of the ravine appeared tremendous; it was black, and the Crags were awful.

We now proceeded homeward—by Stye head Tarn along the road into Borrowdale. Before we reached Stonethwaite a few stars had appeared, and we travelled home in our Cart by Moonlight.

I ought to have described the last part of our ascent to Scaw Fell pike. There, not a blade of grass was to be seen—hardly a cushion of moss, & that was parched & brown; and only growing rarely between the huge blocks & stones which cover the summit & lie in heaps all round to a great distance, like Skeletons or bones of the earth not wanted at the creation, & there left to be covered with never-dying lichens, which the Clouds and dews nourish; and adorn with colours of the most vivid and exquisite beauty, and endless in variety—No gems or flowers can surpass in colouring the beauty of some of these masses of stone which no human eye beholds except the Shepherd or Traveller is led thither by curiosity; and how seldom must this happen. The other eminence is that which is visited by the adventurous Traveller, and the Shepherd has no temptation to go thither in quest of his sheep for on the *Pike* there is no food to tempt them.

We certainly were singularly fortunate in the day; for when we were seated on the Summit our Guide, turning his eyes thoughtfully round, said to us, "I do not know that in my whole life I was ever at any season of the year so high upon the Mountains on so clear a day." Afterwards, you know, we had the storm which exhibited to us the grandeur of earth & heaven commingled, yet without terror; for we knew that the storm would pass away; for our prophetic Guide assured us. I forgot to tell you that I espied a Ship upon the glittering Sea while we were looking over Eskdale. "Is it a Ship?" replied the Guide. "A Ship! Yes it can be nothing else don't you see the shape of it?" Miss Barker interposed, "It is a Ship, of that I am certain—I cannot be mistaken, I am so accustomed to the appearance of Ships at Sea—" The Guide dropped the argument; but a Minute was scarcely gone when he quietly said—"Now look at your Ship, it is now a horse"—So indeed it was, with a gallant neck and head—We laughed

138 Shepherd . . . curiosity D: Shepherd is led thither by chance or the Traveller by curiosity G.   146 clear D: calm G.   you know D: *del.* G. 152–63 a Ship . . . Hutchinson J: *the last legible page of* D *ends:* "It is a Ship," [? *del.*]. *The final loose fragment is so badly torn that only scattered letters and phrases remain:* to/ of/ our/ mon performances on/ ker & I each wrote a/ Top of the Pike of Scaw Fell/ distant friend, Sar[a] Hutchi/ South Wales/ October 21st—1818/ Went up Scaw Fell on Wednesday the 7th October—1818. *Cf.* JOURNALS, i. 430; *minor differences suggest that de Selincourt here followed a manuscript now lost.*

heartily, and I hope when I am again inclined to positiveness I may remember the Ship and the horse upon the glittering Sea; and the calm confidence, yet submission of Our Wise Man of the Mountains; who certainly had more knowledge of *Clouds* than we, whatever might be our 160 knowledge of *Ships*.—To add to our uncommon performances on this Day Miss Barker and I each wrote a letter from the top of the Pike [*tear*] to our far distant Friend in South Wales—Sara Hutchinson.

II

[Ullswater Excursion]

November 1805

W I L L I A M A N D M A R Y returned from Park House by the Patterdale road on Sunday Novr 4th (along with M^r & Mrs Clarkson) having made a

1–10 William . . . needments D: *del*. G.   1–24 William . . . a time, and D: We left the Vale of Grasmere on the 7th of November on a damp & gloomy morning. [Though *del*.] [The season was so far advanced *del*.] [the weather had been so mild that the trees upon the larger Island of Rydal the ⟨?contrast⟩ wh *del*.] The season had been [peculiar *del*.] unusually favorable to the beauty of foliage, and though it was so far advanced the trees [on the lar *del*.] had not lost their gorgeous colouring. Those on the larger Island at Rydal, [with the grey ro *del*.] [were peculiarly splendid ⟨?⟩ by *del*.] in particular had a splendour which did not [require *del*.] [?need] the heightening of sunshine & [the bushes & shrubs *del*.] & the line of its grey rocky shore shaggy with bright bushes & shrubs, & spotted & striped with purplish brown heath indistinguishably blended with its reflexion in the still water [strikingly resembled the magnified image *del*.] [one of those large *del*.] [called to mind & indeed appeared like a gigantic *del*.] strikingly resembled a richly coated gigantic Catterpillar—[a magnified *del*.] one of those which by Children are called Woolly Boys—as it might appear through a magnifying glass of extraordinary power.—The mists [gather *del*.] thickened in the valley as we went along & all the way to Patterdale we had rain if it may be called so; for not a drop appeared upon our hair or cloathes larger than the smallest pearls upon a Lady's ring. [We had been disheartened by the *del*.] When we reached the top of Kirkstone we were thankful we had not been discouraged by the [gloomy *del*.] apprehension of bad weather. Though we could not see fifty yards before we were more than contented. At such a time & [*Written in pencil right over the text on this page of the MS. is* Set off from Grasmere on Wednesday Nov^r] W: We left G.mere Vale on the 7th of November on a damp & gloomy morning. The season [weather *inserted but no deletion made*] had been unusually favourable to the preservation & beauty of Foliage, and, [though it was so far advanced at this late period *del*.] and far advanced as it was, the trees [had not lost their gorgeous colouring. Those trees *del*.] on the larger Island at Rydal in particular [had *del*.] retained a splendour which did not need the heightening of sun-shine, & the line of the grey rocky shore of the same Island shaggy with bright bushes & shrubs, & spotted & striped with purplish brown heath indistinguishably blending [*altered from* blended] with its [reflection *del*.] image reflected in the still water startlingly resembled a richly-coat [*sic*] gigantic catterpillar—[one of those which by Children are called Woolly Boys *del*.] as it might appear thro' a magnifying glass of extraordinary power. The mists gathered in the Valley as we went along, and all the way to Patterdale we had *rain* [if it might be called so ⟨?⟩ *del*.] or rather drizzling Vapour for there was not a drop on our hair or clothes larger than the smallest pearls upon a Lady's Ring. When we reached the top of Kirkstone we were thankful we had not been dis-

delightful excursion of three days. They had engaged that W^m and I
should go to Mr Luff's on the Wednesday or Thursday if the weather 5
continued favorable. It was not very promising on Wednesday; but having
been fine for so long a time we thought there would not be an entire change
all at once; therefore, on a damp & gloomy morning we set forward; W^m
on foot, and I upon the pony, with W's great Coat slung over the saddle
crutch, and a Wallet containing our bundle of needments. As we went 10
along the mists gathered upon the Vallies, & it even *rained* all the way
to Patterdale; but there was never a drop upon my habit larger than the
smallest pearls upon a Lady's ring. The trees upon the larger Island on
Rydale Lake were of the most gorgeous colours, the whole Island reflected
in the water, as I remember once, in particular, to have seen it with dear 15
Coleridge when either he or W^m observed that the rocky shore, spotted &
streaked with purplish brown heath, & its image in the water together,
were like an immense catterpillar, such as when we were children we used
to call *Woolly Boys* from their hairy coats. I had been a little cowardly
when we left home, fearing that heavy rains might detain us at Patterdale; 20
but, as the mists thickened our enjoyments encreased & my hopes grew
bolder; and when we were at the top of Kirkstone (though we could not
see fifty yards before us) we were as happy Travellers as ever paced side
by side on a holiday ramble. At such a time, and in such a place every
scattered stone the size of one's head becomes a companion. There is a 25
fragment of an old wall at the top of Kirkstone, which, magnified yet
obscured as it was by the mist, was scarcely less interesting to us when
we cast our eyes upon it than the view of a noble monument of ancient
grandeur has been.—Yet this same pile of stones we had never before even
observed. When we had descended considerably, the fields of Hartsop 30
below Brothers water were first seen, like a lake coloured by the reflection
of yellow clouds. I mistook them for the water; but soon after we saw the
lake itself gleaming faintly with a grey steelly brightness; then, appeared
the brown oaks and the birches of splendid colour, and, when we came near

couraged by the apprehension of bad weather. Though [we could ⟨*undel.*⟩ not then
del.] then not able there to see [more than *del.*] fifty yards before us we were more
than contented. At such a time The surprize & hurry of spirits which a transforma-
tion of this kind—No gaiety can be felt in such a situation, but a [surprize & *del.*]
hurry of spirits [which is ⟨?⟩ *del.*] not a little delightful [is ⟨?⟩ *del.*] accompanies the
surprize occasioned by [the transformations ⟨?⟩ seeing *del.*] objects transformed
dilated or distorted as they are when seen thro' such a medium. [Some *del.*] Many
of the fragments of rock on the top & slope of K. & similar things in this Country
are fantastic enough of themselves; but [to be ⟨? over *or* ever⟩ *del.*] the full effect of
[this *del.*] such impressions can only be had in a state of weather when it is not
likely to be sought for. W^2 (*cf. Guide*, 2958–85).

8 all D: *del.* G.   12–13 upon . . . upon [*first*] D: on . . . on G.
13 G *corrects to* pearls: pears D.   upon [*second*] D: on G.   15 dear C: [?]
D: *del.* G.   17 together D: indistinguishably blended *inserted but without a
caret* G.   21 enjoyments D: enjoyment G.   21–2 & my hopes grew
bolder D: *del.* G.   22 we were D: *del.* G.   27–8 when . . . upon it C:
[?] D: *del.* G.   28 noble D: some G.   29 has been D: *del.* G.
31 coloured D: tinged G.   33 grey D: *del.* G.   then, D: then, as we
descended G.   34 splendid colour D: lively yellow G.   34–5 when . . .
valley D: *del.* G.

to the valley the cottages, and the lowly old Hall of Hartsop with its long   35
roof and elegant chimnies. We had eaten our dinner under the shelter of
a sheep-fold by a bridge near the foot of the mountain, having tethered
the pony at the entrance, where it stood without one impatient beating of
a foot. I could not but love it for its meekness; and indeed I thought we
were selfish to enjoy our meal so much while its poor jaws were confined   40
by the curb bridle. We reached Luff's about two hours before tea-time.

Thursday Novr 8th

The next morning incessant rain till eleven o'clock when it became fair,
and W^m and I walked to Blowick. Luff joined us by the way. The wind was
strong; and drove the clouds forward along the side of the hill above our   45
heads—four or five goats were bounding among the rocks; the sheep
moved about more quietly; or cowered under their sheltering places. Two
storm-stiffened black Yew trees on the Crag above Luff's house were
striking objects close under, or seen through the flying mists. I do not
know what to say of Blowick; for to attempt to describe the place would   50
be absurd, when you for whom I write have either been there, or may go
thither as soon as you like. When we stood under the naked Crag upon
the Common overlooking the woods and bush-besprinkled fields, the Lake,
Clouds, and Mists were all in motion to the sound of sweeping winds—the
Church & Cottages of Patterdale, scarcely visible from the brightness of   55
the mist. Looking backwards towards the foot of the Lake, the scene less
visionary.—Place Fell steady and bold as a lion. The whole Lake driving
down like a great river—waves dancing round the small islands. We walked
to the house: the Owner was salving sheep in the Barn—an appearance
of poverty & decay every where visible:—he asked us if we wanted to   60

35 old D: *del.* G.   36 elegant D: ancient G.   36–41 We had . . .
bridle D: *del.* G.   41 about . . . tea-time D: in the afternoon *inserted but with
no deletion* G.   44 W^m . . . the way D: *with irregular deletions, G inserts
and alters to* we walked along the Eastern shore of the lake towards the farm of
Blowick   was D: blew G.   47 places. Two *Edd.*: places; [the *del.*]
Two D.   *For insertion after* places (*cf. Guide,* 3002–6), W *writes:* [This might
del.] [Goats *del.*] This is the only part of the Country in which goats are now
found, but before I had seen these I was this morning reminded of that picturesque
animal by 2 Rams of mountain breed both with Ammonian Horns & with beards
almost as majestic as that which M. Angelo has given to the Statue of Moses.
[Animals with *del.*] This reverend appendage cannot I think be common to the
[⟨?Rams⟩ among *del.*] native Breed of Sheep on these Mountains as I have not
observed it anywhere else   48–9 Luff's . . . seen through D: *without deletions,
G inserts and alters to* our friends house fixed our notice as they were seen [?] the
edge of the under the edge of [*sic*] (*cf. Guide,* 2999–3000).   49–52 I . . . like D: *del.*
G.   53 the woods D²: its woods D: G *twice scribbles in pencil above the line*
of Blowick (*the intention was probably to have the phrase follow* fields *in* 53).
56 backwards . . . foot of D: down G.   57 as a lion D: *del.* G.   58 down
D: onward G.   58–61 We . . . Estate D: *del.* G.   58–62 We . . .
beauty D: W *writes for insertion* (*cf. Guide,* 3014–19) The Farm house of Blowick
was the Boundary of our walk & we returned lamenting to see so uncomfortable &
poverty-stricken a residence in a [spot so beautiful *del.*] place so favored by nature.
But these regrets were dispelled by the pleasure we had in beholding the exquisite
beauty   60 decay every where visible D: decay in every [?] G.

purchase the Estate. We could not but stop frequently, both in going &
returning, to observe the exquisite beauty of the woods on the opposite
side of the Lake. The general colour of the trees was brown, rather that
of ripe hazle nuts; but towards the water there were yet beds of green;
and in some of the hollow places in the highest parts of the woods the trees   65
were of a yellow colour, and, through the glittering light, they looked
like masses of clouds, as you see them gathered together in the west and
tinged with the golden light of the sun. After dinner we walked with
Mrs Luff *up* the Vale; I had never had an idea of the extent and width of
it in passing through on the other side. We walked along the path which   70
leads from house to house—two or three times it took us through some
of those copses or groves that cover every little hillock in the middle of the
lower part of the vale, making an intricate and beautiful intermixture of
lawn and wood. We left William to prolong his walk and when he came
into the house he told us he had pitched upon a spot where he should like   75
better to build a Cottage than in any other he had yet seen. Mrs Luff went
with him by moonlight to view it. The Vale looked as if it were filled with
white light when the moon had climbed up to the middle of the sky; but,
long before we could see her face, while all the near hills were in black
shade, those on the opposite side were almost as bright as snow. M^rs   80
Luff's large white Dog lay in the moonshine upon the round knoll under
the old Yew Tree—a beautiful and romantic image—the dark Tree with
its dark shadow, and the elegant Creature as fair as a Spirit.

Friday 9th Nov^r

It rained till near ten o'clock, but a little after that time, it being likely   85
for a tolerably fine day, we packed up bread and cold meat, and, with Luff's

66 colour D: [?] G.   69 Mrs Luff D: *del.* G.   never D, G²: never before G.   72 every little hillock D: the little hillocks G.   74–83 We
. . . Spirit D: *after making revisions recorded in the following notes, G deletes entirely.*
74–77 We . . . view it D: Our fancies could not resist the temptation & we fixed
upon a spot for a cottage which we [built *del.*] began to build & finished as easily as
castles are raised in the air. We visited the same spot by moonlight that evening.
G.   76–83 M^rs . . . Spirit D: I shall say nothing of the [situation which ⟨pleased
me so *del.*⟩ charmed me so much in the afternoon *del.*] moonlight aspect, but [on
my return to our Friends' house *del.*] I wish you had been with me when on returning to our Friends house we espied his Ladys large white Dog lying in the moonshine upon the round knoll under the old yew tree in the garden—a beautiful &
romantic image—The dark tree with its dark Shadow & the elegant Creature as
fair as a Spirit—The torrents [were falling *del.*] murmured [*altered from* murmur-
ing] softly [? *del.*] the mountains down which they fall [furnished *del.*] did not to my
sight furnish a back-ground for this Ossianic picture; but I had [an ⟨? impression⟩
del.] a consciousness [that *del.*] of the depth of the seclusion, & that Mountains
were embracing us on all sides.

I saw not but I felt that they were there. W.

77 looked D: looked at that time G.   78 when . . . had climbed D: G
alters to the moon having climbed   up D: up [? *del.*] G.   79 long . . . could
D: before we had been able to G.   in D: covered with G.   80 were D:
had been G.   84 G *scribbles some insertions*: Rain as before We [?] for to
visit the same spot by moonlight   85–9 It . . . we saw D: *after making
revisions recorded below, G deletes entirely.*   85 It . . . but a little D: Rained
till ten o'clock A little G.   86–7 Luff's Servant D: a man G.

Servant to help to row, set forward in the Boat. As we advanced the day
grew finer—clouds and sunny gleams on the mountains. In the grand
Bay under Place Fell we saw three Fishermen dragging a net, and rowed
up to them. They had just brought the net ashore, and hundreds of fish   90
were leaping in their prison. They were all of one kind; what are called
Skellies. After we had left them the Fishermen continued their work, a
picturesque group—under the lofty and bare crags.—The whole scene was
very grand—a raven croaking on the mountain above our heads. Landed
at Sanwick; the Man took the Boat home, and we pursued our journey   95
towards the Village along a beautiful summer path—at first through a
coppice by the Lake side; then through green fields.—The Village and
Brook very pretty; shut out from Mountains and Lakes—it reminded me
of Somersetshire.—Passed by Harry Hibson's House—I longed to go in
for the sake of old times—Wᵐ went up one side of the Vale and we up the   100
other, and he joined us again after having crossed the one-arched Bridge
below the Church, with its "bare ring of mossy wall," and single Yew
Tree. At the last house in the Dale we were kindly greeted by the Master
who was sitting at the door salving sheep—He invited us to go in and see
a room built by Mʳ Hazel for his accommodation at the yearly Chace of Red   105
Deer in his Forests at the head of these Dales. The Room is fitted up in the
Sportsman's style, with a single cupboard for bottles and glasses &c.—some
strong chairs, and a large dining-table, and ornamented with the Horns
of the Stags caught at these Hunts for many years back, with the length
of the last race they run recorded under each. We ate our dinner here. The   110
good woman treated us with excellent butter and new oaten Bread, and
after drinking of Mʳ Hazel's strong ale we were well prepared to face
the mountain, which we began to climb almost immediately. Martindale
divides itself into two dales at the head. In one of these (that to the left)

88 the grand D²: a grand D: the G.   89 saw three D: Three G.
89–90 and . . . them D: *del.* G.   91–2 of one . . . Skellies D: of kind;
called Skellies a sort of fresh water herring G.   92 After . . . them D: *del.* G.
continued their work, a D: made a G.   93–4 The . . . grand D: around
which G.   94 croaking . . . heads. D: was croaking. G.   95 at D:
near to G: in the Bay of G².   the Man . . . home D: *del.* G.   98–101 Brook
. . . crossed D: Brook shut out from Mountains and Lakes—Crossed G.
103 kindly D: *del.* G.   104 salving D: with sheep collected round him one
of which he was smearing with tar for protection against the winter cold G.
go in and see D: enter his house for the purpose of seeing G.   105 his
accommodation D: [?the] accommodation of his Friends G.   110 they run
D: each had run G.   each D: his stately antlers G.   111 new oaten
Bread D: oaten Cake new & crisp G.   111–12 and after . . . face D: We
faced G. G *also inserts above the line, but without a caret to indicate position,* on our
return to Patterdale   112–14 we were . . . head D: While we had remained
in the Boat our course had [lain *del.*] as you know followed the Base of Place Fell &
[?we now *del.*] [?thus] refreshed we prepared for our return to Patterdale by a
road which would complete the circuit of the mountain. [Martindale *del.*] The
[Village *del.*] Bay of Sanwick [stands *del.*] is at the foot of Martindale, along the
gentle slope of which dale we had [come *del.*] ascended since we left the Boat.
The Valley is thinly peopled & towards the head splits into two parts—It receives a
stream from Boardale [at *del.*] near its lower extremity—& towards its head splits
W.   114 divides . . . head D: splits into two dales G.

there is no house nor any building to be seen but a cattle-shed on the side 115
of a hill which is sprinkled over with wood, evidently the remains of a
Forest, formerly a very extensive one. At the bottom of the other dell
is the house I have mentioned; and beyond the enclosures of this Man's
Farm there are no other. A few old trees remain, relicks of the Forest,
a little stream passes in serpentine windings through the uncultivated 120
valley, where many Cattle were feeding. The Cattle of this country are
generally white, or light-coloured; but those were mostly dark brown or
black which made the scene resemble many parts of Scotland. When we
sate on the hill-side, though we were well contented with the quiet every-
day sounds—the lowing of the Cattle, bleating of sheep, & the very gentle 125
murmuring of the Valley-Stream yet we could not but think what a grand
effect the sound of the bugle horn would have among these Mountains. It
is still heard once every year at the Chace I have spoken of, a day of festivity for all the Inhabitants of this district, except the poor Deer, the most
ancient of them all. The ascent, even to the very top of the mountain is 130
very easy. When we had accomplished it we had some exceedingly fine
mountain views, some of the mountains being resplendent with sunshine
& others partly hidden by clouds. Ulswater was of a dazzling brightness
bordered by black hills. The Plain beyond Penrith smooth & bright, or
rather gleamy, as the Sea or Sea-sands. Looked into Boar Dale, above 135
Sanwick—deep and bare—a stream winding through it. After having
walked a considerable way along the tops of the hills came in view of
Sanwick, Glenridden and the Mountains at the head of Grisdale. Luff then
took us aside, before we had begun to descend, to a small Ruin, which was
formerly a Chapel, or place of worship where the Inhabitants of Martindale 140
and Patterdale were accustomed to meet on Sabbath days. There are now
no traces by which you could distinguish that the Building had been
different from a common Sheep-fold; the loose stones, & the few which
yet remain piled up are the same as those which lie elsewhere on the
mountain; but the shape of the Building, being oblong, is not that of a 145
common Sheep-fold; and it stands East & West. Whether it was ever
consecrated ground or not, I do not know; but the place may be kept holy
in the memory of some now living in Patterdale; for it was the means of
preserving the life of a poor old Man last summer who, having gone up
the mountain to gather peats together, had been overtaken by a storm, and 150

117 a very D²: a [? *del.*] D. 123 made the scene resemble D: heightened
the resemblance which this scene bears to G. 124 sate on D: paused to rest
upon G. 126 yet D: *del.* G. 131–2 some . . . views D: exceedingly fine views
G. 135 into D: down into G. 135–6 above Sanwick D: *del.* G. 138 Sanwick
D: *del.* G. 138–9 Luff . . . us D: Our companion turned G. 140 where D:
where it is said G. 144 same D: same in appearance G. 146 West.
Whether D: *after* West G *inserts a large* X: [Nothing but a *del.*] The piety must
have been more habitual & the zeal more fervent than I fear now prevails in any
part of Great Britain which could have rendered a situation so exposed & lofty of
any use for the purposes of devotion—The psalmody must have had the accompaniment of many a wildly whistling [wind *del.*] [Crag *del.*] Blast—& what storms in
this high place must have often drowned the voice of the Preacher W. (*Cf. Guide*
3135–40.)

could not find his way down again. He happened to be near the remains of
the old Chapel, and in a corner of it he contrived, by laying turf, & ling,
and stones in a corner of it from one wall to the other, to make a shelter
from the wind, and there he sate all night. The Woman who had sent him
on his errand began to grow uneasy towards evening, & the Neighbours   155
went to seek him. At that time the old Man had housed himself in his nest,
& he heard the voices of the Men; but could not make himself heard, the
wind being so loud; & he was afraid to leave the spot, least he should not
be able to find it again, so he remained there all night, and they returned
to their homes, giving him up for lost; but the next morning the same   160
persons discovered him, huddled up in the sheltered nook. He was at first
stupefied, & unable to move, yet after he had eaten and drunk, & recol-
lected himself a little he walked down the Mountain, and his health did not
afterwards seem to have suffered. As we descend the Vale of Patterdale
appears very simple and grand with its two heads, Deep dale, & Brothers-   165
water or Hartsop. It is remarkable that two pairs of Brothers should have
been drowned in that Lake. There is a tradition, at least, that it took its
name from two who were drowned there many years ago; and it is a fact
that two others did meet that melancholy fate about twenty years since.
It was upon a New-year's day. Their Mother had set them to thresh some   170
corn, and they (probably thinking it hard to be so tasked when all others
were keeping holiday) stole out to slide upon the ice and were both
drowned. A neighbour who had seen them fall through the ice, though not
near enough to be certain, *guessed who* they were, & went to the Mother
to enquire after her Sons. She replied that "they were threshing in the   175
Barn"."Nay," said the Man, "they are not there, nor is it likely today." The
Woman went with him to the Barn, and the Boys were gone. He was then
convinced of the truth, and told her that they were drowned. It is said that
they were found locked in each other's arms. I was exceedingly tired when

153 a corner D: *inadvertently del.* G.   165 its D: *del.* G.   166–73 It
is . . . drowned D: That Lake is named Broader Water & probably rightly so;
for Bassenthwaite Lake at this day is familiarly called Broad water; but the
change in the appellation if it be a corruption may have been assisted by some
tragic accident similar to what happened about 20 years ago when two Brothers
were drowned there [*hereafter* W *deletes, inserts, and repeats so erratically that our
reading must be conjectural*] [upon a New Year's Day while taking their holiday
pleasure upon the ice *del.*] [having gone out to take their holiday pleasure upon the
ice on a New-years *del.*] in the Lake while taking their holiday pleasure together
on the Ice upon a New Years day W. (*Cf. Guide*, 3143–50.)   169 did . . .
about D: [did *undel.*] so perished G.   172 both D: *del.* G.   179–90 I
was . . . Penrith D: [A fine moonlight night *del.*] Descended to our Friends house
by a steep & rough peat-track—Another fine moonlight night—But a thick fog
rising from the neighbouring River [hid the *undel.*] [wood-covered *del.*] [rocky *del.*]
[completely *del.*] enveloped the rocks & wood-crested knoll on [*altered from* upon]
which my fancy cottage had been erected—& [? *del.*] under the damp cast upon my
feelings I consoled myself by moralizing upon the folly of hasty decisions in matters
of importance & the necessity of having [a *del.*] at least one years knowledge of a
place before you realize any airy suggestions in solid stone.—A beautiful morning—
Received the tidings of Lord Nelson's Death & the Victory of Trafalgar—
Sequestered as we were from [general *del.*] the sympathy of a crowd we were
shocked to hear that the Bells had been ringing merrily at Penrith to celebrate the

we reached Mr Luff's house, owing to the steepness and roughness of the 180
peat-track down which we descended. I lay down on the Sofa, & was asleep
in three minutes.—A fine moonlight night—a thick fog in the middle
of the Vale, which disheartened William respecting the situation of his
house.—Supped upon some of the Fish caught by the Fishermen under
Place Fell, & thought them excellent. 185

Saturday 10th Nov^r

A beautiful morning.—When we were at breakfast heard the tidings of
Lord Nelson's Death, & the Victory at Trafalgar—Went to the Inn to make
further inquiries. I was shocked to hear that there had been great rejoicings
at Penrith. Returned by William's rock & grove, & were so much pleased 190
with the spot that he determined to buy it, if possible, therefore we prepared to set off to Park House, that W^m might apply to Thomas Wilkinson
to negotiate for him with the Owner. We went down that side of the Lake
opposite to Stybarrow Crag. I dismounted & we sate some time on the
same Rock as before above Blowick. Owing to the brightness of the sun- 195
shine the Church and other buildings were even more concealed from us
than by the Mists two days before. It had been a sharp frost in the night,
and the grass and trees were yet wet. We observed the lemon-coloured
leaves of the birches in the wood below, as the wind turned them to the
sun, sparkle, or rather *flash* like diamonds. The day continued unclouded to 200
the end. We had a delightful Ride and walk, for it was both to both of us.
We led the horse under Place Fell, and though I mostly rode when the way
was good, yet William sometimes mounted to rest himself. Called at
Eusemere—the Miss Greens not yet settled in their house.—Went by
Bower Bank, intending to ford the Emont at the Mill, but the Pony could 205
not carry us both; so after many attempts, I rode over myself & a Girl
followed upon another Horse to carry back the Pony to William.—Very
cold before we reached Park House—Carpets & chairs spread upon the

Victory. Sixty years ago there was [? *del*.] no road for wheels to Patterdale & [this *del*.]
such news [as *del*.] might at that time have been long in [reaching *del*.] penetrating
so far into the Mountains; but Travellers for pleasure or Felicity-hunters, as they are
called by some, are now becoming as active as and more numerous than those who
formerly left their [? houses *or* ? homes] for purposes of gain. [In Lapland the *del*.]
The Priest on the Banks of the remotest stream of Lapland [who *Edd*.] [? will]
[? talk] familiarly of Buonaparte's last conquests and discuss even the minutiae of
the French Revolution [gets *del*.] acquires information from adventurers impelled
by curiosity alone & will [? talk] [? familiarly] &— W. (*Cf. Guide*, 3151–74.)

186 Novr D: *after* Novr G *inserts* Next [?]   193–5 We . . . Blowick D:
G, *without making deletions, inserts* At 10 o'clock we pursued our way on foot on
the same side of the Lake [as we came from on the day before *del*.] which we had
coasted in a Boat the day before   195 above Blowick D: G, *without making
deletions, inserts* [?] above the farm of   195–7 Owing . . . before D: G *alters
to* The brightness of the sunshine concealed from us the Church and other buildings
even more than the haze & vapour had done [the day before *del*.] two days before
201–54 We had . . . the sun D: *after a few emendations recorded below,* G *deletes
the whole passage and substitutes* & I shall not describe [either *del*.] the scene or relate
our little adventures [but *undel*.] & will only add that on the afternoon of the 13 we
returned [from *del*.] along the banks of Ulswater by the usual road. The morning
had been wet but now the sun   203 yet D: *del*. G.

grass—Derwent ran out to meet us. Sate in the kitchen till the parlour fire was lighted; & then enjoyed a comfortable cup of tea. After tea Wᵐ 210 went to Thomas Wilkinson's & to Brougham.

Monday Novʳ 12ᵗʰ

The morning being fine, we resolved to go to Lowther, & accordingly Sara mounted Tom's horse, I the pony & William & Miss Green set out on foot; but she had not walked far before she took a Seat behind Sara.— 215 Crossed the Ford at Yanworth. We found Thomas Wilkinson at work in one of his fields: he chearfully laid down his spade, & walked by our side with William. We left our horses at the Mill below Brougham, & walked through the woods till we came to the [?old] Quarry where the road ends, the very place which has been the Boundary of some of the happiest of the 220 walks of my youth. The sun did not shine when we were there; & it was mid-day, therefore if it *had* shone, the light could not have been the same; yet so vividly did I call to mind those walks, that when I was in the wood I almost seemed to see the same rich light of evening upon the trees which I had seen in those happy hours. My heart was full; and I could not but 225 grieve that any strangers were with us. At this time the Path was scarcely traceable by the eye, all the ground being strewn with withered leaves, which I was very sorry for, William having described the beauty of it with so much delight after having been at Lowther in the summer.

Scrambled along, under the Quarry—then came to T. Wilkinson's new 230 path. We spent three delightful hours by the River-side & in the woods. We were received with much kindness by Richard Bowman & his Wife— dinner was presently prepared; & we were officiously [waited] upon by little Hannah, whose light motions and happy looks plainly expressed the hospitality of the house.—Went with Miss Green to Penrith—drank tea 235 at Mʳˢ Ellwoods—Read Collingwood's dispatches—Went to Mʳ James's Shop, & called upon Miss Monkhouse at Mʳˢ Coupland's. Mary Monkhouse & Sara mounted at the George—I walked with Wᵐ through the town to Mʳˢ Ellwood's door—the first time I have been in Penrith streets at that time of the night, since Mary & her Sister Margaret, and I used to 240 steal out to each other's houses, and when we had had our *talk* over the kitchen fire to delay the moment of parting, paced up one street and down another by moon or star light. S. and I stopped at Red Hills while William went over the Ford to T. Wilkinson's—the house untidy & not comfortable—a little Girl never ceased rocking a Baby in the Cradle. We asked 245 if it would not sleep without being rocked, & the Mother answered "No; for it was used to it."—Reached Park House at ten o'clock—Joanna had waited dinner and tea for us.

Tuesday Novr 13th

A very wet morning—no hope of being able to return home. W^m read 250
in a Book lent him by T. Wilkinson—I read Castle Rackrent—The day
cleared at one o'clock & after dinner at a little before three we set forward.
The pony was bogged in Tom's field, & I was obliged to dismount. Went
over Soulby Fell—Before we reached Ulswater the sun shone, and only
a few scattered clouds remained on the hills except at the tops of the very 255
highest—the Lake perfectly calm. We had a delightful journey. At the
beginning of the first Park William got upon the pony, and, betwixt a
walk and a *run*, I kept pace with him while he trotted to the next gate—
then I mounted again. We were joined by two Travellers, like ourselves
with one white horse between them. We went on in company till we came 260
near to Patterdale, trotting all the time. The trees in Gowbarrow Park
were very beautiful, the hawthorns leafless, their round heads covered
with rich red berries and adorned with arches of green brambles and
Eglantine hung with glossy hips—Many birches yet tricked out in full
foliage of bright yellow—oaks brown or leafless—the smooth branches of 265
the Ashes bare—most of the Alders green as in spring. I think I have more
pleasure in looking at deer than any other animals; perhaps chiefly from
their living in a more natural state. At the end of Gowbarrow Park a large
troop of them were either moving slowly or standing still among the fern.
I was grieved when our Companions startled them with a whistle, disturb- 270
ing a beautiful image of grave simplicity & thoughtful enjoyment, for I
could have fancied that even *they* were partaking with me a sensation of the
solemnity of the closing day. The sun had been set some time though we
could only just perceive that the day-light was fading away from the hills,
and the lake was more brilliant than before. I dismounted again at Sty- 275
barrow Crag, & William rode till we came almost to Glenriddin. Found
the Luffs at Tea in the kitchen. After Tea set out again. Luff accompanied
me on foot into the lane, & W^m continued to ride till we came to Brothers-
water Bridge—a delightful evening—The Seven Stars close to the hill tops
in Patterdale—All the stars seemed brighter than usual. The steeps were 280
reflected in Brothers-water, and above the Lake appeared like enormous
black perpendicular walls. The torrents of Kirkstone had been swoln by
the rains, & filled the mountain Pass with their roaring, which added
greatly to the solemnity of our walk. Behind us, when we had climbed very

256–61 At the beginning . . . time D: *after deleting* again (259), G *then deletes
the whole passage.*   262 very beautiful D: *without making any deletions,* G
inserts in that state when what is gained in interest by the disclosure of their
Bark & Brambles compensates [for *undel.*] [loss in foliage *del.*] almost for the loss
of foliage [in this ⟨? period *or* ? point⟩ *del.*] they exhibited [all *del.*] that variety which
characterises the point of time between autumn & winter   265 branches D:
silver branches G.   266–8 I think . . . state D: *del.* G.   270 our Companions D: a chance Companions [*sic*] who had joined us by the way G.
273–5 though . . . was more D: but as the lake under a luminous sky was more
brilliant than before we could . . . G: and we could . . . hills, but the lake under
a luminous sky was more G².   277 Tea [*second*] D: Tea at Patterdale G.
281 Brothers-water, C: Brother s-water; D.

high, we saw one light in the Vale at a great distance, like a large star, a solitary one, in the gloomy region—all the chearfulness of the scene was in the sky above us.

Found Mary & the Children in bed—no fire—luckily W^m was warm with walking, & I not cold, having wrapped myself up most carefully, & the night being mild—Went to bed immediately after Supper.

285 one D²: only D.   large D: large red G.   290 *After* Supper G *writes in ink* Reached home an hour before *and then in pencil* Reached home at midnight

COMMENTARY: *GUIDE*

1–11. In emphasizing that his 'principal wish', or 'primary object', is to provide 'a Guide or Companion for the *Minds* of Persons of Taste', Wordsworth announces immediately that his work is not simply another guide-book to the Lakes (cf. E. de S., p. [167]). In 1835 the point needed to be made, for the new title, *A Guide through the District of the Lakes*, in contrast to earlier titles (e.g. *A Description of the Scenery of the Lakes*), and the appearance for the first time of the 'Directions and Information for the Tourist' at the front of the volume could have been misleading. Even by the pagination for this newly expanded section (pp. [i]–xxiv), Wordsworth further indicates that the directions for the tourist are merely prefatory to the main work.

8–96. For Wordsworth's earlier remarks on the various approaches to the Lake District cf. *S.V.* 1–30, 115–35, textual n. 135/6, and *U.T.* 1–356. In *S.V.* and *U.T.* he treats first the approaches from the north and then those from the south, whereas in the *Guide* he reverses that order. In *U.T.* the discussion is longer because the approaches from the south include a separate notice of Lancaster and Lancaster Castle (98–200) and another of the Sands and Furness Abbey (202–356).

18–28. The Traveller . . . Stanemoor] From Greta Bridge, Wordsworth and Coleridge went over Stainmore on Coleridge's first trip to the Lakes (*E.Y.*, p. 271; *C.N.B.* i. 495; Moorman, i. 448).

29–31. The second . . . Jervaux Abbey] In the summer of 1789, 'making eager quest of scenes / For beauty famed', Wordsworth had roamed 'through Yorkshire's splendid Vales' (*Prel.* VI (A²C), 208–9).

31–5. up the vale . . . Kendal] On their first journey to their home in Grasmere, in December 1799, Dorothy and William walked this route. A few days later Wordsworth in a long letter to Coleridge described in detail this part of their journey, paying particular attention to the water-falls (*E.Y.*, pp. 277–80). This winter journey is also recalled in *The Recluse*, i. 152–70 (*P.W.* v. 319). When in October 1802 they retraced the route with Mary, then a new bride, Dorothy in her journal constantly compared the experiences of the two trips (*Journals*, i. 179–82). See also I.F. note to *Miscellaneous Sonnets*, Part II, xi (*P.W.* iii. 427).

33–4. Hardraw . . . drawing] 'Hardraw Scar' is one of twenty engravings which Turner made for Thomas D. Whitaker's *History of Richmondshire* (London, 1823). It was the first plate to be finished, and was published separately in 1818 (C. F. Bell, 'Turner and his Engravers', *The Genius of J. M. W. Turner*, ed. Charles Holme (London, 1903), E, p. v, and Illustration E 4), but Wordsworth probably saw it first in Whitaker's *History*. He had long been an admirer of Whitaker's work (see his note to *The White Doe*, *P.W.* iii. 535; I.F. note to 'The Force of Prayer', *P.W.*

iv. 421; *M.T*. i. 167, 270), but his praise of Turner is unusual and note-worthy (cf. n. 2582–6 below).

36–48. In July 1807, in the company of the Marshalls, with whom they had spent a weekend at Kirkstall, William and Dorothy rode to Bolton, where they visited the Abbey and the surrounding countryside. From Bolton they walked on alone to Burnsall, Gordale Scar, Malham, Settle, and Kendal (*M.T*. i. 158 and Moorman, ii. 108). For scenes of Bolton Abbey see *The White Doe* (*P.W*. iii. 281–340) and 'The Force of Prayer' (*P.W*. iv. 88–90), as well as Wordsworth's notes attached to these poems (*P.W*. iii. 535–56 and iv. 420–1).

45. Gordale . . . Gray's Tour] In September 1769 Gray and his friend Thomas Wharton set off for a tour of Yorkshire and the Lakes, but at Brough illness compelled Wharton to turn home and Gray continued the tour alone. The journal which he kept was not intended for publication, but was made solely for Wharton's amusement; after his tour, Gray transcribed the journal and sent it in a series of letters to Wharton. (See *Correspondence of Thomas Gray*, ed. P. Toynbee and L. Whibley (Oxford, 1935), pp. 1074–81, 1087–91, 1094–110.) When William Mason prefixed his *Memoirs* of Gray to his edition of *The Poems of M*ʳ· *Gray* (York, 1775) he printed the letters continuously; he also omitted, inserted, and rewrote passages. Although Wordsworth owned a copy of Mason's 1776 edition (Rydal Mount Catalogue, lot 545), he would have found it convenient in writing the *Guide* to turn to Thomas West's *Guide to the Lakes*, where, in the second and subsequent editions, Gray's journal was reprinted among the 'Addenda'. The 'Addenda' were first collected by William Cockin, who brought out the second edition of West's *Guide* in 1780. A copy of the ninth edition (Kendal, 1807) with Wordsworth's name and the date '1814' inscribed on the title-page is in the Berg Collection of the New York Public Library (John D. Gordan, *William Wordsworth* (New York, 1950), p. 4; cf. Rydal Mount Catalogue, lot 175). Since the date on the title-page does not preclude Wordsworth's having used, earlier than 1814, either this copy or another copy of the same edition, and since it was the most recent when he was composing *Select Views*, we shall ordinarily cite the 1807 edition, not only for West as revised by Cockin and for Gray as edited by Mason, but also for other writers included in the 'Addenda'.

Of Gordale Scar Gray writes:

From thence [Malham] I was to walk a mile over very rough ground, a torrent rattling along on the left hand; on the cliffs above hung a few goats; one of them danced, and scratched an ear with its hind foot, in a place where I would not have stood stock-still

For all beneath the moon.

As I advanced, the crags seemed to close in, but discovered a narrow entrance turning to the left between them; I followed my guide a few paces, and the hills opening [*sic*] again into no large space; and then all further way is barred by a stream that at the height of about fifty feet, gushes from a hole in the rock, and spreading in large sheets over its broken front, dashes from steep to steep, and then rattles away in a torrent down the valley[;] the rock on the left rises perpendicular, with stubbed yew-trees and shrubs starting from its sides, to the height of at least 300 feet; but these are not the thing; it is the rock to the right, under which you stand to see the fall that forms the principal horror of the place. From its very base it begins to slope forward over you in one black or solid mass without any crevice in its surface, and overshadows half the area below its dreadful canopy: when I stood at (I believe) four yards distant from its foot, the drops which perpetually distill from its brow, fell on my head; and in one part of its top, more exposed to the weather, there are loose stones that hang in the air, and threaten visibly some idle spectator with instant destruction; it is safer to shelter yourself close to its bottom, and trust to the mercy of that enormous mass, which nothing but an earthquake can stir. The gloomy uncomfortable day well suited the savage aspect of the place, and made it still more formidable; I stayed there, not without shuddering, a quarter of an hour, and thought my trouble richly paid; for the impression will last for life [West, *Guide*, pp. 220–1].

54. Weathercote Cave] Cf. *Prel*. VIII. 711–41. For three sonnets 'Suggested by Mr. W. Westall's Views of the Caves, etc., in Yorkshire' see *P.W*. iii. 36–7; one of the sonnets is on 'Malham Cove', and another on 'Gordale'. Wordsworth visited the Yorkshire caves and Gordale Scar in May 1800 with his brother John (*E.T*., p. 298 and Moorman, i. 476), and in November 1821 with Edward Quillinan (*M. W., Letters*, p. 82).

75–80. there is . . . found] The view which Gray mentioned as being 'indeed charming' is described in greater detail by Mason in his footnote to Gray's sentence (West, *Guide*, p. 218). In his own text West quotes part of Mason's description, to which Cockin then adds *his* footnote (p. 25): 'As several mistakes have been made respecting this station, it is necessary to point it out more precisely. About a quarter of a mile beyond . . .' etc., as quoted by Wordsworth, except for minor variations in punctuation.

85–96. It is . . . enough] Returning from Carlisle in August 1833, Wordsworth 'came home up the banks of the Eden, by Corby and Nunnery, both charming places' (*L.T*., p. 667). As he makes plain in sonnet XXXVIII of *Poems Composed or Suggested During a Tour, in the Summer of 1833*, he had until then 'viewed' Eden 'By glimpses only' (*P.W*. iv. 45); in notes to sonnet XLI, he tells of having become 'acquainted with the walks of Nunnery when a boy', during his summer holidays in Penrith, and writes admiringly of the 'magnificent viaduct' at Corby (*P.W*. iv. 409–10).

89–90. In the Church . . . Nollekens] Cf. Daniel and Samuel Lysons, *Magna Britannia* (London, 1816), iv. 167. The series cited in the preceding note contains two sonnets (XXXIX and XL) on the 'Monument of Mrs. Howard' by Nollekens (*P.W*. iv. 45–6). In the I.F. note to sonnet XXXIX (ibid., p. 409), Wordsworth recalls Nollekens's showing him this piece of sculpture while it was still in his studio. Joseph Nollekens died in 1823 (*D.N.B*.), and in 1834 Wordsworth said that his visit to Nollekens in London had occurred 'many years ago' (*L.T*., p. 708).

97–286. For excursions in the southern region of the Lake District cf. *S.V*. 31–326 and textual nn., and *U.T*. 357–1591. In the *Guide* the exploration of this region begins with the centre at Bowness and then moves to Coniston; in *S.V*. the itinerary is simply the reverse, with excursions first around Coniston and then around Windermere; altogether, the excursions range as far to the north-east as the Vale of St. John and as far to the south-west as Duddon Sands. Despite its much greater length, *U.T.* has, for this section of the Lake District, a continuous treatment only of Coniston and its neighbouring vales to the north and west, Hawkshead, and the road from Hawkshead to the western shore of Windermere.

In our commentary on what Wordsworth calls the 'approaches' to the Lake District, we have noted some of his visits to places comparatively remote from his native regions; but when it comes to the three main areas of the District, as outlined in 97–286, 287–353, and 354–495, it should be recognized that since his youth Wordsworth had known in varying degrees of intimacy all the places he mentions or describes. On this account, we do not note the many other references in his letters and poetry to specific places within the District, except occasionally for some particular reason. On Wordsworth's early wanderings in the north Mark L. Reed (*Wordsworth: the Chronology of the Early Years* (Cambridge, Mass., 1967)) is especially helpful.

99–101. Bowness . . . WINDERMERE] Cf. *Prel.* II. 145–80.

103. Storrs Hall] The country seat of John Bolton of Liverpool. For Wordsworth's friendship with Bolton see our Introduction to *Bowness*, iii. 287.

108–12. The view . . . wood] Cf. *Guide*, 1776–80, *S.V.* 96–114, and nn. John Christian (1756–1828), who in 1782 married Isabella Curwen of Workington Hall, and some years later assumed her surname, was a wealthy owner of mines and farmland. A Whig, he was for many years M.P. for Carlisle, and in 1820 he was elected County Member. (See Edward Hughes, *North Country Life in the Eighteenth Century* (London, 1952–65), ii. 110–388.) In 1808 Curwen was on Wordsworth's side in the *Cintra* controversy (see i.196–8), but they were opponents in the electoral campaign of 1818 (see iii.141); in 1830 Wordsworth's eldest son, John, married Curwen's granddaughter.

In 1781, the year before her marriage, Isabella Curwen had purchased Belle Isle on Windermere from Mr. Thomas English for 1,640 guineas (Hughes, ii. 132, and Clarke, p. 138). In 1786 Curwen purchased 'some property' near the Ferry on the western shore, but the seller's title to the property was disputed, and a settlement was not reached until some years later; in 1790 he entered negotiations with 'interested proprietors' for a much larger holding in Claife, which he seems finally to have acquired in 1799, when he 'owed the proprietors and landowners in Claife £663 6s. 8d. for lands called the Heald, &c.' (Hughes, ii. 216 and *The Victoria History of . . . Lancaster* (London, 1966), p. 376). In 1809 Curwen was awarded a gold medal by the Society of Arts for 'having planted in a single year over a million larches and other forest trees' (Hughes, ii. 237).

112–40. Windermere . . . inexhaustible] With only a few changes, the *Guide* preserves *S.V.* 173–200.

115, textual n.] Cf. *Prel*. II. *56–65*, quoted in our n. to 952–60. The Ferry Inn property on the western shore was called the 'Great Boat', perhaps to distinguish its ferry, which carried packhorses and wagons, from the one for foot passengers only which ran from Miller Ground to Belle Grange (H. S. Cowper, *Hawkshead* (London, 1899), pp. 248–9).

123–7. the close . . . supplied] The River Brathay, which flows down from Great Langdale. The alteration in textual n. 147–83, from 'two Streams at its head' to 'two vales at its head', was made for the sake of accuracy: the Rothay, flowing through Grasmere and Rydal, enters the Brathay near its influx into Windermere.

140, fn. William Green, *The Tourist's New Guide, Containing A Description of the Lakes, Mountains, and Scenery in Cumberland, Westmorland, and Lancashire* (2 vols., Kendal, 1819). For Wordsworth's interest in Green and his admiration of Green's drawings of the Lake country see Introduction, pp. 124–5, and *M.T.* i. 195, 258.

151–2. then . . . Blea Tarn] The Wordsworths occasionally stayed at Hackett, a cottage overlooking Little Langdale, and in 1818 Wordsworth was a co-purchaser of Ivy How in Little Langdale, a farm bought for the sake of dividing the freehold (Moorman, ii. 359). For other descriptions, in prose and verse, of Little Langdale see 'Epistle to Sir George Beaumont', ll. 203–49 (*P.W.* iv. 148–50 and nn., pp. 433–4); *Exc*. V. 670–826 (and nn., *P.W.* v. 442); *Miscellaneous Sonnets*, Part I, viii (*P.W.* iii. 5 and n., p. 420); *M.T.* i. 447, 500; *M. W., Letters*, p. 40.

156–77. *Exc*. II. 327–48, with minor variations in punctuation. See also I.F. note, *P.W.* v. 376. The Langdale valleys, Loughrigg Fell, and Grasmere form the principal scenes in *Exc*. II–IX.

184–9. The Stranger . . . led] With only slight alterations, this sentence has persisted from 1810 (*S.V.* 15–21) through *U.T.* (209–15) and the editions of 1822 and 1823, to the final text of 1835. Leven Sands, Chapel Island, and the surrounding shores are the setting for *Prel*. X. 475–567. The hazardous journey over the Sands was described by most of the popular writers on the Lakes (see Norman Nicholson, *The Lakers* (London, 1955), pp. 76–88); W. Cockin's description, which was added in a long footnote to West's own (*Guide*, pp. 29–31), is perhaps the best. Like Wordsworth, Gilpin (i. 130–1) had stressed the value of a gradual introduction to these 'grand scenes'.

201. Colonel Mudge] William Mudge (1762–1820); in 1798 Director of the Ordnance Trigonometrical Survey and a Fellow of the Royal Society; lieutenant-colonel in 1804; major-general in 1819; supervised the publication of survey maps and published numerous geodetic works (*D.N.B.*). From the I.F. note to *Inscriptions*, VI (*P.W.* iv. 199 and 442), it appears that E. de S. (p. 170) was mistaken in thinking that the 'geographic Labourer' of whom Wordsworth wrote in Inscription VI was Mudge himself.

204–15. Charles Farish, *The Minstrels of Winandermere* (London, n.d.), pp. 33–4. The dedicatory letter to Richard Clark, Esq., is dated 29 June

1811 (p. xv). Wordsworth has corrected 'Holkar's' to 'Holker's', as well as one obvious misprint; he has also slightly varied the punctuation.

In his long poem Farish frequently alludes to his schooldays at Hawkshead (see our note to *S.V.*, textual n. 135/6); like Wordsworth, he went from Hawkshead School to Cambridge, where he eventually became a Fellow of Queens' College (cf. E. de S., p. 170). When writing this section of the *Guide* in 1822, Wordsworth had already composed two poems of his own on Black Comb ('View from the Top of Black Comb', *P.W.* ii. 289–90, and *Inscriptions*, VI, *P.W.* iv. 199) and had given nine lines to it at the beginning of a third poem ('Epistle to Sir George Howland Beaumont', *P.W.* iv. 142). But as early as *U.T.* 505, his intention apparently had been to quote his schoolfellow's verses on Black Comb.

216. Broughton] For Wordsworth's visits to Broughton and its neighbourhood during his college years and later see Mark L. Reed, *Wordsworth: the Chronology of the Early Years* (Cambridge, Mass., 1967), pp. 84–5, 93, 157, and *E.T.*, pp. 121, 129. In the I.F. note to *The River Duddon* (*P.W.* iii. 504–5), Wordsworth recalls his first acquaintance with the Duddon when he was a schoolboy at Hawkshead, and his later visits to it when he was 'several times resident in the house of a near relative [Mary Wordsworth Smith, daughter of Richard Wordsworth of Whitehaven] who lived in the small town of Broughton'.

224–5. the Author's . . . Notes] *The River Duddon, P.W.* iii. 244–61 and 503–24.

230. as before mentioned] i.e. *Guide,* 133–7.

247. Fox How] The house built by Thomas Arnold, and his summer residence from 1834 onward (see our n. to *Guide,* 1553–63).

249–53. The Waterfalls . . . private] The falls at Rydal are described by Gilpin, i. 169–71; Mason, in a note to Gray's Journal (West, *Guide,* p. 212); West, *Guide,* pp. 76–7. Wordsworth wrote of them in *An Evening Walk,* 1793 (*P.W.* i. 8–11); in *U.T.*, textual n. 1591/2, he mocked the tourists who pause for one brief look at these 'celebrated' falls as they ride posthaste from Ambleside to Keswick.

253–6. A foot road . . . Ambleside] A favourite walk of the Wordsworths; see, for example, 'To the Clouds', ll. 53–7 (*P.W.* ii. 318–19 and I.F. note, p. 524), and *Journals,* i. 137.

257. as before mentioned] i.e. *Guide,* 141–4.

258. the high road] *The Waggoner* (*P.W.* ii. 176–205) opens with the sound of Benjamin's wain heard moving along the banks of Rydal; thereafter, Benjamin's accustomed route along the high road to Keswick is described in vivid and memorable detail.

277. the bridge that divides the Lake] Thirlmere, sometimes still called Wythburn Water or Leathes Water, is now the main reservoir for Manchester. The dam at the foot has raised and widened the lake, and the bridge that formerly spanned the narrowest point is gone.

287–353. Cf. *S.V.* 327–552, where Keswick is the centre for excursions in the northern and western regions of the Lake District. In addition to such far-ranging excursions as those to Loweswater, Wasdale, and Scafell, *S.V.* describes in detail some of the smaller valleys branching off from the main vale of Keswick. In *U.T.* Wordsworth finished only one part on this northern region, a description of Borrowdale (1592–787).

Wordsworth's recommended tours in the north and west were ones on which he had conducted Coleridge in 1799 (*C.N.B.* i. 536–41), Dorothy in 1804 (*E.T.*, pp. 507–8), and Mary in 1807 (*M.T.* i. 164).

297. from the side of Latrigg] Windy Brow, the cottage where William frequently lodged in 1793–4 and to which he brought Dorothy for a visit in the spring of 1794, is on the side of Latrigg above the Greta; in a letter from Windy Brow (*E.T.*, pp. 114–15), Dorothy described the view from the window of the room where she was writing. Cf. also Wordsworth's note to his sonnet 'To the River Greta, near Keswick', *P.W.* iv. 400. The view from Latrigg is particularly commended by West (*Guide*, pp. 103–4).

298. Ormathwaite] For a description of Ormathwaite by Dorothy Wordsworth see *M.T.* i. 381–2. Until 1804 Joseph Wilkinson of *Select Views* had lived at Ormathwaite (see Introduction, p. 124).

Applethwaite] After a visit to Keswick in the summer of 1803 Sir George Beaumont presented Wordsworth with a property in Applethwaite, consisting of 'a few old houses with two small fields attached to them'. Sir George had hoped that Wordsworth would move to Applethwaite and thus be nearer Coleridge at Greta Hall. (See *C.L.* ii. 973, and *E.T.*, pp. 406–9, 427; see also *M.T.* i. 76; *L.T.*, p. 1318.) Wordsworth's sonnet 'At Applethwaite, near Keswick' (*P.W.* iii. 3) expresses his gratitude to Sir George for this gift.

304. Armathwaite] In 1794 William and Dorothy paid several visits to the Speddings at Armathwaite Hall (*E.T.*, pp. 115–16, 122, and Moorman, i. 243). West (*Guide*, pp. 115–17) also praised the views from Armathwaite.

328. Mr. Marshall's woods] Cf. *S. H.*, *Letters* (14 July 1816), p. 93: 'William and I spent three days, the week before last, with Mr [John] Marshall at Scale Hill, Lowess Water, Buttermere, & Crum[m]ock, viewing his estates and manor there, and planning his proposed plantations and Improvements. He is going to plant very largely by the side of the two last lakes—and, as he will only plant native wood, and in no wise sacrifice beauty to convenience, we expect that his labours will not only be profitable but ornamental.'

332–7. Turn back . . . upon it] Cf. Wordsworth's note to *Guide*, 2418.

354–495. Cf. *Guide*, 2958–3229 and *S.V.* 553–712 for excursions in the eastern region of the Lake District. In addition to Ullswater and the valleys which immediately surround it, the itineraries extend north to Dalemain, east to Lowther Park, south to Haweswater, and west to Helvellyn and the roads leading south and west from Patterdale.

358. the Pass of Kirkstone] Cf. *Guide*, 3234–325.

362–489. a magnificent . . . that mansion] Except for a few stylistic alterations and an occasional omission or insertion, the *Guide* follows closely the text of *S.V.* 557–712. In 1823 Dorothy Wordsworth's Ullswater excursion (2958–3230) made its first appearance and necessitated the changes indicated in textual nn. 474–5.

363. Ara-force] For verses on Airey Force see 'The Somnambulist' (*P.W.* iv. 49–54) and 'Airey-Force Valley' (*P.W.* ii. 209).

377–82. The Church-yard . . . office] Old Church—as well as Hallsteads, the home of the John Marshalls, where the Wordsworths frequently visited—is on Skelly Nab, a promontory on the Cumberland side of Ullswater. Wordsworth's historical information may have been drawn from (1) Clarke's *Survey* and (2) Nicolson and Burn:

> (1) The chapel at Gowbarrow being destroyed by the Scots, this place was without any place of worship till some years afterwards, when a chapel was built about a mile from the water: this was consecrated in the year 1558, (as appears from a memorandum in an old Bible,) by Bishop Oglethorpe when on his road to crown Queen Elizabeth [Clarke, p. 26]. (2) In 1558, when Heath archbishop of York, and all the rest of the bishops, refused to crown queen Elizabeth (the see of Canterbury being then void), bishop Oglethorp was with much ado prevailed upon to set the crown on her head. For which fact, when he saw the issue of the matter, and both himself (saith Anthony a-Wood) and all the rest of his sacred order deprived, and the church's holy laws and faith against the conditions of her consecration and acception into that royal office violated, he sore repented him all the days of his life, which were for that special cause both short and wearisome [Nicolson and Burn, ii. 280].

390–1. Dacre . . . Bede] Bede, *Opera Historica*, ed. J. E. King (Loeb Classical Library), ii. 192: '. . . in monasterio quod iuxta amnem Dacore constructum ab eo cognomen accepit'. Bede is the earliest example cited for the *Dacre* in E. Ekwall, *The Concise Oxford Dictionary of English Place-Names*, 3rd edition.

400–1. Matterdale, before spoken of] i.e. *Guide*, 361.

404. a powerful Brook] i.e. the Airey.

412–16. At the outlet . . . picturesque] In 1808 Wordsworth told the Beaumonts that he had bought a sketch of the cottage at Glencoyne done by William Green, 'which I think has great merit, the materials being uncommonly picturesque' (*M.Y.* i. 195).

421–32. and the Stream . . . master] In April 1805 Charles Gough, a young man who had come to Patterdale 'for the sake of angling', accidentally suffered a fatal fall from Striding Edge on Helvellyn; three months later, near Red Tarn, his remains were found still being guarded by his faithful dog. (See I.F. note to 'Fidelity', *P.W.* iv. 417; Moorman, ii. 56–7, who quotes an unpublished contemporary account by Charles Danvers; H. D. Rawnsley, *Literary Associations of the English Lakes* (Glasgow, 1894), ii. 39–41, who quotes Thomas Wilkinson's account.) Almost immediately after the discovery Wordsworth received from the Luffs, his friends in Patterdale, a report of the event (*E.T.*, pp. 611–12). Although 'Fidelity', which tells the story of Gough and his dog, centres on the faithfulness of the dog, the finest stanzas are given to the 'silent Tarn in the recesses of Helvellyn' (*Guide*, 423); one of the stanzas is quoted by Wordsworth in *Guide*, 1053–9.

For other verses on Helvellyn and its near neighbourhood see thirty-six lines of a manuscript draft originally intended for 'Michael', but never used (MS. 2, passage *d*, in *P.W.* ii. 483–4); *Prel*. VIII. 1–61 and 228–44 (the latter passage is quoted in our n. to 433–53 below); 'Inmate of a mountain-dwelling' (*P.W.* ii. 286–7, and quoted by Wordsworth in *Guide*, 2911–49); *Recluse*, I. 517–20: 'And if those Eagles to their ancient Hold / Return, Helvellyn's Eagles! with the Pair / From my own door I shall be free to claim / Acquaintance as they sweep from cloud to cloud' (*P.W.* v. 331). In 'Musings Near Aquapendente', ll. 27–52 (*P.W.* iii. 203–4), Wordsworth writes of Helvellyn in recollection of the happy August day in 1805 when he and Walter Scott, along with Humphry Davy, had 'scrambled along that horn of the mountain called "Striding Edge"' (I.F. note, *P.W.* iii. 491). Scott in his poem *Hellvellyn* (*Poetical Works* (London, 1913), pp. 703–4) also tells the story of Gough and his dog.

433–53. At the head . . . scenery] Just below Grisedale Tarn where the foot road led down to Patterdale, William and Dorothy made what proved to be their last farewell to their brother John. For Wordsworth's recollection of this parting see 'Elegiac Verses', *P.W.* iv. 263–5 (cf. *E.T.*, p. 598).

In lines originally intended for 'Michael', *The Prelude* tells of a shepherd and his son searching for a sheep lost in this neighbourhood:

> And now, at sun-rise sallying out again
> Renew'd their search begun where from Dove Crag,
> Ill home for bird so gentle, they look'd down
> On Deep-dale Head, and Brothers-water, named
> From those two Brothers that were drown'd therein,
> Thence, northward, having pass'd by Arthur's Seat,
> To Fairfield's highest summit; on the right
> Leaving St. Sunday's Pike, to Grisdale Tarn
> They shot, and over that cloud-loving Hill,
> Seat Sandal, a fond lover of the clouds;
> Thence up Helvellyn, a superior Mount
> With prospect underneath of Striding-Edge,
> And Grisdale's houseless Vale, along the brink
> Of Russet Cove, and those two other Coves,
> Huge skeletons of crags, which from the trunk
> Of old Helvellyn spread their arms abroad,
> And make a stormy harbour for the winds.
>   (*Prel*. VIII. 228–44.)

Dorothy Wordsworth describes going over Fairfield with William in July 1812, and tells of her fear and dizziness just above Dove Crag (*M.T.* ii. 36).

448. a Stream] Hartsop Beck.

451. the gleaming surface of Brotherswater] Cf. Dorothy's Ullswater excursion, quoted in *Guide*, 2988: 'that Lake gleaming faintly with a steelly brightness'. See also 'Written in March While Resting on the Bridge at the Foot of Brother's Water', *P.W*. ii. 220 and nn., p. 508.

456. one of which] Goldrill Beck.

459. The other] Howe Grain.

491. the Lowther] Cf. dedicatory sonnet 'To the Right Honourable William, Earl of Lonsdale', *P.W*.v.1; and 'Lines Written in the Album of the Countess of Lonsdale', ll. 22–6, *P.W*. iv. 178.

492. Brougham Hall] Brougham Hall is on the Lowther, and just north of it, where the Lowther joins the Eamont, is Brougham Castle. For Wordsworth's recollections of early visits in this neighbourhood see *Prel*. VI. 218–45.

506, textual n. Wordsworth visited Lucerne on his Continental tour of 1790 (*E.Y*., p. 34); in August 1820 he spent three days at Lucerne (*M.Y*. ii. 640), where he apparently found the panorama still being shown.

528–31. It is hoped ... scenery] The sentence implies dissatisfaction with a great many books devoted to the 'local scenery'; for a selective 'Picturesque Bibliography' on the Lakes, prior to 1810, see Norman Nicholson, *The Lakers* (London, 1955), pp. 224–8.

532–41. To begin . . . wheel] On 10 May 1810, in a letter to Lady Beaumont, who had congratulated him on his Introduction to *Select Views*, Wordsworth evinced the pleasure and pride of an original writer who had had a happy idea and succeeded in expressing it well:

I am very happy that you have read the Introduction with so much pleasure, and must thank you for your kindness in telling me of it. I thought the part about the Cottages well-done; and also liked a sentence where I transport the Reader to the top of one of the Mountains, or rather to the Cloud chosen for his station, and give a sketch of the impressions which the Country might be supposed to make on a feeling mind, contemplating its appearance before it was inhabited [*M.Y*. i. 404].

Despite this letter, Wordsworth's originality in using the image of a wheel to make clear the topography of the Lake District has been challenged by Norman Nicholson (*The Lakers* (London, 1955), pp. 7–8) and questioned by Mary Moorman (ii. 160). Nicholson writes: 'This comparison to the wheel was first made popular by Wordsworth, who took it from William Green, though John Briggs, writing in *The Lonsdale Magazine* about 1821, said that he had heard the same analogy made by a farmer in Little Langdale:

"This", observed my uncle, "is very like the account given by Mr. Wordsworth, in his late publication. Have you ever seen this book?" "No," replied the old man, "I see no books. But if we were on Bowfell, I could let you see down all these vallies in a two hours' walk; though I am so plagued with rheumatism now, I don't think I could get up so high." "Are we to suppose", said my uncle, "that Mr. Wordsworth has borrowed this idea from an old dalelander, and then published it as his own?" "Oh, no," said my father, "Mr. Wordsworth will call it a coincidence of ideas!"'

Nicholson then concludes: 'Briggs is probably inventing this episode since, like many others, he was rather suspicious of Wordsworth, but at least his comments seem to show that the image of the wheel was fairly well known by this time.' Mrs. Moorman, who writes sensitively about the 'aptness' of the simile, summarizes the same story about the Little Langdale farmer. She cites as her source G. A. Cooke, *Excursions to the Lakes of Cumberland* (1840), and draws the conclusion that 'Wordsworth's use of the image is either a pure coincidence or possibly borrowed from the common talk of the dalesmen.'

We can accept neither Nicholson's assertion that the comparison originated with William Green, nor the implication made in the story of the Little Langdale farmer. The comparison does not appear in the one work by Green which antedates the first edition of the *Guide*: *Seventy-eight Studies from Nature* (London and Ambleside, 1809); nor does it appear in Green's second work, which might have antedated Wordsworth by a matter of months: *A Description of Sixty Studies from Nature ... Comprising a General Guide to the Beauties of the North of England* (London, 1810). The story of the Little Langdale farmer first appeared in the seventh of a series of 'Letters from the Lakes', published over the name of 'Leonard Atkins', in *The Lonsdale Magazine*, ed. J. Briggs, ii (July 1821), 243–8; in this letter—as jocose as its predecessors—the author jeers lightly at Wordsworth's 'artless lays' on 'Cock Robin and Mother Hubbard and several others', and lets the farmer, William Tyson, parody at tedious length Wordsworth's comparison:

'I can compare the lake mountains,' said William Tyson, 'to nothing so natural as a cart wheel, with nine spokes; only they are some of them crooked. I call the hills Bowfell, Scawfell, and the Pikes, the *nave* of the wheel, and the long ridges which run from them, I call the *spokes*. I will begin on the east side; and I will mark them on this flag with this piece of burnt wood. . . . The ninth, is a smaller spoke, and divides Borrowdale from Leaths water.'

When these remarks are found similar to 'the account given by Mr. Wordsworth, in his late publication', the publication alluded to is obviously the second edition of the *Guide*, published in the *River Duddon* volume, July 1820; unaware of Wilkinson's *Select Views*, where Wordsworth's comparison first appeared, 'Leonard Atkins' is some ten years too late in casting his sly aspersion. Possibly John Briggs had heard the comparison sometime before 1820, but if he had, the ultimate source was surely the anonymous work of Wordsworth in 1810.

542, fn. E. Ekwall (s.v. Langdale, *Concise Oxford Dictionary of English Place-Names*, 3rd edn.) would support Wordsworth's observation: he cites three twelfth-century examples (*Langedenlittle, Langedena, Langedala*) and one thirteenth-century example (*Langedal*), all meaning 'Long valley'.

556–7. Muncaster . . . Penningtons] Cf. Daniel and Samuel Lysons, *Magna Britannia* (London, 1816), iv. 139: 'The manor is known to have belonged to the Pennington family as early as the reign of Henry II'; its holder in 1816 was General Lowther Pennington, then Lord Muncaster.

562–5. or an array . . . sand] The image of mathematical and geometric symbols drawn upon the sand had attracted Wordsworth at least as early as 1804, for it occurs in *Prel.* VI. 160–74, where he tells of a shipwrecked man who on a remote island would 'draw his diagrams / With a long stick upon the sand'.

572. Egremont . . . castle] Cf. 'The Horn of Egremont Castle', *P.W.* iv. 169–72 and 439.

587–8. four or five miles eastward] Wordsworth underestimates the aerial distance by about three or four miles.

603–4. from elegance . . . sublimity] Cf. *Guide*, 2411–18 and n.

615–29. Hence . . . atmosphere] For one of Wordsworth's earliest treatments of the light thrown by the setting sun on the Lakeland hills cf. 'Dear native regions' (*P.W.* i. 2), lines which were later expanded into *Prel.* VIII (1850), 462–75.

638, textual n. The 1820 revision may reflect the definitions attempted in *Subl. and Beaut.*

658–65. Cf. Gilpin's analysis of mountains from the 'picturesque' point of view (Gilpin, i. 87–97).

664. like the waves of a tumultuous sea] Cf. *Guide*, 870, 2816–17; *Subl. and Beaut.* 97–8. The phrase 'a tempestuous sea of mountains' appears in Dr. John Brown's frequently reprinted *Description of the Lake at Keswick* (West, *Guide*, p. 196). Brown's metaphor is quoted by Clarke, p. 72; Hutchinson, *An Excursion*, p. 169; Nicolson and Burn, ii. 84. For Wordsworth's later quotation from Brown and his appended note see *Guide*, 1239–62.

675–87. In the ridge . . . neck] For one of his later editions of the *Guide* Wordsworth tried to persuade Adam Sedgwick to contribute an essay or note on the geology of the Lake District. He had probably met Sedgwick through Christopher Wordsworth, Master of Trinity College, for Sedgwick was a Fellow of that College, as well as Woodwardian Professor of Geology since 1818. In an unpublished letter to Wordsworth, dated 26 March 1842 and now in the Wordsworth Library, Sedgwick wrote:

> My dear Sir / I have heard, from Kendal, that a new Edition of your beautiful little work on the Lake Country was in the press; & I have been asked to contribute a short essay. . . . I promised to do so nearly twenty years since; & if you [?] my promise and do not fear to forfeit your inspiration, by seeming to league yourself with one on whom the nine sisters have never so much as smiled, I will send a short essay to your printer.

Sedgwick's 'Three Letters upon the Geology of the Lake District', which first appeared in Hudson's *Complete Guide to the Lakes* (Kendal, 1842), were, in the third edition of 1846, supplemented by a fourth letter (see Healey, items 522 and 532). Although the letters are essentially scientific papers, Sedgwick in the opening of the first letter and in the conclusion of the third recalls his earlier associations with Wordsworth ('when I had the happiness of rambling with you through some of the hills and valleys of your native country'), pays tribute to his philosophical views on 'the universality of nature's kingdom', and rejoices 'in the thought of having at length performed a promise, made to you many years since, but claimed by you only now' (*A Complete Guide to the Lakes*, Edited by the Publisher, 3rd edn. (Kendal, 1846), pp. 165 and 214).

683–7. The iron . . . dove's neck] The statement that 'The iron is the principle of decomposition in these rocks' is somewhat obscure, but we believe that de Selincourt's paraphrase is sufficiently accurate: 'the crumbling of the rocks is caused by the presence of iron in their composition' (E. de S., p. xxii). For the simile of the hues of a dove's neck cf. *S.V.* 496–9 and n.

694–8. The brilliant . . . decay] Cf. 2341–2 and n.

701–3. the mountains . . . aërial hues] Cf. *Exc.* II. 92–5, where 'mountains stern and desolate' are 'in the majesty of distance, now / Set off, and to our ken appearing fair / Of aspect, with aërial softness clad'. In her note to these lines (*P.W.* v. 415) Helen Darbishire quotes Dyer's *Grongar Hill* ll. 123–6, as having possibly influenced Wordsworth's observation on the contrasting appearance of mountains seen close by and at a distance.

740–62. It is extracted . . . distance] *C.N.B.* i. 1812, dated by Coleridge 'Friday, Jan. 5, 1804'. Miss Coburn does not mention Wordsworth's quotation of this entry, but from her summary of the period during which Coleridge used this notebook (see *Notes*, pp. xxxviii–xxxix), we deduce that the revised copy was made either within a week after Coleridge entered it, or five years later, when Wordsworth was composing *Select Views*. On 13 January 1804 Coleridge set off from Grasmere on his journey to the Mediterranean; since he took this notebook with him, there were only seven, or possibly eight, days in 1804 when the entry might have been copied. The later date seems to us much more likely. Coleridge was living with the Wordsworths in November 1809, just when Wordsworth was composing the Introduction to *Select Views* (see *M.Y.* i. 372). Having witnessed this particular winter scene together, it would seem perfectly natural for either one to remind the other of it, and for Coleridge to turn back to his notebook and offer Wordsworth the record he had made while the memory of it was still fresh. Since Wordsworth's revisions are numerous, we quote, except for the deletions, the entire entry:

Friday, Jan. 5, 1804. I observed the beautiful Effects of *drifted Snow* upon the mountains / the divine Tone of Color from the Top of the Mountain downward, from the powderiness Grass, a rich olive Green warmed with a little Brown / & in this way harmonious & combined by insensible Gradation with the white—The Drifting took away all the monotony of Snow; & the whole Vale of Grasmere seen from the Terrace Wall in Easedale, called Lankrigg, was as varied, perhaps more so, than even in the pomp of Autumn—In the distance was Loughrigg Fell the bason wall of the Lake / this from the Summit down ward was a rich Orange Olive, then the Lake a bright Olive Green (very nearly the same Tint as the Snow-powdered Mountain Tops & high Slopes in Easedale—then the Church with its Firs, the centre of the View—the Firs looked divine & carried the Eye back to some Firs in Brother's Wood on the Left Side of the Lake / (we looking toward Loughrigg) ⟨next to the Church & its firs⟩ came 9 distinguishable Hills, six of them with woody Sides turned towards us, all of these Oak Copses with their bright red Leaves & snow powdered Twigs / these Hills all distinguishable indeed from the Summit downward, but none seen all the way down—so as to give the strongest sense of number with unity / & these Hills so variously situated to each other, & to the view in general, so variously powdered, some only enough to give the Herbage a rich brown Tint, one intensely white, & lighting up the whole of the others, & yet so placed as in the most inobtrusive manner to harmonize by Contrast with a perfect naked, snowless bleek summit in the far distance on the Left— / from this variety of Site, of colour, of woodiness, of the situation of the woods, etc etc made it not merely number with unity, but Intricacy with Unity / —

769–76. For they . . . plain] De Quincey ('Early Memorials of Grasmere', *Collected Writings*, ed. D. Masson (Edinburgh, 1890), xiii. 127) says that Wordsworth was the first to draw attention to this difference between the valleys of Wales and those of northern England.

775–6. rocks . . . the plain] Cf. lines on Grasmere written for *The Recluse* but not used (*P.W.* v. 347): 'The multitude of little rocky hills, / Rocky or green, that do like islands rise / From the flat meadow lonely there'.

795–7. The form . . . river] Gilpin (i. 192) preferred 'the winding sweep of Windermere' to the circular shape of Derwent Water, but added that 'Some people object to this [Windermere's sweep], as touching rather on the character of the river.'

807–11. *Prel.* V. 409–13, except for a comma following 'heaven' (810) and the absence of italics (811).

813–16. Winandermere . . . river] Cf. *Prel.* (1850), IV. 5–6: 'I overlooked the bed of Windermere, / Like a vast river, stretching in the sun.'

858–906. John R. Nabholtz ('Wordsworth's *Guide to the Lakes* and the Picturesque Tradition', *M.P.*, lxi (1964), 288–97) argues that here particularly, but also elsewhere in the *Guide*, Wordsworth's 'characteristic method of analyzing the natural operations producing surface appearances' and his recognition of a 'natural development from sublimity to beauty' have been influenced by Uvedale Price's *Essays on the Picturesque* and Thomas Whitaker's *History and Antiquities of the Deanery of Craven*.

871–5. Sublimity . . . whole] E. de S. (pp. xx–xxi) discerns in this passage the influence of Coleridge on Wordsworth's 'criticism of landscape', and he quotes from a well-known passage in Coleridge's third essay *On the Principles of Genial Criticism*: '*The sense of beauty subsists in simultaneous intuition of the relation of parts, each to each, and of all to a whole*' (*Biog. Lit.* ii. 239). Cf. our n. to *Subl. and Beaut.* 24–6.

877–8. lie . . . stranded ships] Cf. *U.T.* 1699, where Wordsworth writes of Bowder Stone 'lying like a stranded Vessel'.

905–6. water-lilies . . . wave] Cf. *Epitaphs and Elegiac Pieces*, XIII (*P.W.* iv. 270): 'Or lily heaving with the wave / That feeds it and defends'.

907–18. In a note on Wordsworth's feeling for the birds that 'enliven the waters', E. de S. (pp. 175–6) refers the reader to 'The Wild Duck's Nest' (*P.W.* iii. 9); to this reference might be added ll. 186–90 in 'The Blind Highland Boy' (*P.W.* iii. 94). From 'Lines Left upon a Seat in a Yew-tree' (*P.W.* i. 93) E. de S. quotes l. 27: 'The stone-chat, or the glancing sand-piper', which is a revision of 'The stone-chat, and the Sand-lark, restless Bird / Piping along the margin of the lake'. For a passage descriptive of herons, E. de S. quotes from 'Farewell Lines' (*P.W.* ii. 104):

> So when the rain is over, the storm laid,
> A pair of herons oft-times have I seen,
> Upon a rocky islet, side by side,
> Drying their feathers in the sun, at ease.

For another passage, on the duck, the swan, and the heron, see *An Evening Walk* (1793), ll. 301–8 (*P.W.* i. 28 and 30).

Wordsworth's longest verse description of swans also occurs in *An Evening Walk* (1793), ll. 199–240 (*P.W.* i. 22 and 24), while the I.F. note to this poem is largely given over to recollections of the swans on Esthwaite and Windermere. But the finest descriptions of swans are probably those in *The Recluse*, I. 238–64 (*P.W.* v. 322–3), and in the rejected stanza of 'Dion' (*P.W.* ii. 272–3). In *U.T.* 1435–65 Wordsworth again writes at length of the swans on Esthwaite and Windermere.

919–45. 'Water Fowl', *P.W.* ii. 288–9, except for a comma after 'sound' (936), 'show' for 'shew' 940), and minor variations in punctuation that do not affect the meaning. The critical notes (*P.W.* ii. 522) comment upon the Miltonic phrasing in these lines. First published in the 1823 *Guide* (see textual n. 907–45), and from 1827 onwards printed among *Poems of the Imagination*, the lines were drawn from *The Recluse*, I. 203–29 (*P.W.* v. 321). In *The Recluse* the lines introductory to this passage read:

> But the gates of Spring
> Are opened; churlish Winter hath given leave
> That she should entertain for this one day,
> Perhaps for many genial days to come,
> His guests, and make them jocund. They are pleased,
> But most of all the Birds that haunt the flood,
> With the mild summons; inmates though they be
> Of Winter's household, they keep festival
> This day, who drooped, or seemed to droop, so long;
> They shew their pleasure, and shall I do less?
> Happier of happy though I be, like them
> I cannot take possession of the sky,
> Mount with a thoughtless impulse, and wheel there,
> One of a mighty multitude, whose way
> Is a perpetual harmony, and dance
> Magnificent. Behold, how with a grace
> Of ceaseless motion . . .

946–74. For more detailed descriptions of the islands of Windermere and Derwent Water see *S.V.* 152–89 and *Guide*, 1721–80.

952-60. Every one . . . Winandermere] In 1822 Wordsworth's foot-note to *Guide*, 115 (see textual n.) mentioned the 'Chapel or Oratory' on Chapel-Holm. In 1823 the note was removed, probably because of the expansion made here. E. de S. (p. 176) recognizes in this expansion Wordsworth's growing interest in ecclesiastical history. According to Clarke (p. 140), the Chapel of St. Mary Holm, at the time of Henry VIII, belonged to the Abbey of Furness.

In Wordsworth's poetry a memorable passage on the islands of Winder-mere occurs in *Prel.* II. 56-65:

> When summer came
> It was the pastime of our afternoons
> To beat along the plain of Windermere
> With rival oars, and the selected bourne
> Was now an Island musical with birds
> That sang for ever; now a Sister Isle
> Beneath the oaks' umbrageous covert, sown
> With lillies of the valley, like a field;
> And now a third small Island where remain'd
> An old stone Table, and a moulder'd Cave,
> A Hermit's history.

In the 1850 text, the final lines of this passage read:

> where survived
> In solitude the ruins of a shrine
> Once to Our Lady dedicate, and served
> Daily with chaunted rites.

An even finer passage on the islands of Windermere is that of *Prel.* II. 170-80, where Wordsworth recalls rowing away from one of the islands on which 'the Minstrel of our troop' had been left and hearing the sound of his flute across the water. The islands of Windermere also appear in *An Evening Walk* (1849), ll. 9-10 and 232-43 (*P.W.* i. 5 and 25).

Wordsworth writes of St. Herbert's Island in Derwent Water in *Inscriptions*, XV (*P.W.* iv. 206-8).

960-1. the solitary . . . forgotten] Grasmere's solitary island is not forgotten in the poetry of Wordsworth: see, for example, *An Evening Walk* (1793), ll. 13-14 (*P.W.* i. 4); *The Recluse*, I. 119 (*P.W.* v. 317); *Poems on the Naming of Places*, VI. 91-3 (*P.W.* ii. 122); *Inscriptions*, V (*P.W.* iv. 198).

964. *Paradise Lost*, XI. 835 (noted by E. de S.): 'The haunt of Seals and Orcs, and sea-mews' clang'. For another juxtaposition of the sea-mew and the cormorant see *Ecclesiastical Sonnets*, Part I. iii (*P.W.* iii. 342). On his first journey into the Lake District, under the guidance of Wordsworth, Coleridge mentioned in his notebook Ennerdale and its island: 'Leeza R. pours into the water of Ennerdale, the Enn flows out of it—On the Island of Rock in the Lake there the blackheaded Sea mews build in May / follow the Ploughman in sewing Time, & pick up the worms / being quite harmless. Mr Syms won't let them be destroyed' (*C.N.B.* i. 540).

966–74. It may be . . . world] The 'Floating Island' on Derwent Water attracted the attention of early writers on the Lakes, who tried ingeniously to explain its appearance and disappearance (e.g. Hutchinson, *Excursion*, pp. 150–1; Clarke, pp. 73–4; Green, ii. 49–52—who had a special account written for his book by Jonathan Otley). Norman Nicholson (*The Lakers* (1955), p. 90) summarizes a late nineteenth-century study which estimated that between 1753 and 1888 the 'island' appeared 'about forty times'. The account of it in the latest *Encyclopædia Britannica* (1959) is very brief: 'The "Floating Island" appears at intervals on the southern end of the lake near the mouth of the beck, and is formed by the accumulation of decayed vegetable matter floating on the water' (s.v. Derwentwater). Of Wordsworthian verses illustrative of this remarkable 'island' we know only these in *Prel.* III. 340–4:

> A floating island, an amphibious thing,
> Unsound, of spungy texture, yet withal,
> Not wanting a fair face of water-weeds
> And pleasant flowers.

In *U.T.* 1386–96 Wordsworth writes of the 'moving Island' at the head of Esthwaite. It is probably Esthwaite's 'island', and not Derwent's as E. de S. implies (p. 176), that Dorothy Wordsworth describes in her poem 'Floating Island' (*P.W.* iv. 162–3), for unlike the mass of matted weeds at Derwent, her island is adorned with a 'crest of trees'.

975–6. *Idyllia Heroica Decem, Librum Phaleuciorum Unum* (Pisa, 1820), p. 66. To the phrase 'umbras terrasque natantes' Landor attaches a footnote: '*Natant* in eo profundissimo lacu parvæ cum arbustis quibusdam insulæ.'

Wordsworth's flattering quotations of Landor, here and in his note to 2644 below, first appear in the 1823 edition of the *Guide*. The quotations were almost certainly introduced in response to compliments which Landor had recently paid Wordsworth. In the volume which Wordsworth cites there is a long Latin essay, *De Cultu atque Usu Latini Sermonis*, in which Landor extols Wordsworth ('vir, civis, philosophe, poeta, præstantissime', p. 215), and condemns his critics. Wordsworth probably received his copy in February 1821, for that is when Southey in Keswick received his (see John Forster, *Walter Savage Landor* (Boston, 1869), p. 288). In March Landor wrote to Southey about a second essay, one which is now lost: 'I have finished . . . my translation of Wordsworth's criticisms, saying in the preface that I had taken whatever I wanted from him, with the same liberty as a son eats and drinks in his father's house' (ibid., p. 291).

On 3 September 1821 Wordsworth thanked Landor for his copy of *Idyllia Heroica*; by then he had 'several times' read 'with great pleasure' the essay, but regretted that recent trouble with his eyes had prevented him from reading the poems; he then went on to argue the superiority of English over Latin for 'works of taste and imagination'; in concluding with thanks for 'the honourable mention' made of him in the essay, he wrote: 'It could not but be grateful to me to be praised by a Poet who has written verses of which I would rather have been the Author than of any produced in our time' (*L.Y.*, pp. 47–9). Heeding the advice to return to the use of English, Landor did not publish his Latin essay on Wordsworth's critical writings; instead he planned for a while to dedicate to Wordsworth his forthcoming work, *Imaginary Conversations*. To his announcement of that intention Wordsworth responded in a letter of 20 April 1822: 'I am happy to hear of any intended Publication of yours and shall be proud to receive any public testimony of your esteem' (*L.Y.*, p. 68). Landor, however, soon decided that 'a dedication would embarrass Wordsworth' (R. H. Super, *Walter Savage Landor* (New York, 1954), p. 160), and he therefore put his views on Wordsworth into an *Imaginary Conversation* between Southey and Porson. Publication of this volume was delayed, but an advance printing of this particular dialogue appeared in the *London Magazine*, July 1823. For Wordsworth's responses in 1824 see *L.Y.*, pp. 134 and 166. For a summary of their relations after 1836, when Landor suffered a sudden revulsion of feeling, see *P.W.* v. 428–9.

980. *vivi lacus*] Vergil, *Georgics*, II. 469: 'speluncae vivique lacus et frigida Tempe'. Vergil's phrase had been used by Gilpin (i. 101) in a context almost identical with Wordsworth's:

From the brisk circulation of fluid through these animated bodies of water, a great master of nature has nobly styled them, *living lakes*:

——————————Speluncae
Vivique lacus. ——————

and indeed nothing, which is not really alive, deserves the appellation better. For besides the vital stream, which principally feeds them, they receive a thousand gurgling rills which trickling through a thousand veins, give life, and spirit to every part.

987–90. which Carver . . . one] E. de S. (pp. 176–7) rightly observes that Carver in the passage to which Wordsworth refers was writing not of Lake Erie or Ontario, but of Lake Superior.

The water in general appeared to lie on a bed of rocks. When it was calm, and the sun shone bright, I could sit in my canoe, where the depth was upwards of six fathoms, and plainly see huge piles of stone at the bottom, of different shapes, some of which appeared as if they were hewn. The water at this time was as pure and transparent as air; and my canoe seemed as if it hung suspended in that element. It was impossible to look attentively through this limpid medium at the rocks below without finding before many minutes were elapsed, your head swim, and your eyes no longer able to behold the dazzling scene [Jonathan Carver, *Travels through the Interior Parts of North-America* (London, 1778), pp. 132–3].

Cf. 'To H. C., Six Years Old' (*P.W.* i. 247):

> Thou faery voyager! that dost float
> In such clear water, that thy boat
> May rather seem
> To brood on air than on an earthly stream;
> Suspended in a stream as clear as sky,
> Where earth and heaven do make one imagery.

In a note to these lines Wordsworth refers to the same passage in Carver (ibid., p. 364).

1013–23. Of this class . . . domain] For other descriptions of Loughrigg Tarn ('Diana's Looking-glass') see 'Epistle to Sir George Beaumont', ll. 164–94 (*P.W.* iv. 147–8) and I.F. note (ibid., p. 435); Wordsworth's note to 'Upon Perusing the Foregoing Epistle' (*P.W.* iv. 151).

1034–6. huge stones . . . came thither] Cf. 'Resolution and Independence' (*P.W.* ii. 237):

> As a huge stone is sometimes seen to lie
> Couched on the bald top of an eminence;
> Wonder to all who do the same espy,
> By what means it could thither come, and whence.

1053–9. 'Fidelity', *P.W.* iv. 81, with minor variations in punctuation.

1075–9. this . . . described] Wordsworth writes descriptively of the River Derwent in *An Evening Walk* (1793), ll. 3–6 (*P.W.* i. 4); *Prel.* I. 271–304; 'To the River Derwent' (*P.W.* iv. 22). His writing on the Duddon, 'my favourite river' (*L.Y.*, p. 6), both in prose and verse, is fairly extensive: see, for example, *S.V.* 34–65; *U.T.* 367–542; *The River Duddon* (*P.W.* iii. 244–61, and nn., pp. 503–24); *Ecclesiastical Sonnets* Part I. i (*P.W.* iii. 341).

1085–8. The Woods . . . rocks] E. de S. (p. 179) quotes in illustration *Poems on the Naming of Places*, I. 30–3 (*P.W.* ii. 112):

> Green leaves were here;
> But 'twas the foliage of the rocks—the birch,
> The yew, the holly, and the bright green thorn,
> With hanging islands of resplendent furze.

In commenting on Wordsworth's fondness for the native holly, E. de S. also quotes from his letter to Sir George Beaumont, 10 Nov. 1806 (*M.Y.* i. 93): 'Among the Barbarisers of our beautiful Lake-region, of those who bring and those who take away, there are few whom I have execrated more than an extirpator of this beautiful shrub, or rather tree the Holly.'

1093, fn. In view of the distances involved, the stories which Wordsworth heard from 'the old people of Wytheburn' are as modest as those which James Clarke heard in his day. In his *Survey*, Clarke tells two similar stories—one being set in Grisedale (p. xxxvi) and the other in Keswick (p. 63); we quote the latter:

The road [from Keswick] to the Lake [Derwent Water] lies by *Crow-Park* . . . which was covered with wood thirty-five years ago: the trees were all oak, about 17 yards high, of a most proportionable thickness, and so equal in height, that when in full leaf their tops appeared as close and smooth as a bowling-green: so close indeed did they grow, that many persons now alive have gone from one side of the wood to the other among the branches of the trees without ever coming to the ground.

1106–9. but the sycamore . . . dwellings] E. de S. (p. 180) compares *Exc.* VII. 612 ff.:

> Yon household fir,
> A guardian planted to fence off the blast,
> But towering high the roof above, as if
> Its humble destination were forgot—
> That sycamore, which annually holds
> Within its shade, as in a stately tent
> On all sides open to the fanning breeze,
> A grave assemblage, seated while they shear
> The fleece-encumbered flock.

1114–17. The neighbourhood . . . forest] Cf. *Guide*, 485–9; *S.V.* 226–38, 709–12. In 1805 and again in 1809 Dorothy Wordsworth writes with indignation of the tree-felling in the neighbourhood of Grasmere and Rydal (*E.Y.*, p. 638 and *M.Y.* i. 338).

1122–4. the broom . . . blossoms] E. de S. (p. 180) quotes from 'To Joanna' (*P.W.* ii. 113): 'when the broom, / Full flowered, and visible on every steep, / Along the copses runs in veins of gold'.

1133. "skiey influences"] *Measure for Measure*, iii. i. 8–9: 'a breath thou art, / Servile to all the skyey influences'.

1139. flagging] *O.E.D.*, s.v. *flag*, v[1], 5b: 'To allow or cause to become languid . . . to deprive of vigour . . . to depress'.

1153–7. the feelings . . . ancestors] Cf. James Thomson's note to 'Winter', line 875 in *Poetical Works* (Aldine Edition), i. 177: 'M. de Maupertuis, in his book on the Figure of the Earth, after having described the beautiful lake and mountain of Niëmi, in Lapland, says, "From this height we had occasion several times to see those vapours rise from the lake, which the people of the country call Haltios, and which they deem to be the guardian spirits of the mountains." '

1178–84. when that soft air . . . habitations] As early as 1815, in *E.S.* 609, Wordsworth had—at least by implication—ranked George Buchanan with Dunbar, Thomson, and Burns as pre-eminent among Scottish writers. But the tribute introduced in the 1823 text of the *Guide* was perhaps inspired by an anonymous article in *Blackwood's Magazine*, iii (June 1818), 251–8. The article, entitled 'Observations on the Writings of George Buchanan', discussed at length, and in an interesting way, the use of Latin by 'modern' English poets; it treated, therefore, a question central to Wordsworth's correspondence with Landor in 1821 and 1822 (see our n. to *Guide*, 975–6). Before quoting Buchanan's 'Ode to the first of May', the anonymous essayist wrote:

We doubt, indeed, whether Wordsworth himself has ever touched with a more masterly hand, that secret chord of sympathy which connects the meditative soul of man with the external manifestations of nature,—or called up to dignify and consecrate the enjoyment of the senses, thoughts more profound, and aspirations more sublime. It is a glorious triumph of "the Vision and the Faculty Divine" [*Exc.* I. 79]. It mingles all the graces of youth and love, with the gravity of philosophy, and the energy of faith.—The exquisite version which we place by its side is from the classical pen of Mr [Francis] Wrangham.

In February 1819 Wrangham, a lifelong friend, wrote to Wordsworth: 'I hope you see Blackwood's Magazine—perhaps write in it' (Michael Sadleir, *Archdeacon Francis Wrangham*, Supplement to the Bibliographical Society's *Transactions*, 1937, p. 13). Wordsworth's reply was immediate (19 Feb. 1819):

I know little of Blackwood's Magazine, and wish to know less. I have seen in it articles so infamous that I do not chuse to let it enter my doors. The Publisher sent it to me some time ago, and I begged (civilly you will take for granted) not to be troubled with it any longer. . . . the three Sonnets advertised in Blackwood's Magazine as from my pen were truly so [cf. Healey, item 470], but they were not of my sending. [In a postscript he added:] Perhaps I ought to have mentioned that the articles in B[*lackwood*]'s *Magazine* that disgusted me so, were personal,—referring to myself and friends and acquaintances, especially Coleridge [*M.T.* ii. 522–4].

Since the evidence is plain that Wordsworth knew exactly what was in the recent numbers of *Blackwood's*, we may safely assume that he no more missed the praise given him in June 1818 in the article on Buchanan than that he missed the highly favourable review of *The White Doe* in the following month (*Blackwood's*, iii. 369–81).

Because the text seems more nearly accurate than that given in *Blackwood's*, we quote from George Buchanan, *Opera Omnia* (Edinburgh, 1715), ii. 105–6:

Calendæ Maiæ

Salvete sacris deliciis sacræ
Majæ Calendæ, lætitiæ & mero,
　　Ludisque dicatæ, jocisque,
　　　　Et teneris Charitum choreis.

Salve voluptas, & nitidum decus
Anni recurrens perpetua vice,
　　Et flos renascentis juventæ
　　　　In senium properantis ævi.

Cum blanda veris temperies novo
Illuxit orbi, primaque secula
　　Fulsere flaventi metallo,
　　　　Sponte sua sine lege justa;

Talis per omnes continuus tenor
Annos tepenti rura Favonio
　　Mulcebat, & nullis feraces
　　　　Seminibus recreabat agros.

Talis beatis incubat insulis
Felicis auræ perpetuus tepor,
　　Et nesciis campis senectæ
　　　　Difficilis, querulique morbi.

> Talis silentum per tacitum nemus
> Levi susurrat murmure spiritus
> Lethenque juxta obliviosam
> Funereas agitat cupressos.
>
> Forsan supremis cum Deus ignibus
> Piabit orbem, lætaque secula
> Mundo reducet, talis aura
> Æthereos animos fovebit.
>
> Salve fugacis gloria seculi
> Salve secunda digna dies nota
> Salve vetustæ vitæ imago,
> Et specimen venientis ævi.

For another example, undated, of Wordsworth's praise of 'Calendæ Maiæ' see Christopher Wordsworth, *Memoirs* (London, 1851), ii. 469. E. de S. (pp. 180–1) quotes part of the text of Buchanan as it appears in P. Hume Brown, *George Buchanan: Humanist and Reformer* (Edinburgh, 1890), p. 178; he also quotes Brown's translation, ibid., p. 179.

1196–215. The reason . . . subject] Writing of this section in the Introduction to his edition, E. de S. (p. xxv) says that it 'is perhaps the subtlest and most finely wrought passage in the book'. Wordsworth's pleasure in images reflected in still water is evident elsewhere in the *Guide* (see 2663–738) as well as in numerous passages of his poetry; among the best are *The Recluse*, I. 570–9 (*P.W.* v. 332); *Prel.* IV. 247–61 and V. 409–13.

1220–1. Milton . . . itself] *Paradise Lost*, IV. 606–7 (noted by E. de S.): 'the Moon / Rising in clouded majesty'.

1224–33. The stars . . . sensibly felt] E. de S. (pp. 182–3) comments on Wordsworth's responsiveness to 'the peculiar beauty of the stars in a mountainous district'; he cites as examples 'If thou indeed derive thy light from Heaven', with its accompanying I.F. note (*P.W.* i. 1 and 317), and 'It is no Spirit' (*P.W.* ii. 263). From the first chapter of Samuel Johnson's *Rasselas* E. de S. quotes two passages describing the 'happy valley' which must have appealed to Wordsworth. Cf. also *Prel.* (1850), VI. 614–16 and 661–2 ('confined as in a depth / Of Abyssinian privacy').

1239–62. The Fragment . . . night] Cf. *Guide*, 1697–700, and *S.V.* 327–9. In his own day, Dr. John Brown (1715–66) was best known for an immensely popular work entitled *An Estimate of the Manners and Principles of the Times* (London, 1757); after his death, however, he became important among writers on the Picturesque for his brief, but impressive, description of the region around Keswick: *A Description of the Lake at Keswick (and the Adjacent Country) in Cumberland: Communicated in a Letter to a Friend, by a Late Popular Writer* (Kendal, 1770). This prose description, which seems to have been first published in Newcastle, 1767 (Donald D. Eddy, *A Bibliography of John Brown* (New York, 1971), pp. 119–20), became widely known, mainly because from 1780 onwards it was reprinted as the first item in the Addenda of West's *Guide*.

Brown's 'fragment', which Wordsworth quotes in its entirety, was first published in Richard Cumberland, *Odes* (London, 1776), p. 5. In his dedicatory letter to George Romney, Cumberland says:

I have been favoured with a Manuscript of the late ingenious Dr. Browne, which I had the priviledge of inserting in this publication, and should so have done, but that I found it had already got forth into the world, and was in print: It is touched with great spirit, and in a glowing stile, which gradually kindles till it breaks forth into the following rhapsody, which I believe hath hitherto escaped publication [ibid., pp. 4–5].

(We have here gone into some detail, partly because of de Selincourt's misleading errors in referring to Brown's verses and prose description: see E. de S., p. 183, and *P.W.* i. 323.) In West's *Guide* (p. 113), as well as many other books on the Lakes, Brown's verses were reprinted in the section on Keswick.

1260. Unheard . . . heard] De Selincourt (*P.W.* i. 323) recognizes in Brown's line a source for *An Evening Walk* (1793), ll. 433–4, 'The song of mountain streams unheard by day, / Now hardly heard'. He cites also Gray's Journal, 'At a distance were heard the murmurs of many water-falls, not audible in the day-time' (West, *Guide*, p. 206), and referring to *The White Doe*, 964–5 (*P.W.* iii. 312) and *Exc.* IV. 1173–4, remarks that the observation was a favourite with Wordsworth.

1262, fn. In 1823 Wordsworth had said that Brown was born in Cumberland (see textual n.); 'was in his infancy brought up in Cumberland' is a correction made in 1835. John Brown was born in Rothbury, Northumberland, on 5 November 1715; at the end of that year his father was made vicar at Wigton in Cumberland (*D.N.B.*).

Thomas Tickell (1685–1740) was born at Bridekirk, two miles north-west of Cockermouth; his poem *Kensington Garden* was published in London in 1722. In *U.T.* 1605–11 Wordsworth had spoken of Kensington Garden as a strange subject for a poet 'whose birthplace was within a short walk of the banks of one of the most romantic rivers in the world, this very Derwent'. The same thought seems reflected in an 1800 notebook of Coleridge's: 'Tickell, Auth. of Kensington Garden, born two miles from Cockermouth' (*C.N.B.* i. 725). In her note to this entry Miss Coburn incorrectly says that Coleridge is mistaken, and that Tickell 'was born at Brydekirk, near Carlisle'; Robert Anderson, *A Complete Edition of the Poets of Great Britain* (London, 1794), viii. 403, makes the same error about Tickell's birthplace. For the place and date of Tickell's birth see Richard Eustace Tickell, *Thomas Tickell* (London, 1931), pp. xiv and 15.

In November 1823, the same year in which he added this note, Wordsworth wrote to Allan Cunningham (*L.T.*, pp. 128–9):

I have been indebted to the North for more than I shall ever be able to acknowledge. Thomson, Mickle, Armstrong, Leyden, yourself, Irving (a poet in spirit), and I may add Sir Walter Scott were all Borderers. . . . The list of English Border poets is not so distinguished, but Langhorne was a native of Westmoreland, and Brown the Author of the *Estimate of Manners and Principles*, etc.,—a poet as his letter on the vale of Keswick, with the accompanying verses, shows—was born in Cumberland. So also was Skelton, a demon in point of genius; and Tickell in later times, whose style is superior in chastity to Pope's, his contemporary. Addison and Hogarth were both within a step of Cumberland and Westmoreland, their several fathers having been natives of those counties. . . . It is enough for me to be ranked in this catalogue.

1288–94. When . . . beasts] Thomas West, *The Antiquities of Furness* (London, 1774), p. xlvii: 'Such was the ancient face of Furness; such was the condition in which the first settlers found it. The forest-trees, the fir, the oak, and birch, had skirted the fells, tufted the hills, and shaded the valleys, through many centuries of silent solitude: the beasts and birds of prey reigned over the meeker species, and the "bellum inter omnia" maintained the balance of nature in the empire of beasts.'

In 1810, when Wordsworth first extracted his quotations from West's *Antiquities*, there were, as far as we can discover, only two editions for him to choose from: *The Antiquities of Furness* (London, 1774), and *The Antiquities of Furness*, ed. William Close (Ulverston, 1805). Although the Rydal Mount Catalogue, lot 175, shows that he owned a copy of the 1805 edition, and although in 1822 he may have used that edition for *Guide*, 2770–2, he seems to have used the earlier edition for his own first edition, for twice, when the 1805 text is improved, he continues to quote the 1774 text (cf. *Guide*, 1364, 1368–9, and West, 1774 edn., p. xxiv, versus 1805 edn., p. 23). In our note immediately following, if we have correctly identified Wordsworth's source, it is clear that in 1810 he was oblivious to, if not ignorant of, the 1805 edition.

The British Museum Catalogue lists a second edition by William Close (Ulverston, 1813); this edition we have not seen. Our textual notes show, however, that after 1810 Wordsworth introduced only one minor change in his quotations from West's *Antiquities* (textual n. 1356), and thus an edition of 1813 would be too late to explain his numerous, and sometimes radical, departures from the text he is quoting.

1298–9. the leigh . . . extinct] In a note to *The River Duddon*, II (*P.W.* iii. 246), Wordsworth again writes of the *leigh*: 'The deer alluded to is the Leigh, a gigantic species long since extinct.' In *P.W.* iii. 506 there is no editorial comment on Wordsworth's note, but his source is almost certainly West's *Antiquities* (1774), p. xlvi:

the buck, doe, wild boar, and legh, roamed in Furness at large when the Britons first took possession of it, and the three first remained till the thirteenth century. That the legh was a native of Furness, is evident from the heads of those animals frequently found in Furness. In the year 1766 three heads of horns were taken up on Duddon sands, of a size much superior to those of any deer now known, and supposed to be the horns of the Scofe stag.

In a footnote attached to 'Scofe', West identifies it as 'A place in High Furness, noted for a breed of large deer or leghs'.

Where *Antiquities* (1774) three times prints 'legh', *Antiquities* (1805), p. 41, invariably prints 'segh'; among the notes at the end of the volume the editor, William Close, gives a note on the word (p. 425): 'Segh signifies an Ox at present: in an old Irish glossary it is interpreted *Savage Deer*'; Close follows this note with a reference to Dr. Whitaker's *History of*

Manchester. It is hard to imagine that Wordsworth could have written as confidently as he did about the 'leigh', if he had read this section of the 1805 edition (cf. our note immediately preceding). No creature called *leigh*, *legh*, or *segh* is to be found in the *O.E.D.*, Wright's *English Dialect Dictionary*, or in the Index to the *Encyclopædia Britannica*, 11th edn. If, as we think, Wordsworth drew on West for his information about the 'leigh', it is possible that he altered the spelling because he associated the name with the name of Charles Leigh, who in his *Natural History of Lancashire, Cheshire, and the Peak in Derbyshire* (Oxford, 1700) had also described the finding of huge red-deer antlers. Drawing upon the same passage in *Antiquities* (1774), Ann Radcliffe (*A Journey Made in the Summer of 1794 . . . To Which Are Added Observations During A Tour To The Lakes*, 2nd edn. (London, 1795), ii. 383) preserves West's spelling, and writes of 'a remarkably large breed of deer, called Leghs, the heads of which have frequently been found buried at a considerable depth in the soil'.

1312. a few circles . . . Druids] The erroneous notion that Stonehenge and other stone circles of Britain were temples built for Druidic worship was first put forth by John Aubrey in his *Monumenta Britannica*, a 'Discourse' which he presented to Charles II. Although existing only in manuscript, Aubrey's work was known to William Stukeley, who in 1740 published *Stonehenge, A Temple Restored to the British Druids*; this volume, according to R. J. C. Atkinson, *Stonehenge* (New York, 1956), p. 188, 'was to become the leading source-book for more than a hundred years'. Writing of the 'spate of guide-books' which followed Stukeley, Atkinson says that 'In most of these accounts the Druidical associations so fervently canvassed by Stukeley were accepted without question' (ibid., p. 189). Certainly, the guide-books with which Wordsworth was familiar invariably attributed to the Druids the stone circles of the north. In a note to one of Wordsworth's early poems de Selincourt observes that 'the Druids haunted his imagination long before his fateful visit to Stonehenge in 1793' (*P.W.* i. 367). The most important references to the Druids in Wordsworth's poetry are conveniently collected by R. D. Havens in *The Mind of a Poet* (Baltimore, Md., 1941), ii. 342. For remarks on the Druids in Wordsworth's prose see *Guide*, 1746–59, 3135–7, and *U.T.* 477–83.

1312, fn. When Wordsworth added this footnote in 1822, Thomas Wilkinson of Yanwath on the Eamont had been a friend of his for many years (see Moorman, i. 519; *E.T.*, p. 626). In the I.F. note to his poem on Wilkinson, 'To the Spade of a Friend', Wordsworth repeats the story of Wilkinson's discovery (*P.W.* iv. 416–17). It is a story most fully presented by H. Rossiter Smith in 'Thomas Wilkinson, Antiquary', *N. & Q.* cci (1956), 394–5. Smith publishes two letters of Wilkinson; in the first, written in June 1800, Wilkinson tells of his uncovering 'a complete Druidical place of worship, consisting of a perfect circle of thirty one large stones standing erect, many of them as much as two horses could draw. Within the circles was a level clay floor and something of an altar in the middle.' The following year Wilkinson exchanged this piece of property for another belonging to his neighbour; in the second letter to the same correspondent, Wilkinson writes: 'My Druidical place of Worship, which had stood the shock of twenty centuries is annihilated. I exchanged the field where it stood and stipulated what I could for it remaining. . . . Thou sees some people have no taste for anything but their victuals.' At the end of his article Smith not only disassociates the Druids from the stones of Yanwath, but also rejects the notion that they formed a diminutive stone circle; it was, he thinks, a Neolithic tumulus: 'The stones discovered would perhaps have formed the revetment to the burial mound and would naturally have been hidden from view until Wilkinson's spade unearthed them. The Sanctum Sanctorum to which Wordsworth refers would be the larger stone of the burial chamber at the centre of the monument.'

When Wordsworth says that Wilkinson's circle had 'the same sort of relation to Stonehenge . . . that a rural chapel bears to . . . one of our noble cathedrals', he is employing a figure which perhaps he had seen quoted from John Aubrey, although it is also possible that the similarity is co-incidental: speaking of Avebury, Aubrey said that it 'did as much excell of Stoneheng as a Cathedral does a Parish Church' (*Aubrey's Brief Lives*, ed. Oliver Lawson Dick (Ann Arbor, Mich., 1962), p. xlvi).

Some stones from Karl Lofts are to be seen in Shap, but the destruction of the monument itself was completed in 1844 when the railway was driven through it (S. W. Partington, *A Gossiping Guide to Shap and Haweswater* (London, 1923), p. 18). That Karl Lofts was Danish was a view held by Thomas Pennant (*A Tour in Scotland*, 4th edn. (London, 1776), p. 277). Long Meg and her Daughters, which consists of a monolith standing outside a great circle, belongs to the Early-to-Middle Bronze Age. Wordsworth's measurements for this monument are drawn from Nicolson and Burn (ii. 448): 'The circle is about 80 yards in diameter, and consists of about 72 stones, from above three yards high to less than so many feet.' Although Long Meg is only six miles north-east of Penrith, Wordsworth had not seen it until the winter of 1820–1; in a letter to Beaumont, 6 Jan. 1821, he described his first sudden and unexpected sight of it (*L.T.*, p. 6).

The sonnet, which had its first publication here, was later revised and re-published, first among the *Miscellaneous Sonnets* and finally in the *Poems Composed or Suggested During a Tour, in the Summer of 1833*; in a note to the sonnet (*P.W.* iv. 410), Wordsworth again made observations similar to those he had earlier sent to Beaumont.

1312, fn. textual n. The quotation is from Nicolson and Burn, i. 477; Wordsworth spells out the Arabic numerals; he alters, probably by accident, 'immense weight' to 'immense height'; he introduces a few variations in spelling and punctuation.

1334–7. upon the skirts . . . Dacres] On the southern periphery, near Dalton-in-Furness, stood Furness Abbey and, about three miles to the east of it, Gleaston Castle; on the western periphery, about four miles south of Egremont, stood Calder Abbey; on the northern periphery, about twelve miles north-east of Carlisle and just below the Roman Wall, stood Lanercost Priory. Although the manor of Muchland, or Aldingham, had earlier been held by the Flemings, it was settled upon Sir John de Harrington in the fourteenth century, and there Gleaston Castle was built by Sir Robert de Harrington some time before 1389 (*The Victoria History of . . . Lancaster* (London, 1966), pp. 300–1, 321–4). Westmorland castles of the Cliffords were, notably, Brougham, on the river Lowther, and Appleby and Pendragon, on the river Eden; Cumberland castles of the De Lucis were Egremont and Cockermouth; Cumberland castles of the Dacres were Dacre Castle, south-west of Penrith, and Naworth in the district of Lanercost.

1348–73. The old division of lands, which in Wordsworth's eyes produced such aesthetically pleasing consequences (1344–7), was for West a source of regret, for, as he saw it, efficient agricultural development was thereby impeded. In his quotation from *The Antiquities of Furness* (1774), pp. xxiii–xxiv, Wordsworth has not only cast two paragraphs into one, but also altered the text in other ways. We omit the concluding sentences of the second paragraph.

One general obstacle to the improvement of Furness, and the advancement of agriculture in it, is the mixed lands or township fields. Every whole tenement, besides the customary annual rent, was charged with the obligation of having in readiness a man completely armed for the king's service, on the border or elswhere. Of these there were sixty in Plain Furness. When the abbot of Furness franchised his villains, and raised them to the dignity of customary tenants, the lands they had cultivated for their lord were divided into whole tenements, which were again subdivided into four equal parts: each villain had one, and the party tenant contributed his share in supporting the man at arms and other burthens. These divisions were not properly distinguished; the land remained mixed: each tenant had a share through all the arable and meadow land, and common of pasture over all the wastes; was deemed a principal tenant, and paid a fine upon his admittance. These sub-tenements were judged sufficient for the support of so many families, and no farther division was permitted.

These divisions and subdivisions were convenient at the time for which they were calculated: the land so parcelled out was of necessity more attended to, and the industry greater where more persons were to be supported by the produce of it: the frontier of the kingdom (within which Furness was considered) was in a constant state of attack or defence; more hands were therefore necessary to guard the coast, repel an invasion from Scotland, (from whence it was constantly expected) or make reprisals on the hostile neighbour. The dividing the lands in such manner as has been shewn, increased the number of inhabitants, and kept them at home till called for: and the land being mixed, and several tenants united in equipping a plough, the absence of the fourth man was no prejudice to the cultivation of his land, which was committed to the care of three. And this seems the most that can be said in favour of these mixed lands.

1374–87. Contrary to its appearance in the *Guide*, this paragraph was not originally an immediate continuation of those quoted in our preceding note. Instead, it is derived from two paragraphs, separated from each other by a third, and found some twenty pages later, i.e. *The Antiquities of Furness* (1774), p. xlv.

Whilst the villains of Low Furness were employed in all the useful arts of agriculture, the woodlanders of High Furness were charged with the care of the flocks and herds, which pastured the verdant sides of the fells, to guard them from the wolves which lurked in the thickets below; and, in winter, to browse them with the tender sprouts and sprigs of the hollies and ash. This custom has never been discontinued in High Furness; and the holly-trees are carefully preserved for that purpose, where all other wood is cleared off; and large tracts of common pasture are so covered with these trees, as to have the appearance of a forest of hollies. At the shepherd's call the flock surround the holly-bush, and receive the croppings at his hand, which they greedily nibble up, and bleat for more. . . .

The abbots of Furness permitted the inhabitants to inclose quillets to their houses, for which they paid encroachment rent.

(*O.E.D.*, s.v. *quillet*, sb.[1], sense 1: 'A small plot or narrow strip of land'.) For Wordsworth on the holly of the north see our n. on 1085–8 above.

1407–8. which portions . . . distribute] *O.E.D.*, s.v. *Dale*[2] ('The northern phonetic variant of *Dole*'), sense 1: 'A portion or share of land, *spec.* a share of a common field, or portion of an undivided field indicated by landmarks but not divided off'. The cognate O.E. verb is *dǽlan*, 'to divide'. In 1810 (see textual n., 1408) Wordsworth was perhaps influenced by Clarke, pp. xxv–xxvi, who includes '*deilen*, to divide' in his list of 'Dutch' words that appear in the 'Northern dialect' of England.

1452–8. Sir Launcelot . . . wars] Nicolson and Burn, i. 498: 'This Sir Lancelot the son was wont to say, he had three noble houses . . .' etc., as given by Wordsworth, except for variations in punctuation and Wordsworth's introduction of the parenthesis in 1457.

1480–3. E. de S. (p. 187) for comparison refers to *Guide*, 2262–6 and 'Michael', ll. 82–5 (*P.W.* ii. 83).

1486–9. They had . . . them] Cf. Wordsworth's *Memoir of the Rev. Robert Walker*, *P.W.* iii. 510–22.

1497–508. Accordingly . . . themselves] We have not found the source of Wordsworth's quotation, but West summarizes the same history of the bloomeries in Furness, in *The Antiquities of Furness* (London, 1774), p. xxxvii:

The land about Hawkshead is fitter for pasture, sheep-walks, and wood, than for agriculture. The last article is become a great object since the beginning of this century, by the reintroduction of furnaces and forges for making and working of iron: It is related, in its proper place [i.e. Appendix IX: *A Decree for the abolishing of* BLOOMERIES *in* HIGH FURNES], how the blomaries were suppressed in High Furness, at the common request of the tenants of Hawkshead and Colton, that the tops and croppings of their woods might be preserved for the nourishment of their cattle in winter: since that they have found the means of improving part of their lands into meadows, and preserving their woods for the use of the furnaces; which has raised the value of the land, within these fifty years, to many times the value it was of before.

1520–1. habitations . . . beasts] Cf. *Inscriptions*, V. 14–30 (*P.W.* iv. 198).

1526–9. *The Recluse*, I. 122–5 (*P.W.* v. 317), where line 1528 reads 'glancing at'.

1533–6. rough-cast . . . variegated] Cf. *Guide*, 1953–5.

1541–5. these humble . . . rock] E. de S. (p. 187) compares this statement with the description of a cottage in *Exc.* VI. 1143–6:

> Ye might think
> That it had sprung self-raised from earth, or grown
> Out of the living rock, to be adorned
> By nature only.

1553–63. Nor will . . . air] Cf. *U.T.* 681–5. E. de S. (p. 187) quotes
H. D. Rawnsley, *Reminiscences of Wordsworth among the Peasantry of
Westmoreland* (*Transactions of the Wordsworth Society*, VI, p. 170); the
speaker is recalling Wordsworth's advice to Dr. Thomas Arnold, when
Arnold was building Fox How, near Ambleside:

> Wudsworth was a great un for chimleys, had summut to say in the making of a deal
> of 'em hereabout. There was 'most all the chimleys Rydal way built after his mind.
> I 'member he and the Doctor had great arguments about the chimleys time we was
> building Foxhow, and Wudsworth sed he liked a bit o'colour in 'em. And that the
> chimley coigns sud be natural headed and natural bedded, a little red and little
> yallar. For there is a bit of colour in the quarry stone up Easedale way. And heèd
> a great fancy an' aw for chimleys square up hauf way, and round the t'other. And
> so we built 'em that how.

1575–85. Add the little . . . nature] E. de S. (p. 188) cites for comparison
Exc. I. 713–30 and VI. 1149–55, 1161–73.

1611, fn. Wordsworth quotes Horace, *Epistles*, II. ii. 55. This note was
added in 1823; the very recent improvement which Wordsworth notices
may reflect some of the influence which he himself had exerted. Another
Westmorland builder whose reminiscenses were recorded by Rawnsley
(see our n. on 1553–63) said of Wordsworth: 'He was not maade much
count of at first either in this country, but efter a time folks began to tak
his advice, ye kna, about trees, and plantin', and cuttin', and buildin'
chimleys, and that sort o' thing. He had his saäy at most of the houses in
these parts' (*Transactions of the Wordsworth Society*, VI, p. 177).

1619, fn. In a long note to *The River Duddon*, which includes his *Memoir
of the Rev. Robert Walker*, Wordsworth tells how Walker taught school in
Seathwaite Chapel: 'His seat was within the rails of the altar; the communion table was his desk; and, like Shenstone's schoolmistress, the
master employed himself at the spinning-wheel, while the children were
repeating their lessons by his side' (*P.W.* iii. 515). At the conclusion of
this note Wordsworth also records 'a few memoranda' from the parish
register at Loweswater, where Walker, as a young man, had also taught
school (ibid., p. 522). The story of the youth from Borrowdale appears in
U.T. 1716–25; it was perhaps one of the 'affecting little things' which
Dorothy (*Journals*, i. 61) says that William had 'observed' in Borrowdale
in 1800. In the phrase 'short and simple annals' Wordsworth is quoting
Gray's *Elegy Written in a Country Churchyard*, l. 32.

1643–4. The edifice . . . near it] Cf. *Prel.* VII. 354–8, where the Buttermere chapel is spoken of as 'the little rock-like Pile'.

1657–62. where may yet . . . commands] Cf. *U.T.* 1112–70, and our n. to *U.T.* 1116–22.

1666. a perfect Republic of Shepherds] E. de S. (p. 189) compares *Prel.* IX. 217–35.

1689–92. A practice . . . scenery] Evelyn Cecil, *A History of Gardening in England*, 3rd edn. (New York, 1910), pp. 243–65, describes the pioneer work of William Kent (1684–1748), 'founder of the School of Landscape-Gardening', and the more influential work of Lancelot ('Capability') Brown (1715–1783). For the formal garden of straight lines they substituted landscaped gardens of artfully contrived effects. Opposition to this art, which Wordsworth glances at in 1691, was an opposition to the extremes of Brown's landscaping, led chiefly by William Gilpin, Sir Uvedale Price, and Richard Payne Knight.

1697–700. Dr. Brown . . . Enthusiast] See our n. on 1239–62 above.

1700–13. Gray . . . attire] Although he died only two years later (30 July 1771), Gray was in better health and spirits than usual when he made his northern tour in October 1769 (see R. W. Ketton-Cremer, *Thomas Gray* (Cambridge, 1955), p. 219). Wordsworth's somewhat sentimental view of Gray in the Lake country (cf. *U.T.* 1633–41) may be partly attributable to William Mason: not only did Mason alter the tone of the journal by omitting Gray's ordinary casual details, but he also commented, apropos the years 1770–1, on Gray's declining health and 'spirits only supported by the frequent summer excursions, during this period' (*The Poems of M*[r.] *Gray, To which are prefixed Memoirs of his Life and Writings* (York, 1775), p. 395). Gray himself, in two passages, both of which deeply impressed Wordsworth, recalled suffering an apprehensiveness during his tour which might easily suggest ill health; one passage is on Gordale Scar (cf. 45 above), and the other is on Borrowdale (cf. *U.T.* 1633–41 and *Railway*, 116–19). Finally, Wordsworth's tender sympathy may veil an indirect rebuke of James Clarke, and perhaps others like him, who taunted Gray for his timidity. Clarke scoffingly tells two wildly apocryphal stories: one (p. 143) is about Gray's having himself blindfolded before he could cross Windermere on the ferry and then being too terrified to return; the other (pp. 99–100) is about his travelling out from Keswick to view Skiddaw:

he no sooner came within sight of those awful rocks than he put up the blinds of his carriage: In this dark situation, trembling every moment lest the mountains should 'fall and cover him,' he travelled to Ouzebridge: he thus avoided seeing, not only the horrors, but the beauties of the place. . . . It is indeed a question whether, if Mr Gray had wrote the history of his *terrors*, it would not have been as entertaining, at least as curious, as his journal.

Wordsworth's quotation from Gray's journal differs only slightly from Mason's edition (York, 1775), p. 365 ('. . . garden-walls, break . . . neatest most . . .'), and from that in West's *Guide*, p. 211 ('. . . gentleman's flaring . . . walls, break . . . neatest, most . . .'). The sentence was obviously one of his favourites: he is recalling it when in *U.T.* 1171–2 he writes: 'or break in upon its composure by flaring edifices placed injuriously to the feelings of others'; he refers to it in *L.T.*, p. 1089 (Aug. 1841); he quotes it in *Railway*, 511–12.

1724–76. the Islands . . . behind] For other comments on the islands of Derwent Water and Windermere see *Guide*, 952–60 and n.; *S.V.* 152–81; *Railway*, 127–40.

Bede (*Opera Historica*, IV. xxix) is perhaps the first to tell of St. Herbert's retiring to one of the islands of Derwent Water. Hutchinson (*Excursion*, pp. 136–41, and *History*, ii. 170–3) writes at length of St. Herbert's association with the island that bears his name (cf. Wordsworth's *Inscriptions*, XV, *P.W.* iv. 206–8); Nicolson and Burn (ii. 86), citing a bishop's register of 1374, record that 'an indulgence of forty days' was granted to those inhabitants of Crosthwaite who 'should attend the vicar to St. Herbert's island on the 13th of April yearly, and there celebrate mass in memory of St. Herbert'. The latter also inform us that the forest trees on the island were cut 'about the year 1761' by Sir Wilfred Lawson, who then 'planted the island anew'. In 1819, the year before Wordsworth added this section (see textual n. 1727–81), Green (ii. 53–5) had complained of the 'impervious' wood which gave a 'lumpish' appearance to the island; he also told of Lawson's having erected, 'about twenty years ago', near the site of the hermitage, a one-storey building 'from a design by the Rev. Mr. Wilkinson, who then resided at Ormathwaite'. (This is the Revd. Joseph Wilkinson of *Select Views*; see our Introduction, p. 124.)

Derwent Isle, sometimes called Vicar's Island because it had formerly belonged to Fountains Abbey in Yorkshire, became, after the Dissolution, the property successively of several families (Nicolson and Burn, ii. 86); in 1778, according to William Green (ii. 63), the island was purchased by Joseph Pocklington, who is identified in Hutchinson's *History* (ii. 165 and 168) as Joseph Pocklington of Carlton House, near Newark, Nottinghamshire (cf. *Railway*, 135–40). Pocklington's 'improvements' consisted, *inter alia*, of an imposing Georgian house, neat gravelled walks, a ruined chapel, a small Druidic circle, and several forts with cannons, which were used to exhibit the echoes over the lake. Hutchinson, who in his *Excursion* (p. 134) had been indignant over the tree-felling on Vicar's Island, which had occurred shortly before his first visit, was in his *History* noticeably reserved in his comments on the 'improvements': 'On a late visit, we found this island highly ornamented with modern buildings, the face of the rising ground smoothened and laid out for the pleasure of its new lord, Mr. *Pocklington*, who has expended a large sum, not only to ornament the scene, but also in support of annual festivals, to induce many visitors to resort to Keswick' (ii. 166–7). We note, in passing, that Pocklington, who supplied Hutchinson with illustrative engravings of his island, is listed among Hutchinson's wealthy subscribers. In his remarks on 'King Pocky' and his 'mock church' Coleridge, in a notebook of 1799, was under no such restraint as Hutchinson may have felt (see *C.N.B.* i. 541–2, where in the note to 541 Pocklington's given name is erroneously said to have been 'John'). As far as we know, James Clarke (p. 84) was one of the few admirers of Pocklington's work: as he saw it, the island was 'beautifully ornamented by its spirited owner'; he relished particularly 'the appearance of a *chapel*, which consists of only *one* wall and a steeple: the steeple contains a room, not furnished with bells, but good roast-beef and claret'. By 1807, when Southey published his *Letters from England: by Don Manuel Alvarez Espriella* (ed. Jack Simmons (London, 1951)), General William Peachy had become the owner of Derwent Isle; his alterations—or, as Wordsworth calls it, his ridding 'the spot of its puerilities'—are enumerated by Southey: 'The present owner has done all which a man of taste could do in removing these deformities: the church is converted into a toolhouse, the forts demolished, the batteries dismantled, the stones of the druidical temple employed in forming a bank, and the whole island planted' (p. 238). In 1819 Green (ii. 64) commented enigmatically on General Peachy's tree-planting: 'Amongst the trees added by Mr. Peachy, were many larches. These larches, like the firs planted by Mr. Pocklington, have, from the main land, been grievous eye-sores for many years; notwithstanding which, the General has shewn an extraordinary degree of fine taste in the management of the trees upon his island, but more with a view to local, than to distant appearances.'

When Wordsworth speaks, in 1756–7, of 'the ancient Druids who officiated at the circle upon the opposite hill', he is referring to the stone circle on Castlerigg, one mile south-east of Keswick. Cf. our n. to *Guide*, 1312.

Wordsworth's 'regret for the changes that have been made upon the principal Island at Winandermere' (1764–5) sounds like the regret of one who had himself witnessed these changes and could remember a former beauty. But Holme-house, which once stood in the middle of Belle Isle—or Great Holme or Long Holme, as it was variously called—was demolished in 1774, and the house built in its stead by Mr. Thomas English was nearly completed by the time it was described by Nicolson and Burn in 1777 (i. 185 and 624–5). In the Addenda to their history the 'very curious edifice [which] hath been erected by Mr. English the present owner' is described in detail (i. 624–5): 'The building is a perfect circle fifty-four feet in diameter. The roof thereof is a dome, slated with fine blue slate. . . . The building is four stories high, exclusive of the garrets, which are in the roof, which is somewhat remarkable it being a dome. . . . the proprietor proposes planting different kinds of trees in clumps . . . which will form four vistas from the building.' As early as 1776 Hutchinson (*Excursion*, pp. 187–8) had been sharp in his strictures on the changes introduced by Mr. English:

The few natural beauties of this island are wounded and distorted by some ugly rows of firs set in right lines, and by the works now carrying on by Mr English, the proprietor, who is laying out gardens on a square plan, building fruit walls, and preparing to erect a mansion-house. . . . For pleasure, or ornament, a narrow foot path is cut round the margin of the island, and laid with white sand, resembling the dusty paths of foot passengers over Stepney Fields.

Others followed Hutchinson in deploring the various 'projects' on Belle Isle (e.g. Gilpin, i. 146–7; West, *Guide* (1802), pp. 59–60; Green, i. 209–

25), although James Clarke (p. 139), who had no patience with the 'cant' of Gilpin and other such 'gentlemen', made a hearty and amusing defence of Mr. English.

When John Christian Curwen acquired the island (see our n. to *Guide*, 108–12), it was expected that he would restore it to its natural beauty, and he did in fact satisfy West's editors; a footnote to West's *Guide* (1802), p. 60, expresses satisfaction, and in the next edition West's own strictures were omitted entirely (West, *Guide*, p. 59). But the Wordsworths continued to lament every change. On 8 June 1802 (*Journals*, i. 155) Dorothy found the island 'no better than it was . . . neither one thing or another—neither *natural*, nor wholly cultivated and artificial, which it was before'. When he was composing *Select Views*, Wordsworth made almost a direct appeal to Curwen to heed 'the principles which have been enforced in these pages' (*S.V.* 157–8), but the plea 'Could not the margin of this noble island be given back to nature' (1770–1), which was first made in 1810 (*S.V.* 167–8), was repeated without change in every edition of the *Guide*.

1729–31. the whole island . . . winds] Cf. *Guide*, 1580–1; 2098–102 and n.

1741. warren-house] Neither the *O.E.D.* nor Wright's *English Dialect Dictionary* gives this compound, and we can offer no definition more explicit than what is implied in the text.

1776–80. As to . . . general] For Wordsworth's later discussion of 'plantations' see 2034–252; cf. also *Guide*, 108–12 and n. The proprietor referred to in Wordsworth's note is again John Christian Curwen.

1786–8. All gross . . . ideas] J. R. Nabholtz (*M.P.* lxi (1964), 295) thinks that Uvedale Price may have influenced Wordsworth here; in his *Essay on the Picturesque* (London, 1796), i. 261–2, Price wrote: 'I will make a few observations on what I look upon as the great general defect of the present system. . . . That defect, the greatest of all . . . is want of connection—a passion for making every thing distinct and separate. All the particular defects I shall have occasion to notice, in some degree arise from this original sin, and tend towards it.'

1797–800. the perception . . . form] E. de S. (p. 191) cites in comparison *E.S.* 579–80: 'In nature every thing is distinct, yet nothing defined into absolute independent singleness.'

1801–4. The hill . . . avenue] Cf. Gilpin, ii. 80: 'Shaped with conic exactness; planted uniformly with Scotch firs; and cut as uniformly into walks verging to a center, it [Dunmallet] becomes a vile termination of a noble view.'

1813–922. Wordsworth's letters of 1805–6 written to the Beaumonts, when they were building at Coleorton, contain extensive comments on the proper laying-out of grounds and the appropriate relationship between the house and the kind of countryside in which it is placed; in his letter of 17 October 1805 (*E.T.*, pp. 622–9) and in subsequent explication of a part of it

(*M.T.* i. 8), Wordsworth expounds his principles in a way that frequently parallels this section of the *Guide*:

Setting out from the distinction made by Coleridge which you mentioned, that your House will belong to the Country and not the Country be an appendage to your House, you cannot be wrong. . . . In times when the feudal system was in its vigor . . . there might have been something imposing to the imagination in the whole face of a district testifying, obtrusively even, its dependence upon its Chief. Such an image would have been in the spirit of the society, implying power, grandeur, military state and security. . . . Painters and Poets have had the credit of being reckoned the Fathers of English Gardening; they will also have hereafter the better praise of being fathers of a better taste. . . . It was a misconception of the meaning and principles of poets and painters which gave countenance to the modern system of gardening, which is now I hope on the decline; in other words we are submitting to the rule which you at present are guided by, that of having our houses belong to the Country; which will of course lead us back to the simplicity of nature. . . .Let a man of wealth and influence shew by the appearance of the country in his neighbourhood that he treads in the steps of the good sense of the age, and occasionally goes foremost . . . in that part of his estate devoted to park and pleasure ground let him keep himself as much out of sight as possible; let nature be all in all, taking care that every thing done by man shall be in the way of being adopted by her. . . . Laying out grounds, as it is called, may be considered as a liberal art, in some sort like Poetry and Painting; and its object like that of all the liberal arts is, or ought to be, to move the affections under the controul of good sense; that is, those of the best and the wisest; but speaking with more precision it is to assist Nature in moving the affections [*E.T.*, pp. 623–7]. There were some parts in the long Letter which I wrote about laying out grounds, in which the expression must have been left imperfect. I like splendid mansions in their proper places, and have no objection to large or even obtrusive houses in themselves. My dislike is to that system of gardening which, because a house happens to be large or splendid and stands at the head of a large domain, establishes it therefore as a principle that the house ought to *dye* all the surrounding country with a strength of colouring, and to an extent proportionate to its own importance. This system I think is founded in false taste, false feeling, and its effects disgusting in the highest degree [*M.T.* i. 8].

1814–16. the common feelings . . . imagery] i.e. 'the pleasure which [the mind] receives from distinct ideas, and from the perception of order, regularity, and contrivance' (1787–9). For the substitution of *imagery* for *scenery* in 1816 (see textual n.) and similar alterations in 2036, 2477, 2666, cf. *Railway*, 91–2 and n.

1825–30. The craving . . . houses] Cf. *U.T.* 1173–5: 'I have already protested against that craving for extensive prospect which would prompt the builder to fix his habitation where it may stare & be stared at.'

1838–41. I have . . . nature] See 1522–85.

1855–72. *Faerie Queene*, III. v. 39–40. The first of these two stanzas was quoted by Gilpin, ii. 35, as being appropriate to the Vale of St. John.

1873–4. not obvious . . . retired] *Paradise Lost*, VIII. 504.

1888–900. Kilchurn Castle . . . thy age] The first three lines of 'Address to Kilchurn Castle, Upon Loch Awe' (*P.W.* iii. 78–9, and nn., p. 445), which Wordsworth quotes in 1898–900, were, according to the I.F. note, 'thrown off at the moment I first caught sight of the Ruin [31 Aug. 1803] . . . the rest was added many years after'. As E. de S. (p. 193) observes, the thought and even the phraseology of the poem are close to the prose passage: for example, lines 9–28:

> What art Thou, from care
> Cast off—abandoned by thy rugged Sire,
> Nor by soft Peace adopted; though, in place
> And in dimension, such that thou might'st seem
> But a mere footstool to yon sovereign Lord,
> Huge Cruachan, (a thing that meaner hills
> Might crush, nor know that it had suffered harm;)
> Yet he, not loth, in favour of thy claims
> To reverence, suspends his own; submitting
> All that the God of Nature hath conferred,
> All that he holds in common with the stars,
> To the memorial majesty of Time
> Impersonated in thy calm decay!
>
> Take, then, thy seat, Vicegerent unreproved!
> Now, while a farewell gleam of evening light
> Is fondly lingering on thy shattered front,
> Do thou, in turn, be paramount; and rule
> Over the pomp and beauty of a scene
> Whose mountains, torrents, lake, and woods, unite
> To pay thee homage.

1922–6. Sir Joshua . . . literally] We have not found 'this precept' in any published work, but since it is said that Reynolds used to repeat it in conversation, Wordsworth may simply have heard it quoted by a friend of Reynolds—possibly Beaumont. For example, Allan Cunningham, in *The Lives of the Most Eminent British Painters, Sculptors, and Architects* (London, 1846), vi. 140, writes: 'Sir George, in his conversations and letters, generally introduced something about the art he loved; and even in the shortest note he would slip in an anecdote, personal or professional, of Wilson, of Claude, of Reynolds, or Gainsborough. "My friend, Sir Joshua," he thus writes to one of the brethren . . .' etc.

Despite his strictures against white in landscape (1968–2033), the roads of N. Leicestershire justified Wordsworth's recommendation that a bower in the winter garden at Coleorton should 'be paved with different-coloured pebbles chiefly white, which are to be found in great plenty sprinkling the sandy Roads of the Country' (*M.Y.* i. 118).

1954–5. where the glare . . . weather-stains] When in 1809 De Quincey took up residence at Dove Cottage, the front of the cottage was, he said, covered with roses which 'with as much jassamine and honeysuckle as could find room to flourish . . . performed the acceptable service of breaking the unpleasant glare that would else have wounded the eye from the white-wash; a glare which, having been renewed . . . against my coming to inhabit the house, could not be sufficiently subdued in tone for the artist's eye until the storm of several winters had weather-stained and tamed down its brilliancy' (*Collected Writings*, ed. D. Masson (Edinburgh, 1889), ii. 361–2).

1968–2033. Wordsworth's objections to whitewash in the mountainous north were fixed as early as 1799, if, as Miss Coburn thinks, it was he who, at least for a while, imbued Coleridge with the same opinions (see *C.N.B.*, Notes, i. 836, and the quotation from Coleridge in our note to *S.V.* 222–42). E. de S. (p. 194) in commenting on this section quotes from *Inscriptions*, VII, published in 1800 (*P.W.* iv. 200–1):

> But if thou art one
> On fire with thy impatience to become
> An inmate of these mountains,—if, disturbed
> By beautiful conceptions, thou hast hewn
> Out of the quiet rock the elements
> Of thy trim Mansion destined soon to blaze
> In snow-white splendour,—think again.

In striking contrast to these opinions are the lines on Hawkshead Church in *Prel.* IV. 13–15: 'I saw the snow-white Church upon its hill / Sit like a thronèd Lady, sending out / A gracious look all over its domain.' In *U.T.* textual n. 1248–59, Wordsworth admitted, however, that the whitewashed houses of Hawkshead produced a 'glare' that needed to be softened with trees.

2000–6. The objections . . . distance] Wordsworth has turned back to Gilpin's early work, *Observations on the River Wye, And Several Parts of South Wales, &c.*, 2nd edn. (London, 1789), pp. 94–8, a copy of which is listed in Rydal Mount Catalogue, lot 540. (E. de S., p. 194, mistakenly thinks that Wordsworth is referring to Gilpin's *Observations . . . Cumberland and Westmoreland*.) Because Gilpin's criticism of white in landscape made such a strong and long-lasting impression on Wordsworth, we quote the relevant sentences as they appear in the general context of his argument; by the use of bracketed line-numbers, we also refer to other echoes of Gilpin in the *Guide*:

In general, the Welsh gentlemen, in these parts, seem fond of whitening their houses, which gives them a disagreeable glare. A *speck* of white is often beautiful; but white, in *profusion* [2000–1], is, of all tints, the most inharmonious. A white seat, at the corner of a wood, or a few white cattle grazing in a meadow, inliven a scene perhaps more, than if the seat, or the cattle, had been of any other colour. They have meaning, and effect [1981–5]. But a front, and two staring wings . . . and a variety of other large objects, which we often see daubed over with white, make a disagreeable appearance; and unite ill with the general simplicity of nature's colouring.

Nature never colours in this offensive way. Her surfaces are never white. The chalky cliff is the only permanent object of the kind, which she allows to be her's; and this seems rather a force upon her from the boisterous action of a furious element. . . .

In these remarks I mean only to insinuate—that *white* is a hue, which nature seems studious to expunge from all her works, except in the touch of a flower, an animal, a cloud, a wave, or some other diminutive, or transient object [2002–4]— and that *her mode* of colouring should always be the model of *our's*.

In animadverting however on *white objects*, I would only censure the mere raw tint. It may easily be corrected, and turned into stone-colours [2031] of various hues; which tho light, if not too light, may often have a good effect.

Mr. Lock, who did me the favour to overlook these papers, made some remarks on this part of my subject, which are so new, and so excellent, that I cannot without impropriety, take the credit of them myself.

". . . I partake however of your general dislike to the colour; and though I have seen a very *splendid effect* from an *accidental light* on a white object; yet I think it a hue, which oftener injures, than it improves the scene. It particularly disturbs the air in it's office of graduating distances [2005–6]; shews objects nearer, than they really are; and by pressing them on the eye, often gives them an importance, which from their form, and situation, they are not intitled to.

"The white of snow is so active, and refractory, as to resist the discipline of every harmonizing principle [2568–70]. I think I never saw Mont Blanc, and the range of snows, which run through Savoy, in union with the rest of the landscape, except when they were tinged by the rays of the rising, and setting sun; or participated of some other tint of the surrounding sky. In the clear, and colourless days so frequent in that country, the Glaciers are always out of tune."

2005. Mr. Locke, of N——] William Lock of Norbury; for Lock's contribution to Gilpin's work see Carl P. Barbier, *William Gilpin* (Oxford, 1963), p. 133.

2019–20. it is . . . complained of] But see *An Evening Walk* (1849), ll. ~~s~~ ~~w~~ i. 13 and 15).

2022–5. Wh~~i~~ ~~g~~round . . . cheerful] Cf. Dorothy Wordsworth to Lady Beaumont, 2~~8~~ 1804 (*E.Y.*, pp. 520–1):

the mountains have a th~~in~~ ~~co~~vering of snow which makes our white houses and white church even look w~~hi~~ ~~b~~ut it is a sad pity that the storms do not make a more successful war against wh~~ite~~ wash, for though it is tolerable when there is any quantity of snow and by moo~~nl~~ight, at other times the Church seems absolutely to disturb the proportions of the Vale by its starting forward, at least to us who have known it otherwise.

Cf. also *Guide*, 3036–9 and n.

2028. flaring] Cf. Wordsworth's quotation from Gray, *Guide*, 1710–13 and n.

2033, fn. Cf. 1611, fn. ('the gentry *recently* have copied the old models') and our n. *ad loc.*

2037. the management . . . plantations] Cf. *E.Y.*, pp. 622–9, part of which is quoted in our n. to 1813–922; for Wordsworth's planting at Allan Bank, see Moorman, ii. 109.

2040–203. Larch . . . their situation] The disagreeable regularity of new plantations—especially plantations of firs—was censured by almost all writers who valued 'picturesque' landscape; but, except for Uvedale Price, who also found fault with the pointed larch (*An Essay on the Picturesque* (London, 1796), i. 293–7), Wordsworth seems to have been alone in his severe condemnation of those who had brought the Alpine larch into the north of England.

2098–102. The Scotch fir . . . the house] Cf. *Guide*, 1580–1, 1729–31.

That the fir needs space and should not be 'stifled' in thick plantations is a 'Theory' of Wordsworth's which Coleridge recalls in *C.N.B.* i. 515 and 1496. (In her note to 1496, Coburn mistakenly thinks that the 'Theory' refers to plantations of larches.)

2117–211. indiscriminately . . . could prevail] Wordsworth's own copy of *Select Views in Cumberland, Westmoreland, and Lancashire,* presented to him by Joseph Wilkinson, is now in the possession of Miss Margaret Goalby, of Ambleside. Miss Goalby refused us permission to examine the book and record its manuscript variants. We describe, however, two pages (xxx–xxxi, corresponding to *Guide,* 2117–211) which were on public display at Rydal Mount in the summer of 1970; we do not know how far they are typical of other pages.

Despite the descriptive label in the Rydal Mount exhibit case which asserted that 'This copy has Wordsworth's own pencilled corrections and additions', we are inclined to think that the hand is Mary Wordsworth's, and not William's. On page xxx are two ampersands, which in Wordsworth's hand are invariably a long straight line with a small hook at the top (φ); the ampersands on page xxx lack that distinctive characteristic and have, like Mary's, a rounded turn at the bottom (ϕ); in other respects also, the hand seems to us much more like Mary's than William's. The brief descriptive label further asserted that the pencilled emendations were made for the 1820 edition; this is probably correct, but it is also possible that they may have been made for the earlier *Unpublished Tour* (see *U.T.* textual n. 203–6: 'Here take up Wilkinson Book').

A good many changes eventually introduced into the 1820 edition were not made on pp. xxx–xxxi: revisions of 1820 *not* pencilled in are those recorded in textual notes 2123, 2128, 2133 (the misprint in 2134, however, is corrected), 2138, 2143, 2147, 2159 [*second*] 2175–6, 2179 [*second*], 2183, 2196 [*first*], 2200.

If we ignore—as we do elsewhere—variants in pointing, spelling, and the use of the ampersand, we find that five of the revisions produce immediately a text identical with that of 1820, as recorded in textual notes 2127, 2136, 2139 (except that 'limits' is substituted for a deleted 'restricts'), 2159 [*first*], 2160.

Four revisions are either unique or achieve identity with the 1820 text only after some variation:

(1) 'we have described' is deleted (textual n. 2155–6); a second 'which' is inserted, with the result that the text is garbled to read 'which which as'; in the same sentence (textual n. 2155–6), 'cause' is deleted; 'source of' is inserted; and thus the sentence is further garbled to read 'source of of'.

(2) 'it makes a speck and deformity' is deleted (textual n. 2167); 'wherever it [appears *del.*] shews itself a disagreeable speck is produced' is inserted.

(3) 'it' in 2168 is deleted; 'the larch' is inserted.

(4) 'appears absolutely . . . the forest' (textual n. 2169–72) is deleted; the first substitution reads, 'for though their [? boughs] are bare

they do not seem withered, and one might almost say that [? their] winter [*altered from* wintery] [appearance *del.*] [? look] differs as much from that of the larch as sleep from death'; the second substitution makes the text identical with 2169–72 ('is still more . . . dead').

2153. spiky tree] Cf. *S.V.*, textual n. 151 and our n. ad loc.

2184–91. where, without interruption . . . contribute] J. T. Boulton recognizes in this passage principles clearly inherited from Edmund Burke (*A Philosophical Enquiry into the Origin of our Ideas of the Sublime and Beautiful* (London, 1958), pp. c–ci); cf. *Subl. and Beaut.* 97–101, 140–4 and nn.

2197–200. Let me . . . tracts] Cf. *Guide*, 2055–7, and Dorothy Wordsworth, 18 Oct. 1807 (*M.T*. i. 169).

2212–17. This is . . . annoyance] Cf. *Guide*, 1715–21.

2225–31. 'Degenerate Douglas', ll. 8–14, *P.W.* iii. 83 (noted by E. de S.). In *Exc.* VII. 590–602 the Vicar regrets the 'works of havoc' performed by the woodman of 'these vales':

> Full oft his doings leave me to deplore
> Tall ash-tree, sown by winds, by vapours nursed,
> In the dry crannies of the pendent rocks;
> Light birch, aloft upon the horizon's edge,
> A veil of glory for the ascending moon;
> And oak whose roots by noontide dew were damped,
> And on whose forehead inaccessible
> The raven lodged in safety.

2250–2. and impress . . . change] Cf. *Subl. and Beaut.* 67–9: if analysed, a sensation of sublimity 'would be found to resolve itself into three component parts: a sense of individual form or forms; a sense of duration; and a sense of power'.

2256–97. About the same . . . natives] Cf. Wordsworth's letter to Charles James Fox, 14 Jan. 1801 (*E.T.*, pp. 312–15), in which he recommends to Fox's attention 'The Brothers' and 'Michael', because they illustrate the values to the nation of the 'small independent *proprietors* of land here called statesmen, men of respectable education who daily labour on their own little properties'. Wordsworth's comments on the social and economic changes occurring about the turn of the century are substantiated in C. M. L. Bouch and G. P. Jones, *A Short Economic and Social History of the Lake Counties* (Manchester, 1961), pp. 228–39.

2305–7. a sort . . . enjoy] In 1967 the National Trust owned in the Lake District 73,069 acres and had protective covenants over another 15,500 acres; these properties are all in the Lake District National Park, which was established in 1951. In *Railway*, 606–8, Wordsworth echoes the phrasing of the *Guide*: the beauty and retirement of the district should be protected 'for the sake of every one . . . who coming hither shall bring with him an eye to perceive, and a heart to feel and worthily enjoy'; both prose sentences perhaps echo 'and bring with you a heart / That watches and receives' ('The Tables Turned', *P.W*. iv. 57).

2310–12. Mr. West . . . August] West, *Guide*, p. 7.

2314–58. But that . . . summer] For earlier remarks on the seasonal colourings see *Guide*, 687–762, 1118–29.

2322–3. those deluges . . . Nile] Cf. *Prel*. (1850), VI. 614–16: 'Like the mighty flood of Nile / Poured from his fount of Abyssinian clouds / To fertilise the whole Egyptian plain'.

2341–2. the mountain-sides . . . colours] Cf. *Prel*. (1850), VI. 10–11: 'the coves and heights / Clothed in the sunshine of the withering fern'.

2353–4. the golden . . . intervened] E. de S. (p. 198) cites in comparison 'To Joanna', ll. 38–40 (*P.W*. ii. 113), lines quoted in our note to 1122–4.

2363–6. The number . . . protection] E. de S. (p. 199) notices that the same observation had been made by Gray after he had reached Kendal (West, *Guide*, p. 213): 'The air mild as summer . . . and the sky-larks singing aloud (by the way, I saw not one at Keswick, perhaps because the place abounds in birds of prey).'

2366–7. It is not . . . vales] Commenting upon the textual revision of 1820 (textual n. 2366–7), E. de S. (p. 199) says: 'This significant change suggests that between 1810 and 1820, Wordsworth had heard the nightingale at Grasmere; but . . . all the authority of naturalists is against him.' According to an ornithological article in W. G. Collingwood, *The Lake Counties* (London, 1932), p. 186, 'The nightingale has its extreme north-western limit in Cheshire.'

2371–4. There is . . . country] E. de S. (p. 199) cites in comparison 'Yes, it was the mountain Echo', and quotes Wordsworth's annotation to those lines (*P.W*. ii. 265–6 and 518). References may also be made to 'O Blithe New-comer' (*P.W*. ii. 207–8 and notes, pp. 502–3); 'To the Cuckoo' (*P.W*. iii. 45); 'The Cuckoo at Laverna' (*P.W*. iii. 218–22 and nn., pp. 495–6); *Exc*. II. 346–8.

2377–86. The herbage . . . food] Cf. *Prel*. VIII. 366–75, XIII. 152–6.

2411–18. it will appear . . . excitement] Cf. *S.V*. 23–30, *U.T*. 218–29. West (*Guide*, pp. 54–5) makes a similar comment: 'Windermere-water, like that of Coniston, is viewed to the greatest advantage by facing the mountains, which rise in grandeur on the eye, and swell upon the imagination as they are approached.'

In his unpublished journal the Revd. J. Pering recalls a conversation with Wordsworth in June 1808 (see *M.T*. i. 271, n. 1); Pering had expressed surprise that Gray 'had not done . . . justice' to the 'Sublimity' of the vale of Grasmere and had not mentioned its island.

'Your observations,' replied Mr Wordsworth, 'are for the most part very just, but some allowance should be made. When you first looked down upon Grasmere, you had not seen half the beauties that our Lakes of Westmoreland and Cumberland afford, whilst the Poet was returning from having viewed almost all; and consequently his imagination had been so familiarized with mountainous prospects, that the impressions had become less vivid: moreover, the view he describes is from a point [Town Head] opposite to your own, & perhaps not quite so striking; and the Island could not be clearly distinguished.'

2438. the *mind*] A similar emphasis appears in *Guide*, 5–6; cf. also *Subl. and Beaut.* 288–344. In a letter of 17 January 1825 Wordsworth said that his wish was 'to teach the *Touring World*, which is become very numerous, to look through the clear eye of the Understanding as well as through the hazy one of vague Sensibility' (*L.Y.*, p. 173).

2443. qui *bene . . . docet*] We have not been able to identify this quotation.

2444–6. yet fastidiousness . . . pleased] Cf. *C.N.B.* i. 519: 'Modern Poetry & Landscape—vice of judging from defects not from excellencies'. In her note to 518, Coburn identifies this entry as one of those made in November 1799, 'during the cold wet storm-stayed days at Grasmere with Wordsworth'.

2446–51. For example . . . agitated] E. de S. (p. 200) quotes in comparison from the I.F. note to 'The Forsaken' (*P.W.* ii. 473).

2464–5. 'The Pass of Kirkstone', ll. 39–40 (*P.W.* ii. 279); the whole poem is quoted in 3234–325 (noted by E. de S.).

2466–75. E. de S. (p. 201) cites in comparison 'The Simplon Pass' (*P.W.* ii. 212–13), lines which were first published in *Railway*, 532–51. Among the textual variants to this same passage in *The Prelude* (VI. 562) are lines focusing on the evidence of destructive power: 'And ever as we halted, or crept on, / Huge fragments of primæval mountain spread / In powerless ruin, blocks as huge aloft / Impending, nor permitted yet to fall'.

2482–3. It is . . . rain] Cf. West's *Guide*, p. 75: 'In mountainous countries, cascades, water-falls, and cataracts, are frequent, but only to be seen in high perfection, when in full torrent, and that is in wet weather, or soon after it.'

2489–90. the breath . . . water] E. de S. (p. 201) notices the echo of this phrase in the I.F. note to 'Lines Written in Early Spring' (*P.W.* iv. 411–12): 'The brook fell down a sloping rock so as to make a waterfall considerable for that country [Alfoxden], and across the pool below had fallen a tree. . . . from the underside of this natural sylvan bridge depended long and beautiful tresses of ivy which waved gently in the breeze that might poetically speaking be called the breath of the waterfall.'

2505–788. In 1820 William, Mary, and Dorothy, in the company of a few others, made a long tour of the Continent, devoting most of their time to Alpine scenery ('Switzerland was our end and aim', *Journals*, ii. 23). In her journal Dorothy often compared and contrasted the scenes abroad with those at home; William too must have drawn numerous comparisons, both abroad and on his return home (for example, see his letter to Beaumont, 6 Jan. 1821, *L.Y.*, p. 7). But after writing this section for the 1822 edition, he seems to have felt some qualms about it; as early as April

1822 he wrote to Richard Sharp (*L.T.*, p. 66): 'I have in the press a little book on the Lakes, containing some illustrative remarks on Swiss scenery. If I have fallen into any errors, I know no one better able to correct them than yourself, and should the book . . . meet your eye, pray point out to me the mistakes. The part relating to Switzerland is new.' By 1825 Wordsworth was ready to confess a fault; writing to Jacob Fletcher, who had sent him a manuscript comparing the scenery of North Wales and Scotland, he said (*L.T.*, p. 172):

I object to nothing which you say upon the scenery of N.W. [North Wales] considered per se. Your analysis of it is, as far as it goes, undeniably just—but it seems next to impossible to discriminate between the claims of two countries to admiration with the impartiality of a *Judge*; in one's mind one may be just to both, but something of the advocate will creep into the language—as an office of this kind is generally undertaken with a view to rectify some injustice. This was the case with myself with respect to a comparison which I have drawn between our Mountains &c and the Alps; the general impression is, I am afraid, that I give the preference to my native region, which was far from the truth. But I wished to shew advantages which we possessed that were generally overlooked, and *dwelt* upon those, slightly adverting only to the points in which the Alps have the superiority. The result then is, that I may *appear* to have dealt unfairly with that marvellous portion of the Earth that is presented to view in the Swiss and Italian Vallies.—In like manner you have the *appearance* of being unjust to Scotland.

2530–2. we have . . . elevation] The highest mountain in England is Scafell Pike at 3,210 feet; Mont Blanc is 15,781 feet; the Finsteraarhorn, 14,026; the Jungfrau, 13,667.

2537–43. after a certain . . . atmosphere] Originally Wordsworth had written, 'after a certain point, the sense of sublimity depends more upon form and relation of objects to each other than upon their actual magnitude' (see textual n. 2538–9). This generalization was obviously based on observations of particular scenes, such as that in Dorothy's description of Thun (*Journals*, ii. 105): 'Mountains and lake seemed to bear nearly the same proportion to each other as at Derwent-water, and this diminishes the effect of the mighty difference in bulk and space.' By 1828, however, Wordsworth wanted to modify his statement in the *Guide*:

In the Book of the Lakes, which I have not at hand—is a passage rather too vaguely expressed where I content myself with saying—that after a certain point of elevation—the effect of Mountains depends much more upon their form than their absolute Height—This point which ought to have been defined, is the one to which fleecy clouds (not thin & watery vapours) are accustomed to descend.—I am glad you are so much interested with this tract—it could not have been written without long experience [*Some Letters of the Wordsworth Family*, ed. L. N. Broughton (Ithaca, N.Y., 1942), p.11].

In 1835 the text was accordingly revised.

2562–4. Among the . . . gardens] Cf. *Journals*, ii. 127: 'The monkshood of our gardens, growing at a great height on the Alps, has a brighter hue than elsewhere. It is seen in tufts, that to my fancy presented fairy groves upon the green grass, and in rocky places, or under trees.'

2567–91. When Wordsworth says that 'the colouring of Switzerland' and the forms of the Swiss Alps are 'ill suited to the pencil' and that 'our scenes are better suited to painting', it might be inferred that in this respect he thinks the English scenes superior, although at the end of the paragraph there seems to be something of a warning against our drawing such a conclusion. In 1793, in a note to *Descriptive Sketches* (*P.W*. i. 62), Wordsworth was much plainer, and not at all deprecatory in writing of the Alpine scenes in this same connection:

I had once given to these sketches the title of Picturesque; but the Alps are insulted in applying to them that term. Whoever, in attempting to describe their sublime features, should confine himself to the cold rules of painting would give his reader but a very imperfect idea of those emotions which they have the irresistible power of communicating to the most impassive imaginations. The fact is, that controuling influence, which distinguishes the Alps from all other scenery, is derived from images which disdain the pencil.

2579–82. yet Titian . . . Alps] Titian (1489–1576) was born at Pieve, in Cadore, a district in the Venetian Alps; from his youth onwards he resided chiefly in Venice; in 1548 he crossed the Alps to paint at the court of Charles V in Augsburg.

Nicolas Poussin (1594–1665) was born at Villers near Andelys, in Normandy; his early years were spent chiefly in Paris; about 1621 he set off for Rome, but got only as far as Florence before having to return to Paris; but from 1623 until his death he resided in Rome, except for the years 1640–2, when he again painted in Paris.

Gaspard Dughet (1615–75), called Gaspard Poussin after his brother-in-law, Nicolas, was born in Rome, where he resided most of his life. For the sake of the views, he rented, in his later years, four houses—two on the highest hills of Rome; one at Rivoli, where he had a view of the Alps; and one at Frascati.

Claude Gellée (1600–82), called Claude de Lorrain, was born at Champagne on the Moselle, near Mirecourt; he resided in Rome almost all his life. About 1625 he returned to France for a visit, going from Venice by way of the Tyrol; he returned to Rome by ship from Marseilles.

Pellegrino Tibaldi (1527–96) was born in Puria in the Valsolda; his early work was done in Rome; for nine years he resided in Spain; upon his return to Italy, he settled permanently in Milan.

Little is known of the life of Bernardino Luini (*c*. 1475–1532); it is believed that he was born in Luino on the Lago Maggiore. He painted in Milan and neighbouring towns; his best known works are the frescoes at Sarrono.

(Our authority for this note has been E. Bénézit, *Dictionnaire critique et documentaire des peintres, sculpteurs, dessinateurs et graveurs*, nouvelle édition, 1952.)

2582–6. A few . . . attempt] Besides one or more artists unknown to us, Wordsworth is here almost surely alluding to Turner. In 1802 Turner returned from his first trip to Switzerland, and within the next few years he exhibited numerous oils and water-colours of Alpine scenes: e.g.

Bonneville with Mont Blanc (1803); *Glacier and Source of the Arveron* (1803); *Devil's Bridge, Pass of St. Gothard* (1804); *Fall of the Rhine at Schaffhausen* (1806); *Valley of Chamouni* (1806); *Mer de Glace with Blair's Hut* (1806); *Lausanne, Lake Geneva* (1807). Engravings of Alpine landscapes also appeared in his *Liber Studiorum*, published irregularly between 1807 and 1819. By 1822, however, when Wordsworth first published this section of the *Guide*, Turner was again painting mainly English landscapes. (See A. J. Finberg, *The Life of J. M. W. Turner, R.A.* (Oxford, 1939), pp. 84–5, 465–8; A. J. Finberg, *The History of Turner's Liber Studiorum* (London, 1924), pp. 367–9; R. H. Wilenski, *English Painting* (London, 1964), pp. 182–4.)

We know of only one brief statement of Wordsworth's in praise of a work by Turner, and even this does not appear until the 1835 edition of the *Guide* (33–4). His attitude towards Turner—or, at least, his silence— probably reflects the influence of Sir George Beaumont; as early as 1803 Beaumont was finding fault with Turner, and from 1813 until his death in 1827 his attacks and strictures on Turner were 'incessant' (see Finberg, *Life*, pp. 99, 194–6, 207–8, 212, 220–6, 234). In 1835 Crabb Robinson observed that Wordsworth did not spare even Turner when he was condemning other modern painters (*H.C.R.*, p. 459); we note too that in thanking Samuel Rogers for his *Italy* (1830) and *Poems* (1834), both illustrated with engravings by Turner and Stothard, Wordsworth, without mentioning Turner by name, was markedly lukewarm in his appreciation of the 'embellishments' (see *L.T.*, pp. 514, 664, 684, 691).

2610, textual n. The quotation marks, added in 1823, were perhaps intended to indicate the author's awareness of a witty contrast between the products of uncultivated nature in the north of England and the agricultural products of northern Italy, particularly the olive and grape as they are described immediately below.

2624, fn. *De Rerum Natura*, V. 1370–8 (noted by E. de S.).

2627. hoariness of hue] E. de S. (p. 201) compares *Hamlet*, IV. vii. 166–7: 'There is a willow grows aslant a brook, / That shows his hoar leaves in the glassy stream.'

2635–7. such wild . . . day] For having aided the rebellion of 1715 Sir James Radcliffe, third Earl of Derwentwater, was beheaded in 1716. The Radcliffe lands on Derwent Water were then 'vested in the king for the use of the public, and settled upon Greenwich hospital by act of Parliament'; the trustees of the hospital had the timber cut (Nicolson and Burn, ii. 79–80). For other comments on the woods of Gowbarrow Park, Lowther, and Rydal, cf. *Guide*, 403–8, 485–95, 1114–17, and 3193–205.

2641–2. first, as . . . landscape] Cf. 2501–4 above.

2644, fn. 'Ad Larium', *Idyllia Heroica Decem, Librum Phaleuciorum Unum* (Pisa, 1820), p. 161. Wordsworth corrects 'Cœco' to 'Cæco'. To 'Æstivas' Landor attaches a footnote: 'In lacu Lario tempestates æstate violentiores.' Cf. *Guide*, 975–6 and n.

2663–7. During two . . . here] Cf. *Journals*, ii. 249.

The 'two comprehensive tours among the Alps' were made in 1790 and 1820. From 7 August 1790 when they entered the Savoy Alps until they reached Basel on 21 September, Wordsworth and his friend Robert Jones toured on foot the French, Swiss, and Italian Alps and the Lombard lakes. (See Mark L. Reed, *Wordsworth: the Chronology of the Early Years* (Cambridge, Mass., 1967), pp. 103–13; Reed, pp. 97–114, cites the important references to this trip in Wordsworth's own writings.) In 1820 Wordsworth and his party arrived at Schaffhausen 1 August; from then until 24 September, when they left Geneva, they toured many of the places he had visited in 1790; they also went as far south as Milan (*Journals*, ii. 85–306; *H.C.R.*, pp. 243–53).

2677–8. The subject . . . upon] i.e. 2446–57, 2482–501.

2682–3. excepting . . . Schaffhausen] Cf. *Subl. and Beaut.* 236–55 and *Journals*, ii. 88–90.

2685–701. The 'singular phenomenon' which Wordsworth is recalling occurred not on 'a calm September morning' but on 17 November 1799, when he was conducting Coleridge on his first trip to the Lake District. *C.N.B.* i. 553 also describes the event:

the fog begins to clear off from the Lake, still however leaving straggling Detachments on it—, & clings viscously to the Hill / —all the objects on the opposite Coast are hidden, and all those hidden are reflected in the Lake, Trees, & the Castle, ⟨Lyulph's Tower,⟩ & the huge Crag that dwarfs it!—Divine!—The reflection of the huge pyramidal Crag is still hidden, & the image in the water still brighter / / but the Lyulph's Tower gleams like a Ghost, dim & shadowy—& the bright Shadow thereof how beautiful it is cut across by that Tongue of *breezy* water—now the Shadow is suddenly gone—and the Tower itself rises emerging out of the mist, two-thirds wholly hidden, the turrets quite clear—& a moment all is snatched away—Realities & Shadows—.

Wordsworth's comments about regretting his own 'previous knowledge of the place' and the 'pleasing astonishment' which a 'stranger to the spot' would have experienced are perhaps veiled recollections of Coleridge's response that day. (The editorial note on *C.N.B.* i. 553 does not mention Wordsworth's having preserved in the *Guide* his recollections of the same experience.)

Lyulph's Tower in Gowbarrow Park is a castellated edifice built by the Duke of Norfolk towards the end of the eighteenth century; though still ornate, it is less so than in Wordsworth's day (W. T. Palmer, *The English Lakes* (London, 1930), p. 202).

2709–38. We can neither date the occasion nor identify the friend.

2739–50. Having dwelt . . . astonishing] J. T. Boulton quotes this passage as an example of how fundamental to Wordsworth was Burke's distinction between the sublime and the beautiful (*A Philosophical Enquiry into the Origin of our Ideas of the Sublime and Beautiful* (London, 1958), pp. xcix–c). Cf. *Subl. and Beaut.* 21–2 and n.

2767–88. Wordsworth may have derived his knowledge of West's biography from William Close's editorial additions to *The Antiquities of Furness* (Ulverston, 1805), pp. 409–10:

Thomas West... received the earliest part of his education in the public schools in Edinburgh. Having a taste for learning, and a great desire to investigate the truths of religion, he entered the English College at St. Omers [then at Liège], where he went through his studies with application and brilliancy: and after having entered the holy Order of Priest-hood, and residing some years on the Continent, he came to England, and was much respected in his station of life, as for being a studious antiquarian.

In England, West lived first at Dalton in Furness and then at Ulverston; he died in 1779 at Sizergh Hall near Kendal.

In his quotation from West, *Guide*, pp. 4–5, Wordsworth has corrected 'summit' to 'summits' (2785) and altered the opening sentence ('As there are few people, in easy circumstances, but may find a motive for visiting this extraordinary region, so more especially those who intend', etc.).

2791. SCAWFELL] Actually Scafell Pike; cf. 2824–6 and n.

2793–8. Wordsworth refers to *U.T.*, where throughout he is concerned for the most favourable approaches to the various scenes, and where occasionally (e.g. *U.T.* 1079–87) he regrets his having to diminish the traveller's pleasure through anticipation.

2803–906. Wordsworth gives an extensively altered version of Dorothy Wordsworth's own 'extract' from a letter which she had written to William Johnson, 21 Oct. 1818; Dorothy's 'extract' is printed in our Appendix, pp. 364–8, where we also describe the two manuscripts in which it survives. William Johnson was curate and schoolmaster at Grasmere in 1811; in 1812, largely upon Wordsworth's recommendation, he was appointed by Dr. Andrew Bell to serve as headmaster at the Central School in London (C. C. Southey, *The Life of The Rev. Andrew Bell* (London, 1844), ii. 398–403; *M.Y.* i. 487 and n.; ii. 270 and n.).

In a letter to Jane Marshall (14 Oct. 1818) Dorothy briefly describes the same excursion (*M.Y.* ii. 495).

2804. we ascended] For Dorothy's companions see Scafell Pike Excursion, 19–36, in Appendix, p. 364; for Dorothy's connections with Miss Mary Barker prior to their ascent of Scafell Pike, 7 Oct. 1818, see *M.Y.* ii. 42, n. 3 and 129, n. 1.

2817. Mountains . . . in tumult] Cf. *Guide*, 664 and n.

2820. We had . . . journey] The top of Esk Hause had originally been the goal of the day's excursion (see Scafell Pike Excursion, 19–22, 60–1, in Appendix, pp. 364–5).

2824–6. another . . . Scawfell Head] Scafell Pike, which until recently was called simply the *Pikes*, is the highest summit in England (3,210 feet); it is divided from Scafell (3,162 feet) by Mickledore ridge.

2826. the Stone Man] Cf. 'Rural Architecture', *P.W.* i. 244 and the I.F.

note (p. *363*) on the cairn, or Stone Man, which was frequently built on a conspicuous point 'among our hills'.

2841. Grasmire] i.e. Grassmoor. Cf. Scafell Pike Excursion, 85, in Appendix, p. 366.

2846–50. on its highest . . . snow] Wordsworth verbally echoes *S.V.* 531–8; there is nothing comparable in Dorothy's 'extract'.

2911–49. *P.W.* ii. 286–7. We follow de Selincourt (ibid., p. 521) and earlier editors of Wordsworth's poetry in regarding 'coral' (textual n. 2938) as a misprint for 'choral'.

2953–4. the journal . . . country] From Dorothy's letters to Lady Beaumont written during, and immediately after, this excursion (*E.Y.*, pp. 636–40, 648–51), de Selincourt (*Journals*, i. xiv–xv) infers that the journal was written for Lady Beaumont. The fact that a fine copy of the journal has since been found among the Coleorton papers would further support his inference (see Appendix, p. 361). But Dorothy may at first have written the journal simply for herself and her immediate family; we note that some details in her notebook which would not have been significant to Lady Beaumont are omitted in the Coleorton manuscript (e.g. Ullswater Excursion, textual n. 233, Appendix, p. 376).

2958–3230. Wordsworth revises extensively Dorothy's journal of the Ullswater Excursion. For Dorothy's original version and the earliest revisions made for the *Guide* see Appendix, pp. 368–78. Dorothy also describes briefly the excursion in several letters (*E.Y.*, pp. 636–7, 647, 649–51). For Wordsworth's own descriptions of the same region see *S.V.* 553–712 and *Guide*, 354–495.

Throughout Dorothy's account the dates are one day off (cf. *E.Y.*, p. 637, n. 1). William and Dorothy left Grasmere on Wednesday the sixth; they spent three nights with their friends the Luffs at Patterdale; on the ninth they went to Park House, Tom Hutchinson's farm near Dalemain, where they stayed until Tuesday, 12 November, when they returned to Grasmere. Accordingly, the dates of the excursion (*Guide*, 2958, 3044, 3159, 3190, and Dorothy's Ullswater Excursion, *passim*) should all be moved back one day.

3003. where goats are now found;*] The footnote would suggest that Wordsworth in 1823 was glossing a statement made in 1805, but actually the statement itself, to which the note is appended, was composed for the 1823 *Guide*, and represents, therefore, what might have been said in 1805 (see Ullswater Excursion, textual n. 47). For a reference to the wild goats inhabiting these mountains E. de S. (p. 203) cites *Exc.* IV. 500.

3005. Ammonian horns] Cf. *Memorials of a Tour on the Continent*, XXXII. 19–27 (*P.W.* iii. 191 and notes, p. 485).

3031–3. we fixed . . . evening] It was for the purchase of Broad How, a nineteen-acre farm near the Luffs' cottage, that William and Dorothy extended their excursion in order to see Thomas Wilkinson at Yanwath about negotiations with the owner; although Wordsworth owned the property until 1834, he did not build there (Moorman, ii. 59–62).

3036–9. his lady's . . . spirit] De Selincourt recognizes in this image the source for *The White Doe*, 972–1002 (*P.W.* iii. 312–13, 554).

3039–43. The torrents . . . there."] There is nothing comparable in Dorothy's text. The concluding quotation (noted by E. de S.) is adapted from *Exc.* II. 872: 'I saw not, but I felt that it was there.'

Thinking perhaps of Wordsworth's scorn for Macpherson's *Ossian*, as expressed in *E.S.* 552–611, E. de S. (p. 203) finds 'strange and unexpected' Wordsworth's characterizing this scene as 'Ossianic'. But the epithet was surely intended only to suggest that quality of landscape associated in Scotland with the traditional Ossian. The sentence, written for the 1823 edition of the *Guide* (cf. Ullswater Excursion, textual n. 76–83), provides an interesting example of the way Wordsworth's memory works, for in 1805 he had, in a sense, associated Ossian's Glen Almond with Patterdale. Writing to Sir Walter Scott from the Luffs' house, 7 Nov. 1805, he copied out his poem 'Glen Almain' (*P.W.* iii. 75), which he thus introduced: 'I will transcribe Glenalmond, do I spell right? which you will like better as coming from Patterdale whence I now write. . . . "In this still place, remote from men / Sleeps Ossian in the Narrow Glen" ', etc. (*E.T.*, p. 643). Scott had been with Wordsworth in Patterdale that summer (Moorman, ii. 57 and *Guide*, n. 421–32); it is possible that together they had noted an 'Ossianic' quality in the glens of Patterdale, or it may be that Wordsworth in his letter is simply reminding Scott of their pleasant time together that he may be well disposed towards the poem. But more importantly, if Wordsworth's letter is correctly dated (cf. *Guide*, n. 2958–3230, he copied the verses on Ossian within hours of witnessing the moonlight scene, and years later, revising Dorothy's journal for the *Guide*, he introduces into the scene the 'Ossianic' allusion.

3048–58. A raven . . . destroyer] Wordsworth expands Dorothy's brief comment, 'a raven croaking on the mountain above our heads' (Ullswater Excursion, 94). For 'the iron tone of the raven's voice' E. de S. (p. 203) cites in comparison *Exc.* IV. 1178–81:

> the solitary raven, flying
> Athwart the concave of the dark blue dome,
> Unseen, perchance above all power of sight—
> An iron knell!

From his introducing recollections 'when a boy' (3055), it is apparent that Wordsworth thought that the reader would assume the journalist to be a man. For his own boyish plundering of the raven's nest see *Prel.* I. 335–50. Hawkshead records show that the reward for destroying ravens was 4*d.* a bird, and that the greatest number killed during Wordsworth's days at Hawkshead was twenty-four in 1780 (Henry S. Cowper, *Hawkshead* (London, 1899), p. 434).

3063–4. the chevin . . . Walton] The *chevin* is more commonly called the *chub*; in *The Compleat Angler* (Everyman's Library, 1939) Walton takes pains 'to recover the lost credit of the poor despised Chub' (p. 56), attributing its loss of reputation to 'ill cookery' (p. 165). In an obsolete transferred sense, *chub* also means 'a lazy spiritless person' (*O.E.D.*, s.v. *chub*, sb.²).

3069–70. "retiredness . . . majesty"] We have not been able to identify this quotation.

3079–80. "bare ring of mossy wall"] Originally said of the chapel at Ennerdale in 'The Brothers' (*P.W.* ii. 1), but thereafter quoted apropos the chapel at Martindale (Ullswater Excursion, 102; *S.V.* 692; *Guide*, textual n. 474).

3084–5. Mr. Hasell] Edward Hasell (1765–1825), squire of Dalemain, possessed the Martindale chase; the Hasells were long known for their hunts (see Hutchinson, *Excursion*, pp. 82–6; *The Victoria History of . . . Cumberland*, ed. James Wilson (London, 1905), ii. 423).

3128–35. Before we . . . west] According to Dorothy's Ullswater Excursion, 138–64, Luff pointed out the ruined chapel and told the story associated with it, a story which Wordsworth later developed in *Exc.* II. 730–895 (I.F. note, pp. 417–18).

3135–7. Scarcely . . . elements] Cf. *Guide*, n. 1312.

3143–50. Brotherswater . . . new-year's day] Cf. Clarke, pp. 153–4: 'In *Broadwater*, or *Brotherwater*, two young men, (brothers) were drowned together in December 1785, by the ice breaking with them. The inhabitants have a tradition that it received its name of Brotherwater from the like circumstance happening once before.'

3159–63. At the . . . triumph] Cf. Dorothy's letter to Lady Beaumont, 29 Nov. 1805 (*E.Y.*, pp. 649–50).

3190–229. we returned . . . above us] The Wordsworths traversed countless times the 'usual road' on the Cumberland side of Ullswater; the fullest descriptions are Dorothy's Ullswater Excursion, 251–87 and her Grasmere journal for 15 April 1802 (*Journals*, i. 131–2). In his boyish 'Outline of a Poem descriptive of the lakes' (1792), Christopher Wordsworth planned a detailed treatment of the same side (Z. S. Fink, *The Early Wordsworthian Milieu* (Oxford, 1958), pp. 105–7).

3234–325. *P.W.* ii. 278–80. De Selincourt once thought that 'raised' (3255) was a misprint for 'raz'd' (E. de S., p. 203), but in his edition of the poem for *The Poetical Works* he preserved 'raised', and noted that 'the MS. and all edd. revised by W. have "raised", which is quite intelligible' (*P.W.* ii. 278 and 520).

COMMENTARY: *SELECT VIEWS*

1–30. On the various approaches to the District cf. *Guide*, 8–96; *S.V.* 92–6, 115–35, textual n. 135/6; *U.T.* 1–356. (See our n. to *Guide*, 8–96.)

2–50. It is . . . Seathwaite] For passages echoed and expanded in *U.T.* see our n. to *U.T.* 2–425.

5–6. by the way of Stainmoor] See our n. to *Guide*, 18–28.

9–11. Mr. West . . . Coniston] West, *Guide*, pp. 10–53.

15–21. And further . . . introduced] See our n. to *Guide*, 184–9.

23–30. And I . . . accordingly] Cf. *Guide*, 2411–18 and n.

25. given in the Introduction] The 'Introduction' to *S.V.*, as well as 'Section I', is now represented in the text of the *Guide*, 501–2406, and in the accompanying textual notes.

31–326. For descriptions of the southern and south-eastern regions of the Lake District cf. *Guide*, 97–286 and *U.T.* 357–1591. (See our n. to *Guide*, 97–286.)

46–8. This little . . . Duddon] In writing his long note to *The River Duddon*, XVII and XVIII (*P.W.* iii. 508–22), Wordsworth used portions of *U.T.* 358–557, which in itself is an expansion of *S.V.* 31–83. As a result, this sentence is echoed in the *River Duddon* note ('first descending into a little circular valley, a collateral compartment of the long winding vale through which flows the Duddon', *P.W.* iii. 509). For references to Wordsworth's writing on the River Duddon see our n. to *Guide*, 1075–9.

47 and 52, textual nn. For the reason given immediately above, the *River Duddon* note (*P.W.* iii. 509–10) occasionally echoes the manuscript for *S.V.* In textual n. 52 Wordsworth quotes from Gray's description of the eastern shore of Windermere (West, *Guide*, p. 213): 'no flat marshy grounds, no osier beds, or patches of scrubby plantations on its banks'; the sentence on Grasmere which Wordsworth so much admired in Gray's journal has almost the same kind of negative construction (see our n. to *Guide*, 1700–13). The innkeeper's anecdote, given in the same textual n., was probably not original, for H. S. Cowper (*Hawkshead* (London, 1899), p. 338) quotes a similar saying popular in High Furness: 'The towns are finished and the country unfinished.' At the end of the textual n. Wordsworth quotes the opening lines of *The River Duddon*, XIV (*P.W.* iii. 251–2).

59. Broughton] See our n. to *Guide*, 216.

85. a fine view . . . Etchings] 'Estwaite-water, from below Belle-mount', published 1 July 1810, No. 8 in Wilkinson's CONTENTS. On Wordsworth's somewhat puzzling and erratic way of referring to the plates, see our Introduction, pp. 126–7.

96–114. Before the Traveller . . . architecture] For Curwen's property on Windermere see our n. to *Guide*, 108–12. In the 1799 edition of West's

Guide a footnote is appended to the description of the 'Station' above the ferry: 'In consequence of the act for inclosing Claif common, the Rev. W. Brathwaite purchased the ground including this station, and has erected an elegant and commodious building thereon, for the entertainment of his friends, called *Belle Vieu*; he has also planted the adjoining grounds, and altered the direction of the road, which was rugged and unsafe, and rendered it more convenient by carrying it nearer the margin of the lake' (West, *Guide* (London, 1799), p. 56). In the 1802 edition a revised foot-note refers to 'the late Rev. W. Brathwaite' and adds that 'This place has since been purchased by Mr. Curwen' (West, *Guide* (Kendal, 1802), p. 56). Since the Act for the Enclosure of Claife Commons was passed in 1794 (*The Victoria History of . . . Lancaster* (London, 1966), p. 380), the 'elegant and commodious building' must have been built between 1794 and 1799. Green (i. 228) tells us that it had 'dining and other rooms' on the ground floor and a drawing-room on the floor above, but Southey's description of it in 1807 is the more vivid: from Bowness

we crossed to an inn called the Ferry, on the opposite bank,—a single house, over-shadowed by some fine sycamore trees, which grow close to the water side. We were directed to a castellated building above the inn, standing upon a craggy point, but in a style so foolish, that, if any thing could mar the beauty of so beautiful a scene, it would be this ridiculous edifice. This absurdity is not remembered when you are within, and the spot is well chosen for a banqueting-house. The room was hung with prints, representing the finest similar landscapes in Great Britain and other countries, none of the representations exceeding in beauty the real prospect before us. The windows were bordered with coloured glass, by which you might either throw a yellow sunshine over the scene, or frost it, or fantastically tinge it with purple [Robert Southey, *Letters from England,* ed. Jack Simmons (London, 1951), p. 229].

In the I.F. note to 'Lines left upon a Seat in a Yew-tree' (*P.W.* i. 329) Wordsworth recalls with nostalgia the appearance of the 'Station' when he was a schoolboy at Hawkshead, 1779–87. For his later mockery of the hyperbolic praises made by visitors to this site see 'Written in the Strangers' Book at "The Station," Opposite Bowness', *P.W.* iv. 387–8.

117–30. I would . . . Landscape] Cf. 'On the Projected Kendal and Windermere Railway', quoted in *Railway*, 4–17. The approach to Winder-mere from Staveley was the one taken by William and Dorothy on their way to Grasmere in 1799, and again in 1802, when they were bringing the bride Mary Wordsworth to her new home (*Journals*, i. 182).

124, textual n. In *Prel.* IV (1850), 10, the phrase 'with instantaneous burst', used to describe the first sight of Windermere from Orrest Head, is reminiscent of the earlier prose comment on the same scene ('an instan-taneous map-like burst'). Wordsworth also uses *burst* substantively in *S.V.* 94, 473; *U.T.* 485, 1079. Although the *O.E.D.* cites Coleridge's 'Fears in Solitude', 215, as the first example of the word used for 'a sudden opening on the view' (s.v., *burst*, sb.[3]), Gilpin had also frequently used the word in this same sense (e.g. of Windermere, 'the whole burst of that magnificent scene', i. 142).

125–6. the sublime mountains . . . at the head of the Lake] i.e. the Langdale Pikes, which the tourist in 'The Sublime and the Beautiful' is invited to look at (*Subl. and Beaut.* 56–67; cf. also ibid. 362–6).

135. Inn of Bowness] Cf. *Prel.* II. 145–70.

135/6, textual n. The absence of introductory quotation marks, or the inadvertent presence of the concluding ones ('these Hampdens . . . fields" '), is Wordsworth's, who is adapting Gray, *Elegy Written in a Country Church-yard*: 'Some village-Hampden, that with dauntless breast / The little Tyrant of his fields withstood'.

In abridging Nicolson and Burn, i. 51–9, Wordsworth sometimes skilfully summarizes and sometimes directly copies. For example, in the third sentence from the end of the abridgement ('In short, the matter . . . of the lord'), he gives accurately and succinctly the gist of approximately four long pages of various complex legal documents (ibid., pp. 55–9). On the other hand, he is careful to preserve any striking figurative language; thus in quoting the tenants' remonstrance, he keeps the bit about the 'greedy eagle or devouring vulture' and that about the 'poor bird and weaker cattle', but adds to the parenthesis '(say they)' his own comment: 'making use of an image natural to Mountaineers'. As an example of a typical abridgement, we quote for comparison with Wordsworth's third sentence the following sentences from Nicolson and Burn (i. 51):

In consequence of this doctrine, the prince of Wales, in the 16th year of the said king, exhibited his bill in chancery, complaining, that the tenants claimed by colour of a tenant-right estate, under certain yearly rents, to have an estate of inheritance in the respective tenements; whereas it was conceived, that their estates in the premisses were of no such force in law as they pretended. The tenants put in their answer. But from the hazard of contesting with the king, who had the judges both of law and equity, in a considerable degree, at his devotion, and Sir Francis Bacon lord Verulam presiding then in the court of chancery (who, notwithstanding his greatness in other respects, was as tame, submissive, and obedient to orders, as any courtier could be), and at the same time, a good round sum in hand appearing to be not unacceptable to the prince, the matter was compromised, and for the sum of 2700 l. he agreed to confirm unto them their custom, as set forth in their answer: Which was in these words,——'That they and their ancestors, and all those whose estates they severally and respectively had or claimed to have in the several messuages, lands, tenements, meadows, pastures, closes, improvements' [etc., etc.].

The 'Native' who rebuilt Ings Chapel was Robert Bateman, whom William and Dorothy both mistakenly refer to as Richard Bateman; 'Michael', 258–70 (*P.W.* ii. 88–9 and 484) tells the story of his success and his benefactions (cf. Nicolson and Burn, i. 141). Describing the activities of Hawkshead schoolboys, Charles Farish, a schoolfellow of Wordsworth's (see our n. to *Guide*, 204–15), also remembered Bateman and the suspicions about his death (*Minstrels of Winandermere* (London, n.d.), p. 10):

> Then downward to the Great-boat tree
> The little pilgrims lightly bound,
> Telling what wonders they shall see
> What time they reach Ings' holy ground.

> "Great was his heart!—the marble floor,
> "Table and pulpit marble too,
> "Marble the very pulpit's door!"—
> —"And did they poison one so true?"

In 1802 the Wordsworths stopped at Ings Chapel on their way home from the wedding at Gallow Hill, and Wordsworth is now recalling the occasion, one which Dorothy had recorded in her journal (*Journals*, i. 182–3):

The door [of Ings Chapel] was open, and we went in. It is a neat little place, with a marble floor and marble communion table, with a painting over it of the last supper, and Moses and Aaron on each side. The woman told us that "they had painted them as near as they could by the dresses as they are described in the Bible", and gay enough they are. The marble had been sent by Richard Bateman from Leghorn. The woman told us that a man had been at her house a few days before, who told her he had helped to bring it down the Red Sea, and she had believed him gladly!

148. the last five and thirty years] Some of the changes which Wordsworth regrets would have occurred before 1779 when he first entered Hawkshead Grammar School.

151, textual n. For Wordsworth's disquisition on the faults of larch plantations see *Guide*, 2040–203 and n. The observations on church spires to which Wordsworth refers were made by Coleridge in *The Friend*, No. 14 (23 Nov. 1809), p. 223:

An instinctive taste teaches men to build their churches in flat countries with spire-steeples, which as they cannot be referred to any other object, point as with silent finger to the sky and stars, and sometimes when they reflect the brazen light of a rich though rainy sun-set, appear like a pyramid of flame burning heaven-ward. I remember once, and once only, to have seen a spire in a narrow valley of a mountainous country. The effect was not only mean but ludicrous, and reminded me against my will of an *extinguisher*; the close neighbourhood of the high mountain, at the foot of which it stood, had so completely dwarfed it, and deprived it of all connection with the sky or clouds.

Cf. *Biog. Lit.* ii. 145. In a note to *Exc.* (*P.W.* v. 456), Wordsworth quotes, although without quotation marks, part of the same comment from *The Friend*.

153–72. Upon the largest . . . behind] For the work of Mr. English, Windermere Island's first 'Improver', followed by that of J. C. Curwen, see *Guide*, 1724–76 and n. In a footnote to his second edition (i. 146–7), Gilpin had already expressed a sentiment very much like Wordsworth's: 'Since this view of Windermere island was taken, it hath been under the hands of improvement. The proprietor I have been told spent six thousand pounds upon it; with which sum he has contrived to do almost every thing, that one would wish had been left undone. It is now in other hands, which may probably restore it's beauty.'

167–72. Could not . . . behind] Preserved with only a few verbal changes in *Guide*, 1770–6.

173–2010. Preserved with few verbal changes in *Guide*, 112–40.

201. AMBLESIDE, &c.] The presence of this heading is explained in our Introduction, p. 126.

222–42. From this Bridge . . . seen] Cf. *Guide*, 249–53 and n. Instead of taking the public road up to the falls at Rydal, Wordsworth and Coleridge in 1799 apparently walked along the hillside of Rydal Park, then the residence of Sir Michael le Fleming. Coleridge, who had come to share Wordsworth's views on the use of white in landscapes (see *Guide*, 1968–2033), records in his journal the consequences of their trespass (*C.N.B.* i. 514): 'While at Sir Fleming's a servant, red-eyed &c, came to us, to the Road before the Waterfall to reprove us for having passed before the front of the House— / = by our Trespass of Feet with the Trespass on the Eye by his damned White washing!'

227–40. this may . . . roosting-place] On the tree-felling in Rydal see *Guide*, 1114–17 and n. The verse quotation is from *As You Like It*, iv. iii. 104–5: 'Under an oak, whose boughs were moss'd with age, / And high top bald with dry antiquity'.

248. a sublime Unity] Cf. *Subl. and Beaut.* 140–4, and n.

260. Langdale Chapel] For the sake of its accuracy, Wordsworth might have drawn attention to Wilkinson's etching of 'Langdale Chapel, Vale of Langdale', published 1 May 1810, No. 12 in the CONTENTS. Was he perhaps writing this part before he had seen the print? (See our Introduction, pp. 126–7.)

270–4. 'The Idle Shepherd-Boys; or, Dungeon-Ghyll Force', 51–5 (*P.W.* i. 240); Wordsworth has altered 'a chasm' to 'the chasm'.

280–2. Blea Tarn . . . fields] See *Guide*, 151–77 and nn.

296–7. the Bridge . . . Clappersgate] No etching is so identified by title, nor is any such etching listed in the CONTENTS, but 'Brathay-bridge, near Ambleside', published 1 Dec. 1810, No. 14 in the CONTENTS, was probably misentitled by Wilkinson, for the artist seems to have been looking southward with Ambleside on his left.

307/8, textual n. Reasons why Wordsworth did not finish this manuscript and why in *S.V.* he scanted the whole region between Ambleside and Thirlmere are suggested in our Introduction, pp. 126–7.

The verse quotation is from *The Recluse*, ll. 142–52 (*P.W.* v. 318). A fragment on Grasmere written for *The Recluse*, but not incorporated into it, may be compared with the first complete prose paragraph in our textual n.:

> A mighty vale,
> Fresh as the freshest field, scoop'd out, and green
> As is the greenest billow of the sea:
> The multitude of little rocky hills,
> Rocky or green, that do like islands rise
> From the flat meadow lonely there—
> Embowering mountains, and the dome of Heaven
> And waters in the midst, a second Heaven.
>
> (*P.W.* v. 347)

Towards the end of the part on Grasmere, and just before the description of the ascent towards Wythburn by Dunmail Raise, Wordsworth mentions 'a view from Grasmere Lake [? seen] from the edge of Easedale'; there is no such etching in Wilkinson's collection. Almost at the end of the textual n. there is a reference to an etching of the 'lower division' of Thirlmere; the etching is 'Therl-mere or Leath-water', published 1 Feb. 1810, No. 17 in the CONTENTS.

327–552. For excursions in the northern and western regions of the Lake District see *Guide*, 287–353 and nn. Cf. also *C.N.B*. i. 536–42, and Dorothy Wordsworth to Lady Beaumont, Oct. 1804 (*E.T*., pp. 507–8), for tours led by Wordsworth.

329. Dr. Brown . . . Gray] On Brown's description see our n. to *Guide*, 1239–62; on Gray's, see our nn. to *Guide*, 45 and 1700–13.

335–6. Applethwaite . . . and 24] 'Derwent-water from Appelthwaite' [*sic*], published 1 Jan. 1810, No. 22 in the CONTENTS; 'Part of Skiddaw, from Appelthwaite Gill', published 1 June 1810, No. 23; 'Cottages in Appelthwaite [*sic*], looking from Skiddaw', published 1 Feb. 1810, No. 24. For Wordsworth's associations with Applethwaite see our n. to *Guide*, 298.

352–4. Valley of . . . Views] 'View in the Vale of Newlands', published 1 Feb. 1810, No. 32 in the CONTENTS; 'Cottage in the Vale of Newlands, with Robinson's-crag', published 1 Feb. 1810, No. 30; 'Cottage in the Vale of Newlands, near Stare-bridge', published 1 Mar. 1810, No. 29; 'Cottage in the Vale of Newlands, between Keswick and Buttermere', published 1 Dec. 1810, No. 31; 'Cottages at Braithwaite', published 1 Jan. 1810, No. 25; 'Cottages at Braithwaite', published 1 Apr. 1810, No. 26. From Wordsworth's rather vague references to 'Views' it is not possible to tell whether he had seen more than two or three of these etchings when he was composing his description.

No manuscript survives for this section, but for an explanation of the strange use of the first person singular in 353–4 ('I have given Views') see our Introduction, and cf. textual nn. 464, 510, 705.

375–97. On Borrowdale cf. *U.T*. 1592–787.

391–3. But the noblest . . . detached] Cf. 'Yew-Trees', 13–18 (*P.W*. ii. 210):

> But worthier still of note
> Are those fraternal Four of Borrowdale,
> Joined in one solemn and capacious grove;
> Huge trunks! and each particular trunk a growth
> Of intertwisted fibres serpentine
> Up-coiling, and inveterately convolved.

See also I.F. note, ibid., pp. 503–4.

402, textual n. vale (See No.   )] 'Bassenthwaite Lake from Embleton Vale', published 1 July 1810, No. 38 in the CONTENTS.

410–13 the scenes . . . them] Cf. *Prel*. I. 271–304. Sonnets prompted by these scenes, but not descriptive of them, are *Poems Composed or Suggested During a Tour, in the Summer of 1833*, V–IX, *P.W.* iv. 22–4.

464–5. of which ... Wastdale] 'Ennerdale Broad-water', published 1 Jan. 1810, No. 40 in the CONTENTS; 'View on the Banks of Wast-water', published 1 Apr. 1810, No. 42; 'Wast-water, looking up to Wast-dale Head', published 1 June 1810, No. 41.

487–525. This Water . . . generations] On the possibility that this passage was composed by Dorothy Wordsworth see our Introduction, p. 126, and our description of MS. Prose 29.

496–9. The surface . . . intermingled] After citing Dorothy's letter of 12 November 1810 (*M.T.* i. 449), in which she wrote of helping William by composing 'a description or two for the finishing of his work for Wilkinson', Mary Moorman (ii. 160) goes on to identify this passage as being Dorothy's; her identification is based on the fact that in 1803 Dorothy had used a similar image in describing the Pass of Brander (*Journals*, i. 307):

the long reach of naked precipices on the other side rose directly out of the water, exceedingly steep, not rugged or rocky, but with scanty sheep pasturage and large beds of small stones, purple, dove-coloured, or red, such as are called Screes in Cumberland and Westmoreland. These beds, or rather streams of stones, appeared as smooth as the turf itself, nay, I might say, as soft as the feathers of birds, which they resembled in colour.

Although manuscript evidence further supports Mrs. Moorman's identification, it should be pointed out that, as the parenthesis in 497–8 indicates, Wordsworth himself had already adopted the image for use in *Guide*, 687.

510–11. The Views . . . Wast-water] See our n. to *S.V.* 464–5.

516–17. This Valley . . . Gavel] i.e. *Guide*, 558–69.

531–8. on the highest . . . snow] Cf. *Guide*, 2846–50 and n.

542–3. Stye-Head . . . 43] 'Stye-head Tarn, with Aron, or Great-End, above Borrowdale', published 1 Apr. 1810, No. 43 in the CONTENTS.

550, textual n. Borrowdale] The printer probably misread the scribe's 'Borrowdale' as 'Rovendale'.

550–1. that cluster . . . notice] i.e. *S.V.* 391–3.

553–712. For excursions in the eastern region of the Lake District see *Guide*, 354–495, 2958–3230. Except for a few insertions and omissions, *S.V.* 557–712 ('magnificent . . . mansion') is preserved in *Guide*, 362–489. We comment below on three passages omitted from the *Guide*, but otherwise our commentary on the remainder of *S.V.* will be found in our notes to *Guide*, 362–489.

633–7. the mind ... men] Omitted from *Guide*, 440–1; cf. *Subl. and Beaut.* 67–9: 'if this [a sensation of sublimity] is analyzed, the body of this sensation would be found to resolve itself into three component parts: a sense of individual form or forms; a sense of duration; and a sense of power.'

686–96. This stream . . . herds] Cf. *Guide*, textual n. 474 and our n. to *Guide*, 362–489.

705–6. Hawes-water . . . Etching] 'Hawes-water', published 1 Aug. 1810, No. 47 in the CONTENTS.

COMMENTARY: *UNPUBLISHED TOUR*

1–96. For other discussions of the approaches to the Lake District see *Guide*, 8–96; *S.V.* 1–30, 115–35, textual n. 135/6.

2–425. Before actually adopting two *S.V.* manuscripts (see our descriptions of MSS. Prose 20ᶜ and 20ᵈ, p. 144), Wordsworth in composing *U.T.* occasionally copied, or verbally echoed in expansions, either the printed text of *S.V.* or *S.V.* manuscripts. We list these verbal parallels:

U.T.	*S.V.*
2–11	2–7
39–40	7–9
206–29	12–30
358–84	31–46
422–5	46–50

11–16. A traveller . . . Eden] See our n. to *Guide*, 85–96.

20–37. Persons . . . Carrick] Wordsworth, Dorothy, and Coleridge took this route northward from Keswick, August 1803, on their way to Scotland (*Journals*, i. 195–6; *C.N.B.* i. 1426–7). Rose Castle, nearly demolished during the Civil Wars, was repaired and enlarged by Bishop Edward Rainbow, who took up residence there in 1665, and by his next successors (Nicolson and Burn, ii. 290–1, 312–16). In 29–31, Wordsworth draws directly on Dorothy's journal (i. 195): 'Passed Rose Castle upon the Caldew, an ancient building of red stone with sloping gardens, an ivied gateway, velvet lawns, old garden walls, trim flower-borders with stately and luxuriant flowers.' The stream at Caldbeck (33–5), with its limestone rocks and caves, seems to have been a favourite with Coleridge, who had visited it earlier (in addition to i. 1426–7, see *C.N.B.* i. 828, 1519–20).

52–71. The nearest . . . 12 miles] See our n. to *Guide*, 36–48.

58–62. Gordale Scar . . . Caves] Cf. *Prel.* VIII. 711–41 and our n. to *Guide*, 54.

72–4. 3 miles . . . recommended] Cf. *Guide*, 75–80 and n.

74–9. Hackfall . . . Kendal] See our nn. to *Guide*, 29–31, 31–5.

80–92. I will . . . about] Cf. *Guide*, 18–28 and n.

98–123. Lancaster . . . allow] Cf. 'Suggested by the View of Lancaster Castle (On the Road from the South)', *P.W.* iv. 135. West (*Guide*, pp. 13–25) had similarly opened his tour with a description of Lancaster.

Since the twelfth century, Lancaster Castle had housed the county gaol as well as courts of law. As a result of an act of Parliament for the improvement of prisons, extensive alterations and additions were made to the Castle in 1788–98; the Crown Hall and County Hall, which were then erected, are notable examples of the Gothic revival. The turret rising ten feet above the parapet of the Norman keep, though popularly called John of Gaunt's Chair (103), is now thought to have been added in the fifteenth century. In Wordsworth's time insolvent debtors from all parts of the county were sent to Lancaster Castle prison. (We have drawn on *The Victoria History of the County of Lancaster* (London, 1966), viii. 5–10.)

145–52. Edmund Spenser, *Muiopotmos*, ll. 209–16, *Poetical Works* (Oxford, 1926), p. 518. The editors of Wordsworth's poetry have noted the influence of this passage on *The Recluse*, ll. 31–8 (*P.W.* v. 314 and 476); *Prel.* X. 838–9 (p. 606); 'Beggars', l. 18 (*P.W.* ii. 223 and 509).

156. Mʳ Harrison] For a list of bridges and important public buildings at Lancaster, Chester (cf. 180), and elsewhere designed by Thomas Harrison (1744–1829), see H. M. Colvin, *A Biographical Dictionary of English Architects, 1660–1840* (London, 1954).

158–79. the impression . . . the third] John Britton (*The Beauties of England and Wales* (London, 1807), ix. 61–2) has high praise for the 'elegant and correct architectural decorations' in the County Hall of Lancaster Castle; he commends the 'fidelity and truth' which distinguish J. Allen's full-length portraits of Colonel Stanley and Mr. Blackburne, Lancashire's county members in Parliament; between their portraits a panel was being reserved for James Northcote's 'grand' portrait of George III, 'seated on a charger, with a view of Lancaster Castle and Church in the back ground'.

188–200. R. Duppa, *The Life and Literary Works of Michel Angelo Buonarroti* (London, 1806), p. 144, fn. In addition to introducing abbreviations and careless errors in punctuation, Wordsworth inadvertently alters 'prisoners' to 'the prisoners' (193–4) and 'not afterwards easy' to 'not easy after' (199). (Copies of Duppa's first edition are rare; the one we have used is in the Boston Public Library.) Both Wordsworth and Southey, who had long been a friend of Richard Duppa, contributed translations of Michael Angelo's poetry for Duppa's biography (see *P.W.* iii. 14–15 and 423; *New Letters of Robert Southey*, ed. Kenneth Curry (New York, 1965), ii. 488–9).

202–6. The little . . . Lakes] Cf. West, *Guide*, p. 10: 'for such company as come by Lancaster, it will be more convenient to begin the visit with Coniston-water. By this course, the lakes lie in an order more agreeable to the eye, and grateful to the imagination. The change of scenes is from what is pleasing, to what is surprising; from the delicate touches of Claude, verified on Coniston lake, to the noble scenes of Poussin, exhibited on Windermere-water; and, from these, to the stupendous, romantic ideas of Salvator Rosa, realized on the lake of Derwent.'

203–6, textual n. The manuscript direction to take up the 'Wilkinson Book' or *S.V.* is commented upon in our Introduction, p. 130.

209–15. & further . . . introduced] See our n. to *Guide*, 184–9.

230–4. The detail . . . notes] Apparently it was Wordsworth's intention to print in an appendix an abridgement of West's *Guide*, pp. 25–31, including, no doubt, Cockin's long and interesting footnote on the journey over the Sands. Other notes in the appendix would probably have abridged descriptions of the Abbey drawn from West's *Antiquities* as well as those from his *Guide*.

239–85. With the possible exception of 239, the verses are all quoted from a poem in manuscript by an unknown author. In writing *Ecclesiastical Sonnets*, Wordsworth turned to the same manuscript and adapted some of the lines quoted in *U.T.* for three different sonnets: thus, verses 270–5 appear in *Sonnet* II. xx. 3–14; verses 284–5 in *Sonnet* II. xxi. 7–8; verse 259 in *Sonnet* III. xxxv. 13 (*P.W.* iii. 371–2, 402). In a note to lines 7–8 of *Sonnet* II. xxi ('And the green lizard and the gilded newt / Lead unmolested lives, and die of age'), Wordsworth described his source (though not so fully as one would like): 'These two lines are adopted from a MS., written about the year 1770, which accidentally fell into my possession. The close of the preceding Sonnet on monastic voluptuousness is taken from the same source, as is the verse, "Where Venus sits", etc., and the line, "Once ye were holy, ye are holy still", in a subsequent Sonnet' (*P.W.* iii. 565–6). Because *U.T.* makes it perfectly clear that verses 241 and following are all from the same poem, we now can see that lines 480–4 of *The Tuft of Primroses* (*P.W.* v. 359) were also drawn from the same manuscript:

> nor less tenacious of her rights
> Stands Fountains Abbey, glorious in decay,
> Before the pious Traveller's lifted eye
> Threatening to outlive the ravages of Time
> And bear the cross till Christ shall come again.

Except for Wordsworth's brief note, we know nothing about the author nor can we identify the quotation in 239 ('The triumphal Arch of time'); on the one hand, it is possible that the unknown author wrote not only of Fountains Abbey but also of Furness Abbey and that this phrase is also his; but on the other hand, it may derive from some other source. Wordsworth mentions the 'fractured Arch' of Furness Abbey in *Prel*. II. 112.

286–93. Among these . . . adventurers] Wordsworth seems to be drawing entirely on oral tradition, probably stories he heard as a boy at Hawkshead. Close in his 'Supplementary Notices' to West's *Antiquities* (1805), pp. 363–4, tells of a staircase in a ruined wall which 'was formerly an object of much vulgar attention, many a "tale of wonder" being told of the immoveable iron door at the bottom', but his stories are unlike Wordsworth's and far less lurid. Henry S. Cowper (*Hawkshead* (London, 1899), pp. 337–8) mentions a popular belief in a subterranean passage which was supposed to run 'from beneath Hawkshead Hall to Furness Abbey, nearly nineteen miles as the crow flies'.

307–15. The situation . . . sides] Wordsworth follows very closely *Antiquities* (1774), pp. 93–4.

317–21. James Thomson, *The Castle of Indolence*, I. v (*Complete Poetical Works*, ed. J. L. Robertson (London, 1908), p. 254).

332–4. On the crown . . . Beacon] Cf. West, *Guide*, p. 38: 'To prevent surprise, and call in assistance, a beacon was placed on the crown of an eminence that rises immediately from the abbey, and is seen over all Low-Furness.'

347–51. the line . . . fancy] Writing from a seaside cottage near Bootle, 28 Aug. 1811, Wordsworth tells Beaumont of the 'amusement' he has had from watching the clouds over the Isle of Man, which 'is right opposite our Window', and he goes on to describe in detail one cloud formation that looked 'like a magnificent grove in winter when whitened with snow' (*M.T*. i. 508); cf. also 'Epistle to Sir George Howland Beaumont,' ll. 77–84 (*P.W*. iv. 144) and *Itinerary Poems of 1833*, XII (*P.W*. iv. 30–1).

353–6. *The Castle of Indolence*, I. vi (*Complete Poetical Works* (London, 1908), p. 255). Wordsworth alters 'gay castles' to 'airy castles'.

357–557. For some of Wordsworth's other writings on the Duddon see our n. to *Guide*, 1075–9.

367–70. Donnerdale . . . *upon*] In 1802 at a farmhouse in Eskdale, Coleridge learned that '*er* signifies "upon" . . . Donnerdale—a contraction of Duddon-er-dale the Dale upon the River Duddon' (*C.L*. ii. 845), Ekwall's *Oxford Dictionary of English Place-Names* does not support this etymology.

380–421. any Person . . . beneath him] This passage, which is an expansion of MS. Prose 20[b] (see *S.V*. textual n. 47), was itself later expanded and altered for Wordsworth's note to *The River Duddon*, XVII and XVIII (*P.W*. iii. 509).

382–3. the aftergrass . . . green] Cf. *Guide*, 2338: 'the tender green of the after-grass'.

396. scite] The sixteenth- to nineteenth-century spelling of *site* is Mary Wordsworth's; cf. 1145, 1512.

426–42. One of . . . decaying] Cf. *The River Duddon*, XVIII (*P.W*. iii. 253) and Wordsworth's note on the Revd. Robert Walker (ibid., pp. 510–22). In 437–8 Wordsworth refers to four letters in *The Annual Register, or a View of the History, Politicks, and Literature, of the Year 1760* (London, 1761), pp. 19–22.

442, textual n. The details about Robert Walker in 426–42 and the presence in MSS. Prose 20 of two manuscripts (MSS. Prose 20[g] and 20[h]) written for Wordsworth's note to *The River Duddon*, XVII and XVIII (*P.W*. iii. 508–22) suggest that a *U.T*. manuscript continuing the text of MS. Prose 20[f] was withdrawn for alteration and expansion when the *River Duddon* note was being composed.

443–76. Cf. *The River Duddon*, XXXI (*P.W.* iii. 259–60). For Wordsworth's afternoon at Ulpha Kirk in 1811, see our Introduction, pp. 128–9. The I.F. note to *The River Duddon* (ibid., p. 505) concludes with what appears to be another reference to this same day: 'I have many affecting remembrances connected with this stream. Those I forbear to mention: especially things that occurred on its banks during the later part of that visit to the seaside of which the former part is detailed in my Epistle to Sir George Beaumont.'

452–8. From the text and from textual n. 453/4 it may be conjectured that the first of the 'three great classes' of vales is represented by the Duddon, where the *rocks* and perhaps the rocky stream form the dominating impression. In the second class 'the upper part of Wastdale' may illustrate the majestic unity derived from the simple grandeur of the *mountains* surrounding it (cf. *S.V.*, textual n. 307/8, where Wordsworth emphasizes the unity of Grasmere vale as derived from the mountains which encircle it). The third class is clear enough, for the word lost in 457 must surely be *lake*.

477–539. This wild . . . account, and for] In 477–8 ('This wild . . . stones'), Wordsworth is copying the last surviving sentence in MS. Prose 20ᶜ (see *U.T.*, textual n. 461). We suppose that in 478–539 Wordsworth is partly expanding matter lost from the bottom 7 in. of page [2ʳ] in MS. Prose 20ᶜ. In 528–39 ('towards Broughton . . . account, and for'), the *U.T.* manuscript verbally echoes *S.V.* 58–66, for which no *S.V.* manuscript survives.

477–83. This wild . . . Ravenglass] Cf. *The River Duddon*, XVII, 12–14 (*P.W.* iii. 253) and Wordsworth's accompanying note, ibid., p. 508. On Wordsworth's interest in the stone circles of the north and his allusions to the Druids, see our n. to *Guide*, 1312.

501–5. ascend . . . Poem] Cf. *Guide*, 200–15 and our nn. to 201, 204–15.

515–26. Under it . . . shore] Gordon Wordsworth concluded his transcript of 459–557 with the following note: 'In writing as he does of Millom Churchyard W. W. would have in mind the numerous graves it contains of the Myers family with which he was connected, and also that of his brother John in the portion of Wyke Regis Churchyard formerly set aside for the interment of shipwrecked mariners—His Father was also connected with Millom Castle as Coroner or Bailiff of the Seignieurie or Lordship.' Millom Castle, the ancient seat of the Hudlestons, was purchased by Sir James Lowther in 1774 (Daniel and Samuel Lysons, *Magna Britannia* (London, 1816), iv. 136–7).

541. the general rule] i.e. that vales should be approached towards the head.

543. Broughton] For Wordsworth's summer visits to his relatives in Broughton see our n. to *Guide*, 216.

547–52. the morning . . . Yewdale] In August 1816 Wordsworth sent

Crabb Robinson brief but explicit directions on the best approach to the Lakes; his single paragraph could serve as a summary of the itinerary in *U.T.* (*M.T.* ii. 333–4): Lancaster ('the Castle is extremely well worth your notice'), the Sands to Ulverston, Furness Abbey, Coniston ('the morning rowing upon the water, the afternoon walking up and through Eugh-dale into Tilberthwaite'), Hawkshead, the Ferry-House upon Windermere, Bowness, Rydal Mount ('Here you will have further directions').

554. a dashing [*tear*]t] The word lost was probably 'torrent'.

576. still waters] Ps. 23 : 2. The textual emendation ('margin' for 'side') suggests that Wordsworth perhaps intended to avoid the echo.

591–6. Timothy Dwight, *The Conquest of Canäan* (Hartford, Conn., 1785), ii. 57–62, except that Wordsworth alters 'years . . . years' to 'year . . . year'. A 1788 edition of this work is listed in the Rydal Mount Catalogue, lot 559. In 1822 Southey said that 'some forty years ago' *The Conquest of Canaan* had been 'puffed and reprinted in London', and added, 'Its stilted versification was admired in those days, but it had little or no merit' (*Life and Correspondence*, ed. C. C. Southey (London, 1849–50), v. 125).

599–600. *Paradise Lost*, V. 171–2.

616. Grosvenor Square] The London address for Sir George and Lady Beaumont (see, for example, *E.T.*, pp. 465, 475, 580, 597).

653. aiery colors] Cf. our n. to *Guide*, 701–3.

669, textual n. We assume that 'frigeneous' is a scribal error for 'ferruginous'.

676–85. Conistone Hall . . . design] For a history of Coniston Hall and an architectural description, with drawings and photographs, see *The Victoria History of the County of Lancaster*, viii. 366–9. In MSS. V and U intended for *Prel.* II (p. 582), Wordsworth writes with nostalgia of his visits to Coniston Hall from Hawkshead. For his later interest in the design of chimneys see our n. to *Guide*, 1553–63; Coleridge also mentions the chimneys of Coniston Hall (*C.N.B.* i. 1228).

690–700. Grasmere Abbey . . . exists] Charlotte Smith begins her novel *Ethelinde, or The Recluse of the Lake*, 5 vols. (London, 1789): 'On the borders of the small but beautiful lake called Grasmere Water, in the county of Cumberland, is Grasmere Abbey, an old seat belonging to the family of Newenden'; Sir Edward Newenden, the 'present possessor' of the Abbey, is the uncle of the heroine, Ethelinde Chesterville. The Minerva Press, which from 1773–1820 was 'the chief purveyor of the circulating-library novel', was commonly scorned by sophisticated critics at the turn of the century (Dorothy Blakey, *The Minerva Press* (Oxford, 1939), p. 1).

715–18. Cottage Maidens . . . odours] Cf. *The Tuft of Primroses*, ll. 206–10 (*P.W.* v. 353).

731. Calgarth] Calgarth Hall, three miles south of Ambleside, was partly in ruin when in 1789 Richard Watson, Bishop of Llandaff, built his mansion near by. One version of the Calgarth ghost-story appears in Christopher Wordsworth's early notebook (*The Early Wordsworthian Milieu*, ed. Z. S. Fink (Oxford, 1958), pp. 88, 134–5).

735–8. aged sycamores . . . cloister] Cf. *Prel.* VIII (1850), 458–62:

> A grove there is whose boughs
> Stretch from the western marge of Thurston-mere
> With length of shade so thick, that whoso glides
> Along the line of low-roofed water, moves
> As in a cloister.

Thurston-mere was another name for Coniston Lake.

791/2, textual n. For *S.V.* 76–88 ('From the Valley . . . night') no manuscript survives; conceivably Wordsworth had, at *U.T.* 791, a *S.V.* manuscript, now lost, which he planned to draw upon.

804–10. When we . . . contrast] Cf. 'Epistle to Sir George Howland Beaumont', ll. 223–32 (*P.W.* iv. 149) and I.F. note, pp. 433–4.

815–44. The Sheep . . . suffered] On the labours of the northern shepherd, 'wedded to his life of hope / And hazard', cf. *Prel.* VIII. 215–428. The description of the father and son in 830–8 suggests 'Michael' (*P.W.* ii. 80–94) and *Prel.* VIII. 222–311, but the details and setting are different.

888–9. *Paradise Lost*, VII. 577–8: 'A broad and ample . . .' etc.

915. Blessy Crag] There are quarries on both sides of Tilberthwaite vale, but we have not been able to identify 'Blessy Crag', which Wordsworth says is 'about a mile' from Tilberthwaite.

916–34. The quarrymen . . . abyss] Cf. *An Evening Walk* (1793), ll. 139–50 (*P.W.* i. 16 and 18):

> I love to mark the quarry's moving trains,
> Dwarf pannier'd steeds, and men, and numerous wains:
> How busy the enormous hive within,
> While Echo dallies with the various din!
> Some, hardly heard their chissel's clinking sound,
> Toil, small as pigmies, in the gulph profound;
> Some, dim between th' aereal cliffs descry'd,
> O'erwalk the viewless plank from side to side;
> These by the pale-blue rocks that ceaseless ring
> Glad from their airy baskets hang and sing.

935–57. Cf. *Prel.* VIII. 504–10. Jonathan Yewdale, at whose house in Hackett the Wordsworths sometimes stayed, was a quarryman; *Exc.* V. 670–837, depicts his way of life ('He quits / His door in darkness nor till dusk returns'); see also *M.Y.* i. 501; ii. 409. The miner of Patterdale in *Exc.* VI. 212–54, is an eccentric, rather than a representative of his class.

962–71. Things are . . . Children] Cf. *Guide*, 1563–75, to which Wordsworth himself apparently refers in 968 ('as we . . . noticed').

Like 1170–5 below, the reference provides further evidence that Wordsworth's intention was to print first the 'Introduction' to *S.V.* and to follow it with *U.T.*

972–3. the main . . . a gill] Tilberthwaite Gill descends into Yewdale Beck, the main stream of Tilberthwaite.

981–8. Among sensations . . . insecurity] Cf. *Subl. and Beaut.* 96–102, where Wordsworth again writes of sublime sensations excited by such opposites as those named here. The qualities of the scene are not unlike those of the Simplon Pass as described in *The Prelude* (VI. 551–72).

1030, textual n. Possibly the intention was to insert a corrected version of the interesting passage deleted at 988 (see textual n. 988, which begins 'It is an awful . . .').

1043–7. Weather lam . . . exposed] E. Ekwall (*The Place-Names of Lancashire* (Manchester, 1922), p. 193), offering no etymology, comments on the strange absence of the name *Wetherlam* from early sources; he finds the first mention of *Weatherlom* in Yates's map of 1786, and cites as his third instance *Wetherlam* in the map to Wordsworth's *Description of the Scenery of the Lakes* (London, 1822).

1048–9. Scattered . . . abandoned] In the sixteenth century, German miners were working the copper mines of the Coniston Fells (*Victoria History of . . . Lancaster*, viii. 365).

1060–1. Hannibal . . . Alps] Livy, xxi. 37; cf. *E.S.* 700–1.

1065. (Note)—] Wordsworth was probably planning an Appendix of miscellaneous historical items (cf. our n. to 230–4).

1079–87. I much . . . done] See *Guide*, 2793–7, where Wordsworth attributes his having abandoned *U.T.* to his fear of lessening the traveller's pleasure through anticipation.

1116–22. Tall fir . . . road] For other descriptions of clipped trees in the neighbourhood of Coniston and Esthwaite, see *C.N.B.* i. 511 and 1228. Topiary works became widely popular in the Tudor and Jacobean eras; Evelyn Cecil (*A History of Gardening in England*, 3rd edn. (New York, 1910), p. 106) quotes a gardening manual of 1618 by William Lawson: ' "Your Gardiner can frame your lesser wood to the shape of men armed in the field, ready to give battell: or swift-running Grey Hounds to chase the Deere, or hunt the Hare. This kind of hunting shall not waste your corne, nor much your coyne." ' Addison in 1712 (*The Spectator*, No. 414) and Pope in 1713 (*The Guardian*, No. 173) were among the first to object to ornamental gardening (ibid., pp. 227–8).

1170–5. I have . . . stared at] Wordsworth refers to the 'Introduction' of *S.V.*, or *Guide*, 1688–917. The phrase 'flaring edifice' in 1172 recalls his quotation from Gray's journal in *Guide*, 1710–13; the comment on 'that craving for extensive prospect' which leads to the building of houses that 'stare' and are 'stared at' verbally echoes *Guide*, 1825–30.

1189–206. In the first . . . adorn it] The Baptist Chapel dates from 1678; it is thought that the building was originally an ancient cottage. The income-producing land was Sawrey Ground, a farm with which the Chapel was endowed in 1707; in the burying-ground, which was still being used at the beginning of this century, the earliest stone is dated 1750. (See Henry S. Cowper, *Hawkshead* (London, 1899), pp. 21, 122–3; *Victoria History of . . . Lancaster*, viii. 380.) In a note dated October 1922 and appended to his transcript of Wordsworth's manuscript, Gordon Wordsworth wrote: 'The dipping pool . . . lies in a garden adjoining the Cemetery—It measures about 6 feet by 3, and is formed of large slate slabs, and provided with steps for ingress—The runner still flows into [it], but a neighbour informs me it has now quite fallen out of use.'

1220–4. gill . . . ghyll] Gordon Wordsworth in his transcript of this passage notes that *gill* is Mary Wordsworth's spelling, and *ghyll* Wordsworth's.

1234–5. Ezek. 37 : 3.

1236–376. As our textual n. to 1186–241 indicates, 1187–240 was written later and marked for insertion at the end of 1186. But no adjustments were made for the insertion, and as a result an awkward repetition occurs in 1236–7 ('we are soon after greeted by the white Church of Hawkshead standing conspicuously on a Hill') and 1254–5 ('On the top of the hill . . . stands the Church, overlooking the Valley').

1236–7. we are . . . salutation] Cf. *Prel*. IV. 13–15.

1241–8. The fifteenth-century gate-house may possibly be a rebuilding of the earlier manor house built by the monks of Furness; although later reconstructed, the south wing, containing the hall and solar, was also fifteenth-century; this wing was pulled down about 1870 (*Victoria History of . . . Lancaster*, viii. 377–9).

In 1244–8 Wordsworth follows almost verbatim West's *Antiquities* (1774), pp. xxxvi–xxxvii ('There is, at a small distance from Hawkshead, the house wherein the abbot of Furness kept residence', etc., except for variants in punctuation and the alteration of 'abbots' to 'Abbot' (1248).

1248–59, textual n. The Vestry, of which Wordsworth complains, was added to the Church in 1793–5 (T. W. Thompson, *Hawkshead Church, Chapelry, and Parish*, 2nd edn. (Hawkshead, 1959), pp. 16–17).

1249–51. Passing . . . Abbot] 'it is always supposed, and probably correctly, that the monastic "furca" was on Gallow-barrow' (H. S. Cowper, *Hawkshead* (London, 1899), p. 226).

1251–3. we arrive . . . hills] The phrasing oddly echoes Clarke (p. 146): 'Hawkshead, a little market-town about four miles from Ambleside, pleasantly situated at the foot of a range of small mountains, covered chiefly with wood'.

1258. Archbishop Sandes] Edwin Sandys (1516–1588) was probably born at Esthwaite Hall, his father's estate; an extreme Protestant, he was imprisoned in the Tower for having supported Lady Jane Grey's claim to the throne in 1553, and was later self-exiled to the Continent until the succession of Elizabeth. He was made Bishop of Worcester in 1559, Bishop of London in 1570, and Archbishop of York in 1575. Royal Letters Patent for the founding of the Grammar School were issued in 1585; Sandys drew up his Statutes for the school three months before his death in 1588. (See *Victoria History of . . . Lancaster*, viii. 371; H. S. Cowper, *Hawkshead* (London, 1899), pp. 463 ff.) Wordsworth paid tribute to the founder of his school in 'Lines Written as a School Exercise at Hawkshead' (*P.W.* i. 260): 'Then noble Sandys, inspir'd with great design, / Reared Hawkshead's happy roof, and call'd it mine.'

1266–94. A fisherman . . . comynwealth] Clarke (p. 147) touches briefly on the Pilgrimage of Grace in 1536 and then goes on to say that the people of Hawkshead 'chose for their General one Robert Aske, a man of low parentage, and one Rudston for his assistant: others they had of the same stamp; as a fisherman from this town, who stiled himself (and very justly) the *Earl of Poverty*; he always went by that name, and signed himself so'. Clarke (p. 148) quotes the unsigned announcement, or 'Summons', which Wordsworth copies with only minor differences (the parenthesis in 1278 is an interpolation of Wordsworth's). According to Clarke, the 'pilgrims' got as far as Doncaster where they were met by the Duke of Norfolk, who agreed to carry their demands to the king; Henry refused the demands, but granted a general pardon and the 'pilgrims' dispersed. Clarke (p. 151) then concludes: 'the year following, Robert Ask the General, Lord Dacres, the Abbot and Prior of Saurey near Hawkshead, &c. rising again, were taken and beheaded. I have inserted this for nothing more than to shew what illiterate warlike people this northern part of England was inhabited by.' For a briefer account, see *Victoria History of . . . Lancaster*, viii. 299.

1302, textual n. Caprice . . . skill] This fragmentary sentence, which is deleted from the bottom of page [2ʳ] and the top of page [2ᵛ], MS. Prose 23ᵇ, apparently derives from some other context, unknown to us.

1303–9. Along the . . . beneath] Cf. *Prel.* V. 423–31. The stone seat is today unchanged.

1314–20. Upon a . . . mystery] Cf. Gilpin, i. 96: 'how deep and determined the shadows are at noon'. For martial figures seen in the clouds, cf. *Prel.* II, textual n. 181–3 (3), and p. 522; 'To the Clouds', ll. 11–14 (*P.W.* ii. 317).

1325–64. The table tomb to the memory of William Sandys and his wife Margaret is described in *Victoria History of . . . Lancaster*, viii. 372–3, which also quotes the Latin inscription.

In his memoir of Elizabeth Smith (1776–1806), De Quincey, who did not know the Smiths until after Elizabeth's death, deplored the simplicity of the marble tablet to her memory: 'After mentioning her birth and age (twenty-nine), it closes thus:—"She possessed great talents, exalted virtues, and humble piety." Anything so unsatisfactory or so commonplace I have rarely known' (*Collected Writings*, ed. D. Masson (Edinburgh,

1889), ii. 418; De Quincey's essay was first published in *Tait's Magazine*, June 1840). Wordsworth, who also did not know Elizabeth Smith, probably acquired his information from his friend Thomas Wilkinson, who was a close friend of the Smiths and a great admirer of Elizabeth's. If Wordsworth had read the memoirs to which he refers, he would have found that Elizabeth's unusual linguistic attainments (French, German, Hebrew, Arabic, Persian) were well known in her lifetime. The 'memoirs', compiled by Henrietta Maria Bowdler, are entitled *Fragments, in Prose and Verse: By a Young Lady, Lately Deceased. With Some Account of her Life and Character, by The Author of "Sermons on the Doctrines and Duties of Christianity"* (London, 1808); a second edition in two volumes was published in Bath, 1809. The Smiths, whose home was originally at Piercefield Park in Monmouthshire, moved to Patterdale in 1800 and to Coniston in 1801; at Coniston, Elizabeth sometimes walked twelve to fourteen hours a day (*Fragments* (1808), p. 179) and Thomas Wilkinson in his letter and verses published by Mrs. Bowdler in the *Fragments* (pp. 203–9) makes much of her mountain climbing. From a letter written by her mother soon after her death, and also published in the *Fragments*, we learn that in her last invalid year Elizabeth rested on warm days in a tent pitched near the house and that there she once responded to a proposal that she spend the winter months in Cornwall with the words, 'If I cannot live here, I am sure I can no where else' (*Fragments*, p. 190). As late as the I.F. note to 'To the Spade of a Friend' (*P.W.* iv. 416), Wordsworth recalls Thomas Wilkinson's having been honoured by the friendship of Elizabeth Smith.

1376/7, textual n. Gordon Wordsworth's insertion here of the first paragraph given in our textual n. 1248–59 not only seems to lack the authority of any manuscript direction, but also would seem to come much too late in the description, since the point of view in textual n. 1248–59 is that of a traveller approaching the village from Hawkshead Hall, a little to the north of Hawkshead.

1389–96. a floating grove . . . diminishes] Cf. *Guide*, 966–74 and n. The 'island', which has now disappeared, was described by John Housman, *A Descriptive Tour, and Guide to the Lakes, Caves, Mountains, and Other Natural Curiosities, in Cumberland, Westmoreland, Lancashire* (Carlisle, 1800), p. 180 and mentioned by John Britton, *The Beauties of England and Wales* (London, 1807), ix. 95.

1397–417. Adjoining . . . stood] That an 'Ecclesiastic' had drowned in the pool at the head of Esthwaite Water seems to have been a tradition not founded on fact; from the name *Priest Pot*, Henry S. Cowper (*Hawkshead* (London, 1899), p. 43) infers that the pool had once been 'a private fishery pertaining to Hawkshead Hall'.

In 1672 Thomas Lancaster was hanged for having poisoned his wife and several members of her family. 'The place where the gibbet stood at Pool Stang is yet called Gibbet Moss, and lies just beyond the pool bridge going to Colthouse on the right hand of the road. Although we are unaware of any record of any other hanging taking place here, and although it would appear from the entry [in the Parish Register Book] that a special gibbet was placed here for Lancaster, it is a fact that elderly people can still remember the stump of the gibbet standing; nay more, superstitions had grown up connected with it' (Cowper, p. 226); although no apparition was connected with Gibbet Moss, the place was thought to be haunted and 'so long as the stumps of the grim gibbet were standing . . . people dreaded it even by daylight' (ibid., p. 326).

Wordsworth's description of Gibbet Moss will for most readers evoke one of the most famous 'spots of time' recorded in *The Prelude* (XI. 279–316). The scenery around Hawkshead in the late eighteenth century could well accord with that given in *The Prelude*, especially if one of the near-by eminences had then had a beacon on its summit; although we know of no beacon near Hawkshead, we recall a possibly relevant statement in West's *Antiquities* (1774), p. xi and (1805), p. 11: 'Furness is surrounded with beacons, which might receive the alarm from those at a distance in any quarter; but whether they be ancient or modern cannot be determined.' We also recall that in neighbouring Westmorland beacons were numerous everywhere ('There has scarcely been five miles without a beacon. . . . Many of them still retain the name of beacons as indicative of their original designation' (*Lonsdale Magazine*, iii (1822), 250)). The descriptions of the area around Penrith Beacon as given by Hutchinson (*Excursion*, pp. 52–3), Gilpin (ii. 85), and Clarke (p. 22) would seem to make Cowdrake Quarry, near Penrith Beacon, which Gordon Wordsworth identified as the setting for the episode in *The Prelude* (*Prel.*, p. 614) less likely than the neighbourhood of Gibbet Moss. Nevertheless Wordsworth himself plainly connected the event in *The Prelude* with Penrith Beacon (cf. *Prel.* VI. 239–45 and XI. 317–23), and accordingly we are inclined to believe that later experiences at Hawkshead modified his recollection of a gibbet seen near Penrith when he was 'not six years old' (*Prel.* VI. 280). One sign, in particular, of a modification is that in MS. V, *Prel.* XI. 290, Wordsworth wrote that the man who was hanged was 'the murderer of his wife' and this statement is true of Thomas Lancaster at Hawkshead, but not true of the murderer near Penrith (*Prel.*, p. 614).

1404. in the solitudes of Salisbury Plain] Cf. the Sailor's experience on Salisbury Plain in *Guilt and Sorrow*, 76–81 (*P.W.* i. 98):

> Now, as he plodded on, with sullen clang
> A sound of chains along the desert rang;
> He looked, and saw upon a gibbet high
> A human body that in irons swang,
> Uplifted by the tempest whirling by;
> And, hovering, round it often did a raven fly.

1410–11. the Bittern . . . 1740] From the statement here we assume that line 25 in *An Evening Walk* (1793) has a literary, rather than a factual, origin: 'when first the vales the bittern fills' (*P.W.* i. 6).

1435–65. Cf. our n. to *Guide*, 907–18. The history of the two pairs of swans on Esthwaite and of those brought by John Christian Curwen to Windermere is repeated in the I.F. note to *An Evening Walk* (*P.W.* i. 319).

1466–84. Cf. 'Lines left upon a Seat in a Yew-tree' (*P.W.* i. 92–4). In *U.T.* Wordsworth repeats details which he had given in the poem and adds others which he was to repeat in the I.F. note to the poem (*P.W.* i. 329). For example, in the poem the 'aged Tree' had been 'taught . . . With its dark arms to form a circling bower' (cf. 1474–6), and from this seat the recluse would look out on 'barren rocks, with fern and heath,/And juniper and thistle, sprinkled o'er' (cf. 1477–8). The effects of the 'obnoxious enclosure' (1471), a 'slip of poor cultivated land' (1466–7), are at the beginning of the I.F. note similarly deplored: 'the slip of Common on which it [the yew-tree] stood, that ran parallel to the lake, and lay open to it, has long been enclosed; so that the road has lost much of its attraction' (cf. 1466–71). The man of 'solitary humour' (*U.T.*, textual n. 1467–504) is, in the I.F. note, identified as 'a gentleman of the neighbourhood . . . who had been educated at one of our Universities, and returned to pass his time in seclusion on his own estate. He died a bachelor in middle age.' In addition to the seat in the yew-tree on Esthwaite's north-eastern shore, he was induced 'by the beauty of the prospect' to build 'a small summer-house on the rocks above the peninsula on which the [Windermere] ferry-house stands' (I.F. note).

The builder of the yew-tree seat has been identified as the Revd. William Braithwaite of Satterhow, Far Sawrey, who according to the Hawkshead Parish Register died at Hawkshead, 8 February 1800, aged forty-six (Moorman, i. 312; W. J. B. Owen, ed., *Lyrical Ballads* (London, 1967), pp. 127–8; Mark L. Reed, *Wordsworth: The Chronology of the Early Years* (Cambridge, Mass., 1967), p. 291). The identification, based on the fact that Braithwaite built the 'Pleasure-house' above the ferry (cf. *S.V.* 96–114 and n.), seems somewhat surprising, if not improbable: in the poem, published in 1798, the recluse is said to have died 'In this deep vale . . . this seat his only monument' (*P.W.* i. 93); before his death, Braithwaite had acquired the piece of land on the shore of Esthwaite (Moorman, i. 312) whose alteration would have offended the 'contemplative Man' of *U.T.* On the other hand, we have not been able to discover any evidence that 'a small summer-house' had once stood on the site where in the late nineties Braithwaite built his house, although a remark in the I.F. note (*P.W.* i. 329) about a time 'some years before the first pleasure-house was built' might imply such a building.

Of the yew-tree, Henry S. Cowper (*Hawkshead* (London, 1899), pp. 416–17) writes: 'although the real tree was destroyed by Mr. Braithwaite Hodgson, of Green End, in Wordsworth's lifetime, another stands not far from the site, and has been called by the name of, and we believe is pointed out as, "Wordsworth's Yew" '.

1469–71. it has . . . lake] In the I.F. note referred to in our preceding n., Wordsworth, after remarking that the road 'has lost much of its attraction', adds that 'This spot was my favourite walk in the evenings during the latter part of my school-time'. Mark L. Reed (op. cit., p. 291) misreads the I.F. note and says that it was to this spot that the boy Wordsworth led a child of his own age for the sake of witnessing the child's pleasure upon first seeing the view; this episode, which Wordsworth recalls in the I.F. note (*P.W.* i. 329), occurred not near the yew-tree seat, but on the 'Station' overlooking the more spectacular view of Windermere and its islands.

1490–2. We have . . . distance] i.e. 1377–80 above.

1504–8. But it . . . Strickland-ears] Cf. *Prel.* V. 456–8: 'I chanced to cross / One of those open fields, which, shaped like ears, / Make green peninsulas on Esthwaite's Lake.'

1512–13. the Stranger . . . quoted] Apparently it had been Wordsworth's intention to quote the praise of some 'Stranger' to Hawkshead parish.

1556. black & steep as a wall] Cf. *An Evening Walk* (1793), 1. 372 (*P.W.* i. 34): 'Like a black wall, the mountain steeps appear'.

1556–9. Above . . . the lake] Cf. textual n. 1205–6.

1560–9. Cf. *An Evening Walk* (1793), ll. 339–50 (*P.W.* i. 32):

> —'Mid the dark steeps repose the shadowy streams,
> As touch'd with dawning moonlight's hoary gleams,
> Long streaks of fairy light the wave illume
> With bordering lines of intervening gloom,
> Soft o'er the surface creep the lustres pale
> Tracking with silvering path the changeful gale.
> —'Tis restless magic all; at once the bright
> Breaks on the shade, the shade upon the light,
> Fair Spirits are abroad; in sportive chase
> Brushing with lucid wands the water's face,
> While music stealing round the glimmering deeps
> Charms the tall circle of th' enchanted steeps.

The variants in our text are not recorded in the textual apparatus of *P.W.* i. 32–3, nor are they preserved in the final text of 1849, ll. 291–304, *P.W.* i. 33.

1562. The word *faint* is inserted without any further alteration to the line.

1591/2, textual n. We do not know the date of the fragment, but when Wordsworth speaks of 'the Book which he has undertaken to write', we are reminded of his letter to Pering quoted in our Introduction (p. 123), where he mentions an attempt he had made to describe a tour taken with Mary in 1807. The Salutation is today one of the principal hotels at Ambleside.

1592–787. In our Introduction (p. 131), we discuss the possibility that the description of Borrowdale was written as early as 1807; if it was, it should be noted that in 1809–10 Wordsworth did not draw upon it in writing his brief description of Borrowdale for *S.V.* 375–97 and that he may not have planned on using it for *U.T.* In *Guide*, 289–315, Borrowdale is merely recommended as a place to be visited in excursions from Keswick.

1593–8. Thomas Tickell, 'To a Lady Before Marriage', reprinted in Robert Anderson's *A Complete Edition of the Poets of Great Britain*

(London, 1794), viii. 438, where, in addition to variations in punctuation, Anderson reads 'travell'd' for Wordsworth's 'wandered'. In the I.F. note to 'Yarrow Visited' (*P.W*. iii. 450–1), Wordsworth tells of his early dependence on Anderson's collection for his knowledge of the older English writers. The lady of Tickell's poem is addressed as 'Clotilda'; 'Lycoris' (*U.T*. 1602) appears in Vergil's *Eclogue* X; Wordsworth employs the same name in his 'Ode to Lycoris', *P.W*. iv. 94.

1605–13. Alas . . . recesses] Cf. *Guide*, fn. 1262 and our note ad loc. In 1830 (*L.T*., p. 478), Wordsworth again mentions Tickell, 'of whom Goldsmith rightly observes that there is a strain of ballad-thinking through all his Poetry, and it is very attractive'; in his prefatory life of Tickell, Robert Anderson (op. cit. viii. 407) wrote: 'Of Tickell, it has been said by Goldsmith, that through all his poetry, there is a strain of *Ballad-thinking* to be found: The remark is just, and to that strain he is not a little indebted for the reception he has met with.'

1623–32. Samuel Daniel, *The Queenes Arcadia*, ll. 1022–32, in *The Complete Works in Verse and Prose*, ed. A. B. Grosart (reissued, New York, 1963), iii. 250, where, in addition to differences in spelling and punctuation, the text occasionally differs verbally from Wordsworth's: e.g. 'For this poor corner . . . all t'earth beside . . . Have had no intertrading . . . Ambition, or desire . . . They live as if still in the golden age . . . his pupillage'. Daniel's masque does not appear in Robert Anderson's *The Works of the British Poets* (Edinburgh, 1793), iv. 109–251.

1633–41. Cf. Gray's Journal (West, *Guide* (Kendal, 1802), p. 204):

Soon after we came under Gowdar-crag, a hill more formidable to the eye, and to the apprehension, than that of Lowdore; the rocks at top deep-cloven perpendicularly by the rains, hanging loose and nodding forwards, seen [*sic*] just starting from their base in shivers. The whole way down, and the road on both sides, is strewed with piles of the fragments, strangely thrown across each other, and of a dreadful bulk; the place reminds me of those passes in the Alps, where the guides tell you to move with speed, and say nothing, lest the agitation of the air should loosen the snows above, and bring down a mass that would overwhelm a caravan. I took their counsel here, and hastened on in silence.

Non ragioniam di lor, ma guarda, e passa.

Wordsworth recalls this same passage in *Railway*, 116–19, where he translates Gray's quotation from Dante (*Inferno*, III. 51). For West's excerpts from Gray's Journal see our n. to *Guide*, 45; for Wordsworth's view of Gray's 'mind somewhat weakened by ill health' cf. *Guide*, 1700–13 and n.

1645–51. It is . . . conductors] In September 1800, when he was too ill to continue an excursion on horseback to Buttermere, etc., Wordsworth turned back at Borrowdale, 'and crossed the mountains home' (*E.T*., pp. 295, 301; see also *Journals*, i. 61).

1652–63. While they . . . escape] Cf. Clarke, p. 75: '*Borrowdale*, till within these last thirty years, was hardly in a state even of civilization; the surface of the ground was very little cultivated, for agriculture was not understood there, and the inhabitants were a proverb, even among their unpolished neighbours, for ignorance. A thousand absurd and improbable stories are related concerning their stupidity. . . . The people of Borrowdale have been, on account of the old commonplace-joke of walling in the cuckow, called Borrowdale *Gowks*; the word gowk being the Scottish name for a cuckow.'

1668–714. Borrowdale is mentioned three times in Song XXX of *Poly-Olbion* (ll. 150, 166, 175), but has no song of her own (*The Works of Michael Drayton*, ed. J. William Hebel (Oxford, 1961), iv. 575). Some lines of Song XXX 'recurred' to Wordsworth's memory on seeing the Cumberland mountains from Scotland in 1803 (see *Journals*, i. 201 and *P.W.* iii. 441), and Coleridge (*Biog. Lit.* ii. 82) heard echoes of it in Wordsworth's poem 'To Joanna' (*P.W.* ii. 112–14 and 448).

1687, textual n. The words *north* and *south* are frequently difficult to distinguish in the *U.T.* manuscripts.

1696. the Trossachs or Loch Katrine] Visited by William, Dorothy, and Coleridge in August 1803 (see *Journals*, i. 261–74). Coleridge also compared the Trossachs and Borrowdale (*C.N.B.* i. 1471 and 1610).

1699. Bowder Stone . . . Vessel] The simile was commonly applied to Bowder Stone (see Clarke, p. 82). Cf. also *Exc.* III. 51–5.

1717–25. I was . . . companions] Cf. Wordsworth's note to *Guide*, 1619, and our n. ad loc.

1732–8. The Chamois chaser . . . career] Cf. *Descriptive Sketches* (1793), ll. 366–413 (*P.W.* i. 64–8).

1743–5. James Beattie, *The Minstrel*, I. xi, *Poetical Works* (London, 1831), p. 11.

1757–84. But it . . . found again] Eighteenth-century writers were fairly copious in treating the black lead, or wad, mines of Borrowdale, and almost invariably they remarked that before various, and more valuable, uses were discovered, wad was used by the natives for marking sheep (e.g. Nicolson and Burn, ii. 80; Thomas Pennant, *A Tour in Scotland*, 2nd edn. (London, 1776), i. 45–8; Hutchinson, *Excursion*, pp. 161–5; Clarke, p. 82; Gilpin, i. 213–14). In his *History* (ii. 212–20) Hutchinson gives perhaps the fullest account, including some stories of extensive pilfering, but nowhere have we found any references to the gambling of Borrowdale yeomen, such as Wordsworth describes in 1726–42.

1786–7. as if . . . virtue] Cf. *Areopagitica* in *The Works of John Milton* (New York, 1931): 'that which purifies us is triall, and triall is by what is contrary' (iv. 311); 'Wherefore did [God] creat passions within us, pleasures round about us, but that these rightly temper'd are the very ingredients of vertu' (iv. 319).

COMMENTARY:
SUBLIME AND BEAUTIFUL

1–58. amongst them . . . Pikes] It is, we think, impossible to estimate the amount of text lost from the beginning of MSS. Prose 28. In our description of the manuscripts (see pp. 148–9), we have suggested that page [2ʳ] of MS. Prose 28ᵇ was originally the first page of that particular leaflet; in any case, pages [1ʳ] and [1ᵛ] of MS. Prose 28ᵇ are blank and the text of this leaflet begins, on page [2ʳ], with the rejected passage which is recorded in textual n. 39–58. The revised and amplified version which was substituted for this rejected passage begins seven lines from the bottom of page [1ᵛ] and ends 3 in. from the bottom of page [2ʳ] in MS. Prose 28ᵃ. Since the extant text of MS. Prose 28ᵃ (*Subl. and Beaut.*, 1–58) is entirely coherent, we suppose that just as 39–58 ('making us . . . Pikes') is substituted for the rejected passage in MS. Prose 28ᵇ, so 1–38 ('amongst them . . . precedes the beautiful in') must be a substitution for a rejected passage immediately preceding the one that still survives. In other words, we believe that MS. Prose 28ᵃ is a revised draft, written for insertion in MS. Prose 28ᵇ.

The question then of what has been lost from the opening turns out to be a double-barrelled one: first, what preceded the deletion now preserved in textual n. 39–58, and secondly, what preceded the phrase 'amongst them' in the opening of the revised extant text? If the recurrent '3' in the manuscript page-numbering (see our description of the manuscripts, pp. 148–9) indicates either a third leaflet or a third section, then the loss may have been fairly extensive; but from the statements made in 40–1 and 51–5, it would seem that the loss from the discussion of the sublime and the beautiful has, at least, been minimal.

1–7. It is . . . knowledge] Wordsworth is rejecting eighteenth-century views stemming from Addison's theory that the '*new* or *uncommon*' is a characteristic of objects pleasurable to the imagination (*The Spectator*, ed. D. F. Bond (Oxford, 1965), No. 412, iii. 540–2); for example, John Baillie had maintained that 'Admiration, a Passion always attending the Sublime, arises from *Uncommonness*, and constantly decays as the Object becomes more and more familiar' (*An Essay on the Sublime* (1747), The Augustan Reprint Society, No. 43 (1953), p. 12). In insisting that 'astonishment . . . is the effect of the sublime in its highest degree', Burke implied a similar view (*A Philosophical Enquiry into the Origin of our Ideas of the Sublime and Beautiful*, ed. J. T. Boulton (London, 1958), p. 57).

13–14. love . . . the one] Cf. Burke, *Enquiry*, p. 91: 'By beauty I mean, that quality or those qualities in bodies by which they cause love, or some passion similar to it.'

21–22. the same object . . . beautiful] Cf. Wordsworth's letter to Jacob Fletcher quoted in our n. to 257–78. Whereas Addison (*The Spectator*, No.

412, iii. 541, 544) recognized the superiority of those objects in which the sublime and the beautiful are united, Burke implied that because of their antithetical differences, the two qualities almost never occur in the same object (e.g. *Enquiry*, pp. 5, 124–5, 156–7, 160); in his second edition he commented upon the occasional exception: 'In the infinite variety of natural combinations we must expect to find the qualities of things the most remote imaginable from each other united in the same object. . . . If the qualities of the sublime and beautiful are sometimes found united, does this prove, that they are the same, does it prove, that they are any way allied, does it prove even that they are not opposite and contradictory? Black and white may soften, may blend, but they are not therefore the same. Nor when they are so softened and blended with each other, or with different colours, is the power of black as black, or of white as white, so strong as when each stands uniform and distinguished' (*Enquiry*, pp. 124– 5). On finding beauty and sublimity united at Ullswater, Gilpin (ii. 53–4) sharply protested against Burke's general position. Despite his statement above, Wordsworth in the *Guide* (e.g. 2543–9, 2739–44) tends to preserve the distinction which Burke habitually stressed.

24–6. the mind . . . other] Cf. Burke, *Enquiry*, p. 160: 'the sublime and beautiful are built on principles very different, and . . . their affections are as different: the great has terror for its basis; which, when it is modified, causes that emotion in the mind, which I have called astonishment; the beautiful is founded on mere positive pleasure, and excites in the soul that feeling, which is called love.' In *Prel*. XIII. 143–7, Wordsworth attributes to sublime and beautiful forms his own early apprehension of the universe as 'divine and true':

> To fear and love,
> To love as first and chief, for there fear ends,
> Be this ascribed; to early intercourse,
> In presence of sublime and lovely Forms,
> With the adverse principles of pain and joy.

The sense of beauty and the sense of sublimity are 'opposite to each other' in yet another respect: 'The primary element in the sense of beauty is a distinct perception of parts' (textual n. 26), whereas the sense of sublimity occurs 'without a conscious contemplation of parts' (142). Wordsworth's recognition of this difference may owe something to Coleridge, who in a note for one of his lectures of 1808 wrote: 'What then if . . . we should define beauty to be a pleasurable sense of the many (by many I do not mean comparative multitude, but only as a generic word opposed to absolute unity) reduced to unity by the correspondence of all the component parts to each other, and the reference of all to one central point. . . . Now if we receive this definition, we shall at once understand why in correct language beauty has been appropriated to the objects of the eye and ear, for these senses are the only ones that present a whole to us combined with a consciousness of its parts' (*Shakespearean Criticism*, ed. T. M. Raysor (London, 1960), i. 162–3). In the *Guide* (871–5) Words- worth adds an interesting modification to the antithesis between beauty and sublimity: 'Sublimity is the result of Nature's first great dealings with the superficies of the earth; but the general tendency of her subsequent operations is towards the production of beauty, by a multiplicity of symmetrical parts uniting in a consistent whole.'

32. the present work] See our Introduction to the *Guide*, pp. 131–2.

33–9. Sensations . . . its presence] Cf. *Prel*. XIII. 214–32, where Wordsworth recognizes the precedence which sublimity took over beauty in impressing his own youthful mind.

51–5. These shall . . . landscape] The work of Wordsworth's predecessors who wrote on the sublime and beautiful in the landscape of the Lake District has been described and evaluated by Christopher Hussey (*The Picturesque* (London, 1927)), W. M. Merchant ('Introduction' to Wordsworth's *Guide Through the District of the Lakes* (London, 1951)), and Norman Nicholson (*The Lakers* (London, 1955)).

68–9. a sense of . . . power] Cf. *S.V.* 632–7; *U.T.* 981–4; *Guide*, 871–2, 2251–2. Neither individual form nor duration figures in discussions of the sublime in natural scenery before Wordsworth, perhaps because the ocean, which is often cited as the ultimate in sublimity, would preclude individuality of form, while storms and similar 'sublime' disturbances would preclude duration. Burke does, however, mention 'momentary duration' in connection with beauty ('the flowery species, so remarkable for its weakness and momentary duration . . . gives us the liveliest idea of beauty, and elegance' (*Enquiry*, p. 116)), and throughout his work he emphasizes power as an element of the sublime (e.g. p. 64: 'I know of nothing sublime which is not some modification of power').

69. a sense of power] W. J. B. Owen in *Wordsworth as Critic* (Toronto, 1969), pp. 195–215, has made an interpretative and critical study of Wordsworth's concept of 'power' as a major element in the 'sublime'; see especially pp. 203–10, where important passages of MSS. Prose 28 (i.e. 57–69, 89–102, 140–60, 220–40, 248–55) are quoted and analysed.

89–107. But . . . the sun, &c.] Cf. *Prel*. VII. 716–29.

90–1. impressions . . . elevated] Cf. Burke, *Enquiry*, pp. 50–1: 'Now whatever either on good or upon bad grounds tends to raise a man in his own opinion, produces a sort of swelling and triumph that is extremely grateful to the human mind; and this swelling is never more perceived, nor operates with more force, than when without danger we are conversant with terrible objects, the mind always claiming to itself some part of the dignity and importance of the things which it contemplates.'

96–8. These lines . . . sea] Gilpin (i. 88–90) discusses the same mountain lines in relation to picturesque beauty. Cf. *Guide*, 664 and n.

96–7. danger & sudden change] Cf. Burke, *Enquiry*, p. 39: 'Whatever is fitted in any sort to excite the ideas of pain, and danger, that is to say, whatever is in any sort terrible, or is conversant about terrible objects, or operates in a manner analogous to terror, is a source of the sublime'; cf. also ibid., pp. 51, 57–8.

97–100. they may . . . not less sublime] Cf. *Guide*, 2184–91 and n.; Burke, *Enquiry*, p. 63: 'hardly any thing can strike the mind with its greatness, which does not make some sort of approach to infinity'; ibid., p. 73: 'Another source of the sublime, is *infinity*. . . . Infinity has a tendency to fill the mind with that sort of delightful horror, which is the most genuine effect, and truest test of the sublime . . . the eye not being able to perceive the bounds of many things, they seem to be infinite, and they produce the same effects as if they were really so.'

103. its] The faulty pronominal reference is the result of abortive re-writings; from textual nn. 102, 104–6, it would seem that Wordsworth originally had intended to write: 'this sense of power is imparted to the mind by the individual Mountain or a cluster of Mountains . . . by the torrents . . . by the clouds . . . by the stature . . .', etc.

104–5. the stature . . . sky] *Paradise Lost*, IV. 988 ('His stature reacht the Skie'), quoted and praised in *P. 1815*, 361–6. James Scoggins (*Imagination and Fancy* (Lincoln, Nebraska, 1966), p. 162) observes that in 1803 Dorothy Wordsworth had used the same phrase to characterize sublime mountain forms (*Journals*, i. 332).

107, textual n. these outlines also affect us . . . active force] Cf. *Prel.* I. 406–12 ('a huge Cliff,/As if with voluntary power instinct,/Uprear'd its head. . . / And, growing still in stature. . . / Strode after me'); *Prel.* XIII. 45 ('A hundred hills their dusky backs upheaved').

125–6. an individual cloud . . . body] Although it is not included among Blake's songs copied into Wordsworth's Commonplace Book, dated 'Grasmere Janʳʸ 1800' (Wordsworth Library, MS. Prose 31), Wordsworth may be remembering, among other 'tales & pictures', the introductory poem to *Songs of Innocence*: 'On a cloud I saw a child, / And he laughing said to me'.

138. starting trees] In his description of Gordale Scar, quoted in our n. to *Guide*, 45, Gray similarly used the word *starting*: 'with stubbed yew-trees and shrubs starting from its sides'. Cf. *O.E.D.*, s.v. *start*, 3.d ('Of a plant: To spring up suddenly. *rare*').

139–40. if personal fear . . . bounds] The observation is commonplace in discussions of the sublime: e.g. Addison, *The Spectator*, No. 418, iii. 568, and Burke, *Enquiry*, p. 136; W. J. B. Owen (*Wordsworth as Critic*, n. 29, p. 204) cites in this connection Richard Payne Knight, *An Analytical Inquiry into the Principles of Taste* (2nd edn., London, 1805), pp. 55–6.

140–4. For whatever . . . sublime] Cf. 24–6 and n.; *S. V.* 245–8; *Guide*, 2188–90: 'For sublimity will never be wanting, where the sense of innumerable multitude is lost in, and alternates with, that of intense unity'; Burke, *Enquiry*, p. 57: 'The passion caused by the great and sublime in *nature* . . . is Astonishment; and astonishment is that state of the soul, in which all its motions are suspended, with some degree of horror. In this case the mind is so entirely filled with its object, that it cannot entertain

any other, nor by consequence reason on that object which employs it';
Alexander Gerard, *Essay on Taste* (London, 1759), p. 19: 'Objects exciting
terror are . . . in general sublime; for terror always implies astonishment, occupies the whole soul, and suspends all its motions'.

149–53. Power . . . upon it] Cf. Addison, *The Spectator*, No. 412, iii. 540:
'Our Imagination loves to be filled with an Object, or to graspe at any
thing that is too big for its Capacity'; Gerard, *Essay on Taste*, p. 14:
'We always contemplate objects and ideas with a disposition similar to
their nature. When a large object is presented, the mind expands itself to
the extent of that object, and is filled with one grand sensation, which
totally possessing it, composes it into a solemn sedateness, and strikes it
with deep silent wonder and admiration: it finds such a difficulty in spreading itself to the dimensions of its object, as enlivens and invigorates its
frame: and having overcome the opposition which this occasions, it sometimes imagines itself present in every part of the scene, which it contemplates'.

159. the head & the front] *Othello*, i. iii. 80; cf. *Cintra*, 2609–10.

163. takes place of] 'takes precedence over'; cf. *Cintra*, 2889; *R.M.*
444–5; *Guide*, 1976.

175–9. Belial . . . Eternity?] *Paradise Lost*, II. 146–8: 'for who would
lose,/Though full of pain, this intellectual being,/Those thoughts that
wander through eternity . . .?'

183–6. how industrious . . . despite] Cf. *E.E.* III. 11–12: 'Now, vice
and folly are in contradiction with the moral principle which can never
be extinguished in the mind'; the sentence following contains a reference
to Milton's Satan.

192. As I . . . before] i.e. 140–4.

198–9. our moral Nature . . . violated] Cf. 'Prospectus', 19–22, to
The Excursion, quoted in our n. to 280–2.

199–200. The point . . . carried] Wordsworth should have written: 'The
point to which apprehensions . . . may be carried', or 'The point beyond
which apprehensions . . . may not be carried'. Cf. 144–5: 'if personal fear
be strained beyond a certain point, this sensation [of the sublime] is
destroyed'; 222–3: 'To what degree consistent with sublimity power
may be dreaded has been ascertained'.

203–7. But if . . . law] The thought seems essentially stoical: reason,
which is the ruling principle in man, discovers what things are within our
power and what are not; it directs our exertions towards that which is
within our power; obedience to reason preserves inviolate our moral
nature (198–9) and culminates in repose. Cf. 'Ode to Duty' (*P.W.* iv.
83–6); *Exc.* III. 359–406; *R.M.* 422–40; on Wordsworth's stoicism,
both ancient and modern, see Jane Worthington, *Wordsworth's Reading
of Roman Prose* (New Haven, Conn., 1946), pp. 60–9, and N. P. Stall-
knecht, *Strange Seas of Thought*, 2nd edn. (Bloomington, Indiana, 1958),
pp. 204–22, 276–81.

226–7. as has been determined] i.e. 140–4.

236–47. If the . . . vivid] In 1790 Wordsworth wrote to Dorothy of the fall of the Rhine at Schaffhausen, which he had just seen for the first time: 'Magnificent as this fall certainly is I must confess I was disappointed in it. I had raised my ideas too high' (*E.Y.*, p. 35). In the passage in our text, written some twenty years later and long before he had seen the fall for the second time, he illustrates an observation which Coleridge was to make in 1813: 'The sense of sublimity arises, not from the sight of an outward object, but from the reflection upon it; not from the impression, but from the idea. Few have seen a celebrated waterfall without feeling something of disappointment: it is only subsequently, by reflection, that the idea of the waterfall comes full into the mind, and brings with it a train of sublime associations' (*Shakespearean Criticism*, i. 224). The 'fall of the Rhine', but not the rock, is described in *Ecclesiastical Sonnets*, II. xliii (*P.W.* iii. 382–3). Cf. also *Guide*, 2681–4; *Journals*, ii. 88–92; *M. W., Letters*, p. 63.

247–55. Yet to return . . . unity] See W. J. B. Owen, *Wordsworth as Critic*, pp. 208–10; Owen cites, in illustration of Wordsworth's generalization, *Prel.* VI. 556–72.

254–5. infinity, which is a modification of unity] Cf. *Guide*, 2184–91 and n.; Kant, *The Critique of Judgement*, J. C. Meredith, tr. (Oxford, 1957), p. 90: 'the sublime is to be found in an object even devoid of form, so far as it immediately involves, or else by its presence provokes, a representation of *limitlessness*, yet with a super-added thought of its totality'; Burke quoted above in nn. 97–100, 140–4.

257–78. the main source . . . affected] Cf. Wordsworth to Jacob Fletcher, 25 Feb. 1825 (*L.Y.*, p. 184): 'our business is not so much with objects as with the law under which they are contemplated. The confusion incident to these disquisitions has I think arisen principally from not attending to this distinction. We hear people perpetually disputing whether this or that thing be beautiful or not—sublime or otherwise, without being aware that the same object may be both beautiful and sublime, but it cannot be felt to be such at the same moment'; see also *L.Y.*, pp. 194–5. In general, eighteenth-century critics analysed the effects on the mind rather than the qualities of the objects (W. J. Hipple, Jr., *The Beautiful, The Sublime, & The Picturesque in Eighteenth-Century British Aesthetic Theory* (Carbondale, Illinois, 1957), pp. 81, 84), but later Gilpin, Uvedale Price, and numerous topographical writers fixed their attention upon the external object and its qualities; John R. Nabholtz ('Wordsworth's *Guide to the Lakes* and the Picturesque Tradition', *M.P.* lxi (1964), 288–97) has pointed out how Wordsworth himself in the *Guide* frequently follows the latter course.

263–6. To talk . . . absurd] Cf. Kant, *The Critique of Judgement*, p. 104: 'true sublimity must be sought only in the mind of the judging Subject, and not in the Object of nature that occasions this attitude by the estimate

formed of it', but according to Kant this statement could not be applied
to beauty.

280–2. to power . . . eternity] For the extent of the manuscript loss see
textual n. 280. The governing 'intelligence of law & reason' again suggests a stoical philosophy (cf. our n. to 203–7). On the basis of lines 19–22
of the 'Prospectus' to *The Excursion* (*P.W.* v. 3), we believe that the lost
antecedent of 'her' in 282 may have been 'the individual Mind' or a
semantic equivalent. (The textual n. to ll. 20–22 of the 'Prospectus' implies
that the lines we quote may be a late revision.)

> Of the individual Mind that keeps her own
> Inviolate retirement, subject there
> To Conscience only, and the law supreme
> Of that Intelligence which governs all.

With 280–2 cf. also *Exc.* IV. 69–76:

> "Possessions vanish, and opinions change,
> And passions hold a fluctuating seat:
> But, by the storms of circumstance unshaken,
> And subject neither to eclipse nor wane,
> Duty exists;—immutably survive,
> For our support, the measures and the forms,
> Which an abstract intelligence supplies;
> Whose kingdom is, where time and space are not."

285. influences] Although the word is plainly written, Wordsworth
probably intended 'inferences'; if so, 'the *means*' in 283 should perhaps be
regarded as the antecedent of 'them' in 286.

288–302. I have . . . cause] Cf. *Guide*, 2476–80; *Railway*, 148–56.

302–7. Such would . . . perceiving] Wordsworth summarizes Sir Joshua
Reynolds's recollections of his disappointment upon first seeing the paint-
ings of Raphael in the Vatican and then of his gradually acquiring from
them 'a new taste and new perceptions'. Wordsworth's source was one of
Reynolds's 'loose papers' quoted by Edmund Malone in *The Works of Sir
Joshua Reynolds . . . To Which is Prefixed, An Account of the Life and
Writings of the Author* (London, 1797), i. x–xii. Cf. *Ad. L.B.* 32–5,
P.L.B. 744–7, and nn.

307–20. I have heard . . . lifeless] On 21 September 1803 Sir Walter
Scott told the Wordsworths this anecdote; in retelling it here, Wordsworth seems, in 314–20, to draw verbally on Dorothy's account: 'She used
to say that in the new world into which she was come nothing had disappointed her so much as trees and woods; she complained that they were
lifeless, silent, and, compared with the grandeur of the ever-changing
ocean, even insipid' (*Journals*, i. 402).

324. Glencoe] Visited by William and Dorothy, September 1803
(*Journals*, i. 330–6).

328–31. the chaotic . . . unfinished] Cf. *S.V.* textual n. 52, and our n. to *S.V.*, textual nn. 47 and 52.

335–6, textual n. The word 'in' is clear, but it is perhaps an error for 'of'.

335–40. that intermixture . . . afflictions] Cf. Coleridge on *Hamlet*: 'The terrible, however paradoxical it may appear, will be found to touch on the verge of the ludicrous. Both arise from the perception of something out of the common nature of things. . . . These complex causes will naturally have produced in Hamlet the disposition to escape from his own feelings of the overwhelming and supernatural by a wild transition to the ludicrous' (*Shakespearean Criticism*, ii. 224–5).

349–51. it is . . . sublimity] Cf. 36–9 and our n. to 33–9.

354–68. But I . . . mind] In *Prel.* XI. 148–64, Wordsworth recalls his own brief submission to the false aesthetic theories of the age:

> through presumption, even in pleasure pleas'd
> Unworthily, disliking here, and there,
> Liking, by rules of mimic art transferr'd
> To things above all art.
>
> (XI. 152–5)

According to Gilpin (*Observations on the River Wye*, 2nd edn. (London, 1789), p. 31), nature succeeds in harmonizing colours, but 'is seldom so correct in composition, as to produce an harmonious whole. Either the foreground, or the background, is disproportioned: or some awkward line runs across the piece: or a tree is ill-placed: or a bank is formal: or something or other is not exactly what it should be'; some years later, writing of Windermere, he found fault with both the east and west shores, and although the Langdale Pikes at the head were 'grand', he concluded that because of its extensiveness, 'This great scene . . . surveyed thus from a centre, was rather amusing, than picturesque' (Gilpin, i. 153).

365. *picturesque*] Uvedale Price, whose own landscaping exhibited for Wordsworth too 'delicate and fastidious' a taste (*M.Y.* i. 505–6, but see also *M.Y.* i. 3), had made the *picturesque* a category distinct from the sublime and the beautiful (*An Essay on the Picturesque* (London, 1796), i. 46–61, 229–43). For Wordsworth's definition of the word *picturesque* see *L.Y.*, pp. 173, 183–4.

In 1812 Dorothy Wordsworth wrote of the Revd. C. J. Blomfield: 'B's views of everything he sees are contracted by his love of the picturesque— his amiable disposition and his sensibility will I have little doubt in time overcome this—and after a few visits to the North he will find that there is a wider range of enjoyment here than he at present conceives' (*M.Y.* ii. 41).

ADDENDUM

After this edition had gone into page proof, we learned that the Cornell University Library had recently acquired an additional manuscript for its Wordsworth Collection:

AM *A Description of the Scenery of the Lakes in the North of England*
Fragments of the work and related materials, some in the hand of Mary Wordsworth; including six lines of doggerel verse, "Samuel Barber from his Arbour."
17 pieces, some of which are made up of several leaves sewn or glued together.

Except for two leaves, this manuscript of 1822 was actually sent to the printer, for it contains not only the author's directions to the printer but also a note by the publisher or printer on the type to be used and occasionally, in marginal notation, the name of the typesetter assigned to this or that portion of the text. The two leaves not sent are (1) a fragment in the hand of Wordsworth, recorded in n. 1 below; and (2) a leaf containing the stray sentences recorded in nn. 555–8 and 2441–3, and the doggerel verses, here omitted as being irrelevant.

In the main, the manuscript offers variant readings to three sections of the *Guide*: 1–500, which in 1822 was printed as the final chapter (cf. *Guide*, textual n. 1–500); 2517–641; and 2803–906. It also contains the printed fly title of 1820 (*Topographical Description of the Country of the Lakes in the North of England*), cut from *The River Duddon . . . and Other Poems* (Healey, item 52) and revised for the new separate edition; a table of CONTENTS; a leaf from the *River Duddon* volume (pp. 303–4) bearing two emendations (*Guide*, textual nn. 2215–16, 2235) and the introduction of a particularizing title at the head of the page ('Planting', here substituted for 'DESCRIPTION OF THE COUNTRY OF THE LAKES', the comprehensive running title which in 1820 had been spread over facing pages).

Since the textual notes to the *Guide* already include the variants of 1822, we record the manuscript variants to that edition only. Unfortunately, some variants cannot now be recovered because they have been deleted by revised slips firmly pasted over them, but occasionally, where the edge of a slip is loose, we have been able to record either the beginning or the end of a variant so deleted. In the following notes, we ignore, as we do elsewhere, differences in spelling, capitalization, punctuation, the use of the ampersand, and the immediate restoration of cancelled words and phrases. This editorial practice, incidentally, accounts for the fact that a lemma giving the text of 1822 may differ in spelling or punctuation from the final text of 1835.

The line numbers refer to the text of the *Guide*, pp. 155 ff.

1 *An incomplete sentence in Wordsworth's hand occupies one side of a torn leaf*: Though it is chiefly as [an *del.*] a Guide to [?the mind] that this little Book is offered to the [Public *del.*] notice of those who [may be *del.*] are about to explore the District of the Lakes, [the Tourists *del.*] the pleasure of the Tourist [, and the *del.*] will be most effectively promoted, and the Authors purpose best answered by beginning with particular directions for [seeing *del.*]

4–101, textual n. This Lake 1822: The Lake MS.
by Orrest-head MS.², 1822: Troutbeck Bridge MS.

103 Fell-fort 1822: Fell-foot MS.

104–5 which elsewhere along MS.², 1822: along which MS.

105–6 To one . . . ascended MS.², 1822: Another fine view in this division of the lake presents itself to a Person ascending MS.

108 Mountains MS.², 1822: Mountains seen from this point MS.

115, textual n. *This 1822: *Note— This MS.
Islands. Among 1822: Islands— [of *del.*] among MS.

115 and its having MS.², 1822: & to a circumstance in which this Lake differs from all the rest, viz. that of MS.

117 grandeur MS.², 1822: whole grandeur MS.

120 evening MS.², 1822: evening at least MS.

126 whence MS.², 1822: from which MS.

127 by which it is supplied 1822: of which it is composed MS.

128 during MS.², 1822: in MS.

132 if entered MS.², 1822: if it were entered MS.

136 beautiful MS.², 1822: a pleasing MS.

139 numerous directions MS.², 1822: almost every direction MS.

140, fn. *Mr. 1822: *note Mr MS.

144 church of Grasmere MS.², 1822: Grasmere Church MS.

147–83, textual n. quitting the high road at MS.², 1822: quitting the high road [?under] MS.
Pelter Bridge, 1822: Pelter Bridge, &, MS.
when he has advanced MS.², 1822: upon advancing MS.
the sixth short of 1822: the 6ᵗʰ from MS.
in front. Having 1822: in front; & having MS.
he must cross MS.², 1822: the Traveller must cross MS.

183 by entering MS.², 1822: by those who enter MS.
over MS.², 1822: from MS.

184 those 1822: these MS.

185 traffic MS.², 1822: the traffic MS.

189–94 From the Inn . . . the South. 1822: *not in* MS., *although a large caret, possibly marking the place for an insertion, follows* led. (189).

194–6, textual n. From Coniston . . . its effect. 1822: *not in* MS.
   If the Lake of Coniston MS.², 1822: If this Lake MS.
   (*er* signifies *upon*) 1822: (er signifying upon) MS.

197 rocks MS.², 1822: point MS.

202 point MS.², 1822: part MS.

204 *After the centred line of verse* MS. *inserts on the right margin*: See Wordsworth's Poems, Vol. 2.

216–94, textual n. Details of this Vale, [*sic*] are to be found in the 1822: *at the top of a page* MS. *deletes* [?gives *or* given], *leaves undeleted the two words* in the *which immediately follow, and inserts above the line* Details of this Vale are with
   In the Vale of Esk is MS., 1822: The Vale of Esk is MS.² [*sic*].
   Birker 1822: Birker's MS.
   ridge of Scawfell MS.², 1822: part of Scawfell MS.
   approach. Wastdale is 1822: Approach, & certainly the scenery on the Lake is MS.
   no part . . . sublimity 1822: *not in* MS.
   Pedestrians 1822: foot Travellers MS.

311 They 1822: Those MS.

354–63, textual n. Is finely approached from Keswick* [*with fn. appended*] 1822: Is finely approached (by [the *del.*] foot or horse Travellers) from Keswick MS.

364 road. MS.², 1822: road, but you are separated from it by the Park wall MS.

364–5 If Ullswater . . . a mile 1822: In a carriage, Ullswater is best approached from Penrith. A mile MS.

374 They MS.², 1822: The Person MS.

378 survives MS.², 1822: remains MS.

385 marauders 1822: notice MS.

391–2 This stream . . . below 1822: *not in* MS.

397 with 1822: & with MS.

398 in front, MS.², 1822: in front of it, MS.

409 for 1822: of MS.

418 crossed. 1822: crossed, this, if followed up, would lead to Red Tarn & the recesses of Helvellyn. MS.

428 perished some MS.², 1822: perished [?here] a few MS.

432 master MS.², 1822: dead master MS.

441 the Stream 1822: this Stream MS.

450 but, from MS.², 1822: but, whether MS.

450–1 whoever looks MS.², 1822: whether you look MS.

452 Dove Crag, &c. will MS.², 1822: the mountains, you will MS.

455 Cumberland MS.², 1822: western MS.

456–9 would lead . . . The other MS.², 1822: flows [?] Village of Hartsop near the foot of Brothers-water & the other MS.

467 scenes MS.², 1822: those scenes MS.

470 track MS.², 1822: track, by which a horse may be led, but with difficulty MS.

473 estates MS.², 1822: houses MS.

476 bringing MS.², 1822: bringing into MS.

483 Hawes-water MS.², 1822: [?Of *del*.] Hawes-water MS.

486 had 1822: *not in* MS.

555–8 *Deleted from a corner of a folio leaf*: [?Passing *del*.] Its stream [after gl *del*.] passes [*altered from* passing] under the [woods of *del*.] steeps on which stands Muncaster Castle, the antient seat of the Penningtons it enters the Sea below the [small *del*.] little town of Ravenglass.

2441–3 *Written at right angles to the sentence given immediately above is the following, perhaps an early draft of* 2441–3: It is not unusual for Travellers visiting this Country to compare its scenery with that of Scotland [Ireland *del*.] & Switzerland— & [as the objects here are upon a smaller scale it too often happens that their recollections *del*.] it too often happens that prejudices supported by recollections of those countries where the Lakes & Mountains are upon a larger scale [interferes *del*.] prevents the pleasure which they might otherwise derive from the scenes before them. [For genuine feeling is apt *del*.]

2517–18 *A manuscript fragment numbered 5 begins*: [heights covered with snow, & *del*.] from pikes . . . *etc*.

2519 would be MS.², 1822: would have been MS.

2520 perfect MS.², 1822: striking MS.
  around MS.², 1822: along MS.

2521 leave MS.², 1822: left MS.

2522–5 But the . . . summer MS.², 1822: In late spring & early autumn the resemblance which the scenes among these lakes often [*slip glued over*] is most obvious MS.

2530 perennial MS.², 1822: enduring MS.

2531 little MS.², 1822: scarcely MS.

2532 14,000 . . . 10,000 1822: 14 or 15,000, —& 8, or 10,000 MS.

2533 tracts of . . . water MS.², 1822: woods & waters MS.

2534 absolute MS.², 1822: permanent MS.

2535 height MS.², 1822: elevation MS.

2544 superiority of the Alps MS.², 1822: inferiority [?in] region[?s] of the Alps in respect to [its *del.*] the mountains as visual objects MS.

2549 distinguished MS.², 1822: diversified MS.

2553 the MS.², 1822: [?this] MS.

2553–4 gratification MS.², 1822: gratifications MS.

2555 other. Besides, 1822: other; [?it *del.*] besides, MS.

2556 cattle animate MS.², 1822: Cattle or Sheep are seen animating MS.

2556–9 and, though . . . colour are 1822: the pastures [indeed *del.*] of the higher regions where [Cattle *del.*] they feed during the summer [?where *del.*] are left in [a *del.*] their natural state of flowery herbage [they are *del.*] but these are so [? *del.*] remote that their texture & colour [?will *del.*] are MS.

2564 plant of deep MS.², 1822: plant lifting its tall head of deep MS.
   as tall as MS.², 1822: & taller than [?*del.*] it [?even *or* ever] seen MS.

2565 where MS.², 1822: which MS.

2577–8 they have . . . landscape 1822: there does not exist a single landscape from [any of *del.*] their hands MS.

2579 Alps; yet Titian 1822: Alps. Titian MS.

2581 aspects 1822: aspect MS.

2582 among 1822: in the midst of MS.
   Alps. A few 1822: Alps. Yet none of these were ever tempted to exercise their skill in composing pictures from those materials. A few MS.
   experiments MS.², 1822: successful experiments MS.

2583 by Englishmen MS.², 1822: to overcome these obstacles MS.

2588–9 its fitness . . . more MS.², 1822: it renders it more MS.

2592 Deeming . . . British MS.², 1822: Deeming those points of superiority which the scenery of the Alps has over [our British landscape *del.*] ours MS.

2594–5 triumphing MS.², 1822: flourishing MS.

2595 pomp . . . of MS.², 1822: majesty of [?*del.*] MS.
   have, in general*, neither 1822: have neither MS.

2596 exist MS.², 1822: be found MS.

2601 common; and the oaks 1822: *the typesetter read what appears to be an* X *as an ampersand, but the text may read* common. X The oaks

2602 those of Britain 1822: the British MS.

2608 Alps MS.², 1822: Alps [?*del.*] MS.

2641 those of the] *The manuscript here breaks off.*

2798–803 *The top of a manuscript page, numbered 21, begins:*
                    To the Printer

The conclusion of the last sent copy must run thus— "These objections will not be found applicable to the following extract from a letter to a Friend, giving an account" &c.—(going on as already sent) "This district in comparison with the Alps."
Having left Rossthwaite &c.

2803 *Before* "Having left MS. *deletes* -doned. *The opening quotation mark is omitted from* 1822 (*cf.* 2905–6 *below*).

2804 ascended from Seathwaite to MS.², 1822: clomb to MS.

2811 Ingleborough MS.², 1822: after a long, long distance, Ingleborough MS.

2812 *that* MS.², 1822: it MS.

2815 pre-eminent MS.², 1822: [?& others] MS.

2817 to our right MS.², 1822: and MS.

2819 *After* base MS. *deletes* very grand [?] a grand object

2820 this MS.², 1822: our MS.

2825 has been estimated MS.², 1822: the Measurers of Mountains estimate MS.

2826 Scawfell Head, where MS.², 1822: Scawfell & where MS.

2829 Borrowdale:— on MS.², 1822: Borrowdale:— at MS.

2830–1 Pike . . . there was MS.⁴, 1822: Pike there was MS.: Pike which we gained [after *del.*] with some toil MS.²: Pike which we gained with considerable toil MS.³.

2832 containing . . . rock MS.³, 1822: which we spread out containing our refreshment which we ate in summer warmth; & MS.: containing our refreshment which we [here *del.*] had spread out upon a rock MS.².

2834 could MS.², 1822: was to MS.

2836 yet 1822: still MS.

2840 a 1822: the MS.

2842 *After* beyond MS. *deletes*: While we were [looking *del.*] gazing around after [?dinner] our Guide said that we must not linger long; for [we should have a storm *del.*] a storm was coming. *Above the deletion is written*: See the loose [?]. *Cf.* 2851 *and* 2864–5.

2843 Gladly MS.², 1822: We ate our meal in summer warmth, and gladly MS.

2847 which MS.², 1822: [?that is not] a spring but MS.

2853 "It can . . . cannot 1822: "a Ship! it can be nothing else," interposed my Companion, ["it can be nothing else *del.*] "it *is* a Ship; I cannot MS.

2856 changed into MS.², 1822: like MS.

2864 moving 1822: moving away MS.

2866 signs MS.², 1822: traces MS.
were MS.², 1822: were all MS.

2868 vapour MS.², 1822: cloudy mist MS.

2878 struggles of gloom MS.², 1822: goings on of the storm MS.

2880 Rainbows. Before 1822: Rainbows: we were [truly *del.*] glad to see *them* & the clouds disappear from *that mountain* as we knew [?that *del.*] some of our Friends [*altered from* Friends of ours] were to be upon Skiddaw at that time. Before MS.

2881 every MS.², 1822: on our return every MS.

2883–6 mentioned . . . to a great 1822: described the last part of the ascent to Scaw-fell Pike. There not a blade of grass was to be seen; but a few cushions or tufts of moss, parched and brown, appeared between the huge blocks and stones, which cover the summit, and lie in heaps all round to a great MS.

2887 needed MS.², 1822: wanted MS.

2889 vivid MS.², 1822: the most vivid MS.
    feathers MS.², 1822: [?of] feathers MS.

2890 colouring MS.², 1822: beauty MS.

2891 be MS.², 1822: is MS.

2905–6 and we . . . moonlight. MS.², 1822: and we travelled [?to] home by moonlight." MS.